TITLE IX

CONTEMPORARY DECISIONS

Volume 2

* * *

A LandMark Publication

Litigator Series

Title IX
Contemporary Decisions
Volume 2

Copyright © 2020
by LandMark Publications. All rights reserved.

Published in the United States of America
by LandMark Publications.
www.landmark-publications.com

Publication Date: December 2020;
Subject Heading: Education Law;
Audience: Law Professionals.

Character Set: ISO 8859-1 (Latin-1);
Language Code: EN;
Interior Type: Text; Monochrome.

Help us serve you better.
Write to landmarkpx@live.com with
your requests, comments and suggestions.

ISBN: 979-8579610690

SUMMARY OF CONTENTS

FOREWORD 1

TABLE OF CASES

SIXTH CIRCUIT DECISIONS 5
   Chisholm v. St. Marys City School District Board, 947 F. 3d 342 (6th Cir. 2020) 7
   Doe v. University of Kentucky, 959 F. 3d 246 (6th Cir. 2020) 21
   Bose v. Bea, 947 F. 3d 983 (6th Cir. 2020) 27
   Kollaritsch v. Michigan State University, 944 F. 3d 613 (6th Cir. 2019) 41
   Doe v. Miami University, 882 F. 3d 579 (6th Cir. 2018) 55
   Doe v. Baum, 903 F. 3d 575 (6th Cir. 2018) 79
   Doe v. University of Cincinnati, 872 F. 3d 393 (6th Cir. 2017) 97
   Doe v. University of Kentucky, 860 F. 3d 365 (6th Cir. 2017) 111

SEVENTH CIRCUIT DECISIONS 119
   Doe v. Columbia College Chicago, 933 F. 3d 849 (7th Cir. 2019) 121
   Doe v. Purdue University, 928 F. 3d 652 (7th Cir. 2019) 129
   Doe No. 55 v. Madison Metropolitan School Dist., 897 F. 3d 819 (7th Cir. 2018)
   145
   Wetzel v. Glen St. Andrew Living Community, LLC, 901 F. 3d 856 (7th Cir. 2018)
   151
   Burton v. Bd of Regents of University of WI System, 851 F. 3d 690 (7th Cir. 2017)
   163
   Whitaker v. Kenosha Unified School District, 858 F. 3d 1034 (7th Cir. 2017) . 171

EIGHTH CIRCUIT DECISIONS 191
   Rossley v. Drake University, 958 F. 3d 679 (8th Cir. 2020) 193
   Maher v. Iowa State University, 915 F. 3d 1210 (8th Cir. 2019) 201
   Doe v. Dardanelle School Dist., 928 F. 3d 722 (8th Cir. 2019) 205
   DM by Bao Xiong v. MN State High School League, 917 F. 3d 994 (8th Cir. 2019)
   211
   Pearson v. Logan University, 937 F. 3d 1119 (8th Cir. 2019) 219
   Fryberger v. University of Arkansas, 889 F. 3d 471 (8th Cir. 2018) 229
   KT v. Culver-Stockton College, 865 F. 3d 1054 (8th Cir. 2017) 235
   Roe v. St. Louis University, 746 F. 3d 874 (8th Cir. 2014) 241

NINTH CIRCUIT DECISIONS ... 253
Parents for Privacy v. Barr, 949 F. 3d 1210 (9th Cir. 2020) ... 255
Karasek v. Regents of the University of California, 948 F. 3d 1150 (9th Cir. 2020) ... 283
Austin v. University of Oregon, 925 F. 3d 1133 (9th Cir. 2019) ... 303
Doe v. Regents of the University of California, 891 F. 3d 1147 (9th Cir. 2018) 311
US v. County of Maricopa, Arizona, 889 F. 3d 648 (9th Cir. 2018) ... 319
Campbell v. Hawaii Dept. of Educ., 892 F. 3d 1005 (9th Cir. 2018) ... 325
Stilwell v. City of Williams, 831 F. 3d 1234 (9th Cir. 2016) ... 343

TENTH CIRCUIT DECISIONS ... 361
Doe v. University of Denver, 952 F. 3d 1182 (10th Cir. 2020) ... 363
Farmer v. Kansas State University, 918 F. 3d 1094 (10th Cir. 2019) ... 383
Ross v. University of Tulsa, 859 F. 3d 1280 (10th Cir. 2017) ... 397
Hiatt v. Colorado Seminary, 858 F. 3d 1307 (10th Cir. 2017) ... 413
Levy v. Kansas Dept. of Social & Rehab. Services, 789 F. 3d 1164 (10th Cir. 2015) ... 431
Varnell v. Dora Consol. School Dist., 756 F. 3d 1208 (10th Cir. 2014) ... 441

ELEVENTH CIRCUIT DECISIONS ... 451
Doe v. Valencia College, 903 F. 3d 1220 (11th Cir. 2018) ... 453
JS v. Houston County Bd. of Education, 877 F. 3d 979 (11th Cir. 2017) ... 469
Hill v. Cundiff, 797 F. 3d 948 (11th Cir. 2015) ... 481
Doe v. School Bd. of Broward County, Fla., 604 F. 3d 1248 (11th Cir. 2010) .. 515

Prologue

Title IX provides: "No person in the United States shall, on the basis of sex, be excluded from participation in, be denied the benefits of, or be subjected to discrimination under any education program or activity receiving federal financial assistance." 20 U.S.C. § 1681(a). Though the statute contains no express private right of action, the Supreme Court has held that individuals may sue funding recipients for violating Title IX. *See Cannon v. Univ. of Chi.,* 441 U.S. 677, 717, 99 S.Ct. 1946, 60 L.Ed.2d 560 (1979); *Franklin v. Gwinnett Cty. Pub. Schs.,* 503 U.S. 60, 76, 112 S.Ct. 1028, 117 L.Ed.2d 208 (1992). And the Court has held that this implied right of action includes retaliation claims, explaining that "when a funding recipient retaliates against a person *because* he complains of sex discrimination, this constitutes intentional 'discrimination' 'on the basis of sex,' in violation of Title IX." *Jackson v. Birmingham Bd. of Educ.,* 544 U.S. 167, 174, 125 S.Ct. 1497, 161 L.Ed.2d 361 (2005).

The Supreme Court's decision in *Jackson* did not spell out the elements of a Title IX retaliation claim, and no published case in this circuit has decided the question. In unpublished authority, however, we have analogized to Title VII retaliation claims, stating that a Title IX plaintiff must show "that (1) [s]he engaged in protected activity, (2) [the funding recipient] knew of the protected activity, (3) [s]he suffered an adverse school-related action, and (4) a causal connection exists between the protected activity and the adverse action." *Gordon v. Traverse City Area Pub. Schs.,* 686 F. App'x 315, 320 (6th Cir. 2017). Our sister circuits apply similar tests. *See, e.g., Emeldi v. Univ. of Or.,* 698 F.3d 715, 724 (9th Cir. 2012); *Papelino v. Albany Coll. of Pharmacy of Union Univ.,* 633 F.3d 81, 89 (2d Cir. 2011); *Frazier v. Fairhaven Sch. Comm.,* 276 F.3d 52, 67 (1st Cir. 2002).

Bose v. Bea, 947 F. 3d 983 (6th Cir. 2020)

Foreword

THIS CASEBOOK contains a selection of U. S. Court of Appeals decisions that analyze, interpret, and apply provisions of Title IX of the Education Amendments Act of 1972. Volume 2 of the casebook covers the Sixth through the Eleventh Circuit Court of Appeals.

Tom Rossley is an alumnus and former Trustee of Drake University, a non-profit, private university in Des Moines, Iowa. In the fall of 2015, the University investigated an allegation of sexual misconduct against Rossley's son, Thomas Rossley, Jr. In the course of the Title IX investigation, Rossley Jr. was found responsible for the alleged sexual misconduct, and after an appeal process, was expelled from the University. *See Rossley v. Drake University*, 958 F. 3d 679 (8th Cir. 2020).

During this process, Rossley was critical of how the University handled his son's case. Rossley made phone calls, sent emails, and participated in conversations with other members of the Board of Trustees (the Board), University alumni, University administrators, and donors about the situation. Specifically, Rossley complained that the University did not accommodate his son's disabilities during its investigation. Since childhood, Rossley Jr. suffered from ADHD, anxiety, and language-based disabilities, which "inhibit his ability to communicate effectively."

In March of 2016, Rossley sent an email to the University's Vice President of Finance, as well as Rossley's wife, and the University's bond attorney, stating "please let this email serve as my disclosure that my son may be initiating litigation against Drake University in the event that his hearing verdict is not overturned on appeal." When this email was sent, Rossley Jr.'s expulsion appeal was still pending.

The University president sent an email to the Board of Trustees advising it to hold a special meeting to vote on how to address Rossley's conflict of interest related to his son's Title IX case. The Board met, determined Rossley had a conflict of interest, and referred the matter back to the Board of Trustee's Board Affairs Committee ("BAC") to recommend a course of action. The BAC determined Rossley's conflict of interest was sufficient to amount to a "for cause" removal from the Board, and recommended removal upon a vote of the Board. The Board voted to remove Rossley due to his "pervasive conflict of interest," and "his insistence on using his position as trustee to advocate" on his son's behalf, who had "certainly threatened litigation" against the University.

In response, Rossley sued the University and the Board asserting various causes of action. The district court granted various motions to dismiss, motions for judgment on the pleadings, and summary judgment motions.

Rossley appeals the dismissal of his Title IX retaliation claim.

Affirmed — Rossley cannot hold the University liable under Title IX for the decision of the Board regarding its own internal affairs. When it voted to remove Rossley as a member, the Board was acting in a manner separate and distinct from the University. *Rossley v. Drake University, ibid.*

* * *

The district court dismissed Rossley's Title IX retaliation claim against the University for lack of standing. Under Title IX "[n]o person in the United States shall, on the basis of sex, be excluded from participation in, be denied the benefits of, or be subjected to discrimination under any education program or activity receiving Federal financial assistance." 20 U.S.C. § 1681(a). The Supreme Court has interpreted Title IX to provide a private right of action for students complaining about teachers or peer-to-peer sexual harassment; it also allows individuals employed by federally-funded institutions to sue their employers. *See Davis ex rel. LaShonda D. v. Monroe Cty. Bd. of Educ.*, 526 U.S. 629, 643, 119 S.Ct. 1661, 143 L.Ed.2d 839 (1999) (finding a plaintiff could sue under Title IX for student-on-student sexual harassment); *Gebser v. Lago Vista Indep. Sch. Dist.*, 524 U.S. 274, 290-91, 118 S.Ct. 1989, 141 L.Ed.2d 277 (1998) (finding a student could sue for sexual harassment by a teacher); *N. Haven Bd. of Educ. v. Bell*, 456 U.S. 512, 520-21, 102 S.Ct. 1912, 72 L.Ed.2d 299 (1982) (finding employees are covered by Title IX regulations when the employer directly participates in federal programs or benefits from federal grants, loans, or contracts). Additionally, some federal courts have entertained causes of action for parents on behalf of their minor children or deceased adult children under Title IX. *See, e.g., Lopez v. Regents of Univ. of Cal.*, 5 F. Supp. 3d 1106, 1114 (N.D. Cal. 2013) (noting "parents *do* have standing to assert Title IX claims on behalf of a student," but "in general, non-students such as parents do not have a *personal* claim under Title IX.").

Title IX also protects individuals who suffer retaliation after reporting instances of sex discrimination. *Jackson v. Birmingham Bd. of Educ.*, 544 U.S. 167, 173-74, 125 S.Ct. 1497, 161 L.Ed.2d 361 (2005). The Supreme Court explained in *Jackson* that "[w]here the retaliation occurs because the complainant speaks out about sex discrimination, the 'on the basis of sex' requirement is satisfied." *Id.* at 179, 125 S.Ct. 1497. According to Rossley, this language from *Jackson* indicates that any Title IX advocate has a cause of action when retaliated against, regardless of whether the advocate is an employee, student, or individual subjected to discrimination under an education program or activity. We disagree. Retaliation "on the basis of sex" is not a sufficient condition for Title IX standing. The plain text of 20 U.S.C. § 1681(a) provides protection for persons from actions taken "on the basis of sex" only if it causes the prospective plaintiff to be "excluded from participation in, be denied the benefits of, or be subjected to discrimination under any education program or activity receiving Federal financial assistance." 20 U.S.C. § 1681(a). Therefore, if the action taken "on the basis of sex" against the person did not exclude, deny, or subject the person to discrimination under an education program or activity, then the action cannot be brought under § 1681(a).

Here, then, we must resolve whether Rossley's removal from the Board constitutes exclusion from or denial of an educational program or activity. Title IX informs us that "program or activity" means "all of the operations of" various institutions, including "a college, university, or other postsecondary institution, or a public system of higher education." 20 U.S.C. § 1687(2)(A). But this broad category of "all of the operations" in § 1687 is narrowed by the descriptor "*education* program or activity" in § 1681(a). Because Rossley does not appeal his action against the Board — only his claim against the University — we need not determine whether a Board of Trustees is an educational program or activity. Even assuming, but not deciding the work of the Board is an educational program, we are left to consider only whether the alleged retaliation can be attributed to the University itself, undoubtedly a federally-funded education program.

Rossley specifically argues the University retaliated against him by: (1) removing him from the Board by a vote; (2) prohibiting him from serving as his son's advocate during the Title IX hearings; and (3) directing him not to visit a tavern near campus. None of these acts support a Title IX retaliation claim against the University.

First, we do not believe Rossley's removal from the Board can support a Title IX retaliation claim against the University. This was an internal vote of a Board of Trustees to remove one of its members. When taking this action, the Board was acting in a manner separate and distinct from the University itself. Therefore, we conclude, as a matter of law, Rossley cannot hold the University liable under Title IX for the separate decision of the Board regarding its own internal affairs.

Next, we consider Rossley's claim that the University retaliated against him by prohibiting him from serving as his son's advocate during the campus hearings. Taking the facts in the amended complaint as true, this claim fails. The amended complaint informs us that the University Code of Conduct allows an accused to have a "personal representative" present during a disciplinary hearing who may, but is not required to be, an attorney. The complaint also informs that Rossley's son had a "newly-retained attorney" who had "got[ten] involved." Rossley's complaint goes on to assert that his "disabled son [was forced] to be his own advocate and act as his own legal representative." And finally, it asserts that Rossley and his wife were not allowed to attend the hearings. But at no time does the complaint allege that Rossley Jr. requested his father to serve as his "personal representative" under the Code of Conduct, nor that such a request was denied by the University. Further, even if Rossley was prevented from attending his son's Title IX hearing, the complaint contains no facts showing a nexus between this inability to attend the hearing and Rossley's alleged complaints to the Board. Without such a nexus, a claim of Title IX retaliation by the University must fail as a matter of law.

And finally, we consider Rossley's argument that the University's direction to Rossley to not frequent an off-campus tavern could support a retaliation claim. This request, while perhaps beyond the bounds of the University's power, did not deny Rossley access to any education activity or program. Instead, it was a request to not frequent an establishment outside the University's control. As such, none of the actions Rossley alleges the University took against him in retaliation were part of an education program or activity, and therefore he lacks standing to bring suit under 20 U.S.C. § 1681(a).

Rossley invites our court to expand Title IX's reach such that "any advocate has standing to bring a retaliation claim under Title IX, and to establish such a claim a plaintiff need only show that he was retaliated against *because* he complained of sex discrimination." Because neither the statutory text nor the precedent supports such an expansion, we affirm the district court's dismissal of Rossley's Title IX retaliation claim for lack of standing.

SIXTH CIRCUIT DECISIONS
Title IX

Chisholm v. St. Marys City School District Board, 947 F. 3d 342 (6th Cir. 2020) 7
Doe v. University of Kentucky, 959 F. 3d 246 (6th Cir. 2020) 21
Bose v. Bea, 947 F. 3d 983 (6th Cir. 2020) 27
Kollaritsch v. Michigan State University, 944 F. 3d 613 (6th Cir. 2019) 41
Doe v. Miami University, 882 F. 3d 579 (6th Cir. 2018) 55
Doe v. Baum, 903 F. 3d 575 (6th Cir. 2018) 79
Doe v. University of Cincinnati, 872 F. 3d 393 (6th Cir. 2017) 97
Doe v. University of Kentucky, 860 F. 3d 365 (6th Cir. 2017) 111

947 F.3d 342 (2020)

Dane CHISHOLM and Reid Linninger, former student-athletes of St. Marys City Schools, Plaintiffs-Appellants,

v.

ST. MARYS CITY SCHOOL DISTRICT BOARD OF EDUCATION, Shawn Brown, James Hollman, and Paul Douglas Frye, Defendants-Appellees.

Nos. 19-3034/3100.

United States Court of Appeals, Sixth Circuit.

Argued: October 17, 2019.

Decided and Filed: January 7, 2020.

Appeal from the United States District Court for the Northern District of Ohio at Toledo. Nos. 3:16-cv-02849; 3:16-cv-02853—James G. Carr, District Judge.

ARGUED: Mark A. Weiker, ALBEIT WEIKER, LLP, Columbus, Ohio, for Appellants. Tabitha Justice, SUBASHI, WILDERMUTH & JUSTICE, Dayton, Ohio, for Appellees St. Marys, Shawn Brown, and James Hollman. William V. Beach, ROBISON, CURPHEY & O'CONNELL, LLC, Toledo, Ohio, for Appellee Paul Douglas Frye. ON BRIEF: Mark A. Weiker, ALBEIT WEIKER, LLP, Columbus, Ohio, for Appellants. Tabitha Justice, Brian L. Wildermuth, SUBASHI, WILDERMUTH & JUSTICE, Dayton, Ohio, for Appellees St. Marys, Shawn Brown, and James Hollman. William V. Beach, Amy J. Luck, ROBISON, CURPHEY & O'CONNELL, LLC, Toledo, Ohio, for Appellee Paul Douglas Frye.

Before: ROGERS, WHITE, and READLER, Circuit Judges.

READLER, Circuit Judge, delivered the opinion of the court in which ROGERS, Circuit Judge, joined, and WHITE, Circuit Judge, joined in part. ROGERS, Circuit Judge, (pg. 355), delivered a separate concurring opinion in which WHITE, Circuit Judge, joined in all but the first sentence. WHITE, Circuit Judge (pp. 355-56), delivered a separate opinion dissenting from Part II(B) of the majority opinion.

OPINION

CHAD A. READLER, Circuit Judge.

Playing football is not for the fainthearted. During games, players risk physical injury in the name of beating an opponent. Even at practice, players put their physical wellbeing at risk to compete for starting positions and to gain an edge for an upcoming game.

These competitive desires are often spurred on by a team's coach. As much as in any sport, football coaches push their players to achieve, often in the face of adversity. Through their words and actions, many coaches push quite hard. Sometimes, their efforts can cross lines of decency. Can they also cross legal lines drawn by Title IX of the Education Amendments Act?

All of this sets the backdrop for today's contest, one fought not on the field, but in the courtroom. We are asked to decide whether federal or state law limits the types of verbal motivational tactics a high school football coach may employ. In separate suits below, two former players for the St. Marys (Ohio) Memorial High School Football Team brought claims for federal Title IX violations and state-law intentional infliction of emotional distress against their coach, Defendant Doug Frye. The players claim that Frye harassed them by using numerous derogatory terms—most notably, the term "pussy"— with the intent to insult (and presumably to motivate) the two in front of their teammates. Plaintiffs also sued the St. Marys school board, superintendent, and athletic director for failing to address Frye's conduct. In both suits, the district court entered summary judgment in favor of Defendants. Plaintiffs now bring separate appeals, which we have consolidated for review.

As a matter of decency, Frye's conduct was distasteful, and no doubt offensive to many. But as a matter of law, his conduct did not constitute sex-based discrimination, in violation of Title IX, nor was it conduct intolerable in a civilized society, in violation of Ohio tort law. Accordingly, we AFFIRM the judgment of the district court.

I. BACKGROUND

Baseball may forever be considered "America's pastime"—Levi Stahl, *When and how baseball became America's Pastime*, The Chicago Blog (Oct. 4, 2018), https://pressblog.uchicago.edu/2018/10/04/when-and-how-baseball-became-americas-pastimean-interview-with-david-rapp.html —but by most every measure, football has become the nation's most popular team sport. Of America's professional sporting leagues, the National Football League enjoys the highest viewer ratings, with its annual championship game, the "Super Bowl," among any year's most viewed television programs of any kind. By total attendance figures, college football surpasses its professional counterpart, with fans filling over 100 collegiate stadiums every fall Saturday. High school football similarly p.346 captures the interest of fans in communities across the nation, typically on Friday nights, as a precursor to collegiate football Saturdays and professional football Sundays.

That widespread adulation informs at least two underlying features of today's case. First, football's popularity can be attributed in part to the sport's physical nature. Dating back to the violent gladiator games of Ancient Rome, and likely much earlier, spectators have long enjoyed tests of strength, speed, and aggression, even when the participants risk their health and wellbeing. More than any other modern team sport, football highlights these same traits—strength, speed, and aggression. It draws upon the combative nature of its participants and their coaches, with the sport enjoying a competitive, confrontational, and motivational foundation not seen in other team activities.

Second, football's popularity feeds a strong desire for team success. At the professional and collegiate levels, on-field success translates directly into notoriety for teams, players, and coaches, and significant revenue for the respective professional organization or university. Even in the more localized high school setting, community pride and year-long bragging rights are at stake when one's team takes the field. Facing this pressure to succeed, football teams are sometimes willing to take chances on troubled yet talented players, decisions that may otherwise be difficult to rationalize. And the same can be said of coaches, whose sometimes crude or outlandish antics are tolerated in favor of on-the-field success. Today's case reflects one such example.

A. Frye Has A Turbulent Background As A High School Football Coach.

Doug Frye has been coaching high school football in northern Ohio for a quarter-century. Allegations that Frye harassed players under his watch are nearly as old. The first came in 1995. While coaching at Bucyrus City Schools, Frye was given a written reprimand for "using unacceptable obscene language" and "becoming physical with one of the players."

That conduct repeated itself when Frye took a coaching position at St. Marys City Schools, starting in 1998. Just a year into the job, Frye was rebuked in writing by members of his coaching staff for subjecting his players to degrading language and pushing them to play through injuries. One of those coaching colleagues was James Hollman, then an assistant football coach, now the athletic director of St. Marys City Schools.

Frye left his position at St. Marys in the spring of 2010. That fall, he took a position as head high school football coach in neighboring Wapakoneta. And once again, Frye's behavior became the source of player grievances. In 2012, Frye was accused of harassing Wapakoneta players. Several students even went so far as to file a criminal complaint against Frye. These allegations were supported by a recording of Frye swearing repeatedly and calling his players "pussies," among other derogatory names.

An investigation by the Ohio Department of Education, or "ODE," ensued. That investigation resulted in ODE and Frye entering into a consent agreement. Under the agreement, Frye retained his teaching license and coaching permit. But Frye's employer, for two years, was required to submit quarterly reports to ODE addressing Frye's behavior and treatment of students. Wapakoneta then renewed Frye's position as head coach for the 2013 season. But following the season, Frye voluntarily resigned.

p.347 B. Frye Returns To St. Marys And Becomes Plaintiffs' Coach.

As events unfolded in Wapakoneta, ten miles away at St. Marys Memorial High School, Plaintiffs Dane Chisholm and Reid Lininger began their high school football careers. Both players were highly involved in the school football program. Chisholm played on the offensive and defensive lines for the varsity team while Lininger was the starting quarterback for the junior varsity team.

During Plaintiffs' early years, the team struggled. Over the 2012 and 2013 seasons, the team went winless, posting a record of 0-20. And by and large, these games were not close. During those two seasons, St. Marys was outscored by a collective margin of nearly 3:1.

On the heels of that futility, the St. Marys School Board decided to replace the head coach. To fill the position, the Board turned to Frye, who was well known to St. Marys from his prior coaching tenure at the school and reputation for running a winning program. With full knowledge of Frye's history of disciplinary incidents, superintendent Shawn Brown signed off on Frye's rehiring due to Frye's continued successful employment for several years at other schools following complaints made against him.

The decision, however, divided the St. Marys community. Some community members enthusiastically supported Frye's rehiring. But others opposed rehiring Frye, given his troubled past. Mindful of these concerns, Brown resolved to monitor Frye's behavior. Brown tasked himself, along with Hollman, the district athletic director, to undertake that supervision.

C. In His New Role, Frye Clashes With Lininger.

Lininger claims that his negative relationship with Frye began immediately upon Frye's arrival at St. Marys. During the first months of Frye's renewed tenure, Lininger attended off-season weight-lifting sessions. At those sessions, Lininger stated that Frye called him soft and entitled. Though Frye also said similar things to other players, Lininger felt that Frye targeted him specifically by criticizing him in front of the entire team.

As the 2014 season kicked off, Frye did not relent. On a daily basis, Frye called Chisholm, Lininger, and their teammates various names, including "pussy, bitch, and pretty boy." Frye also continued to make an example of Lininger, complaining that it was impossible to win with players who wasted their talents like Lininger. Some of Lininger's teammates even joined in, calling Lininger a "pussy" and "soft."

Lininger eventually told his parents about the incidents. Lininger's mother contacted Hollman to ask how she could make a formal complaint against Frye. Hollman responded that he did not know how the complaint process worked, referring Ms. Lininger to Brown, the superintendent. Brown in turn referred Ms. Lininger back to Hollman. Ms. Lininger and Hollman never ended up speaking.

Ms. Lininger also separately contacted Travis Kuenning, a member of the St. Marys Board of Education, to inquire about the complaint process. Though Kuenning met with Ms. Lininger and offered to set up a one-on-one meeting between her and Frye, no such meeting ever took place.

D. Frye Has A Contentious Relationship With Chisholm.

Unlike Lininger, Chisholm did not clash with Frye during Frye's first season back at St. Marys. But Chisholm had other problems. Off the field, he got into trouble at school. And on the field, he was ejected p.348 from a game for punching a player on the opposing team "a couple of times." Chisholm was even briefly removed from the team after he was caught smoking on school grounds. Though Chisholm was ultimately allowed back on the team, Frye made clear that similar conduct would not be tolerated. To his credit, Chisholm for a time heeded this warning, improving his behavior and becoming a team captain for the 2015 season, his senior year.

But his relationship with Frye quickly soured. According to Frye, Chisholm started openly questioning Frye's coaching methods. Frye responded by again calling Chisholm names at practice. This conflict came to a head after the penultimate game of St. Marys' season, when Frye and some team members accused Chisholm of throwing the game by intentionally misdirecting a snap. Following this incident, Chisholm's teammates "voted him off" the team, a decision Frye and Hollman, the athletic director, allowed to stand.

E. Plaintiffs' Fathers File A Formal Complaint, And The School Board And ODE Investigate.

Following Chisholm's removal from the team, Chisholm's father contacted Lininger's father to discuss Frye's treatment of their sons. Chisholm's father also reached out to other members of the team, finding some who agreed with the two fathers' complaints. After speaking with other parents about Frye's conduct, the two fathers decided to engage an attorney. At the fathers' behest, their attorney sent a letter to Brown and Hollman requesting the removal of Frye and his staff, both as coaches and teachers. The fathers also submitted a similar complaint to ODE.

The St. Marys School Board initiated an investigation into Frye's conduct. The Board retained Dr. Ted Knapke, the former superintendent of two Ohio school districts, who had previously conducted a similar investigation for another district. *Lininger v. St. Marys City Sch. Dist. Bd. of Educ.,* No. 3:16-cv-2853, 2019 WL 188050, at *4 (N.D. Ohio Jan. 14, 2019). On behalf of the Board, Knapke interviewed eleven players and some of their parents, along with most of the coaching staff. But he did not interview Lininger or his father. In his report, Knapke concluded that the allegations against Frye, while serious, were unsupported by the findings of the investigation. Coaches and students acknowledged Frye's intermittent swearing, but, Knapke concluded, they did not believe Frye's conduct was inappropriate. Despite these findings, Knapke recommended that Hollman "remain very closely involved with" the football program.

Plaintiffs' fathers wrote a letter to Brown to request an appeal. Brown brought the letter to the attention of the Board, but no additional investigation was conducted. Two months later, ODE concluded its investigation. In its final report, ODE determined that no disciplinary action against Frye was necessary.

Following the controversy, Frye remained the head coach at St. Marys. Chisholm finished his senior year and enlisted in the Army. Still a junior, Lininger transferred to nearby Anna High School, where he played receiver for the varsity football team and was chosen for the homecoming court. Despite those achievements, Lininger claims that he suffered severe emotional distress for the remainder of his time in high school.

F. Plaintiffs File Suit Against Various Members Of The St. Marys School District.

Through the same counsel, Plaintiffs filed separate complaints in federal court. Each alleged federal Due Process, Equal Protection, 42 U.S.C. § 1983, and Title IX p.349 claims along with state-law claims for intentional and negligent infliction of emotional distress against the same defendants —the St. Marys Board of Education, Brown, Hollman, and Frye. Following discovery in each case, the district court granted summary judgment to Defendants on all claims. Both Plaintiffs appealed, pursuing only their claims for Title IX violations and intentional infliction of emotional distress. We consolidated the cases for resolution on appeal.

II. ANALYSIS

Viewing the record in the light most favorable to Plaintiffs, the district court concluded that Plaintiffs' Title IX and intentional infliction of emotional distress claims were insufficient as a matter of law. Reviewing those conclusions de novo, we agree. *Patterson v. Hudson Area Sch.*, 551 F.3d 438, 444 (6th Cir. 2009) (citing *DiCarlo v. Potter*, 358 F.3d 408, 414 (6th Cir. 2004)). Even accepting Plaintiffs' factual allegations as true, they are nonetheless insufficient as a matter of law to warrant relief.

A. Plaintiffs Are Not Entitled To Title IX Relief Because They Were Not The Target Of Sex-Based Discrimination.

1. Inspired by the Civil Rights Act of 1964, Congress passed another groundbreaking antidiscrimination law, Title IX, a few years later, in 1972. In enacting Title IX, Congress sought to curb discrimination in federally funded educational institutions (such as public high schools and universities) left unaddressed by the Civil Rights Act. 20 U.S.C. § 1681(a). Unlike its landmark predecessor, however, Title IX prohibits only discrimination "on the basis of sex": "No person in the United States shall, *on the basis of sex,* be excluded from participation in, be denied the benefits of, or be subjected to discrimination under any education program or activity receiving Federal financial assistance." *Id.* (emphasis added). Other forms of discrimination, while they may run afoul of another safeguard, do not implicate Title IX. *See id.*

To sustain a claim under Title IX, a plaintiff must first show that a person or entity affiliated with a federally funded education program engaged in some form of sex-based discrimination against the plaintiff. Once those threshold matters are established, the plaintiff must make three additional showings: (1) the sex-based harassment was so severe, pervasive, and objectively offensive that it could be said to deprive the plaintiff of access to the educational opportunities or benefits provided by the school; (2) the school had actual knowledge of the harassment; and (3) the school was deliberately indifferent to the harassment. *Patterson*, 551 F.3d at 444-45 (citing *Davis v. Monroe Cnty. Bd. of Educ.*, 526 U.S. 629, 633, 119 S.Ct. 1661, 143 L.Ed.2d 839 (1999)).

Plaintiffs' Title IX theory is somewhat unusual. It hinges entirely on Frye's use of the term "pussy." Plaintiffs say the use of that term was a form of sex discrimination due to its gender-based connotations. To Plaintiffs' mind, the term portrayed them as "feminine" and thus seemingly less valuable teammates in the "masculine" setting of football, revealing Frye's favoritism of one sex over the other. And because, Plaintiffs add, Frye's repeated use of the term ultimately denied them educational benefits at St. Marys, Frye's conduct ran afoul of Title IX. We therefore must decide whether a high school football coach's use of the term "pussy"—in the context of football-related activities—is enough to implicate Title IX protections.

2. We start with the traditional understanding of sex discrimination. In crafting p.350 our framework for analyzing Title IX claims, we have looked to the Title VII landscape for guidance, as both statutes prohibit discrimination on the basis of sex. *Compare* 20 U.S.C. § 1681(a) (forbidding educational discrimination "on the basis of sex"), *with* 42 U.S.C. § 2000e-2 (forbidding employment discrimination "because of [an] individual's ... sex"). Indeed, on more than one occasion, we have drawn parallels between sex discrimination in the educational setting under Title IX and sex discrimination in the workplace under Title VII. *See, e.g., Doe v. Miami Univ.*, 882 F.3d 579, 590 (6th Cir. 2018) (citing *Doe v. Claiborne Cnty.*, 103 F.3d 495, 515 (6th Cir. 1996)). Accordingly, we begin our analysis by borrowing from our Title VII precedent to examine whether Frye's comments constituted discrimination "on the basis of sex," for purposes of Title IX.

In the Title VII context, a plaintiff customarily may use any one of three evidentiary routes to show that workplace discrimination occurred on the basis of sex: (1) the defendant made sexual advances or acted out of a sexual desire; (2) the defendant was motivated by general hostility to the presence of one sex in the workplace; or (3) the defendant treated members of each sex differently in a mixed-sex workplace. *Vickers v. Fairfield Med. Ctr.*, 453 F.3d 757, 765 (6th Cir. 2006) (citing *Oncale v. Sundowner Offshore Servs., Inc.*, 523 U.S. 75, 80-81, 118 S.Ct. 998, 140 L.Ed.2d 201 (1998)). Replacing the workplace setting with an educational one, the same three considerations provide a legal structure for examining Title IX sex-discrimination claims.

Viewed through this Title VII-inspired lens, Plaintiffs' allegations fail to satisfy any of the three traditional routes for establishing Title IX liability. Start with the first route—whether Frye made sexual advances or acted out of sexual desire. Even when viewing the record in the light most favorable to Plaintiffs, that type of evidence is absent. In fact, no allegation regarding sexual desire has been raised in this case. The same is true of the second route—whether Frye was motivated by a general hostility to the presence of men. If anything, the evidence is much to the contrary. Frye, after all, dedicated many years of his life to coaching and developing the male student athletes he supervised. So too for the third route—whether Frye treated men and women differently in a mixed-sex environment. That the St. Marys football team had no female members seems to foreclose this route to Title IX relief. And even looking beyond the football field to school activities more broadly, Plaintiffs have not presented any evidence that Frye treated male and female students any differently.

Of course, Plaintiffs cannot be faulted for finding Frye's use of the term "pussy" offensive, even in a football setting. But crude or vulgar language alone does not rise to the level of a Title IX violation. After all, Title IX, like Title VII, is not a "general civility code." *See Oncale,* 523 U.S. at 81, 118 S.Ct. 998. Plaintiffs may also be correct that Frye used the term as an assault on their masculinity. To Frye, the term was a vehicle for criticizing male athletes for not acting in an aggressive or "tough" manner. Yet the mere use of an offensive or gendered term does not in itself rise to the level of discrimination on the basis of sex. *See Oncale,* 523 U.S. at 81, 118 S.Ct. 998 ("[The plaintiff] must always prove that the conduct at issue was not merely tinged with offensive sexual connotations, but actually constituted *discrimina[tion]*... because of ... sex.") (original emphasis). Here, Frye's aim was to chide Plaintiffs for not acting with the forcefulness Frye believed was called for on the football field. Critically, there is no p.351 evidence of Frye favoring one sex over the other in that respect. That shortcoming dooms any claim for relief under the traditional understanding of Title IX. *Cf. Seamons v. Snow*, 84 F.3d 1226, 1233 (10th Cir. 1996) (holding that a football coach's use of offensive gendered language toward a player was not sex-based discrimination for purposes of Title IX).

3. Outside of these traditional applications of Title VII and Title IX, a plaintiff can also demonstrate sex discrimination by showing that he or she was mistreated for failing to conform to traditional sex stereotypes. The seminal Supreme Court case on that score, *Price Waterhouse v. Hopkins,* involved a female employee of an accounting firm who was explicitly instructed to look and act more feminine to improve her chances of a promotion. 490 U.S. 228, 235, 109 S.Ct. 1775, 104 L.Ed.2d 268 (1989). Among those clichéd instructions, the employee was told to "walk more femininely, talk more femininely, dress more femininely, wear make-up, have her hair styled, and wear jewelry," and to behave less "aggressively" with firm staff. *Id.* These traits, of course, had no relevance to the performance of her job duties. And, it bears noting, these traits were not expected of the firm's male employees. *Id.* Rather, this "advice" and the ensuing adverse employment outcome were the result of Price Waterhouse's stereotypical views about how a woman should look and behave in the workplace. In that way, the company's conduct likely ran afoul of federal protections against sex discrimination. That is, unless Price Waterhouse could prove that it would have denied the plaintiff a promotion absent the discrimination, the plaintiff was entitled to Title VII relief on the basis of impermissible "sex stereotyping." *Id.* at 250-51, 109 S.Ct. 1775.

Following *Price Waterhouse*'s lead, we granted relief to a transgender plaintiff who was mistreated by her employer, the City of Salem, while transitioning. *Smith v. City of Salem,* 378 F.3d 566, 573 (6th Cir. 2004). As Smith took progressive steps to appear and act more feminine, Smith's city co-workers complained that Smith's appearance was "not masculine enough." *Id.* at 572. Ultimately, top city officials conspired to constructively terminate Smith by ordering Smith to undergo multiple psychological examinations, which they hoped Smith would refuse, leading to Smith's removal. *Id.* at 569. As the city's actions emanated from their formulaic thinking about how men should appear and behave in the workplace, their conduct toward Smith, we concluded, violated Title VII's prohibition on sex stereotyping. *Id.* at 575.

For today's purposes, and again borrowing from our Title VII jurisprudence in interpreting Title IX, *Smith* instructs us to consider whether Plaintiffs' gender non-conforming appearance or behavior motivated Frye's comments, giving rise to a potential violation of Title IX. *See Vickers,* 453 F.3d at 763 (citing *Smith,* 378 F.3d at 573). We can quickly rule out the former; Plaintiffs have not alleged that they did not have a traditionally male appearance. So we are left to consider whether Frye's gendered comments about Plaintiffs' behavior might implicate Title IX's prohibition of sex stereotyping, as a form of sex discrimination. In our view, they do not.

Today's case falls well short of *Price Waterhouse* and *Smith* terrain, for two reasons. First, the comments at issue in those cases specifically targeted the plaintiffs' perceived failure to appear and act like a woman (in *Price Waterhouse*) or like a man (in *Smith*). In other words, those comments dealt with specific proscriptive p.352 gender norms that the plaintiffs were perceived to have violated—for example, that men do not wear feminine clothing. But compare those gender-based comments with Frye's.

Frye criticized Chisholm and Lininger in a crude, foul-mouthed way because they, in his view, were not "tough" enough. Toughness, while sometimes celebrated in men, is certainly not discouraged in women, especially in a professional or team setting. Indeed, in sports, law enforcement, business, law, politics, the armed services, and myriad other activities and professions, women are called upon to be as tough as men. And in many instances, women outpace their male colleagues in that respect. By the same token, were women to join Frye's team, he undoubtedly would demand nothing less of them than their male teammates. This is worlds apart, then, from the gender-inspired expectations about appearance (such as wearing makeup, jewelry, or certain hairstyles) that loomed large in *Price Waterhouse* and *Smith*.

Second, and of even greater significance, the qualities complained of in *Price Waterhouse* and *Smith* were not related to the plaintiffs' abilities to perform well in their jobs. Here, by comparison, Frye's abusive language targeted a fundamental requirement for football players—toughness. By his remarks, Frye was not offering a commentary on whether Chisholm and Lininger were exemplars of their sex. For better or worse, Frye's comments were about playing football, not gender roles. Frye thought that Lininger's performance as a quarterback suffered because of Lininger's fear of being hit by players on the opposing team. And Frye criticized Lininger for sitting out games and practices due to injury. To Frye's somewhat boorish mind, a "pussy" was a wimp or coward, perhaps a "snowflake" in the current lexicon, but, critically, not a feminine individual. As previously mentioned, gut-wrenching hits and other brutal interactions are part and parcel of football. With such interactions come pain and, all too often, injury. Resilience, a strong will, and possibly even a measure of disregard for one's physical well-being, are necessary ingredients for success in football. And that is true for male and female players alike.

That resilience is the trait Frye sought to draw out of Lininger and Chisholm. While beneath the dignity of a teacher and youth mentor, Frye's use of an offensive, gendered insult to motivate his players does not put this case across the Title IX goal line. *See Vickers*, 453 F.3d at 764 (citing *Smith*, 378 F.3d at 575).

4. Even if the use of the word "pussy," standing alone, could constitute a form of sex-based discrimination, Plaintiffs have still failed to meet the remaining elements of a Title IX claim. Title IX does not protect against all sex discrimination. Rather, it protects only against sex discrimination that is so "severe, pervasive, and objectively offensive that it could be said to deprive the plaintiff of access to the educational opportunities or benefits provided by the school." *Patterson*, 551 F.3d at 444-45 (citing *Davis*, 526 U.S. at 633, 119 S.Ct. 1661).

To make that assessment, we must consider the context in which Frye made these comments. *Oncale*, 523 U.S. at 82, 118 S.Ct. 998. Plaintiffs were high school football players, and Frye was their coach. Though the record suggests that Frye's use of profanity in general, and the term "pussy" in particular, was pervasive, Plaintiffs have not shown that Frye's statements were sufficiently severe or objectively offensive to merit Title IX relief. On the football field, where emotions and adrenaline can run high, it is not unheard of for coaches and players alike to use offensive or gendered language, especially in the heat of a game. Viewed in this light, Frye's conduct, while less than laudable, does not meet the high bar for severe, pervasive, and objectively offensive conduct. *See Pahssen v. Merrill Cmty. Sch. Dist.*, 668 F.3d 356, 360, 363 (6th Cir. 2012) (holding that three separate occasions of sexual harassment—a male student shoving a female student into a locker, demanding that she perform oral sex on him, and making obscene sexual gestures at her—was not "severe, pervasive, and objectively offensive").

This conclusion, of course, might be different in another setting. Conduct considered blasé on the gridiron might very well shock the conscience of the chess club or debate team. The Supreme Court made precisely this observation in *Oncale*, when it stated that the evaluation of conduct as sex-based discrimination "depends on a constellation of surrounding circumstances, expectations, and relationships which are not fully captured by a simple recitation of the words used or the physical acts performed." 523 U.S. at 82, 118 S.Ct. 998. The constellation of circumstances surrounding today's case simply does not give rise to Title IX liability. And as a result, we need not consider whether the remaining Defendants were deliberately indifferent to Frye's conduct. *Pahssen*, 668 F.3d at 364.

B. Plaintiffs' State-Law Claims Likewise Fail Because Frye's Conduct Was Not Sufficiently Outrageous, And Any Anguish Experienced by Plaintiffs Was Not Sufficiently Severe.

In addition to their federal Title IX claim, Plaintiffs also claim that Frye's conduct amounted to intentional infliction of emotional distress, an Ohio state-law claim. According to Plaintiffs, Frye's conduct caused Lininger to develop depression and anxiety, which made it more difficult for him to make friends at his new school. Likewise, Plaintiffs say that Frye's comments and failure to reinstate Chisholm following his dismissal from the team disrupted his home life and caused him to be skeptical of adult leadership.

Under Ohio common law, a claim for intentional infliction of emotional distress requires Plaintiffs to meet a four-factor test:

(1) that the actor either intended to cause emotional distress or knew or should have known that actions taken would result in serious emotional distress to the plaintiff;
(2) that the actor's conduct was so extreme and outrageous as to go beyond all possible bounds of decency and was such that it can be considered as utterly intolerable in a civilized community;
(3) that the actor's actions were the proximate cause of the plaintiff's psychic injury; and
(4) that the mental anguish suffered by the plaintiff is serious and of a nature that no reasonable man could be expected to endure it.

Burkes v. Stidham, 107 Ohio App.3d 363, 668 N.E.2d 982, 989 (1995). For purposes of argument, we assume that Frye, by his derogatory comments, intended to cause Plaintiffs emotional distress, the first in Ohio's four-factor test. We likewise assume the third factor—that Frye's conduct was the proximate cause of Plaintiffs' alleged mental anguish. Neither Lininger nor Chisholm, however, can show that Frye's conduct was "so extreme and outrageous as to go beyond all possible bounds of decency," let alone conduct "considered as utterly intolerable in a civilized community," as required by the second factor. *Id.* Nor, for that matter, can either one show that the mental anguish resulting from Frye's conduct was so severe that no reasonable p.354 player could be expected to endure it, as required by the final factor. *Id.*

Ohio law sets a high bar for establishing an emotional-distress claim. To clear that bar, a plaintiff must show "out-rageous" conduct by the defendant. Hurt feelings caused by insults, threats, and other indignities are not "outrageous" as a matter of Ohio law. *Reamsnyder v. Jaskolski,* 10 Ohio St.3d 150, 462 N.E.2d 392, 394 (1984). Rather, as Ohio courts have recognized, and as we have all experienced, the world is not always kind, meaning that, for common-law tort purposes, the average person is expected to be somewhat thick-skinned. *Id.* With that understanding in mind, Ohio courts routinely deny claims for intentional infliction of emotional distress, even in cases of egregious conduct. *See, e.g., Silvers v. Clay Twp. Police Dep't,* 117 N.E.3d 954, 965-67 (Ohio App. 2018) (denying relief to a plaintiff who, at the hands of her co-worker, was repeatedly teased about the sudden death of her sister, her weight, and her own health problems); *Pierce v. Woyma,* No. 97545, 2012 WL 3758631, at *6 (Ohio App. Aug. 20, 2012) (denying relief to a woman who was verbally berated by an off-duty police officer). That is true for everyday circumstances, let alone in the rough-and-tumble world of football.

That is not to say we condone Frye's comments. They are offensive and inappropriate at best. But they are also not unheard of on the gridiron, where the foul-mouthed coach is something of an unfortunate cultural cliché. All things considered, Frye's statements were not "utterly intolerable in a civilized community." *Burkes,* 668 N.E.2d at 989.

For similar reasons, we cannot say, as required by the final factor, that any emotional anguish Plaintiffs experienced was "serious and of a nature that no reasonable man could be expected to endure it." *Id.* As we have said, Frye's comments were harsh, pointed, and intended to demean. Yet even intense name-calling is not something "no reasonable man could be expected to endure," especially on the football field. *Id.*

All of this is particularly true with respect to Chisholm's claim regarding his removal from the team. As a starting point, it is unlikely that Chisholm's removal from participating in a voluntary team sport, even if wrongful, could be sufficient grounds for an emotional-distress claim. Ohio courts have denied emotional-distress claims brought by *paid employees* terminated even under the most acrimonious and embarrassing circumstances. *Peitsmeyer v. Jackson Twp. Bd. of Trs.,* No. 02AP-1174, 2003 WL 21940713, at *5-6 (Ohio App. Aug 14, 2003) (denying emotional-distress relief to a firefighter who was forced to sort through his personal belongings in front his co-workers after his locked office was emptied without notice). The same must be true of an unpaid recreational activity that was not Chisholm's means of supporting himself. Although Chisholm was likely humiliated when he was removed from the team, Ohio tort law does not reach all indignities. For better or worse, "embarrassment and humiliation are part of everyday life to which the law provides no remedy." *Id.* at *5.

This is perhaps especially so when the embarrassment and humiliation result from a justified action—here, Chisholm's removal from the team. Chisholm had been removed once before for smoking on school grounds. When he returned to the team, Chisholm punched an opponent multiple times during a game and engaged in other violent misconduct at school. And, keep in mind, it was Chisholm's own teammates who chose to remove him from the team after he was accused of throwing a game. Frye merely ratified this decision. Even if p.355 a more fulsome investigation might reveal that Chisholm's removal was unfair, it certainly was not so unfair as to be "utterly intolerable in a civilized community." *Burkes,* 668 N.E.2d at 989.

III. CONCLUSION

For these reasons, we AFFIRM the judgment of the district court.

CONCURRENCE

ROGERS, Circuit Judge, concurring.

I concur in full. Title IX, a federal sex discrimination statute, simply does not prohibit abuse of students merely because a coach uses coarse language with a sexual connotation, like "pussy."

This of course is not to excuse abusive conduct like that attributed to defendant in this case. Such conduct should not be tolerated in our high schools. Motivation by humiliation, ridicule, and shaming is counterproductive, and sends terrible messages to our young people. Good training can be very stressful, and tough—very tough— without such abuse. Moreover, constant coarse language, a sign of insecurity, engenders disrespect more often than respect. The way to root out such bad practices, however, is to rely on school boards, administrators, school councils, PTAs, and parents. It is not to create a federal court action to curb such practices. As the majority opinion explains, Congress has not done so.

DISSENTING IN PART

HELENE N. WHITE, Circuit Judge, dissenting in part.

I concur in the court's opinion except as to section II(B), from which I respectfully dissent. I also join in all but the first sentence of Judge Rogers's concurrence.

I agree that consideration of the context surrounding Frye's behavior is necessary in determining whether Frye's treatment of Plaintiffs was extreme and outrageous. *See, e.g., Stepien v. Franklin,* 39 Ohio App.3d 47, 528 N.E.2d 1324, 1330 (Ohio App. 1988). However, the majority overlooks important aspects of that context. This is not a case of a professional or collegiate football coach employing tough coaching methods to motivate consenting adults. Viewing the facts in the light most favorable to Plaintiffs, it appears instead that Frye used his position of authority to degrade, name-call, and single out minor students over an extended time and on a near-daily basis. Frye engaged in this name-calling in front of other impressionable students, who mimicked his behavior on and off the field. In Lininger's case, students followed in Frye's footsteps by calling Lininger "pussy" and "soft" or confronting him in the school hallway to tell him that "Coach Frye says you're a pussy." (R. 39, PID 1358, 1372.)[1] At times, Frye's name-calling was precipitated by what he apparently perceived to be a lack of toughness or, in Chisholm's case, insubordination; at others, Frye appeared to single Plaintiffs out for reasons having nothing to do with their efforts on the field. Viewed as a whole, Frye's behavior constitutes more than "mere insults, indignities, threats, annoyances, petty oppressions, or other trivialities." *Reamsnyder v. Jaskolski,* 10 Ohio St.3d 150, 462 N.E.2d 392, 394 (1984). I therefore conclude that there is sufficient evidence from which to conclude that Frye's actions were so extreme and outrageous as to fall outside the bounds of decency. *Burkes v. Stidham,* 107 p.356 Ohio App.3d 363, 668 N.E.2d 982, 989 (1995).

As the majority describes, Frye has a long history of similar abusive behavior toward student athletes in other districts and in St. Marys. Frye was reprimanded for using obscene language and physicality as early as 1995. During Frye's first tenure at St. Marys, members of his own coaching staff wrote a letter to the St. Marys Board of Education expressing their concerns about Frye's treatment of students. When Frye moved to Wapakoneta schools, his behavior gave rise to several students filing a criminal complaint against him and a consent agreement with the Ohio Department of Education. In short, during each of Frye's coaching tenures on the record, his actions gave rise to serious concerns, disciplinary actions, or formal complaints. This supports the conclusion that his treatment of Plaintiffs fell outside the bounds of decency. *Burkes,* 668 N.E.2d at 989.

As to the element of intent, the vulgar and derogatory nature of Frye's persistent targeted name-calling is alone enough for a jury to conclude that he intended to cause Plaintiffs emotional distress. *See Meyers v. Hot Bagels Factory, Inc.,* 131 Ohio App.3d 82, 721 N.E.2d 1068, 1075 (1999) ("The outrageousness of a defendant's conduct in and of itself can demonstrate his intent to cause emotional distress."). If he did not so intend, his history of receiving complaints and reprimands as a result of the same behavior he displayed toward Plaintiffs put him on notice that his actions would cause serious emotional harm. Likewise, Plaintiffs have created a factual dispute as to causation. As the majority apparently concedes, Frye's treatment of Plaintiffs directly resulted in their emotional distress. Although there may be factual issues as to what degree Frye's actions—as opposed to other events, including student bullying— caused that distress, those issues should be left to a jury to decide.

Finally, Plaintiffs have presented evidence sufficient to allow a reasonable jury to conclude "that the emotional distress actually suffered" as a result of Frye's behavior "reached the level of serious or debilitating emotional distress." *Meyers,* 131 Ohio App.3d at 94, 721 N.E.2d at 1076. Frye's treatment of Lininger had repercussions on and off the field, including bullying by his peers and loss of friends. Eventually, he felt compelled to leave St. Marys and moved to a different school for his senior year. The expert psychologist who examined Lininger reported that Lininger shared that he was "depressed," "withdrawn," "isolated," and "ostracized" from the St. Marys community. (Appellant Lininger's Br. at 30 (citing R. 59).) Lininger described feeling panic and anxiety as a result of Frye's treatment of him. Lininger further testified that he was prescribed antidepressants and sought a counselor to help him cope with his feelings of anger and sadness. Similarly, Chisholm testified that the events underlying this case strained his relationships and caused him to distrust adults. He described feelings of sadness and being unable to enjoy anything in his hometown. The expert psychologist concluded that Chisholm experienced mental-health and psychological problems as a result of Frye's and the school's treatment of him.

In sum, there is sufficient evidence to support a finding in Plaintiffs' favor on each element of their intentional infliction of emotional distress claims against Frye, and I would reverse the district court's grant of summary judgment to Frye on those claims.

[1] All record citations are to the appellate record in Case No. 19-3100, *Lininger v. St. Marys School District Board of Education, et al.*

959 F.3d 246 (2020)

Jane DOE, Plaintiff-Appellant,
v.
UNIVERSITY OF KENTUCKY, et al., Defendants-Appellees.

No. 19-5156.

United States Court of Appeals, Sixth Circuit.
Argued: October 16, 2019.
Decided and Filed: May 18, 2020.

Appeal from the United States District Court for the Eastern District of Kentucky at Lexington, No. 5:17-cv-00345—Joseph M. Hood, District Judge.

ARGUED: Tad Thomas, THOMAS LAW OFFICES, PLLC, Louisville, Kentucky, for Appellant. Bryan H. Beauman, STURGILL, TURNER, BARKER & MOLONEY, PLLC, Lexington, Kentucky, for Appellees. ON BRIEF: Tad Thomas, Lindsay Cordes, THOMAS LAW OFFICES, PLLC, Louisville, Kentucky, for Appellant. Bryan H. Beauman, Jessica R. Stigall, STURGILL, TURNER, BARKER & MOLONEY, PLLC, Lexington, Kentucky, William E. Thro, UNIVERSITY OF KENTUCKY, Lexington, Kentucky, for Appellees.

Before: BATCHELDER, DONALD, and READLER, Circuit Judges.

OPINION

ALICE M. BATCHELDER, Circuit Judge.

Jane Doe alleges that the University of Kentucky (UK) violated Title IX of the Education Amendments of 1972 (Title IX), 86 Stat. 373, *codified at* 20 U.S.C. § 1681, *et seq.*, by responding with deliberate indifference to her accusations of student-on-student harassment. Because Jane Doe failed to show that UK's response subjected her to further actionable harassment that caused Title IX injuries, we AFFIRM the district court's grant of summary judgment.

I.

During her freshman year at UK, Jane Doe reported two separate rapes to UK, accusing two different male UK students of raping her on two different nights.[1] Her Title IX claims are based on UK's response to those accusations.

Jane Doe's Accusations Against John Doe: On August 20, 2016, Jane Doe attended a fraternity party where she met John Doe. John Doe and Jane Doe left the party together, holding hands on their way back to his apartment. Once they arrived, they drank vodka and orange juice in the living room. John Doe eventually kissed her, and the two moved to his bedroom. As their physical intimacy continued, Jane Doe asked if he had a condom and they began to have sex. Jane Doe remembers asking him to stop mid-intercourse; John Doe denies that she made such a request. Later that night, John Doe walked her home, asked for her number, and kissed her goodnight.

Jane Doe subsequently told several friends that John Doe had raped her. On September 13, 2016, one of these friends reported the incident to UK, and representatives from UK's Title IX office immediately met with Jane Doe. On October 6, 2016, UK issued a no-contact order that directed John Doe to "cease any and all contact" with Jane Doe and began its investigation into the alleged rape. R. 13-5, PagID# 508.

Throughout the investigation, Jane Doe reported several encounters with John Doe. In November 2016, Jane Doe left a fraternity tailgate party feeling "extremely uncomfortable and unsafe" because John Doe stood "within mere feet" of her and "stared her down several times," and, a day after the party, John Doe followed her home from class. R. 18-1, PageID#: 703, 784. The Title IX office questioned John Doe about both incidents and determined that the no-contact order had not been violated.

Months later, Jane Doe saw John Doe again while she was walking to class. Jane Doe said that he "looked right at [her]" and it "caused [her] to have a panic attack." R. 18-1, PageID#: 762. She said that his eye contact made her feel "incredibly intimidated, terrified, and quite frankly stalked." *Id.* She also reported that John Doe habitually sat in her vicinity at the library, forcing her to leave on multiple occasions. Jane Doe described feeling "terrified all the time" and that she went to the library "from midnight — 8 am because that was the only time that [she] felt safe[.]" *Id.* at 62. Jane Doe asked UK to ban John Doe from a certain floor in the library, but UK declined to "restrict the movement of either [student] within an academic building." *Id.* at 60-61.

UK's investigation of the alleged rape involved interviewing Jane Doe and John Doe, as well as several student-witnesses. UK also reviewed documentary evidence, including text messages between relevant parties. UK initially concluded that the evidence was insufficient to proceed to a hearing before the school's Sexual Misconduct Hearing Panel (Panel). But when UK informed Jane Doe of this decision, she became "extremely upset and emotional" and "plea[ded]" with the Title IX office to reconsider. R.1, PageID#: 10. UK acquiesced and the Panel held a hearing on March 3, 2017.

According to UK's administrative regulations, the accuser and the accused are each entitled to assistance by two "support persons" during the hearing. R. 18-5, PageID#: 1181-82. Although these support persons may be attorneys, they cannot "represent, speak on behalf of, delay, disrupt, or otherwise interfere" with the proceedings. *Id.* at 1178, 1181-82. John Doe had two attorneys represent him. Nicholas Kehrwald, UK's Interim Dean of Students, acted as the complainant and presented evidence to the Panel on Jane Doe's behalf.

Jane Doe alleges that Kehrwald failed to adequately represent her interests at the hearing. She says that Kehrwald failed to object when John Doe's attorneys actively participated at the hearing by examining and cross-examining witnesses. Jane Doe also says that Kehrwald did not introduce evidence of a voicemail that she left her friend on the night of the alleged rape. And when Jane Doe asked the Panel officer to include the voicemail as evidence, John Doe's attorneys successfully argued against its admission.

The Panel found John Doe innocent of the alleged sexual misconduct by a preponderance of the evidence. Jane Doe filed an appeal with the Sexual Misconduct Appeals Board (Appeals Board), arguing that her due process rights were violated and that the hearing was fundamentally unfair. The Appeals Board disagreed and upheld the Panel's decision.

Jane Doe's Accusations Against James Doe: On October 8, 2016,[2] Jane Doe attended a football tailgate hosted by James Doe's fraternity. Jane Doe, who had been drinking heavily, accepted James Doe's invitation to accompany him back to his apartment. But she says that once they reached James Doe's apartment, she had p.250 difficulty staying awake and that James Doe raped her while she was incapacitated.

Jane Doe reported the assault to the UK Police Department and her friends notified UK's Title IX office. The Title IX office immediately met with Jane Doe and issued a no-contact order. On November 11, 2016, Jane Doe requested that James Doe be removed from their shared classes because he stared at her and made her uncomfortable. The Title IX office called and sent several emails to James Doe, notifying him that he needed to move sections. But James Doe ignored the correspondence and continued to attend classes with Jane Doe.

UK began a formal investigation into the alleged rape in January 2017. A month later, the Title IX office presented its investigative report and a hearing was held in April. Despite being served with notice of the hearing, James Doe failed to appear, and the Panel found that he violated UK's sexual misconduct policy. James Doe was subsequently dismissed from UK.

Jane Doe brought two Title IX claims against UK and several UK officials, arguing that the school's response to student-on-student harassment was clearly unreasonable because it caused a hostile educational environment and vulnerability to further harassment. She also alleged that the school demonstrated deliberate indifference by failing to follow UK's policies throughout the investigation and hearing processes.

UK moved to dismiss Jane Doe's complaint pursuant to Federal Rule of Civil Procedure 12(b)(6) and attached to its motion certain items from the disciplinary proceedings and investigations. Because the district court considered matters outside the pleadings, it treated UK's Rule 12(b)(6) motion as one for summary judgment under Federal Rule of Civil Procedure 56, *see Doe v. Univ. of Ky.*, 361 F. Supp. 3d 687, 689 (E.D. Ky. 2019) (citing *Song v. City of Elyria*, 985 F.2d 840, 842 (6th Cir. 1993)), and found that Jane Doe failed to allege a triable issue of fact as to whether UK was deliberately indifferent to student-on-student harassment and granted UK's motion. *Id.* at 698, 702-03.

II.

In *Davis v. Monroe County Board of Education*, 526 U.S. 629, 643, 119 S.Ct. 1661, 143 L.Ed.2d 839 (1999), the Supreme Court held that "in certain limited circumstances" a federally funded university may be directly liable under Title IX for its inadequate response to allegations of student-on-student harassment. The *Davis* Court held that a university may be liable "only where [it is] deliberately indifferent to sexual harassment, of which [it has] actual knowledge, that is so severe, pervasive, and objectively offensive that it can be said to deprive the victims of access to the educational opportunities or benefits provided by the school." *Id.* at 650, 119 S.Ct. 1661.

We recently considered and re-articulated *Davis*'s pleading standard in *Kollaritsch v. Michigan State University Board of Trustees,* 944 F.3d 613, 620-24 (6th Cir. 2019). There, we explained that a plaintiff must plead "actionable sexual harassment," which is sexual harassment that is severe, pervasive, and objectively offensive. *Id.* at 620 (citing *Davis,* 526 U.S. at 651, 119 S.Ct. 1661). Severe means "something more than just juvenile behavior"; pervasive means "*multiple* incidents of harassment"; and objectively offensive means "behavior that would be offensive to a reasonable person under the circumstances, not merely offensive to the victim, personally or subjectively." *Id.* at 620-21.

A plaintiff must also allege that the school committed a deliberate-indifference p.251 intentional tort, which comprises four elements: (1) knowledge, (2) an act, (3) injury, and (4) causation. *Id.* at 621. The first two elements are satisfied if the school had "actual knowledge" of actionable sexual harassment and responded in a way that was "'clearly unreasonable in light of the known circumstances,' thus demonstrating the school's deliberate indifference to the foreseeable possibility of *further* actionable harassment of the victim." *Id.* (internal citation omitted) (quoting *Davis,* 526 U.S. at 648, 650, 119 S.Ct. 1661). The third element—injury—means the deprivation of "access to the educational opportunities or benefits provided by the school." *Id.* at 622 (quoting *Davis,* 526 U.S. at 650, 119 S.Ct. 1661).

But it is the element of causation on which this case turns. In *Kollaritsch,* we explained that, pursuant to *Davis,* a plaintiff must show: (1) that a school's clearly unreasonable response subjected the student to further actionable harassment and (2) that the further harassment caused the plaintiff's Title IX injury. *Id.* at 622-24. So, the school's response "must bring about or fail to protect against the further harassment." *Id.* at 622. A clearly unreasonable response might "be a detrimental action, thus fomenting or instigating further harassment." *Id.* at 623. Or it might be "an insufficient action (or no action at all)" that makes "the victim vulnerable to, meaning unprotected from, further harassment." *Id.*

In short, a Title IX cause of action in the student-on-student-harassment context comprises both actionable sexual harassment and a deliberate indifference intentional tort. A school may be liable only if a plaintiff shows "an incident of actionable sexual harassment, the school's actual knowledge of it, some further incident of actionable sexual harassment, that the further actionable harassment would not have happened but for the objective unreasonableness (deliberate indifference) of the school's response, and that the Title IX injury is attributable to the post-actual-knowledge further harassment." *Id.* at 623-24.

Here, Jane Doe's deliberate indifference claim fails as a matter of law.[3] She argues that she adequately alleged harassment of a severe, pervasive, and objectively offensive nature because rape "constitutes a severe form of sexual harassment that can create a hostile educational environment." Appellant Br. at 18. She says that she notified UK of several post-rape interactions with John Doe and James Doe but UK failed to adequately alleviate her distress. Her essential argument then is that she adequately pleaded actionable harassment because she alleged rape in the pre-actual-knowledge period compounded by interactions with the accused students in the post-actual-knowledge period.

But allegations of rape in the pre-actual-knowledge period cannot alone show actionable sexual harassment. The relevant inquiry is whether UK's *response* to Jane Doe's accusations subjected her to *further* actionable sexual harassment. And Jane Doe has not pleaded any incident of actionable harassment in the post-actual-knowledge period. She does assert that John Doe stared at her, stood by her at a party, p.252 followed her home, and sat near her in the library. She similarly alleges that James Doe stared at her during their shared classes. Nothing about these allegations, however, suggest *sexual* harassment, let alone sexual harassment that is of a severe, pervasive, and objectively offensive nature.[4] *Cf. M.D. ex rel. DeWeese v. Bowling Green. Indep. Sch. Dist.,* 709 F. App'x 775, 778 (6th Cir. 2017) (finding no actionable sexual harassment when the student-victim said that in the post-actual-knowledge period she saw the perpetrator "in the hallway and at a handful of school events").

Even if the post-actual-knowledge interactions could amount to actionable harassment, Jane Doe failed to show that UK's response was clearly unreasonable and that it caused the further harassment. UK met with Jane Doe upon learning of the alleged rapes and took "proactive steps to reduce opportunities for further harassment" by issuing no-contact orders. *See Stiles ex rel. D.S. v. Grainger Cty.,* 819 F.3d 834, 849 (6th Cir. 2016). When Jane Doe reported that the no-contact orders were violated, UK immediately investigated. And UK "promptly and thoroughly" investigated the alleged rapes by reviewing documentary evidence, questioning the accuser and the accused, and interviewing other student-witnesses. *See id.* After determining that insufficient evidence existed to proceed to a sexual misconduct hearing, UK even acquiesced to Jane Doe's plea to conduct the hearing anyway. The record simply fails to establish that UK took "insufficient action," which made Jane Doe "vulnerable to, meaning unprotected from, further harassment." *See Kollaritsch,* 944 F.3d at 623.

Nor does UK's non-compliance with its own administrative policies amount to deliberate indifference. *Cf. Gebser v. Lago Vista Indep. Sch. Dist.,* 524 U.S. 274, 292, 118 S.Ct. 1989, 141 L.Ed.2d 277 (1998) (holding that "the failure to *promulgate* a grievance procedure does not itself constitute 'discrimination' under Title IX") (emphasis added). First, and most importantly, Jane Doe does not allege that UK's failure to follow the administrative policies caused her further harassment. Second, school administrators are not required to "engage in particular disciplinary action" and courts should not "second-guess[ ] the disciplinary decisions made by school administrators." *Davis,* 526 U.S. at 648, 119 S.Ct. 1661. Third, we have been quite clear that "if a public university has to choose between competing narratives to resolve a case, the university must give the accused student or his agent an opportunity to cross-examine the accuser and adverse witnesses in the presence of a neutral fact-finder." *See Doe v. Baum,* 903 F.3d 575, 578 (6th Cir. 2018). UK's Panel officer therefore reasonably determined that due p.253 process required the limited participation of John Doe's attorneys.

III.

Because Jane Doe did not plead any further actionable sexual harassment after UK took remedial action in the post-actual-knowledge period, she failed to state a Title IX deliberate indifference claim under *Davis*. She also failed to state material facts that would raise genuine disputes as to whether UK's response was objectively unreasonable or caused any further harassment. We therefore AFFIRM the district court's grant of summary judgment to UK.

[1] The parties and the district court have used the names "Jane Doe" for the plaintiff and "John Doe" and "James Doe" for the accused students. For consistency and ease of reference, we do likewise.

[2] This was two days after Jane Doe had requested and obtained the no-contact order against John Doe.

[3] Count 2 of Jane Doe's complaint alleges a violation of Title IX under a hostile environment theory. Hostile environment claims are distinct from deliberate indifference claims. *Doe v. Miami Univ.*, 882 F.3d 579, 589 (6th Cir. 2018). Jane Doe did not develop her hostile environment argument below and failed to raise the claim on appeal. She therefore forfeited the claim and we will not consider it. *See United States v. White*, 920 F.3d 1109, 1114 (6th Cir. 2019).

[4] In *Foster v. Board of Regents of University of Michigan*, 952 F.3d 765, 781 (6th Cir. 2020), *opinion vacated and reh'g granted by* No. 19-1314, 2020 WL 2510398 (6th Cir. May 15, 2020) (order), the panel held that in making the actionable-sexual-harassment determination, courts may consider "the full scope" of the accused's behavior—"meaning his harassment before and after" the school had actual notice. But that is not what we said in *Kollaritsch*. Rather, plaintiffs must show at least two incidents of actionable sexual harassment to satisfy the pervasive element. One incident may have occurred in the pre-actual-knowledge period; the other in the post-actual-knowledge period. But both incidents must be severe and objectively offensive. So, if a plaintiff alleges that the school's deliberate indifference caused her to suffer from further harassment, that further harassment must be both severe and objectively offensive. Hence, contrary to *Foster*, the Sixth Circuit requires "independent proofs" of severe and objectively offensive harassment "both before *and* after the school had actual knowledge." *See Foster*, 952 F.3d at 782.

947 F.3d 983 (2020)

Prianka BOSE, Plaintiff-Appellant,

v.

Roberto de la Salud BEA; Rhodes College, Defendants-Appellees.

No. 18-5936.

United States Court of Appeals, Sixth Circuit.

Argued: May 9, 2019.

Decided and Filed: January 28, 2020.

Bose v. Bea, 947 F. 3d 983 (6th Cir. 2020)

Appeal from the United States District Court for the Western District of Tennessee at Memphis. No. 2:16-cv-02308—John Thomas Fowlkes, Jr., District Judge.

ARGUED: Adam W. Hansen, APOLLO LAW LLC, Minneapolis, Minnesota, for Appellant. Lisa A. Krupicka, BURCH, PORTER & JOHNSON, PLLC, Memphis, Tennessee, for Appellees. ON BRIEF: Adam W. Hansen, Eleanor E. Frisch, APOLLO LAW LLC, Minneapolis, Minnesota, Bryce Ashby, DONATI LAW, PLLC, Memphis, Tennessee, for Appellant. Lisa A. Krupicka, Gary S. Peeples, Sarah E. Smith, BURCH, PORTER & JOHNSON, PLLC, Memphis, Tennessee, for Appellees.

Before: SILER, LARSEN, and NALBANDIAN, Circuit Judges.

OPINION

LARSEN, Circuit Judge.

Rhodes College expelled Prianka Bose after her organic chemistry professor, Dr. Roberto de la Salud Bea, accused her of cheating on tests and quizzes. Bose says that Bea fabricated these charges after she confronted Bea regarding inappropriate comments and questions Bea had posed to her. Bose brought numerous claims against both Rhodes and Bea, including a Title IX claim against Rhodes and a state law defamation claim against Bea. We agree with the district court that Bose's Title IX claim cannot succeed, but with respect to the defamation claim, we conclude that the district court erred by holding that Bea's statements were subject to absolute privilege under Tennessee law. Accordingly, we AFFIRM in part and REVERSE in part.

I.

We recite the facts in the light most favorable to Bose. Rhodes College is a liberal arts institution in Memphis, Tennessee that receives federal funds. In the fall of 2013, Bose enrolled as a freshman at Rhodes. During her sophomore year, she was accepted into the early selection program for George Washington University's medical school. The program guaranteed Bose admission, without taking the MCAT, if she met certain requirements, including maintaining a 3.6 GPA and receiving at least a B- in required science courses.

In the spring semester of her sophomore year, Bose successfully completed Bea's course, Organic Chemistry I. The following summer, Bea approached Bose in a parking lot on campus, where the two struck up a conversation. After exchanging pleasantries, Bea began asking more personal questions: he asked Bose how she liked to spend her evenings and free time, whether she spent time with friends, and whether she spent time with her boyfriend. As he asked her questions, Bea moved closer to Bose, who eventually stepped backward to create space between them. Bose, who had never mentioned having a boyfriend to Bea, said she had to leave. Bea then asked her whether she would like to have dinner and catch up. Bose later testified that she believed Bea was asking her out on a date, which made her uncomfortable. Bose declined the dinner invitation and left.

Bose took Bea's Organic Chemistry II class the following fall semester as she had planned. Throughout the term, Bea called Bose "pretty" or "beautiful" and would compliment her clothing. During this same p.986 semester, Bose took a corresponding lab course with a different professor. Bea regularly visited the lab, starting conversations with Bose and offering to help her; he did not give the same attention to other students. Once, Bea called Bose to his office after class and asked her whether she would like to be his research assistant; Bose said she would think about it. Bea then asked Bose if she liked to party on campus. When Bose left, Bea followed her and said he would walk her wherever she needed to go. Although Bose said that was not necessary, Bea walked her out anyway.

Throughout the semester, Bea gave all of his students the option to take tests and quizzes early. Bose often used this option. She would arrive at Bea's office around 7:30 or 7:45 a.m.; Bea would give her the test and leave shortly before 8:00 a.m. to teach another class. When he left, Bea would leave his laptop running without logging off, which meant the laptop could be accessed without his password.

In early November 2015, Bose took a quiz in Bea's office. Bose testified that Bea was in the office with her nearly the entire time she took the quiz, leaving only momentarily to collect class evaluations. Bea testified that when he returned to his office, he noticed that the answer key was open on his laptop in a larger view or "zoom" level than he typically uses. Bea explained that he then began to suspect Bose was cheating.

On November 19, 2015, Bose was sitting with a friend in the school cafeteria when Bea approached. Bea leaned over Bose's shoulder and asked sternly whether she was texting her boyfriend. Bose did not answer; Bea smiled and walked away. Later that same day, Bose and her friend approached Bea. Bea seemed happy to see Bose, but that changed when Bose confronted him, saying: "[L]ook, Dr. Bea, I don't know if you mean it this way, but I feel really uncomfortable when you ask me questions about my boyfriend, when you ask me anything about my family, I don't want personal questions, I want to keep our relationship strictly professional." Bea said nothing, looked at the ground, and walked away.

An Organic Chemistry exam was scheduled for the next day (Exam 3). Bose, who woke with a cough and fever, asked to take the exam in Bea's office to avoid disturbing the other students. Bea printed out the exam and tossed it on the desk without saying anything to Bose, which was out of character for him. Bea also logged out of his laptop before leaving the office.

When Bea returned, he found his office door shut, which caused it to lock automatically, though the door was usually left ajar when a student took a test in the office. Bea used his key to open the door and found Bose standing beside his desk. Bose testified that she had risen to open the door when she heard Bea trying to come in. Bea asked Bose whether she needed scratch paper; she said no, and Bea left. Distracted by maintenance noise near Bea's office, Bose finished the exam with the rest of the class. Bose scored 74 points out of 100, approximately 20 points lower than her score on any other quiz or test in Organic Chemistry II, but Bea recorded her score as 47.

The next week, Bose attempted to ask Bea about some practice problems before class began, but he refused to respond to her; when he eventually acknowledged her, he just shrugged his shoulders. Bose had regularly asked for help with practice problems in the past, and Bea had never refused to respond. Feeling uneasy with his changed behavior, Bose went to Bea's office after class; but Bea was again unresponsive. Eventually, Bose broke the silence by relaying her impression that Bea had seemed disinterested in teaching or p.987 helping her since she had spoken to him about the cafeteria incident. Bea still said nothing, so Bose left.

Around this time, Bea told a colleague that he suspected a student of cheating. The colleague advised Bea to create a fake answer key and stay logged in on his computer to see whether the student used it. Bea testified that he took this advice, creating a document entitled "Answer Key," with credible, though incorrect, answers to an upcoming quiz (Quiz 5). Shortly thereafter, Bose took Quiz 5 in Bea's office. Her answers matched the fake answer key precisely. Later that day, Bea emailed several administrators and accused Bose of cheating and of changing her grades in his grade roster. Bose would later deny these claims, maintaining that Bea must have matched his "fake answer key" to her actual answers, rather than the other way around.

Rhodes College Proceedings. Student academic conduct at Rhodes is governed by an Honor Code, administered by students elected to serve on an Honor Council. Two days after Bose took Quiz 5, the Honor Council president emailed Bose to tell her she was under investigation for cheating "on multiple assignments in Organic Chemistry II." After an investigation and hearing, the Honor Council determined that Bose had violated the Honor Code. Among other things, the Honor Council "found clear and convincing evidence that [Bose] had stolen answers, most convincingly on Quiz 5, from Dr. Bea's computer and used them to cheat." Because of the "nature and severity" of the underlying offense, as well as what the Council deemed Bose's "egregious lies" during the hearing, the Honor Council voted to expel her.

Bose appealed her expulsion to the Faculty Appeals Committee. The Appeals Committee upheld the Honor Council's finding but remanded for reconsideration of the penalty, in light of new evidence in the form of tests and quizzes that Bose had previously lost.[1] On remand, the Honor Council upheld Bose's expulsion.

In February 2016, Bose filed an internal Title IX complaint alleging sexual harassment by Bea. A Title IX investigator determined that the allegations of sexual harassment could not be sustained.

The Lawsuit. In May 2016, Bose filed this lawsuit against Rhodes and Bea. Against Rhodes she alleged, among other claims, breach of contract for failing to investigate pursuant to Rhodes' Title IX handbook, and retaliation in violation of Title IX, 20 U.S.C. §§ 1681-88. Against Bea she alleged, among other claims, defamation under Tennessee law for Bea's statements that Bose had violated the Honor Code.

Rhodes and Bea filed a motion to dismiss. Bea argued that his accusations of cheating and the documentary evidence submitted to the Honor Council were made as part of "quasi-judicial proceedings" and were therefore subject to an absolute privilege under Tennessee defamation law. The district court agreed and dismissed the defamation claim against Bea. But the district court allowed the Title IX and breach of contract claims to proceed to discovery.

After discovery, Rhodes moved for summary judgment on the breach of contract and Title IX claims. The court denied the motion on the breach of contract claim. p.988 The court granted summary judgment to Rhodes on the Title IX claim, however. Bose's Title IX theory was that Bea had reported her to the Honor Council in retaliation for her opposing his advances. But Title IX does not provide for individual liability; only "a recipient of federal funds may be liable in damages under Title IX" and "only for its own misconduct." *Davis v. Monroe Cty. Bd. of Educ.,* 526 U.S. 629, 640, 119 S.Ct. 1661, 143 L.Ed.2d 839 (1999); *see also Soper v. Hoben,* 195 F.3d 845, 854 (6th Cir. 1999). Accordingly, Bose asked the court to impute Bea's retaliatory motive to Rhodes using a "cat's paw" theory of causation, which links the discriminatory motive of one actor to the adverse action of another.[2] The district court declined to do so, reasoning that the cat's paw theory depends on principles of respondeat superior and constructive notice that do not apply to Title IX claims. Bose later voluntarily dismissed her breach of contract claim with prejudice. She appeals only the district court's decisions dismissing her Title IX and defamation claims.

II.

We first address the district court's grant of summary judgment to Rhodes on Bose's Title IX claim. We review de novo, viewing the facts in the light most favorable to the non-moving party. *Hunt v. Sycamore Cmty. Sch. Dist. Bd. of Educ.,* 542 F.3d 529, 532, 534 (6th Cir. 2008).

A.

Title IX provides: "No person in the United States shall, on the basis of sex, be excluded from participation in, be denied the benefits of, or be subjected to discrimination under any education program or activity receiving federal financial assistance." 20 U.S.C. § 1681(a). Though the statute contains no express private right of action, the Supreme Court has held that individuals may sue funding recipients for violating Title IX. *See Cannon v. Univ. of Chi.,* 441 U.S. 677, 717, 99 S.Ct. 1946, 60 L.Ed.2d 560 (1979); *Franklin v. Gwinnett Cty. Pub. Schs.,* 503 U.S. 60, 76, 112 S.Ct. 1028, 117 L.Ed.2d 208 (1992). And the Court has held that this implied right of action includes retaliation claims, explaining that "when a funding recipient retaliates against a person *because* he complains of sex discrimination, this constitutes intentional 'discrimination' 'on the basis of sex,' in violation of Title IX." *Jackson v. Birmingham Bd. of Educ.*, 544 U.S. 167, 174, 125 S.Ct. 1497, 161 L.Ed.2d 361 (2005).

The Supreme Court's decision in *Jackson* did not spell out the elements of a Title IX retaliation claim, and no published case in this circuit has decided the question. In unpublished authority, however, we have analogized to Title VII retaliation claims, stating that a Title IX plaintiff must show "that (1) [s]he engaged in protected activity, (2) [the funding recipient] knew of the protected activity, (3) [s]he suffered an adverse school-related action, and (4) a causal connection exists between the protected activity and the adverse action." *Gordon v. Traverse City Area Pub. Schs.*, 686 F. App'x 315, 320 (6th Cir. 2017). Our sister circuits apply similar tests. *See, e.g., Emeldi v. Univ. of Or.*, 698 F.3d 715, 724 (9th Cir. 2012); *Papelino v. Albany Coll. of Pharmacy of Union Univ.*, 633 F.3d 81, 89 (2d Cir. 2011); *Frazier v.* p.989 *Fairhaven Sch. Comm.*, 276 F.3d 52, 67 (1st Cir. 2002). And the parties have litigated this case under that framework, which we apply here.

In this case, Bose cannot make out the fourth element—causation. Bose's theory is that after she opposed Bea's unwelcome attention by confronting him in the cafeteria and asking him to "keep things professional,"[3] he retaliated by taking her to the Honor Council on false allegations of cheating. But there is no individual liability under Title IX, so Bose cannot use Title IX to sue Bea directly for his alleged retaliatory act. *See Soper,* 195 F.3d at 854. Moreover, the "adverse school-related action" she alleges is her expulsion, and Rhodes itself did that, not Bea. Yet there is no evidence that Rhodes itself (or the Honor Council or the Faculty Advisory Committee) harbored any discriminatory motive against Bose. To draw the required connection between Bose's opposition to Bea's unwelcome conduct and Rhodes' act of expelling her, Bose seeks to impute Bea's retaliatory motive to Rhodes using a cat's paw theory.

We have explained the cat's paw theory this way:

> "[T]he term 'cat's-paw' refers to 'one used by another to accomplish his purposes.' In the employment discrimination context, 'cat's paw' refers to a situation in which a biased subordinate, who lacks decisionmaking power, uses the formal decisionmaker as a dupe in a deliberate scheme to trigger a discriminatory employment action." *EEOC v. BCI Coca-Cola Bottling Co. of Los Angeles,* 450 F.3d 476, 484 (10th Cir. 2006) (citations omitted). A plaintiff alleging liability under the cat's paw theory seeks "to hold his employer liable for the animus of a supervisor who was not charged with making the ultimate employment decision." *Staub v. Proctor Hosp.,* 562 U.S. 411, 415, 131 S.Ct. 1186, 179 L.Ed.2d 144 (2011).

Marshall v. The Rawlings Co., 854 F.3d 368, 377 (6th Cir. 2017) (alteration in original). This court has applied the cat's paw theory to a variety of claims, including a Family Medical Leave Act discrimination claim, a Title VII race discrimination claim, and an Age Discrimination in Employment Act claim. *See id.* (collecting cases). Our question today is whether the cat's paw theory can apply in Title IX cases. We hold that it cannot.

Our conclusion follows from the Supreme Court's decision in *Gebser v. Lago Vista Independent School District,* 524 U.S. 274, 118 S.Ct. 1989, 141 L.Ed.2d 277 (1998). In *Gebser,* the Court considered whether a school district could be held liable under Title

IX for failing to stop a teacher's sexual harassment of a high school student. *Id.* at 277, 118 S.Ct. 1989. Though the school had been unaware of the harassment, Gebser argued that Title IX imposed liability on the school under either a respondeat superior or constructive notice theory. *Id.* at 282, 118 S.Ct. 1989. The Court disagreed, concluding that p.990 Title IX imposed liability only for a funding recipient's "own official decision[s]" and not "for its employees' independent actions." *Id.* at 290-91, 118 S.Ct. 1989. Accordingly, the Court held, "a damages remedy will not lie under Title IX unless an official who at a minimum has the authority to address the alleged discrimination and to institute corrective measures on the recipient's behalf has actual knowledge of discrimination" and responds with "deliberate indifference." *Id.* at 290, 118 S.Ct. 1989.

The Court gave several reasons for its holding. First, it noted that while "agency principles guide the liability inquiry under Title VII," that conclusion derives from Title VII's text, which "explicitly defines" a liable "'employer' to include 'any agent.'" *Id.* at 283, 118 S.Ct. 1989 (quoting 42 U.S.C. § 2000e(b)). By contrast, "Title IX contains no comparable reference to an educational institution's 'agents,' and so does not expressly call for application of agency principles." *Id.* Moreover, the Court concluded, "[I]t would frustrate the purposes of Title IX to permit a damages recovery against a school district ... based on principles of respondeat superior or constructive notice." *Id.* at 285, 118 S.Ct. 1989 (emphasis and quotation marks omitted).

The Court noted that, under Title IX's express means of enforcement, through administrative action, "an agency may not initiate enforcement proceedings until it 'has advised the appropriate person or persons of the failure to comply with the requirement and has determined that compliance cannot be secured by voluntary means.'" *Id.* at 288, 118 S.Ct. 1989 (quoting 20 U.S.C. § 1682). The Court concluded that "[i]t would be unsound ... for a statute's *express* system of enforcement to require notice to the recipient and an opportunity to come into voluntary compliance while a judicially *implied* system of enforcement permits substantial liability without regard to the recipient's knowledge or its corrective actions upon receiving notice." *Id.* at 289, 118 S.Ct. 1989. "Congress," the Court held, "did not envision a recipient's liability in damages in that situation." *Id.* at 287-88, 118 S.Ct. 1989.

Cases since *Gebser* have reinforced its message: a "recipient of federal funds may be liable in damages under Title IX only for its own misconduct." *Davis,* 526 U.S. at 640, 119 S.Ct. 1661. Accordingly, it is inappropriate to use "agency principles to impute liability to [a school] for the misconduct of its teachers," *id.* at 642, 119 S.Ct. 1661; liability instead requires that the institution itself be "deliberately indifferent to known acts of ... discrimination," *id.* at 643, 119 S.Ct. 1661. *See also Jackson,* 544 U.S. at 181, 125 S.Ct. 1497 ("Title IX's enforcement scheme also depends on individual reporting because individuals and agencies may not bring suit under the statute unless the recipient has received 'actual notice' of the discrimination." (quoting *Gebser,* 524 U.S. at 288, 118 S.Ct. 1989)). Cat's paw liability, therefore, has no place in Title IX actions.

Under a cat's paw theory, the decisionmaker need not have notice of the subordinate's discriminatory purpose. The cat's paw theory, rather, imputes knowledge and discriminatory intent—the cat's paw is the "unwitting tool" of those with the retaliatory motive. *Seoane-Vazquez v. Ohio State Univ.,* 577 F. App'x 418, 427

(6th Cir. 2014); *see also Henderson v. Chrysler Grp., LLC,* 610 F. App'x 488, 496 (6th Cir. 2015); *Shazor v. Prof. Transit Mgmt., Ltd.,* 744 F.3d 948, 955-56 (6th Cir. 2014) (explaining that a cat's paw theory requires proof only that the subordinates intended to cause the discriminatory employment action and that those actions proximately p.991 caused the ultimate action). Indeed, we have referred to cat's paw as an application of "agency principles," *Marshall,* 854 F.3d at 378; *see also Voltz v. Erie County,* 617 F. App'x 417, 423 (6th Cir. 2015), and have even called it the "rubber-stamp" theory. *Bishop v. Ohio Dep't of Rehab. and Corr.,* 529 F. App'x 685, 696 (6th Cir. 2013); *see also Goodsite v. Norfolk S. Ry. Co.,* 573 F. App'x 572, 586 (6th Cir. 2014). Cat's paw liability does not require either actual notice to the funding recipient or any "official decision" by it; to hold a cat's paw theory applicable to Title IX claims then would be inconsistent with the Supreme Court's decisions in *Gebser, Davis,* and *Jackson. See also M.D. ex rel. Deweese v. Bowling Green Ind. Sch. Dist.,* 709 F. App'x 775, 779 (6th Cir. 2017) (recognizing that a plaintiff raising a Title IX retaliation claim cannot use agency principles to impute liability to a funding recipient for the misconduct of its employees).

Bose suggests that the cat's paw theory does not require the application of respondeat superior principles. Rather, says Bose, "the cat's paw theory is a doctrine of causation; it simply draws a causal link between the discriminatory animus of one individual and the adverse action of another." According to Bose, cat's paw does not impute liability; it is merely a "conduit theory." *See Christian v. Wal-Mart Stores, Inc.,* 252 F.3d 862, 878 (6th Cir. 2001). We fail to see the distinction. The Supreme Court in *Gebser* held that an educational institution is responsible under Title IX only for its "own official decision[s]." 524 U.S. at 290-91, 118 S.Ct. 1989. Bose argues that she seeks to hold Rhodes liable for its own decision—expelling her. But that decision only violated Title IX if it was made "on the basis of sex"—that is, if the decision was taken for a discriminatory reason. Bose has no evidence of any discriminatory motive on Rhodes' part; she, therefore, asks us to hold Rhodes responsible for *Bea's* retaliatory animus. But that would be to hold Rhodes liable "for its employees' independent actions"—precisely what *Gebser* forbids.[4]

Bose asks us to follow the Second Circuit's decision in *Papelino v. Albany College of Pharmacy of Union University,* 633 F.3d 81 (2d Cir. 2011), which she reads as applying a cat's paw theory to a Title IX retaliation claim. There, a college's Honor Code Panel expelled Papelino after concluding that he had cheated on an exam. *Id.* at 87. Papelino claimed that a professor had initiated the Honor Code proceedings in retaliation for his having reported the professor's sexual harassment to the College's Associate Dean for Student Affairs, Albert White. Papelino brought a Title IX retaliation suit against the College. *Id.* at 88. The Second Circuit allowed the retaliation claim to proceed to trial. *Id.* at 92.

p.992 Some aspects of the Second Circuit's decision can indeed be read as invoking a cat's paw theory, though the court never uses the term. The court concluded, for example, that, "even if the [Honor Code] Panel members were themselves unaware that Papelino had engaged in protected activity," a reasonable jury could find that "they were acting on [the professor's] explicit encouragement, or that they acted without information that White should have imparted to them." *Id.* at 92-93. Read this way, the Second Circuit may have seen the Honor Code Panel as the cat's paw, unwittingly manipulated by the retaliatory animus of either the professor or Dean

White, or both. To the extent *Papelino* embraces the cat's paw theory of causation for Title IX claims, we find it inconsistent with *Gebser, Davis,* and *Jackson* and decline to follow it.

Yet other aspects of *Papelino* suggest a different theory of Title IX liability—that the College was on notice of, and was deliberately indifferent to, the professor's retaliation. There, the student had reported his professor's sexual harassment to Dean White.[5] The court considered this act of reporting to be both the "protected activity," and evidence that the College knew that Papelino had engaged in protected activity. *Id.* at 92. There was also evidence that the Dean had informed the professor of Papelino's complaint against her and that the Dean knew that the professor had initiated the Honor Code proceedings against Papelino shortly after she learned of Papelino's complaint. Yet despite the fact that Dean White was "a high-ranking member of the College's administration who was 'responsible for the administration of the Student Code,'" *id.* at 89, he "did nothing even after the cheating charges were lodged against Papelino," *id.* at 92; *see also id.* at 93 (suggesting that Dean White—perhaps because of his supervisory role with respect to the Honor Code—had a duty to "impart[ ]" his knowledge of the professor's retaliatory act to the Honor Code panel). Read this way, it was the College's *own* behavior—its deliberate indifference to the professor's known retaliatory act—that subjected the College to Title IX liability in *Papelino*.

In her reply brief on appeal, Bose attempts to raise a similar theory: that Rhodes had actual notice of Bea's retaliation against her for opposing his unwanted advances but was deliberately indifferent to it. According to Bose, she told the Honor Council in her closing statement about possible retaliation by Bea and repeated her claim to the Faculty Appeals Committee and the Title IX investigator; yet none took any action. But if she ever previously presented such a theory of Title IX liability in this litigation, she has since abandoned it.

In its motion for summary judgment, Rhodes asked the district court to dismiss Bose's Title IX claim in full. In response, Bose raised the cat's paw theory of liability but made no mention of any deliberate indifference by Rhodes to Bea's retaliation. In its reply, Rhodes stated that Bose had abandoned any deliberate indifference claim she might have pled. The district court's order dismissing Bose's Title IX claim in full did discuss, and dismiss, p.993 Bose's claim that Rhodes had been deliberately indifferent to Bea's *sexual harassment;* Bose did not appeal that decision. The district court did not, however, discuss any theory whereby Rhodes would be liable for its own deliberate indifference to Bea's *retaliation*. With respect to the retaliation claim, the district court discussed the cat's paw theory, which it rejected.[6] If Bose believed she had an out-standing theory of Title IX liability that the district court had failed to consider, then would have been the time to raise it, given that the district court had just dismissed her Title IX claim in full. Yet, Bose did not file a motion for reconsideration, alerting the district court that it had failed to consider an alternate theory of liability. Nor did she make any mention of a deliberate-indifference-to-retaliation theory in her opening brief in this court; her opening brief advanced only the cat's paw theory. Only after Rhodes again noted, in its responsive brief on appeal, that Bose had "forfeited" any deliberate indifference claim did Bose make any attempt to develop the theory that Rhodes should be held liable for its own deliberate indifference to Bea's retaliation. That was too late. And even then, at oral argument,

Bose's counsel seemed to retreat, arguing that the cat's paw theory is "the only theory of causation there could be in this case." We conclude, therefore, that Bose has forfeited any argument that Rhodes had actual notice of Bea's retaliation but was deliberately indifferent to it. *See Am. Trim, LLC v Oracle Corp.*, 383 F.3d 462, 477 (6th Cir. 2004) ("This argument was raised for the first time in [appellant's] reply brief, and this court has consistently held that we will not consider such arguments."); *Coach Servs., Inc. v. Source II, Inc.*, 728 F. App'x 416, 417-18 (6th Cir. 2018) (finding that the defendants forfeited arguments where they failed to raise them both in response to a motion for summary judgment and in their motion for reconsideration of the district court's summary judgment ruling).

We do not speculate whether the out-come would have been different had Bose pursued a theory that Rhodes was deliberately indifferent to Bea's known retaliation. But had Bose pursued such a theory in the district court, we imagine that a number of questions would have been joined. For example: was the Honor Council, the Faculty Advisory Committee, or the Title IX investigator an "appropriate person" to notify, within the meaning of Title IX? *See Gebser*, 524 U.S. at 289, 118 S.Ct. 1989. Assuming so, did Bose adequately inform those entities of the alleged retaliation? And, if so, was Rhodes' response "clearly unreasonable" in light of what Rhodes knew? *Williams ex rel Hart v. Paint Valley Local Sch. Dist.*, 400 F.3d 360, 367-68 (6th Cir. 2005). And, for that matter, is deliberate indifference to retaliation even actionable under Title IX? *See M.D. ex rel. Deweese*, 709 F. App'x at 779 ("M.D. has failed to cite any authority applying the ... deliberate indifference framework to a Title IX retaliation claim."); *but see Feminist Majority Found. v. Hurley*, 911 F.3d 674, 695 (4th Cir. 2018) ("[W]e are satisfied that an educational institution can be liable for acting with deliberate indifference toward known instances of student-on-student retaliatory harassment."). Bose's failure to advance a deliberate-indifference-to-retaliation theory below deprives us of the ability to review these questions on appeal.

p.994 Throughout this litigation, Bose chose to argue that the cat's paw theory applies to Title IX claims. We conclude that it does not. The cat's paw theory, which imputes the discriminatory animus of another to the funding recipient, is inconsistent with Title IX principles requiring that a funding recipient be held liable "only for its own misconduct." *Davis*, 526 U.S. at 640, 119 S.Ct. 1661. As a result, we affirm the district court's order granting summary judgment to Rhodes on the Title IX claim.

III.

We next turn to the district court's dismissal of Bose's defamation claim for failure to state a claim. We review such decisions de novo, accepting all factual allegations as true and construing the complaint in the light most favorable to the plaintiff. *Stein v. Regions Morgan Keegan Select High Income Fund, Inc.*, 821 F.3d 780, 785 (6th Cir. 2016).

The district court granted Bea's Rule 12(b)(6) motion on the ground that Bea's statements were absolutely privileged under Tennessee defamation law because they were made in a quasi-judicial proceeding. We cannot agree. Tennessee does recognize an absolute privilege for statements made in quasi-judicial proceedings. *See Lambdin Funeral Serv. Inc. v. Griffith*, 559 S.W.2d 791, 792 (Tenn. 1978); *Logan's Super Mkts., Inc. v. McCalla*, 208 Tenn. 68, 343 S.W.2d 892, 894-95 (1961). But the Tennessee cases have applied this privilege only to statements made before public bodies. In *Evans v.*

Nashville Banner Public Co., for example, the court clarified that Tennessee had expanded the quasi-judicial absolute privilege to "proceedings conducted by *state* departments and agencies." No. 87-164-II, 1988 WL 105718, at *3 (Tenn. Ct. App. Oct. 12, 1988) (emphasis added). And in *Jones v. Trice,* the Tennessee Supreme Court approvingly cited the English rule, which specified that the absolute privilege is "limited to legislative and judicial proceedings *and other acts of state.*" 210 Tenn. 535, 360 S.W.2d 48, 51 (1962) (emphasis added).

The rationale underlying the Tennessee decisions supports limiting this privilege to statements made to public entities. Time and again, the Tennessee courts have emphasized that a benefit to the public is what drives the privilege. In *Independent Life Insurance Co. v. Rodgers,* 165 Tenn. 447, 55 S.W.2d 767 (1933), the Tennessee Supreme Court concluded that statements made in a letter to the state insurance commissioner were absolutely privileged as part of a quasi-judicial license revocation proceeding. *Id.* at 768. According to the Court, the insurance commissioner had been clothed by statute "with attributes similar to those of a court"; the statute had thereby made "of him a court to determine this matter of revocation." *Id.* at 769. The Court recognized that "absolute privilege... has been extended to many inquiries that are not conducted before courts of justice or courts of record," including "to statements made in a court martial; to statements made in an extradition proceeding before the Governor; to proceedings before the interstate commerce commission; to affidavits for a search warrant made before a justice of the peace; to preliminary statements of a witness made to counsel before trial; and ... to statements made upon the hearing of applications for pardon to the Governor." *Id.* (internal citations omitted). Common to all these proceedings is that they were public.

In *Lambdin,* the Tennessee Supreme Court extended an absolute privilege to statements made to the Tennessee Board of Funeral Directors and Embalmers, which concerned "the occupation for which [the plaintiffs] had been licensed by the Board." 559 S.W.2d at 792. As in *Rodgers,* p.995 the Court in *Lambdin* emphasized that the basis of this privilege was public need. *Id.* And in *Evans,* the Tennessee Court of Appeals emphasized the benefit of free dialogue in statements before zoning boards. 1988 WL 105718 at *4. The court explained that "[t]he policy underlying the privilege is to encourage the public to speak freely at public, governmental hearings," as "[l]ocal boards of zoning appeals take actions which affect not only homes and neighborhoods but also the quality of people's lives" and "[w]hen these boards hold hearings, all interested persons should feel free to express their views without fear of a recriminating lawsuit." *Id.*

A common theme emerges from the cases in which Tennessee has recognized an absolute privilege—a strong benefit to the public, often tied to a statute or to powers which the Tennessee legislature had specifically granted to the tribunal at issue. *See id.; see also Rodgers,* 55 S.W.2d at 770 ("The design of [the statute at issue] will be obstructed if those instituting or participating in proceedings to bring about the revocation of the license of an unworthy agent may be subjected by reason of their statements to a suit for libel or a suit for slander."); *Logan's Super Mkts., Inc.,* 343 S.W.2d at 894 ("The privilege belongs to the public, not to the individual, and the public should not stand to lose the benefit it derives....").

Bea cannot point to a similar *public* benefit to Rhodes' disciplinary proceedings. While Bea claims that the public has an interest in a college's academic misconduct proceedings, and that private colleges have an interest in encouraging faculty members and students to report allegations of academic misconduct, whether a student is disciplined by a private college does not affect the citizens of the state in the same fashion as, for example, revoking a business's publicly conferred license, passing zoning laws, or drafting legislation in response to public testimony.

Bea discusses at length the procedural safeguards required in an Honor Council proceeding, but we see nothing in the Tennessee cases that would suggest that procedural safeguards alone are enough to cloak participants in a private proceeding with an absolute privilege under Tennessee law. Bea refers us to *Brundage v. Cumberland County*, 357 S.W.3d 361, 370 (Tenn. 2011), in which the Tennessee Supreme Court declared that "[t]he application of pre-defined standards, the requirement of a hearing, and the requirement of a record are earmarks of quasi-judicial proceedings." But the proceedings at issue in *Brundage* were plainly public— "a local legislative body's land use decision." *Id.* at 363. Moreover, the question in *Brundage* had nothing to do with whether an absolute privilege applied to statements made in such proceedings. *Brundage* instead concerned the standards for seeking judicial review of such decisions under a particular Tennessee statute. *Id.* at 371. Along the way, the Court noted that the proceedings at issue were a "hybrid" between "essentially 'legislative'" and "'quasi-judicial' decisions," and discussed the characteristics of each. *Id.* at 370. But as the question there concerned the procedures for obtaining judicial review of plainly *public* proceedings, and did not concern the availability of an absolute privilege in *any* kind of proceeding, we cannot find in *Brundage* any indication that Tennessee would extend its absolute privilege beyond the realm of public proceedings where it has previously resided.

Finally, Bea notes that in *Myers v. Pickering Firm, Inc.*, 959 S.W.2d 152, 161 (Tenn. Ct. App. 1997), the Tennessee Court of Appeals said that "our Supreme Court [has] strongly endorsed a liberal p.996 application of the absolute privilege accorded to publication of defamatory matters in connection with judicial proceedings." But the key word there is "judicial." In *Myers,* the court discussed whether an expert report made "in anticipation of" the defendant's role as an expert witness in state court litigation was absolutely privileged. *Id.* The court repeated the policy underlying absolute privilege for statements made in a *judicial* proceeding:

> Underlying this general doctrine of absolute immunity from liability in libel and slander for statements made in the course of a judicial proceeding is a policy decision by the courts that access to the judicial process, freedom to institute an action, or defend, or participate therein without fear of the burden of being sued for defamation is so vital and necessary to the integrity of our judicial system that it must be made paramount to the right of an individual to a legal remedy where he has been wronged thereby.

Id. (quoting *Jones,* 360 S.W.2d at 51). Thus, "liberal application" means only that courts should liberally apply the absolute privilege when a statement is connected to a judicial or quasi-judicial proceeding, not that courts should be generous in deciding what proceedings fit that definition.

To our knowledge, Tennessee has never cloaked defamatory statements made to private entities with an absolute privilege, and we see in the Tennessee cases no indication that its rationale for maintaining the privilege would compel an extension. Of course, the Tennessee legislature or the Tennessee courts might, in the future, choose another path. But "[o]ur respect for the role of the state courts as the principal expositors of state law counsels restraint by the federal court in announcing new state-law principles." *Angelotta v. Am. Broad. Corp.,* 820 F.2d 806, 809 (6th Cir. 1987). We conclude that Bea has failed to show that Tennessee would provide absolute immunity to statements made in Rhodes' Honor Council proceedings.[7] Accordingly, we reverse the district court's decision dismissing Bose's defamation claim on this ground.

* * *

We AFFIRM the district court's grant of summary judgment as to Bose's Title IX claim but REVERSE and REMAND regarding Bose's defamation claim.

[1] Bea had testified before the Honor Council that Bose had received a 47 on Exam 3 (though Bose actually received a 74). Bose could not dispute this, as she had lost the graded exam in an airport. Sometime after the hearing, the person who had found her exam mailed it back to her.

[2] According to the Supreme Court, "[t]he term 'cat's paw' derives from a fable conceived by Aesop.... In the fable, a monkey induces a cat by flattery to extract roasting chestnuts from the fire. After the cat has done so, burning its paws in the process, the monkey makes off with the chestnuts and leaves the cat with nothing." *Staub v. Proctor Hosp.,* 562 U.S. 411, 415 n.1, 131 S.Ct. 1186, 179 L.Ed.2d 144 (2011).

[3] In the Title VII context, we have held that under that statute's "opposition clause," 42 U.S.C. § 2000e-3(a), an employee's "demand that a supervisor cease his/her harassing conduct constitutes protected activity covered by Title VII." *EEOC v. New Breed Logistics,* 783 F.3d 1057, 1067 (6th Cir. 2015). Noting that "the language of the opposition clause does not specify to whom protected activity must be directed," we rejected the suggestion that "communication directed solely to a harassing supervisor does not constitute protected activity." *Id.* at 1068 (noting disagreement with *Frank v. Harris County,* 118 F. App'x 799, 804 (5th Cir. 2004)). The parties have not questioned whether this view of protected activity also applies to claims brought under Title IX, and we express no position on that question here.

[4] Bose argues that this court has permitted liability under a cat's paw theory for claims brought under 42 U.S.C. § 1983, despite the fact that respondeat superior liability does not apply to such claims. Although Bose offers two cases in support, neither case held, in a binding, considered opinion, that the cat's paw theory applies to § 1983 claims. In *DeNoma v. Hamilton County Court of Common Pleas,* 626 F. App'x 101 (6th Cir. 2015), a panel of this court applied a cat's paw theory to the plaintiff's § 1983 claim. The opinion, however, is unpublished, and it does not appear that the court had occasion to consider whether a cat's paw theory was appropriate for § 1983 claims, given that the lower court and the parties had proceeded as if it were. *See id.* at 105. Likewise, in *Arendale v. City of Memphis,* 519 F.3d 587 (6th Cir. 2008), this court seemed to assume the applicability of the cat's paw theory to § 1983 claims. *See id.* at 604 n.13. But the court resolved the case on other grounds—that the plaintiff "has

not demonstrated that he was treated differently than similarly situated non-white employees." *Id.* at 604.

[5] The court, in another part of the opinion, expressed its view that reporting to the Dean satisfied *Gebser*'s requirement that notice be given to an "appropriate person"—"a school official with 'authority to address the alleged discrimination and to institute corrective measures.'" *Papelino,* 633 F.3d at 89; *see also id.* (finding that Papelino's complaint to Dean White put the College on "actual notice" of the harassment because "White was a high-ranking member of the College's administration who was 'responsible for the administration of the Student Code'").

[6] The district court also rejected Bose's argument that the court was bound by its causation ruling at the preliminary injunction stage, correctly noting that "the findings of a district court in the context of a preliminary injunction do not bind th[e] court in subsequent proceedings."

[7] Bea argues, for the first time on appeal, that Bose's defamation claim fails because she cannot show publication, an element of defamation under Tennessee law. But because the defamation claim was dismissed at the Rule 12(b)(6) stage, it was never subject to discovery. Counsel for Bea admitted at argument that publication is a fact-specific issue, and there has been little factual development of this claim. We decline to address this issue for the first time on appeal.

944 F.3d 613 (2019)

Emily KOLLARITSCH, et al., Plaintiffs-Appellees,

v.

MICHIGAN STATE UNIVERSITY BOARD OF TRUSTEES; Denise Maybank, in her individual and official capacity as Vice President for Student Affairs, Defendants-Appellants.

Nos. 17-2445/18-1715.

United States Court of Appeals, Sixth Circuit.

Argued: March 20, 2019.

Decided and Filed: December 12, 2019.

Appeal from the United States District Court. for the Western District of Michigan at Grand Rapids. No. 1:15-cv-01191—Paul Lewis Maloney, District Judge.

ARGUED: Michael E. Baughman, PEPPER HAMILTON LLP, Philadelphia, Pennsylvania, for Appellants. Alexander S. Zalkin, THE ZALKIN LAW FIRM, P.C., San Diego, California, for Appellees. ON BRIEF: Michael E. Baughman, Hedya Aryani, PEPPER HAMILTON LLP, Philadelphia, Pennsylvania, for Appellants. Alexander S. Zalkin, THE ZALKIN LAW FIRM, P.C., San Diego, California, for Appellees. Seanna R. Brown, BAKER & HOSTETLER LLP, New York, New York, for Amicus Curiae.

Before: BATCHELDER, ROGERS, and THAPAR, Circuit Judges.

BATCHELDER, Circuit Judge, delivered the opinion of the court in which THAPAR, Circuit Judge, joined, and ROGERS, Circuit Judge, joined in part. THAPAR, Circuit Judge (pp. 627-30), delivered a separate concurring opinion. ROGERS, Circuit Judge, (pg. 630), delivered a separate opinion concurring in part and in the result.

OPINION

ALICE M. BATCHELDER, Circuit Judge.

A victim of "student-on-student sexual harassment" has a private cause of action against the school under Title IX of the Education Amendments of 1972 (Title IX), 86 Stat. 373, codified as 20 U.S.C. § 1681, *et seq.*, based on the formula first set out in *Davis v. Monroe County Board of Education*, 526 U.S. 629, 119 S.Ct. 1661, 143 L.Ed.2d 839 (1999). Under that formula, the sexual harassment must meet a certain standard and the evidence must satisfy the elements for an intentional tort. Our particular focus in this appeal is on the requirements that the harassment must be "pervasive" and the school's response must "cause" the injury. In short, we hold that a student-victim plaintiff must plead, and ultimately prove, that the school had actual knowledge of actionable sexual harassment and that the school's deliberate indifference to it resulted in further actionable sexual harassment against the student-victim, which caused the Title IX injuries. A student-victim's subjective dissatisfaction with the school's response is immaterial to whether the school's response caused the claimed Title IX violation. Because none of the plaintiffs in this case suffered any actionable sexual harassment *after* the school's response, they did not suffer "pervasive" sexual harassment as set out in *Davis* and they cannot meet the causation element. We also find that the individual defendant is entitled to qualified immunity. Altogether, we REVERSE the district court's order and REMAND for entry of a final judgment dismissing these claims.

I.

This lawsuit stems from four student-on-student sexual assaults at Michigan State University. In each case, a male student sexually assaulted a female student and she reported it to campus police and to the proper administrative authorities, which undertook a response beginning with an investigation. The plaintiffs are the female student victims: Emily Kollaritsch, Shayna Gross, Jane Roe 1, and Jane Roe 2. But this lawsuit is not about the sexual assaults, nor is it directed at the perpetrators; it is directed at the University administration and its response. The plaintiffs contend that the administration's response was inadequate, caused them physical and emotional harm, and consequently denied them educational opportunities. They sued the Michigan State University Board of Trustees (hereinafter "MSU") and Vice President for Student Affairs Denise Maybank, among several others, claiming violations of Title IX, Due Process and Equal Protection under 42 U.S.C. § 1983, and Michigan law.

The defendants moved to dismiss the claims pursuant to Federal Rule of Civil Procedure 12(b)(6). Following a hearing and the plaintiffs' withdrawal of several claims, the district court dismissed all but four claims: the claims by Kollaritsch, Gross, and Roe 1 that MSU violated Title IX, and the § 1983 claim by Gross that Maybank violated her right to equal protection. *See Kollaritsch v. Mich. State Univ. Bd. of Tr.*, 298 F. Supp. 3d 1089, 1096 (W.D. Mich. 2017).

Maybank filed an interlocutory appeal of the district court's denial of her assertion of qualified immunity. *See Mitchell v. Forsyth*, 472 U.S. 511, 530, 105 S.Ct. 2806, 86 L.Ed.2d 411 (1985) (providing a defendant the right to an interlocutory appeal of the "denial of a claim of qualified immunity, to the extent that it turns on an issue of law"). Meanwhile, MSU moved the district court to certify its order for interlocutory appeal pursuant to 28 U.S.C. § 1292(b) (providing for interlocutory appeal of qualifying issues at the courts' discretion) and, upon certification, moved this court to permit the appeal. We granted the motion, explaining that "whether a plaintiff must plead further acts of discrimination to allege deliberate indifference to peer-on-peer harassment under Title IX" is a controlling question of law warranting immediate appeal. We consolidated the appeals.

From a procedural posture, a § 1292(b) interlocutory appeal such as this one is unusual in that it arises from a denial rather than a grant of a Rule 12(b)(6) motion to dismiss the complaint, so "we are not governed by the Rule 12(b)(6) standard of review" for granted motions. *Foster Wheeler Energy Corp. v. Metro. Knox Solid Waste Auth., Inc.*, 970 F.2d 199, 202 (6th Cir. 1992). This is a review "limited to pure questions of law." *Id.*; *but see Yamaha Motor Corp., U.S.A. v. Calhoun*, 516 U.S. 199, 205, 116 S.Ct. 619, 133 L.Ed.2d 578 (1996) (explaining that we are not limited to only the specifically certified *question* but may "address any issue fairly included within the certified order"). We do not make any determination of any facts, even by implication; the analyses and decisions herein leave all questions of fact unresolved and all allegations still merely alleged. *See Sheet Metal Emp'rs Indus. v. Absolut Balancing Co.,* 830 F.3d 358, 361 (6th Cir. 2016). This same limitation applies to the facts accepted as true for purposes of our deciding the qualified-immunity claim.

II.

By design and effect, the *Davis* Court's Title IX private cause of action against a school for its response to student-on-student sexual harassment is a "high standard" that applies only "in certain limited circumstances." *Davis,* 526 U.S. at 643, 119 S.Ct. 1661. The school is "properly held liable in damages only where [it is] deliberately indifferent to sexual harassment, of which [it] has actual knowledge, that is so severe, pervasive, and objectively offensive that it can be said to deprive the victims of access to the educational opportunities or benefits provided by the school." *Id.* at 650, 119 S.Ct. 1661.

Ordinarily, we state the *Davis* standard as a three-element test and ordinarily that is enough.[1] But, even without the careful parsing that follows, the *Davis* formula clearly has two separate components, comprising separate-but-related torts by separate-and-*un*related tortfeasors: (1) "actionable harassment" by a student, p.620 *id.* at 651-52, 119 S.Ct. 1661; and (2) a deliberate-indifference intentional tort by the school, *id.* at 643, 119 S.Ct. 1661. The critical point here is that the *Davis* formulation requires that the school had actual knowledge of some actionable sexual harassment and that the school's deliberate indifference to it resulted in further actionable harassment of the student-victim.

Actionable Sexual Harassment. We can conservatively describe "harassment," without additional qualification, as some type of aggressive and antagonistic behavior that, from the victim's perspective, is uninvited, unwanted, and non-consensual. For student-on-student sexual harassment to be *actionable* under *Davis*'s Title IX private-cause-of-action formulation, it must be (a) severe, (a) pervasive, and (c) objectively offensive. *Id.* at 651, 119 S.Ct. 1661; *see, e.g., Pahssen v. Merrill Cmty. Sch. Dist.,* 668 F.3d 356, 363 (6th Cir. 2012) (holding that harassment comprising a shove into a locker, an "obscene sexual gesture," and a "request for oral sex" did "not rise to the level of severe, pervasive, and objectively offensive conduct" (quotation marks omitted)).

"Severe" means something more than just juvenile behavior among students, even behavior that is antagonistic, non-consensual, and crass. The *Davis* Court made an explicit admonishment that "simple acts of teasing and name-calling" are not enough, "even where these comments target differences in gender." *Davis,* 526 U.S. at 651, 119 S.Ct. 1661; 652 ("It is not enough to show ... that a student has been teased or called offensive names." (quotation marks and editorial marks omitted)).[2]

"Pervasive" means "systemic" or "widespread," *id.* at 652-53, 119 S.Ct. 1661, but for our purposes, it also means *multiple* incidents of harassment; one incident of harassment is not enough. *Id.* (explaining that this cause of action does not cover "claims of official indifference to a single instance of one-on-one peer harassment"). The *Davis* Court hypothesized that a single incident could be sufficiently *severe* that it would result in the articulated injury —and we do not doubt that a sexual assault would be such a severe incident— but the Court held that a single incident would nonetheless fall short of Title IX's requirement of "systemic" harassment. As the Court put it:

> Although, in theory, a single instance of sufficiently severe one-on-one peer harassment *could be said to have such an effect, we think it unlikely* that Congress would have thought such behavior sufficient to rise to this level in light of the inevitability of student misconduct and the amount of litigation that would be invited by entertaining claims of official indifference to a single instance of one-on-one peer harassment. By limiting private damages actions to cases having a *systemic effect* on educational programs or activities, we reconcile the general principle that Title IX prohibits official indifference to known peer sexual harassment with the practical realities of responding to student behavior, realities that Congress could not have meant to be ignored.

Id. at 652-53, 119 S.Ct. 1661 (emphasis added). The *Davis* dissent offered its view of this passage, which the majority did not dispute: "The majority appears to intend [the pervasiveness] requirement to do no more than exclude the possibility that a single act of harassment perpetrated by one student on one other student can form the basis for an actionable claim." *Id.* at 677, 119 S.Ct. 1661 (Kennedy, J., dissenting). That a single incident is insufficient on its own to state a claim correspondingly adds further support to the requirement that at least one more (*further*) incident of harassment, after the school has actual knowledge and implements a response, is necessary to state a claim.[3]

"Objectively offensive" means behavior that would be offensive to a reasonable person under the circumstances, not merely offensive to the victim, personally or subjectively. *Id.* at 651, 119 S.Ct. 1661. "Whether gender-oriented conduct rises to the level of actionable harassment thus depends on a constellation of surrounding circumstances, expectations, and relationships, including, but not limited to, the ages of the harasser and the victim and the number of individuals involved." *Id.* (quotation marks omitted). The victim's perceptions are not determinative. "Indeed, the [*Davis* majority] ... suggests that the 'objective offensiveness' of a comment is to be judged by reference to a reasonable child at whom the comments were aimed." *Id.* at 678, 119 S.Ct. 1661 (Kennedy, J., dissenting).

Deliberate Indifference Intentional Tort. Even upon establishing actionable student-on-student harassment, a plaintiff must also plead and prove four elements of a deliberate-indifference-based intentional tort: (1) knowledge, (2) an act, (3) injury, and (4) causation.

"Knowledge" means that the defendant school had "actual knowledge" of an incident of actionable sexual harassment that prompted or should have prompted a response. *Id.* at 650, 642, 119 S.Ct. 1661 (rejecting an imputed-knowledge standard under agency principles or a should-have-known standard based in negligence); *see McCoy v. Bd. of Educ.*, 515 F. App'x 387, 392 (6th Cir. 2013) ("[T]here is a connection between what school officials know and whether their response is clearly unreasonable."). Ordinarily, "deliberate indifference" means that the defendant both knew and consciously disregarded the known risk to the victim. *See Bd. of Cty. Comm'rs v. Brown*, 520 U.S. 397, 410, 117 S.Ct. 1382, 137 L.Ed.2d 626 (1997).

An "Act" means a response by the school that was "clearly unreasonable in light of the known circumstances," *Davis,* 526 U.S. at 648, 119 S.Ct. 1661, thus demonstrating the school's deliberate indifference to the foreseeable possibility of *further* actionable harassment of the victim. *Id.* at 643, 119 S.Ct. 1661 ("Deliberate indifference makes sense as a theory of direct liability under Title IX only where the [school] has some control over the alleged harassment ... [and] authority to take remedial action."); *but see id.* at 667, 119 S.Ct. 1661 (Kennedy, J., dissenting) ("Yet the majority's holding would appear to apply with equal force to universities, which do not exercise custodial and tutelary power over their adult students."). Because the further harassment must be p.622 inflicted against the same victim, the plaintiff "cannot ... premise the [further harassment] element of her Title IX claim on conduct [by the perpetrator] directed at third parties." *Pahssen,* 668 F.3d at 363; *see also Patterson v. Hudson Area Sch.,* 551 F.3d 438, 452 (6th Cir. 2009) (Vinson, J., dissenting) ("Obviously, the school district is not responsible for failing to stop harassment of which it was not made aware, nor can it be held responsible for failing to punish harassment by unknown individuals.").

"Injury" in this Title IX context means the deprivation of "access to the educational opportunities or benefits provided by the school," *Davis,* 526 U.S. at 650, 119 S.Ct. 1661, which the fifth-grade victim in *Davis* described as her inability "to concentrate on her studies" (causing her grades to deteriorate), her fear of attending school (telling her mother "at one point ... that she didn't know how much longer she could keep [the perpetrator] off her"), and eventually a suicide note, *id.* at 634, 119 S.Ct. 1661 (quotation marks, editorial marks, and citations omitted). *See also Vance v. Spencer Cty. Pub. Sch. Dist.,* 231 F.3d 253, 259 (6th Cir. 2000) (describing the victim's injuries as her having to "complet[e] her studies at home" and her deteriorating grades due to her being "diagnosed with depression"). Emotional harm standing alone is not a redressable Title IX injury.

"Causation" means the "Act" caused the "Injury," such that the injury is attributable to the post-actual-knowledge *further* harassment, which would not have happened but for the clear unreasonableness of the school's response. *Davis,* 526 U.S. at 644, 119 S.Ct. 1661. Importantly, *Davis* does not link the deliberate indifference directly to the injury (i.e., it does *not* speak of subjecting students to *injury*); *Davis* requires a showing that the school's "deliberate indifference 'subject[ed]' its students to *harassment,*" necessarily meaning further actionable harassment. *Id.* (emphasis added); *see also Thompson v. Ohio State Univ.,* 639 F. App'x 333, 343-44 (6th Cir. 2016) (relying on further harassment in finding that "Thompson did not raise any further harassment or discrimination with OSU's HR office, nor did OSU have any other reason to believe that its efforts to remediate were ineffective or disproportionate" (quotation and editorial marks omitted)). But the occurrence of further harassment is not enough by itself; the response's *unreasonableness* must have caused the further harassment. *Stiles ex rel. D.S. v. Grainger Cty.,* 819 F.3d 834, 851 (6th Cir. 2016) ("Although the school's efforts did not end [the victim's] problems, Title IX does not require school districts to eliminate peer harassment."). The school's response must be clearly unreasonable *and* lead to further harassment. But the critical point is that the response must bring about or fail to protect against the further harassment, which the Court stated as: "[T]he deliberate indifference must, at a minimum, cause students to undergo harassment or make them liable or vulnerable to it." *Davis,* 526 U.S. at 645, 119 S.Ct. 1661 (quotation marks, editorial marks, and citations omitted).

The plaintiffs contend that the isolated phrase *make them vulnerable* means that post-actual-knowledge *further* harassment is not necessary—that vulnerability alone is its own causal connection between the Act and the Injury. They point to *Davis*'s causation statement that "the deliberate indifference must, at a minimum, [1] cause students to undergo harassment *or* [2] make them liable or vulnerable to it," *id.* (emphasis added), from which they argue: this statement poses two alternatives (cause *or* make vulnerable); the first (cause) clearly requires some further harassment; therefore, the second must *not* require further harassment or else it would be redundant and surplusage. But this logical argument is predicated on a faulty unstated premise: that the two alternatives are necessarily between further harassment and no further harassment. That is a misreading of *Davis* as a whole and the causation element in particular. *See* Zachary Cormier, *Is Vulnerability Enough? Analyzing the Jurisdictional Divide on the Requirement for Post-Notice Harassment in Title IX Litigation*, 29 Yale J.L. & Feminism 1, 23 (2017) (concluding from a "natural reading" of *Davis* that, "[r]ather than beginning an entirely separate idea, the vulnerability component completes the idea that began within the causation component").

A plain and correct reading of that two-part causation statement, *Davis,* 526 U.S. at 645, 119 S.Ct. 1661, particularly when read in conformity with the overall opinion, reveals that the two alternatives are actually two possible ways that the school's "clearly unreasonable" response could lead to further harassment: that response might (1) be a detrimental action, thus fomenting or instigating further harassment, or it might (2) be an insufficient action (or no action at all), thus making the victim vulnerable to, meaning unprotected from, further harassment. Stated in a more articulate way:

> The *Davis* Court described wrongful conduct of both *commission* (directly causing further harassment) and *omission* (creating vulnerability that leads to further harassment). The definition presumes that post-notice harassment *has* taken place; vulnerability is simply an alternative pathway to liability for harassment, not a freestanding alternative ground for liability. In sum, the vulnerability component of the ... 'subjected' definition was not an attempt at creating broad liability for damages for the *possibility* of harassment, but rather an effort to ensure that a student who experiences post-notice harassment may obtain damages regardless of whether the harassment resulted from the institution *placing* the student in a position to experience that harassment or *leaving* the student vulnerable to it.

Cormier, 29 Yale J.L. & Feminism at 23-24. We find this explanation persuasive.

The plaintiffs cite several cases that rely on their same misreading of *Davis* to support that same inapt logical argument. But none of those cases is controlling. And, because we find none of them persuasive, we decline to address them specifically or discuss them here.

Finally, the plaintiffs argue that a Title IX student-on-student cause of action cannot require *further* harassment because, they contend, a single, sufficiently severe sexual assault is enough to state a viable action. But that too is a misreading of *Davis,* as was explained, *supra,* in the analysis of the "pervasive" element, which quoted and relied on *Davis,* 526 U.S. at 652-53, 119 S.Ct. 1661. A single assault— particularly before any notice or response —does not state a claim under *Davis.*

A Title IX private cause of action against a school for deliberate indifference to student-on-student sexual harassment comprises the two components of actionable sexual harassment by a student and a deliberate-indifference intentional tort by the school, along with the underlying elements for each. We hold that the plaintiff must plead, and ultimately prove, an incident of actionable sexual harassment, the school's actual knowledge of it, some further incident of actionable sexual harassment, that the further actionable harassment would not have happened but for the objective unreasonableness (deliberate indifference) p.624 of the school's response, and that the Title IX injury is attributable to the post-actual-knowledge further harassment.

III.

In a § 1292(b) interlocutory appeal, we decide "pure questions of law," *Foster Wheeler,* 970 F.2d at 202, regarding "any issue fairly included within the certified order," *Yamaha Motor Corp.,* 516 U.S. at 205, 116 S.Ct. 619. The next question in this appeal is whether the perpetrators' behavior after the school's response, as pleaded in the Complaint, satisfies the causation element, *supra,* or whether that post-response behavior could not, as a matter of law, satisfy the standard for *actionable* sexual harassment and, consequently, could not satisfy the causation element.

In January 2012, Emily Kollaritsch reported to MSU that a male student had sexually assaulted her, which triggered MSU's response. MSU completed an investigation in August 2012 and disciplined the perpetrator in November 2012 by placing him on probation and forbidding him any contact with Kollaritsch. But Kollaritsch subsequently encountered him at least nine times—she says that he "stalked, harassed and/or intimidated" her at least nine times. Kollaritsch also says that when she filed a formal "retaliation complaint" in March 2013, the MSU administrator said "there was a difference between retaliation and just seeing [him,] and consistently suggested that Kollaritsch needed mental health services." MSU nonetheless conducted an investigation, which determined that no retaliation had occurred.

Kollaritsch has not pleaded further actionable sexual harassment. She did not provide any details or assert any facts about these encounters to show—or even suggest—that they were sexual, or that they were severe, pervasive, or objectively unreasonable. In describing her encounters in the Complaint, she suggested that these were merely their mutual presence at the same location:

> [The perpetrator] and Kollaritsch lived in the same dormitory and frequented the same cafeteria and public areas around the dormitory. Kollaritsch actually encountered [him] on multiple occasions, subsequent to filing her official report. On more than one instance, Kollaritsch encountered [him] at a dormitory cafeteria. On each of these occasions, Kollaritsch experienced a panic attack, and was forced to leave the building, often crying, lightheaded, and significantly distraught.

Kollaritsch characterized the nine encounters as "stalking, harassing, and intimidating," but those conclusory statements, without supporting facts, are meaningless. In the Complaint, Kollaritsch expressed her indignation at the MSU administrator for discounting the encounters as nothing more than her "just seeing him," but she did not provide any rebuttal that would describe the encounters as something more (i.e., something sexual, severe, pervasive, or objectively offensive).[4] *See Gordon v. Traverse City Area Pub. Sch.*, 686 F. App'x 315, 325 (6th Cir. 2017) (because plaintiffs "offer no details on the nature of this additional harassment, when it occurred, or how [defendant] responded," "these missing pieces doom [their] case").

p.625 We hold as a matter of law that Kollaritsch's allegations, as stated in her Complaint, do not plead actionable further sexual harassment and, therefore, she has not pleaded and cannot show causation necessary to state a viable deliberate-indifference claim under Title IX and *Davis*.

In February 2014, Shayna Gross reported to MSU that a male student had sexually assaulted her, which triggered MSU's response. MSU completed an investigation in October 2014, finding sexual assault, and disciplined the perpetrator in January 2015 by expelling him from the university. MSU denied his first appeal, but his second appeal led to a new investigation by an outside law firm, which found no sexual assault, and MSU presumably reinstated him. At no point after the initiation of MSU's response did that male student have any contact with or commit any *further* harassment of Gross. In the Complaint, Gross said only that she "could have encountered him at any time" due to his "mere presence ... on campus." Gross did not plead any facts that would show any post-response encounter, much less any further sexual harassment that was actionable.

We hold as a matter of law that Gross's allegations, as stated in her Complaint, do not plead actionable further sexual harassment and, therefore, she has not pleaded and cannot show causation necessary to state a viable deliberate-indifference claim under Title IX and *Davis*.

In February 2014, Jane Roe 1 reported to MSU that a male student had sexually assaulted her, which triggered MSU's response. MSU completed an investigation in November 2014, declining to find sexual assault due to insufficient evidence. At no point after the initiation of MSU's response did the male student have any contact with or commit any further harassment of Roe 1; in fact, he withdrew from the university in April 2014. There is no indication that he ever returned. In her Complaint, Roe 1 said that the male student "could return to campus without [her] knowledge," and that his "mere presence... on campus, after [she] made her report to MSU ... created a hostile environment for [her] and made her vulnerable to further harassment." She did not plead any facts that would show any post-response encounter, much less any further sexual harassment that was actionable.

We hold as a matter of law that Roe 1's allegations, as stated in her Complaint, do not plead actionable further sexual harassment and, therefore, she has not pleaded and cannot show causation necessary to state a viable deliberate-indifference claim under Title IX and *Davis*.

IV.

When Shayna Gross reported that a male student had sexually assaulted her, MSU undertook an investigation that found sexual assault and it ordered the male student expelled from the University. The male student appealed and MSU denied his first appeal, but when he appealed again, Denise Maybank, MSU's Vice President for Student Affairs, set aside the previous findings and ordered that a new investigation be conducted by an outside law firm, which found no sexual assault. Gross claimed that Maybank's response was deliberately indifferent and violated her clearly established right to equal protection, making Maybank liable to Gross under § 1983. Maybank moved to dismiss the claim, asserting qualified immunity, but the district court denied the motion, holding that Gross had stated an "equal protection right to be free from student-on-student discrimination" that was "well-established." *Kollaritsch,* 298 F. Supp. 3d at 1109 (quotation marks and citation omitted). Although the Complaint was not so specific, the district court reasonably determined that the claim centered on Maybank's decision to set aside the initial investigation's finding of sexual assault and order a new investigation by outside counsel. *Id.* at 1107.[5] The district court did not elaborate further on the specifics, but emphasized that, "[a]t least in the [C]omplaint, no explanation for this decision is provided," and declared the decision "unreasonable under the circumstances as a response to Gross's allegation of a sexual assault." *Id.*

Qualified immunity shields government officials from standing trial for civil liability in their performance of discretionary functions, unless their actions violate clearly established rights. *Cahoo v. SAS Analytics Inc.,* 912 F.3d 887, 897 (6th Cir. 2019). To survive a motion to dismiss based on qualified immunity, the complaint must allege facts that, if proven to be true, would show the violation of a right so clearly established that a reasonable official would necessarily have recognized the violation. *Id.* at 898. "[D]amage claims against government officials arising from alleged violations of constitutional rights must allege, with particularity, facts that demonstrate what each defendant did to violate the asserted constitutional right." *Id.* at 899. The Supreme Court has been emphatic and explicit in what it means by "clearly established":

> [T]he legal principle [must] clearly prohibit the offic[ial]'s conduct in the particular circumstances before him. The rule's contours must be so well defined that it is clear to a reasonable offic[ial] that his conduct was unlawful in the situation he confronted. This requires a high degree of specificity.... [C]ourts must not define clearly established law at a high level of generality, since doing so avoids the crucial question [of] whether the official acted reasonably in the particular circumstances that he or she faced. A rule is too general if the unlawfulness of the offic[ial]'s conduct does not follow immediately from the conclusion that the rule was firmly established.

District of Columbia v. Wesby, 583 U.S. ___, 138 S. Ct. 577, 590, 199 L.Ed.2d 453 (2018) (quotation marks, editorial marks, and citations omitted). And, as we have said, "[t]here does not need to be a case directly on point, but existing precedent must have placed the constitutional question beyond debate." *Cahoo,* 912 F.3d at 898 (quotation marks, editorial marks, and citation omitted).

Gross claims that Maybank's decision to set aside the initial investigation's finding of sexual assault (and the initial order of expulsion) and, without explanation or citation to authority, order a new investigation by outside counsel, violated her clearly established equal-protection right to be free from student-on-student discrimination. Gross cites two cases for support, *Shively v. Green Local School District Board of Education,* 579 F. App'x 348, 358 (6th Cir. 2014), and *Doe v. Forest Hills School District,* No. 1:13-cv-428, 2015 WL 9906260, at *14 (W.D. Mich. Mar. 31, 2015), but neither case addresses with a "high degree of specificity" anything like Maybank's act of setting aside one investigation in favor of another without explanation or apparent authority, much less under these "particular circumstances," as is required by *Wesby,* 138 S. Ct. at 590.

p.627 Moreover, Gross's theory fundamentally contradicts *Davis,* 526 U.S. at 648, 119 S.Ct. 1661. *Davis* explained that "[s]chool administrators will continue to enjoy the flexibility they require" in conducting investigations and imposing discipline, and "courts should refrain from second-guessing the disciplinary decisions made by school administrators." *Id.* at 648, 119 S.Ct. 1661 (citation omitted). Particularly prescient here is the *Davis* dissent's comment that "[o]ne student's demand for a quick response to her harassment complaint will conflict with the alleged harasser's demand for due process," putting the school in a position where it is "beset with litigation from every side." *Id.* at 682, 119 S.Ct. 1661 (Kennedy, J., dissenting). Such were Maybank's "particular circumstances," as she was caught between Gross's demand for judgment and punishment on one side and the accused male student's appeal for additional due process on the other. *See also M.D. v. Bowling Green Indep. Sch. Dist.,* 709 F. App'x 775, 777 (6th Cir. 2017) ("Often, school administrators face the unenviable task of balancing victims' understandable anxiety with their attackers' rehabilitation.").

Gross is clearly dissatisfied with Maybank's decision to overturn the male student's punishment (expulsion), which also served as Gross's remedy.[6] But Gross has no "right" to her preferred remedy. *Davis* expressly denied the prospect "that administrators must engage in particular disciplinary action," and stressed that the victim does *not* "have a Title IX right to make particular remedial demands." *Id.* at 648, 119 S.Ct. 1661; *see also Stiles,* 819 F.3d at 848; *M.D.,* 709 F. App'x at 777. Gross claimed a right to be free from student-on-student discrimination and predicated the alleged violation of that right on her belief that Maybank's decision about the punishment (her remedy) was deliberately indifferent. But Gross has pointed us to no legal principle or precedent that clearly prohibits Maybank's otherwise discretionary decision under these "particular circumstances." *See Wesby,* 138 S. Ct. at 590. Gross has not claimed a violation of any other right.

The Complaint does not allege facts showing that Maybank violated Gross's clearly established constitutional right to equal protection. Maybank is entitled to qualified immunity.

V.

For the foregoing reasons, we REVERSE the district court's order denying the defendants' motion to dismiss the Complaint and REMAND for entry of judgment dismissing these claims.

THAPAR, Circuit Judge, concurring.

CONCURRENCE

I join the majority opinion in full. But since the question here has divided our sister circuits, I write separately to explain why.

To begin with, I should emphasize that the allegations in this case are troubling. The plaintiffs allege facts suggesting that Michigan State University seriously mismanaged its Title IX process. And that matters to everyone involved—the victims, the accused, their families and friends, and the broader University community. Everyone has an interest in a timely, fair, and transparent process for resolving claims of sexual assault. So long as we expect universities to adjudicate such claims, we should expect them to do better.

p.628 But this case is not about whether the University mismanaged its Title IX process. Rather, the question here is whether Michigan State University "subjected" the plaintiffs to "discrimination" (as those terms are used in Title IX). To answer that question, the parties agree, we should look to the Supreme Court's decision in *Davis v. Monroe County Board of Education*, 526 U.S. 629, 119 S.Ct. 1661, 143 L.Ed.2d 839 (1999). There, the Court decided that a school may be held liable for "student-on-student harassment" only if the school "acts with deliberate indifference to known acts of harassment in its programs or activities" and that harassment is "severe, pervasive, and objectively offensive." *Id.* at 633, 119 S.Ct. 1661. The parties also agree that *Davis* established a causation requirement. The Court made clear that a school "may not be liable for damages unless its deliberate indifference 'subjects' its students to harassment." *Id.* at 644, 119 S.Ct. 1661 (alteration adopted). Yet the parties—as well as our sister circuits —disagree about what this requirement entails.

That confusion has arisen based on the Supreme Court's definition of the term "subjects." In *Davis*, the Court said that the school's deliberate indifference must "'cause students to undergo' harassment or 'make them liable or vulnerable' to it." *Id.* at 645, 119 S.Ct. 1661 (alteration adopted) (quoting *Random House Dictionary of the English Language* 1415 (1966); *Webster's Third New International Dictionary* 2275 (1961)). Some courts have read this language broadly. Students must allege only that the school's deliberate indifference made harassment more likely, not that it actually led to any harassment. *See, e.g., Farmer v. Kan. State Univ.*, 918 F.3d 1094, 1103-04 (10th Cir. 2019); *Fitzgerald v. Barnstable Sch. Comm.*, 504 F.3d 165, 172 (1st Cir. 2007), *rev'd on other grounds*, 555 U.S. 246, 129 S.Ct. 788, 172 L.Ed.2d 582 (2009). Other courts have read the language more narrowly. Students must allege that the school's deliberate indifference actually led to harassment, not that it only made such harassment more likely. *See, e.g., K.T. v. Culver-Stockton Coll.*, 865 F.3d 1054, 1057-58 (8th Cir. 2017); *Escue v. N. Okla. Coll.*, 450 F.3d 1146, 1155-56 (10th Cir. 2006); *Reese v. Jefferson Sch. Dist. No. 14J*, 208 F.3d 736, 740 (9th Cir. 2000).

Today, our circuit adopts the latter view, and I think rightly so. Under Title IX, schools can "subject" their students to harassment in two different ways. First, the school can "cause" the harassment directly. Imagine, for instance, that the school sent disparaging emails to just its female students. In that scenario, we would have no trouble saying that the school had "subjected" the students to harassment. After all, the school's conduct quite directly led to the harassment. Yet *Davis* also said that schools can "subject" their students to harassment in a second way: the school can make its students "vulnerable" to harassment. Take the facts of *Davis* itself. There, the school "subjected" a student to harassment because it failed to take any effort to prevent or end ongoing harassment by another student. *Davis,* 526 U.S. at 635, 654, 119 S.Ct. 1661. Unlike in the first scenario, the school's conduct did not directly cause the harassment. But still the Court concluded that the school had "effectively caused" the harassment. *Id.* at 642-43, 119 S.Ct. 1661 (cleaned up). And that's because the school's conduct indirectly led to the harassment: it left the student vulnerable to her harasser.

But in either scenario, we wouldn't say that the school had "subjected" its students to harassment if the students never experienced any harassment as a result of the school's conduct. To be "subjected" to a harm, as a matter of ordinary English, p.629 requires that you experience that harm. And that holds true whether someone directly causes the harm or simply makes you vulnerable to it.

That more precise reading also makes sense when you consider the specific statutory text. Under Title IX, "[n]o person in the United States shall, on the basis of sex... be *subjected to discrimination* under any education program or activity receiving [federal funding]." 20 U.S.C. § 1681(a) (emphasis added). If a person can be "subjected to harassment" without experiencing any harassment as a result of the defendant's conduct, then a person can also be "subjected to discrimination" without experiencing any discrimination as well. And that surely can't be right. The Supreme Court has long debated whether the phrase "subjected to discrimination" (used in various statutes) requires the plaintiff to prove a discriminatory intent. *See, e.g., Guardians Ass'n v. Civil Serv. Comm'n of City of New York,* 463 U.S. 582, 103 S.Ct. 3221, 77 L.Ed.2d 866 (1983). But no one has questioned whether the plaintiff must prove some discriminatory *effect*.

Consider also the statutory context. The phrase "subjected to discrimination" appears in a parallel list with the phrases "excluded from participation" and "denied the benefits." 20 U.S.C. § 1681(a). To "exclude" means to "shut out," "hinder the entrance of," or "expel." *Random House Dictionary of the English Language* 497 (1966); *Webster's Third New International Dictionary* 2275 (1961). So to be "excluded from participation" means that something blocked your participation—not just that something made it more likely that you wouldn't be able to participate. To "deny" (as relevant here) means "to withhold" or "refuse to grant." *Random House Dictionary of the English Language* 387 (1966); *Webster's Third New International Dictionary* 603 (1961). So to be "denied [] benefits" means that something held the benefits back—not just that something made it more likely that you wouldn't be able to receive them. This context reinforces the point. To be "subjected to discrimination" means that something led you to experience discrimination—not just that something made it more likely that you would face it.

And if you're still not convinced, two more points favor this reading. First, Congress enacted Title IX under the Spending Clause. *See Gebser v. Lago Vista Indep. Sch. Dist.,* 524 U.S. 274, 287, 118 S.Ct. 1989, 141 L.Ed.2d 277 (1998). In effect, Congress offered the states a deal: they would receive federal funding so long as they complied with the requirements of Title IX. But the states could not knowingly accept that offer if they didn't know its terms. So Congress had to identify any condition on its funding "unambiguously." *Pennhurst State Sch. & Hosp. v. Halderman,* 451 U.S. 1, 17, 101 S.Ct. 1531, 67 L.Ed.2d 694 (1981). And if it didn't, then the states may not be held liable for a violation. *See Gebser,* 524 U.S. at 287-88, 118 S.Ct. 1989.

So even if there were any ambiguity, that very ambiguity would require us to adopt the less expansive reading of Title IX.

Second, the opinion in *Davis* itself supports this reading. There, the Court went to great lengths to emphasize the narrowness of its decision. *See Davis,* 526 U.S. at 648-49, 652-53, 119 S.Ct. 1661. And it expressly warned against any "characterization" of its opinion that would "mislead courts to impose more sweeping liability" than Title IX requires. *Id.* at 652, 119 S.Ct. 1661. But some of our sister circuits have adopted just such a characterization. To hold schools liable for any act or omission that makes students "vulnerable to" harassment is to hold schools liable for a wide range of decisions. Could a university be held liable for reducing its Title IX staff p.630 as a result of budget cuts? What about for allowing a bar to open on campus? Or for expanding coed housing options? All these decisions could make students vulnerable to harassment. Yet surely Title IX does not make schools liable for these everyday decisions. In short, I would not read the term "subjects" so broadly as to erase the causation requirement enacted by Congress and confirmed by the Supreme Court.

Of course, all this does not resolve what should count as "discrimination" under Title IX. But the plaintiffs in this case premised their suit on student-on-student harassment. And *Davis* made clear that "discrimination" in such cases means "severe, pervasive, and objectively offensive" harassment—not just the risk of harassment. *Id.* at 650, 119 S.Ct. 1661. We have no authority to say otherwise.

For these reasons, the plaintiffs have failed to state a claim under Title IX. The plaintiffs have not adequately alleged that they experienced any harassment *after* Michigan State University had notice of their complaints. As a result, they cannot show that the University "subjected" them to harassment.

ROGERS, Circuit Judge, concurring.

CONCURRENCE

I join parts I, III, and IV of the majority opinion, and concur in the result. I agree with the analysis in support of our holding that a Title IX sexual harassment plaintiff must plead post-notice sexual harassment, and that mere vulnerability to sexual harassment after the school has actual notice is not enough.

There is no reason, however, for us to address what a plaintiff must show to establish the required actual notice. What constitutes actual notice in this case is not at issue, and in particular was not an issue discussed by the parties on appeal. The plaintiffs here all allege sufficiently severe sexual assault, plus reporting to MSU, to demonstrate that they meet the actual notice requirement under Title IX. Any statement by us that notice must, as one example, be notice of "actionable" sexual harassment is accordingly not necessary to our decision and, whether right or wrong, is usefully avoided and in any event not controlling on future panels.

Judge Leval, in his timeless 2005 Madison Lecture, tellingly criticized the tendency of judges "to promulgate law through utterance of dictum made to look like a holding—in disguise, so to speak. When we do so, we seek to exercise a lawmaking power that we do not rightfully possess." Pierre Leval, *Judging Under the Constitution: Dicta about Dicta,* 81 N.Y.U. L. Rev. 1249, 1250 (2006).

[1] *See, e.g., Gordon v. Traverse City Area Pub. Sch.,* 686 F. App'x 315, 323 (6th Cir. 2017); *Stiles ex rel. D.S. v. Grainger Cty.,* 819 F.3d 834, 848 (6th Cir. 2016); *Pahssen v. Merrill Cmty. Sch. Dist.,* 668 F.3d 356, 362 (6th Cir. 2012); *Patterson v. Hudson Area Sch.,* 551 F.3d 438, 444-45 (6th Cir. 2009); *Vance v. Spencer Cty. Pub. Sch. Dist.,* 231 F.3d 253, 258-59 (6th Cir. 2000); *Soper v. Hoben,* 195 F.3d 845, 854 (6th Cir. 1999).

[2] We do not imply that "severe" requires physical contact, or that *Davis* holds that it does. *See Davis,* 526 U.S. at 653, 119 S.Ct. 1661 (describing the harassment in that case). Obviously, verbal harassment can exceed teasing and name-calling, and the severity of harassment on social media is virtually boundless. But we have no such scenario in this case.

[3] In *Vance v. Spencer County Public School District,* 231 F.3d 253, 259 n.4 (6th Cir. 2000), we mistakenly opined that a single incident of sexual harassment could satisfy a Title IX claim. But the *Vance* plaintiff had presented several instances of severe and pervasive sexual harassment, *id.,* making the assertion dicta, so we are not bound by it. Regardless, *Davis* holds that a single incident cannot constitute pervasive harassment under Title IX.

[4] It is noteworthy that the plaintiffs' overall theory and argument is that *further* actionable harassment is not necessary, arguing in their appellate brief that "a victim need not suffer actual, subsequent harassment in order to state a claim[, but] [r]ather, a vulnerability to additional harassment ... is sufficient." That is an unnecessary theory if the facts and circumstances of these encounters *could* demonstrate actionable further sexual harassment.

[5] On appeal, Gross has described the violation as: "Maybank, without authority in the policies or procedures of MSU[,] nullified the prior investigation of [Gross's] assailant and voided his sanctions on an unsanctioned second appeal by the assailant." We can accept this description for our purposes.

[6] Gross is also dissatisfied with Maybank's decision to set aside the initial investigation's findings and order a new investigation to be conducted by an outside law firm, but Gross would have little, if any, genuine complaint if the new investigation had upheld the initial investigation and led Maybank to sustain the initial punishment.

882 F.3d 579 (2018)

John DOE, Plaintiff-Appellant,
v.
MIAMI UNIVERSITY; Steven Elliot; Rose Marie Ward; Alana Van Grundy-Yoder; Jayne Brownell; Susan Vaughn, Defendants-Appellees.

No. 17-3396.

United States Court of Appeals, Sixth Circuit.
Argued November 29, 2017.
Decided and Filed February 9, 2018.

Doe v. Miami University, 882 F. 3d 579 (6th Cir. 2018)

Appeal from the United States District Court for the Southern District of Ohio at Cincinnati. No. 1:15-cv-00605—Michael R. Barrett, District Judge.

ARGUED: Eric John Rosenberg, ROSENBERG & BALL CO. LPA, Granville, Ohio, for Appellant. Evan T. Priestle, TAFT STETTINIUS & HOLLISTER LLP, Cincinnati, Ohio, for Appellees. ON BRIEF: Eric John Rosenberg, ROSENBERG & BALL CO. LPA, Granville, Ohio, for Appellant. Evan T. Priestle, Doreen Canton, TAFT STETTINIUS & HOLLISTER LLP, Cincinnati, Ohio, for Appellees.

Before: GUY, MOORE, and ROGERS, Circuit Judges.

OPINION

KAREN NELSON MOORE, Circuit Judge.

In the fall of 2014, John Doe and Jane Doe[1] were students at Miami University, a public university located in Oxford, Ohio. The two students knew each other and had engaged in several consensual "physical encounters." This case arises from an incident between John and Jane on September 14, 2014. Both parties had consumed alcohol, and John states that he was so intoxicated that he cannot remember what occurred. According to Jane's statement, the two engaged in some consensual sexual acts, but at some point Jane stopped consenting and John continued to engage in then non-consensual sexual acts for some period of time before he stopped. This accusation of sexual misconduct was evaluated by Miami University, and John was found responsible for violating the school's sexual-assault policy. He was initially suspended for approximately eight months, but this suspension was reduced by the University on appeal to four months. After the University's appeals process affirmed the original finding of responsibility, John brought suit against Jane, Miami University, and individual University employees who had been part of the disciplinary process. John voluntarily dismissed his claims against Jane after the two parties reached a settlement. The other defendants moved to dismiss John's six remaining claims under Title IX and § 1983 pursuant to Federal Rule of Civil Procedure 12(b)(6), and the district court granted their motion.

On appeal, John argues that the district court erred in granting the defendants' motion to dismiss. We AFFIRM the district court's dismissal of John's Title IX hostile-environment claim, Title IX deliberate-indifference claim, and § 1983 substantive-due-process claim. Furthermore, we AFFIRM in part and REVERSE in part the district court's dismissal of John's p.585 § 1983 procedural-due-process and equal-protection claims and related finding of qualified immunity. We REVERSE the district court's holding that John did not sufficiently plead his Title IX erroneous-outcome claim. We REMAND for further proceedings consistent with this opinion.

I. BACKGROUND

On the evening of September 13, 2014, John and his roommate attended "a party where John Doe consumed approximately six beers."[2] R. 39 (Am. Compl. ¶ 22) (Page ID #1977). John then proceeded to "a bar and drank at least two more beers and four shots of alcohol before leaving the bar in the early morning hours of September 14, 2014." *Id.* At this point, John was sufficiently intoxicated that he cannot clearly remember what happened for the remainder of the night. *Id.* ¶¶ 22, 24 (Page ID #1977, 1978). Based on text messages he later found on his cellphone, John knows that he called Jane and "exchanged text messages with" her after he left the bar. *Id.* ¶ 23 (Page ID #1978).

John recalls Jane getting into his bed some time before dawn on September 14. *Id.* ¶ 24 (Page ID #1978). His next memory is when he awoke the morning of September 14. *Id.* Jane was upset that her cellphone was "ruined." *Id.* ¶ 25 (Page ID #1978). "Because John Doe believed that he had been the last person to handle Jane Doe's phone, John Doe offered to buy her a new one." *Id.* During their trip to the store, Jane told John that "she was uncomfortable that he began to perform oral sex on" her. *Id.* ¶ 26 (Page ID #1978). John apologized for whatever he may have done, but informed Jane that he could not remember anything about his interactions with her the prior night. *Id.* "After John Doe purchased a new phone for Jane Doe, she told him that she forgave him and still wanted to be friends." *Id.*

John attached to his complaint Jane's written statement about what occurred that night and stated that this is the only information he has about what happened besides his own incomplete recollection. *Id.* ¶ 6 (Page ID #1975); R. 39-2 (Pl. Ex. 1: Jane Doe Statement) (Page ID #2036-37). In her statement, Jane recalled that on the evening of September 13 she was out with a group of friends. R. 39-2 (Pl. Ex. 1: Jane Doe Statement at 1) (Page ID #2036). As she and her friends walked back home, she ran into John and his roommate, whom Jane had previously dated. *Id.* Jane described herself as a "little drunk." *Id.* Jane and one of her friends returned to John and his roommate's dorm room. *Id.* Once there, Jane's friend told her that she was going to sleep in Jane's room that evening. *Id.* John and his roommate then offered to let Jane stay in their room, and she accepted. *Id.* In her statement, Jane then describes a sexual encounter with John that transitioned between consensual and non-consensual acts:

> I had made out with [John] a couple of times before then, so I decided to stay with them, I had just kind of assumed we might make out again. I did not know [his roommate] was going to stay there. At the time I thought I gave [my friend] my ID to get into my dorm to stay there. And she left. At this point I was kinda sobered up and thought [John] and [his roommate] were too. So they gave me a change of clothes and told me to pick a bed. I picked [John's] bed, because I

thought that would be p.586 less weird. We got in bed and turned of [sic] the lights and we thought [the roommate] was asleep, [John] started kissing me and that was okay and what I expected and fine. He had asked me to do things before, and I had said no, and he had kept pressuring me to do things and I kept saying no, no, no. And he asked me again, if he could finger me and I said fine, because I was tired of him asking me. I am a virgin and Christian, and I don't do that. So he started doing that, and it was hurting. I said "[John] stop it is hurting." He said "Oh it will hurt at first, you will be fine in a couple of minutes." I said "Okay fine, whatever." It kept hurting and never got better. I kept saying stop and it hurts. [John] kept telling me to be quite [sic] because I would wake up [his roommate]. I finally got him to stop doing it, after telling him I pushed him away. We went back to kissing. He asked to eat me out. And I said no you are not doing that. We were kissing and then he just did it. I never said no. I pushed him away. He rolled over and went to sleep.

Id.

Jane discussed the incident with several of her friends. *Id.* at 2 (Page ID #2037); R. 39 (Am. Compl. ¶ 28) (Page ID #1979). One of her friends informed a Resident Advisor ("RA") that John had sexually assaulted Jane. R. 39 (Am. Compl. ¶ 28) (Page ID #1979). The RA informed her superiors at Miami about the alleged sexual assault and also expressed concern that John might harm himself because of the accusation. *Id.* ¶ 29 (Page ID #1979).

On September 16, 2014, Miami University's Associate Vice President and Dean of Students Michael Curme emailed John and informed him that the University had received a report that he had sexually assaulted another student two days before. R. 39-2 (Pl. Ex. 3: Summ. Hr'g Notification at 4) (Page ID #2042). Curme told John that he was required to attend a summary suspension hearing the following day. *Id.* Following that hearing, the University imposed several restrictions on John, including one that prohibited him from contacting Jane. R. 39 (Am. Compl. ¶ 31) (Page ID #1980); R. 39-2 (Pl. Ex. 4: Summ. Hr'g Dec. at 5) (Page ID #2047).

On or about September 19, 2014, Miami University's Emergency Case Manager Tim Parsons met with John to explain the disciplinary process at Miami. R. 39 (Am. Compl. ¶ 34) (Page ID #1980). John applied for, and received, a Medical Leave of Absence from the University, effective September 23, 2014, because of his psychological distress resulting from the accusations. *Id.* ¶¶ 37-38 (Page ID #1981).

Also on September 23, 2014, defendant Susan Vaughn, the Director of the University's Office of Ethics and Student Conflict Resolution, provided John a Notice of Alleged Violation. *Id.* ¶ 39 (Page ID #1981); R. 39-2 (Pl. Ex. 6: Notice of Alleged Violation) (Page ID #2052). The notice informed John that there was an allegation that he had "sexually assaulted a female resident while both she and you were intoxicated." R. 39-2 (Pl. Ex. 6: Notice of Alleged Violation) (Page ID #2052). According to the notice, this was an alleged violation of Section 103 of Miami University's Student Conduct Regulations. *Id.*; R. 39-2 (Pl. Ex. 8: Miami Univ. Student Handbook at 39-40) (Page ID #2095-96). The notice informed John that he must attend a Procedural Review meeting the following day. R. 39 (Am. Compl. ¶ 39) (Page ID #1981). The purpose of the meeting was to review with John the alleged violation and potential consequences. R. 39-2 (Pl. Ex. 6: Notice of Alleged Violation) (Page ID #2052). At that meeting, John denied that he had committed a violation and requested that the violation be p.587 adjudicated by an Administrative Hearing Panel. R. 39 (Am. Compl. ¶ 43) (Page ID #1982).

On October 1, 2014, Procedural Hearing Officer Kelly Ramsey informed John and Jane that the hearing panel would convene on October 7. *Id.* ¶ 50 (Page ID #1984); R. 39-3 (Pl. Ex. 11: John Doe Notice of Hr'g at 1) (Page ID #2193); R. 39-3 (Pl. Ex. 12: Jane Doe Notice of Hr'g at 1) (Page ID #2196). Ramsey further informed John and Jane of the identity of the panel members and that objections to their inclusion based on bias could be filed by October 3. R. 39-3 (Pl. Ex. 11: John Doe Notice of Hr'g at 1) (Page ID #2193); R. 39-3 (Pl. Ex. 12: Jane Doe Notice of Hr'g at 1) (Page ID #2196). The panel members were defendants Vaughn, Professor Alana Van Gundy-Yoder, and Professor Steve Elliott. *Id.* John alleges that he had insufficient time to investigate the proposed panel members and contest their inclusion before the deadline. R. 39 (Am. Compl. ¶ 52) (Page ID #1985). Ramsey also told John he had to submit a witness list, supporting documents, and any written statements by noon on October 3. R. 39-3 (Pl. Ex. 11: John Doe Notice of Hr'g at 1-2) (Page ID #2193-94). Jane received the same instructions. R. 39-3 (Pl. Ex. 12: Jane Doe Notice of Hr'g at 1) (Page ID #2196). The University did not, however, hold Jane to the October 3 deadline and allowed her to submit a written statement on October 6. R. 39 (Am. Compl. ¶ 51) (Page ID #1984-85).

Miami University held the Administrative Hearing Panel on October 7. *Id.* ¶ 55 (Page ID #1985). John alleges that he was not provided the names of the witnesses who testified against him prior to the hearing or a summary of their proposed testimony. *Id.* ¶ 57 (Page ID #1986). He also alleges that he was not given access to the disciplinary report compiling the evidence against him. *Id.* ¶ 102 (Page ID #2001). John describes Vaughn—who had been the person responsible for initially reviewing the evidence against him and choosing to pursue disciplinary action—as dominating the hearing and trying "to deflate John Doe's credibility while inflating Jane Doe's credibility." *Id.* ¶ 58 (Page ID #1986). John also describes Vaughn's body language during the hearing as "suggesting she believed John was lying" and alleges that she told him "I'll bet you do this [i.e., sexually assault women] all the time." *Id.* ¶ 66 (Page ID #1988-89).

The hearing panel found John responsible for violating Section 103 of the Student Conduct Regulations. *Id.* ¶ 61 (Page ID #1987); R. 39-3 (Pl. Ex. 15: Admin. Panel Hr'g Dec.) (Page ID #2233). The totality of the panel's fact-finding is reproduced below:

> You stated that you and [Jane] were friends and have spent time together in the past. Both of you agreed to go to your residence hall room, where you engaged in consensual kissing and some consensual sexual contact. However, at some point, [Jane] indicated she did not want to have oral sex and asked you to stop but the act continued.

R. 39-3 (Pl. Ex. 15: Admin. Panel Hr'g Dec.) (Page ID #2233). The panel sanctioned John by suspending him for three terms—fall, winter, and spring—until May 2015. R. 39 (Am. Compl. ¶ 61) (Page ID #1987); R. 39-3 (Pl. Ex. 15: Admin. Panel Hr'g Dec.) (Page ID #2233). Upon John's re-enrollment, he was to be placed on disciplinary probation for one year. R. 39-3 (Pl. Ex. 15: Admin. Panel Hr'g Dec.) (Page ID #2233).

On October 13, John appealed the hearing panel's decision to the Chair of the University Appeals Board, defendant Rose Marie Ward. R. 39 (Am. Compl. ¶ 69) (Page ID #1989-90); R. 39-4 (Pl. Ex. 18: p.588 Oct. 13, 2014 Appeal Ltr.) (Page ID #2237-38). On November 11, 2014, Ward informed John via letter that the University Appeals Board had denied his appeal. R. 39 (Am. Compl. ¶ 73) (Page ID #1991); R. 39-4 (Pl. Ex. 20: Appeals Bd. Dec.) (Page ID #2242). John then appealed this decision to Vice President of Student Affairs, defendant Jayne Brownell. R. 39 (Am. Compl. ¶ 75) (Page ID #1991-92); R. 39-4 (Pl. Ex. 21: Nov. 14, 2014 Appeal Ltr.) (Page ID #2243-44). Brownell affirmed the University Appeals Board's decision to uphold the hearing panel's finding of responsibility, but reduced his suspension period such that it ended on January 23, 2015. R. 39 (Am. Compl. ¶ 77) (Page ID #1993); R. 39-4 (Pl. Ex. 23: Brownell Dec. at 1) (Page ID #2249).

John filed suit against the University and several individual defendants in the United States District Court for the Southern District of Ohio on September 17, 2015. R. 1 (Complaint) (Page ID #1-55). John voluntarily dismissed the two state-tort claims that he brought against Jane after the two parties reached a settlement. R. 32 (Voluntary Dismissal) (Page ID #1873). The remaining defendants moved to dismiss all claims under Federal Rule of Civil Procedure 12(b)(6). R. 42 (Mot. to Dismiss at 6) (Page ID #3139). The district court granted the defendants' motion. *Doe v. Miami Univ.*, 247 F.Supp.3d 875, 896-97 (S.D. Ohio 2017). John now appeals the district court's judgment with respect to Counts 3 through 7.

II. STANDARD OF REVIEW

We review de novo a district court's grant of a motion to dismiss for failure to state a claim. *Jackson v. Ford Motor Co.*, 842 F.3d 902, 906 (6th Cir. 2016). "To survive a motion to dismiss, a complaint must contain sufficient factual matter, accepted as true, to 'state a claim to relief that is plausible on its face.'" *Ashcroft v. Iqbal*, 556 U.S. 662, 678, 129 S.Ct. 1937, 173 L.Ed.2d 868 (2009) (quoting *Bell Atl. Corp. v. Twombly*, 550 U.S. 544, 570, 127 S.Ct. 1955, 167 L.Ed.2d 929 (2007)). "A claim has facial plausibility when the plaintiff pleads factual content that allows the court to draw the reasonable inference that the defendant is liable for the misconduct alleged." *Id.* On a motion to dismiss, "[w]e must construe the complaint in the light most favorable to the plaintiff and accept all allegations as true." *Keys v. Humana, Inc.*, 684 F.3d 605, 608 (6th Cir. 2012).

We have previously applied the *Twombly/Iqbal* standard of pleading without modification in Title IX cases. *See, e.g., Tumminello v. Father Ryan High Sch., Inc.*, 678 Fed.Appx. 281, 283-84 (6th Cir. 2017); *Doe v. Cummins*, 662 Fed.Appx. 437, 443 (6th Cir. 2016). In other words, a complaint alleging Title IX violations must plead sufficient factual allegations to satisfy *Twombly* and *Iqbal*. *See Keys*, 684 F.3d at 609-10.

Nevertheless, John argues that we should adopt the Second Circuit's recent decision in *Doe v. Columbia University*, 831 F.3d 46 (2d Cir. 2016), which modified the pleading standard for Title IX claims. Appellant Br. at 28-34. In *Columbia University*, our sister circuit considered what a plaintiff asserting a Title IX claim must allege in order to plead sufficiently the required element of discriminatory intent. *Columbia Univ.*, 831 F.3d at 56. The Second Circuit analogized between what it required of plaintiffs in Title VII employment-discrimination cases and what it should require of plaintiffs alleging Title IX claims. *Id.* It concluded that a complaint under Title IX "is sufficient with respect to the element of discriminatory intent . . . if it pleads specific facts that support a minimal plausible inference of p.589 such discrimination." *Id.* This modified pleading standard "reduces the facts needed to be pleaded under *Iqbal.*" *Id.* at 54 (quoting *Littlejohn v. City of New York*, 795 F.3d 297, 310 (2d Cir. 2015)).

Whatever the merits of the Second Circuit's decision in *Columbia University*, to the extent that the decision reduces the pleading standard in Title IX claims, it is contrary to our binding precedent. *Columbia University* is partially premised on the Second Circuit's decision in *Littlejohn*, 795 F.3d 297. In that case, the Second Circuit reconciled *Twombly* and *Iqbal* with the Supreme Court's holding in *Swierkiewicz v. Sorema N.A.*, 534 U.S. 506, 122 S.Ct. 992, 152 L.Ed.2d 1 (2002), by holding that "[t]o the same extent that the *McDonnell Douglas* temporary presumption reduces the facts a plaintiff would need to show to defeat a motion for summary judgment prior to the defendant's furnishing of a non-discriminatory motivation, that presumption also reduces the facts needed to be pleaded under *Iqbal.*" *Littlejohn*, 795 F.3d at 310. In contrast, we reconciled these cases differently in *Keys*, 684 F.3d at 609-10, and held that a plaintiff asserting a Title VII claim must plead sufficient factual allegations to satisfy *Twombly* and *Iqbal* in alleging the required element of discriminatory intent. Thus, the foundational analogy in *Columbia University* lacks support from our precedent. Accordingly, in this Circuit, John must meet the requirements of *Twombly* and *Iqbal* for each of his claims in order to survive a Rule 12(b)(6) motion to dismiss.

III. TITLE IX CLAIMS

Title IX states that "[n]o person in the United States shall, on the basis of sex, be excluded from participation in, be denied benefits of, or be subjected to discrimination under any education program receiving Federal financial assistance. . . ." 20 U.S.C. § 1681(a). "Title IX is enforceable through a judicially implied private right of action, through which monetary damages are available." *Klemencic v. Ohio State Univ.*, 263 F.3d 504, 510 (6th Cir. 2001).

We have recognized, although never explicitly adopted in a published opinion, at least four theories of liability that a student who is "attacking a university disciplinary proceeding on grounds of gender bias," *Yusuf v. Vassar Coll.*, 35 F.3d 709, 715 (2d Cir. 1994), can potentially assert under Title IX. These theories are: (1) "erroneous outcome," (2) "selective enforcement," (3) "deliberate indifference," and (4) "archaic assumptions." *Cummins*, 662 Fed.Appx. at 451-52 & n.9; *Mallory v. Ohio Univ.*, 76 Fed.Appx. 634, 638-39 (6th Cir. 2003). Here, John argues that the defendants are liable under Title IX under the first three of these theories, as well as under a hostile-environment theory. The hostile-environment theory of liability has been recognized in other Title IX cases, *see, e.g., Doe v. Claiborne Cty.*, 103 F.3d 495, 515 (6th Cir. 1996), although not one in which a student who was disciplined for sexual misconduct has brought suit against a university.

A. Count 3: Hostile Environment

In Counts 3 and 4 of his complaint, John alleges a violation of Title IX under a hostile-environment theory and a deliberate-indifference theory. R. 39 (Am. Compl. ¶¶ 138-62) (Page ID #2012-19). The district court analyzed both as asserting claims under the deliberate-indifference theory. *Miami Univ.*, 247 F.Supp.3d at 885 n.3. While the district court was correct that John's allegations overlap substantially between Counts 3 and 4, a hostile-environment claim and deliberate-indifference claim require the plaintiff to allege different elements.

p.590 A Title IX hostile-environment claim is analogous to a Title VII hostile-environment claim. *Claiborne Cty.*, 103 F.3d at 515; *see also Tumminello*, 678 Fed.Appx. at 284. Under this theory of liability, the plaintiff must allege that his educational experience was "permeated with discriminatory intimidation, ridicule, and insult that is sufficiently severe or pervasive [so as] to alter the conditions of the victim's" educational environment. *Harris v. Forklift Sys., Inc.*, 510 U.S. 17, 21, 114 S.Ct. 367, 126 L.Ed.2d 295 (1993) (internal citations and quotation marks omitted).

John argues that his allegations of gender bias in the University's sexual-assault disciplinary process suffice to constitute a viable hostile-environment claim. Appellant Br. at 35. John does not allege facts that support a reasonable inference that his educational experience was "permeated with discriminatory intimidation, ridicule, and insult." *Harris*, 510 U.S. at 21, 114 S.Ct. 367 (citation and internal quotation marks omitted). Thus, we affirm the district court's grant of the defendants' motion to dismiss as to Count 3. *Cf. La. Sch. Emps.' Ret. Sys. v. Ernst & Young, LLP*, 622 F.3d 471, 477 (6th Cir. 2010) (stating that on de novo review of a district court's grant of a motion to dismiss, this court "may affirm the judgment of the district court on any ground supported by the record").

B. Count 4: Deliberate Indifference

John's second theory of Title IX liability is deliberate indifference: He argues that the University was deliberately indifferent to the gender discrimination that he faced during the disciplinary process and the sexual misconduct perpetrated against him by Jane. Appellant Br. at 35-36. Under the deliberate-indifference theory, a plaintiff must "demonstrate that an official of the institution who had authority to institute corrective measures had actual notice of, and was deliberately indifferent to, the misconduct." *Mallory*, 76 Fed.Appx. at 638. Furthermore, a deliberate-indifference claim premised on student-on-student misconduct must allege "harassment that is so severe, pervasive, and objectively offensive that it effectively bars the victim's access to an educational opportunity or benefit." *Davis v. Monroe Cty. Bd. of Educ.*, 526 U.S. 629, 633, 119 S.Ct. 1661, 143 L.Ed.2d 839 (1999); *see also Patterson v. Hudson Area Schs.*, 551 F.3d 438, 444-45 (6th Cir. 2009).

In *Mallory*, we did not explicitly state whether a deliberate-indifference claim in this context requires the plaintiff to plead that the misconduct alleged is sexual harassment, because we only assumed arguendo that this theory applied. *Mallory*, 76 Fed.Appx. at 638-39; *see also Cummins*, 662 Fed.Appx. at 451 n.9 (declining to decide whether the deliberate-indifference theory was applicable to this kind of case because the plaintiff did not argue that it was).[3] John asserts no rationale why deliberate-indifference claims in this kind of case do not require allegations of sexual harassment when such an allegation is a required element of a prima facie case of deliberate indifference in other Title IX cases. *See Horner v. Ky. High Sch. Athletic Ass'n*, 206 F.3d 685, 691-93 (6th Cir. 2000) (summarizing the three Supreme p.591 Court cases that articulate the deliberate-indifference theory of liability in Title IX cases and noting that "all address deliberate indifference to sexual harassment"); *Doe v. Univ. of the South*, 687 F.Supp.2d 744, 758 (E.D. Tenn. 2009) (dismissing a plaintiff's Title IX deliberate-indifference claim because he "fail[ed] to allege any facts to support a finding that the University's actions were at all motivated by [his] gender or sex or constituted gender harassment or sexual harassment"). *But see Plummer v. Univ. of Houston*, 860 F.3d 767, 778 (5th Cir. 2017) (dismissing plaintiffs' deliberate-indifference claim, but implying that the misconduct need not be sexual harassment, but rather could be constitutional deficiencies in the disciplinary process). Thus, to plead sufficiently a Title IX deliberate-indifference claim the misconduct alleged must be sexual harassment.

John's argument, therefore, that he has sufficiently alleged a deliberate-indifference claim based solely on the gender discrimination he asserts occurred throughout the disciplinary process, Appellant Br. at 35-36, fails because the alleged gender discrimination is not tethered to a claim of sexual harassment. John, however, also argues that the defendants were deliberately indifferent to the sexual misconduct that Jane perpetrated against him. Appellant Br. at 36. The district court rejected this argument because John did not allege that he had initiated his own sexual-misconduct complaint against Jane and only one incident of sexual misconduct does not rise to the level of being "severe, pervasive, and objectively offensive." *Miami Univ.*, 247 F.Supp.3d at 886.

The district court was incorrect to suggest that John needed to have made a formal complaint about Jane in order to plead a deliberate-indifference claim. We require only that "the funding recipient had actual knowledge of the sexual harassment," and not that the plaintiff followed a formal procedure to put the funding recipient on notice. *Patterson*, 551 F.3d at 445. The University did have actual knowledge that Jane had kissed John while John was so intoxicated that he could not remember the events of the night the next morning—indicating that John was inebriated to the extent that he could not consent under Miami University's policies.[4] R. 39-2 (Pl. Ex. 1: Jane Doe Statement at 1) (Page ID #2036); R. 39-2 (Pl. Ex. 6: Notice of Alleged Violation) (Page ID #2052). Thus, John's failure to initiate his own complaint against Jane for her sexual misconduct has no impact on the actual knowledge of the defendants.[5]

However, one incident of allegedly non-consensual kissing—while unacceptable—does not rise to the level of "sexual harassment [that is] so severe, pervasive, and objectively offensive that it could be said to deprive the plaintiff of access to the educational opportunities or benefits provided by the school." *Patterson*, 551 F.3d at 444-45. Rather, we have required a plaintiff alleging deliberate indifference to establish an extensive pattern of sexually offensive behavior, and this one incident of kissing is insufficient. *Pahssen v. Merrill Cmty. Sch. Dist.*, 668 F.3d 356, 360, 363 (6th Cir. 2012) (holding that three separate p.592 occasions of sexual harassment—a male student shoving a female student into a locker, demanding that she perform oral sex on him, and making obscene sexual gestures at her—did not constitute sexual harassment that rose to the level of "severe, pervasive, and objectively offensive").

Thus, we affirm the district court's judgment with respect to John's Title IX deliberate-indifference claim.

C. Count 5: Erroneous Outcome

Count 5 of John's complaint alleges that Miami University violated Title IX under an erroneous-outcome theory of liability. R. 39 (Am. Compl. ¶¶ 169-76) (Page ID #2019-21). To plead an erroneous-out-come claim, a plaintiff must allege: "(1) 'facts sufficient to cast some articulable doubt on the accuracy of the outcome of the disciplinary proceeding' and (2) a 'particularized. . . causal connection between the flawed outcome and gender bias.'" *Cummins,* 662 Fed.Appx. at 452 (quoting *Yusuf,* 35 F.3d at 715). The district court held that John had alleged sufficient facts to "cast doubt on the accuracy of the out-come of the Administrative Hearing." *Miami Univ.,* 247 F.Supp.3d at 886. The district court, however, held that John had not sufficiently pleaded the second part of an erroneous-outcome claim: causation between the disciplinary proceeding's out-come and gender bias. *Id.* at 889-90. Thus, the district court held that John had failed to state a claim under Title IX based on an erroneous-outcome theory. *Id.* at 890.

We agree with the district court that John has pleaded sufficient facts to cast "some articulable doubt on the accuracy" on the outcome of his disciplinary hearing. He alleges that he was so intoxicated that he cannot recall the critical events in question. R. 39 (Am. Compl. ¶¶ 6, 22) (Page ID #1975, 1977). Thus, John's only knowledge of what occurred is drawn from Jane's description. *Id.* ¶ 6 (Page ID #1975). In her written statement, Jane describes a series of sexual acts between herself and John, some of which were consensual and some of which were not. R. 39-2 (Pl. Ex. 1: Jane Doe Statement at 1) (Page ID #2036). She states that she initially agreed to digital penetration, but at some point told John to stop. *Id.* John did stop, but only after some period of time had passed. *Id.* Then John asked Jane if he could engage in oral sex. *Id.* According to Jane, she said no, but John proceeded anyway and Jane responded by pushing him away, rather than re-verbalizing her denial of consent. *Id.* John then stopped. *Id.* Jane also states, however, that "I never said no." *Id.*

The Administrative Hearing Panel found John responsible for sexual misconduct on the basis of the following finding of fact: "However, at some point, [Jane] indicated she did not want to have oral sex and asked you to stop but the act continued." R. 39-3 (Pl. Ex. 15: Admin. Panel Hr'g Dec.) (Page ID #2233). This one-sentence finding of misconduct holds John responsible for non-consensual oral sex only, and not non-consensual digital penetration. But Jane's statement is internally inconsistent with regard to her description of the oral sex: she states both that "I said no" and "I never said no." R. 39-2 (Pl. Ex. 1: Jane Doe Statement at 1) (Page ID #2036). The Administrative Hearing Panel does not explain how it resolved this inconsistency. Additionally, the panel's terse statement does not elucidate why it found the oral sex to be non-consensual when it appears to have found that the digital penetration was consensual. Furthermore, John alleges that Vaughn, a hearing-panel member, was mistaken about the applicable standard of consent, and that she erroneously believed Miami University required affirmative consent, as evidenced by a quote attributed to p.593 Vaughn explaining the University's policy in a local newspaper article. R. 39 (Am. Compl. ¶ 108) (Page ID #2004); R. 41 (Pl. Ex.

59: Dayton Daily News Article) (Page ID #2804). Affirmative consent is a more stringent requirement than what is actually articulated in the University's Title IX policy and student handbook. R. 39-2 (Pl. Ex. 8: Miami Univ. Student Handbook at 39) (Page ID #2095); R. 39-2 (Pl. Ex. 9: Miami Univ. Title IX Policy at 3-4) (Page ID #2170-71). At the motion-to-dismiss stage, where all reasonable inferences must be drawn in favor of the plaintiff, the unresolved inconsistency in Jane's statement, the unexplained discrepancy in the hearing panel's finding of fact, and the alleged use of an erroneous definition of consent creates "some articulable doubt" as to the accuracy of the decision.

In order to survive a motion to dismiss on this claim, John must also allege facts showing "a 'particularized . . . causal connection between the flawed outcome and gender bias.'" *Cummins,* 662 Fed.Appx. at 452 (quoting *Yusuf,* 35 F.3d at 715). "Such allegations might include, inter alia, statements by members of the disciplinary tribunal, statements by pertinent university officials, or patterns of decision-making that also tend to show the influence of gender." *Yusuf,* 35 F.3d at 715. The district court concluded that John had not sufficiently pleaded this second part of his claim. *Miami Univ.,* 247 F.Supp.3d at 890. We disagree.

Taken together, the statistical evidence that ostensibly shows a pattern of gender-based decision-making and the external pressure on Miami University supports at the motion-to-dismiss stage a reasonable inference of gender discrimination.[6] John alleges facts showing a potential pattern of gender-based decision-making that "raise a reasonable expectation that discovery will reveal" circumstantial evidence of gender discrimination. *See Twombly,* 550 U.S at 556, 127 S.Ct. 1955. He asserts that every male student accused of sexual misconduct in the Fall 2013 and Spring 2014 semesters was found responsible for the alleged violation, R. 39 (Am. Compl. ¶ 151) (Page ID #2016), and that nearly ninety percent of students found responsible for sexual misconduct between 2011 and 2014 have male first-names, *Id.*; R. 40-4 (Pl. Ex. 42: Public Record Request of Sexual Misconduct Violations) (Page ID #2613) (listing twenty students' first-names, only two of which are traditionally female names). Additionally, John incorporated an affidavit from an attorney who represents many students in Miami University's disciplinary proceedings, which describes a pattern of the University pursuing investigations concerning male students, but not female students. R. 39 (Am. Compl. ¶ 85) (Page ID #1996); R. 41-5 (Pl. Ex. B: Meloy Affidavit at 1-2) (Page ID #3132-33). Lastly, John points to his own situation, in which the University initiated an investigation into him but not Jane, as evidence that Miami University p.594 impermissibly makes decisions on the basis of a student's gender. R. 39 (Am. Compl. ¶¶ 80-83) (Page ID #1994-95). Discovery may reveal that the alleged patterns of gender-based decision-making do not, in fact, exist. That information, however, is currently controlled by the defendants, and John has sufficiently pleaded circumstantial evidence of gender discrimination. *See Brown Univ.,* 166 F.Supp. at 189; *Marshall v. Ind. Univ.,* 170 F.Supp.3d 1201, 1210 (S.D. Ind. 2016).

John also asserts that Miami University faced external pressure from the federal government and lawsuits brought by private parties that caused it to discriminate against men. Specifically, he argues that pressure from the government to combat vigorously sexual assault on college campuses and the severe potential punishment—loss of all federal funds—if it failed to comply, led Miami University to discriminate against men in its sexual-assault adjudication process. R. 39 (Am. Compl. ¶¶ 76, 86-92) (Page ID #1992-93, 1996-98); R. 40 (Pl. Ex. 30: White House "Not Alone" Report at 17) (Page ID #2315); R. 40-2 (Pl. Ex. 32: Miami Univ. Training at 49-54) (Page ID #2504-09); R. 39-4 (Pl. Ex. 22: ATIXA Tip of the Week Apr. 24, 2014 at 1-2) (Page ID #2245-46); *see also* "Dear Colleague" Letter from Russlynn Ali, Assistant Sec'y for Civil Rights, U.S. Dep't of Educ. (Apr. 4, 2011), https://www2.ed.gov/about/offices/list/ocr/letters/colleague-201104.pdf; Emma Ellman-Golan, Note, *Saving Title IX: Designing More Equitable and Efficient Investigation Procedures*, 116 MICH. L. REV. 155, 162-66, 173-74 (2017). Additionally, John contends that Miami University was facing pressure to increase the zealousness of its "prosecution" of sexual assault and the harshness of the sanctions it imposed because it was a defendant in a lawsuit brought by a student who alleged that she would not have been assaulted if the University had expelled her attacker for prior offenses. R. 39 (Am. Compl. ¶ 100) (Page ID #2000-01); R. 40-4 (Pl. Ex. 43: Media Reports of Lawsuit at 5-7) (Page ID #2618-2620); R. 40-4 (Pl. Ex. 44: 2013 Lawsuit against Miami Univ.) (Page ID #2621-61).

Considering all of these factual allegations relating to Miami University's pattern of activity respecting sexual-assault matters and the asserted pressures placed on the University, John has pleaded sufficient specific facts to support a reasonable inference of gender discrimination. At the pleading stage, John's allegations need only create the plausible inference of intentional gender discrimination; although alternative non-discriminatory explanations for the defendants' behavior may exist, that possibility does not bar John's access to discovery. *See 16630 Southfield Ltd. P'ship v. Flagstar Bank, F.S.B.*, 727 F.3d 502, 505 (6th Cir. 2013) ("[T]he mere existence of more likely alternative explanations does not automatically entitle a defendant to dismissal"); *Watson Carpet & Floor Covering, Inc. v. Mohawk Indus., Inc.*, 648 F.3d 452, 458 (6th Cir. 2011) ("Often, defendants' conduct has several plausible explanations. Ferreting out the most likely reason for the defendants' actions is not appropriate at the pleadings stage."). Consequently, we reverse the district court's grant of the defendants' motion to dismiss Count 5 of John's complaint and remand for further proceedings.

D. Selective Enforcement

In his appellate brief, John argues in passing that he sufficiently alleged a Title IX claim premised on the theory of selective enforcement. Appellant Br. at 18-19. John did not assert this as a theory of liability in his complaint or in his opposition to the defendants' motion to dismiss. To the extent that John is now trying to assert a Title IX selective-enforcement claim, he has forfeited this argument. *Guyan Int'l, Inc. v. Prof'l Benefits Adm'rs, Inc.*, 689 F.3d 793, 799 (6th Cir. 2012) ("If a party fails to raise an issue to the district court, then that party 'forfeits the right to have the argument addressed on appeal.'" (quoting *Armstrong v. City of Melvindale*, 432 F.3d 695, 699-700 (6th Cir. 2006))).

IV. SECTION 1983 CLAIMS

John brought claims pursuant to 42 U.S.C. § 1983 against the individual defendants in their official capacities for injunctive relief and in their personal capacities for monetary damages. R. 39 (Am. Compl. ¶¶ 177-207) (Page ID #2021-26). He alleges that the individual defendants violated the Due Process Clause and the Equal Protection Clause of the Fourteenth Amendment. *Id.* The district court held that John had failed to state a claim under either of these clauses and granted the defendants' motion to dismiss. *Miami Univ.*, 247 F.Supp.3d at 891, 895, 896. The district court also held that the individual defendants were entitled to qualified immunity. *Id.* at 896.

"To state a claim under 42 U.S.C. § 1983, a plaintiff must set forth facts that, when construed favorably, establish (1) the deprivation of a right secured by the Constitution or laws of the United States (2) caused by a person acting under the color of state law." *Heyne v. Metro. Nashville Pub. Sch.*, 655 F.3d 556, 562 (6th Cir. 2011) (quoting *Marvin v. City of Taylor*, 509 F.3d 234, 243 (6th Cir. 2007)). Here, the defendants do not dispute that they were acting under the color of state law; thus, the issue is whether John has sufficiently alleged that he has been deprived of a constitutional right. Because part of John's due-process claim is premised on his equal-protection claim, we will address the two counts in the opposite order from how they are presented in his complaint.

A. Count 7: Equal Protection

To establish an equal-protection violation, a plaintiff must allege that the state made a distinction which "burden[ed] a fundamental right, target[ed] a suspect class, or intentionally treat[ed] one differently from others similarly situated without any rational basis for the difference." *Radvansky v. City of Olmsted Falls*, 395 F.3d 291, 312 (6th Cir. 2005). John alleges three instances when the defendants treated him differently from those similarly situated without any rational basis for the treatment. Only the last of the three asserted occasions of differential treatment sustains a viable-equal protection claim.

First, John argues that he faced unequal treatment because Jane was given "limited amnesty" for underage drinking. Appellant Br. at 39-40. Although the district court considered this an allegation of unequal treatment, *Miami Univ.*, 247 F.Supp.3d at 895-96, John's complaint does not support his argument that he faced an unequal application of Miami University's policy against underage drinking. John asserts that Jane received "limited amnesty" for her violation of the prohibition on underage drinking, R. 39 (Am. Compl. ¶ 49) (Page ID #1983-84), but he does not allege that the University proceeded against him for violating the underage drinking policy. John was found responsible by the University for sexual misconduct, not underage drinking. R. 39-3 (Pl. Ex. 15: Admin. Panel Hr'g Dec.) (Page ID #2233). The grant of "limited amnesty" to one student who admitted underage drinking and the non-prosecution of another student who also admitted underage drinking does not give rise to a claim of unequal treatment in violation of the Equal Protection Clause.

p.596 Second, John alleges that Jane was allowed to submit her written statement on October 6, 2014, three days after the deadline that the University had stated. R. 39 (Am. Compl. ¶ 51) (Page ID #1984-85). John does not, however, allege that he attempted to submit materials after the deadline, much less that the University refused to accept such materials or would not have provided an extension to him as well. Thus, John's allegations do not give rise to a reasonable inference that he faced unequal treatment.

Lastly, John argues that the defendants' failure to discipline Jane for sexual misconduct, when he faced discipline, was unequal treatment. Appellant Br. at 40; R. 39 (Am. Compl. ¶ 65) (Page ID #1988). The gravamen of John's argument is that Miami University, acting through Vaughn, pursued disciplinary action against him because he was a man, whereas it did not do so with respect to Jane because she was a woman.[7] Appellant Reply Br. at 4. In order to plead this claim sufficiently, John must allege that Vaughn was operating under "the same set of operative facts" when she decided not to initiate the disciplinary process against Jane. *Doe v. Ohio State Univ.*, 239 F.Supp.3d 1048, 1083 (S.D. Ohio 2017); *see also Perry v. McGinnis*, 209 F.3d 597, 601 (6th Cir. 2000) (holding that for individuals to be similarly situated there must be "relevant similarity," but there need not be "exact correlation").

Vaughn, the individual allegedly responsible for deciding whether or not to charge students with sexual-misconduct violations, R. 39 (Am. Compl. ¶ 58) (Page ID #1986), had received a report that John had engaged in non-consensual sexual acts against Jane. R. 39-2 (Pl. Ex. 6: Notice of Alleged Violation) (Page ID #2052). Vaughn also allegedly knew that Jane had engaged in non-consensual sexual acts against John, when John was so intoxicated he was unable to provide consent—as defined by Miami University's consent policy—and Jane had "kinda sobered up." R. 39 (Am. Compl. ¶¶ 24, 63) (Page ID #1978, 1988); R. 39-2 (Pl. Ex. 6: Notice of Alleged Violation) (Page ID #2052); R. 39-2 (Pl. Ex. 8: Miami Univ. Student Handbook at 39-40) (Page ID #2095-96); R. 39-2 (Pl. Ex. 1: Jane Doe Statement at 1) (Page ID #2036). The non-consensual acts Jane allegedly perpetrated—kissing John—are a type of prohibited sexual misconduct under the University's policies. R. 39-2 (Pl. Ex. 1: Jane Doe Statement at 1) (Page ID #2036); R. 39-2 (Pl. Ex. 9: Miami Univ. Title IX Policy at 3) (Page ID #2170). Thus, Vaughn knew that Jane had potentially violated the University's sexual misconduct provisions at the same time she reviewed the allegations against John. Neither Jane nor John initiated a formal complaint themselves regarding the other's conduct, R. 39-2 (Pl. Ex. 1: Jane Doe Statement at 2) (Page ID #2037), but Vaughn chose to pursue disciplinary action against John, but not Jane.

These alleged facts sufficiently show at the motion-to-dismiss stage that John and Jane were similarly situated. Vaughn had credible information that both students had potentially violated the University's sexual misconduct policy. Vaughn, however, chose not to pursue disciplinary action against the female student, but only against the male student. We note that the exact alleged sexual misconduct of each student is not the same. John, while extraordinarily inebriated, apparently engaged in non-consensual digital penetration and oral sex. Jane, apparently p.597 mostly sober, purportedly kissed John when he was incapacitated and unable to consent. But we have not previously required a plaintiff to allege that the misconduct giving rise to an allegedly discriminatory disciplinary outcome be of the same type and degree. *See Heyne*, 655 F.3d at 571 (holding that the plaintiff sufficiently pleaded an equal-protection claim when he alleged that he was punished more harshly for running over another student's foot with his vehicle than the other student was for threatening the plaintiff's life because of the different races of the two students).

The instance of unequal treatment that John sufficiently pleads arises out of Vaughn's failure to initiate the University's disciplinary process with respect to Jane after receiving credible information that Jane may have violated the sexual-misconduct policy. *Cf. Reese v. Jefferson Sch. Dist. No. 14J*, 208 F.3d 736 (9th Cir. 2000) (affirming the grant of summary judgment for the defendants on plaintiffs' § 1983 equal-protection claim when the asserted disparate treatment was that the female plaintiffs were suspended after being caught violating the school rules, whereas the male students were not punished because the school had no notice of misconduct on their part). But equal protection does not require John and Jane to have received the same sanctions when the underlying alleged misconduct of the two was different; if Miami University had initiated disciplinary proceedings against Jane, this process may have led to a finding of not responsible or the imposition of a lesser sanction. None of these hypotheticals, unless impermissibly motivated by gender, would establish an equal-protection violation.

John must also allege that the different treatment he received was based on "purposeful or intentional" gender discrimination. *Smith v. City of Salem*, 378 F.3d 566, 577 (6th Cir. 2004). John asserts the same facts that undergirded his Title IX claims of gender discrimination to buttress his § 1983 claim. Appellant Br. at 40. For the same reasons that we held that John had sufficiently pleaded facts demonstrating discriminatory intent under his Title IX erroneous-outcome claim, John has alleged sufficient facts to show circumstantial evidence of gender discrimination with respect to his equal-protection claim. *See* Section III.C *supra*.

"[C]onstru[ing] the complaint in the light most favorable to the plaintiff," *Keys*, 684 F.3d at 608, John has sufficiently pleaded an equal-protection claim. Of course this case is before us at the motion-to-dismiss stage, and discovery may disprove John's allegation that the reason he was treated differently than Jane was because of his gender and not because of other, legitimate reasons. But given the procedural posture in which the case currently stands, however, we must presume John's allegations to be true.

Thus, we reverse the district court's grant of the defendants' motion to dismiss Count 7 with respect to Vaughn and remand for further proceedings. As the remaining individual defendants—Van Gundy-Yoder, Elliott, Ward, and Brownell—played no role in the decision to initiate disciplinary proceedings against John, but not Jane, we affirm the district court's grant of the defendants' motion to dismiss Count 7 with respect to them.

B. Count 6: Substantive Due Process

Substantive-due-process claims are "loosely divided into two categories: (1) deprivations of a particular constitutional guarantee; and (2) actions that shock the conscience." *Valot v. Southeast Local Sch. Dist. Bd. of Educ.*, 107 F.3d 1220, 1228 (6th Cir. 1997) (internal quotation marks p.598 omitted). Here, John has pleaded both types of substantive-due-process claims.

1. Deprivation of Constitutional Guarantee

In his complaint, John alleges that his substantive-due-process rights were violated because he was deprived of two constitutionally protected property interests: a property interest in continuing his education and a property interest in a transcript "unmarred" by the finding of responsibility for sexual misconduct. R. 39 (Am. Compl. ¶¶ 182, 197) (Page ID #2021, 2024). In his response to the defendants' motion to dismiss before the district court and in front of this court, John has asserted only his property interest in continuing his education. R. 25 (Dist. Ct. Op. at 22) (Page ID #3592); Appellant Br. at 41.

"As an initial matter, we note that the Supreme Court never has held that the interest in continued education at a public university constitutes a fundamental property or liberty interest that finds refuge in the substantive protections of the Due Process Clause." *Martinson v. Regents of Univ. of Mich.*, 562 Fed.Appx. 365, 375 (6th Cir. 2014). "[O]ur own precedent suggests that the opposite is true," although this court has not definitively decided the issue. *Id.* A consensus on this issue does not appear to have emerged among our sister circuits either. *See, e.g., Williams v. Wendler,* 530 F.3d 584, 589 (7th Cir. 2008) (holding that a suspension from a public university is not a deprivation of constitutional property); *Butler v. Rector & Bd. of Visitors of Coll. of William & Mary,* 121 Fed.Appx. 515, 518-19 (4th Cir. 2005) (assuming, without deciding, that a student had "a property interest in continued enrollment" in a master's program "that is protected by the Due Process Clause").

In *Bell v. Ohio State University,* 351 F.3d 240, 251 (6th Cir. 2003), we held that, because a medical student had not established that her expulsion from medical school was an equal-protection violation, "we c[ould] see no basis for finding that [her] interest in continuing her medical school education is protected by substantive due process." *See also Rogers v. Tenn. Bd. of Regents,* 273 Fed.Appx. 458, 463 (6th Cir. 2008). The holding in *Bell* relied on our earlier decision in *Gutzwiller v. Fenik,* 860 F.2d 1317, 1329 (6th Cir. 1988), where we noted that in "certain situations. . . a violation of one [clause] will constitute a violation of the other."

John relies on *Bell* to argue that because he has asserted an equal-protection violation, he has sufficiently pleaded a substantive-due-process violation. Appellant Br. at 42; Appellant Reply Br. at 23. But "[t]he spheres of protection offered by the two concepts [equal protection and substantive due process] are not, to be sure, coterminous." *Gutzwiller,* 860 F.2d at 1328. For a substantive-due-process claim to lie, the interest that John allegedly was deprived of must fall within the ambit of substantive due process. *Id.* at 1329. Here, John offers no argument for why we should recognize an independent property interest in pursuing a post-secondary education continuously, free from a suspension of less than four months. *Cf. Bell,* 351 F.3d at 249-50 ("The interests protected by substantive due process are of course much narrower than those protected by procedural due process. . . . [Substantive due process] protects those fundamental rights and liberties which are, objectively, deeply rooted in this Nation's history and tradition, and implicit in the concept of ordered liberty, such that neither liberty nor justice would exist if they were sacrificed."). On the alleged facts and arguments presented to us in this case, John has not sufficiently pleaded a substantive-due-process claim premised on a deprivation p.599 of a constitutionally protected guarantee.

2. Actions that "Shock the Conscience"

John also alleges that the defendants violated the substantive component of the Due Process Clause because they engaged in an "arbitrary abuse of executive power so egregious that it shocks the conscience of the public." R. 39 (Am. Compl. ¶ 190) (Page ID #2023). The district court held that John had forfeited this argument because he did not raise it in his opposition to the defendants' motion to dismiss. R. 25 (Dist. Ct. Op. at 22) (Page ID #3592). John vigorously contests the district court's conclusion that he has abandoned this part of his substantive-due-process claim. Appellant Br. at 41 & n.11. But even if John has not forfeited this claim, he cannot survive a motion to dismiss on this claim.

Executive action shocks the conscience when it is "arbitrary, or conscience shocking, in a constitutional sense." *Handy-Clay v. City of Memphis*, 695 F.3d 531, 547 (6th Cir. 2012) (quoting *Cty. of Sacramento v. Lewis*, 523 U.S. 833, 847, 118 S.Ct. 1708, 140 L.Ed.2d 1043 (1998)). "Moreover, this characterization applies to only the most egregious official conduct, conduct that is so brutal and offensive that it [does] not comport with traditional ideas of fair play and decency." *Id.* at 547-48 (alteration in original) (internal citations and quotation marks omitted). Even viewing John's complaint in the most favorable light, the defendants' alleged actions do not constitute constitutionally arbitrary or conscience-shocking conduct. *See, e.g., Flaim v. Med. Coll. of Ohio*, 418 F.3d 629, 643 (6th Cir. 2005) (describing an example of conscience-shocking conduct drawn from a case in which two African-American students were expelled from Alabama State College, without notice or a hearing, "for seeking to purchase lunch at a publicly owned grill in the basement of the Montgomery, Alabama, county courthouse" (citing *Dixon v. Ala. State Bd. of Educ.*, 294 F.2d 150 (5th Cir. 1961))).

"Where government action does not deprive a plaintiff of a particular constitutional guarantee or shock the conscience, that action survives the scythe of substantive due process so long as it is rationally related to a legitimate state interest." *Valot*, 107 F.3d at 1228. Here, the defendants' imposition of sanctions on John is rationally related to Miami University's legitimate interest in investigating alleged violations of its student code of conduct and disciplining those found responsible. Consequently, we affirm the district court's grant of the defendants' motion to dismiss with respect to John's § 1983 substantive-due-process claim.

C. Count 6: Procedural Due Process

"Procedural due process imposes constraints on governmental decisions which deprive individuals of 'liberty' or 'property' interests within the meaning of the Due Process Clause of the Fifth or Fourteenth Amendment." *Mathews v. Eldridge*, 424 U.S. 319, 332, 96 S.Ct. 893, 47 L.Ed.2d 18 (1976). Procedural due process is "implicated by higher education disciplinary decisions." *Flaim*, 418 F.3d at 633; *see also Doe v. Univ. of Cincinnati*, 872 F.3d 393, 399 (6th Cir. 2017). "Suspension 'clearly implicates' a protected property interest, and allegations of sexual assault may 'impugn [a student's] reputation and integrity, thus implicating a protected liberty interest.'" *Univ. of Cincinnati*, 872 F.3d at 399 (quoting *Cummins*, 662 Fed. Appx. at 445).

Because John's suspension implicates a constitutionally protected interest, "the question remains what process is p.600 due." *Morrissey v. Brewer*, 408 U.S. 471, 481, 92 S.Ct. 2593, 33 L.Ed.2d 484 (1972); *see also Univ. of Cincinnati*, 872 F.3d at 399. We evaluate the nature of the procedure that is due under the three-factor framework articulated by the Supreme Court in *Mathews,* 424 U.S. at 334-35, 96 S.Ct. 893; *see also Flaim,* 418 F.3d at 634. These "three distinct factors" are: (1) "the private interest that will be affected by the official action"; (2) "the risk of an erroneous deprivation of such interest through the procedures used, and the probable value, if any, of additional or substitute procedural safeguards"; and (3) "the Government's interest, including the function involved and the fiscal and administrative burdens that the additional or substitute procedural requirement would entail." *Mathews,* 424 U.S. at 335, 96 S.Ct. 893.

The private interest at stake in this case is substantial. "A finding of responsibility for a sexual offense can have a 'lasting impact' on a student's personal life, in addition to his 'educational and employment opportunities,' especially when the disciplinary action involves a long-term suspension." *Univ. of Cincinnati,* 872 F.3d at 400 (quoting *Cummins,* 662 Fed.Appx. at 446); *see also* Ellman-Golan, *Saving Title IX: Designing More Equitable and Efficient Investigation Procedures, supra,* at 175 (An individual accused of sexual misconduct "will see his own rights curtailed. He may be forced, even as an interim measure, to move out of university housing or to withdraw from certain classes or to avoid a certain dining hall during certain periods of time. He may be suspended or expelled from school. . . . And as some states . . . begin to pass legislation requiring schools to note on a student's transcript whether the student was suspended or expelled for sexual misconduct, he may face severe restrictions, similar to being put on a sex offender list, that curtail his ability to gain a higher education degree." (internal citations omitted)). Thus, the effect of a finding of responsibility for sexual misconduct on "a person's good name, reputation, honor, or integrity" is profound. *See Goss v. Lopez,* 419 U.S. 565, 574, 95 S.Ct. 729, 42 L.Ed.2d 725 (1975).

When a student faces the possibility of suspension, we have held that the minimum process a university must provide is "notice of the charges, an explanation of the evidence against the student, and an opportunity to present his side of the story before an unbiased decision maker." *Univ. of Cincinnati,* 872 F.3d at 399-400. "In some circumstances [such as] where factual issues are disputed [and the student is not permitted to attend the adjudication proceeding], notice might also be required to include the names of witnesses and a list of other evidence the school intends to present." *Flaim,* 418 F.3d at 635. Furthermore, if the credibility of an alleged victim is at issue, the university must provide a way for the adjudicative body to evaluate the victim's credibility and "to assess the demeanor of both the accused and his accuser." *Univ. of Cincinnati,* 872 F.3d at 406. But the protections afforded to an accused, even in the face of a sexual-assault accusation, "need not reach the same level . . . that would be present in a criminal prosecution." *Id.* at 400 (quoting *Doe v. Univ. of Ky.,* 860 F.3d 365, 370 (6th Cir. 2017)); *see also Flaim,* 418 F.3d at 635 n.1 ("A university is not a court of law, and it is neither practical nor desirable it be one." (quoting *Gomes v. Univ. of Me. Sys.,* 365 F.Supp.2d 6, 16 (D. Me. 2005))).

On appeal, John does not ask for additional procedures beyond what we have already held to be required. Rather, John suggests that these procedures should be strengthened considering the significance p.601 of the private interest at stake. Appellant Br. at 44-46.

1. Unbiased Decision-Maker

John's main argument is that his procedural-due-process rights were violated because he was not given the opportunity to present his side of the story to an unbiased decision-maker. Appellant Br. at 45. "[S]chool officials responsible for deciding whether to exclude a student from school must be impartial." *Heyne*, 655 F.3d at 567. However, "[i]t is also well established that school-disciplinary committees are entitled to a presumption of impartiality, absent a showing of actual bias." *Cummins*, 662 Fed.Appx. at 449.

John alleges that Vaughn, one of three members of his Administrative Hearing Panel, was biased against him because: (1) she was his investigator, prosecutor, and judge; and (2) she had pre-determined his guilt. Appellant Br. at 46. "[D]ue process is not necessarily violated when the school official who initiates, investigates, or prosecutes charges against a student plays a role in the decision to suspend the student." *Heyne*, 655 F.3d at 567 (first citing *Lamb v. Panhandle Cmty. Unit Sch. Dist. No. 2*, 826 F.2d 526, 529-30 (7th Cir. 1987); and then citing *Brewer ex rel. Dreyfus v. Austin Indep. Sch. Dist.*, 779 F.2d 260, 264 (5th Cir. 1985)). Due process may, however, be violated when "a school official's involvement in an incident created a bias such as to preclude his affording the student an impartial hearing." *Brewer*, 779 F.2d at 264 (internal quotation marks omitted).

Here, John argues that Vaughn's dual roles undermined her neutrality enough to overcome the presumption of impartiality afforded school officials. Appellant Br. at 46. For support, John alleges that Vaughn dominated the hearing and that her remarks were designed to reduce John's credibility while bolstering Jane's credibility. R. 39 (Am. Compl. ¶ 58) (Page ID #1986). Vaughn's alleged dominance on the three-person panel raises legitimate concerns, as she was the only one of the three with conflicting roles. Furthermore, John alleges that Vaughn announced during the hearing that "I'll bet you do this [i.e., sexually assault women] all the time." *Id.* ¶ 66 (Page ID #1988). This statement implies that Vaughn had determined prior to the hearing that John was responsible for the misconduct alleged in this incident and had a propensity for engaging in sexual misconduct. Thus, although an individual's dual roles do not per se disqualify him or her from being an impartial arbiter, here John has alleged sufficient facts plausibly indicating that Vaughn's ability to be impartial "had been manifestly compromised." *Heyne*, 655 F.3d at 568.

John also alleges that the two other members of his Administrative Hearing Panel (Van Gundy-Yoder and Elliott) and the two individuals who decided his appeals (Ward and Brownell) were not neutral decision-makers. Appellant Br. at 47. He argues that Van Gundy-Yoder and Ward were biased due to their research interests. R. 39 (Am. Compl. ¶¶ 54, 74) (Page ID #1985, 1991). But merely being a feminist or researching topics that affect women does not support a reasonable inference that a person is biased. John also alleges that all of these individual defendants faced institutional pressures to find him responsible due to external influence from the federal government and lawsuits brought by private parties. R. 39 (Am. Compl. ¶¶ 86-100) (Page ID #1996-2001); R. 40 (Pl. Ex. 30: White House "Not Alone" Report at 22) (Page ID #2315); R.40-2 (Pl. Ex. 32: Miami Univ. Training at 49-54) (Page ID #2504-09).

These generalized allegations of institutional pressure, however, do not suffice to show that Van Gundy-Yoder, Elliott, Ward, and Brownell were actually biased, thus overcoming the presumption of impartiality afforded to them. *See*

Cummins, 662 Fed.Appx. at 449. John's complaint is silent as to how the public pressure to combat sexual misconduct on college campuses and the governmental pressure to comply with Title IX affected these individual defendants' decisions. This is not, for example, a case in which individual decision-makers were instructed by a superior to alter their disciplinary decisions based on the identity of the student. *See, e.g., Heyne,* 655 F.3d at 569 (holding that a plaintiff had alleged sufficient facts to support the inference that two arbiters were, although not personally biased against the plaintiff, partial because they had been instructed by the school principal "to enhance both the charges against and the discipline imposed on" the plaintiff because of his race). One could imagine a case in which the pressure placed on a university caused employees to feel that they must reach certain outcomes in the institution's adjudicative process in order to protect their own career prospects. But that is not what is alleged in this case. Consequently, John has not alleged sufficient facts to overcome the presumption of impartiality afforded to these four defendants.[8]

p.603 2. Notice of the Charges and Explanation of the Evidence

John's second-due process argument is that Miami University did not provide sufficient notice or an explanation of the evidence against him. Appellant Br. at 44-45. John's argument that the University provided him insufficient notice is unavailing. The timeline of the multiple communications Miami University had with John prior to his hearing, detailed in Section I *supra,* demonstrates that John had notice of the charges against him two days after the incident occurred and that the University explained the allegations against him in an in-person meeting eight days later. As the district court noted, *Miami Univ.,* 247 F.Supp.3d at 893, the type and timing of the notice John received is very similar to the notice in *Cummins,* which we held "was sufficiently formal and timely to satisfy due-process requirements and provide appellants with a meaningful opportunity to prepare a defense," 662 Fed.Appx. at 447.

John also argues that Miami University did not sufficiently explain the evidence against him because it withheld his disciplinary file from him. Appellant Br. at 45; R.39 (Am. Compl. ¶ 102) (Page ID #2001). John asserts that it is the University's policy for its Title IX investigator to interview individuals connected to the incident in question, compile written statements, police reports, and any other relevant documentation into a report. R. 39 (Am. Compl. ¶ 101) (Page ID #2001); R. 40-4 (Pl. Ex. 45: Minutes of Title IX Training at 3) (Page ID #2664). This report is then sent to the Office of Ethics and Student Conflict Resolution "for appropriate disciplinary action." R. 39 (Am. Compl. ¶ 101) (Page ID #2001); R. 40-4 (Pl. Ex. 45: Minutes of Title IX Training at 3) (Page ID #2664). John alleges that Miami University refused to provide this report, or the evidence against him contained within the report, even though the University's policies state that he was allowed access to this evidence. R. 39 (Am. Compl. ¶ 102) (Page ID #2001-02); R. 39-2 (Pl. Ex. 9: Miami Univ. Title IX Policy at 15) (Page ID #2182). The district court was correct to note that a mere failure by the University to follow its own internal guidelines does not give rise to a procedural-due-process violation. *Miami Univ.,* 247 F.Supp.3d at 893; *see, e.g., Cummins,* 662 Fed.Appx. at 445 n.2. The Constitution does require, however, that the student be provided the evidence against him. *Univ. of*

Cincinnati, 872 F.3d at 399-400. Thus, to the extent any of the evidence contained within this report was used by the Administrative Hearing Panel to adjudicate John's claim, and John was not provided this evidence, he has alleged a cognizable due-process violation. Because John has alleged that this report was held by the Office of Ethics and Student Conflict Resolution, it is plausible to infer that Vaughn, as director of that office, had control of this report and could have provided him access. John does not allege, however, that any of the other individual defendants he has sued had control over the report. Thus, John has sufficiently pleaded allegations with respect to this aspect of his procedural-due process claim as to Vaughn, but not as to the other individual defendants.

* * *

To summarize, John has sufficiently pleaded a procedural-due-process claim against Vaughn based on the claims that p.604 she was not an impartial adjudicator and that she did not fully provide him the evidence used against him. Thus, we reverse the district court with respect to these claims against Vaughn. We affirm, however, the district court's dismissal of John's procedural-due-process claims against Van Gundy-Yoder, Elliott, Ward, and Brownell.

D. Qualified Immunity

The district court also found that the individual defendants were entitled to qualified immunity from all of John's § 1983 claims on the basis that he had failed to state a claim that his constitutional rights were violated. *Miami Univ.,* 247 F.Supp.3d at 896. There is "a two-part test [that] determines whether qualified immunity applies: '(1) whether, considering the allegations in a light most favorable to the party injured, a constitutional right has been violated, and (2) whether that right was clearly established.'" *Heyne,* 655 F.3d at 562 (quoting *Colvin v. Caruso,* 605 F.3d 282, 290 (6th Cir. 2010)). These two prongs may be addressed in any order. *Courtright v. City of Battle Creek,* 839 F.3d 513, 518 (6th Cir. 2016). If either prong is not met, then the government officer is entitled to qualified immunity. *Id.*

As John has failed to state a claim that his substantive-due-process rights have been violated, qualified immunity shields all of the individual defendants from this claim against them. We therefore affirm the district court's holding that the individual defendants are entitled to qualified immunity from John's substantive-due-process claim. Furthermore, because John has failed to state a claim that Van Gundy-Yoder, Elliott, Ward, or Brownell violated his procedural-due-process or equal-protection rights, we affirm the district court's holding that these four defendants are entitled to qualified immunity with respect to Count 6 and 7 of John's complaint.

John has, however, sufficiently alleged a claim under § 1983 that Vaughn violated his equal-protection and procedural-due process rights. *See* Section IV.A and C *supra.* All of these rights were clearly established in the fall of 2014. John's "right to freedom from invidious [gender] discrimination under the Equal Protection Clause was certainly clearly established at all times pertinent to this action. . . ." *Rondigo, L.L.C. v. Twp. of Richmond,* 641 F.3d 673, 681 (6th Cir. 2011). John's procedural-due-process right to an impartial adjudicator and access to the evidence used against him was also clearly established. First, viewing the allegations in the light most favorable to John, we conclude that a reasonable person in Vaughn's position should have known that she was partial and that she could not, therefore, sit on John's Administrative Hearing Panel. "The impropriety of [Vaughn's] alleged conduct in failing to disqualify [her]self should have been apparent based on *Goss*[, 419 U.S. at 579-84, 95 S.Ct. 729], *Newsome*[*v. Batavia Local Sch. Dist.,* 842 F.2d 920, 927 (6th Cir. 1988)], and other precedent directly on point." *Heyne,* 655 F.3d at 568. Second, John's right to view all of the evidence against him is clearly established. *Id.* at 565 (citing *Goss,* 419 U.S. at 582, 95 S.Ct. 729). Thus, we reverse the district court's holding that Vaughn is entitled to qualified immunity from John's equal-protection and procedural-due-process claims.

V. CONCLUSION

We AFFIRM the district court's dismissal of John's Title IX hostile-environment claim, Title IX deliberate-indifference claim, and § 1983 substantive-due-process claim. We also AFFIRM the district court's dismissal of John's § 1983 procedural-due-process and equal-protection p.605 claims and related finding of qualified immunity with respect to Van Gundy-Yoder, Elliott, Ward, and Brownell. We REVERSE the district court's holding that John did not sufficiently plead his Title IX erroneous-outcome claim. Furthermore, we REVERSE the district court's dismissal of John's § 1983 procedural-due-process and equal-protection claims against Vaughn, as well as its holding that Vaughn was entitled to qualified immunity. We REMAND for further proceedings consistent with this opinion.

[1] The district court granted John's motion to allow the parties to use pseudonyms. R. 49 (Dist. Ct. Order re Pseudonyms) (Page ID #3270).

[2] These facts are drawn from John Doe's amended complaint and attached exhibits. R. 39 (Am. Compl.) (Page ID #1973-2028). As this case is in front of us on an appeal from the district court's grant of the defendants' motion to dismiss, we presume all factual allegations in the complaint to be true at this stage of the proceedings.

[3] The Fifth Circuit has recognized deliberate indifference as a theory of liability, as have lower courts in this Circuit. *Plummer v. Univ. of Houston,* 860 F.3d 767, 777 (5th Cir. 2017) (implicitly recognizing that plaintiffs could allege a deliberate-indifference claim by holding that their pleading of this claim was insufficient); *Wells v. Xavier Univ.,* 7 F.Supp.3d 746, 752 (S.D. Ohio 2014); *Doe v. Univ. of the South,* 687 F.Supp.2d 744, 757-58 (E.D. Tenn. 2009).

[4] Miami University's Student Handbook states that "[a]n individual cannot consent who is substantially impaired by any drug or intoxicant. . . ." R. 39-2 (Pl. Ex. 8: Miami Univ. Student Handbook at 39-40) (Page ID #2095-96).

[5] It also appears that Jane did not initiate a formal complaint herself, but rather Jane's friend reported the alleged sexual misconduct. R. 39-2 (Pl. Ex. 1: Jane Doe Statement at 2) (Page ID #2037).

[6] We do not rely on John's allegation that Van Gundy-Yoder, one of the members of the Administrative Hearing Panel, is biased against men because she researches "feminist criminological theory" and is affiliated with the Women's, Sexuality, and Gender Studies program at Miami University, R. 39 (Am. Compl. ¶ 54) (Page ID #1985), or that Ward, the chair of the University Appeals Board, was motivated by gender bias because her "research focuses on student alcohol consumption and sexual assault from the perspective of protecting females from males," *id.* ¶ 74 (Page ID #1991). Merely being a feminist, being affiliated with a gender-studies program, or researching sexual assault does not support a reasonable inference than an individual is biased against men. Nor do we rely on Vaughn's statements and body language at the hearing, *id.* ¶ 66 (Page ID #1988-89), which do not support an inference that she was motivated by biases against men as a group.

[7] John does not allege that the other individual defendants—Van Gundy-Yoder, Elliott, Ward, and Brownell—had any role in deciding whether to pursue disciplinary action against Jane. We focus, therefore, on Vaughn's alleged conduct.

[8] The defendants also argue that the partiality or impartiality of Ward and Brownell is not dispositive, because a student has no due-process right to appeal a school's disciplinary decision. Appellees Br. at 41. In support of this proposition, the defendants cite *C.Y. ex rel. Antone v. Lakeview Pub. Sch.*, 557 Fed. Appx. 426, 434 (6th Cir. 2014), and *Flaim*, 418 F.3d at 642. In *Flaim*, we said that "[c]ourts have consistently held that there is no right to an appeal from an academic disciplinary hearing that satisfies due process." *Flaim*, 418 F.3d at 642. However, we then considered whether an appeal was part of the due-process rights to which Flaim was entitled under the *Mathews* framework. *Id.* We concluded that given the "rather unique" circumstances of the case—Flaim was expelled on the basis of a felony conviction—Flaim was not entitled to an appeal. *Id.* at 643. In doing so, "we strongly emphasize[d] that a disciplinary hearing involving a record of conviction is wholly different from a case involving disputes of fact, even if the university believes the evidence to be overwhelming." *Id.* at 643 n.7. *C.Y.*, meanwhile, involved the expulsion of a high school freshman for bringing a knife to school and threatening to stab another student. *C.Y.*, 418 Fed.Appx. at 427. In this unpublished decision, we relied on *Flaim* to reject C.Y.'s claim that she had the right to an appeal. *Id.* at 433.

Neither of these cases forecloses the possibility that in a school discipline case in which the private interest is so significant—a potential lifetime of stigma and preclusion from further educational and employment opportunities—and there is a dispute about the facts of the events in question, due process entitles a student to some type of appeals process. *Cf. Flaim*, 418 F.3d at 642 n.6 ("An appeal is valuable for many reasons, among them being the gravity of the decision to expel a student from medical school, the personal and professional consequences an expelled student will face, the institution's role as an educator and teacher of young people, and more. An appeal also provides additional assurance to the institution that a just result has been reached and provides the student with, irrespective of the outcome, significant participation value."); *Heyne*, 655 F.3d at 569 ("Students have no constitutional right to appeal the decision of school officials *to suspend them for ten days or fewer.*" (emphasis added)). We do not need to reach that question here, because, even assuming due process provides a right to appeal, John has failed to allege a violation of his due-process rights at the appeals level of Miami University's discipline system. As explained above, John's claim that the individual defendants who heard his appeals were not neutral arbiters because of institutional pressures is not viable. Furthermore, although his allegation that he was denied access to a recording of his panel hearing when preparing his appeal might raise a due-process violation, Appellant Br. at 45, John does not allege that any of the individuals he has sued under § 1983 had control of this recording and denied a request to access it. *See* R. 39 (Am. Compl. ¶ 56) (Page ID #1985) (alleging that John requested "Miami provide him a copy of the recording" and that "Miami failed to provide" him the copy).

903 F.3d 575 (2018)

John DOE, Plaintiff-Appellant,

v.

David H. BAUM; Susan Pritzel; Tabitha Bentley; E. Royster Harper; Nadia Bazzy; Erik Wessel; University of Michigan; Board of Regents of the University of Michigan, Defendants-Appellees.

No. 17-2213.

United States Court of Appeals, Sixth Circuit.

Argued: August 1, 2018.

Decided and Filed: September 7, 2018.

Rehearing En Banc Denied October 11, 2018.

Doe v. Baum, 903 F. 3d 575 (6th Cir. 2018)

Appeal from the United States District Court for the Eastern District of Michigan at Detroit. No. 2:16-cv-13174—David M. Lawson, District Judge.

COUNSEL ARGUED: Deborah L. Gordon, Deborah Gordon Law, Bloomfield Hills, Michigan, for Appellant. David W. DeBruin, Jenner & Block, LLP, Washington, D.C., for Appellees. ON BRIEF: Deborah L. Gordon, Irina L. Vaynerman, Deborah Gordon Law, Bloomfield Hills, Michigan, for Appellant. David W. DeBruin, Jenner & Block, LLP, Washington, D.C., Brian M. Schwartz, Miller, Canfield, Paddock, and Stone, P.L.C., Detroit, Michigan, for Appellees.

Before: GILMAN, GIBBONS, and THAPAR, Circuit Judges.

THAPAR, J., delivered the opinion of the court, in which GIBBONS, J., joined, and GILMAN, J., joined in part. GIBBONS, J. (pg. 588), delivered a separate concurrence. GILMAN, J. (pp. 588-93), delivered a separate opinion concurring in part and dissenting in part.

p.578 **OPINION**

THAPAR, Circuit Judge.

Thirteen years ago, this court suggested that cross-examination may be required in school disciplinary proceedings where the case hinged on a question of credibility. *Flaim v. Med. Coll. of Ohio*, 418 F.3d 629, 641 (6th Cir. 2005). Just last year, we encountered the credibility contest that we contemplated in *Flaim* and confirmed that when credibility is at issue, the Due Process Clause mandates that a university provide accused students a hearing with the opportunity to conduct cross-examination. *Doe v. Univ. of Cincinnati*, 872 F.3d 393, 401-02 (6th Cir. 2017). Today, we reiterate that holding once again: if a public university has to choose between competing narratives to resolve a case, the university must give the accused student or his agent an opportunity to cross-examine the accuser and adverse witnesses in the presence of a neutral fact-finder. Because the University of Michigan failed to comply with this rule, we reverse.

I.

John Doe and Jane Roe were students at the University of Michigan. Halfway through Roe's freshman and Doe's junior year, the two crossed paths at a "Risky Business" themed fraternity party. While p.579 there, they had a drink, danced, and eventually had sex. Two days later, Roe filed a sexual misconduct complaint with the university claiming that she was too drunk to consent. And since having sex with an incapacitated person (unsurprisingly) violates university policy, the administration immediately launched an investigation. Over the course of three months, the school's investigator collected evidence and interviewed Roe, Doe, and twenty-three other witnesses. Two stories emerged.

First, Doe told the investigator that Roe did not appear drunk and that she was an active participant in their sexual encounter. According to him, the night went something like this: after he and Roe had a drink, danced, and kissed at the party, the two decided to go upstairs to his bedroom. Once there, they kissed "vigorous[ly]" and eventually made their way onto his bed. R. 16, Pg. ID 332. After they jointly removed their clothing, he asked Roe if she wanted to have sex. She said, "Yeah," and the two proceeded to have intercourse followed by oral sex. *Id.* at Pg. ID 333-34. When they were done, they cuddled until Roe became sick and vomited into a trash can by Doe's bed. Doe rubbed her back for five or so minutes and then left to use the bathroom and talk with friends. By the time he returned, Roe was crying and another female student was helping her gather her things. He asked Roe if she was okay, but Roe's new companion told him to "[g]o away" and the two women walked out of the room. *Id.* at Pg. ID 335. At the time, he assumed that Roe was upset because he had left her alone after they had sex. He asserted that he had no reason to believe that she was drunk or that Roe thought any of his sexual advances were unwelcome.

Roe remembered the night differently. According to her, she was drunk and unaware of her surroundings when she and Doe went to his room. While kissing near the doorway, she told Doe "no sex" before she "flopped" onto his bed. *Id.* at Pg. ID 325-26. Without asking, Doe undressed her and had intercourse with her while she "laid there in a hazy state of black out." *Id.* at Pg. ID 326. And at some point, she passed out and woke up to Doe having oral sex with her. Afterwards, she felt a "spinning sensation" and fell back onto the bed. *Id.* at Pg. ID 327. Doe asked her if she was okay, and she told him that she was not. So Doe placed a trash can by the side of his bed and left the room. She proceeded to vomit into the trash can. Afterward, she attempted to find her clothes but could not get her bearings. Feeling a sense of "desperation and defeat," she tried to catch another female student's attention by making "vomit sounds." *Id.* It worked, and the female student ("Witness 2") helped Roe find her clothes, put them on, and get back to her dorm.

If Doe's and Roe's stories seem at odds, the twenty-three other witnesses did not offer much clarification. Almost all of the male witnesses corroborated Doe's story, and all of the female witnesses corroborated Roe's. For example, Doe's roommate said that Roe "didn't seem like she was hammered or that drunk," although he stated that he did not "want to speculate" about whether she had had some alcohol because he did not talk to her directly or "really interact with [her]" much. *Id.* at Pg. ID 339. Yet he mentioned that in his two interactions with her, he did not smell alcohol on her. *Id.* Doe's roommate further alleged that Roe and Witness 2 were just "rallying against a fraternity guy." *Id.* at Pg. ID 339-41. Another member of Doe's fraternity told the investigator that he saw Doe and Roe "making out" on the dance floor and there was no reason to suspect that either of them had too much to drink. *Id.* at Pg. ID 347. And two others stated that Roe did not appear drunk when she left Doe's room at the end of the night, p.580 although they indicated they had limited observations of Roe.

Roe's sorority sisters, on the other hand, reported that Roe seemed "more than a little buzzed" at the party because her eyes were "open but unfocused" and she "trail[ed] off at the end of sentences." *Id.* at Pg. ID 345-46. The female student who helped Roe leave the party told the investigator that she found Roe crying and "very drunk" in Doe's bed. *Id.* at Pg. ID 342-43. And two other friends provided that when Roe returned to her dorm that night, she sobbed on the floor of her room and said "she thought she'd been raped." *Id.* at Pg. ID 352.

Given the students' conflicting statements, the investigator concluded that the evidence supporting a finding of sexual misconduct was not more convincing than the evidence offered in opposition to it. The investigator did note, however, that Witness 2 might have been a more credible witness because she had no prior connection to Doe, Roe, or their respective Greek organizations. But because Witness 2 only observed Roe after the sexual encounter had ended, the investigator concluded that she could not address the relevant question — Roe's level of intoxication *during* the encounter or what signs of intoxication she manifested at that time. So after three months of thorough fact-finding, the investigator was unable to say that Roe exhibited outward signs of incapacitation that Doe would have noticed before initiating sexual activity. Accordingly, the investigator recommended that the administration rule in Doe's favor and close the case.

Roe appealed. She argued that the evidence did not support the investigator's findings and asked the university to reconsider. The case went up to the university's Appeals Board, and a three-member panel reviewed the investigator's report. After two closed sessions (without considering new evidence or interviewing any students), the Board reversed. Although the Board found that the investigation was fair and thorough, it thought the investigator was wrong to conclude that the evidence was in equipoise. According to the Board, Roe's description of events was "more credible" than Doe's, and Roe's witnesses were more persuasive. R. 6-5, Pg. ID 274-75. As a result, the university set the investigator's recommendation aside and proceeded to the sanction phase. Facing the possibility of expulsion, Doe agreed to withdraw from the university. He was 13.5 credits short of graduating.

Since then, Doe filed a lawsuit claiming that the university's disciplinary proceedings violated the Due Process Clause and Title IX. He argues that because the university's decision turned on a credibility finding, the school was required to give him a hearing with an opportunity to cross-examine Roe and adverse witnesses. He also maintains that the Board violated Title IX by discriminating against him on account of his gender. The university filed a motion to dismiss, which the district court granted in full. Doe now appeals, and we review de novo. *Kottmyer v. Maas,* 436 F.3d 684, 688 (6th Cir. 2006).

II.

To survive a motion to dismiss, a complaint must provide "a short and plain statement of the claim showing that the [plaintiff] is entitled to relief." Fed. R. Civ. P. 8(a)(2). A plaintiff shows that he is entitled to relief by "plausibly suggesting" that he can meet the elements of his claim. *Bell Atl. Corp. v. Twombly,* 550 U.S. 544, 557, 127 S.Ct. 1955, 167 L.Ed.2d 929 (2007). And a plaintiff's suggestion is plausible when it contains enough factual content that the court can reasonably infer that the defendant is liable. *Ashcroft v. Iqbal,* 556 U.S. 662, 678, 129 S.Ct. 1937, 173 L.Ed.2d 868 (2009). Legal conclusions, p.581 "formulaic recitation[s]" of the claim's elements, and "naked assertion[s]" of liability are all insufficient. *Id.* (second alteration in original) (quoting *Twombly,* 550 U.S. at 557, 127 S.Ct. 1955).

When evaluating a complaint's sufficiency, courts use a three-step process. First, the court must accept all of the plaintiff's factual allegations as true. *Logsdon v. Hains,* 492 F.3d 334, 340 (6th Cir. 2007). Second, the court must draw all reasonable inferences in the plaintiff's favor. *Id.* And third, the court must take all of those facts and inferences and determine whether they plausibly give rise to an entitlement to relief. *Iqbal,* 556 U.S. at 679, 129 S.Ct. 1937. If it is at all plausible (beyond a wing and a prayer) that a plaintiff would succeed if he proved everything in his complaint, the case proceeds.

III.

Doe first argues that the university violated his due process rights during his disciplinary proceedings. He claims that because the university's decision ultimately turned on a credibility determination, the school was required to give him a hearing with an opportunity to cross-examine Roe and other adverse witnesses. The district court dismissed this claim, finding that even if credibility was at issue, the university's failure to allow for cross-examination was "immaterial" in Doe's case. R. 74, Pg. ID 2871. We disagree.

When it comes to due process, the "opportunity to be heard" is the constitutional minimum. *Grannis v. Ordean,* 234 U.S. 385, 394, 34 S.Ct. 779, 58 L.Ed. 1363 (1914). But determining what being "heard" looks like in each particular case is a harder question. The Supreme Court has declined to set out a universal rule and instead instructs lower courts to consider the parties' competing interests. *See Mathews v. Eldridge,* 424 U.S. 319, 335, 96 S.Ct. 893, 47 L.Ed.2d 18 (1976); *Goss v. Lopez,* 419 U.S. 565, 579, 95 S.Ct. 729, 42 L.Ed.2d 725 (1975). So, consistent with this command, our circuit has made two things clear: (1) if a student is accused of misconduct, the university must hold some sort of hearing before imposing a sanction as serious as expulsion or suspension, and (2) when the university's determination turns on the credibility of the accuser, the accused, or witnesses, that hearing must include an opportunity for cross-examination. *Univ. of Cincinnati,* 872 F.3d at 399-402; *Flaim,* 418 F.3d at 641.

Due process requires cross-examination in circumstances like these because it is "the greatest legal engine ever invented" for uncovering the truth. *Univ. of Cincinnati,* 872 F.3d at 401-02 (citation omitted).[1] Not only does cross-examination allow the accused to identify inconsistencies in the other side's story, but it also gives the fact-finder an opportunity to assess a witness's demeanor and determine who can be trusted. *Id.* So if a university is faced with competing narratives about potential misconduct, the administration must facilitate some form of cross-examination in order to satisfy due process. *Id.* at 402.

Doe claims that the university ran afoul of this well-established rule in his disciplinary proceedings. And the pleadings in his case suggest that he is right. The university's decision rested on a credibility determination: the Board found Doe responsible after concluding that Roe and p.582 her witnesses were "more credible" than Doe and his. R. 6-5, Pg. ID 274-75. Nevertheless, Doe never received an opportunity to cross-examine Roe or her witnesses — not before the investigator, and not before the Board. As a result, there is a significant risk that the university erroneously deprived Doe of his protected interests.[2] *See Mathews,* 424 U.S. at 335, 96 S.Ct. 893.

This risk is all the more troubling considering the significance of Doe's interests and the minimal burden that the university would bear by allowing cross-examination in Doe's case. *See id.* at 334-35, 96 S.Ct. 893. Time and again, this circuit has reiterated that students have a substantial interest at stake when it comes to school disciplinary hearings for sexual misconduct. *Doe v. Miami Univ.,* 882 F.3d 579, 600 (6th Cir. 2018); *Univ. of Cincinnati,* 872 F.3d at 400; *Doe v. Cummins,* 662 F. App'x 437, 446 (6th Cir. 2016). Being labeled a sex offender by a university has both an immediate and lasting impact on a student's life. *Miami Univ.,* 882 F.3d at 600. The student may be forced to withdraw from his classes and move out of his university housing. *Id.* His personal relationships might suffer. *See id.* And he could face difficulty obtaining educational and employment opportunities down the road, especially if he is expelled. *Id.*

In contrast, providing Doe a hearing with the opportunity for cross-examination would have cost the university very little. As it turns out, the university already provides for a hearing with cross-examination in all misconduct cases other than those involving sexual assault. So the administration already has all the resources it needs to facilitate cross-examination and knows how to oversee the process. *See Univ. of Cincinnati,* 872 F.3d at 406 (noting that a university does not bear a significant administrative burden when it already has procedures in place to accommodate cross-examination). And, importantly, the university identifies no substantial burden that would be imposed on it if it were required to provide an opportunity for cross-examination in this context.

Still, the university offers four reasons why Doe's claim is not as plausible as it seems. None do the trick. First, the university contends that even if Doe did not have a formal opportunity to question Roe, he was permitted to review her statement and submit a response identifying inconsistencies for the investigator. As such, the university claims that there would have been no added benefit to cross-examination. But this circuit has already flatly rejected that argument. In *University of Cincinnati,* we explained that an accused's ability "to draw attention to alleged inconsistencies" in the accuser's statements does not render cross-examination futile. *Id.* at 401-02. That conclusion applies equally here, and we see no reason to doubt its wisdom. Cross-examination is essential in cases like Doe's because it does *more* than uncover inconsistencies — it "takes aim at credibility like no other procedural device." *Id.* Without the back-and-forth of adversarial questioning, the accused cannot probe the witness's story to test her memory, intelligence, or potential ulterior motives. *Id.* at 402. Nor can the fact-finder observe the witness's demeanor under that questioning. *Id.* For that reason, written statements cannot substitute for cross-examination. *See*

Brutus Essay XIII, in *The Anti-Federalist* 180 (Herbert J. Storing ed., 1985) ("It is of great importance in the distribution of justice that p.583 witnesses should be examined face to face, that the parties should have the fairest opportunity of cross-examining them in order to bring out the whole truth; there is something in the manner in which a witness delivers his testimony which cannot be committed to paper, and which yet very frequently gives a complexion to his evidence, very different from what it would bear if committed to writing...."). Instead, the university must allow for some form of *live* questioning *in front of* the fact-finder. *See Univ. of Cincinnati*, 872 F.3d at 402-03, 406 (noting that this requirement can be facilitated through modern technology, including, for example, by allowing a witness to be questioned via Skype "without physical presence").

That is not to say, however, that the accused student always has a right to *personally* confront his accuser and other witnesses. *See Miami Univ.*, 882 F.3d at 600 (noting that "even in the face of a sexual-assault accusation," the protections afforded to an accused "need not reach the same level ... that would be present in a criminal prosecution" (quoting *Univ. of Cincinnati*, 872 F.3d at 400)). Universities have a legitimate interest in avoiding procedures that may subject an alleged victim to further harm or harassment. And in sexual misconduct cases, allowing the accused to cross-examine the accuser may do just that. *See Univ. of Cincinnati*, 872 F.3d at 403. But in circumstances like these, the answer is not to deny cross-examination altogether. Instead, the university could allow the accused student's agent to conduct cross-examination on his behalf. After all, an individual aligned with the accused student can accomplish the benefits of cross-examination — its adversarial nature and the opportunity for follow-up — without subjecting the accuser to the emotional trauma of directly confronting her alleged attacker. *Cf. Maryland v. Craig*, 497 U.S. 836, 857, 110 S.Ct. 3157, 111 L.Ed.2d 666 (1990) (holding that where forcing the alleged victim to testify in the physical presence of the defendant may result in trauma, the court could use an alternative procedure that "ensures the reliability of the evidence by subjecting it to rigorous adversarial testing" through "full cross-examination" and ensuring that the alleged victim could be "observed by the judge, jury, and defendant as they testified"). The university's first argument is therefore unavailing.[3]

Second, the university contends that Doe is not entitled to cross-examination because the university's decision did not depend *entirely* on a credibility contest between Roe and Doe. For support, the university brings our attention back to *University of Cincinnati*, where we emphasized the exclusively "he said/she said" nature of the investigation at issue in that case. 872 F.3d at 395, 402. But the university reads far too much into that point. When we emphasized the exclusively "he said/she said" nature of the *University of Cincinnati* dispute, we were not implying that cross-examination would be less important in cases where the school's finding rested on the credibility of several witnesses instead of one or two. Rather, we merely distinguished that case from others holding that cross-examination was unnecessary when the university's decision did not rely on *any testimonial evidence at* p.584 *all. Id.* at 401, 405 (distinguishing *Plummer v. Houston*, 860 F.3d 767, 775-76 (5th Cir. 2017), which held that cross-examination was unnecessary when conduct depicted in videos and photos was sufficient to sustain a finding of misconduct without resorting to testimonial evidence); *see also Flaim*, 418 F.3d at 641. Accordingly, *University of*

Cincinnati does not stand for the proposition that cross-examination is required only if the university's decision depends solely on the accuser's statement. Instead, *University of Cincinnati* is consistent with our conclusion today: if credibility is in dispute and material to the outcome, due process requires cross-examination. *See* 872 F.3d at 406 (recognizing that credibility disputes might be more common in sexual misconduct proceedings than other university disciplinary investigations).

Third, the university claims that cross-examination was unnecessary in Doe's case because he admitted to the misconduct in a police interview the day after the incident in question. Here, the university is right about the law but wrong about the facts. This court has long held that cross-examination is unnecessary if a student admits to engaging in misconduct. *Flaim,* 418 F.3d at 641. After all, there is little to be gained by subjecting witnesses to adversarial questioning when the accused student has already confessed. But at the motion-to-dismiss stage, we cannot conclude that Doe confessed to the misconduct in this case. To see why, a closer look at the police report is instructive.

During the police interview, a detective asked Doe to describe the previous night's sexual encounter. When doing so, Doe told the detective that Roe performed oral sex on him before they engaged in intercourse, and that when the pair began to have intercourse, Roe was on top. As it turns out, this story was different than the one Roe had reported to the detective earlier that day. According to the detective, Roe claimed that she told Doe "no sex" before making her way to the bed, and that she performed oral sex on Doe after the pair had intercourse. The detective thus relayed Roe's version of the story to Doe, and Doe immediately conceded that Roe was right and that he "got it all wrong." R. 16, Pg. ID 356. Even so, however, Doe reiterated that (1) he never heard Roe say "no sex," (2) he "didn't rape" Roe, and (3) he believed their sexual encounter was consensual. *Id.*

Because the district court made this report part of the pleadings, we must read it in the light most favorable to Doe.[4] *See Logsdon,* 492 F.3d at 340. When we do, we cannot conclude that Doe admitted to any of the critical facts in his case — i.e., that Roe was too drunk to consent to sex, and that he knew or should have known as much. For one, we would have to ignore Doe's claim that the sex was "consensual." R. 16, Pg. ID 356. And for another, because Doe did not mention anything about Roe's level of intoxication in his own account of the night's events, his concession that Roe was correct and that he "got it all wrong" appears to relate only to the points on which the detective said their two accounts actually diverged — the order of the sexual acts. *See id.,* Pg. ID 354-56. This alleged confession thus does not sufficiently rebut the plausibility of Doe's claim.

The university offers one last ditch effort to avoid reversal. It points out that although Doe did not have an opportunity to cross-examine Roe in the university disciplinary process, he recently deposed her in state civil proceedings. According to the university, because Roe's deposition is consistent with what she told the investigator, Doe's inability to cross-examine her during the disciplinary proceedings did not cause any prejudice. To start, Doe disputes whether Roe's deposition is, in fact, consistent with her earlier statements in the disciplinary process. But more importantly, Roe's later deposition has no bearing on this case. As discussed above, the value of cross-examination is tied to the fact-finder's ability to assess the witness's demeanor. *Univ. of Cincinnati,* 872 F.3d at 402. So just as a written response insufficiently substitutes for cross-examination, so too does a written deposition transcript. And, critically, cross-examination for the sake of cross-examination is not what Doe seeks. Rather, Doe seeks cross-examination as part of the credibility assessment *by the university*. That a state court later allowed for cross-examination as a part of *its* fact-finding after the university had already made its decision is beside the point. If anything, the fact that the state court allowed cross-examination only goes to show just how far removed the university's fact-finding procedures are from the tried and true methods invoked by courts. *See id.* at 404-05 (noting that while classrooms are not courtrooms, at the very least a circumscribed version of cross-examination is required (citing *Cummins,* 662 F. App'x at 448)).

In sum, accepting all of Doe's factual allegations as true and drawing all reasonable inferences in his favor, he has raised a plausible claim for relief under the Due Process Clause. We thus reverse the district court's decision to dismiss his claim.[5]

IV.

Doe also sued under Title IX, which prohibits federally-funded universities from discriminating against students on the basis of sex. 20 U.S.C. § 1681(a); *Cannon v. Univ. of Chi.,* 441 U.S. 677, 717, 99 S.Ct. 1946, 60 L.Ed.2d 560 (1979) (recognizing an implied private right of action under Title IX). He advances three theories of liability, claiming that the university (1) reached an erroneous outcome in his case because of his sex, (2) relied on archaic assumptions about the sexes when rendering a decision, and (3) exhibited deliberate indifference to sex discrimination in his disciplinary proceedings.

Erroneous Outcome. A university violates Title IX when it reaches an erroneous outcome in a student's disciplinary proceeding because of the student's sex. *See Miami Univ.,* 882 F.3d at 592. To survive a motion to dismiss under the erroneous-outcome theory, a plaintiff must plead facts sufficient to (1) "cast some articulable doubt" on the accuracy of the disciplinary proceeding's outcome, and (2) demonstrate a "particularized ... causal connection between the flawed outcome and gender bias." *Id.* (alteration in original) (quoting *Cummins,* 662 F. App'x at 452). The district court held that Doe's complaint failed to meet either element and dismissed his claim. We reverse.

First, because Doe alleged that the university did not provide an opportunity for cross-examination even though credibility was at stake in his case, he has p.586 pled facts sufficient to cast some articulable doubt on the accuracy of the disciplinary proceeding's outcome. *See Yusuf v. Vassar Coll.,* 35 F.3d 709, 715 (2d Cir. 1994) (noting the "pleading burden in this regard is not heavy" and can be met by alleging "particular procedural flaws affecting the proof"); *see also Univ. of Cincinnati,* 872 F.3d at 401 ("Few procedures safeguard accuracy better than adversarial questioning."). Second, Doe has pointed to circumstances surrounding his disciplinary proceedings that, accepting all of his factual allegations as true and drawing all reasonable inferences in his favor, plausibly suggest the university acted with bias based on his sex. *See Iqbal,* 556 U.S. at 681-82, 129 S.Ct. 1937.

Around two years before Doe's disciplinary proceeding, the federal government launched an investigation to determine whether the university's process for responding to allegations of sexual misconduct discriminated against women. When news of the investigation broke, student groups and local media outlets sharply criticized the administration. The federal government's investigation and the negative media reports continued for years, throughout the Board's consideration of Doe's case.

This public attention and the ongoing investigation put pressure on the university to prove that it took complaints of sexual misconduct seriously. The university stood to lose millions in federal aid if the Department found it non-compliant with Title IX. The university also knew that a female student had triggered the federal investigation and that the news media consistently highlighted the university's poor response to female complainants. Of course, all of this external pressure alone is not enough to state a claim that the university acted with bias in this particular case. Rather, it provides a backdrop that, when combined with other circumstantial evidence of bias in Doe's specific proceeding, gives rise to a plausible claim. *See Twombly*, 550 U.S. at 570, 127 S.Ct. 1955.

Specifically, the Board credited exclusively female testimony (from Roe and her witnesses) and rejected all of the male testimony (from Doe and his witnesses). In doing so, the Board explained that Doe's witnesses lacked credibility because "many of them were fraternity brothers of [Doe]." But the Board did not similarly note that several of Roe's witnesses were her sorority sisters, nor did it note that they were female. This is all the more telling in that the initial investigator who actually interviewed all of these witnesses found in favor of Doe. The Board, by contrast, made all of these credibility findings on a cold record.

When viewing this evidence in the light most favorable to Doe, as we must, one plausible explanation is that the Board discredited all males, including Doe, and credited all females, including Roe, because of gender bias. And so this specific allegation of adjudicator bias, combined with the external pressure facing the university, makes Doe's claim plausible. Indeed, other courts facing similar allegations have reached the same result. *See, e.g., Miami Univ.*, 882 F.3d at 594 (plaintiff's complaint was sufficient where allegations included that the university faced "pressure from the government to combat vigorously sexual assault on college campuses and the severe potential punishment — loss of all federal funds — if it failed to comply"); *Doe v. Columbia Univ.*, 831 F.3d 46, 56-57 (2d Cir. 2016) (plaintiff's complaint pointing to student group criticism and university statements was sufficient to raise a plausible inference of bias under a "minimal plausible inference" standard); *Doe v. Amherst Coll.*, 238 F.Supp.3d 195, 223 (D. Mass. 2017) (plaintiff's complaint was sufficient where allegations p.587 suggested that university was trying to "appease" a biased, student-led movement); *Doe v. Lynn Univ., Inc.*, 235 F.Supp.3d 1336, 1340-42 (S.D. Fla. 2017) (plaintiff's complaint was sufficient where allegations suggested that university was reacting to "pressure from the public and the parents of female students" to punish males accused of sexual misconduct); *Wells v. Xavier Univ.*, 7 F.Supp.3d 746, 751 (S.D. Ohio 2014) (plaintiff's complaint was sufficient where, taken together, his allegations suggested that university was "reacting against him[] as a male" in response to a Department of Education investigation).

The dissent disagrees, taking a deep and thoughtful dive into the factual record to conclude that there is "no basis to reasonably infer" that Doe was a victim of gender discrimination. But when viewed against the backdrop of external pressure, the

Board's decision to discredit Doe's fraternity brothers in part because they were fraternity brothers, while not holding Roe's witnesses to the same standard, is basis enough at the motion-to-dismiss stage. Of course, anti-male bias is not the only plausible explanation for the university's conduct, or even the most plausible. The university might have been unaffected by the federal investigation or the media's criticism, and the significance of the Board's decision to disregard Doe's witnesses' statements might be overblown. And as the dissent points out, the Board might have ruled the way it did because it believed Witness 2's testimony was more credible. But alternative explanations are not fatal to Doe's ability to survive a Rule 12(b)(6) motion to dismiss. *See 16630 Southfield Ltd. P'ship v. Flagstar Bank*, F.S.B., 727 F.3d 502, 505 (6th Cir. 2013) ("[T]he mere existence of more likely alternative explanations does not automatically entitle a defendant to dismissal."); *Watson Carpet & Floor Covering, Inc. v. Mohawk Indus., Inc.*, 648 F.3d 452, 458 (6th Cir. 2011) (noting that there are often several plausible explanations for a defendant's conduct, but "[f]erreting out the most likely reason for the defendants' actions is not appropriate at the pleadings stage"). Doe's allegations do not have to give rise to the *most* plausible explanation — they just have to give rise to one of them. *See Iqbal*, 556 U.S. at 678, 129 S.Ct. 1937 (stating that there is no "probability requirement" at the pleading stage (quoting *Twombly*, 550 U.S. at 556, 127 S.Ct. 1955)).

As this case proceeds and a record is developed, evidence might very well come to show that today's inference is the least plausible of the bunch. Certain allegations that we must assume are true might be proven false. And with the benefit of exhibits, testimony, and cross-examination, a fact-finder may conclude that the inferences we were required to draw in Doe's favor are simply untenable. But these possibilities cannot affect this court's evaluation of Doe's complaint. Our job is simply to ensure that Doe is not deprived of an opportunity to prove what he has alleged unless he would lose regardless. Because Doe has alleged facts that state a plausible claim for relief, we reverse the district court's decision to dismiss his complaint. Whether he will ultimately succeed is a question for another day.

Archaic Assumptions and Deliberate Indifference. Doe advances two more theories of Title IX liability. First, he maintains that the university relied on archaic assumptions about the sexes when resolving his case. And second, he claims that the university was deliberately indifferent to the Board's sex discrimination. The problem for Doe, however, is that neither of these theories applies in the context of university disciplinary proceedings.

Title IX plaintiffs use the archaic-assumptions theory to show that a p.588 school denied a student an equal opportunity to participate in an athletic program because of historical assumptions about boys' and girls' physical capabilities. *See Mallory v. Ohio Univ.*, 76 F. App'x 634, 638-39 (6th Cir. 2003). This court has never applied the theory outside of the athletic context, and, indeed, we have repeatedly refused litigants' requests to do so. *See Cummins*, 662 F. App'x at 451 n.9. Since Doe has not offered any reason why we should change course and take that step today, we affirm the district court's decision to dismiss on this ground.

The same problem dooms Doe's deliberate-indifference theory. The deliberate-indifference theory was designed for plaintiffs alleging *sexual harassment*. *See Horner v. Ky. High Sch. Athletic Ass'n*, 206 F.3d 685, 693 (6th Cir. 2000) (explaining that the deliberate-indifference test arose from Supreme Court cases that "all address deliberate indifference to sexual harassment"). And though sexual harassment is a form of discrimination for purposes of Title IX, *Davis v. Monroe Cty. Bd. of Educ.,* 526 U.S. 629, 649-50, 119 S.Ct. 1661, 143 L.Ed.2d 839 (1999), we have held that to plead a Title IX deliberate-indifference claim, "the misconduct alleged must be sexual harassment," not just a biased disciplinary process. *Miami Univ.,* 882 F.3d at 591. Because Doe did not allege that actionable sexual harassment occurred during his disciplinary proceedings, he failed to state a claim under Title IX by way of deliberate indifference.

V.

Accordingly, we REVERSE the district court's dismissal of John Doe's procedural due process claim insofar as it is based on the university's failure to provide a hearing with the opportunity for cross-examination, we REVERSE the district court's dismissal of John Doe's Title IX claim insofar as it is based on erroneous outcome, and we REMAND for further proceedings consistent with this opinion.

JULIA SMITH GIBBONS, Circuit Judge, concurring.

CONCURRENCE

I write separately to make one discrete point with respect to the Title IX Claim. I agree that Doe has plausibly alleged a claim of gender bias. The inclusion of materials, other than the complaint, in the record makes a summary judgment standard tempting. The dissent avoids summary judgment language, but its analytical approach is analogous to the process by which a judge determines the existence of a genuine issue of material fact. Yet Doe is entitled to the full benefit of the standard for considering a motion to dismiss. Under that standard, my view is that Doe's complaint survives.

RONALD LEE GILMAN, Circuit Judge, concurring in part and dissenting in part.

CONCURRING IN PART AND DISSENTING IN PART

I concur in the majority's judgment (but not in its discussion) with regard to the disposition of Doe's due process claim. As to Doe's Title IX claim, I would affirm the judgment of the district court because of Doe's failure to plausibly state a claim under Title IX.

I. Due process claim

Although I agree that Doe's due process rights were violated when he was not permitted the opportunity to engage in *any form* of cross-examination of the witnesses against him, I disagree with the majority about the scope of cross-examination mandated by the United States Constitution in p.589 this context. I particularly believe that the majority has traveled "a bridge too far" in mandating that "if the university does not want the accused to cross examine the accuser under any scenario, then it must allow a representative to do so." Maj. Op. at 583 n.3.

This court has found that when witness credibility is at issue, the accused must have an opportunity for at least a "circumscribed form" of cross-examination where he or she is allowed to submit questions to the trier of fact, who will then directly pose those questions to the witnesses. *Doe v. Cummins*, 662 F. App'x 437, 446 (6th Cir. 2016). *Cummins* held that this requirement was met even where the trier of fact did not ask all the questions submitted or allow an opportunity to submit follow-up questions. *Id.* at 448; *see also Doe v. Univ. of Cincinnati*, 872 F.3d 393, 406 (6th Cir. 2017) (emphasizing that the university has only a narrow obligation to provide the trier of fact with an opportunity "to evaluate an alleged victim's credibility, not [to allow] the accused to physically confront his accuser," and that "what matters" is that the trier of fact has the "ability to assess the demeanor of both the accused and his accuser"); *Nash v. Auburn University*, 812 F.2d 655, 664 (11th Cir. 1987) (finding that the due process rights of a student suspended for academic dishonesty were not violated where he was given the opportunity to submit questions to the trier of fact, who would then direct the questions to the witnesses, and that the student did not have a right to "question the adverse witnesses in the usual, adversarial manner").

Although *Cummins* is factually distinguishable because the two accused students faced only suspension and probation rather than expulsion, the majority cites no case that would support its expansion of Doe's cross-examination rights beyond those set forth in *Cummins*. Nor does the majority explain why the *Eldridge* balancing factors would require the added protection of unfettered cross-examination by a representative whenever expulsion from a university is a potential penalty. *See Mathews v. Eldridge*, 424 U.S. 319, 335, 96 S.Ct. 893, 47 L.Ed.2d 18 (1976).

And this expansion, in the absence of a focused and caselaw-supported analysis, leaves many questions unanswered. For example, who is the "representative" that will be allowed to question witnesses on the accused's behalf? Is it an attorney? If so, then this expanded right of cross-examination conflicts with our caselaw making clear that a student has no constitutional right to have an attorney actively participate in his disciplinary hearings, except in very limited circumstances. *See Flaim v. Med. Coll. of Ohio*, 418 F.3d 629, 640 (6th Cir. 2005) (noting that a student has no recognized right to have counsel participate in school disciplinary proceedings except, possibly, where the proceedings are complex or where the university itself utilizes an attorney); *Cummins*, 662 F. App'x at 448-49 (same); *Gorman v. Univ. of Rhode Island*, 837 F.2d 7, 16 (1st Cir. 1988) (noting that "the weight of authority is against [recognizing the right to] representation by counsel at [school] disciplinary hearings, unless the student is also facing criminal charges stemming from the incident in question"); *Donohue v. Baker*, 976 F.Supp. 136, 146 (N.D.N.Y. 1997) (noting that a student in a school disciplinary hearing has a right to counsel only to protect his Fifth Amendment right against self-incrimination, not to affect the outcome of the hearing through cross-examination).

Should the representative instead be a teacher or an administrator? Such an individual would undoubtedly need to be paid for his or her work, imposing an additional burden on the university. Could the representative p.590 be a friend or family member of the accused? And would the rules of evidence apply to the cross-examination? *Cf. Flaim*, 418 F.3d at 635 (observing that "[c]ourts have generally been unanimous... in concluding ... that neither rules of evidence nor rules of civil or criminal procedure need be applied" in school disciplinary hearings). Assuming they would not, who would decide what limits to impose on the representative's questioning and using what criteria?

This court has repeatedly held that "[f]ull-scale adversarial hearings in school disciplinary proceedings have never been required by the Due Process Clause." *Univ. of Cincinnati,* 173 F.Supp.3d at 603 (quoting *Flaim,* 418 F.3d at 640). And the burden of allowing a representative to participate by cross-examining witnesses "in every disciplinary hearing would be significant due to the added time, expense, and increased procedural complexity." *Cummins,* 662 F. App'x at 449; *see also Flaim,* 418 F.3d at 640-41 ("[C]onducting [full adversarial hearings] with professional counsel would entail significant expense and additional procedural complexity."). This would be especially true if the university were also required to provide representation for a student who could not provide his or her own.

Although a university may choose to allow an agent or representative of an accused student to cross-examine the complainant and his or her witnesses, no court has previously held that this is constitutionally required. This court has instead held that the university must provide at least the "circumscribed form" of cross-examination set out in *Cummins,* 662 F. App'x at 446. And because Doe was not provided with even this level of cross-examination, I agree that his due process rights were violated.

I recognize that a case might arise where the Constitution requires more than the procedures that this court approved of in *Cummins,* but we should address that issue only if and when it arises. We need not — and should not — resolve it today because we have been given neither the facts nor the arguments necessary to conduct an adequate analysis. I therefore believe that we should refrain from imposing on all universities a rigid requirement to provide students facing expulsion with an opportunity to have a representative cross-examine adverse witnesses. *See Kremer v. Chem. Constr. Corp.,* 456 U.S. 461, 482, 102 S.Ct. 1883, 72 L.Ed.2d 262 (1982) ("We must bear in mind that no single model of procedural fairness, let alone a particular form of procedure, is dictated by the Due Process Clause.... 'The very nature of due process negates any concept of inflexible procedures universally applicable to every imaginable situation.'" (quoting *Mitchell v. W.T. Grant Co.,* 416 U.S. 600, 609, 94 S.Ct. 1895, 40 L.Ed.2d 406 (1974))); *Gorman v. Univ. of Rhode Island,* 837 F.2d 7, 16 (1st Cir. 1988) ("[O]n review, the courts ought not to extol form over substance, and impose on educational institutions all the procedural requirements of a common law criminal trial.... In all cases the inquiry is whether, under the particular circumstances presented, the hearing was fair, and accorded the individual the essential elements of due process.").

II. Title IX claim

I now turn to Doe's claim under Title IX. Doe contends that the University faced pressure from the United States Department of Education, the general public, and student groups to adequately address sexual-assault complaints made against male students on campus and that, as a consequence, the University erroneously found him responsible for sexual misconduct because of his gender. But no circuit court has ever held that a student plausibly states a claim that deficiencies in his disciplinary p.591 proceedings were motivated by gender bias where the only fact that he alleges to show such bias is general pressure on the university to adequately address allegations of sexual assault. *Cf. Doe v. Miami Univ.*, 882 F.3d 579, 593 (6th Cir. 2018) (noting that to survive a motion to dismiss, a plaintiff must show a "causal connection between the flawed [disciplinary] outcome and gender bias" by alleging, "inter alia, statements by members of the disciplinary tribunal, statements by pertinent university officials, or patterns of decision-making that also tend to show the influence of gender").

In *Miami University,* this court found the complaint sufficient where it alleged facts showing a pattern of gender-based decision-making, in addition to general pressure on the university to take sexual-assault claims seriously. *Id.* at 593. This evidence included "an affidavit from an attorney who represents many students in Miami University's disciplinary proceedings, which describes a pattern of the University pursuing investigations concerning male students, but not female students." *Id.* It also included an allegation that the university investigated the complaint of sexual misconduct made against the male plaintiff but did not investigate his allegation that his female accuser actually perpetrated sexual misconduct against him. *Id.* at 590-91, 593.

The *Miami University* court further noted that the university "was facing pressure to increase the zealousness of its 'prosecution' of sexual assault and the harshness of the sanctions it imposed because it was a defendant in a lawsuit brought by a student who alleged that she would not have been assaulted if the University had expelled her attacker for prior offenses." *Id.* at 594. This alleged pattern of activity relating to sexual-assault matters, combined with the general pressure on the university, was deemed sufficient to "support a reasonable inference of gender discrimination" and therefore to survive a motion to dismiss. *Id.*

Similarly, in *Doe v. Columbia University,* 831 F.3d 46, 57 (2d Cir. 2016), the Second Circuit held that a complaint plausibly alleged gender discrimination when it contended that, "during the period preceding the disciplinary hearing, there was substantial criticism of the University[ ] both in the student body and in the public media [that] accus[ed] the University of not taking seriously complaints of female students alleging sexual assault by male students." *Id.* The complaint further alleged that "the University's administration was cognizant of, and sensitive to, these criticisms, to the point that the President called a University-wide open meeting with the Dean to discuss the issue." *Id.* Moreover, the investigator in that case had been subjected to "personal criticism" by the student body and in news articles "for her role in prior cases in which the University was seen as not taking seriously the complaints of female students." *Id.* at 51, 58.

The investigator in *Columbia University* was thus aware that the university "had been criticized for ... conducting the investigations in a manner that favored male athletes and that was insufficiently protective of sexually assaulted females." *Id.* Finally, the plaintiff in *Columbia University* alleged that the investigator failed to interview key witnesses identified by the plaintiff, that she was hostile to him during interviews, and that she failed to inform him of his right to make a statement at the hearing. *Id.* at 49, 52.

Unlike the plaintiffs in *Miami University* and *Columbia University,* Doe crucially fails to link general pressure on the University of Michigan to the particular proceedings that he faced. *See Doe v. Cummins,* 662 F. App'x 437, 452 (6th Cir. 2016) (noting that "to state an erroneous-outcome p.592 claim, a plaintiff must plead ... a '*particularized* ... causal connection between the flawed outcome and gender bias'" (emphasis and first ellipsis added; second ellipsis in original) (quoting *Yusuf v. Vassar College,* 35 F.3d 709, 715 (2d Cir. 1994))). Nor does Doe allege any facts suggesting a pattern of discriminatory behavior by the University in its response to sexual-assault allegations, or that he made any sexual-misconduct complaints himself that the University ignored, in contrast to the plaintiff's allegations in *Miami University,* 882 F.3d at 590-91, 593. There is also no allegation here that the investigator faced individualized criticism for her handling of previous sexual-assault claims and subsequently manifested hostility toward Doe, in contrast to the plaintiff's contentions in *Columbia University,* 831 F.3d at 49, 51-52, 58. In fact, the investigator here found in favor of Doe, and Doe acknowledged that her investigation was "thorough."

Doe also fails to show how general pressure on the University's administration to pursue and effectively address sexual-assault complaints led the Appeals Board — a board made up of an assistant dean from the law school, a retired professor from the dentistry school, and a student — to take actions against him based on gender bias. He also fails to identify any practice or policy adopted by the University in response to either external or internal pressure that would reflect bias against males. Moreover, the media reports published *after* the Appeals Board decision (which reports allege that the University was continuing to inadequately address sexual-misconduct complaints) would appear to belie any contention that the University had overcorrected by adopting policies or practices biased against male students accused of sexual misconduct.

The majority in fact recognizes that the alleged external pressure on the University alone is not sufficient to plausibly show that a university acted based on gender bias in Doe's particular case. Maj. Op. at 586. But it concludes that this pressure is sufficient when combined with Doe's allegation that the Appeals Board adopted all of the statements made by the female witnesses and rejected all of the statements made by the male witnesses. Maj. Op. at 586-87. More specifically, the majority reasons that "when viewed against the backdrop of external pressure, the Board's decision to discredit Doe's fraternity brothers in part because they were fraternity brothers, while not holding Roe's witnesses to the same standard, is basis enough at the motion-to-dismiss-stage." Maj. Op. at 587. But the majority's observation about the Appeals' Board's alleged disparate treatment of the witnesses is not borne out by the record. (I recognize that the record would not normally be considered at the motion to dismiss stage of the case. But as acknowledged in footnote 4 of the majority opinion, the administrative record was referenced in the complaint and, without objection by either party, considered as part of the pleadings.)

To start with, the Appeals Board discussed statements from only two of Roe's sorority sisters, although additional sorority sisters provided statements that were contained in the investigator's report. The record reflects the following evaluation by the Appeals Board:

> Two witnesses who know [Roe] reported that they observed [Roe] drinking from the wine bag at [Doe's] fraternity and also reported that they perceived she was intoxicated for a variety of reasons (very energetic when she's drunk;

inhibitions were lowered; and speech that was 'not completely clear,' contained 'occasional slurs,' and occasionally trailed off at the end of sentences).

p.593 The Appeals Board provided no further discussion of these statements that would suggest that it was relying on them beyond its observation that Roe's statements were "corroborated by other witnesses, particularly by Witness 2's observations of [Roe's] behavior and physical condition immediately after the sexual encounter." And this observation by the Appeals Board leads directly to the biggest weakness in both Doe's and the majority's position: the Appeals Board's decision to credit the testimony of Roe and Witness 2 (and subsequently to find Doe responsible for sexual misconduct) was based on the considerations that (1) Witness 2 spent significant time with Roe following Roe's sexual encounter with Doe, and (2) Witness 2 had no connection to Doe, Roe, or their respective Greek institutions.

The Appeals Board explained:

> Although there were other witnesses who observed Complainant both prior to and after the sexual encounter with Respondent, many of them were fraternity brothers of Respondent, and all of them only observed Complainant briefly and/or at a distance. For these reasons, we find their statements to be significantly less persuasive than the statements of Complainant and Witness 2. Complainant knew that she consumed an excessive amount of alcohol and recognized that she was not mentally or physically in control. Witness 2 had no previous connection to Complainant and observed her for a lengthy period of time, spanning from a few minutes after Complainant's sexual encounter with the Respondent, through the time she got Complainant into bed at her dorm.

Whether the statements made by Roe's sorority sisters were credible was not discussed. The Appeals Board's decision instead shows that the statements by Doe and his witnesses were disfavored only as compared to the statements of Roe and Witness 2, and that there was no categorical preference shown for or against statements by fraternity brothers versus sorority sisters, or for or against statements by men versus women as such. The Appeals Board also noted that Witness 2's observations were further corroborated by two witnesses who helped Roe into a vehicle outside the fraternity house and who, like Witness 2, had no connection to Doe or Roe.

I therefore find no basis to reasonably infer that the Appeals Board declined to rely on the statements made by Doe and his witnesses *simply because they were men*. This leaves us with only one fact from which to infer that gender bias caused the procedural defects in Doe's disciplinary proceedings — the general pressure on the University to adequately address sexual-assault claims. But as discussed above, this is not sufficient to show the "particularized ... casual connection" required to plausibly allege a claim of gender bias under Title IX. *See Doe v. Miami Univ.*, 882 F.3d 579, 592 (6th Cir. 2018) (quoting *Doe v. Cummins*, 662 F. App'x 437, 452 (6th Cir. 2016)); *Cummins*, 662 F. App'x at 453 (noting that a complaint is insufficient if it shows at most "a disciplinary system that is biased in favor of alleged victims and against those accused of misconduct"). Absent an allegation of some particularized facts linking *gender bias* to the University's disciplinary practices or proceedings, I respectfully dissent as to the viability of Doe's Title IX claim.

[1] Even popular culture recognizes the importance of cross-examination. *See A Few Good Men* (Castle Rock Entertainment 1992) (depicting one of the most memorable examples of cross-examination in American cinema); *My Cousin Vinny* (Palo Vista Productions et al. 1992) (demonstrating that cross-examination can both undermine and establish the credibility of witnesses).

[2] Contrary to the concurrence/dissent's characterization, we apply the *Mathews* factors herein. We consider the seriousness of Doe's deprivation, the burden on the university, and the risk of an erroneous outcome in a process without live cross-examination. *See infra* Part III; *see also Mathews,* 424 U.S. at 335, 96 S.Ct. 893.

[3] The concurrence/dissent poses a number of thoughtful questions about what universities need to do going forward. None of these, however, are currently before us. Doe asks for an opportunity for a hearing with live cross-examination. Due process requires as much. If the university is worried about the accused confronting the accuser, it could consider other procedures such as a witness screen. But if the university does not want the accused to cross-examine the accuser under any scenario, then it must allow a representative to do so.

[4] The district court considered the administrative record (which included the police report) when deciding the motion to dismiss, even though it was not attached to the complaint, because it was referenced in the complaint and integral to Doe's claims. Since neither party objected then or in their appellate briefs, we, like the district court, consider the administrative record as part of the pleadings.

[5] We need not address Doe's argument that the district court abused its discretion in denying his motion to reopen and file an amended complaint. We hold that Doe stated a claim under the Due Process Clause absent the new evidence he seeks to add to the complaint. Should Doe want to introduce that evidence later in this litigation, the district court will need to determine whether, and under what circumstances, it may be used.

872 F.3d 393 (2017)

John DOE, Plaintiff-Appellee,
v.
UNIVERSITY OF CINCINNATI; Aniesha Mitchell; Juan Guardia, Defendants-Appellants.

No. 16-4693.

United States Court of Appeals, Sixth Circuit.
Argued: August 1, 2017.
Decided and Filed: September 25, 2017.

Doe v. University of Cincinnati, 872 F. 3d 393 (6th Cir. 2017)

Appeal from the United States District Court for the Southern District of Ohio at Cincinnati. No. 1:16-cv-00987—Michael R. Barrett, District Judge.

ARGUED: Evan T. Priestle, TAFT, STETTINIUS & HOLLISTER LLP, Cincinnati, Ohio, for Appellants. Joshua Adam Engel, ENGEL & MARTIN, LLC, Mason, Ohio, for Appellee. ON BRIEF: Evan T. Priestle, Doreen Canton, TAFT, STETTINIUS & HOLLISTER LLP, Cincinnati, Ohio, for Appellants. Joshua Adam Engel, ENGEL & MARTIN, LLC, Mason, Ohio, for Appellee.

Before: CLAY, GRIFFIN, and THAPAR, Circuit Judges.

p.396 OPINION

GRIFFIN, Circuit Judge.

On September 6, 2015, University of Cincinnati students John Doe and Jane Roe[1] engaged in sex at John Doe's apartment. John contends that the sex was consensual; Jane claims it was not. No physical evidence supports either student's version.

After considerable delay, defendant University of Cincinnati ("UC") held a disciplinary hearing on Jane Roe's sexual assault charges against graduate student John Doe. Despite Jane Roe's failure to appear at the hearing, the University found John Doe "responsible" for sexually assaulting Roe based upon her previous hearsay statements to investigators. Thereafter, UC suspended John Doe for two years — reduced to one year after an administrative appeal.

Plaintiff Doe appealed his suspension to the district court, arguing that the complete denial of his right to confront his accuser violated his due process right to a fair hearing. In granting a preliminary injunction against Doe's suspension, the district court found a strong likelihood that John Doe would prevail on his constitutional claim. So do we, and for the reasons stated herein, affirm the order of the district court.

The Due Process Clause guarantees fundamental fairness to state university students facing long-term exclusion from the educational process. Here, the University's disciplinary committee necessarily made a credibility determination in finding John Doe responsible for sexually assaulting Jane Roe given the exclusively "he said/she said" nature of the case. Defendants' failure to provide any form of confrontation of the accuser made the proceeding against John Doe fundamentally unfair.

I.

John Doe met Jane Roe on Tinder, and after communicating for two or three weeks, met in person. Thereafter, Doe invited Roe back to his apartment, where the two engaged in sex. Three weeks later, Jane Roe reported to the University's Title IX Office that John Doe had sexually assaulted her that evening in his apartment. Five months later, UC cited Doe for violating the Student Code of Conduct, "most specifically," the University's policies against sex offenses, harassment, and discrimination.

UC resolves charges of non-academic misconduct through an Administrative Review Committee (ARC) hearing process. The process begins when "[a]ny person, department, organization or entity" files a complaint against a student, and the University informs the student of the allegations against him. If the claim involves a potential sexual offense, UC's Title IX Office investigates the matter, interviewing both parties and gathering the evidence. Defendant Aniesha Mitchell, the Director of UC's Office of Student Conduct and Community Standards, discloses the evidence to the accused student before the hearing.

During the hearing, the ARC panelists (a mix of faculty and students) hear the allegations, review the evidence, and question the participating witnesses. Accused students are entitled to present favorable evidence and explain their side of the story in their own words. They may also question witnesses through a "circumscribed form of cross-examination" — one that involves "submitting written questions" to the ARC panelists, "who then determine whether [the] questions are relevant and whether they will be posed to the witness." *Doe v. Cummins,* 662 Fed.Appx. 437, 439, 448 (6th Cir. 2016).

However, there is no guarantee that a witness will appear for questioning. "Witnesses are strongly encouraged to be present for hearings," but UC's Code of Conduct does not require them to be present, regardless of whether they are the accused, the accuser, or a bystander with relevant information. If a witness is "unable to attend," the Code permits him to submit a "notarized statement" to the Committee in lieu of an appearance. At the close of the hearing, the ARC deliberates and determines whether the accused student should be found "responsible" for violating the Code of Conduct.

Defendants planned to follow these procedures at Doe's June 27, 2016, hearing, but modified the process when Jane Roe failed to appear. The Committee Chair explained how the hearing would proceed in her absence:

> So, during the hearing, the Administrative Review Committee and both the respondent and complainant shall have the right to submit evidence and written questions to be asked of all adverse witnesses who testify in the matter. The hearing chair, in consultation with the ARC, has the right to review and determine which written questions will be asked. Questions will be asked in the

order presented by the Chair. And all questions from the complainant and respondent must be submitted in writing for review by the ARC [C]hair.

Again, there is no complainant here and we have no witnesses. So we likely won't have to do any of this.

John Doe claims, and defendants do not dispute, that he was not informed in advance that Jane Roe would not be attending the hearing.

The Chair recited the Code of Conduct violations leveled against Doe and invited him to enter an "understanding" — accepting or denying responsibility for the allegations. Doe entered an understanding of not responsible.

The Chair then read a summary of the Title IX Office's report, which began with Jane Roe's account of the night in question, followed by Doe's account. Each party's account was based on his or her interview statements to the Title IX investigators and included remarks that would be hearsay if introduced in court. The Chair also read a summary of witness statements from four of Jane Roe's friends who were told of the alleged sexual assault through Roe. Once the Chair finished, he gave the Committee members the chance to ask questions regarding the report. They had none.

The Chair then asked whether John Doe had any questions:

[The Chair]: Okay, so the complainant is not here. At this time I would have given Roe time to ask questions of the Title IX report. But again, they [sic] are not here. So we'll move on.
So now, do you, as the respondent Mr. Doe, have any questions of the Title IX report?
[Doe]: Well, since she's not here, I can't really ask anything of the report.
Is this the time where I would enter in like a situation where like she said this and that never could have happened? Because that's just —
[The Chair]: You'll have time here in just a little bit to direct those questions. Just —
[Doe]: Then no, I don't have any questions for the report.

With that, the Chair concluded the "Title IX presentation" portion of the hearing.

"And so now," the Chair explained that if Jane Roe had been present, he would have asked her to "read into the record what happened and [provide] any additional information." "The ARC would then have time to ask clarifying questions" of Roe, followed by Doe's opportunity to ask her questions. "Again," however, the Chair noted Roe was not present and "move[d] onto the next step" — asking Doe to "summarize what happened." Doe challenged a number of Roe's statements, and responded to the Committee's questions. Following this exchange, the Chair read Jane Roe's written closing statement into the record and invited Doe to give a responsive closing statement.

After its deliberations, the Committee submitted its recommended findings to Daniel Cummins, UC's Assistant Dean of Students. It recommended that Cummins find Doe responsible for violating the Student Code of Conduct and issue a two-year suspension. On July 7, Cummins notified John Doe that he had accepted the recommendation.

Doe appealed the decision the next day. The University's Appeals Administrator rejected Doe's appeal of the finding of responsibility, but recommended that his sentence be reduced to a one-year suspension to begin at the end of the fall 2016 semester, and conclude at the end of the fall 2017 semester — meaning Doe could not attempt to re-enroll in his graduate program until January 2018. Defendant Juan Guardia, the Assistant Vice President and Dean of Students, accepted the Administrator's recommendation and informed plaintiff on September 23, 2016, that this was the University's final decision.

II.

Doe then filed this action against UC Administrators Guardia and Mitchell and the University in the district court. Plaintiff Doe claimed that defendants violated his due process rights under the United States and Ohio Constitutions and discriminated against him in violation of Title IX.

On the same day he filed his complaint, Doe moved for preliminary relief enjoining UC from enforcing his suspension. Plaintiff's motion focused solely on defendants' failure "to permit John Doe to confront his accuser." Doe maintained that UC could not constitutionally find him responsible for sexually assaulting Roe without "any opportunity to confront and question" her. The district court agreed.

"In this case," the court reasoned, "the ARC Hearing Committee was given the choice of believing either Jane Roe or Plaintiff, and therefore, cross-examination was essential to due process." *Doe v. Univ. of Cincinnati*, 223 F.Supp.3d 704, 711 (S.D. Ohio 2016). The fact that Doe could have submitted written questions to the Committee Chair, which the Chair could have put to Roe, had she appeared at the hearing, did not convince the district court otherwise. *Id.* at 712. And although UC's Code of Conduct permits absent witnesses who are "unable" to attend the hearing to provide notarized statements, the district court noted that Roe's closing statement was not notarized. Such a "significant and unfair departure[] from an institution's own procedures can," the court explained, "amount to a violation of due process." *Id.* (quoting *Furey v. Temple Univ.*, 730 F.Supp.2d 380, 396-97 (E.D. Pa. 2010) (brackets omitted)).

The district court ruled that plaintiff demonstrated a strong likelihood of success on the merits of his due process claim, and that the remaining preliminary injunction factors weighed in favor of granting preliminary relief. *Id.* at 712. Accordingly, the court entered an order enjoining UC p.399 from suspending plaintiff. *Id.* Defendants timely appealed.

III.

In reviewing a district court's decision to grant a preliminary injunction, "we evaluate the same four factors that the district court does": (1) whether the movant has demonstrated a strong likelihood of success on the merits; (2) whether he would suffer irreparable injury without the injunction; (3) whether the injunction would cause substantial harm to others; and (4) whether issuing the injunction would serve the public interest. *Planet Aid v. City of St. Johns*, 782 F.3d 318, 323 (6th Cir. 2015) (internal quotation marks omitted). "We have often cautioned that these are factors to be balanced, not prerequisites to be met." *S. Glazer's Distributors of Ohio, LLC v.*

Great Lakes Brewing Co., 860 F.3d 844, 849 (6th Cir. 2017). "At the same time, however, we have also held that 'a preliminary injunction issued where there is simply no likelihood of success on the merits must be reversed.'" *Id.* (brackets and citation omitted). And in the case of a potential constitutional violation, "the likelihood of success on the merits often will be the determinative factor." *City of Pontiac Retired Emps. Ass'n v. Schimmel,* 751 F.3d 427, 430 (6th Cir. 2014) (en banc, per curiam) (citation omitted).

We review a district court's legal conclusions de novo, its factual findings for clear error, and its ultimate decision to grant preliminary relief for abuse of discretion. *S. Glazer's,* 860 F.3d at 849. Practically speaking, this means "when we look at likelihood of success on the merits, we independently apply the Constitution, but we still defer to the district court's overall balancing of the four preliminary-injunction factors." *Planet Aid,* 782 F.3d at 323 (citation omitted).

IV.

State universities must afford students minimum due process protections before issuing significant disciplinary decisions. *See Flaim v. Med. Coll. of Ohio,* 418 F.3d 629, 633 (6th Cir. 2005); *see also Jaksa v. Regents of the Univ. of Michigan,* 597 F.Supp. 1245, 1248 (E.D. Mich. 1984), *aff'd* 787 F.2d 590 (6th Cir. 1986) (per curiam, unpublished) ("Whether plaintiff's interest is a 'liberty' interest, 'property' interest, or both, it is clear that he is entitled to the protection of the due process clause."). Suspension "clearly implicates" a protected property interest, and allegations of sexual assault may "impugn [a student's] reputation and integrity, thus implicating a protected liberty interest." *Cummins,* 662 Fed.Appx. at 445 (citations omitted).

Because the Due Process Clause applies, "the question remains what process is due." *Morrissey v. Brewer,* 408 U.S. 471, 481, 92 S.Ct. 2593, 33 L.Ed.2d 484 (1972). "[T]he specific dictates of due process generally require[] consideration of three distinct factors": (1) the nature of the private interest subject to official action; (2) the risk of erroneous deprivation under the current procedures used, and the value of any additional or substitute procedural safeguards; and (3) the governmental interest, including the burden any additional or substitute procedures might entail. *Mathews v. Eldridge,* 424 U.S. 319, 334-35, 96 S.Ct. 893, 47 L.Ed.2d 18 (1976).

At a minimum, a student facing suspension is entitled to "the opportunity to be 'heard at a meaningful time and in a meaningful manner.'" *Cummins,* 662 Fed. Appx. at 446 (quoting *Mathews,* 424 U.S. at 333, 96 S.Ct. 893). While the exact outlines of process may vary, universities must "at least" provide notice of the charges, an explanation of the evidence p.400 against the student, and an opportunity to present his side of the story before an unbiased decision maker. *Id.* (citing *Heyne v. Metro. Nashville Pub. Sch.,* 655 F.3d 556, 565-66 (6th Cir. 2011)).

A student's opportunity to share his version of events must occur at "some kind of hearing," *Goss v. Lopez,* 419 U.S. 565, 579, 95 S.Ct. 729, 42 L.Ed.2d 725 (1975), though that hearing need not "take on ... [the] formalities" of a criminal trial. *Flaim,* 418 F.3d at 635. Education is a university's first priority; adjudication of student disputes is, at best, a distant second. *See Bd. of Curators of the Univ. of Missouri v. Horowitz,* 435 U.S. 78, 88, 98 S.Ct. 948, 55 L.Ed.2d 124 (1978). "Formalizing hearing requirements would divert both resources and attention from the educational process." *Jaksa,* 597 F.Supp. at 1250. Thus, UC is not required to "transform its classrooms into courtrooms" in pursuit of a more reliable disciplinary outcome. *Id.;* see also *Flaim,* 418 F.3d at 635 ("Courts have generally been unanimous... in concluding that hearings need not be open to the public, that neither rules of evidence nor rules of civil or criminal procedure need be applied, and witnesses need not be placed under oath." (citations omitted)). Even in the case of a sexual assault accusation — where "[a] finding of responsibility will ... have a substantial and lasting impact" on the student, *see Cummins,* 662 Fed.Appx. at 446 — the protection afforded to him "need not reach the same level ... that would be present in a criminal prosecution." *Doe v. Univ. of Kentucky,* 860 F.3d 365, 370 (6th Cir. 2017). Review under *Mathews* asks only whether John Doe "had an opportunity to 'respond, explain, and defend,'" not whether a jury could constitutionally convict him using the same procedures. *Cummins,* 662 Fed. Appx. at 446 (quoting *Flaim,* 418 F.3d at 635).

A.

First, Doe contends, and UC does not dispute, that the private interest at stake in this case is significant. A finding of responsibility for a sexual offense can have a "lasting impact" on a student's personal life, in addition to his "educational and employment opportunities," especially when the disciplinary action involves a long-term suspension. *Id.* The "private interest that will be affected by the official action" is therefore compelling. *Mathews,* 424 U.S. at 335, 96 S.Ct. 893.

B.

Next, we consider the risk of erroneous deprivation of this interest under the University's current procedures and the value of any additional procedural safeguards plaintiff requests. *Id.* at 334-35, 96 S.Ct. 893. The only additional procedure Doe requests is one that UC, in theory, already provides: the opportunity to confront and cross-examine Roe by posing questions to her through the Committee Chair.

"The right to cross-examine witnesses generally has not been considered an essential requirement of due process in school disciplinary proceedings." *Winnick,* 460 F.2d at 549. However, general rules have exceptions, and "the very nature of due process negates any concept of inflexible procedures universally applicable to every imaginable situation." *Goss,* 419 U.S. at 578, 95 S.Ct. 729 (citation and parenthetical omitted). The more serious the deprivation, the more demanding the process. And where the deprivation is based on disciplinary misconduct, rather than academic performance, "we conduct a more searching inquiry." *Flaim,* 418 F.3d at 634. "Disciplinarians, although proceeding in utmost good faith, frequently act on the reports and advice of others; and the controlling facts and the nature of the conduct under challenge are often disputed." *Goss,* 419 U.S. at 580, 95 S.Ct. 729. For the student, "[t]he risk of error is not at all trivial, and it should be guarded against... without prohibitive cost or interference with the educational process." *Id.*

Accused students must have the right to cross-examine adverse witnesses "in the most serious of cases." *Flaim,* 418 F.3d at 636. We alluded to what "the most serious of cases" might entail in *Flaim*. If a case "resolve[s] itself into a problem of credibility, cross-examination of witnesses might ... be[] essential to a fair hearing." *Id.* at 641 (quoting *Winnick,* 460 F.2d at 549). We ultimately did not reach that answer, however. It was not essential to Sean Michael Flaim's hearing, because Flaim admitted to the misconduct that prompted the Medical College of Ohio to expel him — his felony drug conviction. *Id.* That "rather unique" fact justified the College's decision to deny his request to cross-examine his arresting officer during Flaim's expulsion hearing. *Id.* at 641, 643.

But the circumstances of the present case pose the credibility contest we contemplated in *Flaim*. John Doe maintains that their sex was consensual; Jane Roe claims that it was not. Importantly, the Committee's finding of responsibility necessarily credits Roe's version of events and her credibility. The Title IX Office proffered no other evidence "to sustain the University's findings and sanctions" apart from Roe's hearsay statements. *Cf. Plummer v. Univ. of Houston,* 860 F.3d 767, 775-76 (5th Cir. 2017) (cross-examination not required where the plaintiffs distributed videos and a photograph of the victim's "degrading and humiliating" assault online, and "[t]he University's case did not rely on testimonial evidence" from the victim).

Defendants insist that Roe's nonappearance did not impact the fairness of the proceedings because Doe still had an opportunity be heard. The ARC panel invited him to "summarize what happened" in his own words, and Doe took advantage of that opportunity. He disputed Roe's overall interpretation of events and a number of her specific claims. Because plaintiff was able to draw attention to alleged inconsistencies in Roe's statements, defendants argue that cross-examination would have been futile. We disagree.

UC assumes cross-examination is of benefit only to Doe. In truth, the opportunity to question a witness and observe her demeanor while being questioned can be just as important to the trier of fact as it is to the accused. "A decision relating to the misconduct of a student requires a factual determination as to whether the conduct took place or not." *Horowitz,* 435 U.S. at 95 n.5, 98 S.Ct. 948 (Powell, J. concurring). "The accuracy of that determination can be safeguarded by the sorts of procedural protections traditionally imposed under the Due Process Clause." *Id.* Few procedures safeguard accuracy better than adversarial questioning. In the case of competing narratives, "cross-examination has always been considered a most effective way to ascertain truth." *Watkins v. Sowders,* 449 U.S. 341, 349, 101 S.Ct. 654, 66 L.Ed.2d 549 (1981) (footnote omitted); *see also Maryland v. Craig,* 497 U.S. 836, 846, 110 S.Ct. 3157, 111 L.Ed.2d 666 (1990) (cross-examination "ensur[es] that evidence admitted against an accused is reliable and subject to the rigorous adversarial testing that is the norm of Anglo-American criminal proceedings").

"The ability to cross-examine is most critical when the issue is the credibility of the accuser." *Doe v. Brandeis Univ.,* 177 F.Supp.3d 561, 605 (D. Mass. 2016). Cross-examination takes aim at credibility like no other procedural device. *Craig,* 497 U.S. at 846, 110 S.Ct. 3157; *Watkins,* 449 U.S. at 349, 101 S.Ct. 654. A cross-examiner may "delve into the witness' story to test the witness' perceptions and memory." *Davis v. Alaska,* 415 U.S. 308, 316, 94 S.Ct. 1105, 39 L.Ed.2d 347 (1974). He may "expose testimonial infirmities such as forgetfulness, confusion, or evasion ... thereby calling to the attention of the factfinder the reasons for giving scant weight to the witness' testimony." *Craig,* 497 U.S. at 847, 110 S.Ct. 3157 (citation and brackets omitted). He may "reveal[] possible biases, prejudices, or ulterior motives" that color the witness's testimony. *Davis,* 415 U.S. at 316, 94 S.Ct. 1105. His strategy may also backfire, provoking the kind of confident response that makes the witness appear more believable to the fact finder than he intended. *Watkins,* 449 U.S. at 345, 348-49, 101 S.Ct. 654; *cf. Davis,* 415 U.S. at 318, 94 S.Ct. 1105 ("On the basis of the limited cross-examination that was permitted, the jury might well have thought that defense counsel was engaged in a speculative and baseless line of attack on the credibility of an apparently blameless witness."). Whatever the outcome, "the greatest legal engine ever invented for the discovery of truth" will do what it is meant to: "permit[] the [fact finder] that is to decide the [litigant]'s fate to observe the demeanor of the witness in making his statement, thus aiding the [fact finder] in assessing his credibility." *Craig,* 497 U.S. at 846, 110 S.Ct. 3157 (quoting in part *California v. Green,* 399 U.S. 149, 158, 90 S.Ct. 1930, 26 L.Ed.2d 489 (1970)).

Given the parties' competing claims, and the lack of corroborative evidence to support or refute Roe's allegations, the present case left the ARC panel with "a choice between believing an accuser and an accused." *Flaim,* 418 F.3d at 641. Yet, the panel resolved this "problem of credibility" without assessing Roe's credibility. *Id.* (citation omitted). In fact, it decided plaintiff's fate without seeing or hearing from Roe at all. That is disturbing and, in this case, a denial of due process.

Even in *Flaim* — where "cross-examination would have been a fruitless exercise" because the plaintiff student admitted the "critical fact[s]" against him — the trier of fact was still able to question the plaintiff's arresting officer, and the plaintiff was still "able to listen to and observe" the officer's testimony. *See id.* at 633, 641 (quoting in part *Winnick,* 460 F.2d at 550). More critically, *the trier of fact* was "able to listen to and observe" the officer's testimony. *Id.* at 633. Evaluation of a witness's credibility cannot be had without some form of presence, some method of compelling a witness "to stand face to face with the [fact finder] in order that it may look at him, and judge by his demeanor upon the stand and the manner in which he gives his testimony whether he is worthy of belief." *Mattox v. United States,* 156 U.S. 237, 242-43, 15 S.Ct. 337, 39 L.Ed. 409 (1895). Cross-examination is "not only beneficial, but essential to due process" in a case that turns on credibility because it guarantees that the trier of fact makes this evaluation on both sides. *Flaim,* 418 F.3d at 641. When it does, the hearing's result is most reliable.

Reaching the truth through fair procedures is an interest Doe and UC have in common. "The Due Process Clause will not shield [a student] from suspensions properly imposed, but it disserves both his interest and the interest of the State if his suspension is in fact unwarranted." *Goss,* 419 U.S. at 579, 95 S.Ct. 729. UC, of course, also has a "well recognized" interest in maintaining a learning environment free of sex-based harassment and discrimination. *Bonnell v. Lorenzo,* 241 F.3d 800, 822 (6th Cir. 2001). To that end, "ensuring allegations of sexual assault on college campuses are taken seriously is of critical p.403 importance, and there is no doubt that universities have an exceedingly difficult task in handling these issues." *Brandeis,* 177 F.Supp.3d at 602 (citation omitted).

But if a university's procedures are insufficient to make "issues of credibility and truthfulness ... clear to the decision makers," that institution risks removing the wrong students, while overlooking those it should be removing. *See Furey v. Temple Univ.,* 884 F.Supp.2d 223, 252 (E.D. Pa. 2012). "The concern would be mostly academic if the disciplinary process were a totally accurate, unerring process, never mistaken and never unfair. Unfortunately, that is not the case, and no one suggests that it is." *Goss,* 419 U.S. at 579-80, 95 S.Ct. 729. Cross-examination, "the principal means by which the believability of a witness and the truth of his testimony are tested," can reduce the likelihood of a mistaken exclusion and help defendants better identify those who pose a risk of harm to their fellow students. *See Newsome v. Batavia Local Sch. Dist.,* 842 F.2d 920, 924 (6th Cir. 1988) (citation omitted).

We are equally mindful of Jane Roe's interest, and the extent to which it conflicts with John Doe's. Roe and other alleged victims have a right, and are entitled to expect, that they may attend UC without fear of sexual assault or harassment. *See* 20 U.S.C. § 1681(a). If they are assaulted, and report the assault consistent with the University's procedures, they can also expect that UC will promptly respond to their complaints. *Cf. Vance v. Spencer Cty. Pub. Sch. Dist.,* 231 F.3d 253, 261 (6th Cir. 2000) (citing *Wills v. Brown Univ.,* 184 F.3d 20, 25 (1st Cir. 1999)). Setting aside the troubling fact that UC's Title IX Office waited a month to interview Roe, another four months to notify Doe of her allegations, and *yet another four* months to convene the ARC hearing, the concern at this point is that UC's inadequate procedures left the ARC's decision vulnerable to a constitutional challenge.[2]

Strengthening those procedures is not without consequence for victims. "Allowing an alleged perpetrator to question an alleged victim directly may be traumatic or intimidating, thereby possibly escalating or perpetuating" the same hostile environment Title IX charges universities with eliminating. *Doe v. Regents of the Univ. of Cal.,* 5 Cal.App.5th 1055, 210 Cal.Rptr.3d 479, 505 (2016) (citation omitted). However, John Doe is not requesting an opportunity to question Jane Roe "directly." In this appeal, he does not challenge our determination in an unpublished decision that UC's "circumscribed form of cross-examination" is constitutional. *Cummins,* 662 Fed.Appx. at 448. Rather, plaintiff asks only to question Roe through the ARC panel — a procedure the Department of Education's Office for Civil Rights previously recommended for the victim's wellbeing. Catherine E. Lhamon, Assistant Secretary for Civil Rights, *Questions and Answers on Title IX and Sexual Violence,* at 31, April 29, 2014, https://www2.ed.gov/about/offices/list/ocr/docs/qa-201404-title-ix.pdf (last visited Aug. 31, 2017). (The Department subsequently withdrew its April 29, 2014, letter, and replaced it with an interim letter. *See* Dep't of Educ., Office for Civil Rights, *Q&A on Campus Sexual Misconduct,* Sept. 22, 2017, https://www2.ed.gov/about/offices/list/ocr/docs/qa-title-ix-201709.pdf (last visited Sept. 22, 2017)).

We acknowledge this procedure may not relieve Roe's potential emotional trauma. Still, a case that "resolve[s] itself into a problem of credibility" cannot itself be resolved without a mutual test of credibility, at least not where the stakes are this high. *Flaim,* 418 F.3d at 641 (quoting *Winnick,* 460 F.2d at 550); *but see Cummins,* 662 Fed.Appx. at 448 (a plaintiff subject to disciplinary probation may be entitled to less process than one subject to suspension). "While protection of victims of sexual assault from unnecessary harassment is a laudable goal, the elimination of such a basic protection for the rights of the accused raises profound concerns." *Brandeis,* 177 F.Supp.3d at 604-05. One-sided determinations are not known for their accuracy. Jane Roe deserves a reliable, accurate outcome as much as John Doe.

Ultimately, the ARC must decide whether Doe is responsible for violating UC's Code of Conduct: whether Roe's allegations against him are true. And in reaching this decision "[t]he value of cross-examination to the discovery of truth cannot be overemphasized." *Newsome,* 842 F.2d at 924. Allowing John Doe to confront and question Jane Roe through the panel would have undoubtedly aided the truth-seeking process and reduced the likelihood of an erroneous deprivation.

C.

UC has a strong interest both "in eliminating sexual assault on its campus and establishing a fair and constitutionally permissible disciplinary system." *Doe,* 860 F.3d at 370. And in defendants' favor, we have recognized that a constitutionally permissible disciplinary system need not follow the rules of evidence. *See Flaim,* 418 F.3d at 635. Cross-examination can "unnecessarily formalize school expulsion proceedings" precisely because it "impos[es] the additional burden on school administrators of applying, to some extent, the rules of evidence." *Newsome,* 842 F.2d at 925 n.4. UC's administrators are "in the business of education, not judicial administration." *Flaim,* 418 F.3d at 640. "To saddle them with the burden of overseeing the process of cross-examination (and the innumerable objections that are raised to the form and content of cross-examination) is to require of them that which they are ill-equipped to perform." *Newsome,* 842 F.2d at 926.

These concerns informed our decision to approve UC's procedure in *Doe v. Cummins,* issued a week after the district court enjoined UC from suspending plaintiff. *See* 662 Fed.Appx. at 448. *Cummins* held that UC's practice of limiting cross-examination to preapproved written questions comported with due process even if the ARC panel "did not ask all of the questions [the accused students] submitted," and did not permit follow-up questions. *Id.* at 448. But that holding gets defendants only so far. Fear of "saddl[ing] school officials with the burden of overseeing ... cross-examination" convinced the *Cummins* court that this "circumscribed form of cross-examination" is sufficient when a student's accuser appears for the hearing. *See id.* (quoting *Newsome,* 842 F.2d at 926, brackets omitted). The court left open the possibility that UC's procedures may nonetheless violate due process as applied to a student whose accuser *fails to appear* for the hearing.[3] Sparing the ARC panel from having p.405 to navigate traditional cross-examination justifies the requirement for written preapproved questions, but it does not justify denying the opportunity to question an adverse witness altogether.

Defendants' better argument is that they cannot compel a witness (adverse or not) to attend the ARC hearing. UC's Student Code of Conduct does not require witnesses to attend the hearing, and even if it did, there is no guarantee the witness would show. Universities do not have subpoena power. What is more, UC refers to cross-examination as an alternative to hearsay evidence, suggesting that the latter cannot be introduced at a disciplinary hearing unless the accused student has an opportunity to conduct the former. While UC's concerns are not unfounded, both arguments lose sight of our limited holding in this case.

For one, defendants are not required to facilitate witness questioning at every non-academic misconduct hearing. *Flaim*'s dictate is narrow: cross-examination is "essential to due process" only where the finder of fact must choose "between believing an accuser and an accused." 418 F.3d at 641. The ARC panel need not make this choice if the accused student admits the "critical fact[s]" against him. *Id.* Another relevant factor is that UC's allegations against Doe rested solely on Roe's statements to investigators. Cross-examination may be unnecessary where the University's case "d[oes] not rely on testimonial evidence" from the complainant. *See, e.g., Plummer,* 860 F.3d at 775-76.

For another, nothing in our decision jeopardizes UC's ability to rely on hearsay statements. *See Crook v. Baker,* 813 F.2d 88, 99 (6th Cir. 1987) ("It is clear that admission of hearsay evidence [at a school disciplinary proceeding] is not a denial of procedural due process."). Hearsay and its exceptions are delineated in the Federal Rules of Evidence, *see* Fed. R. Evid. 801(c), but a university student has "no right to [the] use of formal rules of evidence" at his disciplinary hearing. *Flaim,* 418 F.3d at 635 (citing *Nash v. Auburn Univ.,* 812 F.2d 655, 665 (11th Cir. 1987)). UC may still open the hearing with a Title IX report summary that includes the parties' "out-of-court" statements, and the ARC panel may still rely on those statements in deciding whether Doe is responsible for violating the Code of Conduct — it need not demand that Roe and Doe recite the evening's events from memory. We do not require schools to "transform [their] classrooms into courtrooms" to provide constitutionally adequate due process. *Jaksa,* 597 F.Supp. at 1250.

Plaintiff is likely to succeed on the merits of his due process claim not because defendants introduced hearsay evidence against him, but because the nature of that evidence posed a problem of credibility.[4] *See Flaim,* 418 F.3d at 641. Jane p.406 Roe claimed that John Doe engaged in specific acts without her consent, and John Doe replied that he did not. Although hearsay and credibility disputes often go hand in hand, use of hearsay does not itself trigger the right to question an adverse witness. Were it otherwise, the Medical College of Ohio would have violated Flaim's rights by expelling him on the basis of his "certified record of a recent felony conviction" (i.e., a hearsay record) without permitting him to cross-examine his arresting officer. *See id.* at 643; *see also* Fed. R. Evid. 803(22) (excluding evidence of a judgment of conviction from the general prohibition against the admission of hearsay). That is not *Flaim*'s holding, and it is not our holding here.

That said, we acknowledge that witness questioning may be particularly relevant to disciplinary cases involving claims of alleged sexual assault or harassment. Perpetrators often act in private, leaving the decision maker little choice but to weigh the alleged victim's word against that of the accused. Credibility disputes might therefore be more common in this context than in others. Arranging for witness questioning might also pose unique challenges given a victim's potential reluctance to interact with the accused student. *See Regents of the Univ. of Cal.,* 210 Cal. Rptr.3d at 505. However, we emphasize that UC's obligations here are narrow: it must provide a means for the ARC panel to evaluate an alleged victim's credibility, not for the accused to physically confront his accuser.

The University has procedures in place to accommodate this requirement. A month before the ARC hearing, Mitchell informed Doe and Roe that they could "participate via Skype ... if they could not attend the hearing."[5] Doe did not object to Roe's participation by Skype, and he does not object to this practice on appeal. To the contrary, the record suggests that he or one or more of the ARC panelists in fact appeared at the hearing via Skype. What matters for credibility purposes is the ARC panel's ability to assess the demeanor of both the accused and his accuser. Indisputably, demeanor can be assessed by the trier of fact without physical presence, especially when facilitated by modern technology. *See Craig,* 497 U.S. at 849-50, 857, 110 S.Ct. 3157. That fact mitigates UC's administrative burden.

D.

We are sensitive to the competing concerns of this case. "The goal of reducing sexual assault[] and providing appropriate discipline for offenders" is more than "laudable"; it is necessary. *Brandeis,* 177 F.Supp.3d at 572. But "[w]hether the elimination of basic procedural protections — and the substantially increased risk that innocent students will be punished — is a fair price to achieve that goal is another question altogether." *Id.*

Here, John Doe's private interest is substantial, and the risk of erroneous deprivation under the procedures UC followed at his ARC hearing is unacceptably high. Allowing defendants to pose questions to witnesses at certain disciplinary hearings may impose an administrative burden on UC. Yet on the facts here, that burden does not justify imposition of severe discipline without p.407 any credibility assessment of the accusing student. Accordingly, Doe has demonstrated a strong likelihood of success on the merits of his due process claim. *Planet Aid,* 782 F.3d at 323. This "often ... determinative" factor weighs in favor of preliminary relief. *Schimmel,* 751 F.3d at 430.

V.

The second factor in our preliminary-injunction inquiry asks whether the movant is likely to suffer irreparable harm in the absence of the injunction. *S. Glazer's,* 860 F.3d at 852. In Doe's case, the district court found that he would.

"When constitutional rights are threatened or impaired, irreparable injury is presumed." *Obama for Am. v. Husted,* 697 F.3d 423, 436 (6th Cir. 2012); *Overstreet v. Lexington-Fayette Urban Cty. Gov't,* 305 F.3d 566, 578 (6th Cir. 2002). Defendants' characterization of Doe's injury as "speculative or unsubstantiated" does not rebut that presumption. *Abney v. Amgen, Inc.,* 443 F.3d 540, 552 (6th Cir. 2006) (citation omitted). Were we to vacate the injunction, Doe would be suspended for a year and suffer reputational harm both on and off campus based on a finding rendered after an unfair hearing. Accordingly, this factor weighs in favor of preliminary relief.

Defendants do not challenge the district court's findings regarding the third factor — that the preliminary injunction will not harm others.

But they do contest the fourth: the district court's finding that the preliminary injunction serves the "public good." *Doe,* 223 F.Supp.3d at 712. In rejecting UC's claim that it has an interest in regulating and maintaining the integrity of its disciplinary system, the district court merely reiterated that "part of Plaintiff's claim is that UC failed to follow the procedures outlined in its own disciplinary system" — namely, the requirement that Roe's statement to the ARC panel be notarized. *See id.* That UC did so is irrelevant.

A school's departure from its own hearing rules amounts to a due process violation only when the departure "results in a procedure which itself impinges on due process rights." *Flaim,* 418 F.3d at 640 (quoting *Bates v. Sponberg,* 547 F.2d 325, 329-30 (6th Cir. 1976)). The Committee's review of Roe's non-notarized statement did not "result in a procedure which itself impinge[d]" upon plaintiff's right to a fair hearing. Plaintiff's rights are dictated by the Constitution, "not internal school rules or policies." *Cummins,* 662 Fed. Appx. at 445 n.2 (citing *Heyne,* 655 F.3d at 570, and *Hall v. Med. Coll. of Ohio,* 742 F.2d 299, 309 (6th Cir. 1984)).

The district court may have been nodding to the principle that it is always in the public's interest to prevent a violation of an individual's constitutional rights, which, it is. *Dodds v. United States Dep't of Educ.,* 845 F.3d 217, 222 (6th Cir. 2016). At the same time, while the public has a competing interest in the enforcement of Title IX, that interest can never override individual constitutional rights. U.S. Const. art. VI, cl.2. This factor is, at most, neutral.

VI.

On balance, the preliminary injunction factors favor the grant of preliminary relief. Accordingly, we conclude that the district court did not abuse its discretion in enjoining John Doe's suspension. For these reasons, we affirm the order of the district court.

[1] We use aliases to protect the parties' privacy.

[2] UC encourages victims to report alleged assaults "as soon as reasonably possible" "to ensure that the passage of time does not limit the University's ability to conduct an investigation or locate witnesses, as memory lapses and other time-sensitive factors may impair an investigation." *See* https://www.uc.edu/titleix/procedures.html (last visited Aug. 31, 2017). "[T]ime-sensitive factors" evidently did not motivate the University in the instant case.

[3] The two *Cummins* plaintiffs also faced charges of sexual assault, but successfully appealed the results of their first ARC hearings to UC's Appeals Administrator. After a second round of hearings, UC found each student "responsible" for violating the Student Code of Conduct. It suspended one for a three-year period and placed the other on disciplinary probation. *Cummins,* 662 Fed.Appx. at 438-43. The latter plaintiff argued UC violated his due process rights because his alleged victim did not attend his second ARC hearing, denying him the opportunity to question her through the panel. *Id.* at 448. We found no violation, however, because the accused student had an opportunity to conduct cross-examination at his first hearing, and because UC gave him a lesser punishment — disciplinary probation rather than suspension. *Id. Cummins* did not address whether a student facing suspension who is denied even this modified form of cross-examination suffers a violation of due process.

[4] In arguing against UC's use of Roe's hearsay statements, plaintiff assumes this evidence is necessarily harmful to his defense. Yet Doe's intended strategy is "to question Jane Roe about inconsistencies in her [prior] statements" in order to

demonstrate her claimed lack of credibility. He cannot do that if her previous statements are not presented at the hearing.

[5] UC's Code of Conduct does not define the conditions under which a student might be "unable to attend" an ARC hearing. In any event, this is an individual determination best left to defendants. *See Horowitz,* 435 U.S. at 91, 98 S.Ct. 948 (the niceties of "public education... [are] committed to the control of state and local authorities" (citation omitted)); *see also Goss,* 419 U.S. at 578, 95 S.Ct. 729. In the present case, there was no finding that Jane was unable to attend the hearing.

860 F.3d 365 (2017)

John DOE, Plaintiff-Appellant,

v.

UNIVERSITY OF KENTUCKY, Defendant,

Denise B. Simpson, individually and in her official capacity as Director of the Office of Student Conduct, University of Kentucky; Victor Hazard, in his official capacity as Associate Vice President for Student Affairs and Dean of Students, University of Kentucky, Defendants-Appellees.

No. 16-5170.

United States Court of Appeals, Sixth Circuit.

Argued: April 27, 2017.

Decided and Filed: June 15, 2017.

Doe v. University of Kentucky, 860 F. 3d 365 (6th Cir. 2017)

Appeal from the United States District Court for the Eastern District of Kentucky at Lexington. No. 5:15-cv-00300—Joseph M. Hood, District Judge.

ARGUED: Michael J. Cox, COX LAW, PLLC, Lexington, Kentucky, for Appellant. Bryan H. Beauman, STURGILL, TURNER, BARKER & MOLONEY, PLLC, Lexington, Kentucky, for Appellees. ON BRIEF: Michael J. Cox, COX LAW, PLLC, Lexington, Kentucky, E. Douglas Richards, E. DOUGLAS RICHARDS, PSC, Lexington, Kentucky, for Appellant. Bryan H. Beauman, STURGILL, TURNER, BARKER & MOLONEY, PLLC, Lexington, Kentucky, William E. Thro, UNIVERSITY OF KENTUCKY, Lexington, Kentucky, for Appellees.

Before: GUY, SILER, and DONALD, Circuit Judges.

OPINION

SILER, Circuit Judge.

This case arises out of the federal district court's involvement in an ongoing disciplinary hearing against John Doe[1] at the University of Kentucky. For the reasons contained herein, we affirm the district court's decision to abstain, reverse the district court's dismissal of the claims against Defendant Denise Simpson, and remand to the district court to stay the case pending conclusion of the university proceedings.

I.

After a series of disciplinary hearings, Doe filed suit against the University and Simpson requesting both injunctive and monetary relief. The hearings were initiated after an unidentified individual lodged a complaint against Doe, alleging that he had engaged in nonconsensual sexual activities with a female student, identified as Student A. After conducting an investigation, a Hearing Panel was convened. It found that Doe had violated the Code of Student Conduct and assessed a one-year suspension of Doe. Doe appealed the ruling to the University Appeals Board ("UAB"), which reversed, finding a violation of Doe's due process rights and the Code of Student Conduct due to Simpson's withholding of critical evidence and witness questions from the Hearing Panel. The Hearing Panel held a second hearing, and it again found Doe had violated the University's sexual misconduct policy. Doe appealed, and the UAB reversed the ruling and returned the matter for another hearing. The UAB found multiple due process errors, including Defendants' improper partitioning of Doe and his advisors from Student A, improperly denying Doe the "supplemental proceeding" described in the Student Code, and finding ex parte communications between Student A, Simpson, and the Hearing Panel regarding sanctions.

A third hearing was scheduled, but before it commenced, Doe filed an action in the district court seeking to enjoin Defendants from conducting the hearing based on alleged unconstitutional flaws in the University's policies, and also asserting due process and equal protection claims under the Constitution, 42 U.S.C. § 1983, and Title IX of the Education Amendments Act of 1972, 20 U.S.C. §§ 1681 *et seq.* Defendants responded by arguing that any constitutional problems would be cured in the third hearing, as new procedures would be in place.[2] Defendants also filed a motion requesting the district court to abstain from providing injunctive relief under *Younger* and to find that Simpson is entitled to qualified immunity and to dismiss the damages claims against her. The district court granted both requests.

II.

A.

We review de novo a district court's decision to abstain pursuant to the *Younger* doctrine. *Nimer v. Litchfield Twp. Bd. of Trustees,* 707 F.3d 699, 700 (6th Cir. 2013).

Younger abstention derives from a desire to prevent federal courts from interfering with the functions of state criminal prosecutions and to preserve equity and comity. *Younger v. Harris,* 401 U.S. 37, 44, 91 S.Ct. 746, 27 L.Ed.2d 669 (1971) ("This underlying reason for restraining courts of equity from interfering with criminal prosecutions is reinforced by an even more vital consideration, the notion of 'comity,' that is, a proper respect for state functions, a recognition of the fact that the entire country is made up of a Union of separate state governments, and a continuance of the belief that the National Government will fare best if the States and their institutions are left free to perform their separate functions in their separate ways."). The Supreme Court later clarified that *Younger* abstention can apply to cases that are not criminal prosecutions but noted that such applications are narrow and exist only in a few exceptional circumstances. *New Orleans Pub. Serv., Inc. v. Council of City of New Orleans,* 491 U.S. 350, 368, 109 S.Ct. 2506, 105 L.Ed.2d 298 (1989) ("*NOPSI*") (finding that *Younger* abstention did not apply to state council utility ratemaking procedure as it was essentially a legislative act and not judicial in nature). Regarding the situations to which *Younger* applies, first, *Younger* permits abstention when there is an ongoing state criminal prosecution. *Id.* Next, *Younger* precludes federal involvement in certain civil enforcement proceedings. *Id.* These are proceedings that "are akin to criminal prosecutions." *Sprint Commc'ns, Inc. v. Jacobs,*

___ U.S. ___, 134 S.Ct. 584, 588, 187 L.Ed.2d 505 (2013). Finally, *Younger* pertains to "civil proceedings involving certain orders that are uniquely in furtherance of the state courts' ability to perform their judicial functions," such as contempt orders. *NOPSI,* 491 U.S. at 368, 109 S.Ct. 2506 (citations omitted).

Once the proceeding is found to fit into one of the three *NOPSI* categories listed above, the court evaluates the proceeding using a three-factor test laid out in *Middlesex County Ethics Committee v. Garden State Bar Ass'n,* 457 U.S. 423, 102 S.Ct. 2515, 73 L.Ed.2d 116 (1982). *See Sprint Commc'ns, Inc.,* 134 S.Ct. at 593-94 (clarifying that the *Middlesex* factors are only considered by a court after the court decides that one of the *NOPSI* exceptional circumstances is present). The *Middlesex* test states that abstention may occur when three criteria are met: (1) state proceedings are currently pending; (2) the proceedings involve an important state interest; and (3) the state proceedings will provide the federal plaintiff with an adequate opportunity to raise his constitutional claims. *Middlesex,* 457 U.S. at 432-34, 102 S.Ct. 2515 (holding that abstention from a state bar disciplinary hearing was proper as the state has traditionally exercised control over the conduct of attorneys, and the "judiciary as well as the public is dependent upon professionally ethical conduct of attorneys and thus has a significant interest in assuring and maintaining high standards of conduct of attorneys engaged in practice"); *see also Habich v. City of Dearborn,* 331 F.3d 524, 530 (6th Cir. 2003).

Accordingly, the first issue we must decide is whether the university disciplinary hearing meets one of the exceptional circumstances in *NOPSI*. It is clearly not a criminal prosecution or civil proceeding dealing with the judiciary's ability to enforce its orders, so we must determine if the second circumstance, that is, a civil enforcement proceeding akin to a criminal prosecution, applies to the university disciplinary hearings. In proceedings akin to a criminal prosecution, "a state actor is routinely a party to the state proceeding and often initiates the action," and the procedure is initiated to sanction the federal plaintiff. *Sprint Commc'ns, Inc.,* 134 S.Ct. at 592.[3]

p.370 Here, the disciplinary proceeding was brought to sanction Doe and could have severe consequences, such as expulsion and future career implications. A state actor, the public University, is a party to the proceeding and initiated the action. Additionally, the case against Doe involved a filed complaint, an investigation, notice of the charge, and the opportunity to introduce witnesses and evidence. Although the proceeding lacks some of the due process protections for a criminal trial, such as having an attorney cross-examine witnesses and being able to subpoena witnesses, that does not destroy the applicability of *Younger* abstention. Doe focuses on the fact that an attorney cannot cross-examine witnesses as a key reason why abstention should not apply, but cross-examination is permitted. Doe could submit questions to a hearing officer who would present them to the witness, and counsel can be present. And we have previously stated that school disciplinary proceedings, while requiring some level of due process, need not reach the same level of protection that would be present in a criminal prosecution. *See Doe v. Cummins,* 662 Fed. Appx. 437, 446 (6th Cir. 2016). Thus, while the proceeding may lack all the formalities found in a trial, it contains enough protections and similarities to qualify as "akin to criminal prosecutions" for purposes of *Younger* abstention.

Finding that this case fits into one of the *Younger* exceptional circumstances established in *NOPSI,* we next look at the additional *Middlesex* factors. First, does this case qualify as an ongoing state judicial proceeding? A complaint was filed, a hearing was held, and Doe can call witnesses, have an attorney present, submit questions for cross-examination, and present evidence. Although the hearing failed to include every element of due process in a criminal prosecution, it is still adjudicative in nature. *See Fieger v. Thomas,* 74 F.3d 740, 744 (6th Cir. 1996) ("Because the Board is proceeding against Fieger to enforce its Rules of Professional Conduct, it is performing an adjudicative, as opposed to a legislative, function. It therefore, satisfies the first [*Middlesex*] requirement for *Younger* abstention."). Additionally, the University intends to hold a third hearing once this appeal is resolved, so the process is still ongoing. Second, the state has an interest in eliminating sexual assault on its campus and establishing a fair and constitutionally permissible disciplinary system. *See Middlesex,* 457 U.S. at 432, 102 S.Ct. 2515. Doe's argument that the state lacks any interest simply because the claims were brought under federal law is illogical and has no support. The final factor is whether Doe has an adequate opportunity to raise his constitutional claims in the university proceeding. *See id.* Doe has raised his constitutional claims twice already, and the UAB has overturned the Panel's decisions. Clearly, there is an avenue available to raise such claims, and the UAB has not rubber-stamped the Panel's p.371 decision but has carefully examined it for defects. Doe can appeal after the third hearing, which will involve more protections and procedures, if he believes the hearing still suffers from constitutional error, and he may raise his claims again in federal court once the proceedings have concluded. While the previous system had its flaws, and the University has recognized and attempted to correct this, Doe was still able to raise his constitutional challenges, and he will continue to be able to do so under the new system. As such, we find that the *Middlesex* factors are met and abstention applies.

Even if abstention is warranted, however, a plaintiff still has the opportunity to show that an exception to *Younger* applies. These exceptions include bad faith, harassment, or flagrant unconstitutionality of the statute or rule at issue. *Fieger,* 74 F.3d at 750. For the flagrant unconstitutionality exception, "a statute might be flagrantly and patently violative of express constitutional prohibitions in every clause, sentence and paragraph, and in whatever manner and against whomever an effort might be made to apply it." *Younger,* 401 U.S. at 53-54, 91 S.Ct. 746 (quoting *Watson v. Buck,* 313 U.S. 387, 402, 61 S.Ct. 962, 85 L.Ed. 1416 (1941)). That is not the case here. Showing such flagrant unconstitutionality is a high bar, and the University's policy does not reach that level. Doe's argument that in practice the policy was applied in an unconstitutional manner fails as there must be facial unconstitutionality as well as in application. Furthermore, although the UAB did find that Doe was denied his due process rights, that was because Defendant Simpson was not following the policy, not because the policy itself was flagrantly unconstitutional. As such, Doe cannot meet this exception.

Doe has also failed to show a pattern of bad faith prosecution and harassment against him. It is true that the UAB has twice found problems with the hearings, but Doe's conclusory statements that the University is using him as an example is not enough to show harassment. A complaint was filed and an investigation occurred, and the University will use improved policies in the next hearing. As mentioned above, the hearings have not been ideal, but that does not amount to bad faith and harassment, especially as Doe has succeeded on appeal. The court in *Younger* discussed *Dombrowski v. Pfister,* 380 U.S. 479, 85 S.Ct. 1116, 14 L.Ed.2d 22 (1965), as an example of the harassment exception, because that case involved repeated threats by prosecutors designed to discourage individuals from asserting their constitutional rights. *Younger,* 401 U.S. at 48, 91 S.Ct. 746. Those types of threats, or other similar actions, are not alleged here, and as such, the district court was correct in finding *Younger* abstention precluded its involvement in the case.

B.

Doe next claims that the district court erred in finding that Defendant Simpson was entitled to qualified immunity and subsequently granting Defendants' motion to dismiss after it had decided to abstain from the case. We review a district court's dismissal of claims pursuant to Federal Rule of Civil Procedure 12(b)(6) de novo. *Winget v. JP Morgan Chase Bank, N.A.,* 537 F.3d 565, 572 (6th Cir. 2008).

When deciding whether to rule on the motion to dismiss, the district court looked to *Meyers v. Franklin County Court of Common Pleas,* 23 Fed.Appx. 201, 205-06 (6th Cir. 2001), and stated that the appropriate action after deciding to abstain was to stay the case, rather than decide and dismiss the claims. However, citing *Pearson v. Callahan,* 555 U.S. 223, p.372 231, 129 S.Ct. 808, 172 L.Ed.2d 565 (2009), the district court chose to decide the immunity issue at the earliest possible stage of the litigation. The purpose of *Younger* abstention is to promote equity and comity and allow state officials to proceed with cases uninterrupted by the federal courts. *Younger,* 401 U.S. at 43-46, 91 S.Ct. 746. As such, albeit not in the context of qualified immunity, we have consistently held that if a court abstains under *Younger,* it should stay any claim for damages rather than evaluate the merits and dismiss the case. *See Carroll v. City of Mount Clemens,* 139 F.3d 1072, 1075 (6th Cir. 1998) (holding that when abstaining from damages claims, the proper course of action is a stay of the claim, rather than dismissal); *see also Quackenbush v. Allstate Insurance Co.,* 517 U.S. 706, 721, 116 S.Ct. 1712, 135 L.Ed.2d 1 (1996); *Meyers,* 23 Fed. Appx. at 206 (finding that when claim for injunctive relief was dismissed due to *Younger* abstention, the proper course of action was to stay, rather than dismiss, the related damages claim). Defendant Simpson fails to show this procedure is inapplicable in cases involving qualified immunity.[4]

The concerns that support determining qualified immunity at the earliest stage of litigation are not present here. As qualified immunity is "immunity from suit rather than a mere defense to liability," it becomes essentially meaningless if a case wrongfully goes to trial. *Pearson,* 555 U.S. at 231, 129 S.Ct. 808. To save the costs associated with discovery and ongoing litigation, courts have generally held that such immunity be determined early in a proceeding. *Id.* In this case, however, there are no such concerns. As the district court abstained, there will be no discovery or ongoing litigation costs in the federal court. Nor will Defendant Simpson be forced to undergo a trial or waste extensive time and resources when she ultimately may be entitled to qualified immunity. The disciplinary proceedings will continue at the University level, and as Simpson is no longer involved, she will not be harmed by waiting for the proceedings to be concluded at the state level. Once the hearings are complete, Doe may continue with his federal claims, if he chooses, and the district court can evaluate qualified immunity early in that point of the litigation. As a qualified immunity determination involves analyzing important and difficult issues in the case, finding that it applies after choosing to abstain defeats the purpose of allowing the state proceedings to go forward without interference from the federal courts.

The University also argues that the claims against Defendant Simpson are backwards-looking, and thus, may be determined prior to resolution of all issues. That the claims are not for prospective relief is not determinative. As the district court has rightfully abstained from the case, the University will continue with its hearings. We are not able to assess the full measure of potential damages or evaluate the extent of the harm when another hearing will soon occur. Depending on what p.373 happens at the next hearing, Doe's federal court claim and alleged damages may change. Hopefully, Doe will face a fair proceeding. If not, or if he argues that the harm from the previous hearings still exists regardless of the outcome, he can file an amended complaint based on the final order(s) of the Hearing Panel and UAB, and qualified immunity and its relation to what due process he should be afforded can then be decided. Even though Defendant Simpson is no longer involved with the hearings, calculating the damages associated with the process is premature until the process has concluded. Only at that point can the parties and the court assess the constitutionality of the procedures and the damages, if any, caused by the proceedings as a whole.

Affirmed in part. Reversed and remanded in part.

[1] This is a fictitious name to protect the party.

[2] In the third hearing, Doe will receive a new Hearing Panel; a new Hearing Officer will oversee the proceeding; Doe will be able to have the assistance of counsel; Doe may submit questions for cross-examination of Student A to the Hearing Officer; Doe may call his own witnesses and present evidence, and offer any affirmative defenses he chooses; Doe's alleged violation must be proven by a preponderance of the evidence; and Doe may appeal the result if he is not satisfied.

[3] Although not binding, other courts have held university hearings in varying circumstances qualify as proceedings akin to criminal prosecutions for *Younger* abstention. *See Choudhry v. Regents of the Univ. of Cal.,* No. 16-CV-05281-RS, 2016 WL 6611067, at *3 (N.D. Cal. Nov. 9, 2016) (finding abstention proper in disciplinary action against dean because a state institution initiated the proceedings, a preliminary investigation occurred followed by filing a formal charge, the investigation was designed to sanction Choudhry, and Choudhry faces potential serious consequences); *Sanchez v. Ariz. Bd. of Regents,* No. CV-15-01591-PHX-JAT, 2015 WL 6956288, at *2 (D. Ariz. Nov. 10, 2015) (permitting abstention in student disciplinary hearing when "[e]ach party may offer an opening statement, call witnesses, introduce documents and exhibits into evidence, and generally cross-examine witnesses who are called to testify"); *Cameron v. Ariz. Bd. of Regents,* No. CV-08-1490-PHX-ROS, 2008 WL 4838710, at *3 (D. Ariz. Nov. 6, 2008) ("State university tenure decisions

and subsequent appeals are, indeed, state judicial proceedings as contemplated in *Younger's* progeny.").

[4] Defendants' citation to *Summers v. Leis,* 368 F.3d 881 (6th Cir. 2004), fails to support their argument. In that case, we stated that "[a] district court's determinations of whether it must abstain under *Younger* and whether to grant qualified immunity require the application of separate and distinct legal standards. It is not necessary to decide whether the district court should have abstained under *Younger* in order to review whether it applied the appropriate legal standard and analysis in denying qualified immunity to Sheriff Leis." *Id.* at 889-890. *Summers* differs in a significant way from this case as the district court in *Summers* did not abstain, and we were determining whether we should analyze that decision not to abstain.

SEVENTH CIRCUIT DECISIONS
Title IX

Doe v. Columbia College Chicago, 933 F. 3d 849 (7th Cir. 2019) 121
Doe v. Purdue University, 928 F. 3d 652 (7th Cir. 2019) 129
Doe No. 55 v. Madison Metropolitan School Dist., 897 F. 3d 819 (7th Cir. 2018) 145
Wetzel v. Glen St. Andrew Living Community, LLC, 901 F. 3d 856 (7th Cir. 2018) 151
Burton v. Bd of Regents of University of WI System, 851 F. 3d 690 (7th Cir. 2017) 163
Whitaker v. Kenosha Unified School District, 858 F. 3d 1034 (7th Cir. 2017) . 171

933 F.3d 849 (2019)

John DOE, Plaintiff-Appellant,
v.
COLUMBIA COLLEGE CHICAGO, Defendant-Appellee.

No. 18-1869.

United States Court of Appeals, Seventh Circuit.
Argued April 10, 2019.
Decided August 13, 2019.

Doe v. Columbia College Chicago, 933 F. 3d 849 (7th Cir. 2019)

Appeal from the United States District Court for the Northern District of Illinois, Eastern Division, No. 17 C 00748, Amy J. St. Eve, *Judge*.

Eric J. Rosenberg, Attorney, Rosenberg & Ball, Co. LPA, Granville, OH, for Plaintiff-Appellant.

Scott L. Warner, Attorney, Husch Blackwell LLP, Chicago, IL, for Defendant-Appellee.

Before Bauer, Manion, and Rovner, Circuit Judges.

Bauer, Circuit Judge.

This case arises out of a sexual assault investigation and disciplinary hearing conducted by Columbia College of Chicago ("Columbia"). Jane Roe accused John Doe of sexual assault after the two engaged in what she says were non-consensual sexual relations. Doe was given multiple opportunities to submit exculpatory evidence to Columbia, and after the investigation was complete, Doe was given multiple opportunities to review the investigative materials and the evidence submitted by Roe. After a formal disciplinary hearing a panel weighed the evidence, found that some of Roe's allegations were proven by a preponderance of the evidence, and that some were not. Doe was then suspended from Columbia for an academic year.

Doe filed a complaint in federal court alleging Roe and Columbia violated 20 U.S.C. § 1681 ("Title IX"), breach of contract, promissory estoppel, negligent infliction of emotional distress, intentional infliction of emotional distress, and negligence. The district court ruled that each claim was defective and granted the defendants' motion to dismiss. Because we agree with the well reasoned and thorough opinion of the district court, we affirm.

I. BACKGROUND

Jane Roe and John Doe attended Columbia and had a sexual encounter on December 11, 2015. In February 2016, Roe filed a complaint with Columbia alleging she had not consented to the encounter. Columbia appointed staff member Sarah Shaaban to investigate the matter. She met with Doe on February 3, 2016, to discuss the allegations and provide him with an opportunity to submit whatever evidence he wished. At this time Doe did not provide any exculpatory evidence.

Columbia's Title IX coordinator, Dr. Beverly Anderson, reviewed the investigative report and notified Doe that there was sufficient evidence for a reasonable hearing panel to conclude that Doe had violated the school's sexual misconduct policy. She informed Doe that he would be given written notification of the date, time, and place of the hearing, the names of the hearing officers, and that he had a right to review investigative materials. Anderson also provided Doe with Columbia's hearing procedures policy.

Doe responded by asserting that the allegations were false and that he had been physically assaulted and verbally harassed by Roe and her friends since the incident. Columbia requested the names of the individuals who committed the acts Doe described in his letter; Doe refused to provide Columbia with any.

p.853 Anderson contacted Doe two days later and suggested they meet in person to discuss his concerns, but Doe refused to do so without his attorney being present. Anderson informed Doe that he could bring his attorney. Doe said that two of Roe's friends had "flipped him off" a few days prior. Anderson said she would look into the incident.

The associate vice president for campus safety and security contacted Doe and met with him twice to address his concerns. Campus safety and security was able to identify the student who struck Doe and addressed the issue. Doe was instructed to inform Columbia if he had any other interaction with the student.

On April 19, Anderson provided Doe with a letter addressing each concern that Doe had raised in his March 13 letter. Anderson informed Doe that he and Roe would be provided with the same period of time to review the investigative materials. She reminded Doe that he could submit evidence, but had failed to do so, and that he needed to inform Columbia if he had evidence he intended to present. The letter again provided Doe with the specific conduct alleged against him and the categories of sexual misconduct that the allegations fell into. The letter also stated that Doe had not provided any evidence of gender discrimination and, if he provided any evidence of discrimination or bias by a Columbia employee connected with the investigation, Columbia would promptly investigate it.

Anderson contacted Doe in early April to provide him with an academic advisor who could approve any accommodations Doe might need. Anderson followed up several times advising Doe that she needed more information before she could approve any accommodation. Doe failed to provide her with this information.

On April 26, Columbia provided Doe with a copy of the information that Roe had submitted regarding the sexual assault. Doe responded in writing to her submission.

On May 6, Anderson informed Doe that Columbia would schedule a hearing and again advised him of the allegations and his procedural rights. Doe reviewed a copy of Roe's submissions and the investigation materials on May 9. Doe then submitted his evidence including screen shots of text messages, his April 25 letter, and a toxicology report that he had paid an expert to prepare. All of this evidence was submitted to the hearing panel.

On May 4, Anderson received a report that Doe and another male student made "kissing noises" at Roe when she was leaving her dorm the night before. Anderson requested that she and Doe speak about the incident. Nothing in the record indicates that Doe was disciplined for this behavior.

The hearing took place on May 23 and the panel found by a preponderance of the evidence that Doe violated Columbia's student sexual misconduct policy and procedures. The panel also found there was insufficient evidence to support two of Roe's allegations. The panel suspended Doe for the 2016-17 academic year.

Doe appealed and Anderson appointed an appeals officer to the case—acting chair of the Cinema Arts and Sciences, Joe Steiff. When Doe discovered that Steiff was involved in a documentary titled "How Will I Tell? Surviving Sexual Assault," he requested Steiff's removal from the case; Columbia replaced Steiff with an appeals officer that Doe found to be unobjectionable, but who ultimately upheld the hearing panel's findings and discipline.

Doe filed a complaint in federal court on January 30, 2017, against Roe and Columbia p.854 alleging violations of Title IX and a number of state law claims. The district court granted a motion to dismiss all counts without prejudice and granted Doe's motion for leave to file an amended complaint. On November 7, 2017, Doe filed an amended complaint that was identical in all respects to the original complaint, save the addition of a breach of contract claim against Columbia. Doe explained that he included his previously dismissed claims in the amended complaint to preserve them for appeal and indicated he would not attempt to remedy the deficiencies outlined in the district court's prior ruling.

The district court dismissed Doe's breach of contract claim and now Doe appeals each ruling. Because we agree with the district court, we affirm the dismissal of each of Doe's claims.

II. DISCUSSION

We review a district court's grant of a motion to dismiss pursuant to Federal Rule of Civil Procedure 12(b)(6) *de novo*. *Trujillo v. Rockledge Furniture LLC*, 926 F.3d 395, 397 (7th Cir. 2019). This requires we accept all well-pleaded facts as true and draw all reasonable inferences in favor of the plaintiff. *Id.* To survive a motion to dismiss the complaint must "state a claim for relief that is plausible on its face." *Bell Atlantic Corp. v. Twombly*, 550 U.S. 544, 570, 127 S.Ct. 1955, 167 L.Ed.2d 929 (2007). A plaintiff must plead particularized factual content, not conclusory allegations, that allows the court to plausibly infer the defendant is liable for the alleged misconduct. *Ashcroft v. Iqbal*, 556 U.S. 662, 678, 129 S.Ct. 1937, 173 L.Ed.2d 868 (2009). We may consider documents attached to the pleadings so long as the documents are referred to in the complaint and central to the plaintiff's claims. *See Adams v. City of Indianapolis*, 742 F.3d 720, 729 (7th Cir. 2014). Here, plaintiff attached documents to his complaint related to the investigation, hearing, and other issues central to his claims, and the court considered them in deciding the case.

A. Title IX Claims

Title IX states that "[n]o person in the United States shall, on the basis of sex, be excluded from participation in, be denied the benefits of, or be subjected to discrimination under any educational program or activity receiving Federal financial assistance." 20 U.S.C. § 1681(a). The Supreme Court has interpreted Title IX to provide individual plaintiffs with an implied private right of action to pursue claims of gender discrimination in federal court and has recognized a number of claims that constitute discrimination. *Cannon v. Univ. of Chicago,* 441 U.S. 677, 689, 99 S.Ct. 1946, 60 L.Ed.2d 560 (1979). Doe alleges various discriminatory theories and we will analyze each in turn.

i. Discrimination

A Title IX discrimination claim requires a plaintiff allege (1) the educational institution received federal funding, (2) plaintiff was excluded from participation in or denied the benefits of an educational program, and (3) the educational institution in question discriminated against plaintiff based on gender. *See Doe v. Purdue University,* 928 F.3d 652, 657 (7th Cir. 2019). The parties do not dispute that Columbia received federal funding, nor that Doe was denied the benefits of an educational program, but rather focus on whether Columbia discriminated against Doe because of his gender. Recently, this Court held that tests or categories labeled "erroneous outcome" or "selective enforcement" or "deliberate indifference" or "archaic assumptions" need not be considered because at bottom they all ask the same p.855 question: whether "the alleged facts, if true, raise a plausible inference that the university discriminated ... 'on the basis of sex'?" *Id.* at 668-69.

Doe begins with the 2011 "Dear Colleague" letter from the Department of Education that addressed the problem of sexual violence at educational institutions. *See* United States Department of Education, Office of the Assistant Secretary of Civil Rights, Dear Colleague Letter (2011), https:/www2.ed.gov/print/about/offices/list/ocr/letters/colleague-201104.html. Approximately 20 percent of women and 6 percent of men are victims of completed or attempted sexual assault during college. *Id.* at 2. To address this problem, the letter encouraged schools to publish their discrimination policies, adopt and publish grievance procedures, ensure their employees are trained to report and effectively respond to incidents of harassment, and appoint a Title IX coordinator. *Id.* at 4. The letter also encouraged schools to apply a preponderance of the evidence standard when adjudicating sexual assault cases. *Id.* at 10-11. Despite the fact that the letter applies equally to male and female students accused of sexual assault, Doe argues that Columbia's attempts to comport with the letter's requirements demonstrate an anti-male bias.

Doe alleges events aimed at raising awareness of sexual assault issues and a screening of "The Hunting Ground," a film about sexual assault, demonstrate an anti-male bias on campus. Doe also points to Columbia sanctioned social media posts titled the "Presence of Yes" which included statements like, "Teach boys that they are not entitled to women's bodies" and "Misogyny kills: the sexual entitlement that many men have and the ways in which they objectify women are behind the high rates of sexual violence, abuse, and harassment that women experience."

Doe asserts that the "Dear Colleague" letter, pressure from the Office of Civil Right investigations, and the aforementioned on-campus programming combined to cause Columbia to implement anti-male policies to increase convictions of male students. This, Doe alleges, was done to avoid additional investigations by the Office of Civil Rights, to avoid losing federal funds, and to avoid negative publicity. A plaintiff cannot rely on these generalized allegations alone, however, but must combine them with facts particular to his case to survive a motion to dismiss. *Purdue,* 928 F.3d at 668; *Doe v. Baum,* 903 F.3d 575, 586 (6th Cir.2018).

For example, in *Baum,* the court noted that the hearing panel credited witness testimony based on gender—the panel discredited the testimony of all males, including the accused, and credited the testimony of all females, including the victim. *Id.* at 586. In *Doe v. Purdue,* the plaintiff alleged the University found the victim's story credible (without hearing directly from her), and the plaintiff's story incredible. 928 F.3d at 659. The plaintiff was not provided with a copy of the investigative report nor made aware of its contents before his hearing, and the investigation summary failed to include favorable evidence he had submitted to the University. *Id.* at 657. Additionally,

> Two members of the panel candidly stated that they had not read the investigative report. The one who apparently had read it asked John accusatory questions that assumed his guilt. Because John had not seen the evidence, he could not address it. He reiterated his innocence and told the panel about some of the friendly texts that Jane had sent him after the alleged assaults. The panel refused John permission to present witnesses, including character witnesses and a roommate who would state that he p.856 was present in the room at the time of the alleged assault and that Jane's rendition of events was false.

Id. We found the above allegations made the plaintiff's claim of gender discrimination plausible. But here, Doe does not allege the particularized "something more" that is required to survive a motion to dismiss. Doe was provided with the opportunity to review the investigative materials; was given multiple opportunities to submit evidence; presented affidavits signed by witnesses; and submitted questions to be asked of Roe on cross-examination.[1] Nor did Doe allege any panel member failed to review the applicable materials or demonstrated bias during the hearing. When Doe did voice concerns about potential bias, Steiff, the appeals officer originally assigned to his case, was removed.

Doe argues that restricting his access to documents relevant to the investigation demonstrated an anti-male bias. First, this allegation is divorced from gender—Doe does not allege that females accused of sexual assault were allowed to review materials or that only female victims were allowed to review them. Second, the documents attached to Doe's complaint show that he accessed the investigative materials and information submitted by Roe multiple times before his hearing.

Doe also argues the board's decision was against the weight of the evidence. Again, this allegation does not imply that the board's decision was based on Doe's gender. Moreover, the documents attached to Doe's complaint do not imply the board blindly accepted Roe's allegations while finding Doe incredible. Rather, after considering all of the evidence the hearing panel found some claims were substantiated and others were not. Doe asserts the toxicology report proved that Roe's assertion that she was incapacitated should have been rejected. But the board did not find that Roe was incapacitated during the sexual encounter; it found that she did not consent to many of the acts performed by Roe. This conclusion is supported by the toxicology report which concluded that Roe likely had limited memory of the events that night due to alcohol induced amnesia.

In sum, there is simply no way to plausibly infer that Columbia's investigation or adjudication was tainted by an anti-male bias. Doe fails to allege particularized facts that could lead to a reasonable inference that Columbia denied him an educational benefit because of his sex.

ii. Sexual Harassment

Sexual harassment by a fellow student is actionable under Title IX if a plaintiff demonstrates: (1) the harassment was based on sex, (2) it was at an educational institution that was receiving federal funds, (3) the harassment was so severe, pervasive, and objectively offensive that it deprived the victim of access to educational opportunities, and (4) the school officials had actual knowledge of the harassment and were deliberately indifferent to it. *Doe v. Galster,* 768 F.3d 611, 617 (7th Cir. 2014). We cannot infer from the allegations that the conduct was based on Doe's gender or that Columbia was deliberately indifferent in light of the circumstances.

Doe alleges the following created a hostile environment based on his gender: he was punched by someone who believed he had raped Roe; a social media post stated "boy[s] like [Doe] are the reason #Ineed-Feminism"; two social media posts referred to him as a "rapist" and one as a "predator"; and one post indicated that Doe raped someone. However, these acts were directed at Doe not because of his gender, but because the individuals believed he raped someone. Doe alleges no facts that would cause us to plausibly infer he was harassed because he is a man, rather than because his harassers believed that he raped their friend.

Moreover, Doe does not allege Columbia acted with deliberate indifference. Deliberate indifference is a high bar because "[s]chool administrators must continue to enjoy the flexibility they require in disciplinary decisions unless their response to harassment is clearly unreasonable." *Galster,* 768 F.3d at 619 (quoting *Davis Next Friend LaShonda D. v. Monroe County Bd. of Educ.,* 526 U.S. 629, 643, 119 S.Ct. 1661, 143 L.Ed.2d 839 (1999)) (internal quotation marks omitted).

When alerted to the above posts, Columbia responded quickly and requested the names of the individuals that made the comments so it could address the issue. When Doe alerted Columbia that one of Roe's friends had "flipped him off," Anderson responded quickly and said she would look into the incident. Additionally, the associate vice president for campus safety and security met with Doe on multiple occasions to ensure his complaints were addressed. Columbia also investigated Doe's claim that he was struck by a student, identified who it was, and addressed the issue while instructing Doe to bring to Columbia's attention if she ever interacted with him again. Doe does not allege that the harassment continued after his initial complaints or that Columbia's response was otherwise deficient. We affirm the district court's dismissal of his peer-harassment claim.

iii. Retaliation

Doe also alleges that Columbia unlawfully retaliated against him for defending himself against the sexual assault charge and for complaining about Roe and her friends. To establish a Title IX retaliation claim Doe must show: (1) he engaged in protected activity under Title IX, (2) Columbia took a materially adverse action against him, and (3) there was a but-for causal connection between the two. *Burton v. Bd. of Regents of the Univ. of Wis. Sys.*, 851 F.3d 690, 695 (7th Cir. 2017).

Doe's first claim of retaliation argues that Columbia suspended Doe for an academic year not because it found he violated the school's sexual harassment policy, but because he attempted to defend himself at his disciplinary proceeding. No facts indicate the panel came to its conclusion because it wanted to punish Doe for defending himself at the proceeding. The complaint and attached exhibits demonstrate that Columbia investigated the complaint, considered the evidence presented by Doe, and concluded that he committed some of the acts that Roe alleged. Doe's discipline was based on this conclusion and nothing indicates otherwise.

Doe's second allegation is that Columbia retaliated against him for complaining about Roe and her friends' behavior by failing to discipline them. There is nothing in Doe's complaint that would allow us to infer that Columbia wanted to retaliate against him for complaining about harassment. Contrary to Doe's argument, his complaint and the attached documents show that Columbia was diligent in investigating his complaints, while nothing Doe alleges leads us to believe that Columbia failed to discipline Roe because they were frustrated that Doe complained about the p.858 behavior. This claim was properly dismissed.

B. State Law Claims

i. Breach of Contract

Doe's primary breach-of-contract argument is that Columbia violated its own policies and procedures by failing to provide him with an impartial investigation and adjudication. Doe asserts that he was not provided with access to the documents related to his hearing, that Columbia failed to discipline female individuals who engaged in similar conduct, and that the hearing panel's decision was against the weight of the evidence.

A breach of contract claim requires Doe allege: (1) the existence of a valid and enforceable contractual promise, (2) a breach of that promise, (3) plaintiff performed his contractual obligations, and (4) resultant damages. *Dual-Temp of Illinois, Inc. v. Hench Control, Inc.*, 821 F.3d 866, 869 (7th Cir. 2016). A college and its students have a contractual relationship and its terms are set forth in the school's catalogues and bulletins. *Raethz v. Aurora Univ.*, 346 Ill.App.3d 728, 282 Ill.Dec. 77, 805 N.E.2d 696, 699 (2004). Illinois courts have expressed a reluctance to interfere with academic affairs and have held that a student's breach of contract claim must involve decisions that were arbitrary, capricious, or made in bad faith. *Id.* Columbia would not be liable even if we find it exercised its academic judgment unwisely; rather it must have disciplined a student without any rational basis. *Frederick v. Northwestern Univ. Dental School*, 247 Ill. App.3d 464, 187 Ill.Dec. 174, 617 N.E.2d 382, 387 (1993).

The assertion that Doe was not allowed to review investigative materials is contradicted by the documents attached to his complaint. Nor was Columbia arbitrary or capricious in its response to Doe's complaints about female students. They responded quickly, investigated, and handled his complaints, and encouraged Doe to inform them if any further incidents occurred. Finally, nothing indicates that the investigation or the decision by the hearing panel was arbitrary. Quite the contrary, after a thorough investigation the hearing panel determined that some allegations were established and others were not.

The burden on Doe is high. To find in his favor we must find that Columbia "did not exercise its academic judgment at all, instead acting arbitrarily or in bad faith in its treatment of plaintiff." *Raethz*, 346 Ill.App.3d 728, 805 N.E.2d at 700. Because the record does not support a plausible inference that Columbia was biased against Doe, we affirm the district court's dismissal of Doe's breach of contract claim.

ii. Remainder of Doe's State Law Claims

Doe's arguments related to the remainder of his state law claims are cryptic and undeveloped and we hold he has waived these claims. Without the facts or the law necessary to rule on these issues, we will not attempt to piece together an argument for Doe or guess as to what he meant to argue in his brief. Instead, we uphold the dismissal by the district court.

III. CONCLUSION

The rulings of the district court and its final order are AFFIRMED.

---

[1] As appellees note, all parties were able to submit questions for cross-examination, but only the hearing officers were able to ask questions of witnesses. Thus, it was within the discretion of the hearing officers whether to ask questions on cross-examination of either party, regardless of gender.

928 F.3d 652 (2019)

John DOE, Plaintiff-Appellant,

v.

PURDUE UNIVERSITY, et al., Defendants-Appellees.

No. 17-3565.

United States Court of Appeals, Seventh Circuit.

Argued September 18, 2018.

Decided June 28, 2019.

Doe v. Purdue University, 928 F. 3d 652 (7th Cir. 2019)

Appeal from the United States District Court for the Northern District of Indiana, Hammond Division, No. 2:17-cv-00033-PRC, Paul R. Cherry, Magistrate Judge.

Philip A. Byler, Attorney, NESENOFF & MILTENBERG, LLP, New York, NY, Damon M. Cheronis, Attorney, LAW OFFICES OF DAMON M. CHERONIS, Chicago, IL, for Plaintiff-Appellant.

William Peter Kealey, James Francis Olds, Attorneys, STUART & BRANIGIN LLP, Lafayette, IN, for Defendants-Appellees.

Before Sykes, Barrett, and St. Eve, Circuit Judges.

Barrett, Circuit Judge.

After finding John Doe guilty of sexual violence against Jane Doe, Purdue University suspended him for an academic year and imposed conditions on his readmission. As a result of that decision, John was expelled from the Navy ROTC program, which terminated both his ROTC scholarship and plan to pursue a career in the Navy.

John sued the university and several of its officials, asserting two basic claims. First, he argued that they had violated the Fourteenth Amendment by using constitutionally flawed procedures to determine his guilt or innocence. Second, he argued that Purdue had violated Title IX by imposing a punishment infected by sex bias. A magistrate judge dismissed John's suit on the ground that he had failed to state a claim under either theory. We disagree. John has adequately alleged violations of both the Fourteenth Amendment and Title IX.

I.

We are reviewing the magistrate judge's decision to dismiss John's complaint for failing to state a claim. That means that we must recount the facts as he describes them, drawing every inference in his favor. *See D.B. ex rel. Kurtis B. v. Kopp,* 725 F.3d 681, 682 (7th Cir. 2013). In other words, the story that follows is one-sided because the posture of the case requires it to be. Our task is not to determine what allegations are supported by the evidence but to determine whether John is entitled to relief if everything that he says is true. *See McCauley v. City of Chicago,* 671 F.3d 611, 616 (7th Cir. 2011).

John and Jane were both students in Purdue's Navy ROTC program. They began dating in the fall of 2015, and between October and December, they had consensual sexual intercourse fifteen to twenty times. Jane's behavior became increasingly erratic over the course of that semester, and she told John that she felt hopeless, hated her life, and was contemplating running away. In December, Jane attempted suicide in front of John, and after that incident, they stopped having sex. They continued dating, however, until January, when John tried to get Jane help by reporting her suicide attempt to two resident assistants and an advisor. Jane was upset at John for reporting her, and she distanced herself from him. Soon thereafter, she began dating someone else.

For a few months, things were quiet between John and Jane. That changed in April 2016, which was Sexual Assault Awareness Month. During that month, Purdue hosted over a dozen events to promote the reporting of sexual assaults. Many of the events were sponsored by the Center for Advocacy, Response, and Education (CARE), a university center dedicated to supporting victims of sexual violence. CARE promoted the events on its Facebook page, along with posts containing information about sexual assault. One of its posts was an article from *The Washington Post* titled "Alcohol isn't the cause of campus sexual assault. Men are."

During the first ten days of April, five students reported sexual assault to the university. Jane was one of them. She alleged that in November 2015, she was sleeping with John in his room when she woke to him groping her over her clothes p.657 without her consent. According to Jane, she told John that this was not okay, and John then confessed that he had digitally penetrated her while the two were sleeping in Jane's room earlier that month. Jane told the university that John had engaged in other misconduct as well: she asserted that he had gone through her underwear drawer without her permission, chased her through a hallway while joking about tasering her, gone to her room unannounced after they broke up, and lost his temper in front of her.

John learned about Jane's accusations in a letter from Katherine Sermersheim, Purdue's Dean of Students and a Title IX coordinator. Sermersheim informed John that the university had elected to pursue Jane's allegations even though Jane had not filed a formal complaint. She outlined the school's disciplinary procedures and explained that two employees who reported to her, Erin Oliver and Jacob Amberger, would investigate the case. She also instructed John not to have any contact with Jane. After he received the letter, John was suspended from the Navy ROTC, banned from all buildings where Jane had classes, and barred from eating in his usual dining hall because Jane also used it.

John submitted a written response denying all of Jane's allegations. He asserted that he never had sexual contact with Jane while she was sleeping, through digital penetration or otherwise. He said that there was one night in December, after Jane's suicide attempt, when he touched Jane's knee while she was sleeping on a futon and he was on the floor next to her. But he denied groping her or engaging in any of the harassing behavior of which she had accused him. John also recounted evidence that he thought inconsistent with Jane's claim of sexual assault: she texted and talked to him over the holidays, sent his family a package of homemade Christmas cookies, and invited him to her room when they returned to school in January. He also provided details suggesting that Jane was troubled and emotionally unstable, which he thought might explain her false accusations.

Under Purdue's procedures, John was allowed the assistance of a "supporter" at any meeting with investigators. In late April, John and his supporter met with Oliver and Amberger. As he had in his written response, John steadfastly denied Jane's allegations. He provided the investigators with some of the friendly texts that he thought belied her story, as well as a list of over thirty people who could speak to his integrity.

When the investigators' report was complete, Sermersheim sent it to a three-person panel of Purdue's Advisory Committee on Equity, which was tasked with making a recommendation to her after reviewing the report and hearing from the parties. Sermersheim called John to appear before the panel, but consistent with Purdue's then-applicable procedures, she neither gave him a copy of the report nor shared its contents with him. Moments before his committee appearance, however, a Navy ROTC representative gave John a few minutes to review a redacted version of the report. To John's distress, he learned that it falsely claimed that he had confessed to Jane's allegations. The investigators' summary of John's testimony also failed to include John's description of Jane's suicide attempt.

John and his supporter met with the Advisory Committee and Sermersheim, who chaired the meeting, for about thirty minutes. Jane neither appeared before the panel nor submitted a written statement. Instead, Monica Soto Bloom, the director of CARE, wrote the Advisory Committee p.658 and Sermersheim a letter summarizing Jane's accusations.

The meeting did not go well for John. Two members of the panel candidly stated that they had not read the investigative report. The one who apparently had read it asked John accusatory questions that assumed his guilt. Because John had not seen the evidence, he could not address it. He reiterated his innocence and told the panel about some of the friendly texts that Jane had sent him after the alleged assaults. The panel refused John permission to present witnesses, including character witnesses and a roommate who would state that he was present in the room at the time of the alleged assault and that Jane's rendition of events was false.

A week later, Sermersheim sent John a perfunctory letter informing him that she had found him guilty by a preponderance of the evidence of sexual violence. She suspended John from Purdue for one academic year. In addition, she conditioned John's reentry on his completion of a university-sponsored "bystander intervention training" and his agreement to meet with the Assistant Director of CARE during the first semester of his return.

John appealed this decision to Alysa Rollock, Purdue's Vice President for Ethics and Compliance, who instructed Sermersheim to identify the factual basis of her determination. Sermersheim sent a revised letter to John adding the following:

> Specifically, a preponderance of the evidence supports that:
> 1. [Jane Doe] had fallen asleep on a futon with you on the floor beside her. She woke up and found that you inappropriately touched her over her clothing and without her consent by placing your hand above her knee, between her legs, and moved it up to her "crotch" areas; and

2. On another occasion, while she was sleeping and without her consent, you inappropriately touched [Jane Doe] by digitally penetrating her vagina.

As the basis for these findings, Sermersheim offered: "I find by a preponderance of the evidence that [John Doe] is not a credible witness. I find by a preponderance of the evidence that [Jane Doe] is a credible witness." John appealed to Rollock again, but this time, Rollock upheld Sermersheim's determination of guilt and accompanying sanctions. A few weeks after his second appeal was denied, John involuntarily resigned from the Navy ROTC, which has a "zero tolerance" policy for sexual harassment.

John sued Mitch Daniels, the President of Purdue University; Rollock, the Vice President for Ethics and Compliance; Sermersheim, the Dean and a Title IX coordinator; and Oliver and Amberger, the investigators, in their individual capacities, seeking monetary relief under 42 U.S.C. § 1983.[1] He sued these same defendants, along with the members of Purdue's Board of Trustees, in their official capacities, seeking injunctive relief under *Ex Parte Young*, 209 U.S. 123, 28 S.Ct. 441, 52 L.Ed. 714 (1908), to remedy the Fourteenth Amendment violation. And he sued Purdue University for discriminating against him on the basis of sex in violation of Title IX.

The magistrate judge dismissed John's § 1983 claims with prejudice, holding that the disciplinary proceedings did not deprive John of either liberty or property, so p.659 the Due Process Clause did not apply. He offered an additional reason for dismissing John's § 1983 claim against Daniels: John's theory of liability was based on Daniels's role as supervisor, and there is no supervisory liability under § 1983. As for John's claims for injunctive relief, the magistrate judge dismissed them without prejudice for lack of standing because John had not alleged that the violations posed any threat of future harm. And he dismissed John's claims under Title IX with prejudice on the ground that John had not alleged facts sufficient to show that Purdue discriminated against him on the basis of sex. John appeals each of these rulings.

II.

We begin with procedural due process. According to John, he was punished pursuant to a process that failed to satisfy the minimum standards of fairness required by the Due Process Clause. He alleges the following deficiencies: he was not provided with the investigative report or any of the evidence on which the decisionmakers relied in determining his guilt and punishment; Jane did not appear before the Advisory Committee; he had no opportunity to cross-examine Jane; Sermersheim found Jane credible even though neither Sermersheim nor the Advisory Committee talked to her in person; Jane did not write her own statement for the panel, much less a sworn one; Sermersheim was in charge of both the investigation and the adjudication of his case; the Advisory Committee was blatantly biased against him; and the Advisory Committee refused to allow him to present any evidence, including witnesses.

Yet John cannot recover simply because the procedures were unfair, even if they were. The Due Process Clause is not a general fairness guarantee; its protection kicks in only when a state actor deprives someone of "life, liberty, or property." U.S.

CONST. amend. XIV, § 1. The threshold question, then, is whether John lost a liberty or property interest when he was found guilty of sexual violence and punished. We address whether the procedures satisfied minimum constitutional requirements of fairness only if the answer to that question is yes.

A.

Our precedent involving due process claims in the context of university discipline has focused on whether a student has a protected property interest in his education at a state university. We have explained that "[a] college education—any education—is not 'property' in the usual sense of the word." *Williams v. Wendler,* 530 F.3d 584, 589 (7th Cir. 2008); *see also Charleston v. Bd. of Trs. of Univ. of Ill. at Chi.,* 741 F.3d 769, 772 (7th Cir. 2013) ("[O]ur circuit has rejected the proposition that an individual has a stand-alone property interest in an education at a state university, including a graduate education.").[2] Instead, "we ask whether the student has shown that he has a *legally protected entitlement* to his continued education at the university." *Charleston,* 741 p.660 F.3d at 773 (emphasis in original). High school students (and, for that matter, elementary school students) have a property interest in their public education because state law entitles them to receive one. *Goss v. Lopez,* 419 U.S. 565, 573-74, 95 S.Ct. 729, 42 L.Ed.2d 725 (1975). The same is not true, however, of students at public universities—certainly, John has not contended that Indiana guarantees its residents a college education.

In the context of higher education, any property interest is a matter of contract between the student and the university. *Bissessur v. Ind. Univ. Bd. of Trs.,* 581 F.3d 599, 601 (7th Cir. 2009) (explaining that the "basic legal relation between a student and a private university or college is contractual in nature" (citation omitted)). And to demonstrate that he possesses the requisite property interest, a university student must do more than show that he has a contract with the university; he must establish that the contract entitled him to the specific right that the university allegedly took, "such as the right to a continuing education or the right not to be suspended without good cause." *Id.* at 601. Generalities won't do; "the student's complaint must be specific about the source of this implied contract, the exact promises the university made to the student, and the promises the student made in return." *Charleston,* 741 F.3d at 773.

John has not adequately alleged that Purdue deprived him of property because his complaint does not point to any specific contractual promise that Purdue allegedly broke.[3] To be sure, John asserts that he had a property interest in his continued enrollment at Purdue. But as support for that proposition, his complaint states only that the right arose "from the express and implied contractual relationship" between John and the university. It points to no "identifiable contractual promise that the [university] failed to honor." *Bissessur,* 581 F.3d at 602 (alteration in original) (citation omitted).

His brief does only slightly better. In it, John insists that the Indiana state courts have held that a student enrolled in a public institution has a property interest in continuing his education. He cites *Reilly v. Daly,* in which an Indiana court said: "It is without question that a student's interest in pursuing an education is included within the Fourteenth Amendment's protection of liberty and property and that a student facing expulsion or suspension from a public educational institution is therefore entitled to the protections of due process." 666 N.E.2d 439, 444 (Ind. Ct. App. 1996). But John's reliance on *Reilly* is misplaced. To begin with, this cryptic sentence—the sum of what the case says on the topic—does not specify whether university disciplinary proceedings implicate liberty or property interests. And to the extent that *Reilly* refers to property, it does not purport to identify a state-granted property right to pursue higher education. Instead, it appears to express a view about federal law that we have already rejected: that the Due Process Clause protects a generalized property interest in higher education, irrespective of any specific state entitlement. While Indiana is free to align itself with courts taking that view, *see supra* note 2, our position is clear and to the contrary, *see Williams*, 530 F.3d at 589 (rejecting "the bald assertion that any student who is suspended from college has suffered a deprivation of constitutional property").

p.661 John's failure to establish a property interest does not doom his claim, however, because he also maintains that Purdue deprived him of a protected liberty interest: his freedom to pursue naval service, his occupation of choice. To succeed on this theory, John must satisfy the "stigma plus" test, which requires him to show that the state inflicted reputational damage accompanied by an alteration in legal status that deprived him of a right he previously held. *See Mann v. Vogel*, 707 F.3d 872, 878 (7th Cir. 2013); *see also Paul v. Davis*, 424 U.S. 693, 708-09, 96 S.Ct. 1155, 47 L.Ed.2d 405 (1976); *Hinkle v. White*, 793 F.3d 764, 767-68 (7th Cir. 2015). John argues that he has satisfied this test because he alleges that Purdue inflicted reputational harm by wrongfully branding him as a sex offender; that Purdue changed his legal status by suspending him, subjecting him to readmission requirements, and causing the loss of his Navy ROTC scholarship; and that these actions impaired his right to occupational liberty by making it virtually impossible for him to seek employment in his field of choice, the Navy. *See Lawson v. Sheriff of Tippecanoe Cty., Ind.*, 725 F.2d 1136, 1138 (7th Cir. 1984) ("The concept of liberty in Fourteenth Amendment jurisprudence has long included the liberty to follow a trade, profession, or other calling."); *Townsend v. Vallas*, 256 F.3d 661, 670 (7th Cir. 2001) (Liberty interests are impinged when someone's "good name, reputation, honor or integrity [are] called into question in a manner that makes it virtually impossible for ... [him] to find new employment in his chosen field.").

Purdue insists that John has not adequately alleged "stigma," much less the necessary "plus." The university maintains that it has not and will not divulge John's disciplinary record without his permission. The Navy knows about it only because John signed a form authorizing the disclosure after the investigation began. Because John permitted the disclosure, Purdue says, he cannot complain that Purdue stigmatized him.

Purdue cites no cases in support of its position, but it is presumably trying to draw an analogy between John and a plaintiff who publishes damaging information about himself—because it is true that a plaintiff can't himself spill the beans and then blame the defendant for ruining his reputation. *Olivieri v. Rodriguez* illustrates the point. 122 F.3d 406 (7th Cir. 1997). There, a probationary police officer asserted a procedural due process claim against his superintendent after he was fired for sexually harassing other probationers. *Id.* at 407. We observed that "the defendant [had not] disclosed to anyone the grounds of the plaintiff's discharge." *Id.* at 408. The plaintiff, however, insisted that the defendant's silence didn't matter because the plaintiff would have to tell potential employers why he was fired—and "[i]f he answers truthfully, he will reveal the ground of the termination as effectively as (actually more effectively than) if the Department had taken out a full-page ad in every newspaper in the nation announcing the termination of Felix A. Olivieri for sexually harassing female probationary officers at the Chicago police training academy." *Id.*

We rejected Olivieri's claim, holding that a plaintiff who publicizes negative information about himself cannot establish that the *defendant* deprived him of a liberty interest. *Id.* As an initial matter, we noted that it was uncertain whether Olivieri's prospective employers would ever find out why he was discharged. *Id.* at 408-09 ("A prospective employer might not ask him—might ask only the Chicago Police Department, which for all we know might refuse to disclose the grounds of Olivieri's discharge; many former employers refuse to answer such inquiries, because of fear of p.662 being sued for defamation."). In addition, we explained that "[t]he principle of self-defamation, applied in a case such as this, would encourage [the plaintiff] to apply for a job to every police force in the nation, in order to magnify his damages; and to blurt out to each of the them the ground of his discharge in the most lurid terms, to the same end." *Id.* at 409.

John's case is different. He does not claim simply that he might someday have to self-publish the guilty finding to future employers. Instead, John says that he had an obligation to authorize Purdue to disclose the proceedings to the Navy. That makes John's case more like *Dupuy v. Samuels*, 397 F.3d 493 (7th Cir. 2005), than *Olivieri*. In *Dupuy*, we held that the publication requirement of the stigma-plus test was satisfied when the plaintiffs were obligated to authorize a state agency to disclose its finding that they were child abusers to the plaintiffs' current and prospective employers. 397 F.3d at 510. In contrast to *Olivieri*, where disclosure was voluntary and speculative, it was compelled and certain in *Dupuy*. And in *Dupuy*, unlike in *Olivieri*, the disclosure was not self-published—it came from the defendant, even if the plaintiff had been obligated to authorize it. So too here: Purdue, not John, revealed to the Navy that it had found him guilty of sexual violence, and John had a legal obligation to authorize the disclosure.

Thus, if what John says is true, the university has stigmatized him by telling the Navy about the guilty finding. But the loss of reputation is not itself a loss of liberty, "even when it causes 'serious impairment of one's future employment.'" *Hojnacki v. Klein-Acosta*, 285 F.3d 544, 548 (7th Cir. 2002) (alteration and citation omitted). John must also show that the stigma was accompanied by a change in legal status. In *Paul v. Davis*, for example, the Supreme Court held that the police did not trigger the Due Process Clause by posting flyers falsely asserting that the plaintiff was an active shoplifter. 424 U.S. at 712, 96 S.Ct. 1155. The flyers undoubtedly harmed the plaintiff's professional reputation, but their posting did not alter his legal status. *Id.* at 708-12, 96 S.Ct. 1155. Similarly, in *Hinkle v. White*, looselipped state police officers spread word that they were investigating the plaintiff for child molestation and that he might be guilty of arson to boot. 793 F.3d at 767. But the gossip did not alter his legal status—the plaintiff was not prosecuted, much less found guilty; nor did the county impose a consequence like firing him from his job as county sheriff. *Id.* at 768-69. Even though the rumors made it "virtually impossible" for him to change to a new job in his chosen field, the lack of a status change meant that he could not state a due process claim. *Id.* at 768-70.

John's situation is unlike that of the plaintiffs in *Paul v. Davis* and *Hinkle v. White* because it is not a matter of state-spread rumors or an investigation that was ultimately dropped. After conducting an adjudicatory proceeding, Purdue formally determined that John was guilty of a sexual offense. That determination changed John's status: he went from a full-time student in good standing to one suspended for an academic year. *Cf. Mann,* 707 F.3d at 878 (holding that the state deprived the plaintiff of occupational liberty when, after an investigation, it found that she had violated child-safety laws and suspended her ability to operate her daycare center); *Doyle v. Camelot Care Ctrs.,* 305 F.3d 603, 617 (7th Cir. 2002) (holding that the state deprived the plaintiffs of occupational liberty when, after an investigation, it found that they had neglected a minor and informed their respective employers, who fired them). And it was this official determination of guilt, not the preceding p.663 charges or any accompanying rumors, that allegedly deprived John of occupational liberty. It caused his expulsion from the Navy ROTC program (with the accompanying loss of scholarship) and foreclosed the possibility of his re-enrollment in it. John has satisfied the "stigma plus" test.

B.

Having determined that John has adequately alleged that Purdue deprived him of a liberty interest, we turn to whether he has adequately claimed that Purdue used fundamentally unfair procedures in determining his guilt.

When a right is protected by the Due Process Clause, a state "may not withdraw [it] on grounds of misconduct absent[ ] fundamentally fair procedures to determine whether the misconduct has occurred." *Goss,* 419 U.S. at 574, 95 S.Ct. 729. Determining what is fundamentally fair is always a context-specific inquiry. *See Bd. of Curators of Univ. of Mo. v. Horowitz,* 435 U.S. 78, 86, 98 S.Ct. 948, 55 L.Ed.2d 124 (1978) ("[W]e have frequently emphasized that '[t]he very nature of due process negates any concept of inflexible procedures universally applicable to every imaginable situation.'" (citation omitted)). Thus, for example, a university has much more flexibility in administering academic standards than its code of conduct. *See id.* ("[T]here are distinct differences between decisions to suspend or dismiss a student for disciplinary purposes and similar actions taken for academic reasons which may call for hearings in connection with the former but not the latter."). And even in the disciplinary context, the process due depends on a number of factors, including the severity of the consequence and the level of education. A 10-day suspension warrants fewer procedural safeguards than a longer one, *Goss,* 419 U.S. at 584, 95 S.Ct. 729, and universities are subject to more rigorous requirements than high schools, *Pugel v. Bd. of Trs. of Univ. of Ill.,* 378 F.3d 659, 663-64 (7th Cir. 2004).

John's circumstances entitled him to relatively formal procedures: he was suspended by a university rather than a high school, for sexual violence rather than academic failure, and for an academic year rather than a few days. Yet Purdue's process fell short of what even a high school must provide to a student facing a days-long suspension. "[D]ue process requires, in connection with a suspension of 10 days or less, that the student be given oral or written notice of the charges against him and, if he denies them, an explanation of the evidence the authorities have and an opportunity to present his side of the story." *Goss,* 419 U.S. at 581, 95 S.Ct. 729. John received notice of Jane's allegations and denied them, but Purdue did not disclose its evidence to John. And withholding the evidence on which it relied in adjudicating his guilt was itself sufficient to render the process fundamentally unfair. *See id.* at 580, 95 S.Ct. 729 ("[F]airness can rarely be obtained by secret, one-sided determination of facts decisive of rights. ..." (quoting *Joint Anti-Fascist Refugee Comm. v. McGrath,* 341 U.S. 123, 170, 71 S.Ct. 624, 95 L.Ed. 817 (1951) (Frankfurter, J., concurring))).

John has adequately alleged that the process was deficient in other respects as well. To satisfy the Due Process Clause, "a hearing must be a real one, not a sham or pretense." *Dietchweiler by Dietchweiler v. Lucas,* 827 F.3d 622, 629 (7th Cir. 2016) (citation omitted). At John's meeting with the Advisory Committee, two of the three panel members candidly admitted that they had not read the investigative report, which suggests that they decided that John was guilty based on the accusation rather than the evidence. *See id.* at 630 p.664 (stating that a hearing would be a sham if "members of the school board came to the hearing having predetermined [the plaintiff's] guilt"). And in a case that boiled down to a "he said/she said," it is particularly concerning that Sermersheim and the committee concluded that Jane was the more credible witness—in fact, that she was credible at all—without ever speaking to her in person. Indeed, they did not even receive a statement written by Jane herself, much less a sworn statement.[4] It is unclear, to say the least, how Sermersheim and the committee could have evaluated Jane's credibility.

Sermersheim and the Advisory Committee's failure to make any attempt to examine Jane's credibility is all the more troubling because John identified specific impeachment evidence. He said that Jane was depressed, had attempted suicide, and was angry at him for reporting the attempt. His roommate—with whom Sermersheim and the Advisory Committee refused to speak—maintained that he was present at the time of the alleged assault and that Jane's rendition of events was false. And John insisted that Jane's behavior after the alleged assault—including her texts, gifts, and continued romantic relationship with him—was inconsistent with her claim that he had committed sexual violence against her. Sermersheim and the Advisory Committee may have concluded in the end that John's impeachment evidence did not undercut Jane's credibility. But their failure to even question Jane or John's roommate to probe whether this evidence was reason to disbelieve Jane was fundamentally unfair to John.

John also faults Sermersheim for being in charge of both the investigation and adjudication of his case. We have held, however, that blending these two functions in the university context does not necessarily render a process unfair. *Hess v. Bd. of Trs. of S. Ill. Univ.,* 839 F.3d 668, 675 (7th Cir. 2016). To rebut the presumption that university administrators are "honest and impartial," a plaintiff must "lay a specific foundation of prejudice or prejudgment, such that the probability of actual bias is too high to be constitutionally tolerable." *Id.* This burden is "heavy indeed," typically requiring evidence that "the adjudicator had a pecuniary interest in the outcome of the case, or that he was previously the target of the plaintiff's abuse or criticism." *Id.* (citations omitted). John has made no such allegation here.

C.

To this point, we have analyzed the due process claim without distinguishing between defendants. Now, however, we separate them.

(1)

We begin with John's individual-capacity claim against Mitch Daniels, the president of Purdue. The magistrate judge was right to dismiss this claim. Section 1983 "does not allow actions against individuals merely for their supervisory role of others." *Zimmerman v. Tribble,* 226 F.3d 568, 574 (7th Cir. 2000). To be liable, a supervisor "must know about the conduct and facilitate it, approve it, condone it, or turn a blind eye." *Zentmyer v. Kendall Cty., Ill.,* 220 F.3d 805, 812 (7th Cir. 2000) (quoting *Gentry v. Duckworth,* 65 F.3d 555, 561 (7th Cir. 1995)). John's p.665 complaint asserts nothing more about Daniels than that "'The Buck Stops Here' with him." There is no allegation that Daniels knew about the conduct, much less that he facilitated, approved, or condoned it.

(2)

The individual-capacity claims against Rollock, Sermersheim, Oliver, and Amberger present a different obstacle for John: qualified immunity. For the reasons that we have already explained, John has alleged facts that amount to a constitutional violation. But because the defendants have asserted qualified immunity, John can recover damages from them only if his right to receive procedural due process in the disciplinary proceeding was clearly established. *See Rainsberger v. Benner,* 913 F.3d 640, 647 (7th Cir. 2019). The magistrate judge did not address qualified immunity because he concluded that John had failed to state a due process claim. The defendants raised it below, however, and they press it again here as an alternative ground for affirmance.

John insists that it would be premature for us to address the issue because we are reviewing the magistrate judge's dismissal of his claims under Rule 12(b)(6). As he points out, qualified immunity is generally addressed at summary judgment rather than on the pleadings. *See Alvarado v. Litscher,* 267 F.3d 648, 651 (7th Cir. 2001) ("[A] complaint is generally not dismissed under Rule 12(b)(6) on qualified immunity grounds."); *see also Jacobs v. City of Chicago,* 215 F.3d 758, 765 n.3 (7th Cir. 2000) ("[T]he dismissal of a § 1983 suit under Rule 12(b)(6) is a delicate matter."). Thus, John argues, we should send the case back to the district court for discovery.

There is no hard-and-fast rule, however, against resolving qualified immunity on the pleadings. The reason for deferring it to summary judgment is that an officer's entitlement to qualified immunity often "depend[s] on the particular facts of a given case," *Jacobs,* 215 F.3d at 765 n.3, and the Federal Rules of Civil Procedure do not require a plaintiff to include much factual detail in a complaint, *see* FED. R. CIV. P. 8 (providing that a complaint must contain "a short and plain statement of the claim showing that the pleader is entitled to relief"). *See also Pearson v. Callahan,* 555 U.S. 223, 238-39, 129 S.Ct. 808, 172 L.Ed.2d 565 (2009) ("When qualified immunity is asserted at the pleading stage, the precise factual basis for the plaintiff's claim or claims may be hard to identify."). That said, the existence of qualified immunity is not always dependent on factual development—it is sometimes clear on the face of the complaint that the constitutional right invoked was not clearly articulated in the case law. In that circumstance, the existence of qualified immunity is a "purely legal question" that the court can address on a motion to dismiss. *Jacobs,* 215 F.3d at 765 n.3.

That is the situation here. Qualified immunity is a high standard. It protects government officials from liability for civil damages as long as their actions do not violate "clearly established statutory or constitutional rights of which a reasonable person would have known." *Figgs v. Dawson,* 829 F.3d 895, 905 (7th Cir. 2016) (citation omitted). While the general stigma-plus test is well-settled in our law, *see Hinkle,* 793 F.3d at 768, we have never applied it specifically in the university setting. Instead, our cases in this area have considered only whether students have a *property* interest in their public university education—and to this point, no student has successfully shown the requisite interest. Because this is our first case addressing whether university discipline deprives a student of a *liberty* interest, the relevant legal rule was not "clearly established," p.666 and a reasonable university officer would not have known at the time of John's proceeding that her actions violated the Fourteenth Amendment. We therefore affirm the dismissal of John's individual-capacity claims against Rollock, Sermersheim, Oliver, and Amberger.

(3)

That leaves John's claims for injunctive relief, which he seeks to obtain by suing Daniels, Rollock, Sermersheim, Oliver, and Amberger in their official capacities. *See Ex Parte Young,* 209 U.S. 123, 28 S.Ct. 441, 52 L.Ed. 714 (1908). The magistrate judge dismissed this claim without prejudice on the ground that John lacked standing to bring it. In his complaint, John asked for "an injunction enjoining violations of the Fourteenth Amendment in the process of investigating and adjudicating sexual misconduct complaints." But John doesn't have standing to claim such relief. He has not alleged that he intends to re-enroll at Purdue, much less that he faces a "real and immediate threat" that Purdue would again investigate him for sexual misconduct, much less that any such investigation would violate due process. *See City of L.A. v. Lyons,* 461 U.S. 95, 105, 103 S.Ct. 1660, 75 L.Ed.2d 675 (1983) ("That Lyons may have been illegally choked by the police on October 6, 1976, while presumably affording Lyons standing to claim damages against the individual officers and perhaps against the City, does nothing to establish a real and immediate threat that he would again be stopped for a traffic violation, or for any other offense, by an officer or officers who would illegally choke him into unconsciousness without any provocation or resistance on his part."). What John really seeks to do is champion the rights of other men at Purdue who might be investigated for sexual misconduct using the flawed procedures that he describes in his complaint. That is a no-go: John plainly lacks standing to assert the Fourteenth Amendment rights of other students, even if he had alleged (which he didn't) that the threat of injury to any one of them was "real and immediate." *Id.*

John also seeks to remove the conditions of re-entry imposed by Purdue as part of his discipline. John lacks standing here too. As we already noted, he has not alleged that he intends to return to Purdue—a necessary fact to demonstrate a cognizable injury from the barriers to re-entry. That said, the magistrate judge dismissed this claim without prejudice, so on remand John can seek to remedy his lack of standing by pleading the necessary facts, if he has them.

In his response to the defendants' motion to dismiss, and then again in his brief and at oral argument, John argued that he is also entitled to an injunction ordering university officials to expunge the finding of guilt from his disciplinary record. For this relief, John has standing: John's marred record is a continuing harm for which he can seek redress. *See, e.g., Flint v. Dennison,* 488 F.3d 816, 825 (9th Cir. 2007) (pursuing expungement of university records "serve[s] the purpose of preventing present and future harm"); *Doe v. Cummins,* 662 F. App'x 437, 444 (6th Cir. 2016) (seeking to "remove the negative notation from appellants' disciplinary records" is "nothing more than prospective remedial action"); *Shepard v. Irving,* 77 F. App'x 615, 620 (4th Cir. 2003) (an "F" grade and a plagiarism conviction "constitute[d] a continuing injury to the plaintiff" and an action to remove them was "prospective in nature"). And he claims that if the guilty finding is expunged, a career in the Navy may once again be open to him.

Because John did not specifically request this relief in his complaint, the university p.667 officials object that it is too late for him to raise it now. But Federal Rule of Civil Procedure 54(c) states that "[e]very [] final judgment [other than default judgments] should grant the relief to which each party is entitled, even if the party has not demanded that relief in its pleadings." That means that even though John may not have asked specifically for expungement, he may still be entitled to it. In *Felce v. Fiedler,* for example, the plaintiff did not request injunctive relief but instead— using language similar to that in John's complaint—asked for "other and further relief as the court may deem to be just and equitable." 974 F.2d 1484, 1501 (7th Cir. 1992). The district court in *Felce* had not reached the question of injunctive relief because it had held—as the magistrate judge did in John's case—that the plaintiff had not alleged the necessary liberty interest. On appeal, we concluded that the plaintiff did have a liberty interest and instructed the district court to address the issue of injunctive relief on remand. *Id.* at 1502. We do the same here: having determined that John has pleaded a liberty interest, we instruct the court to address the issue of expungement on remand.

III.

John also asserts a claim against Purdue under Title IX, which provides that "[n]o person in the United States shall, on the basis of sex, be excluded from participation in, be denied the benefits of, or be subjected to discrimination under any education program or activity receiving Federal financial assistance." 20 U.S.C. § 1681(a); *see also Gebser v. Lago Vista Indep. Sch. Dist.,* 524 U.S. 274, 281, 118 S.Ct. 1989, 141 L.Ed.2d 277 (1998) (explaining that Title IX is enforceable through an implied private right of action). It is undisputed that Purdue receives federal funding and that John was "excluded from participation in [or] denied the benefits of ... [an] education program" when Purdue suspended him. 20 U.S.C. § 1681(a). The success of John's claim depends on whether Purdue discriminated against him "on the basis of sex." *Id.*

Some circuits use formal doctrinal tests to identify general bias in the context of university discipline. For example, the Second Circuit channels such claims into two general categories. *Yusuf v. Vassar Coll.,* 35 F.3d 709, 715 (2d Cir. 1994). In what has come to be called the "erroneous out-come" category, the plaintiff must show that he "was innocent and wrongly found to have committed the offense." *Id.* The other category, "selective enforcement," requires a plaintiff to prove that "regardless of [his] guilt or innocence, the severity of the penalty and/or the decision to initiate the proceeding was affected by the student's gender." *Id.; see also Plummer v. Univ. of Hous.,* 860 F.3d 767, 777-78 (5th Cir. 2017) (resolving the case by reference to the *Yusuf* framework); *Doe v. Valencia Coll.,* 903 F.3d 1220, 1236 (11th Cir. 2018) ("[W]e will assume for present purposes that a student can show a violation of Title IX by satisfying the 'erroneous outcome' test applied by the Second Circuit in *Yusuf.*"). The Sixth Circuit has added two more categories to the mix: "deliberate indifference" and "archaic assumptions." *See Doe v. Miami Univ.,* 882 F.3d 579, 589 (6th Cir. 2018) (recognizing "at least four different theories of liability" in this context: "(1) 'erroneous outcome,' (2) 'selective enforcement,' (3) 'deliberate indifference,' and (4) 'archaic assumptions'" (citations omitted)).

We see no need to superimpose doctrinal tests on the statute. All of these categories simply describe ways in which a plaintiff might show that sex was a motivating factor in a university's decision to discipline a student. We prefer to ask the question more directly: do the alleged p.668 facts, if true, raise a plausible inference that the university discriminated against John "on the basis of sex"?

John casts his Title IX claim against the backdrop of a 2011 "Dear Colleague" letter from the U.S. Department of Education to colleges and universities. *See* United States Department of Education, Office of the Assistant Secretary for Civil Rights, Dear Colleague Letter (2011), https:/www 2.ed.gov/print/about/offices/list/ocr/letters/colleague-201104.html. That letter ushered in a more rigorous approach to campus sexual misconduct allegations by, among other things, defining "sexual harassment" more broadly than in comparable contexts, *id.* at 3, mandating that schools prioritize the investigation and resolution of harassment claims, *id.* at 4, and requiring them to adopt a lenient "more likely than not" burden of proof when adjudicating claims against alleged perpetrators, *id.* at 11. The Department of Education made clear that it took the letter and its enforcement very seriously. *See* Examining Sexual Assault on Campus, Focusing on Working to Ensure Student Safety, Hearing Before the S. Comm. on Health, Educ., Labor, and Pensions, 113th Cong. 7 (2014) (statement of Catherine Lhamon, Assistant Secretary for Civil Rights, U.S. Dep't of Educ.) ("[S]ome schools still are failing their students by responding inadequately to sexual assaults on campus. For those schools, my office and this Administration have made it clear that the time for delay is over."). And it warned schools that "[t]his Administration is committed to using all its tools to ensure that all schools comply with [T]itle IX so campuses will be safer for students across the country." *Id.* In other words, a school's federal funding was at risk if it could not show that it was vigorously investigating and punishing sexual misconduct.

According to John, this letter reveals that Purdue had a financial motive for discriminating against males in sexual assault investigations. To protect its federal funds, John says, the university tilted the process against men accused of sexual assault so that it could elevate the number of punishments imposed. The resulting track record of enforcement would permit Purdue to signal its commitment to cracking down on campus sexual assault, thereby fending off any suggestion that it was not complying with the Department of Education's directive. *Cf. Doe v. Columbia Univ.*, 831 F.3d 46, 58 n.11 (2d Cir. 2016) ("A covered university that adopts, even temporarily, a policy of bias favoring one sex over the other in a disciplinary dispute, doing so in order to avoid liability or bad publicity, has practiced sex discrimination, notwithstanding that the motive for the discrimination did not come from ingrained or permanent bias against that particular sex."). And because the Office of Civil Rights—a sub-agency of the Department of Education—had opened two investigations into Purdue during 2016, the pressure on the university to demonstrate compliance was far from abstract. That pressure may have been particularly acute for Sermersheim, who, as a Title IX coordinator, bore some responsibility for Purdue's compliance.

Other circuits have treated the Dear Colleague letter as relevant in evaluating the plausibility of a Title IX claim. For example, in *Doe v. Miami University*, the plaintiff alleged that "pressure from the government to combat vigorously sexual assault on college campuses and the severe potential punishment—loss of all federal funds—if it failed to comply, led Miami University to discriminate against men in its sexual-assault adjudication process." 882 F.3d at 594. The Sixth Circuit held that this allegation, combined with others, "support[ed] a reasonable inference of gender discrimination." *Id.; see also Doe v. Baum,* 903 F.3d 575, 586 (6th Cir. 2018) p.669 (explaining that the pressure of a Department of Education investigation and the resulting negative publicity "provides a backdrop, that, when combined with other circumstantial evidence of bias in Doe's specific proceeding, gives rise to a plausible claim."); *Columbia Univ.,* 831 F.3d at 58 ("There is nothing implausible or unreasonable about the Complaint's suggested inference that the panel adopted a biased stance in favor of the accusing female and against the defending male varsity athlete in order to avoid further fanning the criticisms that Columbia turned a blind eye to such assaults.").

That said, the letter, standing alone, is obviously not enough to get John over the plausibility line. *See Baum,* 903 F.3d at 586 (pressure from the Dear Colleague letter "alone is not enough to state a claim that the university acted with bias in this particular case"). The letter and accompanying pressure gives John a story about why Purdue might have been motivated to discriminate against males accused of sexual assault. But to state a claim, he must allege facts raising the inference that Purdue acted at least partly on the basis of sex in his particular case. *See id.* (the Dear Colleague letter "provides a backdrop that, when combined with other circumstantial evidence of bias in [a] specific proceeding, gives rise to a plausible claim").

John has alleged such facts here, the strongest one being that Sermersheim chose to credit Jane's account without hearing directly from her. The case against him boiled down to a "he said/she said"—Purdue had to decide whether to believe John or Jane. Sermersheim's explanation for her decision (offered only after her supervisor required her to give a reason) was a cursory statement that she found Jane credible and John not credible. Her basis for believing Jane is perplexing, given that she never talked to Jane. Indeed, Jane did not even submit a statement in her own words to the

Advisory Committee. Her side of the story was relayed in a letter submitted by Bloom, a Title IX coordinator and the director of CARE.

For their part, the three panelists on Purdue's Advisory Committee on Equity were similarly biased in favor of Jane and against John. As John tells it—and again, we must accept his account as true—the majority of the panel members appeared to credit Jane based on her accusation alone, given that they took no other evidence into account. They made up their minds without reading the investigative report and before even talking to John. They refused to hear from John's witnesses, including his male roommate who maintained that he was in the room at the time of the alleged assault and that Jane's rendition of events was false. And the panel members' hostility toward John from the start of the brief meeting despite their lack of familiarity with the details of the case—including Jane's depression, suicide attempt, and anger at John for reporting the attempt—further supports the conclusion that Jane's allegation was all they needed to hear to make their decision.

It is plausible that Sermersheim and her advisors chose to believe Jane because she is a woman and to disbelieve John because he is a man. The plausibility of that inference is strengthened by a post that CARE put up on its Facebook page during the same month that John was disciplined: an article from *The Washington Post* titled "Alcohol isn't the cause of campus sexual assault. Men are." Construing reasonable inferences in John's favor, this statement, which CARE advertised to the campus community, could be understood to blame men as a class for the problem of campus sexual assault rather than the individuals who commit sexual assault. And it is pertinent here that Bloom, CARE's director, wrote the letter regarding Jane to which p.670 Sermersheim apparently gave significant weight.

Taken together, John's allegations raise a plausible inference that he was denied an educational benefit on the basis of his sex. To be sure, John may face problems of proof, and the factfinder might not buy the inferences that he's selling. But his claim should have made it past the pleading stage, so we reverse the magistrate judge's premature dismissal of it.

A final note: John seeks both money damages and injunctive relief for his claim under Title IX. Our earlier discussion of his entitlement to injunctive relief for his due process claim applies equally here.

* * *

John has pleaded facts sufficient to state a claim under both the Fourteenth Amendment and Title IX. We therefore REVERSE and REMAND this case to the district court for proceedings consistent with this opinion.

[1] John's complaint also asserted § 1983 claims against Purdue and all other defendants in their official capacities. Before us, he concedes that § 1983 does not permit him either to assert official-capacity claims or to sue Purdue itself. *See Will v. Mich. Dep't of State Police*, 491 U.S. 58, 71, 109 S.Ct. 2304, 105 L.Ed.2d 45 (1989).

[2] The First, Sixth, and Tenth Circuits have recognized a generalized property interest in higher education. *See* Dalton Mott, Comment, *The Due Process Clause and Students: The Road to A Single Approach of Determining Property Interests in Education*, 65 U. KAN. L. REV. 651, 659-60 (2017); *see also, e.g., Flaim v. Med. Coll. of Ohio*, 418 F.3d 629, 633 (6th Cir. 2005) (asserting that "the Due Process Clause is implicated by university disciplinary decisions"). The Fifth and Eighth Circuits have assumed without deciding that such a property interest exists. *See* Mott, *supra*, at 663. The Second, Third, Fourth, Ninth, and Eleventh Circuits join us in making a statespecific inquiry to determine whether a property interest exists. *See id.* at 658.

[3] For simplicity's sake, we will refer to the university and its officers collectively as "Purdue" or "the university."

[4] Citing a recent case from the Sixth Circuit, John also argues that he was entitled to cross-examine Jane. *See Doe v. Baum*, 903 F.3d 575, 581 (6th Cir. 2018). Because John has otherwise alleged procedural deficiencies sufficient to survive a motion to dismiss, we need not address this issue.

897 F.3d 819 (2018)

Jane DOE NO. 55, Plaintiff-Appellant,
v.
MADISON METROPOLITAN SCHOOL DISTRICT, Defendant-Appellee.

No. 17-1521.

United States Court of Appeals, Seventh Circuit.
Argued November 30, 2017.
Decided July 26, 2018.

Appeal from the United States District Court for the Western District of Wisconsin, No. 3:15-cv-00570-bbc, Barbara B. Crabb, *Judge.*

Jeffrey Herman, Stuart Mermelstein, Attorneys, Herman Law, Boca Raton, FL, for Plaintiff-Appellant.

Peggy E. Van Horn, Attorney, Law Offices of Thomas P. Stilp, Milwaukee, WI, for Defendant-Appellee.

Before EASTERBROOK and MANION, Circuit Judges, and LEE, District Judge.[*]

LEE, District Judge.

The allegations in this case are troubling, to say the least. The appellant, Jane Doe, claims that she was sexually assaulted by a security guard at her middle school while she was in eighth grade. Seeking redress, she filed suit against the Madison Metropolitan School District under Title IX of the Education Amendments of 1972, 20 U.S.C. § 1681(a). To obtain damages against the school district, Doe was required to prove, among other things, that a school official had actual knowledge of the alleged conduct. The question in this case is whether a reasonable jury could have found, based upon the summary judgment record, that the principal at Doe's middle school had actual knowledge of the security guard's misconduct. The district court thought not and granted summary judgment in the school district's favor. We affirm.

I. BACKGROUND

Jane Doe attended Whitehorse Middle School in the Madison Metropolitan School District from 2011 to 2014. During that time, Willie Collins was a security assistant at Whitehorse. In that capacity, Collins supervised lunch and recess, oversaw students in detention, and monitored the school for safety and security.

Deborah Ptak was the principal of Whitehorse, and she supervised the entire staff, including Collins. Collins was a larger-than-life presence at the school. Ptak was aware that Collins had been a mentor and confidant to many students. She regularly saw Collins hugging male and female students and observed that most of the hugs were student-initiated.

On a few occasions while Doe was in seventh grade, Ptak saw Collins walk up behind Doe as she was seated at a table in the cafeteria and rub the top of her shoulders with his hands. Collins had not singled Doe out in this regard, however, as he engaged in similar physical contact with many students, boys and girls alike.

Tracy Warnecke, the school's positive behavioral support coach, told Ptak in the spring of 2013 that she was concerned after seeing Doe frequently seek out Collins, initiate hugs with Collins, and sometimes jump and hang onto him. Warnecke informed Ptak that, on one occasion, she saw Doe jump on Collins and kiss him on the cheek. Warnecke did note that when Doe attempted to kiss Collins again, he rebuffed her and spoke to Doe privately. After that, Warnecke did not see Doe attempt to kiss Collins again. At the end of the conversation, Ptak told Warnecke that she would follow up with Collins about Warnecke's concerns.

Around that time, Mary McAuliffe, the school's counselor, notified Ptak that she and Brooke Gritt, one of Doe's teachers, echoed Warnecke's concerns based on their own observations. McAuliffe told Ptak that she and Gritt had seen Collins give Doe a shoulder rub and had seen Doe look for Collins, hug him, jump and hang on him, and on one occasion, attempt to kiss Collins on the cheek. Ptak told McAuliffe that she should speak with Doe and that Ptak would discuss the matter with Collins.

In addition, at a school committee meeting, Karen Wydenven, the school's psychologist, and McAuliffe spoke to Ptak and Warnecke about a group of seventh grade girls who were hanging around Collins. Ptak responded, "That's just Willie's personality, you know, because he's a coach; and you know, the kids know him."

On April 11, 2013, Ptak met with Collins to discuss the issues raised by Warnecke, McAuliffe and Gritt. Ptak expressed concern for Doe's well-being and stated that Doe could have a crush on Collins. Collins told Ptak that Doe merely had been confiding in him about her problematic relationships with her family and peers and that he was providing her with support. Ptak cautioned Collins against hugging and physically touching Doe and told Collins to limit any such conduct. Ptak reiterated that "clear" and "strong boundaries. . . needed to be set" and that "hugging and her jumping on him [wa]s not appropriate." Ptak also instructed Collins to speak to Doe only in common areas when others were around.

Later that month, Gritt reported to McAuliffe that Doe had been intentionally cutting herself. That same day, McAuliffe brought up the matter with Doe, but Doe did not want to talk to McAuliffe. McAuliffe then called Doe's mother to report Doe's actions and advised Doe's mother to obtain counseling for Doe.

During their conversation, Doe's mother told McAuliffe that, after a recent family argument, Doe had run off and deleted some information from her iPad. Doe's mother added that, as a result, she had learned that Doe had been using Collins' name as her iPad password. McAuliffe mentioned to Doe's mother that Doe frequently had been hanging on Collins' arm, and that if Doe's mother believed that Doe had an unhealthy preoccupation with Collins, Doe's mother should schedule a meeting with Ptak and potentially Collins.

Shortly after McAuliffe's conversation with Doe's mother, Ptak met with McAuliffe to discuss McAuliffe's concerns about Doe, including Doe's self-harming, her problems at home and preoccupation with Collins, and the use of Collins' name as her iPad password. McAuliffe told Ptak that she had recommended that Doe's mother seek counseling for Doe. McAuliffe asked Ptak to speak with Doe's mother and Collins, and Ptak reassured McAuliffe that she would. Although it is disputed whether Ptak left a voicemail message for Doe's mother, it is undisputed that the two never spoke about Collins. Nor is there any evidence that Doe's mother spoke to any school administrator about Collins other than her initial conversation with McAuliffe, p.822 or that Ptak spoke to Collins after this discussion with McAuliffe.

Three days after her conversation with McAuliffe, Doe's mother sent Collins an email apologizing to him for "dragging [him] into the drama" with Doe. Doe's mother stated that she was not upset with Collins and thanked him for being so kind to her daughter. The email did not request that Collins cease interacting with Doe.

A week or two later, McAuliffe reported to Ptak that Gritt had seen Collins at one of Doe's tennis matches and that he had stayed for five to ten minutes. During that brief time, Gritt had not seen any contact between Doe and Collins. McAuliffe stated she would follow up with Gritt and never raised this incident with Ptak again.

After April 2013, Ptak noticed a significant decrease in interaction between Doe and Collins. She did not see any physical contact between the two after that point.

In May 2013, McAuliffe informed Ptak and Warnecke that Doe had attempted to get out of class by saying that she needed Collins to help her with a "problem." As recounted by Warnecke, Ptak indicated to them that she had already met with Collins about setting appropriate boundaries between himself and Doe. That same month, Jaime Duckert, the school district's social worker, expressed her own concerns to Ptak that so many students were hugging Collins. But this conversation occurred upon Duckert's return from a three-month maternity leave.

Once Doe started eighth grade in the fall of 2013, Ptak was unaware of any new instances of interaction between Doe and Collins that raised concerns.[1] And, according to the school's staff, Doe was much "calmer" during eighth grade.

Then, in late August 2014, Doe told her cousin that Collins had sexually abused her while she was in eighth grade. Doe's mother learned of the abuse a short time later on Doe's first day of high school. According to Doe, Collins had made sexual comments to her, kissed her, fondled her breasts, rubbed his penis against her clothed body, and digitally penetrated her.

The Madison Police Department was notified and commenced an investigation. School district officials became aware of the allegations against Collins, and he was immediately put on a leave of absence pending the investigation.

II. ANALYSIS

Title IX provides that "No person... shall on the basis of sex, be excluded from participating in, be denied the benefits of, or be subjected to discrimination under any education program or activity, receiving Federal financial assistance." 20 U.S.C. § 1681(a). At bottom, Title IX does not prohibit sexual harassment, but, rather, prohibits school districts from discriminating on the basis of sex in providing educational benefits. *See Davis v. Monroe Cty. Bd. of Educ.*, 526 U.S. 629, 652, 119 S.Ct. 1661, 143 L.Ed.2d 839 (1999).

"[A]s in cases under the Civil Rights Act of 1871, 42 U.S.C. § 1983, a school district sued in a private suit under Title IX cannot be held liable on the ground of respondeat superior for an employee's violation of the statute." *Doe v. St. Francis Sch. Dist.,* 694 F.3d 869, 870 (7th Cir. 2012) (citing *Gebser v. Lago Vista* p.823 *Indep. Sch. Dist.,* 524 U.S. 274, 285, 118 S.Ct. 1989, 141 L.Ed.2d 277 (1998)). Accordingly, a Title IX plaintiff must ultimately prove that "an official who at a minimum has authority to address the alleged discrimination and to institute corrective measures on the recipient's behalf has actual knowledge of discrimination in the recipient's programs and fails adequately to respond" in a way that "amount[s] to deliberate indifference." *Gebser,* 524 U.S. at 277, 291, 118 S.Ct. 1989. To survive summary judgment, a plaintiff "must establish a genuine issue of fact as to whether an appropriate official. . . had (1) actual knowledge of misconduct. . . that created a serious risk to its students, and (2) responded with deliberate indifference to the misconduct." *Hansen v. Bd. of Trs. of Hamilton Se. Sch. Corp.,* 551 F.3d 599, 606 (7th Cir. 2008).

Here, the district court granted summary judgment in favor of the school district, concluding that Doe had failed to raise a genuine issue of material fact as to her assertion that Ptak had actual notice of Collin's sexual abuse. We review a grant of summary judgment *de novo. Brunson v. Murray,* 843 F.3d 698, 704 (7th Cir. 2016).

In *Delgado v. Stegall,* we explored the contours of Title IX's actual notice requirement. 367 F.3d 668, 672 (7th Cir. 2004), *abrogated on other grounds by Fitzgerald v. Barnstable Sch. Comm.,* 555 U.S. 246, 259, 129 S.Ct. 788, 172 L.Ed.2d 582 (2009). There, a former student of Western Illinois University sued the school and a professor, claiming that the professor had sexually harassed her. *Id.* at 670. The district court granted summary judgment in favor of the school, concluding that there were no facts to support the claim that school administrators had actual knowledge of the teacher's misconduct. *Id.* In affirming the decision, we discussed the Supreme Court's holding in *Gebser* that damages are only available against a school district if "an official of the school district . . . has actual notice of, and is deliberately indifferent to, the teacher's misconduct" and observed a "peculiarity of the Supreme Court's formula." *Id.* at 671. "Ordinarily," we noted, "actual notice and deliberate indifference are alternative paths to proving knowledge," with deliberate indifference — like its criminal counterpart recklessness — denoting "shutting one's eyes to a risk one knows but would prefer to ignore." *Id.* at 671. Nevertheless, we concluded that "under the Supreme Court's formula, the plaintiff in a Title IX damages suit based on a teacher's behavior must prove actual knowledge of misconduct, not just actual knowledge of the risks of misconduct." *Id.* at 672.

That said, we recognized that, at times, the line between these two standards may blur. *Id.; see St. Francis Sch. Dist.,* 694 F.3d at 871 (noting "there is less to the conflict in standards than meets the eye, because in practice there is little difference between known and obvious, the former being a natural inference from the latter."). And, indeed, "[w]hen the cases speak of a 'known' or 'obvious' risk that makes a failure to take steps against it reckless they have in mind risks so great that they are almost certain to materialize if nothing is done." *See Delgado* 367 F.3d at 672. "[I]t is only in such cases that recklessness regarding the consequences if the risk materializes merges with intention to bring about the consequences." *Id.* And, by way of illustration, we suggested that if a school official had knowledge that a staff member was a serial harasser, such knowledge might suffice to satisfy the Supreme Court's "actual knowledge" standard, even though the official may not have actual knowledge of the specific harassment against the complainant. *See id.*

This discussion is apropos because, in this case, it is undisputed that Ptak was unaware of Doe's allegations of sexual abuse until *after* Doe had graduated from middle school. Indeed, during Doe's eighth-grade year, when, according to Doe, the sexual abuse occurred, no teacher or staff member had reported any incidents or concerns regarding Collins and Doe to Ptak. Nor does Ptak recall seeing any physical contact between Collins and Doe during that school year. p.824

As a result, the appellant relies on events that occurred during the *previous* school year to establish that Ptak had actual knowledge, not of Collins' abuse of Doe, but of the risk that Collins would do so. For example, appellant points out that Ptak had observed Collins hugging male and female students in the hallways and giving them brief shoulder and back rubs in the cafeteria. Ptak also knew that a group of seventh grade girls was hanging around Collins. As for Collins' interactions with Doe specifically, Ptak had observed Collins give Doe a shoulder rub a few times in the cafeteria and was aware that, on one occasion, Doe had kissed him on the cheek. Ptak also was aware that Collins had allowed Doe to hug him, as well as jump and hang on him, and that Doe had a seeming preoccupation with Collins. And, when Ptak directed Collins to set clear and strong boundaries and refrain from having any physical contact with Doe, Collins informed Ptak that Doe had confided in him about her familial and peer relationships and that he had supported her.

Although such facts certainly could have raised some concern that stricter and more defined boundaries between Collins and Doe might have been advisable during Doe's seventh-grade year (which Ptak did impose), we agree with the district court that a reasonable jury could not find, based on these facts, that Ptak had actual knowledge of any sexual misconduct on the part of Collins that created a serious risk to Doe. Nor could a rational jury find that Ptak had actual knowledge of a risk so great that harm to Doe was almost certain to materialize if nothing were done to stop it.

In this respect, our decision in *St. Francis* is instructive. In that case, an eighth grader sued his school district under Title IX after being sexually abused by his teacher. We affirmed summary judgment in the school district's favor because the student had failed to create a triable issue that the school district superintendent had actual knowledge of the abuse. 694 F.3d at 870, 872. The superintendent was well aware that the teacher's colleagues had complained that the teacher had "blurred the line" by treating students as friends. *Id.* at 872. And one of the teacher's peers told the superintendent that the teacher and the student "had something like an eighth grade girlfriend/boyfriend relationship, like a crush." But no facts were offered to support these suspicions, and when questioned by the superintendent, the fellow teacher denied that the teacher was doing anything "illegal." *Id.* The teacher herself also denied any impropriety when confronted by the superintendent, and the superintendent found her denial to be sincere. *Id.* Indeed, school officials did not find out about the relationship between the teacher and the student until the student's mother discovered text messages from the teacher on her son's phone. *Id.* Such facts, we concluded, were insufficient to establish actual notice because even if the principal and superintendent knew that the teacher's colleagues suspected an improper relationship between her and the student, "to know that someone suspects something is not to know the something and does not mean the something is obvious." *Id.*

The facts of this case are on par with those in *St. Francis*. Here, Ptak observed Collins hugging male and female students, p.825 giving male and female students shoulder rubs in the cafeteria, permitting Doe to kiss him on the cheek on one occasion, and playing the role of mentor and confidant to Doe and other students. Certain staff members also expressed misgivings about Doe's seeming preoccupation with Collins. Such facts may have raised (and, in fact, did raise) cautionary flags, but they are insufficient to bestow upon Ptak actual knowledge that Collins was engaging in sexual misconduct at the time or that there was an almost certain risk that he would do so in the future.

What is more, it is worth iterating that things appeared to have calmed down during the late spring of Doe's seventh-grade year. Ptak did not recall seeing any physical contact between Doe and Collins after that point. And to the extent that others did, they did not report anything to Ptak.

For these reasons, the district court properly determined that a trial was unwarranted because no reasonable jury could find that Ptak possessed actual knowledge of misconduct that created a serious risk of harm to Doe. And because the absence of a genuine issue in this regard is dispositive, we need not reach the other issues raised on appeal.[2] The district court's decision is AFFIRMED.

[*] Of the Northern District of Illinois, sitting by designation.

[1] The appellant points to surveillance recordings from May 28, 2014, to June 11, 2014, showing Collins having various interactions with female students other than Doe to establish Ptak's knowledge that Collins posed a significant risk to Doe. But appellant's counsel conceded at oral argument that it is undisputed that Ptak was unaware of the specific physical interactions depicted in the surveillance recordings.

[2] Doe's lawyer declined an opportunity at oral argument to present facts in the record to show that Doe had been denied equal access to education. *See Gabrielle M. v. Park Forest-Chicago Heights, Ill. Sch. Dist. 163,* 315 F.3d 817, 823 (7th Cir. 2003) (citing *Davis,* 526 U.S. at 652, 119 S.Ct. 1661) ("[A]n action under Title IX lies only where the behavior at issue denies a victim equal access to education."). Because we affirm on a different ground, we need not consider Doe's contention that a denial of equal access to education should be presumed in the case of staff-student sexual harassment.

901 F.3d 856 (2018)

**Marsha WETZEL, Plaintiff-Appellant,
v.
GLEN ST. ANDREW LIVING COMMUNITY, LLC, et al., Defendants-Appellees.**

No. 17-1322.

**United States Court of Appeals, Seventh Circuit.
Argued February 6, 2018.
Decided August 27, 2018.**

Wetzel v. Glen St. Andrew Living Community, LLC, 901 F. 3d 856 (7th Cir. 2018)

Appeal from the United States District Court for the Northern District of Illinois, Eastern Division, No. 16 C 7598, Samuel Der-Yeghiayan, *Judge.*

Karen Lee Loewy, Attorney, Lambda Legal Defense & Education Fund, New York, NY, John L. Litchfield, Attorney, Ellen M. Wheeler, Attorney, Foley & Lardner LLP, Chicago, IL, for Plaintiff-Appellant.

James Hayes Ryan, Attorney, Lindsay A. Watson, Attorney, Gordon & Rees Scully Mansukhani, LLP, Lisa A. Hausten, Attorney, Clausen Miller, Chicago, IL, for Defendants-Appellees.

Dara Smith, Attorney, AARP Foundation Litigation, Washington, DC, for Amici Curiae American Association of Retired Persons, AARP Foundation.

Yiyang Wu, Attorney, Relman, Dane & Colfax PLLC, Washington, DC, for Amicus Curiae National Fair Housing Alliance.

Before WOOD, Chief Judge, and KANNE and HAMILTON, Circuit Judges.

p.859 WOOD, Chief Judge.

Within months of her arrival at Glen St. Andrew Living Community ("St. Andrew"), Marsha Wetzel faced a torrent of physical and verbal abuse from other residents because she is openly lesbian. Time and again, she implored St. Andrew's staff to help her. The staff's response was to limit her use of facilities and build a case for her eviction.

Wetzel sued St. Andrew, alleging that it failed to provide her with non-discriminatory housing and that it retaliated against her because of her complaints, each in violation of the Fair Housing Act (FHA or Act), 42 U.S.C. §§ 3601-3619. St. Andrew insists that the Act affords Wetzel no recourse, because it imposes liability only on those who act with discriminatory animus, an allegation Wetzel had not expressly made of any defendant. The district court agreed and dismissed Wetzel's suit. We read the FHA more broadly. Not only does it create liability when a landlord intentionally discriminates against a tenant based on a protected characteristic; it also creates liability against a landlord that has actual notice of tenant-on-tenant harassment based on a protected status, yet chooses not to take any reasonable steps within its control to stop that harassment. We therefore reverse the district court's grant of St. Andrew's motion to dismiss and remand for further proceedings.

I

After her partner of 30 years died, Wetzel moved into St. Andrew, a residential community for older adults; she continues to live there today. Her tenancy, presumably like that of St. Andrew's other residents, is governed by a form Tenant's Agreement ("Agreement"). Beyond a private apartment, the Agreement guarantees three meals daily served in a central location, access to a community room, and use of laundry facilities. It conditions tenancy at St. Andrew on refraining from "activity that [St. Andrew] determines unreasonably interferes with the peaceful use and enjoyment of the community by other tenants" or that is "a direct threat to the health and safety of other individuals." It also requires compliance with the "Tenant Handbook," which may "be amended from time to time." The Agreement authorizes St. Andrew to institute eviction proceedings against a tenant in breach, and if St. Andrew prevails, the breaching tenant must also reimburse St. Andrew for its attorney's fees. (Indeed, the Agreement requires reimbursement of St. Andrew's fees related to an alleged violation or breach even if suit has not been instituted.)

After arriving at St. Andrew, Wetzel spoke openly to staff and other residents about her sexual orientation. She was met with intolerance from many of them. The following is just a sample of what Wetzel has alleged that she endured. At this early stage of the litigation, we accept her account as true, recognizing that St. Andrew will have the right to contest these assertions at a trial.

Beginning a few months after Wetzel moved to St. Andrew and continuing at least until she filed this suit (a 15-month period), residents repeatedly berated her for being a "fucking dyke," "fucking faggot," and "homosexual bitch." One resident, Robert Herr, told Wetzel that he reveled in the memory of the Orlando massacre at the Pulse nightclub, derided Wetzel's son for being a "homosexual-raised faggot," and threatened to "rip [Wetzel's] tits off." Herr was the primary, but not sole, culprit. Elizabeth Rivera told Wetzel that "homosexuals will burn in hell."

There was physical abuse too. Wetzel depends on a motorized scooter. Herr at one time rammed his walker into Wetzel's scooter forcefully enough to knock her off a ramp. Rivera bashed her wheelchair into a dining table that Wetzel occupied, flipping the table on top of Wetzel. In yet another incident, Wetzel was struck in the back of the head while alone in the mailroom; the blow was hard enough to push her from her scooter, and she suffered a bump on her head and a black eye. She did not see the assailant, but the person said "homo" when attacking her. Following this mugging, Herr taunted Wetzel, rubbing his head and saying "ouch." Wetzel also had two abusive trips in the elevator. During the first, Rivera spat on her and hurled slurs. During the second, Wetzel, Herr, and another resident, Audrey Chase, were together in the elevator when Herr again hit Wetzel's scooter with his walker.

Wetzel routinely reported the verbal and physical abuse to St. Andrew's staff, including Carolyn Driscoll, Sandra Cubas, and Alyssa Flavin (the "management defendants"). Wetzel's initial complaints won her a brief respite, prompting her to draft a thank-you note. But the management defendants, among whom we need not distinguish for purposes of this appeal, otherwise were apathetic. They told Wetzel not to worry about the harassment, dismissed the conduct as accidental, denied Wetzel's accounts, and branded her a liar. Wetzel's social worker accompanied her to one meeting about the harassment; despite that, the managers denounced Wetzel as dishonest.

Had the management defendants done nothing but listen, we might have a more limited case. But they took affirmative steps to retaliate against Wetzel for her complaints. For example, they relegated Wetzel to a less desirable dining room location after she notified them about being trampled by Rivera. Following other complaints, they barred her from the lobby except to get coffee and they halted her cleaning services, thus depriving her of access to areas specifically protected in the Agreement. They falsely accused Wetzel of smoking in her room in violation of St. Andrew's policy. Early one morning, two staff members woke Wetzel up and again accused her of smoking in her room. When she said that she had been sleeping, one of them slapped her across the face. One p.861 month, Wetzel did not receive the customary rent-due notice, though other tenants did. She remembered to pay on time, but she had to pry a receipt from management.

In response, Wetzel changed her daily routine. She ate meals in her room, forgoing those included as part of the Agreement. She stopped visiting the third floor of St. Andrew, where Herr lived. She did not use the laundry room at hours when she might be alone. And she stayed away from the common spaces from which she had been barred by management.

Eventually Wetzel brought this action against the management defendants and the entities that own and operate St. Andrew (the "corporate defendants"). Unless the distinction matters, we refer to the group collectively as defendants or St. Andrew. She alleged that St. Andrew failed to ensure a non-discriminatory living environment and retaliated against her for complaining about sex-based harassment, each in violation of the FHA. The complaint included related state claims.

All of the defendants moved for dismissal, contending that the FHA does not make a landlord accountable for failing to stop tenant-on-tenant harassment unless the landlord's in-action was animated by discriminatory animus. In the alternative, the defendants argued that Wetzel's harassment claim must be dismissed insofar as it relied on 42 U.S.C. § 3604(b) because that section does not cover post-acquisition harassment claims — in other words, harassment claims brought by a tenant already occupying her home. The defendants also asserted that Wetzel's retaliation claim failed because it too lacked an allegation that the defendants were motivated by discriminatory animus. The district court agreed with each of the defendants' arguments and dismissed the harassment claim. It dismissed the retaliation claim without further discussion. With the federal claims gone, the court chose to relinquish supplemental jurisdiction over the state claims. Wetzel appeals the dismissal of her suit.

II

A

As we recognized in *Bloch v. Frischholz*, 587 F.3d 771 (7th Cir. 2009) (*en banc*), the protections afforded by the Fair Housing Act do not evaporate once a person takes possession of her house, condominium, or apartment. The question before us, while an important one, is thus narrow: does the Act cover the particular kinds of post-acquisition discrimination that Wetzel suffered?

Under 42 U.S.C. § 3604(b), it is unlawful "[t]o discriminate against any person in the terms, conditions, or privileges of sale or rental of a dwelling, or in the provision of services or facilities in connection therewith, because of race, color, religion, sex, familial status, or national origin." In addition, the Act makes it unlawful "to coerce, intimidate, threaten, or interfere with any person in the exercise or enjoyment of ... any right granted or protected by section ... 3604 ... of this title." 42 U.S.C. § 3617. Among other things, these sections prohibit discriminatory harassment that unreasonably interferes with the use and enjoyment of a home — by another name, a hostile housing environment. *Krueger v. Cuomo,* 115 F.3d 487, 491 (7th Cir. 1997); *DiCenso v. Cisneros,* 96 F.3d 1004, 1008 (7th Cir. 1996); see also *Bloch,* 587 F.3d at 781 (recognizing that the protections under sections 3604(b) and 3617 may be coextensive).

A hostile-housing-environment claim requires a plaintiff to show that: (1) she endured unwelcome harassment based on a protected characteristic; (2) the harassment was severe or pervasive p.862 enough to interfere with the terms, conditions, or privileges of her residency, or in the provision of services or facilities; and (3) that there is a basis for imputing liability to the defendant. See *DiCenso,* 96 F.3d at 1008; see also *Alamo v. Bliss,* 864 F.3d 541, 549 (7th Cir. 2017) (listing elements of a Title VII hostile-workplace claim); *Honce v. Vigil,* 1 F.3d 1085, 1090 (10th Cir. 1993) (adopting elements of a Title VII hostile-workplace claim for the FHA).

B

St. Andrew agrees that our ruling in *Hively v. Ivy Tech Community College of Indiana,* 853 F.3d 339 (7th Cir. 2017) (*en banc*), holding that discrimination based on sexual orientation qualifies as discrimination based on sex under Title VII, applies with equal force under the FHA. We therefore move directly to the second element of the case: whether the harassment from which Wetzel suffered was severe or pervasive enough to interfere with her enjoyment of her dwelling. Harassment is severe or pervasive if it objectively interferes with the enjoyment of the premises or inhibits the privileges of rental. *DiCenso,* 96 F.3d at 1008. That standard requires us to consider the totality of the circumstances, including the frequency of the discriminatory conduct, its severity, and whether it is physically threatening or humiliating rather than merely offensive. *Alamo,* 864 F.3d at 549-50. There is no "magic number of instances" that must be endured before an environment becomes so hostile that the occupant's right to enjoyment of her home has been violated. *Id.* at 550. While isolated minor affronts are not enough, *DiCenso,* 96 F.3d at 1008, either a small number of "severe episode[s]" or a "relentless pattern of lesser harassment" may suffice, *Alamo,* 864 F.3d at 550 (quoting *Cerros v. Steel Techs., Inc.,* 398 F.3d 944, 951 (7th Cir. 2005)).

Though it need be only one or the other, the harassment Wetzel describes plausibly can be viewed as both severe and pervasive. For 15 months, she was bombarded with threats, slurs, derisive comments about her family, taunts about a deadly massacre, physical violence, and spit. The defendants dismiss this litany of abuse as no more than ordinary "squabbles" and "bickering" between "irascible," "crotchety senior resident[s]." A jury would be entitled to see the story otherwise. (We confess to having trouble seeing the act of throwing an elderly person out of a motorized scooter as one of the ordinary problems of life in a senior facility.) Wetzel has presented far more than "a simple quarrel between two neighbors or [an] isolated act of harassment." See *Halprin v. Prairie Single Family Homes of Dearborn Park Ass'n*, 388 F.3d 327, 330 (7th Cir. 2004).

C

That takes us to the main event: Is there a basis to impute liability to St. Andrew for the hostile housing environment? This question is new to our circuit. Our response begins, as it must, with the text of the statute. *Duncan v. Walker*, 533 U.S. 167, 172, 121 S.Ct. 2120, 150 L.Ed.2d 251 (2001). Again, 42 U.S.C. § 3604(b) makes it unlawful "[t]o discriminate ... because of ... sex," and 42 U.S.C. § 3617 forbids a housing provider to "interfere with any person in the exercise or enjoyment of ... any right granted or protected by section ... 3604 ... of this title." The focus on the actor rather than the benefitted class, St. Andrew deduces, confines the world of possible defendants under these sections to those accused of carrying discriminatory animus. But St. Andrew relies on language defining the substantive contours of an FHA action to ascertain a landlord's potential liability for actionable abuse — in other words, it is looking at p.863 *what* is prohibited, not *who* is subject to those prohibitions. As the Supreme Court's cases in analogous areas demonstrate, the questions are different. See *Davis v. Monroe Cnty. Bd. of Educ.*, 526 U.S. 629, 639, 119 S.Ct. 1661, 143 L.Ed.2d 839 (1999) (distinguishing the scope of behavior proscribed under Title IX from availability of private suit); *Faragher v. City of Boca Raton*, 524 U.S. 775, 788-89, 118 S.Ct. 2275, 141 L.Ed.2d 662 (1998) (separating the analysis of the substantive contours of a forbidden hostile environment claim under Title VII from the rules for determining employer liability); *Meritor Sav. Bank, FSB v. Vinson*, 477 U.S. 57, 72, 106 S.Ct. 2399, 91 L.Ed.2d 49 (1986) (telling lower courts to look to common-law principles for guidance on employer liability under Title VII). True, a sex-harassment claim under the FHA demands sex-based discrimination, but Wetzel has alleged such discrimination. On its face, the Act does not address who may be liable when sex-based discrimination occurs or under what circumstances. *Cf. Burlington Indus., Inc. v. Ellerth*, 524 U.S. 742, 754-55, 118 S.Ct. 2257, 141 L.Ed.2d 633 (1998) (considering proper vicarious liability standard for an employer for purposes of Title VII).

Because the text of the FHA does not spell out a test for landlord liability, we look to analogous anti-discrimination statutes for guidance. One natural point of reference is Title VII, which governs discrimination in employment. It and the FHA have been described as "functional equivalent[s]" to be "given like construction and application." *Kyles v. J.K. Guardian Sec. Servs., Inc.*, 222 F.3d 289, 295 (7th Cir. 2000); see also *Texas Dep't of Hous. & Cmty. Affairs v. Inclusive Communities Project, Inc.*, ___ U.S. ___, 135 S.Ct. 2507, 2516, 192 L.Ed.2d 514 (2015) (comparing section 3604(a) of the FHA to Title VII); *Bloch*, 587 F.3d at 779 (noting that section 3604(b) mirrors Title VII). The Supreme Court's interpretation of Title VII's parallel section is illuminating. That section makes it unlawful "to discriminate against any individual ... because of ... sex." 42 U.S.C. § 2000e-2(a)(1). Under operative language in Title VII identical to that of the 42 U.S.C. § 3604(b), an employer may be liable under some circumstances when its own negligence is a cause of prohibited harassment. *Burlington Indus.,* 524 U.S. at 758-59, 118 S.Ct. 2257. Indeed, "when Congress uses the same language in two statutes having similar purposes, particularly when one is enacted shortly after the other, it is appropriate to presume that Congress intended that text to have the same meaning in both statutes." *Smith v. City of Jackson,* 544 U.S. 228, 233, 125 S.Ct. 1536, 161 L.Ed.2d 410 (2005). The FHA followed Title VII by four years. See Civil Rights Act of 1964 § 703; Civil Rights Act of 1968 § 804. St. Andrew provides no reason why the FHA requires in all instances that the defendant acted with discriminatory animus when an identically worded statute has not been read in such a manner. As a textual matter, we see none.

We recognize, however, that there are some potentially important differences between the relationship that exists between an employer and an employee, in which one is the agent of the other, and that between a landlord and a tenant, in which the tenant is largely independent of the landlord. We thus refrain from reflexively adopting the Title VII standard and continue our search for comparable situations.

That takes us to Title IX of the Education Amendments of 1972, 20 U.S.C. §§ 1681-1688. Like the FHA and Title VII, Title IX aims to eradicate sex-based discrimination from a sector of society — education. The Supreme Court has held that Title IX supports a private right of action on the part of a person who experiences sex discrimination in an education program or activity receiving federal financial p.864 aid. *Cannon v. Univ. of Chicago,* 441 U.S. 677, 688-89, 99 S.Ct. 1946, 60 L.Ed.2d 560 (1979). In *Davis v. Monroe County Board of Education,* the Court confronted the question whether a school district's "failure to respond to student-on-student harassment in its schools can support a private suit for money damages." 526 U.S. at 639, 119 S.Ct. 1661. Because Title IX was enacted pursuant to the Spending Clause, private damages were available against a funding recipient only if it had adequate notice of its potential liability. *Id.* at 640, 119 S.Ct. 1661. Applying that limiting principle, the Court held that the district could be held accountable only for its own misconduct. *Id.* But that is just what the *Davis* plaintiff was trying to do. As the Court put it, "petitioner attempts to hold the Board liable for its *own* decision to remain idle in the face of known studenton-student harassment in its schools." *Id.* at 641, 119 S.Ct. 1661. Indeed, the district itself subjected the plaintiff to discrimination by remaining "deliberately indifferent to known acts of student-on-student sexual harassment [when] the harasser is under the school's disciplinary authority." *Id.* at 646-47, 119 S.Ct. 1661. It emphasized that the recipient of funds exercised substantial control over both the harasser and the premises on which the misconduct took place. *Id.* at 645, 119 S.Ct. 1661.

Much of what the Court said in *Davis* can be applied readily to the housing situation. In *Davis,* the fund recipient's own misconduct subjected the student to actionable sex-based harassment. Here, we need look only to the management defendants themselves, asking whether they had actual knowledge of the severe harassment Wetzel was enduring and whether they were deliberately indifferent to it. If so, they subjected Wetzel to conduct that the FHA forbids. (We say nothing about the situation in a setting that more closely resembles custodial care, such as a skilled nursing facility, or an assisted living environment, or a hospital. Any of those are different enough that they should be saved for another day.) Wetzel may be in unchartered territory, but the Supreme Court's interpretation of analogous anti-discrimination statutes satisfies us that her claim against St. Andrew is covered by the Act.

D

St. Andrew offers several reasons why, in its view, we should not adopt the analysis we have just laid out. We respond to the most important points. It argues that there is no agency or custodial relationship between a landlord and tenant, and from that it reasons that a landlord has no duty to protect its tenants from discriminatory harassment. But we have not gone that far: we have said only that the duty not to discriminate in housing conditions encompasses the duty not to permit *known* harassment on *protected* grounds. The landlord does have responsibility over the common areas of the building, which is where the majority of Wetzel's harassment took place. And the incidents within her apartment occurred precisely because the landlord was exercising a right to enter. More broadly, St. Andrew has a statutory duty not to discriminate. As the Supreme Court said, the FHA "defines a new legal duty, and authorizes the courts to compensate a plaintiff for the injury caused by the defendant's wrongful breach." *Curtis v. Loether,* 415 U.S. 189, 195, 94 S.Ct. 1005, 39 L.Ed.2d 260 (1974). The same is true of an action under Title VII or Title IX. See *Dunn v. Washington,* 429 F.3d 689, 691 (7th Cir. 2005); *Davis,* 526 U.S. at 643, 119 S.Ct. 1661.

We need not address St. Andrew's arguments about vicarious liability, because it is irrelevant here to the management defendants' possible liability. (The Supreme Court has held already that the Act imposes vicarious liability on a corporation, but not upon its officers or owners. See *Meyer v. Holley,* 537 U.S. 280, 285-86, 123 S.Ct. 824, 154 L.Ed.2d 753 (2003).) The management defendants' liability, if any after a full trial, would be direct — the result of standing pat as Wetzel reported the barrage of harassment. Because liability is direct, "it makes no difference whether the person whose acts are complained of is an employee, an independent contractor, or for that matter a customer.... The genesis of inequality matters not; what *does* matter is how the employer handles the problem." *Dunn,* 429 F.3d at 691. A school district's liability under Title IX is the same. *Davis,* 526 U.S. at 640-43, 119 S.Ct. 1661.

St. Andrew complains that it would be unfair to hold it liable for actions that it was incapable of addressing, but we are doing no such thing. We have no quarrel with the idea that direct liability for inaction makes sense only if defendants had, but failed to deploy, available remedial tools. *Id.* at 644, 119 S.Ct. 1661; *Dunn,* 429 F.3d at 691. St. Andrew protests that it can only minimally affect the conduct of its tenants because tenants expect to live free from a landlord's interference.

Control in the absolute sense, however, is not required for liability. Liability attaches because a party has "an arsenal of incentives and sanctions ... that can be applied to affect conduct" but fails to use them. *Id.* St. Andrew brushes aside the many tools for remedying harassment that it has pursuant to the Agreement. For example, the Agreement allows St. Andrew to evict any tenant who "engages in acts or omissions that constitute a direct threat to the health and safety of other individuals" or who "engage[s] in any activity that [St. Andrew] determines unreasonably interferes with the peaceful use and enjoyment of the community by other tenants." The mere reminder that eviction (along with liability for attorneys' fees) was a possibility might have deterred some of the bad behavior. St. Andrew also could have updated the Tenant Handbook to clarify the anti-harassment and anti-abuse provisions. With respect to the common areas, St. Andrew could have suspended privileges for tenants who failed to abide by the anti-harassment policies, instead of taking a blame-the-victim approach.

If liability is possible here, St. Andrew warns, then landlords may just renounce control of the premises altogether. But unless the rental unit is a detached, single-family dwelling, such total abandonment is not a practical possibility. St. Andrew itself had a common living area, a common dining area, common laundry facilities, and hallways. It is hard to believe that a total disclaimer of liability would be in its own best interest. In addition, contract law is not the exclusive source of a landlord's duties or powers. Property law governs landlord-tenant relations as well. A landlord typically must provide its tenants a residence that is free from "interfer[ence] with a permissible use of the leased property by the tenant." RESTATEMENT (SECOND) OF PROP.: LAND. & TEN. § 6.1. The obligation is breached even if a third party causes the interference, so long as the disturbance was "performed on property in which the landlord has an interest" and the "conduct could be legally controlled by [the landlord]." *Id.* § 6.1 cmt. d. Inherent powers spring from that obligation. *Cf. id.* § 6.1 cmt. d, illus. 10-11 (illustrating that a landlord breaches its obligation to a tenant if the landlord fails to act after learning that conduct performed on the owned property interferes with the tenant's permissible use of the leased property). And if need be, there is always the right of exclusion, which is p.866 "[o]ne of the main rights attaching to property." *Byrd v. United States,* ___ U.S. ___, 138 S.Ct. 1518, 1527, 200 L.Ed.2d 805 (2018) (citing 2 W. Blackstone, Commentaries on the Laws of England, ch. 1). The same kinds of steps we already mentioned could have been justified as a matter of property law.

Seeking a broader ruling, Wetzel points to a rule interpreting the FHA that the U.S. Department of Housing and Urban Affairs (HUD) published in 2016. The HUD rule interprets the FHA to make a landlord directly liable for failing to "take prompt action to correct and end a discriminatory housing practice by a third party" if the landlord "knew or should have known of the discriminatory conduct and had the power to correct it." 24 C.F.R. § 100.7(a)(1)(iii). HUD's rule mirrors the scope of employee liability under Title VII for employee-on-employee harassment. We have no need, however, to rely on this rule. As we noted earlier, there are salient differences between Title VII and the FHA. In the end, it is possible that they could be overcome, but more analysis than HUD was able to offer is necessary before we can take that step. It is enough for present purposes to say that nothing in the HUD rule stands in the way of recognizing Wetzel's theory.

It is important, too, to recognize that the facts Wetzel has presented (which we must accept at this stage) go far beyond mere rudeness, all the way to direct physical violence. This case is thus not, as St. Andrew would have it, one about good manners. Courts around the country have policed that line for years in the context of Title VII, for which they have ensured that the standard is "sufficiently demanding to ensure that Title VII does not become a general civility code," and "filter[s] out complaints attacking the ordinary tribulations of the workplace, such as the sporadic use of abusive language, gender-related jokes, and occasional teasing." *Faragher,* 524 U.S. at

788, 118 S.Ct. 2275 (citations omitted). We have no reason not to expect the same discipline here.

III

In the alternative, St. Andrew urges that Wetzel's section 3604(b) claim falls outside the scope of post-acquisition actions available under that section of the FHA. Our treatment of this argument might have little effect on the outcome of this case, because Wetzel's harassment claim invokes the protections of both section 3604(b) and section 3617. And a claim alleging a post-acquisition pattern of harassment can proceed under section 3617 even if there is no route for relief under section 3604. *Halprin*, 388 F.3d at 330. St. Andrew nonetheless maintains that Wetzel's section 3604(b) claim is unavailable post-acquisition.

In *Bloch*, the *en banc* court took a careful look at the availability of post-acquisition claims under section 3604(b). 587 F.3d at 779-81. We identified two situations in which such a claim could proceed: (1) when discriminatory conduct constructively evicts a resident, and (2) when occupancy is governed by discriminatory terms (in that case, a condo association rule that prohibited hanging mezuzot and thus discriminated against Jews). *Id.* at 779-80. As to the first situation, we reasoned that habitation is a "privilege of sale." *Id.* As to the second, the Bloch family's adherence to the discriminatory rule was a "condition of sale." *Id.* St. Andrew reads *Bloch* as identifying the exclusive set of post-acquisition claims that would be possible under section 3604(b). But we said no such thing. Instead, as courts do, we were addressing the case before us, and so we simply noted that those were "two possibilities for relief in [the present] case." *Id.* at 779. St. Andrew's argument also ignores that section 3604(b) protects not only against discrimination in the "terms, conditions, or privileges of sale or rental," but also discrimination "in the provision of services or facilities in connection therewith." As the Ninth Circuit has recognized, the latter language most naturally encompasses conduct that follows acquisition. *Comm. Concerning Cmty. Improvement v. City of Modesto*, 583 F.3d 690, 713 (9th Cir. 2009). Few "services or facilities" are provided prior to the point of sale or rental; far more attach to a resident's occupancy. *Id.*

In this case, Wetzel has alleged that while the management defendants sat on their hands, residents' harassment confined her to her room for prolonged stretches. Regular harassment also impeded her from eating the meals she had paid for at the dining hall, visiting the lobby and other common spaces, and obtaining access to the laundry room. These were concrete violations of the Agreement, which guarantees "three-well balanced meals per day to be served in a central location," a community room, and available laundry facilities. At a minimum then, Wetzel has a cognizable post-acquisition claim because discrimination affected the provision of services and facilities connected to her rental.

Beyond that, the discrimination diminished the privileges of Wetzel's rental. Though she has not been constructively evicted from her apartment, occupancy of the unit is not the only privilege of rental. Use of the totality of the rented premises is another. See RESTATEMENT (SECOND) OF PROP.: LAND. & TEN. § 4.3; A. JAMES CASNER ET AL., 1 AMERICAN LAW OF PROPERTY § 3.49 (1952).

So too is the covenant of quiet enjoyment. See *City of Modesto*, 583 F.3d at 713; CASNER, *supra*, § 3.47.

Contrary to St. Andrew's assertion, this case is unlike *Halprin*. There, the Halprin family sued its homeowners' association because the association's president incessantly harassed them because they were Jewish. *Halprin*, 388 F.3d at 328. The *Halprin* opinion took a limited approach to post-acquisition claims under section 3604(b), and so it had no reason to reach the question whether the harassment was connected to a term, condition, or privilege, or the provision of services, related to homeownership. In *Bloch*, however, the *en banc* court distinguished *Halprin* as a case in which the homeowners' association had no contractual relationship to the Halprin family. *Bloch*, 587 F.3d at 780. St. Andrew tries to use *Halprin* by noting that there was no contractual relationship between Wetzel and any other *tenant*. True enough, but that is not the relevant comparator. It is between Wetzel and St. Andrew, and that relationship was governed by the Agreement and the Tenant Handbook. Nothing in *Halprin* supports the dismissal of Wetzel's case at this time.

IV

Wetzel separately alleged that after she complained about the harassment, the management defendants restricted her access to facilities and common spaces, downgraded her dining seat, halted her cleaning services, and attempted to build a case for her eviction. In doing so, she says, they retaliated against her in violation of 42 U.S.C. § 3617. St. Andrew offers several reasons to affirm the district court's dismissal of this claim. It argues that the alleged retaliatory conduct was not adverse action; if it was adverse, it was not causally related to Wetzel's complaints; and there is no allegation of discriminatory animus. St. Andrew conceded at oral argument that it argued in the district court only that Wetzel's retaliation claim lacked an allegation of discriminatory animus. We thus limit our remark to that argument. *Fednav Int'l Ltd. v. Cont'l Ins. Co.*, 624 F.3d 834, 841 (7th Cir. 2010).

p.868 To prove retaliation, a plaintiff must show that: (1) she engaged in protected activity; (2) she suffered an adverse action; and (3) there was a causal connection between the two. See, *e.g., Owens v. Old Wisconsin Sausage Co., Inc.*, 870 F.3d 662, 668 (7th Cir. 2017) (elements of a Title VII retaliation claim); *Boston v. U.S. Steel Corp.*, 816 F.3d 455, 464 (7th Cir. 2016) (same for ADEA); *Milligan v. Bd. of Trs. of S. Ill. Univ.*, 686 F.3d 378, 388 (7th Cir. 2012) (same for Title IX). Proof of discriminatory animus is not on the list. We have said that a claim under section 3617 requires showing intentional discrimination only when considering an *interference* claim. See *Bloch*, 587 F.3d at 783; *East-Miller v. Lake Cnty. Highway Dep't*, 421 F.3d 558, 562-63 (7th Cir. 2005); see also *Halprin*, 388 F.3d at 330-31 (recognizing that section 3617 creates different types of claims).

Indeed, if we were to read the FHA's anti-retaliation provision to require that a plaintiff allege discriminatory animus, it would be an anomaly. The FHA's anti-retaliation provision makes it unlawful "to coerce, intimidate, threaten, or interfere with any person in the exercise or enjoyment of, or on account of his having exercised or enjoyed, ... any right granted or protected by section 3603, 3604, 3605, or 3606 of this title." 42 U.S.C. § 3617. Like all anti-retaliation provisions, it provides protections not because of who people are, but because of what they do. See

Burlington Northern & Santa Fe Ry. Co. v. White, 548 U.S. 53, 63, 126 S.Ct. 2405, 165 L.Ed.2d 345 (2006).

V

The district court's judgment is REVERSED and the case is REMANDED for further proceedings consistent with this opinion. We also instruct the district court to reinstate the state-law claims that were dismissed for want of jurisdiction.

851 F.3d 690 (2017)

Sabina BURTON, Plaintiff-Appellant,
v.
BOARD OF REGENTS OF the UNIVERSITY OF WISCONSIN SYSTEM, et al., Defendants-Appellees.

No. 16-2982.

United States Court of Appeals, Seventh Circuit.
Argued January 19, 2017.
Decided March 17, 2017.

Burton v. Bd of Regents of University of WI System, 851 F. 3d 690 (7th Cir. 2017)

p.692 Appeal from the United States District Court for the Western District of Wisconsin, No. 14-cv-274, James D. Peterson, Judge.

Kimberly Laura Penix, Attorney, Alderman Law Firm, Madison, WI, for Plaintiff-Appellant.

Steven C. Kilpatrick, Attorney, Office of the Attorney General, Madison, WI, for Defendants-Appellees.

Before FLAUM, MANION, and WILLIAMS, Circuit Judges.

MANION, Circuit Judge.

Sabina Burton, a professor in the criminal justice department at the University of Wisconsin-Platteville, sued the school's Board of Regents and three individual defendants. She claims that her superiors took several retaliatory actions against her over the course of about two years. She seeks relief under Title VII of the Civil Rights Act of 1964 and Title IX of the Education Amendments of 1972. The district court granted summary judgment to the Board and the individual defendants. For the reasons set forth below, we affirm the judgment of the district court.

I. Background

In 2009, Dr. Burton was hired as a tenure-track professor in the criminal justice department at the University of Wisconsin-Platteville. In January 2012, she was promoted to associate professor. Later p.693 that year, a series of events began to unfold that eventually led to this litigation.

First, in October 2012, Burton received a complaint from a student in her department who claimed that another professor had sexually harassed her. The student was upset that the professor had handed her a note during class that read "call me tonight!" and included the professor's phone number. The next day, Burton contacted the Dean of the College of Liberal Arts (which encompasses her department), Elizabeth Throop, regarding the alleged harassment. Burton then spoke with her department chair, Thomas Caywood, who broached the subject with the offending professor.

The professor who wrote the note claimed that it was part of a "breach experiment," or an intentional provocation designed to display to the class social norms by violating them. The student, however, took it seriously. In any event, Burton told Caywood that she thought all faculty members should be made aware whenever a professor conducts such an experiment, but Caywood didn't think that was necessary. A week later, Caywood circulated a memo to the department that altered the procedure for reporting student complaints about faculty members: professors were now to bring students' complaints directly to Caywood, rather than going outside of the department. The next month, Caywood said at a department meeting that the change was necessary because someone had overreacted by bringing a student complaint outside the department. Overall, Caywood became less collegial towards Burton, and she viewed the change in departmental policy as a direct repudiation of her conduct.

Around the same time, Throop and Caywood began to withdraw their support for a cybersecurity curriculum that Burton had been developing. In April 2012, Burton submitted (and Caywood signed) a grant application to the National Science Foundation in an attempt to receive funding for the creation of a cybersecurity curriculum at the University. That application was rejected, but Burton eventually received a modest offer from AT&T of $7,000 to fund the cybersecurity program.

Caywood and Throop hampered this process after Burton had reported the alleged harassment of the student in October 2012. Specifically, in November Caywood failed to respond to Burton's request for a meeting about the grant process. Then on January 24, 2013, both Throop and Caywood objected to the wording in a draft press release prepared by the AT&T representative. In an email chain that included Burton and the AT&T representative, Throop and Caywood expressed their concerns that the press release said too much because Burton had yet to submit formally any course curricula to the appropriate University committees. Caywood also confronted Burton about inaccuracies (which Caywood had never noticed before) on two websites that Burton had created for the proposed cybersecurity program. Nevertheless, Throop and the AT&T representative ironed out the language of the press release and Burton received the grant the next day in a public ceremony attended by the provost of the University.

In the midst of this, in January 2013 Burton submitted her application for tenure. It was unanimously granted two months later. Although Caywood had initially opposed Burton's application, he eventually voted in her favor. Caywood then stepped down as department chair after the 2012 — 13 academic year, seemingly in part because of conflict with Burton. He was replaced by Michael Dalecki, but Burton's troubles did not end there.

On August 13, 2013, Burton filed a charge of discrimination with the Wisconsin p.694 Department of Workforce Development — Equal Rights Division (ERD). In it, Burton alleged that (1) Caywood had discriminated against her because of her sex and retaliated against her for reporting the note incident; (2) both Throop and the University's human resources director (to whom Burton had sent an email complaining of Caywood's retaliation) had discriminated against her; (3) Throop had defamed her (in connection with the AT&T press release); and (4) the University had been deliberately indifferent to her grievances. After she filed that charge, Dalecki and others pressured her on multiple occasions to drop her case. Burton was told that she might have been considered for the positions of dean or department chair, but that she could not expect to advance if she continued to engage in litigious behavior.

On April 14, 2014, Burton filed her initial complaint in this case in the Western District of Wisconsin, alleging both discrimination and retaliation. Then on October 20, 2014, she completed an intake questionnaire with the United States Equal Employment Opportunity Commission (EEOC). Four days later, Throop sent Burton a "letter of direction" which identified seven events that Throop considered examples of inappropriate behavior by Burton.[1] Throop's letter included five specific directions for Burton to follow. Burton, however, rejected the directions and accused Throop of mischaracterizing the facts. Afterwards, Throop filed a complaint against Burton with the chancellor of the Board of Regents pursuant to Wis. Admin. Code UWS § 6.01, asking for a formal letter of reprimand. It is unclear from the record whether this complaint has been resolved.

Finally, on December 4, 2014, Throop accused Burton of canceling class without permission. In response, Burton sent an email to all of her students documenting her issues with Throop and Caywood and asking for the students' help in proving that she had in fact held class on that day. When the students responded that class had occurred, Throop did not discipline Burton. The next day, Burton filed her EEOC charge. She filed the second amended complaint in this case on September 11, 2015, and the district court granted summary judgment to the Board on March 18, 2016.[2] Burton timely appealed.

II. Analysis

A. Standard of Review

We review the district court's decision to grant summary judgment to the Board *de novo*. *Brunson v. Murray*, 843 F.3d 698, 704 (7th Cir. 2016). Summary judgment is appropriate where "there is no genuine dispute as to any material fact and the moving party is entitled to judgment as a matter of law." Fed. R. Civ. P. 56(a). We view all evidence in the light most favorable to Burton, who was the party opposing the motion below. *Brunson*, 843 F.3d at 704. The Board is entitled to summary judgment if Burton cannot present sufficient evidence to create a dispute of material fact regarding any essential element of her legal claims on which she bears the burden of proof. *Celotex Corp. v. Catrett*, 477 U.S. 317, 323, 106 S.Ct. 2548, 91 L.Ed.2d 265 (1986).

p.695 B. Title VII and Title IX Framework

Both Title VII of the Civil Rights Act of 1964 and Title IX of the Education Amendments of 1972 permit plaintiffs to bring causes of action for retaliation. See 42 U.S.C. § 2000e-3(a) (Title VII); *Jackson v. Birmingham Bd. of Educ.*, 544 U.S. 167, 173-74, 125 S.Ct. 1497, 161 L.Ed.2d 361 (2005) (Title IX). The elements of those claims are the same: Burton must produce enough evidence for a reasonable jury to conclude that (1) she engaged in a statutorily protected activity; (2) the Board took a materially adverse action against her; and (3) there existed a but-for causal connection between the two. *Milligan v. Bd. of Trs.,* 686 F.3d 378, 388 (7th Cir. 2012); *Univ. of Tex. Sw. Med. Ctr. v. Nassar,* ___ U.S. ___, 133 S.Ct. 2517, 2533, 186 L.Ed.2d 503 (2013) (causation standard).

C. Waiver of Certain Arguments

One threshold matter that we must address is Burton's attempt to inject more facts into the case on appeal than she presented to the district court. Burton claims that the district court erred by limiting its analysis to certain alleged protected activities and materially adverse actions. She says that if the district court had considered everything, it would have found that she engaged in more protected activities and suffered more significant adverse employment actions.

Burton's problem is that she did not make these broad arguments to the district court. For example, on the Title IX claim she argues that the district court should have considered a litany of potential materially adverse employment actions. Yet she presented only two to the district court: Caywood's reaction to her reporting of the note incident and Caywood's and Throop's supposed withdrawal of support for her cybersecurity curriculum. Throughout her briefing, Burton relies on facts that appear nowhere in her opposition to the Board's motion for summary judgment below. It appears that she made a strategic decision in the district court to focus on the strongest points in her case and omit the rest.

That decision was not necessarily a bad one, but it does preclude her reliance here on the facts omitted below. For one, she had the burden of identifying protected activities and materially adverse actions in opposition to summary judgment before the district court. See *Ellis v. CCA of Tenn. LLC,* 650 F.3d 640, 649 (7th Cir. 2011). The district court was necessarily limited to arguments presented in Burton's opposition brief. After all, "a lawsuit is not a game of hunt the peanut. Employment discrimination cases are extremely fact-intensive, and neither appellate courts nor district courts are 'obliged in our adversary system to scour the record looking for factual disputes....'" *Greer v. Bd. of Educ.,* 267 F.3d 723, 727 (7th Cir. 2001) (quoting *Waldridge v. Am. Hoechst Corp.,* 24 F.3d 918, 921-22 (7th Cir. 1993)).

Instead, "[i]t is a well-settled rule that a party opposing a summary judgment motion must inform the trial judge of the reasons, legal or factual, why summary judgment should not be entered." *Liberles v. Cook Cty.,* 709 F.2d 1122, 1126 (7th Cir. 1983). "If [the nonmoving party] does not do so, and loses the motion, it cannot raise such reasons on appeal." *Id.* This rule prevents Burton from raising specific factual arguments that were absent from her briefing below even though her general claims were plainly before the court. See *Fednav Int'l Ltd. v. Cont'l Ins. Co.,* 624 F.3d 834, 841 (7th Cir. 2010) ("[A] party has waived the ability to make a specific argument for the first time on appeal when the party failed to present that specific argument to the district court, even though the issue may have p.696 been before the district court in more general terms."). Thus, Burton is limited to the facts laid out in Part I above and to the particular protected activities and adverse actions that she argued below. We now proceed to the merits of her Title IX and Title VII claims.

D. Title IX Claim

The Board concedes on appeal that Burton's actions in reporting the allegedly inappropriate in-class note were protected activities under Title IX. As Burton did not raise any further protected activities below, we move on to assess whether any alleged actions by Burton's superiors in the wake of the note incident were materially adverse to her. As noted above, Burton raised two potential adverse actions: (1) the supposed criticisms of Burton after she reported the note; and (2) the apparent withdrawal of support for Burton's cybersecurity initiative.

First, we emphasize that "[n]ot everything that makes an employee unhappy is an actionable adverse action." *Brown v. Advocate S. Suburban Hosp.*, 700 F.3d 1101, 1106 (7th Cir. 2012) (quoting *Stephens v. Erickson*, 569 F.3d 779, 790 (7th Cir. 2009)). Rather, "an adverse action is one that a reasonable employee would find to be materially adverse such that the employee would be dissuaded from engaging in the protected activity." *Silverman v. Bd. of Educ.*, 637 F.3d 729, 740 (7th Cir. 2011) (citations and internal quotation marks omitted); see also *Lucero v. Nettle Creek Sch. Corp.*, 566 F.3d 720, 729 (7th Cir. 2009). In other words, it does not include "those petty slights or minor annoyances that often take place at work and that all employees experience." *Burlington N. & Santa Fe Ry. Co. v. White*, 548 U.S. 53, 68, 126 S.Ct. 2405, 165 L.Ed.2d 345 (2006).

Like the district court, we conclude that neither of Burton's proffered adverse actions rises to the level of materiality necessary to form the basis of a Title IX retaliation claim. With respect to the post-note criticism, the record does not support Burton's claims. Caywood never expressly denounced the way Burton handled the situation. Instead, he merely presented a new policy for handling similar problems in the future. Even if we were to construe Caywood's rollout of the new policy as an implicit reprimand, that would not be sufficient to be a materially adverse action either. See *Chaib v. Indiana*, 744 F.3d 974, 987 (7th Cir. 2014), overruled on other grounds by *Ortiz v. Werner Enters., Inc.*, 834 F.3d 760 (7th Cir. 2016). As in *Chaib*, there was no showing that any reprimand (or any lack of collegiality on the part of Caywood) caused any subsequent consequences for Burton's employment. See also *Lloyd v. Swifty Transp., Inc.*, 552 F.3d 594, 602 (7th Cir. 2009) ("[W]ritten reprimands without any changes in the terms or conditions of [an employee's] employment are not adverse employment actions."). Indeed, Burton unanimously received tenure just months after the incident.

The same is true of the disagreement over the cybersecurity program at the University. The most the record shows is that Throop and Caywood were concerned that the language of the AT&T press release may have been over-representing the progress of the cybersecurity curriculum that Burton had been developing, and that Caywood was concerned about some errors on websites that Burton had created. Yet Throop approved the press release the same day that the dispute began, and Burton received the AT&T grant in a public ceremony attended by the provost and vice chancellor of the University. Once again, Burton received tenure within months of this incident and can point to no material p.697 consequences resulting from it. While she may have perceived that Throop and Caywood had retaliated against her, these actions simply do not rise to the level of a materially adverse employment action protected by Title IX. Therefore, like the district court, we need not engage in any causation analysis. The district court correctly granted summary judgment to the Board on the Title IX retaliation claim.

E. Title VII Claim

With respect to the Title VII claim, the Board concedes both that Burton undertook protected activities (filing charges with the Wisconsin ERD and the EEOC and filing this lawsuit) and was subjected to materially adverse employment actions (Throop's letter of direction and subsequent complaint to the chancellor).[3] Burton didn't raise any other protected activities below, so she has forfeited the chance to do so now. But she did present two further adverse actions to the district court: (1) the repeated pressuring by Dalecki and others to drop the discrimination charges; and (2) Throop's threat of discipline in retaliation for the allegedly canceled class on December 4, 2013. The district court properly concluded that the pressure to drop the suit could not have amounted to a materially adverse action because these statements "did not cause [Burton] any injury." *Dunn v. Washington Cty. Hosp.*, 429 F.3d 689, 692 (7th Cir. 2005).[4] For a similar reason, unfulfilled threats of discipline related to the accusation that Burton canceled class are not actionable. See *Poullard v. McDonald*, 829 F.3d 844, 856-57 (7th Cir. 2016) (recognizing that unfulfilled threats are not materially adverse actions for the purpose of a Title VII retaliation claim).

So we are left with the task of determining whether the record contains enough evidence for a reasonable jury to conclude that the admitted protected activities were the but-for cause of the admitted adverse actions. Without direct evidence of causation, Burton must rely on circumstantial evidence like suspicious timing, ambiguous statements, treatment of similarly-situated employees, and any other relevant information that could permit an inference of retaliation. See *Lambert v. Peri Formworks Sys., Inc.*, 723 F.3d 863, 869 (7th Cir. 2013). It's also true that actions that were not in and of themselves materially adverse, such as unfulfilled threats, may still be evidence of retaliatory motive for actionable actions. *Poullard*, 829 F.3d at 857. But the dispositive question remains whether a reasonable jury could find a but-for causal link between the protected activities and adverse actions at issue. And because the Board has presented non-retaliatory reasons for Throop's conduct, the true question is whether the proffered reasons were pretext for retaliation. See *Majors v. Gen. Elec. Co.*, 714 F.3d 527, 539 (7th Cir. 2013).

We agree with the district court on this point as well. First, the timing p.698 of the letter of direction is not suggestive of retaliatory motive. The last potential protected activity here was the filing of this lawsuit in April 2014, six months before Throop sent the letter of direction. Burton has not provided any evidence that bridges the significant time gap between her final protected activity and Throop's adverse action.[5] While the six-month gap does not preclude Burton's claim as a matter of law, it does substantially weaken it.[6]

Moreover, the record demonstrates that Throop had a factual basis for each of the allegations she leveled against Burton in the letter of direction, and Burton failed to provide evidence that the allegations were pretextual. Indeed, the district court stated that Burton did not dispute the truth of the allegations, only "how Throop *perceived* and *characterized* those events, and whether Throop should have accepted Burton's explanations for each of them." *Burton*, 171 F.Supp.3d at 846. These are exactly the type of personnel management decisions that federal courts do not second-guess. We intervene only where "an employer's reason for [an adverse action] is without factual basis or is completely unreasonable." *Hobgood v. Ill. Gaming Bd.,* 731 F.3d 635, 646 (7th Cir. 2013). This is plainly not such a situation. Burton has not presented sufficient evidence of pretext, and as a result she cannot establish but-for causation.

There is no evidence in the record that Throop's complaint against Burton was retaliation for her protected activity, but there is evidence that Burton decided not to heed any of the "direction" contained in the letter. Then, as now, Burton simply argues that Throop should never have written the letter. But once again, pretext "involves more than just faulty reasoning or mistaken judgment on the part of the employer; it is [a] lie, specifically a phony reason for some action." *Harden v. Marion Cty. Sheriff's Dep't,* 799 F.3d 857, 864 (7th Cir. 2015) (quoting *Argyropoulos v. City of Alton,* 539 F.3d 724, 735 (7th Cir. 2008)). There is no evidence that either the letter of direction or Burton's subsequent complaint were such lies. No reasonable jury could find that either the letter of direction or the subsequent complaint were caused by Burton's protected activities, rather than legitimate disagreements between Burton and Throop. Therefore, the district court properly granted summary judgment to the Board on Burton's Title VII claim.

III. Conclusion

Professor Burton undoubtedly feels that she has been treated unfairly by some of her superiors at the University because p.699 she reported alleged harassment and proceeded with this case. Yet the record does not support her claims. During the relevant period, Burton was granted tenure by a unanimous vote and the University held a public ceremony celebrating Burton's receipt of a grant from AT&T. Dean Throop even sought an upward salary adjustment for her after she had brought a charge with the Wisconsin ERD. Burton's frustrations may be significant, but they do not amount to actionable retaliation under either Title VII or Title IX. Therefore, the district court correctly granted summary judgment to the Board.

AFFIRMED.

---

[1] As Burton conceded at oral argument, the record does not show that Throop or anyone else at the University was aware of the intake questionnaire when the letter of direction was issued.

[2] In her response to the defendants' motion for summary judgment below, Burton dismissed all of her original claims except for retaliation claims under Title VII and Title IX. She also apparently pursues claims only against the Board of Regents, so we will refer to the defendants simply as the Board.

[3] We follow the parties' briefing in presenting the claims separately under Title IX and Title VII. The parties appear to agree that the facts surrounding the in-class note incident would not state a Title VII claim because of the lack of employment relationship between Burton and the reporting student. We need not consider whether they are right, because the elements of a Title VII and Title IX retaliation claim are the same.

[4] Even the comments noting that Burton could have been dean or department chair material if she were not so litigious don't amount to an adverse action. There is no indication that Burton ever sought those positions or that she was otherwise under consideration apart from the stray comments. In other words, the comments caused Burton no injury.

[5] Moreover, as the district court noted, "Throop sought and obtained an equity adjustment to Burton's salary in March 2014." *Burton v. Bd. of Regents,* 171 F.Supp.3d 830, 846 (W.D. Wis. 2016). This occurred between the filing of Burton's ERD charge and the initial complaint in this case. Such positive intervention in between two instances of protected activity at least somewhat undermines Burton's retaliation theory. See *Albrechtsen v. Bd. of Regents,* 309 F.3d 433, 437-38 (7th Cir. 2002).

[6] As indicated in Part I, Burton conceded at oral argument that the record does not indicate that Throop or anyone else at the University knew that Burton had completed an intake questionnaire with the EEOC four days before the letter of direction issued. This gap in the record is particularly harmful to Burton's claim, because in order to be liable for Title VII retaliation, "the employer must have had actual knowledge of the protected activity" at issue. *Nagle v. Vill. of Calumet Park,* 554 F.3d 1106, 1122 (7th Cir. 2009). Without evidence establishing actual knowledge, the timing of the intake questionnaire is irrelevant.

858 F.3d 1034 (2017)

Ashton WHITAKER, BY his mother and next friend Melissa WHITAKER, Plaintiff-Appellee,

v.

KENOSHA UNIFIED SCHOOL DISTRICT NO. 1 BOARD OF EDUCATION, et al., Defendants-Appellants.

No. 16-3522.

United States Court of Appeals, Seventh Circuit.

Argued March 29, 2017.

Decided May 30, 2017.

Whitaker v. Kenosha Unified School District, 858 F. 3d 1034 (7th Cir. 2017)

p.1038 Appeal from the United States District Court for the Eastern District of Wisconsin, No. 2:16-cv-00943-PP, Pamela Pepper, Judge.

Robert Theine Pledl, Attorney, Pledl & Cohn, Milwaukee, WI, Joseph John Wardenski, Sasha M. Samberg-Champion, Attorneys, Relman, Dane & Colfax PLLC, Washington, DC, Shawn Thomas Meerkamper, Ilona M. Turner, Attorneys, Transgender Law Center, Oakland, CA, for Plaintiff-Appellee.

Ronald S. Stadler, Attorney, Mallery & Zimmerman, Milwaukee, WI, for Defendants-Appellants.

Jordan W. Lorence, Attorney, Alliance Defending Freedom, Washington, DC, Gary McCaleb, Jeremy D. Tedesco, Attorneys, Alliance Defending Freedom, Scottsdale, AZ, for Amicus Curiae Alliance Defending Freedom.

Kyle Palazzolo, Attorney, Lambda Legal Defense & Education Fund, Chicago, IL, for Amicus Curiae School Administrators from Twenty-One States and the District of Columbia.

Julia Renee Lissner, Attorney, Akerman LLP, Chicago, IL, for Amici Curiae Forge, Inc., Indianapolis Chapter of P-Flag, Inc., Genders & Sexualities Alliance Network, Gender Expansive Kids and Company.

Maureen Alger, Attorney, Cooley Godward Kronish LLP, Palo Alto, CA, for Amici Curiae Gay Straight Alliance for Safe Schools, Inc., Illinois Safe Schools Alliance, Indiana Youth Group, Inc., Gender Spectrum Charitable Fund.

Charles A. Rothfeld, Attorney, Mayer Brown LLP, Washington, DC, for Amicus Curiae National Women's Law Center.

Mark E. Haddad, Attorney, Sidley Austin LLP, Los Angeles, CA, for Amici Curiae Katherine R Allen, Nadav Antebi-Gruszka, M.V. Lee Badgett.

Before WOOD, Chief Judge, and ROVNER and WILLIAMS, Circuit Judges.

WILLIAMS, Circuit Judge.

Ashton ("Ash") Whitaker is a 17 year-old high school senior who has what would p.1039 seem like a simple request: to use the boys' restroom while at school. However, the Defendants, the Kenosha Unified School District and its superintendent, Sue Savaglio, (the "School District") believe that the request is not so simple because

Ash[1] is a transgender boy. The School District did not permit Ash to enter the boys' restroom because, it believed, that his mere presence would invade the privacy rights of his male classmates. Ash brought suit, alleging that the School District's unwritten bathroom policy[2] violates Title IX of the Education Amendments Act of 1972 and the Fourteenth Amendment's Equal Protection Clause.

In addition to filing suit, Ash, beginning his senior year, moved for preliminary injunctive relief, seeking an order granting him access to the boys' restrooms. He asserted that the denial of access to the boys' bathroom was causing him harm, as his attempts to avoid using the bathroom exacerbated his vasovagal syncope, a condition that renders Ash susceptible to fainting and/or seizures if dehydrated. He also contended that the denial caused him educational and emotional harm, including suicidal ideations. The School District vigorously objected and moved to dismiss Ash's claims, arguing that Ash could neither state a claim under Title IX nor the Equal Protection Clause. The district court denied the motion to dismiss and granted Ash's preliminary injunction motion.

On appeal, the School District argues that we should exercise pendent appellate jurisdiction to review the district court's decision to deny the motion to dismiss. However, we decline this invitation, as the two orders were not inextricably intertwined and we can review the grant of the preliminary injunction without reviewing the denial of the motion to dismiss.

The School District also argues that we should reverse the district court's decision to grant the preliminary injunction for two main reasons. First, it argues that the district court erred in finding that Ash had demonstrated a likelihood of success on the merits because transgender status is neither a protected class under Title IX nor is it entitled to heightened scrutiny. And, because the School District's policy has a rational basis, that is, the need to protect other students' privacy, Ash's claims fail as a matter of law. We reject these arguments because Ash has sufficiently demonstrated a likelihood of success on his Title IX claim under a sex-stereotyping theory. Further, because the policy's classification is based upon sex, he has also demonstrated that heightened scrutiny, and not rational basis, should apply to his Equal Protection Claim. The School District has not provided a genuine and exceedingly persuasive justification for the classification.

Second, the School District argues that the district court erred in finding that the harms to Ash outweighed the harms to the student population and their privacy interests. We disagree. The School District has failed to provide any evidence of how the preliminary injunction will harm it, or any of its students or parents. The harms identified by the School District are all speculative and based upon conjecture, whereas the harms to Ash are well-documented and supported by the record. As a consequence, we affirm the grant of preliminary injunctive relief.

p.1040 I. BACKGROUND

Ash Whitaker is a 17 year-old who lives in Kenosha, Wisconsin with his mother, who brought this suit as his "next friend."[3] He is currently a senior at George Nelson Tremper High School, which is in the Kenosha Unified School District. He entered his senior year ranked within the top five percent of his class and is involved in a number of extracurricular activities including the orchestra, theater, tennis, the National Honor Society, and the Astronomical Society. When not in school or participating in these activities, Ash works part-time as an accounting assistant in a medical office.

While Ash's birth certificate designates him as "female," he does not identify as one. Rather, in the spring of 2013, when Ash was in eighth grade, he told his parents that he is transgender and a boy. He began to openly identify as a boy during the 2013-2014 school year, when he entered Tremper as a freshman. He cut his hair, began to wear more masculine clothing, and began to use the name Ashton and male pronouns. In the fall of 2014, the beginning of his sophomore year, he told his teachers and his classmates that he is a boy and asked them to refer to him as Ashton or Ash and to use male pronouns.

In addition to publicly transitioning, Ash began to see a therapist, who diagnosed him with Gender Dysphoria, which the American Psychiatric Association defines as "a marked incongruence between one's experienced/expressed gender and assigned gender...."[4] *Am. Psychiatric Ass'n, Diagnostic & Statistical Manual of Mental Disorders* 452 (5th ed. 2013). In July 2016, under the supervision of an endocrinologist at Children's Hospital of Wisconsin, Ash began hormone replacement therapy. A month later, he filed a petition to legally change his name to Ashton Whitaker, which was granted in September 2016.

For the most part, Ash's transition has been met without hostility and has been accepted by much of the Tremper community. At an orchestra performance in January 2015, for example, he wore a tuxedo like the rest of the boys in the group. His orchestra teacher, classmates, and the audience accepted this without incident. Unfortunately, the School District has not been as accepting of Ash's requests to use the boys' restrooms.

In the spring of his sophomore year, Ash and his mother met with his guidance counselor on several occasions to request that Ash be permitted to use the boys' restrooms while at school and at school-sponsored events. Ash was later notified that the administration had decided that he could only use the girls' restrooms or a gender-neutral restroom that was in the school's main office, which was quite a distance from his classrooms. Because Ash had publicly transitioned, he believed that using the girls' restrooms would undermine his transition. Additionally, since Ash was the only student who was permitted to use the gender-neutral bathroom in the school's office, he feared that using it would draw further attention to his transition and status as a transgender student at Tremper. As a high schooler, Ash also worried that he might be disciplined if he tried to use the boys' restrooms and that such discipline might hurt his chances of getting into college. For these reasons, p.1041 Ash restricted his water intake and attempted to avoid using any restroom at school for the rest of the school year.

Restricting his water intake was problematic for Ash, who has been diagnosed with vasovagal syncope. This condition renders Ash more susceptible to fainting and/or seizures if dehydrated. To avoid triggering the condition, Ash's physicians have advised him to drink six to seven bottles of water and a bottle of Gatorade daily. Because Ash restricted his water intake to ensure that he did not have to utilize the restroom at school, he suffered from symptoms of his vasovagal syncope, including fainting and dizziness. He also suffered from stress-related migraines, depression, and anxiety because of the policy's impact on his transition and what he perceived to be the impossible choice between living as a boy or using the restroom. He even began to contemplate suicide.

In the fall of 2015, Ash began his junior year at Tremper. For six months, he exclusively used the boys' restrooms at school without incident. But, in February 2016, a teacher saw him washing his hands at a sink in the boys' restroom and reported it to the school's administration. In response, Ash's guidance counselor, Debra Tronvig, again told Ash's mother that he was permitted to only use the girls' restrooms or the gender-neutral bathroom in the school's main office. The next month, Ash and his mother met with Assistant Principal Holly Graf to discuss the school's policy. Like before, Ms. Graf stated that Ash was not permitted to use the boys' restrooms. However, the reason she gave this time was that he was listed as a female in the school's official records and to change those records, the school needed unspecified "legal or medical documentation."

Two letters submitted by Ash's pediatrician, identifying him as a transgender boy and recommending that he be allowed to use male-designated facilities at school were deemed not sufficient to change his designation. Rather, the school maintained that Ash would have to complete a surgical transition ... a procedure that is prohibited for someone under 18 years of age ... to be permitted access to the boys' restroom. Further, not all transgender persons opt to complete a surgical transition, preferring to forgo the significant risks and costs that accompany such procedures. The School District did not give any explanation as to why a surgical transition was necessary. Indeed, the verbal statements made to Ash's mom about the policy have never been reduced to writing. In fact, the School District has *never* provided any written document that details when the policy went into effect, what the policy is, or how one can change his status under the policy.

Fearing that using the one gender-neutral restroom would single him out and subject him to scrutiny from his classmates and knowing that using the girls' restroom would be in contradiction to his transition, Ash continued to use the boys' restroom for the remainder of his junior year.

This decision was not without a cost. Ash experienced feelings of anxiousness and depression. He once more began to contemplate suicide. Nonetheless, the school's security guards were instructed to monitor's Ash's restroom use to ensure that he used the proper facilities. Because Ash continued to use the boys' restroom, he was removed from class on several occasions to discuss his violation of the school's unwritten policy. His classmates and teachers often asked him about these meetings and why administrators were removing him from class.

In April 2016, the School District provided Ash with the additional option of using two single-user, gender-neutral restrooms. These locked restrooms were on the opposite side of campus from where his classes were held. The School District provided only one student with the key: Ash. Since the restrooms were not near his classrooms, which caused Ash to miss class time, and because using them further stigmatized him, Ash again avoided using the bathrooms while at school. This only exacerbated his syncope and migraines. In addition, Ash began to fear for his safety as more attention was drawn to his restroom use and transgender status.

Although not part of this appeal, Ash contends that he has also been subjected to other negative actions by the School District, including initially prohibiting him from running for prom king, referring to him with female pronouns, using his birth name, and requiring him to room with female students or alone on school-sponsored trips. Furthermore, Ash learned in May 2016 that school administrators had considered instructing its guidance counselors to distribute bright green wristbands to Ash and other transgender students so that their bathroom usage could be monitored more easily. Throughout this litigation, the School District has denied that it considered implementing the wristband plan.

A. Proceedings Below

In the spring of 2016, Ash engaged counsel who, in April 2016, sent the School District a letter demanding that it permit him to use the boys' restroom while at school and during school-sponsored events. In response, the School District repeated its policy that Ash was required to use either the girls' restroom or the gender-neutral facilities. On May 12, 2016, Ash filed an administrative complaint with the United States Department of Education's Office for Civil Rights, alleging that this policy violated his rights under Title IX. To pursue the instant litigation, Ash chose to withdraw the complaint without prejudice.

On July 16, 2016, Ash commenced this action and on August 15, he filed an Amended Complaint alleging that the treatment he received at Tremper High School violated Title IX, 20 U.S.C. § 1681, *et seq.*, and the Equal Protection Clause of the Fourteenth Amendment. That same day, Ash, in a motion for preliminary injunction, sought to enjoin the enforcement of the School District's policy pending the outcome of the litigation. The next day, the School District filed a motion to dismiss and filed its opposition to the preliminary injunction shortly thereafter.

After a hearing on the motion to dismiss, the district court denied the motion. The next day, it heard oral arguments on Ash's motion for preliminary injunction. A few days later, the district court granted the motion in part and enjoined the School District from: (1) denying Ash access to the boys' restroom; (2) enforcing any written or unwritten policy against Ash that would prevent him from using the boys' restroom while on school property or attending school-sponsored events; (3) disciplining Ash for using the boys' restroom while on school property or attending school-sponsored events; and (4) monitoring or surveilling Ash's restroom use in any way. This appeal followed.

In a separate appeal, the School District petitioned this court for permission to file an interlocutory appeal of the district court's denial of its motion to dismiss. Although initially the district court certified the order denying the motion to dismiss for immediate interlocutory appeal pursuant to 28 U.S.C. § 1292(b), it revoked that certification when it concluded that it had erred by including the certification language in its initial order. Therefore, we p.1043 denied the School District's petition for interlocutory review of the motion to dismiss for lack of jurisdiction. *See Kenosha Unified Sch. Dist. No. 1 Bd. of Educ. v. Whitaker,* 841 F.3d 730, 731-32 (7th Cir. 2016). In the alternative, the School District urged this court to exercise pendent jurisdiction over the order denying the motion to dismiss because the district court had partially granted the preliminary injunction. But since we lacked jurisdiction to consider the petition for interlocutory appeal, we also lacked a proper jurisdictional basis for extending pendent jurisdiction. *Id.* at 732. Therefore, in this appeal, the School District was directed to seek pendent appellate jurisdiction, which it has now done.

II. ANALYSIS

The School District raises two issues on appeal. First, that this court should assert pendent jurisdiction over the district court's decision to deny its motion to dismiss and second, that the district court erred in granting Ash's motion for preliminary injunction. We will address each issue in turn.

A. Pendent Jurisdiction Is Not Appropriate

Ordinarily, an order denying a motion to dismiss is not a final judgment and is not appealable. *See* 28 U.S.C. § 1291 (providing federal appellate courts with jurisdiction over appeals from all final decisions). But, the School District again urges us to assert pendent appellate jurisdiction to consider the denial of the motion to dismiss. We decline the invitation.

Pendent appellate jurisdiction is a discretionary doctrine. *Jones v. InfoCure Corp.*, 310 F.3d 529, 537 (7th Cir. 2002). It is also a narrow one, *Abelesz v. OTP Bank*, 692 F.3d 638, 647 (7th Cir. 2012), which the Supreme Court sharply restricted in *Swint v. Chambers County Commission,* 514 U.S. 35, 115 S.Ct. 1203, 131 L.Ed.2d 60 (1995). After *Swint,* we noted in *United States v. Board of School Commissioners of the City of Indianapolis,* 128 F.3d 507 (7th Cir. 1997), that pendent appellate jurisdiction is a "controversial and embattled doctrine." *Id.* at 510. Nonetheless, the Supreme Court recognized a narrow path for its use in *Clinton v. Jones,* 520 U.S. 681, 707 n.41, 117 S.Ct. 1636, 137 L.Ed.2d 945 (1997), where it found that a collateral order denying presidential immunity was inextricably intertwined with an order that stayed discovery and postponed trial, and was therefore, reviewable on appeal.

When applicable, the doctrine allows for review of an "otherwise unappealable interlocutory order if it is inextricably intertwined with an appealable one." *Montano v. City of Chicago,* 375 F.3d 593, 599 (7th Cir. 2004) (quoting *Jones,* 310 F.3d at 536) (internal quotation marks omitted). This requires more than a "close link" between the two orders. *Id.* at 600. Judicial economy is also an insufficient justification for invoking the doctrine and disregarding the final-judgment rule. *McCarter v. Ret. Plan For Dist. Managers of Am. Family Ins. Grp.,* 540 F.3d 649, 653 (7th Cir. 2008). Rather, we must satisfy ourselves that based upon the specific facts of this case, it is "practically indispensable that we address the merits of the unappealable order in order to resolve the properly-taken appeal." *Montano,* 375 F.3d at 600 (quoting *United States ex rel. Valders Stone & Marble, Inc. v. C-Way Constr. Co.,* 909 F.2d 259, 262 (7th Cir. 1990)) (internal quotation marks omitted); *see also Abelesz,* 692 F.3d at 647 ("[P]endent appellate jurisdiction should not be stretched to appeal normally unappealable interlocutory orders that happen to be related — even closely related — to the appealable order."). Such a high threshold is required because p.1044 a more relaxed approach would allow the doctrine to swallow the final-judgment rule.

Montano, 375 F.3d at 599 (citing *Patterson v. Portch,* 853 F.2d 1399, 1403 (7th Cir. 1988)).

As we discuss below, the district court determined that Ash sufficiently demonstrated a likelihood of success on the merits of his claims and that preliminary injunctive relief was warranted. In doing so, the district court referenced its decision to deny the School District's motion to dismiss. The School District contends that this rendered the two decisions inextricably intertwined. Therefore, it reasons that pendent jurisdiction is appropriate because to engage in a meaningful review of the preliminary injunction order, the court must also review the denial of the motion to dismiss.

Merely referencing the earlier decision to deny the motion to dismiss, however, did not inextricably intertwine the two orders. Certainly the legal issues raised in the motions overlapped, as both motions challenged, in different ways and under different standards, the likely merits of Ash's claim. Invoking pendent jurisdiction simply because of this overlap would essentially convert a motion for preliminary injunctive relief into a motion to dismiss, which would raise the threshold showing a plaintiff must make before receiving injunctive relief. For all practical purposes, this would mean that every time a motion to dismiss is filed simultaneously with a motion for preliminary injunction, this doctrine would apply. This makes no sense and we do not see a compelling reason for invoking the doctrine here.

B. Preliminary Injunctive Relief Was Proper

A preliminary injunction is an extraordinary remedy. *See Girl Scouts of Manitou Council, Inc. v. Girl Scouts of United States of Am., Inc.,* 549 F.3d 1079, 1085 (7th Cir. 2008) (noting that "a preliminary injunction is an exercise of a very far-reaching power, never to be indulged in except in a case clearly demanding it.") (internal quotation marks and citation omitted). It is never awarded as a matter of right. *D.U. v. Rhoades,* 825 F.3d 331, 335 (7th Cir. 2016). We review the grant of a preliminary injunction for the abuse of discretion, reviewing legal issues *de novo, Jones v. Markiewicz-Qualkinbush,* 842 F.3d 1053, 1057 (7th Cir. 2016), while factual findings are reviewed for clear error. *Fed. Trade Comm'n v. Advocate Health Care Network,* 841 F.3d 460, 467 (7th Cir. 2016). Substantial deference is given to the district court's "weighing of evidence and balancing of the various equitable factors." *Turnell v. CentiMark Corp.,* 796 F.3d 656, 662 (7th Cir. 2015).

A two-step inquiry applies when determining whether such relief is required. *Id.* at 661. First, the party seeking the preliminary injunction has the burden of making a threshold showing: (1) that he will suffer irreparable harm absent preliminary injunctive relief during the pendency of his action; (2) inadequate remedies at law exist; and (3) he has a reasonable likelihood of success on the merits. *Id.* at 661-62. If the movant successfully makes this showing, the court must engage in a balancing analysis, to determine whether the balance of harm favors the moving party or whether the harm to other parties or the public sufficiently outweighs the movant's interests. *Jones,* 842 F.3d at 1058.

1. Ash Likely to Suffer Irreparable Harm

The moving party must demonstrate that he will likely suffer irreparable harm absent obtaining preliminary injunctive relief. *See Michigan v. U.S. Army* p.1045 *Corps of Eng'rs*, 667 F.3d 765, 787 (7th Cir. 2011). This requires more than a mere possibility of harm. *Id.* at 788. It does not, however, require that the harm actually occur before injunctive relief is warranted. *Id.* Nor does it require that the harm be certain to occur before a court may grant relief on the merits. *Id.* Rather, harm is considered irreparable if it "cannot be prevented or fully rectified by the final judgment after trial." *Girl Scouts of Manitou Council, Inc.*, 549 F.3d at 1089 (quoting *Roland Mach. Co. v. Dresser Indus., Inc.*, 749 F.2d 380, 386 (7th Cir. 1984)) (internal quotation marks omitted). Because a district court's determination regarding irreparable harm is a factual finding, it is reviewed for clear error. *Id.* at 1087.

On appeal, the School District argues that the district court erred in finding that Ash established that he would suffer irreparable harm absent a preliminary injunction. Although Ash proffered reports from two different experts regarding the harm caused to him by the School District's policy, the School District contends that neither expert was able to actually quantify this harm. Further, the School District notes that Ash's failure to take advantage of "readily available alternatives," namely the gender-neutral bathrooms, undermines his claim of irreparable harm. Lastly, the School District points to Ash's delay in seeking injunctive relief as indicative of the lack of irreparable harm.

The School District's arguments miss the point. The district court was presented with expert opinions that supported Ash's assertion that he would suffer irreparable harm absent preliminary relief. These experts opined that use of the boys' restrooms is integral to Ash's transition and emotional well-being. Dr. Stephanie Budge, a psychologist who specializes in working with adolescents and adults who have Gender Dysphoria, met with Ash and his mother, and in her report noted that the treatment Ash faced at school "significantly and negatively impacted his mental health and overall well-being."

Dr. Budge also noted that Ash reported current thoughts of suicide and that his depression worsened each time he had to meet with school officials regarding his bathroom usage. Ultimately, she opined that the School District's actions, including its bathroom policy, which identified Ash as transgender and therefore, "different," were "directly causing significant psychological distress and place [Ash] at risk for experiencing life-long diminished well-being and life-functioning." The district court did not clearly err in relying upon these findings when it concluded that Ash would suffer irreparable harm absent preliminary injunctive relief.

Further, the School District's argument that Ash's harm was self-inflicted because he chose not to use the gender-neutral restrooms, fails to comprehend the harm that Ash has identified. The School District actually exacerbated the harm, when it dismissed him to a separate bathroom where he was the only student who had access. This action further stigmatized Ash, indicating that he was "different" because he was a transgender boy.

Moreover, the record demonstrates that these bathrooms were not located close to Ash's classrooms. Therefore, he was faced with the unenviable choice between using a bathroom that would further stigmatize him and cause him to miss class time, or avoid use of the bathroom altogether at the expense of his health.

Additionally, Ash alleged that using the single-user restrooms actually invited more scrutiny and attention from his peers, who inquired why he had access to these restrooms and asked intrusive questions about his transition. This further intensified p.1046 his depression and anxiety surrounding the School District's policy. Therefore, it cannot be said that the harm was "self-inflicted."

Finally, Ash did not delay in seeking injunctive relief. He had used the boys' bathroom for months without incident, and he filed an administrative complaint with the Department of Education in April 2016, just weeks after the school began to enforce its policy once more. He made the decision to withdraw that complaint over the summer and commence the instant litigation instead so that he could pursue injunctive relief prior to beginning his senior year. It is important to note that Ash was on summer break and not subject to the School District's bathroom policy at the time he chose to pursue the litigation. Therefore, Ash's decision to seek injunctive relief over the summer rather than initiate an administrative complaint does not undermine his argument that the policy was inflicting, and would continue to inflict, irreparable harm.

2. No Adequate Remedies at Law

The moving party must also demonstrate that he has no adequate remedy at law should the preliminary injunction not issue. *Promatek Indus., Ltd. v. Equitrac Corp.*, 300 F.3d 808, 813 (7th Cir. 2002). This does not require that he demonstrate that the remedy be wholly ineffectual. *Foodcomm Int'l v. Barry*, 328 F.3d 300, 304 (7th Cir. 2003). Rather, he must demonstrate that any award would be "seriously deficient as compared to the harm suffered." *Id.*

While the School District focuses the majority of its arguments on why Ash's harm is not irreparable, it also argues that any harm he has allegedly suffered can be remedied by monetary damages. We are not convinced. While monetary damages are used to compensate plaintiffs in tort actions, in those situations the damages relate to a past event, where the harm was inflicted on the plaintiff through negligence or something comparable. But this case is not the typical tort action, as Ash has alleged *prospective* harm. He has asserted that the policy caused him to contemplate suicide, a claim that was credited by the expert report of Dr. Budge. We cannot say that this potential harm — his suicide — can be compensated by monetary damages. Nor is there an adequate remedy for preventable "life-long diminished well-being and life-functioning." Therefore, we reject the School District's analogy to tort damages and find that Ash adequately established that there was no adequate remedy of law available.

3. Likelihood of Success on Merits

A party moving for preliminary injunctive relief need not demonstrate a likelihood of absolute success on the merits. Instead, he must only show that his chances to succeed on his claims are "better than negligible." *Cooper v. Salazar*, 196 F.3d 809, 813 (7th Cir. 1999). This is a low threshold. *U.S. Army Corps of Eng'rs*, 667 F.3d at 782. Ash's Amended Complaint contains two claims — one pursuant to Title IX and the other pursuant to the Equal Protection Clause of the Fourteenth Amendment. We will discuss each claim in turn.

i. Title IX Claim

Title IX provides that no person "shall, on the basis of sex, be excluded from participation in, be denied the benefits of, or be subjected to discrimination under any educational program or activity receiving Federal financial assistance...." 20 U.S.C. § 1681(a); *see also* 34 C.F.R. § 106.31(a). Covered institutions are, p.1047 therefore, among other things, prohibited from: (1) providing different aid, benefits, or services; (2) denying aid, benefits, or services; and (3) subjecting any person to separate or different rules, sanctions, or treatment on the basis of sex. *See* 34 C.F.R. § 106.31(b)(2)-(4). Pursuant to the statute's regulations, an institution may provide separate, but comparable, bathroom, shower, and locker facilities. *Id.* § 106.33. The parties agree that the School District receives federal funds and is a covered institution.

The parties' dispute focuses on the coverage of Title IX and whether under the statute, a transgender student who alleges discrimination on the basis of his or her transgender status can state a claim of sex discrimination. Neither the statute nor the regulations define the term "sex." Also absent from the statute is the term "biological," which the School District maintains is a necessary modifier. Therefore, we turn to the Supreme Court and our case law for guidance.

First, under our own case law, we do not see a barrier to Ash's Title IX claim. Although not as often as some of our sister circuits, this court has looked to Title VII when construing Title IX. *See e.g., Smith v. Metro. Sch. Dist. Perry Twp.,* 128 F.3d 1014, 1023 (7th Cir. 1997) (noting that "it is helpful to look to Title VII to determine whether the alleged sexual harassment is severe and pervasive enough to constitute illegal discrimination on the basis of sex for purposes of Title IX."). The School District contends that we should do so here, and relies on our reasoning in *Ulane v. Eastern, Airlines, Inc.,* 742 F.2d 1081 (7th Cir. 1984), to conclude that Ash cannot state a claim under Title IX as a matter of law. Other courts have agreed with the School District's position. *See Etsitty v. Utah Transit Auth.,* 502 F.3d 1215, 1221 (10th Cir. 2007) (relying upon *Ulane* to find that transsexuals are not a protected class under Title VII); *Johnston v. Univ. of Pittsburgh of Commw. Sys. of Higher Educ.,* 97 F.Supp.3d 657, 675-76 (W.D. Pa. 2015) (relying upon *Ulane* to find that a transgender student cannot state a claim under Title IX). We disagree.

In *Ulane,* we noted in dicta that Title VII's prohibition on sex discrimination "implies that it is unlawful to discriminate against women because they are women and against men because they are men." 742 F.2d at 1085. We then looked to the lack of legislative history regarding the meaning of the term "sex" in Title VII and concluded that this prohibition should be "given a narrow, traditional interpretation, which would also exclude transsexuals." *Id.* at 1085-86. This reasoning, however, cannot and does not foreclose Ash and other transgender students from bringing sex-discrimination claims based upon a theory of sex-stereotyping as articulated four years later by the Supreme Court in *Price Waterhouse v. Hopkins,* 490 U.S. 228, 109 S.Ct. 1775, 104 L.Ed.2d 268 (1989).

In *Price Waterhouse*, a plurality of the Supreme Court and two justices concurring in the judgment, found that the plaintiff had adequately alleged that her employer, in violation of Title VII, had discriminated against her for being too masculine. The plurality further emphasized that "we are beyond the day when an employer could evaluate employees by assuming or insisting that they matched the stereotype associated with their group." *Id.* at 251, 109 S.Ct. 1775. Thus, the Court embraced a broad view of Title VII, as Congress "intended to strike at the entire spectrum of disparate treatment of men and women resulting from sex stereotypes." *Id.; see also Sprogis v. United Air Lines, Inc.*, 444 F.2d 1194, 1198 (7th Cir. 1971) ("In forbidding employers to discriminate against individuals p.1048 because of their sex, Congress intended to strike at the entire spectrum of disparate treatment of men and women resulting from sex stereotypes.").

The Supreme Court further embraced an expansive view of Title VII in *Oncale v. Sundowner Offshore Services, Inc.*, 523 U.S. 75, 118 S.Ct. 998, 140 L.Ed.2d 201 (1998), where Justice Scalia, writing for a unanimous Court, declared that "statutory prohibitions often go beyond the principal evil to cover reasonably comparable evils, and it is ultimately the provisions of our laws rather than the principal concerns of our legislators by which we are governed." *Id.* at 79, 118 S.Ct. 998.

Following *Price Waterhouse*, this court and others have recognized a cause of action under Title VII when an adverse action is taken because of an employee's failure to conform to sex stereotypes. *See, e.g., Doe v. City of Belleville*, 119 F.3d 563, 580-81 (7th Cir. 1997), *vacated on other grounds*, 523 U.S. 1001, 118 S.Ct. 1183, 140 L.Ed.2d 313 (1998); *Christiansen v. Omnicom Grp., Inc.*, 852 F.3d 195, 201 (2d Cir. 2017); *Bibby v. Phila. Coca Cola Bottling Co.*, 260 F.3d 257, 263-64 (3d Cir. 2001); *Nichols v. Azteca Rest. Enters., Inc.*, 256 F.3d 864, 874-75 (9th Cir. 2001); *Higgins v. New Balance Athletic Shoe, Inc.*, 194 F.3d 252, 261 n.4 (1st Cir. 1999). Our most recent application occurred when, sitting *en banc*, we held that a homosexual plaintiff can state a Title VII claim of sex discrimination based upon a theory of sex-stereotyping. *Hively v. Ivy Tech Cmty. Coll. of Ind.*, 853 F.3d 339, 351-52 (7th Cir. 2017) (holding that a homosexual plaintiff may state a claim for sex-based discrimination under Title VII under either a sex stereotyping theory or under the associational theory).

The School District argues that even under a sex-stereotyping theory, Ash cannot demonstrate a likelihood of success on his Title IX claim because its policy is not based on whether the student behaves, walks, talks, or dresses in a manner that is inconsistent with any preconceived notions of sex stereotypes. Instead, it contends that as a matter of law, requiring a biological female to use the women's bathroom is not sex-stereotyping. However, this view is too narrow.

By definition, a transgender individual does not conform to the sex-based stereotypes of the sex that he or she was assigned at birth. We are not alone in this belief. *See Glenn v. Brumby*, 663 F.3d 1312 (11th Cir. 2011). In *Glenn*, the Eleventh Circuit noted that "[a] person is defined as transgender precisely because of the perception that his or her behavior transgresses gender stereotypes." *Id.* at 1316. The Eleventh Circuit reiterated this conclusion in a *per curiam* unpublished opinion, noting that "sex discrimination includes discrimination against a transgender person for gender nonconformity." *Chavez v. Credit Nation Auto Sales, LLC*, 641 Fed.Appx. 883, 884 (11th Cir. 2016) (unpub.).

The Sixth Circuit has also recognized a transgender plaintiff's ability to bring a sex-stereotyping claim. In *Smith v. City of Salem,* 378 F.3d 566 (6th Cir. 2004), the plaintiff was diagnosed with Gender Identity Disorder, a condition later renamed Gender Dysphoria. Born a male, the plaintiff began to present at work with a more feminine appearance and mannerisms. He[5] alleged in his complaint that as a result, his employer schemed to take action against him and ultimately subjected him to a pretextual suspension in violation of Title VII. While the district court concluded that because the plaintiff was transsexual he was not entitled to Title VII's protections, the Sixth Circuit disagreed.

Instead, the Sixth Circuit noted that *Price Waterhouse* established that the prohibition on sex discrimination "encompasses both the biological differences between men and women, and gender discrimination, that is, discrimination based on a failure to conform to stereotypical gender norms." *Id.* at 573 (citing *Price Waterhouse,* 490 U.S. at 251, 109 S.Ct. 1775). If Title VII prohibits an employer from discriminating against a woman for dressing too masculine, then, the court reasoned, Title VII likewise prohibits an employer from discriminating against a man who dresses in a way that it perceives as too feminine. In both examples the discrimination would not occur but for the victim's sex, in violation of Title VII. *Id.* at 574. Therefore, the plaintiff's status as transsexual was not a bar to his claim.

Several district courts have adopted this reasoning, finding that a transgender plaintiff can state a claim under Title VII for sex discrimination on the basis of a sex-stereotyping theory. *See Valentine Ge v. Dun & Bradstreet, Inc.,* No. 6:15-CV-1029-ORL-41GJK, 2017 WL 347582, at *4 (M.D. Fla. Jan. 24, 2017); *Roberts v. Clark Cty. Sch. Dist.,* 215 F.Supp.3d 1001, 1014 (D. Nev. 2016), *reconsideration denied,* No. 2:15-CV-00388-JAD-PAL, 2016 WL 6986346 (D. Nev. Nov. 28, 2016); *Fabian v. Hosp. of Cent. Conn.,* 172 F.Supp.3d 509, 527 (D. Conn. 2016); *E.E.O.C. v. R.G. & G.R. Harris Funeral Homes, Inc.,* 100 F.Supp.3d 594, 603 (E.D. Mich. 2015); *Lopez v. River Oaks Imaging & Diagnostic Grp., Inc.,* 542 F.Supp.2d 653, 660 (S.D. Tex. 2008); *Schroer v. Billington,* 577 F.Supp.2d 293, 305 (D.D.C. 2008). Further, courts have applied *Price Waterhouse* and found that transgender plaintiffs can state claims based upon a sex-stereotyping theory under the Gender Motivated Violence Act, *Schwenk v. Hartford,* 204 F.3d 1187, 1200 (9th Cir. 2000), and the Equal Credit Opportunity Act, *Rosa v. Park W. Bank & Trust Co.,* 214 F.3d 213, 215-16 (1st Cir. 2000).

Here, however, the School District argues that this reasoning flies in the face of Title IX, as Congress has not explicitly added transgender status as a protected characteristic to either Title VII or Title IX, despite having opportunities to do so. *See e.g.,* Student Non-Discrimination Act of 2015 S. 439 114th Cong. (2015). The Supreme Court has rejected this argument, stating that congressional inaction "lacks persuasive significance because several equally tenable inferences may be drawn from such inaction, including the inference that the existing legislation already incorporated the offered change." *Pension Benefit. Guar. Corp. v. LTV Corp.,* 496 U.S. 633, 650, 110 S.Ct. 2668, 110 L.Ed.2d 579 (1990) (quoting *United States v. Wise,* 370 U.S. 405, 411, 82 S.Ct. 1354, 8 L.Ed.2d 590 (1962)) (internal quotation marks omitted); *see also Hively,* 853 F.3d at 344 ("[I]t is simply too difficult to draw a reliable inference from these truncated legislative initiatives to rest our opinion on them."). Therefore, Congressional inaction is not determinative.

Rather, Ash can demonstrate a likelihood of success on the merits of his claim because he has alleged that the School District has denied him access to the boys' restroom because he is transgender. A policy that requires an individual to use a bathroom that does not conform with his or her gender identity punishes that individual for his or her gender non-conformance, which in turn violates Title IX. The School District's policy also subjects Ash, as a transgender student, to different rules, sanctions, and treatment than non-transgender students, in violation of Title p.1050 IX. Providing a gender-neutral alternative is not sufficient to relieve the School District from liability, as it is the policy itself which violates the Act. Further, based on the record here, these gender-neutral alternatives were not true alternatives because of their distant location to Ash's classrooms and the increased stigmatization they caused Ash. Rather, the School District only continued to treat Ash differently when it provided him with access to these gender-neutral bathrooms because he was the only student given access.

And, while the School District repeatedly asserts that Ash may not "unilaterally declare" his gender, this argument misrepresents Ash's claims and dismisses his transgender status. This is not a case where a student has merely announced that he is a different gender. Rather, Ash has a medically diagnosed and documented condition. Since his diagnosis, he has consistently lived in accordance with his gender identity. This law suit demonstrates that the decision to do so was not without cost or pain. Therefore, we find that Ash has sufficiently established a probability of success on the merits of his Title IX claim.

ii. Equal Protection Claim

Although we are mindful of our duty to avoid rendering unnecessary constitutional decisions, *ISI Int'l, Inc. v. Borden Ladner Gervais LLP,* 256 F.3d 548, 552 (7th Cir. 2001), *as amended* (July 2, 2001), we will address Ash's Equal Protection claim as the district court determined that Ash also demonstrated an adequate probability of success on the claim to justify the preliminary injunction. The Equal Protection Clause of the Fourteenth Amendment "is essentially a direction that all persons similarly situated should be treated alike." *City of Cleburne v. Cleburne Living Ctr.,* 473 U.S. 432, 439, 105 S.Ct. 3249, 87 L.Ed.2d 313 (1985) (citing *Plyler v. Doe,* 457 U.S. 202, 216, 102 S.Ct. 2382, 72 L.Ed.2d 786 (1982)). It therefore, protects against intentional and arbitrary discrimination. *See Vill. of Willowbrook v. Olech,* 528 U.S. 562, 564, 120 S.Ct. 1073, 145 L.Ed.2d 1060 (2000) (per curiam). Generally, state action is presumed to be lawful and will be upheld if the classification drawn by the statute is rationally related to a legitimate state interest. *City of Cleburne,* 473 U.S. at 440, 105 S.Ct. 3249.

The rational basis test, however, does not apply when a classification is based upon sex. Rather, a sex-based classification is subject to heightened scrutiny, as sex "frequently bears no relation to the ability to perform or contribute to society." *Id.* at 440-41, 105 S.Ct. 3249 (quoting *Frontiero v. Richardson,* 411 U.S. 677, 686, 93 S.Ct. 1764, 36 L.Ed.2d 583 (1973)) (internal quotation marks omitted); *see also J.E.B. v. Alabama ex rel. T.B.,* 511 U.S. 127, 135, 114 S.Ct. 1419, 128 L.Ed.2d 89 (1994). When a sex-based classification is used, the burden rests with the state to demonstrate that its proffered justification is "exceedingly persuasive." *United States v. Virginia,* 518 U.S. 515, 533, 116 S.Ct. 2264, 135 L.Ed.2d 735 (1996); *see also Hayden ex rel. A.H. v.*

Greensburg Cmty. Sch. Corp., 743 F.3d 569, 577 (7th Cir. 2014). This requires the state to show that the "classification serves important governmental objectives and that the discriminatory means employed are substantially related to the achievement of those objectives." *Virginia,* 518 U.S. at 524, 116 S.Ct. 2264 (internal quotation marks omitted). It is not sufficient to provide a hypothesized or *post hoc* justification created in response to litigation. *Id.* at 533, 116 S.Ct. 2264. Nor may the justification be based upon overbroad generalizations about sex. *Id.* Instead, the justification must be genuine. *Id.*

p.1051 If a state actor cannot defend a sex-based classification by relying upon overbroad generalizations, it follows that sex-based stereotypes are also insufficient to sustain a classification. *See J.E.B.,* 511 U.S. at 138, 114 S.Ct. 1419 (rejecting the state's reliance on sex-based stereotypes as a defense to the discriminatory use of peremptory challenges during jury selection); *see Glenn v. Brumby,* 663 F.3d 1312, 1318 (11th Cir. 2011) ("All persons, whether transgender or not, are protected from discrimination on the basis of gender stereotype.").

As a threshold matter, we must determine what standard of review applies to Ash's claim. The School District urges us to apply the rational basis test, arguing that transgender status is not a suspect class. Applying that test, the School District contends that its policy is presumptively constitutional and that requiring students to use facilities corresponding to their birth sex to protect the privacy of all students is a rational basis for its policy. So, the School District maintains that Ash cannot demonstrate a likelihood of success on his Equal Protection Claim.

Ash disagrees. He argues that transgender status should be entitled to heightened scrutiny in its own right, as transgender people are a minority who have historically been subjected to discrimination based upon the immutable characteristics of their gender identities. Alternatively, he argues that even if transgender status is not afforded heightened scrutiny in its own right, the School District's bathroom policy creates a sex-based classification such that heightened scrutiny should apply.

There is no denying that transgender individuals face discrimination, harassment, and violence because of their gender identity. According to a report issued by the National Center for Transgender Equality, 78% of students who identify as transgender or as gender non-conformant, report being harassed while in grades K-12. *See* Jaime M. Grant et al., *Injustice at Every Turn: A Report of the National Transgender Discrimination Survey,* Nat'l Center for Transgender Equality, at 33 (2011), *available at* http://www. transequality.org/sites/default/files/docs/ resources/NTDS_Report.pdf. These same individuals in K-12 also reported an alarming rate of assault, with 35% reporting physical assault and 12% reporting sexual assault. *Id.* As a result, 15% of transgender and gender non-conformant students surveyed made the decision to drop out. *Id.* These statistics are alarming. But this case does not require us to reach the question of whether transgender status is per se entitled to heightened scrutiny. It is enough to stay that, just as in *Price Waterhouse,* the record for the preliminary injunction shows sex stereotyping. We note as well that there is no requirement that every girl, or every boy, be subjected to the same stereotyping. It is enough that Ash has experienced this form of sex discrimination.

Here, the School District's policy cannot be stated without referencing sex, as the School District decides which bathroom a student may use based upon the sex listed on the student's birth certificate. This policy is inherently based upon a sex-classification and heightened review applies. Further, the School District argues that since it treats all boys and girls the same, it does not violate the Equal Protection Clause. This is untrue. Rather, the School District treats transgender students like Ash, who fail to conform to the sex-based stereotypes associated with their assigned sex at birth, differently. These students are disciplined under the School District's bathroom policy if they choose to use a bathroom that conforms to their gender identity. This places the burden p.1052 on the School District to demonstrate that its justification for its bathroom policy is not only genuine, but also "exceedingly persuasive." *See Virginia,* 518 U.S. at 533, 116 S.Ct. 2264. This burden has not been met here.

The School District defends its bathroom policy by claiming it needs to protect the privacy rights of all 22,160 students.[6] The mere presence of a transgender student in the bathroom, the School District argues, infringes upon the privacy rights of other students with whom he or she does not share biological anatomy. While this court certainly recognizes that the School District has a legitimate interest in ensuring bathroom privacy rights are protected, this interest must be weighed against the facts of the case and not just examined in the abstract, to determine whether this justification is genuine.

What the record demonstrates here is that the School District's privacy argument is based upon sheer conjecture and abstraction. For nearly six months, Ash used the boys' bathroom while at school and school-sponsored events without incident or complaint from another student. In fact, it was only when *a teacher* witnessed Ash washing his hands in the restroom that his bathroom usage once more became an issue in the School District's eyes. And while at oral argument, the School District asserted that it had received just one complaint from a parent, this is insufficient to support its position that its policy is required to protect the privacy rights of each and every student. Counsel for the School District cited to Ash's Amended Complaint for this assertion. The Amended Complaint, however, states that "some parents and other Kenosha residents began to speak out in opposition to Ash's right to use the boys' restrooms." Am. Comp. ¶ 77. It further states that several community members spoke at a School Board meeting and voiced their opposition to a policy that would allow transgender students to use gender-appropriate restrooms. *See id.* ("One parent told the Board that he was opposed to permitting transgender students to use gender-appropriate restrooms...."). Nonetheless, neither party has offered any evidence or even alleged that the School District has received any complaints *from other students.* This policy does nothing to protect the privacy rights of each individual student vis-à-vis students who share similar anatomy and it ignores the practical reality of how Ash, as a transgender boy, uses the bathroom: by entering a stall and closing the door.

A transgender student's presence in the restroom provides no more of a risk to other students' privacy rights than the presence of an overly curious student of the same biological sex who decides to sneak glances at his or her classmates performing their bodily functions. Or for that matter, any other student who uses the bathroom at the same time. Common sense tells us that the communal restroom is a place where individuals act in a discreet manner to protect their privacy and those who have true privacy concerns are able to utilize a stall. Nothing in the record suggests that the bathrooms at Tremper High School are particularly susceptible to an intrusion upon an individual's privacy. Further, if the School District's concern is that a child will be in the bathroom with another child who does not look anatomically the same, then it would seem that separate bathrooms also would be appropriate for pre-pubescent and post-pubescent children who do not look alike anatomically. But the School District has not drawn this line. Therefore, this court agrees with the district court that the School District's privacy arguments are insufficient to establish an exceedingly persuasive justification for the classification.

Additionally, at oral argument, counsel for the School District clarified that the only way that Ash would be permitted to use the boys' restroom would be if he were to present the school with a birth certificate that designated his sex as male. But it is important to keep in mind that the School District has not provided a written copy of the policy. Nor is it clear that one even exists. And, before this litigation, Ash's mother was never told that she needed to produce a birth certificate. Instead, when she asked the School District to permit him to use the boys' restroom, the school's assistant principal told her that Ash could use the boys' restroom only if his sex was changed in the school's official records. To do so, Ash would need to submit unspecified legal or medical "documentation." Despite explaining to the assistant principal that Ash was too young to have sex-reassignment surgery and presenting the School District with two letters from Ash's pediatrician, Ash was still not allowed to use the boys' restroom.

Further, it is unclear that the sex marker on a birth certificate can even be used as a true proxy for an individual's biological sex. The marker does not take into account an individual's chromosomal makeup, which is also a key component of one's biological sex. Therefore, one's birth certificate could reflect a male sex, while the individual's chromosomal makeup reflects another. It is also unclear what would happen if an individual is born with the external genitalia of two sexes, or genitalia that is ambiguous in nature. In those cases, it is clear that the marker on the birth certificate would not adequately account for or reflect one's biological sex, which would have to be determined by considering more than what was listed on the paper.

Moreover, while it is true that in Wisconsin an individual may only change his or her designated sex on a birth certificate after completing a surgical reassignment, *see* Wis. Stat. Ann. § 69.15(4), this is not universally the case. For example, as Ash's counsel pointed out during oral argument, in Minnesota, an individual may amend his or her birth certificate to reflect his or her gender identity without surgical reassignment. *See Requirements for documents submitted to support the amendment of a birth record,* MINNESOTA DEP'T OF HEALTH, http://www.health.state.mn.us/divs/chs/osr/reqdocs.html#gender (last visited May 30, 2017). Therefore, a student who is born in Minnesota and begins his transition there, obtaining a modified birth certificate as part of the process, could move to Kenosha and be permitted to use the boys' restroom in one of the School District's schools even though he retains female anatomy.

Additionally, the policy fails to account for the fact that a new student registering with the School District need not even provide a birth certificate. Rather, the School District requires that each new student provide either a birth certificate *or* a passport. *See Registration,* KENOSHA UNIFIED SCH. DIST., http://www.kusd.edu/registration (last visited May 30, 2017). Pursuant to the United States Department of State's policies, an individual may apply for and receive a passport that reflects his or her gender identity by presenting a signed medical certification from a physician. *See Gender Designation Change,* U.S. DEP'T OF STATE, https://travel.state.gov/content/passports/en/passports/information/gender.html#change (last visited May 30, 2017). This process does not p.1054 require that an individual have undergone sex-reassignment surgery. Therefore, the School District's reliance upon a birth certificate's sex-marker demonstrates the arbitrary nature of the policy; so, Ash has met the low threshold of demonstrating a probability of success on his Equal Protection Claim.

4. Balance of Harms Favors Ash

Having already determined that the district court did not err in finding that Ash will suffer irreparable harm absent preliminary injunctive relief, we now must look at whether granting preliminary injunctive relief will harm the School District and the public as a whole. Once a moving party has met its burden of establishing the threshold requirements for a preliminary injunction, the court must balance the harms faced by both parties and the public as a whole. *See Girl Scouts of Manitou Council, Inc. v. Girl Scouts of U.S. of Am., Inc.,* 549 F.3d 1079, 1100 (7th Cir. 2008); *see also Turnell v. CentiMark Corp.,* 796 F.3d 656, 662 (7th Cir. 2015). This is done on a "sliding scale" measuring the balance of harms against the moving party's likelihood of success. *Turnell,* 796 F.3d at 662. The more likely he is to succeed on the merits, the less the scale must tip in his favor. *Id.* The converse, however, also is true: the less likely he is to win, the more the balance of harms must weigh in his favor for an injunction to issue. *Id.* Substantial deference is given to the district court's analysis of the balancing of harms. *Id.*

The School District argues that the district court erred in determining that the balance of the harms weighed in favor of granting the injunction because it ignored the fact that the harm extends to 22,160 students in the School District whose privacy rights are at risk by allowing a transgender student to utilize a bathroom that does not correspond with his biological sex. Granting the injunction, the School District continues, also irreparably harmed these students' parents, who are now denied the right to direct the education and upbringing of their children. Additionally, the School District asserts that the injunction harms the public as a whole, since it forces other school districts nationwide to contemplate whether they must change their policies and alter their facilities or risk being found out of compliance with Title IX. Noncompliance places their federal funding at risk. Based upon this record, however, we find the School District's arguments unpersuasive.

The School District has not demonstrated that it will suffer any harm from having to comply with the district court's preliminary injunction order. Nor has it established that the public as a whole will suffer harm. As noted above, before seeking injunctive relief, Ash used the bathroom for nearly six months *without incident.* The School District has not produced any evidence that any students have ever complained about Ash's presence in the boys' restroom. Nor have they demonstrated that Ash's presence has actually caused an invasion of any other student's privacy. And while the School District claims that preliminary injunctive relief infringes upon parents' ability to direct the education of their children, it offers no evidence that a parent has ever asserted this right. These claims are all speculative.

We are further convinced that the district court did not err in finding that this balance weighed in favor of granting the injunction when considering the statements made by *amici*, who are school administrators from twenty-one states and the District of Columbia. Together, these administrators are responsible for educating approximately 1.4 million students. Each administrator has experience implementing inclusive bathroom policies in their respective schools, and each has grappled with the same privacy concerns that the School District raises here. These administrators uniformly agree that the frequently-raised and hypothetical concerns about a policy that permits a student to utilize a bathroom consistent with his or her gender identity have simply not materialized. Rather, in their combined experience, all students' needs are best served when students are treated equally.

Although the School District argues that implementing an inclusive policy will result in the demise of gender-segregated facilities in schools, the *amici* note that this has not been the case. In fact, these administrators have found that allowing transgender students to use facilities that align with their gender identity has actually reinforced the concept of separate facilities for boys and girls. When considering the experience of this group in light of the record here, which is virtually devoid of any complaints or harm caused to the School District, its students, or the public as a whole, it is clear that the district court did not err in balancing the harms.

III. CONCLUSION

Appellants' motion to have this court assert pendent appellant jurisdiction over the district court's denial of Appellants' Motion to Dismiss is DENIED. The district court's order granting the Appellee's motion for a preliminary injunction is AFFIRMED.

[1] We will refer to the Plaintiff-Appellee as "Ash," rather than by his last name, as this is how he refers to himself throughout his brief.

[2] We will refer to the School District's decision to deny Ash access to the boys' restroom as a "policy," although any such "policy" is unwritten and its exact boundaries are unclear.

[3] Because Ash is a minor without a duly appointed representative, pursuant to Rule 17 of the Federal Rules of Civil Procedure, he may assert these claims only through a "next friend" or guardian ad litem.

[4] We take judicial notice of the Diagnostic and Statistical Manual pursuant to Rule 201 of the Federal Rules of Evidence.

[5] We will use the masculine pronoun to refer to the *Smith* plaintiff for the purpose of clarity, as this is how the Sixth Circuit referred to the *Smith* plaintiff throughout its opinion.

[6] We note that the School District's reliance upon the privacy interests of all of its 22,160 students is odd given that the preliminary injunction order only pertains to

Ash, a student at one of its high schools. Many of the School District's students attend schools other than Tremper and are therefore, totally unaffected by the district court's order.

EIGHTH CIRCUIT DECISIONS
Title IX

Rossley v. Drake University, 958 F. 3d 679 (8th Cir. 2020) 193
Maher v. Iowa State University, 915 F. 3d 1210 (8th Cir. 2019) 201
Doe v. Dardanelle School Dist., 928 F. 3d 722 (8th Cir. 2019) 205
DM by Bao Xiong v. MN State High School League, 917 F. 3d 994 (8th Cir. 2019) 211
Pearson v. Logan University, 937 F. 3d 1119 (8th Cir. 2019) 219
Fryberger v. University of Arkansas, 889 F. 3d 471 (8th Cir. 2018) 229
KT v. Culver-Stockton College, 865 F. 3d 1054 (8th Cir. 2017) 235
Roe v. St. Louis University, 746 F. 3d 874 (8th Cir. 2014) 241

958 F.3d 679 (2020)

Tom ROSSLEY, Plaintiff Appellant
v.
DRAKE UNIVERSITY; Drake University Board of Trustees, Defendants Appellees.

No. 19-1392.

United States Court of Appeals, Eighth Circuit.
Submitted: March 12, 2020.
Filed: May 4, 2020.

Appeal from United States District Court for the Southern District of Iowa — Des Moines

Amy Kathryn Davis, David Harris Goldman, BABICH & GOLDMAN, Des Moines, IA, Andrew Miltenberg, Gabrielle M. Vinci, Diana Warshow, NESENOFF & MILTENBERG, New York, NY, for Plaintiff-Appellant.

Mary Elizabeth Funk, Frank Boyd Harty, NYEMASTER & GOODE, Des Moines, IA, Frances M. Haas, Attorney, NYEMASTER & GOODE, Cedar Rapids, IA, for Defendants-Appellees.

Before ERICKSON, GRASZ, and KOBES, Circuit Judges.

GRASZ, Circuit Judge.

Tom Rossley served on the Drake University (the "University") Board of Trustees ("Board") for many years before the Board voted to remove him because of a purported conflict of interest. He sued the University and the Board, alleging Title IX retaliation, disability retaliation, and breach of contract. The district court[1] dismissed his Title IX retaliation claim on the pleadings, and granted summary judgment to the University and the Board on the contract and disability retaliation claims. Rossley now appeals, and we affirm.

I. Background

Tom Rossley is an alumnus and former Trustee of Drake University, a non-profit, private university in Des Moines, Iowa. In the fall of 2015, the University investigated an allegation of sexual misconduct against Rossley's son, Thomas Rossley, Jr. In the course of the Title IX investigation, Rossley Jr. was found responsible for the alleged sexual misconduct, and after an appeal process, was expelled from the University.

During this process, Rossley was critical of how the University handled his son's case. Rossley made phone calls, sent emails, and participated in conversations with other Board members, University alumni, University administrators, and donors about the situation. Specifically, Rossley complained that the University did not accommodate his son's disabilities during its investigation. Since childhood, Rossley

Jr. suffered from ADHD, anxiety, and language-based disabilities, which "inhibit his ability to communicate effectively." Because Rossley's communications about his son's case form the basis of the Board's actions, we will provide an overview of the exchanges between Rossley, the University, and the Board.

In March of 2016, Rossley sent an email to the University's Vice President of Finance, as well as Rossley's wife, and the University's bond attorney, stating "please let this email serve as my disclosure that my son may be initiating litigation against Drake University in the event that his hearing verdict is not overturned on appeal." When this email was sent, Rossley Jr.'s expulsion appeal was still pending.

Then, in April, Rossley emailed the Dean of Students and the Chairman of the Board with a list of nine specific criticisms of the Dean and the University's investigation of his son. Rossley also addressed an earlier request made by the University that he avoid a popular off-campus establishment when he was in town due to an alleged "staring" incident between Rossley and a student who worked there. This student was a witness in his son's investigation. The tone of Rossley's email was dismissive and mocking. A few weeks later, Rossley sent another email to the Board as well as members of the University's faculty and administration, in which he criticized the University for failing to accommodate his son and selectively enforcing the University's sexual assault policy and Title IX.

A few days after this second email, and during an annual alumni event, Rossley spoke with the Board Chairman and another Board member. They asked Rossley to stop speaking to alumni and donors about his son's disciplinary process and the University's compliance with the law. Rossley admitted to having spoken to at least three alumni or donors in attendance at the event. Later, during his deposition, Rossley expanded the list of persons with whom he discussed his son's case to include "literally hundreds of people that [he] had conversations with, either directly or indirectly." The Chairman and Board member told Rossley that if he wanted to remain a Trustee he would need to "disassociate... from [his] son's issues" and stop talking about the matter. At the time, Rossley agreed to disassociate himself and later sent an "assurance" email recognizing the conflict of interest.

In the same assurance email, Rossley informed the Board his son had engaged the services of an attorney who would help his son "take[ ] his case to the next stage," and "to address this in the courts and, if necessary, the public arena." The Board of Trustee's Board Affairs Committee ("BAC") advised Rossley that his actions created a conflict of interest under the University Bylaws. The BAC was concerned that Rossley could not discharge his fiduciary duty to the Board while also advocating for his son as a parent. To resolve this conflict, the BAC asked Rossley to take a leave of absence from the Board. Rossley responded with a lengthy letter denying a conflict of interest and refusing to take a leave. He also included proposed resolutions, including expunging his son's expulsion, granting his son a diploma p.683 immediately, compensating his son for lost income, and offering his son direct admission to the University's MBA program.

The University president sent an email to the Board advising it to hold a special meeting to vote on how to address Rossley's conflict of interest related to his son's Title IX case. The Board met, determined Rossley had a conflict of interest, and referred the matter back to the BAC to recommend a course of action. The BAC determined Rossley's conflict of interest was sufficient to amount to a "for cause" removal from the Board, and recommended removal upon a vote of the Board. The Board voted to remove Rossley due to his "pervasive conflict of interest," and "his insistence on using his position as trustee to advocate" on his son's behalf, who had "certainly threatened litigation" against the University.

In response, Rossley sued the University and the Board asserting five causes of action. After the district court granted various motions to dismiss, motions for judgment on the pleadings, and summary judgment motions, Rossley now appeals the dismissal of his Title IX retaliation, disability retaliation, and breach of contract claims.

II. Analysis

A. Title IX Retaliation

We first consider the district court's dismissal on the pleadings of Rossley's Title IX retaliation claim against the University. "We review a district court's grant of judgment on the pleadings *de novo.*" *Levitt v. Merck & Co., Inc.,* 914 F.3d 1169, 1171 (8th Cir. 2019). "The movant has the burden of 'clearly establish[ing] that there are no material issues of fact and that [he] is entitled to judgment as a matter of law.'" *Id.* (first alteration in original) (quoting *Porous Media Corp. v. Pall Corp.,* 186 F.3d 1077, 1079 (8th Cir. 1999)). We must view all facts pled as true and grant all reasonable inferences in Rossley's favor. *Id.*

The district court dismissed Rossley's Title IX retaliation claim against the University for lack of standing. Under Title IX "[n]o person in the United States shall, on the basis of sex, be excluded from participation in, be denied the benefits of, or be subjected to discrimination under any education program or activity receiving Federal financial assistance." 20 U.S.C. § 1681(a). The Supreme Court has interpreted Title IX to provide a private right of action for students complaining about teachers or peer-to-peer sexual harassment; it also allows individuals employed by federally-funded institutions to sue their employers. *See Davis ex rel. LaShonda D. v. Monroe Cty. Bd. of Educ.,* 526 U.S. 629, 643, 119 S.Ct. 1661, 143 L.Ed.2d 839 (1999) (finding a plaintiff could sue under Title IX for student-on-student sexual harassment); *Gebser v. Lago Vista Indep. Sch. Dist.,* 524 U.S. 274, 290-91, 118 S.Ct. 1989, 141 L.Ed.2d 277 (1998) (finding a student could sue for sexual harassment by a teacher); *N. Haven Bd. of Educ. v. Bell,* 456 U.S. 512, 520-21, 102 S.Ct. 1912, 72 L.Ed.2d 299 (1982) (finding employees are covered by Title IX regulations when the employer directly participates in federal programs or benefits from federal grants, loans, or contracts). Additionally, some federal courts have entertained causes of action for parents on behalf of their minor children or deceased adult children under Title IX. *See, e.g., Lopez v. Regents of Univ. of Cal.,* 5 F. Supp. 3d 1106, 1114 (N.D. Cal. 2013) (noting "parents *do* have standing to assert Title IX claims on behalf of a student," but "in general, non-students such as parents do not have a *personal* claim under Title IX.").

Title IX also protects individuals who suffer retaliation after reporting instances of sex discrimination. *Jackson v. Birmingham Bd. of Educ.,* 544 U.S. 167, 173-74, 125 S.Ct. 1497, 161 L.Ed.2d 361 (2005). The Supreme Court explained in *Jackson* that "[w]here the retaliation occurs because the complainant speaks out about sex discrimination, the 'on the basis of sex' requirement is satisfied." *Id.* at 179, 125 S.Ct. 1497. According to Rossley, this language from *Jackson* indicates that any Title IX advocate has a cause of action when retaliated against, regardless of whether the advocate is an employee, student, or individual subjected to discrimination under an education program or activity. We disagree. Retaliation "on the basis of sex" is not a sufficient condition for Title IX standing. The plain text of 20 U.S.C. § 1681(a) provides protection for persons from actions taken "on the basis of sex" only if it causes the prospective plaintiff to be "excluded from participation in, be denied the benefits of, or be subjected to discrimination under any education program or activity receiving Federal financial assistance." 20 U.S.C. § 1681(a). Therefore, if the action taken "on the basis of sex" against the person did not exclude, deny, or subject the person to discrimination under an education program or activity, then the action cannot be brought under § 1681(a).

Here, then, we must resolve whether Rossley's removal from the Board constitutes exclusion from or denial of an educational program or activity. Title IX informs us that "program or activity" means "all of the operations of" various institutions, including "a college, university, or other postsecondary institution, or a public system of higher education." 20 U.S.C. § 1687(2)(A). But this broad category of "all of the operations" in § 1687 is narrowed by the descriptor "*education* program or activity" in § 1681(a). Because Rossley does not appeal his action against the Board — only his claim against the University — we need not determine whether a Board of Trustees is an educational program or activity. Even assuming, but not deciding the work of the Board is an educational program, we are left to consider only whether the alleged retaliation can be attributed to the University itself, undoubtedly a federally-funded education program.

Rossley specifically argues the University retaliated against him by: (1) removing him from the Board by a vote; (2) prohibiting him from serving as his son's advocate during the Title IX hearings; and (3) directing him not to visit a tavern near campus. None of these acts support a Title IX retaliation claim against the University.

First, we do not believe Rossley's removal from the Board can support a Title IX retaliation claim against the University. This was an internal vote of a Board of Trustees to remove one of its members. When taking this action, the Board was acting in a manner separate and distinct from the University itself. Therefore, we conclude, as a matter of law, Rossley cannot hold the University liable under Title IX for the separate decision of the Board regarding its own internal affairs.

Next, we consider Rossley's claim that the University retaliated against him by prohibiting him from serving as his son's advocate during the campus hearings. Taking the facts in the amended complaint as true, this claim fails. The amended complaint informs us that the University Code of Conduct allows an accused to have a "personal representative" present during a disciplinary hearing who may, but is not required to be, an attorney. The complaint also informs that Rossley's son had a "newly-retained attorney" p.685 who had "got[ten] involved." Rossley's complaint goes on to assert that his "disabled son [was forced] to be his own advocate and act as his own legal representative." And finally, it asserts that Rossley and his wife were not allowed to attend the hearings. But at no time does the complaint allege that Rossley Jr. requested his father to serve as his "personal representative" under the

Code of Conduct, nor that such a request was denied by the University. Further, even if Rossley was prevented from attending his son's Title IX hearing, the complaint contains no facts showing a nexus between this inability to attend the hearing and Rossley's alleged complaints to the Board. Without such a nexus, a claim of Title IX retaliation by the University must fail as a matter of law.

And finally, we consider Rossley's argument that the University's direction to Rossley to not frequent an off-campus tavern could support a retaliation claim. This request, while perhaps beyond the bounds of the University's power, did not deny Rossley access to any education activity or program. Instead, it was a request to not frequent an establishment outside the University's control. As such, none of the actions Rossley alleges the University took against him in retaliation were part of an education program or activity, and therefore he lacks standing to bring suit under 20 U.S.C. § 1681(a).

Rossley invites our court to expand Title IX's reach such that "any advocate has standing to bring a retaliation claim under Title IX, and to establish such a claim a plaintiff need only show that he was retaliated against *because* he complained of sex discrimination." Because neither the statutory text nor the precedent supports such an expansion, we affirm the district court's dismissal of Rossley's Title IX retaliation claim for lack of standing.

B. Disability Retaliation

We next consider the district court's grant of summary judgment against Rossley's disability retaliation claim. We review the district court's grant of summary judgment de novo, "construing the record in the light most favorable to the nonmoving party." *Wages v. Stuart Mgmt. Corp.*, 798 F.3d 675, 679 (8th Cir. 2015). "Even if not discussed by the district court, we may affirm on any ground supported by the record." *Id.*

The district court granted summary judgement in favor of the University and the Board on Rossley's claim that they retaliated against him in violation of Title III of the Americans with Disabilities Act, § 504 of the Rehabilitation Act, and the Iowa Civil Rights Act. Summary judgment was granted in favor of the University and the Board because the district court concluded Rossley failed to provide any evidence showing the defendants' decisions or actions were pretext for retaliatory animus. On appeal, Rossley argues the district court "did not do justice to [his] retaliation case when it selectively chose to highlight only those actions relied upon by Drake to support its motion for summary judgment," which resulted in a no pretext finding.

For purposes of summary judgment all parties concede that (1) Rossley could state a prima facie case of retaliation, and (2) the University and the Board had a legitimate, non-discriminatory reason for his removal from the Board. Thus, the only question on appeal is whether Rossley could prove the non-discriminatory reason for his removal was actually a pretext for disability retaliation. *Moses v. Dassault Falcon Jet-Wilmington Corp.*, 894 F.3d 911, 924 (8th Cir. 2018). Rossley asserts the district court erred by improperly relying on facts highlighted by the University p.686 and the Board, and that it failed to view the evidence in the light most favorable to him. He also argues the district court erroneously relied on Eighth Circuit precedent in

Mershon v. St. Louis University, because he believes the facts are distinguishable. 442 F.3d 1069 (8th Cir. 2006).

Viewing the facts in the light most favorable to Rossley, we find that the Board voted to remove Rossley from his position of Trustee due to his "[p]ervasive conflict of interest" with the University, and only after Rossley refused to take a leave of absence from the Board. This decision was bolstered by the emails from Rossley intimating he or his son may sue the University. And while Rossley asserts that other Trustees "were previously personally involved in Title IX proceedings at the University" but were not found to have conflicts of interest, we find this suggestion dubious. Nothing suggests these other allegedly personally-involved Trustees sent emails to the University about possible litigation, asked the Board to consider reversing a University disciplinary decision, or spoke to faculty, alumni, and donors about their children's situation. The factual dissimilarities between Rossley and the other interested Board members he identifies do not generate an inference that the Board removed Rossley because of disability-related animus. No question of fact exists for a jury. Rossley has not shown any evidence that the proffered reason — a pervasive conflict of interest — was not the motivation behind his removal from the Board. One cannot reasonably infer that either the University or the Board retaliated against Rossley.

And although it is true the facts in *Mershon* are distinguishable from the actions Rossley and the University undertook here, its principles are nonetheless applicable. In *Mershon,* a former student was prevented from returning to St. Louis University's ("SLU") campus shortly after he allegedly complained of SLU's failure to accommodate his disability. The former student therefore argued that the timing of SLU's action indicated pretext. We disagreed. SLU had explained it prevented the student's return because it believed the student had threatened a professor with violence. 442 F.3d at 1073. The former student's claim that he had complained about his lack of accommodations shortly before his removal did not undercut SLU's proffered explanation, because the university's explanation justified the student's prompt removal. *Id.* at 1075. The same principle applies here. Rossley's removal shortly after his threat of litigation does not undercut the Board's proffered explanation, because the ever-increasing conflict between Rossley's interests and the University's justified Rossley's removal at the time. Therefore the district court did not err in relying on *Mershon* in its analysis.

C. Contract Claim

Finally, Rossley argues the district court erred by granting summary judgment for the University and the Board on his breach of contract claim. Reviewing de novo, we affirm. *Wages,* 798 F.3d at 679.

Under Iowa law, a breach of contract is proven by showing there was capacity to contract, the existence of certain elements of a contract, and a showing of breach. *Magnusson Agency v. Pub. Entity Nat'l Co. Midwest,* 560 N.W.2d 20, 25 (Iowa 1997). At the heart of such a claim is the existence of a contract, which requires an offer and acceptance. *Id.* at 26. "The test for an offer is whether [the alleged offer] induces a reasonable belief in the recipient that he or she can, by accepting, bind the sender." *Id.* "If an offer is not definite, there is no intent to be bound." *Id.*

p.687 Here, Rossley claims he entered a contract with the University and the Board when he was asked to serve as a Trustee of the University and he then accepted this unpaid, volunteer position. But Rossley offered no evidence of a definite contractual offer. He does not recall receiving a written contract governing his service with the Board, nor did he present any evidence of a verbal contract with definite terms or conditions. Rossley admits the Trustees were unpaid volunteers and the Bylaws do not include any specific provisions requiring certain promises in exchange for service on the Board.

Rossley readily concedes he and the other Board members "voluntarily accepted" their positions to serve on the Board of Trustees. Under Iowa law, "if the promisor did not seek anything in exchange for the promise made," then there is no consideration to support the alleged contract. *Margeson v. Artis,* 776 N.W.2d 652, 655-56 (Iowa 2009). The only evidence of an exchange Rossley can point to is that, in return for his service as a Trustee, he was provided with liability insurance as well as free meals and entertainment on certain occasions. However, the mere provision of liability insurance for Trustees without any evidence that such insurance was a part of the bargained for exchange — that is, a part of the offer made to Rossley — is insufficient to constitute contractual consideration under Iowa law. Viewing the evidence in the light most favorable to Rossley, we can only determine that he was asked to serve on the Board as an unpaid, uncompensated volunteer. There was no consideration present in Rossley's alleged contract with the University and the Board, and as such the breach of contract claim fails as a matter of law. The district court properly granted summary judgment.

III. Conclusion

For the foregoing reasons, we affirm the decision of the district court.

---

[1] The Honorable Rebecca Goodgame Ebinger, United States District Judge for the Southern District of Iowa.

915 F.3d 1210 (2019)

Melissa MAHER, Plaintiff-Appellant
v.
IOWA STATE UNIVERSITY, Defendant-Appellee.

No. 18-1559.

United States Court of Appeals, Eighth Circuit.
Submitted: January 15, 2019.
Filed: February 15, 2019.

Appeal from United States District Court for the Southern District of Iowa — Des Moines.

Andrew J. Zbaracki, NEWBROUGH LAW FIRM, Ames, IA, for Plaintiff-Appellant.

Hayley Elizabeth Hanson, Michael T. Raupp, Derek T. Teeter, HUSCH & BLACKWELL, Kansas City, MO, Natasha N. Wilson, ATTORNEY GENERAL'S OFFICE, Des Moines, IA, for Defendant Appellee.

Before GRUENDER, WOLLMAN, and SHEPHERD, Circuit Judges.

GRUENDER, Circuit Judge.

Melissa Maher appeals the district court's[1] grant of Iowa State University's ("ISU") motion for summary judgment. She argues that her action is not barred by the applicable statute of limitations and that ISU was deliberately indifferent. We affirm.

Patrick Whetstone sexually assaulted Maher in March 2014. Both Maher and Whetstone were ISU students at the time. Maher reported the assault to ISU, and ISU began an investigation after Maher identified her assailant in May 2014. ISU subsequently issued a no-contact order that prohibited Whetstone from interacting with Maher.

When Maher returned to ISU in the late summer of 2014, she discovered that Whetstone lived in a building close to her own. Maher, her parents, and her roommate met with ISU administration to discuss a housing change on August 20, 2014. At that meeting, ISU explained that it could not move Whetstone until the investigation and hearing process concluded. ISU presented at least two alternative housing arrangements for Maher.[2] She declined both. On September 19, 2014, ISU's investigative report concluded that Whetstone sexually assaulted Maher. Maher withdrew from ISU shortly after. On July 22, 2015, an administrative judge found that Whetstone was responsible for violating ISU's Code of Conduct and expelled him.

Maher filed a Title IX action against ISU on September 9, 2016. 20 U.S.C. § 1681(a). She argued that she was "excluded from participation in and denied the benefits of the educational programs at ISU as a result of ISU's response to the sexual assault." ISU filed a motion for summary judgment, which the district court granted.

The district court concluded that Maher's claim was time barred by Iowa's two-year statute of limitations because it accrued on August 20, 2014, the day ISU administration met with Maher, her parents, and her roommate to discuss the housing situation.[3] The district court also held that Maher had not raised a material question of fact as to whether ISU was deliberately indifferent and that she had not "demonstrated a genuine issue of material fact as to whether ISU engaged in severe, pervasive, and objectively offensive discrimination against Maher because of her sex." Maher appeals, arguing that her action was not time barred and that there is a genuine dispute as to a material fact—whether ISU was deliberately indifferent.

"We review a district court's grant of summary judgment de novo, viewing the evidence in the light most favorable to the nonmoving party." *Ridenour v. Boehringer Ingelheim Pharm., Inc.,* 679 F.3d 1062, 1065 (8th Cir. 2012). "[A] court shall grant summary judgment if the movant shows that there is no genuine dispute as to any material fact and the movant is entitled to judgment as a matter of law." Fed. R. Civ. P. 56(a).

We assume, without deciding, that Maher's claim survives Iowa's statute of limitations. Thus, we consider Maher's Title IX claim on the merits. Title IX requires that "[n]o person in the United States shall, on the basis of sex, be excluded from participation in, be denied the benefits of, or be subjected to discrimination p.1213 under any education program or activity receiving Federal financial assistance." 20 U.S.C. § 1681(a). Maher's Title IX claim must demonstrate that ISU was "(1) deliberately indifferent (2) to known acts of discrimination (3) which occurr[ed] under its control." *K.T. v. Culver-Stockton College,* 865 F.3d 1054, 1057 (8th Cir. 2017). We conclude that there is no genuine dispute as to whether ISU was deliberately indifferent.

Maher argues that "[i]t wasn't until [ISU] refused to move the man it admitted raped Maher and offered no comparable housing that.... [ISU] was deliberately indifferent to Maher." In other words, Maher argues that ISU's handling of the housing situation became deliberately indifferent only after ISU's investigative report concluded that Whetstone sexually assaulted Maher. A school is deliberately indifferent when its "response to the harassment or lack thereof is clearly unreasonable in light of the known circumstances." *Davis Next Friend LaShonda D. v. Monroe Cty. Bd. of Educ.,* 526 U.S. 629, 648, 119 S.Ct. 1661, 143 L.Ed.2d 839 (1999). "This clearly unreasonable standard is intended to afford flexibility to school administrators." *Estate of Barnwell by and through Barnwell v. Watson,* 880 F.3d 998, 1007 (8th Cir. 2018) (internal quotation marks omitted). "[V]ictims of peer harassment" do not "have a Title IX right to make particular remedial demands." *Davis,* 526 U.S. at 648, 119 S.Ct. 1661.

Before the conclusion of ISU's investigative report, ISU had offered Maher at least two reasonable housing alternatives that would have resolved Maher's objection to the housing situation: a converted housing den or a room at the Memorial Union Hotel. But Maher declined both of those options, and dissatisfaction with the school's response does not mean the school's response can be characterized as deliberate indifference. *See Ostrander v. Duggan,* 341 F.3d 745, 751 (8th Cir. 2003). After ISU's investigative report concluded that Whetstone sexually assaulted Maher, there was no reason for ISU to think that Maher's dissatisfaction with its proposed housing alternatives would have changed.

And while Maher's preference was that ISU move Whetstone, it was not deliberately indifferent for ISU to wait to take such action until the hearing process concluded because ISU was respecting Whetstone's procedural due process rights. *See Keefe v. Adams,* 840 F.3d 523, 535 (8th Cir. 2016) (explaining that when conduct "that leads to an adverse academic decision is of a disciplinary nature, due process *may* require ... procedural protections."); *Davis,* 526 U.S. at 649, 119 S.Ct. 1661 ("[I]t would be entirely reasonable for a school to refrain from a form of disciplinary action that would expose it to constitutional or statutory claims."). Further, ISU instituted a no-contact order between Whetstone and Maher in May 2014, and there is no evidence that it was violated. Thus, there is no genuine dispute that ISU was deliberately indifferent after its investigative report concluded that Whetstone sexually assaulted Maher because ISU was not clearly unreasonable in light of the known circumstances. *See id.* at 648, 119 S.Ct. 1661. The district court properly granted ISU's motion for summary judgment.

For the foregoing reasons, we affirm.

[1] The Honorable Helen C. Adams, Chief Magistrate Judge, United States District Court for the Southern District of Iowa, to whom the case was referred by consent of the parties pursuant to 28 U.S.C. § 636(c).

[2] ISU claims it presented three options to Maher, including a room reserved for emergency situations. But Maher claims that "[t]he facts establish that [ISU] generally maintains a small number of beds for emergency situations, but not that any were available for Maher or that one was offered to Maher." On a motion for summary judgment, we construe the record in the light most favorable to Maher. *See Scott v. Harris,* 550 U.S. 372, 378, 127 S.Ct. 1769, 167 L.Ed.2d 686 (2007).

[3] Title IX does not include a statute of limitations. Instead, Title IX claims are "governed by the state's personal injury statute of limitations." *Walker v. Barrett,* 650 F.3d 1198, 1205 (8th Cir. 2011). Iowa's personal injury statute of limitations is two years. Iowa Code Ann. § 614.1(2).

928 F.3d 722 (2019)

Jane DOE, (originally named as John Doe individually and as a parent and next friend to Jane Doe, a minor) Plaintiff-Appellant,

v.

DARDANELLE SCHOOL DISTRICT Defendant-Appellee.

No. 18-2816.

United States Court of Appeals, Eighth Circuit.

Submitted: April 18, 2019.
Filed: June 27, 2019.

Doe v. Dardanelle School Dist., 928 F. 3d 722 (8th Cir. 2019)

Appeal from United States District Court for the Eastern District of Arkansas — Little Rock

Mason Boling, Jenna R. Fogleman, George McAllaster Rozzell, KEITH & MILLER, Rogers, AR, for Plaintiff-Appellant.

George Jay Bequette, Jr., William Cody Kees, BEQUETTE & BILLINGSLEY, Little Rock, AR, for Defendant-Appellee.

Before COLLOTON, GRUENDER, and ERICKSON, Circuit Judges.

p.724 GRUENDER, Circuit Judge.

Jane Doe appeals the district court's[1] grant of Dardanelle School District's ("Dardanelle") motion for summary judgment and its partial denial of her motion for leave to amend her complaint. We affirm.

While Doe was a student at Dardanelle, she claims that another student, R.C., sexually assaulted her at least twice. The first incident took place in October 2014 during a kickball game. While running the bases, R.C. ran into Doe, who was standing on second base. Doe testified that R.C.'s upper arm "bump[ed]" her breast and that he called her a bitch. Doe said she did not know why R.C. called her a bitch but that she may have been "blocking his way" and that the comment may have been "out of frustration."

The second incident took place in October 2015. Doe and R.C. were seated next to each other while watching a movie with the lights off in a home economics class. Doe testified that R.C. reached up her shorts and touched the outside of her "private parts." After Doe pushed him away, R.C. attempted to force Doe to touch his groin. Doe pulled her arm away, and R.C. "grabbed" Doe's breast over her shirt. Doe testified that nobody else at the table at which she and R.C. sat saw or heard what happened.

Doe reported both incidents to Dardanelle administrators, who discussed them with R.C. Alleging that Dardanelle was p.725 deliberately indifferent, Doe filed a complaint under 20 U.S.C. § 1681 *et seq.* ("Title IX") and 42 U.S.C. § 1983 in May 2017. Doe later moved to amend the complaint, and the district court denied her motion in part. Dardanelle moved for summary judgment, and the district court granted its motion. Doe appeals both orders.

We review a grant of summary judgment *de novo*, considering the facts "in the light most favorable to the nonmoving party." *Hiland Partners GP Holdings, LLC v. Nat'l Union Fire Ins. Co. of Pittsburgh, PA*, 847 F.3d 594, 597 (8th Cir. 2017). A motion for summary judgment will be granted where "the movant shows that there is no genuine dispute as to any material fact and the movant is entitled to judgment as a matter of law." Fed. R. Civ. P. 56(a). "Only disputes over facts that might affect the outcome of the suit under the governing law will properly preclude the entry of summary judgment." *Anderson v. Liberty Lobby, Inc.*, 477 U.S. 242, 248, 106 S.Ct. 2505, 91 L.Ed.2d 202 (1986).

The district court explained that Title IX and § 1983 have the same deliberate indifference standard and concluded that Dardanelle was not deliberately indifferent.[2] It reasoned that the first incident did not put Dardanelle on notice that R.C. might sexually assault Doe and that though Dardanelle might have taken more "prudent" steps after the second incident, it is not liable for "failing to take the most reasonable course of action or even for responding negligently." *Doe v. Dardanelle School District*, No. 4:17cv00359, 2018 WL 3795235, at *4 (E.D. Ark. Aug. 9, 2018). It additionally observed that even if Dardanelle were deliberately indifferent, the harassment was not "so severe, pervasive, and objectively offensive" that it deprived Doe "of access to the educational opportunities or benefits provided by the school." *Id.* (*quoting Davis*, 526 U.S. at 650, 119 S.Ct. 1661). The district court therefore granted Dardanelle's motion for summary judgment.

"Deliberate indifference is a stringent standard of fault that cannot be predicated upon mere negligence." *Doe v. Flaherty*, 623 F.3d 577, 584 (8th Cir. 2010) (internal quotation marks and citation omitted). Under Title IX, Dardanelle is liable only if its "deliberate indifference effectively 'cause[d]' the discrimination." *Davis*, 526 U.S. at 642-43, 119 S.Ct. 1661 (alteration in original). We "should refrain from second-guessing the disciplinary decisions made by school administrators." *Id.* at 648, 119 S.Ct. 1661. Summary judgment is proper unless Dardanelle was "clearly unreasonable in light of the known circumstances." *Id.* at 648-49, 119 S.Ct. 1661.

First, Doe claims that Dardanelle was deliberately indifferent because it had "received at least one other report from a second student, T.R., complaining that R.C. had attempted to touch her inappropriately." R.C. said that he sometimes hit T.R. on the arm. Vice Principal Lynn Balloun discussed T.R.'s complaint with R.C., who promised that he would stop. The record does not indicate when T.R. made the complaint. Even if we assume the complaint came before the first incident with Doe as she claims, we cannot say that Dardanelle's response to the complaint "effectively caused" the first incident with Doe. *See Davis*, 526 U.S. at 642, 119 S.Ct. 1661.

Doe next argues that Dardanelle's "inaction in the face of the first incident involving Doe "led to the second, more severe assault." But Dardanelle did take action after the first incident. Doe reported the first incident to a teacher and to Principal Marcia Lawrence. In response, Balloun and Counselor Cynthia Hutchins discussed the incident with R.C. Both Balloun and Hutchins "sternly" talked to R.C. "about proper behavior."

While Balloun's notes from his discussion with R.C. after the first incident indicate that he believed R.C. had touched Doe several times, Doe testified in deposition and without reservation that R.C. had never touched her before the kickball incident. She also testified that, according to her memory of the 2014 school year, there was only one incident when R.C. touched her. Accepting Doe's statement is not a "failure to apply the proper summary judgment standard," as Doe contends. Rather, the unambiguous testimony of the only witness with firsthand knowledge demonstrates that there is no genuine dispute of fact. *Cf. Prosser v. Ross,* 70 F.3d 1005, 1008 (8th Cir. 1995) ("We have held that a party cannot avoid summary judgment by contradicting his own earlier testimony.")

Dardanelle's response to the allegation that R.C. ran into Doe during a kickball game, hitting her breast with his upper arm and calling her a bitch, is not "clearly unreasonable in light of the known circumstances." *See Davis,* 526 U.S. at 648-49, 119 S.Ct. 1661. Indeed, the "clearly unreasonable standard is intended to afford flexibility to school administrators." *Estate of Barnwell by and through Barnwell v. Watson,* 880 F.3d 998, 1007 (8th Cir. 2018) (internal quotation marks omitted). Thus, Dardanelle's alleged deliberate indifference did not effectively cause the second incident.

Doe additionally argues that Dardanelle's response to the second incident "exacerbated [her] injuries." Dardanelle again took steps to address R.C.'s misconduct. Immediately after the incident, Doe went to the school office to speak with Lawrence. According to Lawrence, Doe did not tell her at that time that R.C. had tried to touch her vagina, but Doe testified that she had told Lawrence.[3] During the conversation, Lawrence asked Doe whether she was "feeling more upset about this than [she was] showing" and called a school counselor to talk with Doe.

Lawrence referred the incident to Balloun, who met with R.C. and the school resource officer, the school's police officer. Balloun testified that he and the resource officer questioned R.C. "extensively," and R.C. denied the incident. Lawrence and Balloun also talked with the home economics teacher "about keeping a light on" during movies and informed her that some "inappropriate touching" had been alleged. They told the teacher to separate Doe and p.727 R.C. in her class. R.C. was eventually moved to a different class in April 2016. Balloun testified that after the second incident, he "tried to pay particular attention, as it was warranted," to R.C. and that Lawrence likewise "was trying to keep an eye on" Doe. In light of the fact that R.C. denied the second incident and nobody else in the home economics class witnessed it, Dardanelle's response was not "clearly unreasonable in light of the known circumstances." *See Davis,* 526 U.S. at 648-49, 119 S.Ct. 1661.

Doe claims that Dardanelle's response to the incidents led to depression, self-harm, and isolation, as evidenced by her counselor's notes. Doe told her counselor that she was afraid that R.C. would "harm her again" and that R.C. "calls her names." But Doe testified that after the October 2015 incident she only interacted with R.C. once and sometimes saw him at Walmart. Further, we agree with the district court that, even if Dardanelle were deliberately indifferent, it was not "deliberately indifferent to sexual harassment... that is so severe, pervasive, and objectively offensive that it can be said to [have deprived Doe] of access to the educational opportunities or benefits provided by the school." *Davis,* 526 U.S. at 650, 119 S.Ct. 1661. Doe's grade point average increased in both her junior and senior years, and she graduated on time. *See also id.* at 652, 119 S.Ct. 1661 ("Damages are not available for simple acts of teasing and name-calling among school children, however, even where these comments target differences in gender."). In sum, the district court properly granted Dardanelle's motion for summary judgment.

Finally, Doe argues that the district court should have granted her motion to amend her complaint in full. Doe sought to add a negligence claim against Dardanelle through a direct action against its insurance provider and a claim that Arkansas Code Annotated section 21-9-301 violates the Arkansas constitution.[4] The district court denied her motion as futile.[5] "We review the denial of leave to amend for abuse of discretion and questions of futility *de novo*." *United States ex rel. Roop v. Hypoguard USA, Inc.*, 559 F.3d 818, 822 (8th Cir. 2009). "Denial of a motion for leave to amend on the basis of futility means the district court has reached the legal conclusion that the amended complaint could not withstand a motion to dismiss under Rule 12(b)(6) of the Federal Rules of Civil Procedure." *Zutz v. Nelson*, 601 F.3d 842, 850 (8th Cir. 2010) (internal quotation marks omitted). "[I]n reviewing a denial of leave to amend we ask whether the proposed amended complaint states a cause of action under the [*Bell Atlantic Corp. v. Twombly*, 550 U.S. 544, 127 S.Ct. 1955, 167 L.Ed.2d 929 (2007),] pleading standard ...." *Id.* at 850-51. Under the *Twombly* standard, a complaint will survive a motion to dismiss if it contains "sufficient factual matter, accepted as true, to state a claim to relief that is plausible on its face." *Ashcroft v. Iqbal*, 556 U.S. 662, 678, 129 S.Ct. 1937, 173 L.Ed.2d 868 (2009) (internal quotation marks omitted).

We agree with the district court that Doe's negligence claim is futile. As the district court correctly noted, Dardanelle's p.728 insurance policy includes an exclusion for claims or suits "alleging Sexual Abuse and Molestation," and Doe does not contest that the policy contains an exclusion against such lawsuits. The court therefore concluded that the plaintiff's proposed amendment to add a direct claim against the insurer is futile.

Doe argues that the district court "erred by drawing inferences in [Dardanelle's] favor." This argument is not persuasive. Though the district court must take her factual allegations as true and draw all inferences in her favor, *see Braden v. Wal-Mart Stores, Inc.*, 588 F.3d 585, 594-95 (8th Cir. 2009), Doe offered no factual basis to support the possibility that the policy exclusion does not exist or does not apply. Thus, we agree with the district court that Doe's negligence claim is futile.

Likewise, the district court correctly determined that Doe's Arkansas constitutional claim is futile. It relied on an Arkansas Supreme Court decision holding that Ark. Code Ann. section 21-9-301 is consistent with the same Arkansas constitutional provisions to which Doe points. *See White v. City of Newport*, 326 Ark. 667, 672, 933 S.W.2d 800 (1996). Doe nevertheless claims that the Arkansas Supreme Court "signaled a sea change" in *Bd. of Trs. of Univ. of Arkansas v. Andrews*, 2018 Ark. 12, 535 S.W.3d 616 (2018). She contends that *Andrews* "singled out [the court's] 1996-era caselaw," which includes *White*, "for failing to strictly construe and enforce constitutional provisions." But *Andrews* involved sovereign immunity, and we see no reason why its dicta affects the holding in *White*. Thus, we agree with the district court that this claim is likewise futile.

For the foregoing reasons, we affirm.

---

[1] The Honorable J. Leon Holmes, United States District Judge for the Eastern District of Arkansas.

[2] Doe does not argue that the district court erroneously applied the same deliberate indifference standard to her Title IX and § 1983 claims. Thus, we do not address whether the district court should have separately considered whether Dardanelle was deliberately indifferent to unconstitutional conduct and the rights of students under Doe's § 1983 claim and to student-on-student harassment under her Title IX claim. *Compare Plamp v. Mitchell School Dist. No. 17-2,* 565 F.3d 450, 459, 461 (8th Cir. 2009) (requiring deliberate indifference to or tacit authorization of unconstitutional misconduct for § 1983 failure-to-act claims and deliberate indifference to the rights of students for § 1983 failure-to-train claims), *with Davis Next Friend LaShonda D. v. Monroe Cty. Bd. of Educ.,* 526 U.S. 629, 633, 119 S.Ct. 1661, 143 L.Ed.2d 839 (1999) (requiring "deliberate indifference to known acts of harassment in ... programs or activities" for Title IX student-on-student harassment claims).

[3] We view the facts "in the light most favorable to" Doe, giving her "the benefit of all reasonable inferences that can be drawn from the record." *Pedersen v. Bio-Med. Applications of Minn.,* 775 F.3d 1049, 1053 (8th Cir. 2015).

[4] Section 21-9-301 provides that school districts "shall be immune from liability and from suit for damages except to the extent that they may be covered by liability insurance."

[5] Doe's motion to amend also included a request to substitute the "parental claim on behalf of Jane Doe with Jane Doe herself." The district court granted that portion of her motion.

917 F.3d 994 (2019)

D.M., a Minor, BY BAO XIONG, the Mother, Legal Guardian, and Next Friend of D.M.; Z.G., a Minor, by Joel Greenwald, the Father, Legal Guardian, and Next Friend of Z.G., Plaintiffs-Appellants

v.

MINNESOTA STATE HIGH SCHOOL LEAGUE; Bonnie Spohn-Schmaltz, in Her Official Capacity as President of the Board of Directors for the Minnesota State High School League; Erich Martens, in His Official Capacity as Executive Director of the Minnesota State High School League; Craig Perry, in His Official Capacity as an Associate Director of the Minnesota State High School League; Bob Madison, p.995 in His Official Capacity as an Associate Director of the Minnesota State High School League, Defendants-Appellees.

Missouri State High School Activities Association; Arkansas Activities Association; Nebraska School Activities Association; North Dakota High School Activities Association; National Federation of State High School Associations, Amici on Behalf of Appellee(s).

No. 18-3077.

United States Court of Appeals, Eighth Circuit.

Submitted: December 12, 2018.

Filed: March 6, 2019.

DM by Bao Xiong v. MN State High School League, 917 F. 3d 994 (8th Cir. 2019)

Appeal from United States District Court for the District of Minnesota.

Anastasia Boden, Timothy R. Snowball, Joshua Paul Thompson, Caleb R. Trotter, PACIFIC LEGAL FOUNDATION, Sacramento, CA, Erick G. Kaardal, MOHRMAN p.998 & KAARDAL, Minneapolis, MN, for Plaintiffs-Appellants.

Kevin Michael Beck, Joseph A. Kelly, Patrick John Kelly, KELLY & LEMMONS, Saint Paul, MN, for Defendants-Appellees.

Mallory V. Mayse, Columbia, MO, for Amicus on Behalf of Appellee(s) Missouri State High School Activities Association.

Edward W. McCorkle, McMILLAN & McCORKLE, Arkadelphia, AR, for Amicus on Behalf of Appellee(s) Arkansas Activities Association.

Rex R. Schultze, PERRY LAW FIRM, Lincoln, NE, for Amicus on Behalf of Appellee(s) Nebraska School Activities Association.

Rachel Bruner, PEARCE & DURICK, Bismarck, ND, for Amicus on Behalf of Appellee(s) North Dakota High School Activities Association.

William E. Quirk, POLSINELLI, PC, Kansas City, MO, for Amicus on Behalf of Appellee(s) National Federation of State High School Associations.

Before LOKEN, MELLOY, and ERICKSON, Circuit Judges.

p.997MELLOY, Circuit Judge.

In 2018, two boys sued their state's high school athletic league and several of its officers for declaratory and injunctive relief under 42 U.S.C. § 1983. The boys alleged that the league violated their rights under the Equal Protection Clause of the Fourteenth Amendment to the U.S. Constitution and under Title IX of the Education Amendments of 1972, 20 U.S.C. §§ 1681-88 ("Title IX"). Specifically, they claimed that the league unlawfully discriminated against them on the basis of sex through its rule prohibiting boys from participating on high school competitive dance teams. The district court denied the boys' motion for a preliminary injunction, and they appealed. Having jurisdiction under 28 U.S.C. § 1292(a)(1), we reverse and direct the district court to enter a preliminary injunction.

I.

Appellants D.M. and Z.G. are sixteen-year-old boys who attend high school in Maplewood and Minnetonka, Minnesota, respectively. Both are in the eleventh grade. Both are passionate about dance and have participated in various dance classes and programs. Both want to dance on their schools' competitive dance teams but, for reasons explained below, have been prohibited from doing so.

Appellee Minnesota State High School League (the "League") is a non-profit corporation that is a voluntary association of high schools. The League exercises authority delegated to it by the high schools to control high school extracurricular activities and sports throughout the state. To obtain and maintain such control, the League passes bylaws and rules that set forth the standards member schools use to regulate and supervise those activities and sports.

The League's Bylaw 412 limits participation on a school's competitive dance team to females. The League claims that the reason for this limitation is that girls' "overall athletic opportunities have previously been limited," whereas boys' have not. To support its claim, the League points to data compiled by Amicus National Federation of High School Athletic Associations ("NFHS"). The League also relies on Minnesota law, which allows for gender-based, athletic limitations in certain circumstances. See Minn. Stat. § 121A.04, subdiv. 3 ("[I]n athletic programs operated by educational institutions or public services and designed for participants 12 years old or older or in the 7th grade or above, it is not an unfair discriminatory practice to restrict membership on p.999 an athletic team to participants of one sex whose overall athletic opportunities have previously been limited."). Pursuant to Bylaw 412, neither D.M. nor Z.G. have been allowed to participate on their schools' competitive dance teams.

D.M. and Z.G. sued the League in July 2018 for allegedly violating Title IX and their rights to equal protection under the Fourteenth Amendment. Shortly thereafter, the boys moved for a preliminary injunction of Bylaw 412 as it pertains to boys and competitive dance teams. The district court denied the motion. Despite finding that the boys suffered irreparable harm and that "the balance of harms may favor" them, the district court concluded that the injunction was not warranted because the boys were not likely to prevail on the merits. The district court also concluded that the public interest, as reflected in Minnesota Statute section 121A.04, favored denying the injunction. The court explained that "[t]he girls-only dance team rule is substantially related to an important governmental objective"—namely, "increasing girls' athletic opportunities." Moreover, the court said that Title IX permits the League to create girls-only athletic teams such as dance teams. The boys timely filed a notice of appeal.

II.

We review "the denial of a preliminary injunction for abuse of discretion." Gresham v. Swanson, 866 F.3d 853, 854 (8th Cir. 2017). A district court abuses its discretion when it "rests its conclusion on clearly erroneous factual findings or erroneous legal conclusions." Jones v. Kelley, 854 F.3d 1009, 1013 (8th Cir. 2017) (per curiam). "We will not disturb a district court's discretionary decision if such decision remains within the range of choice available to the district court, accounts for all relevant factors, does not rely on any irrelevant factors, and does not constitute a clear error of judgment." Richland/Wilkin Joint Powers Auth. v. U.S. Army Corps of Eng'rs, 826 F.3d 1030, 1035 (8th Cir. 2016) (quoting PCTV Gold, Inc. v. SpeedNet, LLC, 508 F.3d 1137, 1142 (8th Cir. 2007)). We review a district court's legal conclusions de novo. Barrett v. Claycomb, 705 F.3d 315, 320 (8th Cir. 2013).

When determining whether to issue a preliminary injunction, the district court considers: "(1) the threat of irreparable harm to the movant; (2) the state of balance between this harm and the injury that granting the injunction will inflict on other parties litigant; (3) the probability that [the] movant will succeed on the merits; and (4) the public interest." Dataphase Sys., Inc. v. C L Sys., Inc., 640 F.2d 109, 114 (8th Cir. 1981) (en banc). Generally, no one of these factors is determinative. Id. at 113. However, "the absence of a likelihood of success on the merits strongly suggests that preliminary injunctive relief should be denied." Barrett, 705 F.3d at 320 (quoting CDI Energy Servs., Inc. v. West River Pumps, Inc., 567 F.3d 398, 402 (8th Cir. 2009)). Consequently, we will begin our review with an analysis of that factor.

A.

There are two standards a district court may apply when assessing a movant's probability of success on the merits. The first, which applies in most instances, directs the district court to ask whether the party requesting a preliminary injunction has a "fair chance of prevailing." Planned Parenthood Minnesota, North Dakota, South Dakota v. Rounds, 530 F.3d 724, 732 (8th Cir. 2008) (en banc). This fair-chance standard does not require the party seeking relief to "show 'a greater than fifty per cent likelihood that he will prevail on the merits.'" Id. at 731 (citation omitted). The second, which we have called a "more rigorous standard," calls on the district court to determine, as a threshold matter, whether the movant is "likely to prevail" on his or her claims. Id. at 733. The likely-to-prevail standard applies when "a preliminary injunction is sought to enjoin the implementation of a duly enacted state statute." Id. at 732. The district court applied the heightened, likely-to-prevail standard because "the challenged policy is supported by a Minnesota statute." The parties dispute whether that was error.

As noted above, the test for determining which standard applies is whether the "preliminary injunction is sought to enjoin the implementation of a duly enacted state statute." Id. We apply a heightened standard in such instances because the duly enacted state statute constitutes "government action based on presumptively reasoned democratic processes," and such action is "entitled to a higher degree of deference and should not be enjoined lightly." Id. at 732 (quoting Able v. United States, 44 F.3d 128, 131 (2d Cir. 1995)). The likely-to-prevail test may also be appropriate when a movant seeks to preliminarily enjoin other forms of government action such as "administrative actions by federal, state or local government agencies." Id. at 732 n.6. However, in those cases, the suggested course of action is to first "evaluate whether 'the full play of the democratic process[ ]' was involved" in the actions and "then determine which standard would be more appropriate." Richland/Wilkin, 826 F.3d at 1040 (quoting Rounds, 530 F.3d at 732 n.6).

Here, Bylaw 412 can, under Eighth Circuit precedent, rightly be considered government action. See Brenden v. Indep. Sch. Dist. 742, 477 F.2d 1292, 1295 (8th Cir. 1973) (determining that the League "act[ed] under color of state law" for purposes of 42 U.S.C. § 1983 in promulgating rules governing high school athletics). However, the bylaw was not based on the "presumptively reasoned democratic processes" that Rounds contemplated. Rounds, 530 F.3d at 732. Indeed, the creation of the bylaw did not involve "the full play of the democratic process." Id. at 732 n.6; see also Richland/Wilkin, 826 F.3d at 1040. There was no lengthy public debate involving both the legislative and executive branches before the formulation of the bylaw and its subsequent enactment. Cf. Able, 44 F.3d at 131-32 (imposing a heightened likelihood-of-success standard upon a motion to enjoin federal legislation and regulation because "Congress and the President [had] engaged in lengthy public debate before formulating" them).[1] And the bylaws are created by League-member schools throughout the state, not by democratically elected officials who must answer to their constituents or face the possibility of not being reelected.

To the extent the League argues that the heightened standard applies because it is implementing a state statute, Minnesota Statute section 121A.04, we reject the argument. Section 121A.04 does not direct the League to do anything; rather, the statute permits the League to discriminate on the basis of sex in limited circumstances —when athletic opportunities for a sex have previously been limited. The League must still show the continuing lack of opportunity and how the challenged policy addresses that inequity. Nothing in this action calls into question the validity of the underlying statute.

Consequently, the heightened, likely-to-prevail standard does not apply to the boys' preliminary injunction motion. We p.1001 ask, instead, whether the boys have a fair chance of prevailing.

B.

We now turn to the merits of the boys' claims, applying the appropriate standard. The boys argue that the League violated their Fourteenth Amendment equal protection rights when it banned them from participating on their high schools' competitive dance teams because they are male. The League contends that it is justified in precluding the boys from the dance teams because doing so constitutes means that are "substantially related to the important governmental interest of redressing past discrimination and providing equal opportunities for women."

On the issue of past discrimination, the parties have submitted a chart that shows, for Minnesota in a given year, the relative percentages of boys and girls enrolled in League-member schools statewide. It then shows the relative percentages of boys and girls among those students participating in interscholastic sports. The underrepresented sex column shows the difference between the percentage of students enrolled and the percentage of students participating in interscholastic sports for whichever gender is underrepresented that year. The chart is reproduced here as follows:

League-Member School Enrollments and Athletes by Gender League League Members Members League League Year Enrollment Enrollment Athletes Athletes Under-represented Boys Girls Boys Girls Sex 2013-14 133,964 127,364 119,034 104,706 Girls (51.3%) (48.7%) (53.2%) (46.8%) (-1.9%) 2014-15 134,879 128,128 118,899 108,084 Girls (51.3%) (48.7%) (52.4%) (47.6%) (-1.1%) 2015-16 136,257 129,394 121,024 110,023 Girls (51.3%) (48.7%) (52.4%) (47.6%) (-1.1%) 2016-17 137,603 130,263 122,269 117,020 Boys (51.4%) (48.6%) (51.1%) (48.9%) (-0.3%) Average 135,676 128,787 120,307 109,958 Girls (51.3%) (48.7%) (52.2%) (47.8%) (-1.0%)

The same data for 2017-18 shows boys were underrepresented by 0.35%.

The Fourteenth Amendment provides that "[n]o State shall ... deny to any person within its jurisdiction the equal protection of the laws." U.S. Const. amend. XIV, § 1. In the context of gender-based discrimination, the U.S. Supreme Court has interpreted that clause to mean that unless a government actor can meet the "demanding" burden of showing an "exceedingly persuasive" justification for treating males differently from females, the differential treatment is unconstitutional. United States v. Virginia, 518 U.S. 515, 533, 116 S.Ct. 2264, 135 L.Ed.2d 735 (1996); see also Duckworth v. St. Louis Metro. Police Dep't, 491 F.3d 401, 406 (8th Cir. 2007). To successfully justify a classification p.1002 based on gender, the actor "must show 'at least that the [challenged] classification serves "important governmental objectives and that the discriminatory means employed" are "substantially related to the achievement of those objectives."'" Virginia, 518 U.S. at 533, 116 S.Ct. 2264 (alteration in original) (quoting Miss. Univ. for Women v. Hogan, 458 U.S. 718, 724, 102 S.Ct. 3331, 73 L.Ed.2d 1090 (1982)).

The Court has explained that "gender-based classification[s] favoring one sex" that are designed to remedy past discrimination can be justified "[i]n limited circumstances." Miss. Univ., 458 U.S. at 728, 102 S.Ct. 3331. Such circumstances exist when the classification "intentionally and directly assists members of the sex that is disproportionately burdened." Id. However, a government actor may "evoke a compensatory purpose to justify an otherwise discriminatory classification only if members of the gender benefited by the classification *actually suffer* a disadvantage related to the classification." Id. (emphasis added). In other words, for a government actor to classify individuals based on gender for the purpose of remedying a prior lack of opportunities, the individuals must continue to lack opportunities or the classification is not constitutionally justified. See id. at 729, 102 S.Ct. 3331 (declaring a public university's women-only policy to be unconstitutional because the university had "made no showing ... that women [were] currently ... deprived of" opportunities to obtain nursing training or positions of leadership); id. at 730, 102 S.Ct. 3331 ("[A]lthough the State recited a 'benign, compensatory purpose,' it failed to establish that the alleged objective is the actual purpose underlying the discriminatory classification.").

The parties agree that girls historically have been underrepresented in Minnesota high school athletics. However, over the past five years, the representation of girls in Minnesota athletics has been almost directly proportional to the number of girls enrolled at Minnesota schools. In fact, in both the 2016-17 and 2017-18 school years, the parties' means of determining representation show that boys have been slightly underrepresented in high school athletics. Thus, the League has not shown that the underlying problem it initially sought to remedy by creating all-girl teams—the overall underrepresentation of girls in high school athletics—continues to exist, at least in Minnesota.[2] Without this underlying problem to remedy, the League cannot prohibit boys from participating on girls' teams unless it has some other "exceedingly persuasive" justification for doing so. Virginia, 518 U.S. at 533, 116 S.Ct. 2264.

The League does not offer any such justification. Instead, it merely argues, in broad terms, that restricting the membership p.1003 of athletic teams to one sex "advances the important government interest of promoting safety, increasing competition, redressing past discrimination, and providing more athletic opportunities for female athletes." The League also cites a Rhode Island Supreme Court case, Kleczek v. R.I. Interscholastic League, Inc., 612 A.2d 734 (R.I. 1992) (per curiam), in which the court held that promoting safety and preserving interscholastic athletic competition for boys and girls are important government interests. Id. at 739. Kleczek, however, in addition to being non-binding, is distinguishable from this case. Kleczek involved a ban on boys participating on girls-only field hockey teams. Id. at 735. The court, understandably, had concerns about participants' safety if boys were allowed on the teams. Id. at 739. Here, the League does not explain how allowing boys to dance on their schools' competitive dance[3] teams would be unsafe or how it would deprive girls of opportunities to compete. Moreover, Kleczek was decided under the Rhode Island constitution, not the U.S. Constitution. Id. at 736. We find the League's asserted other justifications for prohibiting boys from participating on high school competitive dance teams unpersuasive.

Because the League has not asserted an "exceedingly persuasive" justification for keeping boys from participating on high school competitive dance teams, we hold that the boys had more than a fair chance of prevailing on the merits of their case.[4] The district court erred in concluding otherwise.

C.

Because we conclude that the boys have a fair chance of prevailing on the merits of their equal protection claim, we need not address their probability of success on their Title IX claim. See Richland/Wilkin, 826 F.3d at 1040 ("The plaintiff 'need only establish a likelihood of succeeding on the merits of any one of [its] claims.'" (alteration in original) (citation omitted)). We turn now to the other Dataphase factors.

The district court concluded that the boys "sufficiently demonstrated irreparable harm." We agree. Students who are denied the opportunity to join their schools' sports teams because of their sex may suffer irreparable harm. See Bednar v. Neb. Sch. Activities Ass'n, 531 F.2d 922, 923 (8th Cir. 1976) (per curiam). That is especially true here. Both boys are juniors in high school. They love to dance and want to do so competitively as part of a school team. The League's ban has prohibited them from doing so this year. They cannot get that season back. Without injunctive relief or final resolution of their suit, they will be prevented from competing next year as well. These sorts of injuries, i.e., deprivations of temporally isolated opportunities, are exactly what preliminary injunctions are intended to relieve.

Furthermore, we hold that the district court erred in concluding that the public interest favored denying the injunction. The district court reasoned that "[t]he public interest is evidenced in the Minnesota statute allowing girls-only teams that do not violate Title IX or the p.1004 Equal Protection Clause." That statement, while true enough, overlooks the fair probability that the League's bylaw violates the Constitution. "[T]he public is served by the preservation of constitutional rights." Phelps-Roper v. Nixon, 545 F.3d 685, 694 (8th Cir. 2008), overruled on other grounds by Phelps-Roper v. City of Manchester, 697 F.3d 678, 692 (8th Cir. 2012) (en banc); see also Awad v. Ziriax, 670 F.3d 1111, 1132 (10th Cir. 2012) ("[I]t is always in the public interest to prevent the violation of a party's constitutional rights." (quoting G & V Lounge, Inc. v. Mich. Liquor Control Comm'n, 23 F.3d 1071, 1079 (6th Cir. 1994))). As such, the public interest Dataphase factor favors the boys.

Finally, we hold that the balance of harms tips in favor of granting an injunction. The district court alluded that such may be the case in its memorandum and order, and for good reason. If the injunction is granted, the boys may try out for their schools' competitive dance teams. The negative public consequences of such an allowance, if any, will be slight.[5] See Winter v. Nat. Res. Def. Council, Inc., 555 U.S. 7, 24, 129 S.Ct. 365, 172 L.Ed.2d 249 (2008) ("In exercising their sound discretion, courts of equity should pay particular regard for the public consequences in employing the extraordinary remedy of injunction." (quoting Weinberger v. Romero-Barcelo, 456 U.S. 305, 312, 102 S.Ct. 1798, 72 L.Ed.2d 91 (1982))). On the other hand, if the injunction is denied, the boys will continue to suffer irreparable harm—namely, they will be prevented from trying out for and participating on their schools' competitive dance teams in probable violation of their constitutional rights. The balance of harms is decidedly in the boys' favor.

III.

In sum, all of the Dataphase factors favor granting D.M.'s and Z.G.'s motion for a preliminary injunction. We therefore reverse the judgment of the district court and remand for the district court to issue a preliminary injunction in favor of the boys.

[1] Able served as an important guide for us when we adopted our heightened, likely-to-prevail test in Rounds. See Rounds, 530 F.3d at 731-33; see also id. at 732 n.6. Able's treatment of when government action represents "the full play of the democratic processes" is, therefore, significant.

[2] The U.S. Department of Education's Office of Civil Rights, the League, and the NFHS all repeatedly stress that girls are underrepresented in high school athletics nationwide. To support their claims, they point to data that show "[o]ver the last four years 1,218,125 (15.6%) more boys participated nationwide in interscholastic sports, on average, than girls." The problem with the data they cite, however, is that the data do not show the total, nationwide number of students enrolled in schools that offer interscholastic athletic programs. Nor do the data break down how many of those students are boys and how many are girls. Without that information, it is impossible to appreciate the extent to which either gender is over- or underrepresented in interscholastic athletics at the national level. There may be more boys than girls participating in interscholastic sports because there are simply more boys than girls enrolled. Moreover, the alleged fact that girls are underrepresented in sports nationwide does not address the question of whether girls are underrepresented in Minnesota so as to justify a bylaw that prohibits boys from joining high school competitive dance teams in that state.

[3] In many sports, single-sex teams can be justified if boys enjoy a competitive advantage over girls due to their weight and height. The League has not presented any evidence (and does not seem to seriously argue) that boys enjoy any competitive advantage over girls in dance.

[4] Given the lack of justification for the policy, we have no doubt that the boys could even satisfy the heightened, likely-to-prevail standard if it were applicable.

[5] The League argues that "[g]ranting an injunction would fundamentally alter the requirements for MSHSL-sponsored activities and would disregard the unambiguous language of Minn. Stat. § 121A.04." The League worries that were the preliminary injunction to be granted and the boys "subsequently determined ineligible after a trial on the merits," their teams would be required to forfeit "all contests in which [the boys] participated." We do not share the League's concerns. If the injunction is granted, the boys are "eligible" for all intents and purposes. Therefore, we are not convinced that their teams would have to forfeit contests under the League's rules. Moreover, the League's inability to show an "exceedingly persuasive" justification for its discriminatory rule at this stage of the litigation makes a scenario wherein the boys lose at trial highly unlikely.

937 F.3d 1119 (2019)

Morgan Katelin PEARSON; Kirsten Elizabeth Kirkpatrick, Plaintiffs-Appellants

v.

LOGAN UNIVERSITY, doing business as Logan College of Chiropractic, Defendant-Appellee.

No. 18-2764.

United States Court of Appeals, Eighth Circuit.

Submitted: April 17, 2019.
Filed: September 4, 2019.
Rehearing Denied October 10, 2019.

Pearson v. Logan University, 937 F. 3d 1119 (8th Cir. 2019)

Appeal from United States District Court for the Eastern District of Missouri — St. Louis

Daniel F. Harvath, HARVATH LAW GROUP, Webster Groves, for Plaintiffs-Appellants.

Andrew W. Blackwell, Assistant Attorney General, Mark Goodman, Sheila Greenbaum, CAPES & SOKOL, Saint Louis, MO, Justin Gelfand, MARGULIS & GELFAND, Saint Louis, MO, for Defendant-Appellee.

Before SMITH, Chief Judge, KELLY and KOBES, Circuit Judges.

PER CURIAM.

Morgan Katelin Pearson and Kirsten Elizabeth Kirkpatrick each sued Logan University under Title IX of the Education Amendments of 1972, 20 U.S.C. §§ 1681-1688, as well as various state laws, alleging that Logan failed to protect them against stalking and sexual harassment by a fellow student (FS). The district court granted summary judgment for Logan, which Pearson and Kirkpatrick appeal. We affirm.

I

We draw the following background facts from the summary judgment record, viewing the evidence in the light most favorable to Pearson and Kirkpatrick. See Schilf v. Eli Lilly & Co., 687 F.3d 947, 948 (8th Cir. 2012).

In September 2015, Pearson and Kirkpatrick enrolled as undergraduate students at Logan. Logan's academic catalog contains its harassment policy. According to the catalog, a student who wants to complain of stalking or sexual assault should contact Logan's Title IX Coordinator, who will commence an investigation within seven days of notification.

On December 8, 2015, Pearson met with Sandra Periello, Logan's Associate Dean of Students. Pearson complained that FS would come into the library — where she worked — to stare at her, that he would stare at her during chemistry lab, and that he once pressed himself up against her in November in the cadaver lab. Periello told Pearson to write down what happened to her and that Periello would give her statement to Shelley Sawalich, Logan's Dean of Students and Title IX Coordinator. On December 9, Periello emailed Pearson, reminding her to provide a written statement. Pearson responded by asking to meet with Sawalich, stating she believed another dean had allowed FS to take Pearson's same "complete schedule" in the next trimester. Sawalich and Pearson then exchanged emails to set up a meeting that same day.

At their December 9 meeting, Pearson repeated to Sawalich what she had told Periello with respect to FS's conduct and provided the names of four people who she said had witnessed the harassment. Pearson said that she was "terrified of being raped." She also agreed with Sawalich that the November incident in the cadaver lab may have been an accident.

Sawalich labeled Pearson's allegations as harassment and stalking and said that she was required to investigate FS's conduct. Sawalich told Pearson that she had the option to remain anonymous as the complainant. Pearson asked how Sawalich would interview her witnesses while maintaining her anonymity, and Sawalich gave Pearson an example of the kind of question Sawalich would ask. Pearson elected to remain anonymous. Sawalich explained that she was not going to move forward with the investigation at the time because she had another case to "take care of" and Logan's finals and holidays were coming up, but told Pearson that before meeting with FS, she would email Pearson. Sawalich asked Pearson for a written statement, which she expected to receive from Pearson by Monday, December 14. She wanted the written statement "to assist with understanding the situation, interactions, and timeline" of relevant events.

On December 14, Pearson emailed Sawalich that she was "pinched for time" and asked, "Is it okay if I send it to you via email by next Monday?" On December 15, Sawalich responded,"You are welcome to get me the information next week.... What this means, though, is that I won't really be able to move forward until next trimester with the investigation. Is that okay with you?" Pearson did not respond to that question.

On December 21, Pearson sent her written statement to Sawalich. In her statement, Pearson claimed that at the beginning of the semester FS had made several attempts to spend time with her outside of p.1122 class, wanting to study with her and waiting at the end of class to walk out with her. She stated that FS suggested they could drink beer while studying together, which she found inappropriate because he knew she was underage and did not drink. FS was in his early thirties. After she began working at the library, FS would come to the library every day and watch her, trying to find opportunities to interact with her. She claimed that he would always sit at a nearby table and often appear to not be doing homework or other library-related work. She alleged that in class, FS would "try to jump into conversations" she was having with other people. Pearson also stated that she thought FS was trying to take her very same schedule in the next trimester, which made her uncomfortable because she believed he had no good reason to do so. Pearson made no mention in her statement of the November incident in the cadaver lab. Sawalich replied that same day, stating that she would review Pearson's statement and "call [FS] in to talk" after he returned to campus. Sawalich also stated, "I ... want to reiterate that Logan's ability to meaningfully investigate the incident and pursue disciplinary action may be limited because of the attempt to maintain confidentiality."

Sawalich met with FS on January 8, 2016, and again on January 15, 2016, but did not email Pearson in advance of either meeting. Among other things, she told him there had been a complaint filed against him, and reminded him of Logan's policy against retaliation. On January 16, Pearson emailed Sawalich for an update, stating that FS continued to make her feel unsafe on campus. Sawalich responded that same day, telling Pearson she had met with FS twice and asking Pearson to meet on January 19, after the holiday weekend. At that meeting, Pearson told Sawalich that she continued to feel uncomfortable. She believed FS had followed her inappropriately at a school event and had stopped to watch as a female classmate measured her hip bone at the library. Sawalich told Pearson that FS had been very angry at their first meeting and that she had reiterated to FS at the second meeting that retaliation would be "frowned upon." Sawalich explained that she had not interviewed any of Pearson's witnesses because Sawalich did not believe that she could maintain Pearson's anonymity while doing so.

On February 1, Pearson met with Boyd Bradshaw, Vice President for Enrollment Management, to complain about Sawalich's handling of the investigation. On February 3, Pearson met with both Bradshaw and Sawalich to address her concerns and to discuss reopening the case. They also agreed that FS would be asked to stay out of the library and instructed to have no contact with Pearson. Pearson decided to drop her request for anonymity.

Sawalich began reaching out to witnesses. Kirkpatrick was one of those witnesses. Sawalich interviewed Kirkpatrick on February 4. Kirkpatrick told Sawalich that on the first day of school, FS solicited her phone number by saying he was getting everybody's phone numbers, but after she gave him her number it seemed that she was the only one he asked. He started texting that Friday, wanting her to go to the library with him on Saturday. She eventually told him that she had a boyfriend, but FS continued to text her. Kirkpatrick stopped answering. In total, they exchanged approximately 15 texts that day. She told Sawalich that when she first met FS she thought he was "creepy," but she also said she "was fine now." Later, Kirkpatrick explained she said that because she did not want FS to be upset with her when he read Sawalich's findings. She also explained that before Sawalich emailed her, she had no plans to call or go see Sawalich, and that she had never communicated p.1123 any complaints about FS's conduct before her February 4 interview.

On February 6, a Saturday, Pearson emailed Sawalich that she feared FS was retaliating against her because she heard that he was spreading rumors that Pearson had falsely accused another student at her old school of harassing her and that she is overly dramatic. On February 8, Sawalich responded that she was planning to meet with FS that same day and would address the alleged retaliation. When she met with FS, Sawalich told him that he was prohibited from going into the library during the duration of the investigation and from having any contact with Pearson.

On February 22, Sawalich emailed Pearson, explaining that she had talked with witnesses for both Pearson and FS, and that she was putting together information for a written report to Logan's Honor Council. She also asked Pearson for the text messages that Pearson had mentioned in her written statement and for clarification as to whether Pearson ever told FS "in general terms that [Pearson] was not interested in interacting with him at all and that he should ... leave [her] alone." On February 26, Sawalich and Pearson met once more. In response to Sawalich's question, Pearson explained that she had on "countless" occasions told FS not to talk to her and that she would ignore FS and reject his attempts to interact with her. Pearson also told Sawalich that she thought that FS was now blaming her for his poor academic performance. On February 28, Pearson wrote Sawalich that she was unable to retrieve any of the text messages and asked Sawalich to move forward without them.

In early March, Sawalich circulated a written report of her investigation to Logan's Honor Council, Pearson, and FS. Among other things, the written report stated that Sawalich had spoken to both Pearson and FS, that both Pearson and FS had identified potential witnesses, and that Sawalich had interviewed fourteen people in addition to Pearson and FS. The report summarized that "12 of the people said that they witness[ed] no interactions at all between [FS] and [Pearson] or very few interactions; nothing out of the ordinary." According to the report, one of the other witnesses said that she had "witnessed interactions between [FS] and the other girls in their classes that she found uncomfortable and she feels like he takes it further with [Pearson] ... [and] that he is always around and staring." The other witness purportedly said that Pearson seemed "uncomfortable" around FS, and that FS had been asking questions about the work schedules of other students in the library. In addition to the written report, Sawalich also circulated summaries of her witness interviews, including her conversations with Pearson and FS. She did not circulate her handwritten notes.

Pearson believed that Sawalich was trying to blame her for the investigation and omitting information from her witnesses and otherwise twisting their words. She circulated a written response on March 6, and met with Boyd on March 7 to express her disappointment with the written report. Also on March 7, Sawalich interviewed an additional witness. She sent Pearson's and FS's written responses to the report, as well as her notes from the additional witness interview, to the Honor Council. Pearson met with the Honor Council on March 8, and FS met with the Honor Council on March 10. On March 11, the Honor Council issued its decision, determining that there was insufficient evidence to find FS responsible for stalking and harassment. It also stated:

> There is to be no personal contact between you two. Neither of you may contact or attempt to contact the other. Due to the decision, there are no limitations to utilization of common space or campus p.1124 resources. In clarity, you both may use Logan's facilities without limitations (I.e., LRC/Library, hallways, cafeteria, classrooms, etc.) but are prohibited from any personal social contact (i.e., calling, texting, etc.). In social settings, such as Logan sponsored events you should ignore each other.

Sawalich informed Pearson and FS that either student could have the Honor Council's decision reviewed by Kimberly O'Reilly, Logan's Vice President of Academic Affairs.

On March 14, Pearson and her mother met with Bradshaw and O'Reilly to discuss the review process, and on March 15, Pearson submitted a written request to have O'Reilly review the decision. On March 20, Pearson emailed O'Reilly that she did not feel safe on campus and was afraid to return to the library. On March 21, O'Reilly replied, reminding Pearson of the security and safety measures that were available to her on campus and to contact Sawalich immediately if FS violated the no-contact order. O'Reilly also reminded Pearson that—even though she had previously turned it down—she still had the option to switch to a work-study position outside of the library. On March 31, O'Reilly emailed Pearson, explaining that she would stay her decision on the appeal to give Pearson time to get phone records showing the text messages FS sent her. On April 4, Pearson met with O'Reilly and told her that she could not obtain the text messages. That same day, O'Reilly lifted her stay and rendered her decision, finding that "the process outlined in [Logan's harassment policy] was followed and all evidence provided was reviewed [by the Honor Council]." By that fall, both Pearson and Kirkpatrick had transferred schools.

Pearson and Kirkpatrick sued Logan, claiming that Logan failed to adequately respond to their complaints about FS's conduct and that they left Logan in large part due to this inadequate response. Logan moved for summary judgment on all of Pearson's and Kirkpatrick's claims. The district court granted the motion, concluding that Pearson's Title IX claim failed because she could not show that Logan was deliberately indifferent to her plight, Kirkpatrick's Title IX claim failed because Logan never had actual knowledge that she was subject to sex-based discrimination, and their remaining negligence and premises liability claims failed because they did not demonstrate that Logan owed them a duty of care to protect them against student-on-student harassment. Pearson and Kirkpatrick appeal.

II

"We review a grant of summary judgment *de novo,* viewing the facts in the light most favorable to the nonmoving party." Walz v. Ameriprise Fin., Inc., 779 F.3d 842, 844 (8th Cir. 2015). "The non-moving party receives the benefit of all reasonable inferences supported by the evidence, but has the obligation to come forward with specific facts showing that there is a genuine issue for trial." Id. (quoting B.M. ex rel. Miller v. S. Callaway R-II Sch. Dist., 732 F.3d 882, 886 (8th Cir. 2013)).

A

Title IX addresses discrimination on the basis of sex in any educational program that receives federal funding. Roe v. St. Louis Univ., 746 F.3d 874, 881 (8th Cir. 2014). Under its terms, "[n]o person in the United States shall, on the basis of sex, be excluded from participation in, be denied the benefits of, or be subjected to discrimination under any education program or activity receiving Federal financial assistance." 20 U.S.C. § 1681(a). Title IX provides a private right of action, see Cannon v. Univ. of Chi., 441 U.S. 677, 717, p.1125 99 S.Ct. 1946, 60 L.Ed.2d 560 (1979), which extends to suits for compensatory damages against any public or private entity other than a state, Fryberger v. Univ. of Ark., 889 F.3d 471, 475 (8th Cir. 2018). To succeed on a Title IX claim based on harassment by another student, a plaintiff must show that the educational institution was "(1) deliberately indifferent (2) to known acts of discrimination (3) which occur[red] under its control." K.T. v. Culver-Stockton Coll., 865 F.3d 1054, 1057 (8th Cir. 2017) (quoting Ostrander v. Duggan, 341 F.3d 745, 750 (8th Cir. 2003)). "Additionally, the discrimination must be so severe, pervasive, and objectively offensive that it can be said to deprive the victim of access to the educational opportunities or benefits provided by the school." Id. (cleaned up).

1

We begin with Kirkpatrick's Title IX claim, which the district court dismissed because it determined that Kirkpatrick could not show that Logan had actual knowledge that Kirkpatrick was subject to harassment by FS. There is no evidence that Logan knew of any complaints about FS's behavior before September 2015, when the only interactions that made Kirkpatrick uncomfortable occurred. And Kirkpatrick spoke to a Logan administrator about FS's behavior only once, in her February 4 interview with Sawalich. At that meeting, she told Sawalich that, although she used to think FS was creepy, she "was fine now." Viewing the evidence in the light most favorable to Kirkpatrick, she provided after-the-fact notice that she found limited interactions with FS at the beginning of the school year distressing. But such after-the-fact notice of limited interaction is insufficient to satisfy Title IX's actual knowledge requirement. See Culver-Stockton Coll., 865 F.3d at 1058. Because Kirkpatrick cannot satisfy the actual knowledge element, her Title IX claim fails as a matter of law and the district court properly granted summary judgment in favor of Logan on that claim.

2

We turn next to Pearson's Title IX claim, which the district court dismissed because it determined that Pearson could not show that Logan was deliberately indifferent to her complaints. As we have explained, "[a] school is deliberately indifferent when its 'response to the harassment or lack thereof is clearly unreasonable in light of the known circumstances.'" Maher v. Iowa State Univ., 915 F.3d 1210, 1213 (8th Cir. 2019) (quoting Davis ex rel. LaShonda D. v. Monroe Cty. Bd. of Educ., 526 U.S. 629, 648, 119 S.Ct. 1661, 143 L.Ed.2d 839 (1999)), cert denied, ___ U.S. ___, 139 S.Ct. 2763, ___ L.Ed.2d ___, 2019 WL 2256264 (2019). We have cautioned that the "clearly unreasonable" standard is "intended to afford flexibility to school administrators." Roe, 746 F.3d at 882. "[D]issatisfaction with [a] school's response does not mean the school's response can be characterized as deliberate indifference." Maher, 915 F.3d at 1213.

It is undisputed that Logan did investigate Pearson's allegations of stalking and harassment and that, even though its Honor Council ultimately determined that there was insufficient evidence to find FS responsible, it instructed Pearson and FS to have no contact with each other. In Maher, the university's investigative report revealed that the Title IX plaintiff had been sexually assaulted, but the university declined to move the alleged perpetrator before the investigation and hearing process had concluded. Id. at 1212. Nevertheless, we determined that instituting a no-contact order and giving the Title IX plaintiff housing alternatives so that she would not have to live in proximity to her assailant—which she declined—did not p.1126 constitute deliberate indifference. See id. at 1212-13. Here, Logan's investigation did not conclude that FS engaged in stalking or harassment. But Logan still instituted a no-contact order and gave Pearson the option of taking a work-study position at a location other than the library. Pearson made no attempt to enforce that no-contact order or accept an alternative work-study position before leaving Logan. Nonetheless, Pearson contends that Logan was clearly unreasonable in its investigation and adjudication of her complaint.

The summary judgment record reveals no triable issue of fact as to whether Logan's response to and investigation of Pearson's complaint were clearly unreasonable. Any delays in investigating Pearson's complaint do not show that Logan ignored the harassment or stalking that Pearson described. Pearson complained of FS's behavior in December, shortly before the winter holidays. After Pearson described a continuing pattern of conduct that made her feel uncomfortable, Sawalich requested a written statement to better understand "the situation, interactions, and timeline" of relevant events. When Pearson requested additional time to prepare her statement, it was not clearly unreasonable for Sawalich to wait for Pearson before continuing her investigation. Possible student witnesses may also have had limited availability for interviews given that winter break started only five days later, and Pearson's request indicated that she was comfortable delaying the investigation. Indeed, when Sawalich specifically asked if it would be "okay with [Pearson]" if Sawalich began her investigation in earnest after the students had returned to campus, Pearson did not object. And Sawalich asked to speak to FS as soon as classes resumed and did speak to FS in early and mid-January, after which she determined that she could investigate no further while respecting Pearson's request for anonymity.

Pearson contends that Sawalich unreasonably delayed the investigation by not reaching out to other witnesses until Pearson dropped her anonymity in early February, but limiting the scope of an investigation out of respect for a Title IX complainant's desire for confidentiality does not by itself constitute deliberate indifference. See Roe, 746 F.3d at 883 (holding university was not deliberately indifferent where, among other things, university did not inform student's parents or professors of sexual assault out of respect for student's desire for confidentiality); see also Kesterson v. Kent State Univ., 345 F. Supp. 3d 855, 876 (N.D. Ohio 2018) (collecting cases), appeal docketed, No. 18-4200 (6th Cir. Dec. 5, 2018). After Pearson dropped her request for anonymity, Sawalich promptly reached out to witnesses and instructed FS to stay out of the library during her investigation and to have no contact with Pearson.

Similarly, the Honor Council proceedings do not show that Logan was clearly unreasonable in its adjudication of Pearson's allegations against FS. Although Pearson contends that the Honor Council impermissibly relied on several statements in Sawalich's written report that misrepresented Sawalich's investigative findings, Sawalich also circulated summaries of her interviews to the Honor Council that allowed its members to reach their own conclusions. Moreover, Pearson had the opportunity to challenge Sawalich's presentation of the facts—both in writing and in person before the Honor Council— and did so. As for the Honor Council, its members did receive Title IX trainings, and its failure to adopt the Office of Civil Rights's suggested preponderance-of-the-evidence standard alone is insufficient to generate a dispute of material fact that may stave off summary judgment. See Butters v. James Madison Univ., 208 F. Supp. 3d 745, 759 (W.D. Va. 2016) (collecting cases for the proposition that a school's compliance or non-compliance with OCR guidance can be a factor to consider, but is not tantamount to deliberate indifference). Because there is no genuine dispute of material fact as to whether Logan was deliberately indifferent to any stalking or harassment that Pearson experienced, her Title IX claim fails as a matter of law. The district court properly granted summary judgment in Logan's favor on this claim.

III

Finally, we turn to the Missouri premises liability and general negligence claims. The district court dismissed these claims because it determined that Pearson and Kirkpatrick could not establish that Logan owed them a duty of care. We agree.

Under Missouri law, Pearson and Kirkpatrick must show that Logan University had a duty to protect them, breached that duty, and that breach proximately caused an injury. Lopez v. Three Rivers Elec. Coop., 26 S.W.3d 151, 155 (Mo. banc 2000). As the district court correctly explained, whether a duty exists is a question of law. Id. As a general rule, a college does not owe a duty to protect its students. Nickel v. Stephens College, 480 S.W.3d 390, 401 n.8 (Mo. Ct. App. 2015) (acknowledging a "very narrow exception" in cases where a "special relationship" exists between a school and a student when "one party entrusts another for protection and relies upon that party to provide a place of physical safety").

There are two "special circumstances" under which Missouri recognizes an exception to this general rule, but they do not apply here. First, Missouri law recognizes that a "duty may arise when a person, known to be violent, is present on the premises or an individual is present who has conducted himself so as to indicate danger and sufficient time exists to prevent injury." Faheen v. City Parking Corp., 734 S.W.2d 270, 273 (Mo. Ct. App. 1987). Missouri courts have limited this exception to cases presenting "extraordinary danger." Id. at 274. Pearson and Kirkpatrick have not shown any facts in this case that would have alerted Logan to an extraordinary danger posed by FS. The only complaint involving any actual touching by FS was acknowledged to be a possible accident by Pearson. The other complaints involved potentially harassing conduct but nothing that would indicate extraordinary danger.

Second, Missouri law recognizes a duty where "specific incidents of violent crimes on the premises [] are sufficiently numerous and recent to put a defendant on notice, either actual or constructive, that there is a likelihood third persons will endanger the safety of defendant's invitees." Faheen, 734 S.W.2d at 273-74. Pearson and Kirkpatrick have alleged a history of misconduct of varying kinds at Logan. For example, they claim that in 2013 the school "discriminated against a pregnant student by giving her failing grades rather than 'incomplete' grades." But nothing they have alleged approaches the sort of violent, numerous, and recent crimes that would be necessary to put Logan on notice that an unknown third party like FS could pose a danger to Pearson and Kirkpatrick's safety.

For these reasons, we affirm the judgment of the district court.

KELLY, Circuit Judge, concurring in part and dissenting in part.

I concur in Parts I and II of the court's opinion, but respectfully disagree with the court's conclusion in Part III.

In December 2015, Pearson notified Logan University administrators Shelley Sawalich and Sandra Periello that FS was p.1128 stalking and harassing her, and that his conduct made her feel unsafe on Logan's campus. She also explained that FS had pressed himself up against her in the cadaver lab, making her extremely uncomfortable; and she told Sawalich that she was "terrified of being raped." In light of Pearson's complaints, Logan was on notice by December 2015 that FS was engaged in a continuing pattern of conduct that made at least one student feel that she was going to be physically assaulted. And, in January and early February, Pearson reported to Logan administrators that FS's behavior continued to make her feel unsafe on campus.

The fact that Pearson's complaints included only one instance of "actual touching" does not diminish the potential danger inherent in her allegations. Missouri law recognizes that an individual may "conduct[] himself so as to indicate danger" without having engaged in any physical contact. Cf. Faheen v. City Parking Corp., 734 S.W.2d 270, 273 (Mo. Ct. App. 1987). For example, a person seeking a protection order against stalking must demonstrate a "pattern of conduct" that causes "a fear of danger of physical harm." Binggeli v. Hammond, 300 S.W.3d 621, 623-24 (Mo. Ct. App. 2010) (quoting Mo. Ann. Stat. § 455.010). A pattern of conduct, in turn, "may include, but is not limited to, following the other person or unwanted communication or unwanted contact." Id. (quoting Mo. Ann. Stat. § 455.010).

Here, Pearson informed Logan personnel of FS's alleged conduct that included unwanted physical touching, stalking, and harassment. While the record on this issue is admittedly thin, it is sufficient. Viewing the record in the light most favorable to Pearson and Kirkpatrick and giving them the benefit of all reasonable inferences, as we must on summary judgment, I believe they established, if just barely, the existence of a duty of care to protect them against FS. See Walz v. Ameriprise Fin., Inc., 779 F.3d 842, 844 (8th Cir. 2015).

The district court declined to address whether Pearson or Kirkpatrick could satisfy the other elements of their premises liability and negligence claims. Therefore, I would remand for the district court to make those determinations in the first instance. In the alternative, I would leave to the district court's discretion whether it wishes to continue exercising supplemental jurisdiction over the remaining state law claims on remand, in light of the dismissal of all federal claims. See Gregoire v. Class, 236 F.3d 413, 419 (8th Cir. 2000).

889 F.3d 471 (2018)

**Elizabeth FRYBERGER, Plaintiff-Appellee
USA, Intervenor**

v.

UNIVERSITY OF ARKANSAS; Board of Trustees of the University of Arkansas, Defendants-Appellants
State of Arizona, Amicus on Behalf of Appellant(s)
Equal Rights Advocates, Amicus on Behalf of Appellee(s)
State of Arkansas; State of Kansas; State of Louisiana; State of Nebraska; State of South Carolina; State of Texas, Amici on Behalf of Appellant(s)

No. 16-4505.

United States Court of Appeals, Eighth Circuit.

Submitted: February 13, 2018.

Filed: May 2, 2018.

Appeal from United States District Court for the Western District of Arkansas — Fayetteville.

Counsel who presented argument on behalf of the appellant and appeared on the brief was David A. Curran, of Little Rock, AR. The following attorney(s) appeared on the appellant brief; Carmine Joseph Cordi, Jr., of Fayetteville, AR., Matthew Blayne McCoy, of Fayetteville, AR.

Counsel who presented argument on behalf of the appellee and appeared on the brief was Mason Boling, of Rogers, AR. The following attorney(s) appeared on the appellee brief; George McAllaster Rozzell, of Rogers, AR.

The following attorney(s) appeared on the intervenor brief filed by the United States; Tovah Calderon, of Washington, DC., Francesca Lina Procaccini, of Washington, D.C.

The following attorney(s) appeared on the amicus brief of the States of Arizona, Arkansas, Kansas, Louisiana, Nebraska, South Carolina and Texas,; Patrick E. Hollingsworth, AAG, of Little Rock, AR., Lee P. Rudofsky, Arkansas Solicitor General, of Little Rock, AR.

The following attorney(s) appeared on the amicus brief of the Equal Rights Advocates; Rebecca Peterson-Fisher, of San Francisco, CA.

Before LOKEN, BENTON, and ERICKSON, Circuit Judges.

BENTON, Circuit Judge.

Elizabeth Fryberger sued the University of Arkansas and its Board of Trustees. The district court[1] partly denied the University's motion to dismiss. It appeals. Having jurisdiction under 28 U.S.C. § 1291, this court affirms.

Fryberger sued the University over its response to her report of a sexual assault on campus. She sought compensatory and punitive damages for violations of Title IX of the Education Amendments of 1972. Title IX says (with exceptions): "No person in the United States shall, on the basis of sex, be excluded from participation in, be denied the benefits of, or be subjected to discrimination under any education program or activity receiving Federal financial assistance...." 20 U.S.C. § 1681(a).

The University moved to dismiss on the basis of sovereign immunity. The district court refused to dismiss the Title IX claims, citing the "Civil rights remedies equalization" amendment of 1986 (the Remedies Equalization amendment), 42 U.S.C. § 2000d-7, and *Franklin v. Gwinnett County Public Schools*, 503 U.S. 60, 76, 112 S.Ct. 1028, 117 L.Ed.2d 208 (1992).

"[D]enials of motions to dismiss on Eleventh Amendment immunity grounds are immediately appealable." *United States ex rel. Rodgers v. Arkansas*, 154 F.3d 865, 867 (8th Cir. 1998), *citing Puerto Rico Aqueduct and Sewer Auth. v. Metcalf & Eddy, Inc.,* 506 U.S. 139, 147, 113 S.Ct. 684, 121 L.Ed.2d 605 (1993) ("States and state entities that claim to be 'arms of the State' may take advantage of the collateral order doctrine to appeal a district court order denying a claim of Eleventh Amendment immunity."). This court reviews de novo questions of sovereign immunity. *Lors v. Dean*, 746 F.3d 857, 861 (8th Cir. 2014).

Under the Eleventh Amendment and constitutional principles of sovereign immunity, "an unconsenting State is immune from suits brought in federal courts by her own citizens as well as by citizens of another state." *Port Auth. Trans-Hudson Corp. v. Feeney*, 495 U.S. 299, 304, 110 S.Ct. 1868, 109 L.Ed.2d 264 (1990), *quoting Pennhurst State Sch. & Hosp. v. Halderman*, 465 U.S. 89, 100, 104 S.Ct. 900, 79 L.Ed.2d 67 (1984). "A State, however, may choose to waive its immunity in federal court at its pleasure." *Sossamon v. Texas*, 563 U.S. 277, 284, 131 S.Ct. 1651, 179 L.Ed.2d 700 (2011).

"Congress may require a waiver of state sovereign immunity as a condition for receiving federal funds." *Jim C. v. United States*, 235 F.3d 1079, 1081 (8th Cir. 2000) (en banc), *citing College Sav. Bank v. Florida Prepaid Postsecondary Educ. Expense Bd.*, 527 U.S. 666, 119 S.Ct. 2219, 144 L.Ed.2d 605 (1999). However, because "[s]overeign immunity principles enforce an important constitutional limitation on the power of the federal courts," "[a] State's consent to suit must be 'unequivocally expressed' in the text of the relevant statute." *Sossamon*, 563 U.S. at 285, 131 S.Ct. 1651, *quoting Pennhurst*, 465 U.S. at 99, 104 S.Ct. 900. "Only by requiring this 'clear declaration' by the State can we be 'certain that the State in fact consents to suit.'" *Id.* at 284, 131 S.Ct. 1651, *quoting College Sav.*, 527 U.S. at 680, 119 S.Ct. 2219.

Fryberger argues that under the Remedies Equalization amendment, the University consented to this suit by accepting federal funds. The University acknowledges it accepted federal funds. It also does not challenge — and this court does not address — Congress's authority to enact p.474 Title IX or the Remedies Equalization amendment under the Spending Clause. *See Sossamon*, 563 U.S. at 282 n.1, 131 S.Ct. 1651 (declining to address Congress's authority to enact RLUIPA under the Spending Clause). The question is whether the University's consent is unequivocally expressed in the Remedies Equalization amendment, section 2000d-7(a) (emphasis added):

> (1) A State shall not be immune under the Eleventh Amendment of the Constitution of the United States from suit in Federal court for a violation of section 504 of the Rehabilitation Act of 1973..., *title IX of the Education Amendments of 1972* ..., the Age Discrimination Act of 1975 ..., title VI of the

Civil Rights Act of 1964 ..., or the provisions of any other Federal statute prohibiting discrimination by recipients of Federal financial assistance.

(2) In a suit against a State for a violation of a statute referred to in paragraph (1), remedies (including remedies both at law and in equity) are available for such a violation to the same extent as such remedies are available for such violation in the suit against any public or private entity other than a State.

The Remedies Equalization amendment unequivocally expresses the University's consent to suit in federal court for violations of Title IX. *See Sossamon,* 563 U.S. at 291, 131 S.Ct. 1651 ("[Section 2000d-7(a)(1)] expressly waives state sovereign immunity for violations of ... title IX...."); *Lane v. Pena,* 518 U.S. 187, 200, 116 S.Ct. 2092, 135 L.Ed.2d 486 (1996) (referring to § 2000d-7 as "an unambiguous waiver of the States' Eleventh Amendment immunity"). *Cf. Crawford v. Davis,* 109 F.3d 1281, 1283 (8th Cir. 1997) ("Congress has unequivocally expressed its intent to abrogate the states' Eleventh Amendment immunity for Title IX claims, *see* 42 U.S.C. § 2000d-7(a)(1)...."), *citing Egerdahl v. Hibbing Cmty. Coll.,* 72 F.3d 615, 619 (8th Cir. 1995).

The University contends, however, that this consent does not extend to the only relief sought by Fryberger, *damages* in a Title IX suit. The University relies on *Sossamon.* There, the Supreme Court reaffirmed that "a waiver of sovereign immunity 'will be strictly construed, in terms of its scope, in favor of the sovereign.'" *Sossamon,* 563 U.S. at 285, 131 S.Ct. 1651, *quoting Lane,* 518 U.S. at 192, 116 S.Ct. 2092. Accordingly, "a waiver of sovereign immunity to other types of relief does not waive immunity to damages." *Id.* (alteration in original), *quoting Lane,* 518 U.S. at 192, 116 S.Ct. 2092. "The question ... is... whether Congress has given clear direction that it intends to include a damages remedy. The text must 'establish unambiguously that the waiver extends to monetary claims.'" *Id.* at 289, 131 S.Ct. 1651, *quoting United States v. Nordic Village,* 503 U.S. 30, 34, 112 S.Ct. 1011, 117 L.Ed.2d 181 (1992).

The Court in *Sossamon* addressed the waiver provision in the Religious Land Use and Institutionalized Persons Act of 2000 (RLUIPA). *Id.* at 280, 131 S.Ct. 1651. That waiver says, "A person may assert a violation of [RLUIPA] as a claim or defense in a judicial proceeding and obtain appropriate relief against a government." *Id.* at 282, 131 S.Ct. 1651 (alteration in original), *quoting* 42 U.S.C. § 2000cc-2(a). The Court held that "appropriate relief" does not unambiguously include damages. *Id.* at 285, 131 S.Ct. 1651. Strictly construing the waiver in favor of the sovereign, the Court said, "'Appropriate relief does not so clearly and unambiguously waive sovereign immunity to private suits for damages that we can 'be certain that the State in fact consents' to such a suit." *Id.* at 285-86, 131 S.Ct. 1651, *quoting College Sav.,* 527 U.S. at 680, 119 S.Ct. 2219.

In contrast, the Remedies Equalization amendment says that in suits against a state, "remedies *(including remedies* both *at law* and in equity) are available for [violations of Title IX] to the same extent as such remedies are available for such a violation in the suit against any public or private entity other than a state." § 2000d-7(a)(2) (emphasis added). This resolves any possible ambiguity in section 2000d-7(a)(1). Remedies at law include damages. *See SCA Hygiene Prod. Aktiebolag v. First Quality Baby Prod., LLC,* ___ U.S. ___, 137 S.Ct. 954, 960, 197 L.Ed.2d 292 (2017) ("damages" are "a quintessential legal remedy"); *Mertens v. Hewitt Assoc.,* 508 U.S. 248, 255, 113 S.Ct. 2063, 124 L.Ed.2d 161 (1993) ("Money damages are, of course, the classic form of *legal* relief." (emphasis in original)); *Bowen v. Massachusetts,* 487 U.S. 879, 893, 108 S.Ct.

2722, 101 L.Ed.2d 749 (1988) (discussing the "distinction between an action at law for damages ... and an equitable action for specific relief"); *Ventura v. Kyle,* 825 F.3d 876, 887 (8th Cir. 2016) ("damages" are a "remedy at law"). Compensatory damages are available in Title IX suits against any public or private entity other than a state. *Franklin,* 503 U.S. at 76, 112 S.Ct. 1028 (the Title IX implied right of action, recognized in *Cannon v. University of Chicago,* 441 U.S. 677, 717, 99 S.Ct. 1946, 60 L.Ed.2d 560 (1979), extends to suits for compensatory damages). *See Barnes v. Gorman,* 536 U.S. 181, 187, 122 S.Ct. 2097, 153 L.Ed.2d 230 (2002) ("[U]nder Title IX ... a recipient of federal funds is ... subject to suit for compensatory damages"), *citing Franklin,* 503 U.S. at 76, 112 S.Ct. 1028. Thus, the only "plausible interpretation" is that compensatory damages — remedies at law available against non-states — are available against states to the same extent. *Cf. Sossamon,* 563 U.S. at 287, 131 S.Ct. 1651 ("[W]here a statute is susceptible of multiple plausible interpretations, including one preserving immunity, we will not consider a State to have waived its sovereign immunity.").

The University argues that Congress did not intend the waiver to include Title IX suits for damages, because it was unclear in 1986 (when Congress enacted the Remedies Equalization amendment) whether there was a cause of action for damages. In 1986, the Supreme Court had decided *Cannon,* which held there is a private Title IX cause of action, but not *Franklin,* which held that the cause of action extends to suits for compensatory damages.

But this context supports finding a waiver here. First, it shows that Congress intended to create an unambiguous waiver of state sovereign immunity including suits for damages. The Court explained:

> [Section 2000d-7] was enacted in response to our decision in *Atascadero State Hospital v. Scanlon,* 473 U.S. 234 [105 S.Ct. 3142, 87 L.Ed.2d 171] (1985), where we held that Congress had not unmistakably expressed its intent to abrogate the States' Eleventh Amendment immunity in the Rehabilitation Act, and that the States accordingly were not subject to suit in federal court by litigants seeking retroactive monetary relief under § 504.... By enacting [section 2000d-7], Congress sought to provide the sort of unequivocal waiver that our precedents demand.

Lane, 518 U.S. at 198, 116 S.Ct. 2092 (internal quotation marks and citation omitted). Second, it shows Congress intended the waiver to apply in Title IX suits. Congress "was legislating with full cognizance of" *Cannon. See Franklin,* 503 U.S. at 72, 112 S.Ct. 1028 ("[Section 2000d-7] cannot be read except as a validation of *Cannon*'s holding."); *Cf. id.* at 78, 112 S.Ct. 1028 (Scalia, J., concurring) ("42 U.S.C. § 2000d-7(a)(2), must be read, in my view, not only 'as a validation of *Cannon*'s holding,' ... but also as an implicit acknowledgment that damages are available [in Title IX suits]."). Thus, Congress "specifically considered state sovereign immunity," including immunity to Title IX suits for damages, and "intentionally legislated on the matter," conditioning funds on a waiver of that immunity. *See Sossamon,* 563 U.S. at 290, 131 S.Ct. 1651, *citing Spector v. Norwegian Cruise Line Ltd.,* 545 U.S. 119, 139, 125 S.Ct. 2169, 162 L.Ed.2d 97 (2005) ("[C]lear statement rules ensure Congress does not, by broad or general language, legislate on a sensitive topic inadvertently or without due deliberation.").

The University also argues the text of section 2000d-7(a) is ambiguous, because rather than ending with the concept that "damages are available against a state," it continues with "damages are available against a state *to the same extent as a non-state.*" True, a state must look outside the text to *Franklin* in order to determine that compensatory damages are available against non-states. The University concludes the waiver is not "'unequivocally expressed' *in the text of the relevant statute.*" *See id.*, at 285, 131 S.Ct. 1651 (emphasis added). *See also Dellmuth v. Muth*, 491 U.S. 223, 230, 109 S.Ct. 2397, 105 L.Ed.2d 181 (1989) ("[E]vidence of congressional intent must be both unequivocal and *textual.*" (emphasis added)).

The text is not ambiguous. As discussed, it "establish[es] unambiguously that the waiver extends to" the *Cannon-Franklin* cause of action for damages. *See Sossamon*, 563 U.S. at 289, 131 S.Ct. 1651. This satisfies the clear statement rule. *Cf. Sossamon*, 563 U.S. at 289 n.6, 131 S.Ct. 1651 ("Liability against nonsovereigns could not put the states on notice that they would be liable in the same manner, absent an unequivocal textual waiver."). The text of the waiver need not also expressly restate the *Cannon-Franklin* cause of action. *Cf. FDIC v. Meyer*, 510 U.S. 471, 484, 114 S.Ct. 996, 127 L.Ed.2d 308 (1994) (explaining that "whether there has been a waiver" of the federal government's sovereign immunity and whether there is a "cause of action for damages" are "analytically distinct inquiries" (internal quotation marks omitted)). If the University were correct, the Remedies Equalization amendment would be *entirely ineffective*, because it similarly relies on the substantive law of each listed statute without expressly stating a cause of action for any kind of relief. The University rightly does not argue this. *See, e.g., Dinkins v. Correctional Med. Servs.*, 743 F.3d 633, 635 (8th Cir. 2014) (per curiam) ("As to the request for damages, the [state agency] waives sovereign immunity under [section 504 of the Rehabilitation Act] by accepting federal funds."), *citing* § 2000d-7(a).

The University and its amici emphasize the Court's holding in *Lane* that section 2000d-7(a) "is not so free from ambiguity that we can comfortably conclude, based thereon, that Congress intended to subject the Federal Government to awards of monetary damages for violations of § 504(a) of the [Rehabilitation] Act." 518 U.S. at 200, 116 S.Ct. 2092. However, the lack of clarity in *Lane* — whether section 2000d-7(a)(2)'s phrase "public or private entity" included the *federal government* — does not create ambiguity here, where state immunity is at issue. Section 2000d-7(a) speaks clearly to state immunity. *See id.* at 200, 116 S.Ct. 2092 ("Given the care with which Congress responded to our decision in *Atascadero* by crafting an unambiguous waiver of the States' Eleventh Amendment immunity in [42 U.S.C. § 2000d-7(a)(1)], it would be ironic indeed p.477 to conclude that the same provision 'unequivocally' establishes a waiver of the Federal Government's sovereign immunity against monetary damages awards....").

The Remedies Equalization amendment clearly and unambiguously expresses the University's consent to Title IX suits for damages. By accepting federal funds, the University in fact consented to suits for compensatory damages for violations of Title IX. *See Cherry v. University of Wisconsin Sys. Bd. of Regents*, 265 F.3d 541, 555 (7th Cir. 2001) (under 2000d-7(a), state waives sovereign immunity to Title IX suit for compensatory damages by accepting federal funds), *citing Pederson v. LSU*, 213 F.3d 858, 876 (5th Cir. 2000) *and Litman v. George Mason Univ.*, 186 F.3d 544, 555 (4th Cir. 1999). *Cf. Dinkins*, 743 F.3d at 635 (under 2000d-7(a), state waives sovereign immunity to suits seeking damages for violations of section 504 of the Rehabilitation Act).

The district court did not err in refusing to dismiss Fryberger's Title IX claims. Because the University waived its immunity, this court need not consider whether Congress, under section 5 of the Fourteenth Amendment, abrogated it.

This court also need not consider whether *punitive* damages are available. The district court did not rule on this. Neither party raised it on appeal. This court's holding on compensatory damages resolves whether the University is immune *from suit. See Puerto Rico Aqueduct,* 506 U.S. at 141, 144-45, 113 S.Ct. 684 ("district court order denying a claim... to Eleventh Amendment immunity from suit" is "effectively unreviewable on appeal," and thus appealable under the collateral order doctrine, because "the value to the States of their Eleventh Amendment immunity ... is ... lost as litigation proceeds past motion practice"). *See also Espinal-Dominguez v. Commonwealth of Puerto Rico,* 352 F.3d 490, 499 (1st Cir. 2003) (no collateral order jurisdiction where "a State asserts only that a singular remedy, compensatory damages, is precluded by the Eleventh Amendment, yet acknowledges that it is subject to the plaintiff's federal court suit"); *Cherry v. University of Wisconsin Sys. Bd. of Regents,* 265 F.3d 541, 547 (7th Cir. 2001) (declining to address claim that state agency is immune from a punitive damages award on interlocutory appeal because "[a] claim of immunity to a certain class of damages" is different than a claim to immunity from suit); *Burns-Vidlak ex rel. Burns v. Chandler,* 165 F.3d 1257, 1260 (9th Cir. 1999) (no collateral order jurisdiction over claim of immunity to punitive damages where the state "concedes that it is subject to suit").

* * * * * * *

The judgment is affirmed.

[1] The Honorable P.K. Holmes, III, Chief Judge, United States District Court for the Western District of Arkansas.

865 F.3d 1054 (2017)

K.T., Plaintiff-Appellant

v.

CULVER-STOCKTON COLLEGE; A.B.; Lambda Chi Alpha Fraternity; Lambda Chi Alpha Fraternity Inc., Defendants-Appellees.

Women's and Children's Advocacy Project at New England Law Boston, Amicus Curiae.

No. 16-3617.

United States Court of Appeals, Eighth Circuit.

Submitted: April 5, 2017.

Filed: August 1, 2017.

KT v. Culver-Stockton College, 865 F. 3d 1054 (8th Cir. 2017)

Appeal from the United States District Court for the Eastern District of Missouri—St. Louis

Counsel who represented the appellant was James M. Martin, of Saint Louis, MO. Also appearing on appellant's brief was Heidi Lynn Leopold of Saint Louis, MO.

Counsel who represented the appellee was Ian P Cooper, of Saint Louis, MO. A Also appearing on appellees' brief was Katherine L. Nash of Saint Louis, MO.

Before SMITH, Chief Judge, ARNOLD and SHEPHERD, Circuit Judges.

SHEPHERD, Circuit Judge.

K.T. brought a Title IX student-on-student harassment claim against Culver-Stockton College after she was allegedly sexually assaulted by a Culver-Stockton student on campus. The district court[1] dismissed her complaint for failure to state a claim under Federal Rule of Civil Procedure 12(b)(6). We affirm.

I.

Sixteen-year-old K.T., a junior in high school, was invited by Culver-Stockton College to visit campus as a potential recruit to the women's soccer team. While there, K.T. went to a party at an on-campus fraternity house, where she says she was served alcohol before being physically and sexually assaulted by a fraternity member. The alleged assailant was a student of Culver-Stockton College. According to K.T., the incident was reported to College authorities the same weekend of the party, but the College did nothing other than cancel a scheduled conference with K.T. and her parents.

K.T. sued the College in federal court seeking money damages under Title IX of the Education Amendments of 1972.[2] The claim was couched in terms of student-on-student harassment (or peer harassment), a theory first articulated by the United States Supreme Court in Davis ex rel. LaShonda D. v. Monroe County Board of Education, 526 U.S. 629, 119 S.Ct. 1661, 143 L.Ed.2d 839 (1999). Davis held that a federally funded institution may be liable for damages in a private Title IX action if its deliberate indifference to known acts of peer harassment denied the victim access to educational opportunities provided by the institution. Id. at 650, 119 S.Ct. 1661. K.T.'s complaint stated that the College acted with deliberate indifference toward sexual harassment on its campus by failing to (1) take reasonable preventative measures such as supervising K.T. during her visit, and (2) investigate and provide treatment for K.T. once the College received reports of the alleged incident.

The College moved to dismiss the Title IX claim under Federal Rule of Civil Procedure 12(b)(6), arguing that K.T. failed to state a claim because she was not a Culver-Stockton student when the alleged assault occurred. The College averred that the student-on-student harassment doctrine, as its name suggests, applies only in cases where a student sues her own school over harassment by a fellow student. In support, the College quoted language from Davis that a funding recipient is not liable under Title IX "unless its deliberate indifference subject[s] *its students* to harassment." Id. at 644-45, 119 S.Ct. 1661 (alteration in original) (emphasis added) (internal quotation marks omitted). The College further asserted that no federal court has extended Davis's holding to claims by non-students.

The district court agreed with Culver-Stockton. In an order dismissing the Title IX claim, the court first concluded that as a non-student K.T. could not bring a Title IX claim against the College. Even if K.T. could bring such a claim, the district court continued, she failed to plausibly allege p.1057 that (1) an appropriate person at the College had actual knowledge of previous incidents of similar harassment so as to alert it to a substantial risk of further abuse, and (2) the College's response to K.T.'s allegations was deliberately indifferent and caused her to undergo harassment, made her vulnerable to it, or subjected her to further discrimination. The court determined that K.T. therefore failed to state a plausible claim under Title IX.[3]

II.

The parties dispute whether K.T.'s status as a non-student precludes her from asserting a Title IX harassment claim. Assuming arguendo that it does not, we find no merit in K.T.'s appeal because her complaint failed to state a plausible claim to survive dismissal under Rule 12(b)(6). Accordingly, we affirm.

A. Standard of Review

We review the district court's grant of a Rule 12(b)(6) motion to dismiss de novo. Cox v. Mortg. Elec. Registration Sys., Inc., 685 F.3d 663, 668 (8th Cir. 2012). To prevail, K.T. must allege more than "[t]hreadbare recitals of the elements of a cause of action, supported by mere conclusory statements." Ashcroft v. Iqbal, 556 U.S. 662, 678, 129 S.Ct. 1937, 173 L.Ed.2d 868 (2009). The complaint must allege sufficient facts that, taken as true, "'state a claim to relief that is plausible on its face.'" Id. (quoting Bell Atlantic Corp. v. Twombly, 550 U.S. 544, 570, 127 S.Ct. 1955, 167 L.Ed.2d 929 (2007)). A claim is facially plausible when its factual content "allows the court to draw the reasonable inference that the defendant is liable for the misconduct alleged." Id. "We make this determination by considering only the materials that are necessarily embraced by the pleadings and exhibits attached to the complaint." Cox, 685 F.3d at 668 (internal quotation marks omitted).

B. Title IX Student-on-Student Harassment

Title IX provides that "[n]o person in the United States shall, on the basis of sex, be excluded from participation in, be denied the benefits of, or be subjected to discrimination under any education program or activity receiving Federal financial assistance." 20 U.S.C. § 1681(a). Where, as here, the plaintiff's Title IX claim is based on harassment, the school is liable in damages only where it is "(1) deliberately indifferent (2) to known acts of discrimination (3) which occur under its control." Ostrander v. Duggan, 341 F.3d 745, 750 (8th Cir. 2003) (internal quotation marks omitted). Additionally, the discrimination must be "so severe, pervasive, and objectively offensive that it can be said to deprive the victim[] of access to the educational opportunities or benefits provided by the school." Davis, 526 U.S. at 650, 119 S.Ct. 1661.

i. Deliberate Indifference

K.T. failed to plausibly allege that Culver-Stockton acted with deliberate indifference. A funding recipient "may not be liable for damages unless its deliberate indifference *subject[s]* its students to harassment. That is, the deliberate indifference must, at a minimum, *cause* [students] to undergo harassment or make them liable or vulnerable to it." Davis, 526 U.S. at 644-45, 119 S.Ct. 1661 (alterations in original) (emphasis added) (internal quotation marks omitted); see also Shrum ex rel. Kelly v. Kluck, 249 F.3d 773, 782 (8th Cir. 2001) ("[D]eliberate indifference must either directly cause the abuse to occur or make students vulnerable to such abuse.").

In her complaint, K.T. alleged that Culver-Stockton was deliberately indifferent by failing to adopt practices to prevent sexual assault and also failing to investigate and offer medical services to K.T. after it received reports of the alleged incident. But the complaint identified no causal nexus between Culver-Stockton's inaction and K.T.'s experiencing sexual harassment. Rather, the complaint alleged that "as a direct and proximate result of... [Culver-Stockton's] failure to investigate and provide guidance, counseling and treatment, . . . Plaintiff sustained substantial mental and emotional distress and . . . [s]he currently suffers from post-trauma syndrome and psychiatric overlay." At most, these allegations link the College's inaction with emotional trauma K.T. claims she experienced following the assault. The complaint does not, however, allege that Culver-Stockton's purported indifference "subject[ed] [K.T.] to harassment." See Davis, 526 U.S. at 644, 119 S.Ct. 1661. Thus, while K.T. was dissatisfied with Culver-Stockton's response, based on the allegations in the complaint the response cannot be characterized as deliberate indifference *that caused the assault.* See, e.g., Shrum, 249 F.3d at 782. We therefore agree with the district court that K.T. failed to adequately plead deliberate indifference.

ii. Actual Knowledge

We also agree with the district court that K.T. did not plausibly plead that Culver-Stockton had actual knowledge of discrimination. Citing Williams v. Board of Regents of the University System of Georgia, 441 F.3d 1287, 1298 (11th Cir. 2006), *vacated*, 477 F.3d 1282 (11th Cir. 2007), K.T. argues that a plaintiff satisfies the actual knowledge element simply by notifying the school that she was subjected to a sexual assault. Because K.T.'s complaint stated that her assault allegations were reported to Culver-Stockton one to two days after the fraternity party, K.T. argues that she sufficiently pled actual knowledge.

Contrary to K.T.'s contention, the actual knowledge element requires schools to have more than after-the-fact notice of a single instance in which the plaintiff experienced sexual assault. See, e.g., Plamp v. Mitchell Sch. Dist. No. 17-2, 565 F.3d 450, 454, 457 (8th Cir. 2009) (no actual knowledge of discrimination where a high school student's parents "immediately reported" a teacher's sexual harassment of the student). Rather, a plaintiff must allege that the funding recipient had *prior notice* of a substantial risk of peer harassment "in the recipient's programs," see Gebser v. Lago Vista Indep. Sch. Dist., 524 U.S. 274, 290, 118 S.Ct. 1989, 141 L.Ed.2d 277 (1998), based on evidence such as previous similar incidents of assault. In Ostrander, for instance, this court intimated that actual knowledge may be established where the recipient has *prior knowledge* of (1) harassment previously committed by the same perpetrator and/or (2) previous reports of sexual harassment occurring on the same premises. 341 F.3d at 751. Similarly, in Thomas v. Board of Trustees of the Nebraska State Colleges, this court stated that a plaintiff must show that the school "had actual knowledge that [the assailant] posed a substantial risk of sufficiently severe harm to students based on [the assailant's] *previous known conduct*." 667 Fed.Appx. 560, 562 (8th Cir. 2016) (per curiam) (emphasis added). Even in Williams—which K.T. misreads as favoring her case—the Eleventh Circuit on sua sponte rehearing found that school officials had actual knowledge of discrimination in part because they recruited the student-assailant p.1059 despite having "preexisting knowledge" of the student's previous sexual misconduct. 477 F.3d at 1293-94.

K.T.'s complaint lacks any assertion that Culver-Stockton knew—prior to the alleged assault on K.T.—that individuals in the College's soccer recruiting program faced a risk of sexual harassment. As the district court acknowledged, K.T. "makes no factual allegations that the College was aware of invited high-school aged recruits, visitors or College students being assaulted in similar circumstances, or that the College was aware of any prior allegations of sexual assault by [the same alleged perpetrator]." We therefore agree with the district court that K.T. failed to plausibly allege that Culver-Stockton had actual knowledge of discrimination within the meaning of a Title IX peer harassment claim.

iii. Severe, Pervasive, and Objectively Offensive Discrimination

By the language of Title IX itself, liability lies only where the plaintiff is "subjected to discrimination *under any education program or activity* receiving Federal financial assistance." 20 U.S.C. § 1681(a) (emphasis added). The Supreme Court in Davis interpreted this provision to "suggest[] that the behavior be serious enough to have the systemic effect of denying the victim equal access to an educational program or activity." 526 U.S. at 652, 119 S.Ct. 1661. "[I]n theory," the Court explained, "a single instance of sufficiently severe one-on-one peer harassment could be said to have such an effect, [but] we think it unlikely that Congress would have thought such behavior sufficient to rise to this level in light of the . . . amount of litigation that would be invited by entertaining claims of official indifference to a single instance of one-on-one peer harassment." Id. at 652-53, 119 S.Ct. 1661; see also Williams, 477 F.3d at 1297 ("[D]iscrimination must be more widespread than a single instance of one-on-one peer harassment." (internal quotation marks omitted)). Rather, the discrimination must be "severe, pervasive, and objectively offensive." Davis, 526 U.S. at 651, 119 S.Ct. 1661.

K.T.'s complaint is limited to an allegation of a single sexual assault. Although we are sympathetic to K.T.'s circumstances and agree that she has alleged opprobrious misconduct on the part of the fraternity member, K.T.'s singular grievance on its own does not plausibly allege pervasive discrimination as required to state a peer harassment claim. See id. Accordingly, K.T.'s complaint lacks factual content allowing us to conclude that either the alleged misconduct or Culver-Stockton's response to K.T.'s allegations had the required "systemic effect" such that K.T. was denied equal access to educational opportunities provided by Culver-Stockton. See id. at 652, 119 S.Ct. 1661. The complaint therefore failed to state a claim of peer harassment under Title IX.[4]

III.

For these reasons, we affirm the order of the district court granting Culver-Stockton's motion to dismiss for failure to state a claim under Federal Rule of Civil Procedure 12(b)(6).

[1] The Honorable Charles A. Shaw, United States District Judge for the Eastern District of Missouri.

[2] Though Culver-Stockton College is a private Christian school, it receives federal financial assistance and is therefore subject to Title IX's prohibition against sex-based discrimination. 20 U.S.C. § 1681(a).

[3] In the district court, K.T. also brought an assault claim against the alleged assailant, as well as assault and negligent supervision claims against the local fraternity chapter and the fraternity's national organization. After dismissing the Title IX claim against the College, the district court declined to exercise supplemental jurisdiction over the remaining state law claims.

[4] Because K.T. failed to adequately plead the elements of deliberate indifference, actual knowledge, and pervasive discrimination depriving her equal access to an educational program, we need not determine whether she sufficiently alleged the element of Culver-Stockton's "substantial control over both the harasser and the context in which the known harassment occurs." See Ostrander, 341 F.3d at 750.

746 F.3d 874 (2014)

Joan ROE, Plaintiff-Appellant
Mary ROE; John Roe, Plaintiffs
v.
ST. LOUIS UNIVERSITY, Defendant-Appellee.
Sigma Tau Gamma Epsilon Xi Chapter; Sigma Tau Gamma Fraternity, Inc., Defendants.
National Women's Law Center, Amicus on Behalf of Appellant.

No. 13-1206.

United States Court of Appeals, Eighth Circuit.

Submitted: January 16, 2014.
Filed: March 25, 2014.

Roe v. St. Louis University, 746 F. 3d 874 (8th Cir. 2014)

p.877 David J. Fraser, argued, Trabuco Canyon, CA, for Appellant.

Neal Frederick Perryman, argued, Saint Louis, MO (Debbie S. Champion, Sarah Elizabeth Mullen, on the brief), for Appellee.

National Women's Law Center; Neena Chaudhry, Fatima Goss Graves, Devi Rao, Washington, DC, for amicus.

Before LOKEN, MURPHY, and COLLOTON, Circuit Judges.

MURPHY, Circuit Judge.

Joan Roe[1], a student athlete recruited for the field hockey team at Saint Louis University, and her parents brought this case under Title IX, a federal statute banning discrimination on the basis of sex in federally funded educational programs, and Missouri state law. Roe claims deliberate indifference by the University to her rape by another student and state law violations including breach of contract, misrepresentation, and negligence following a back injury she received in training.[2] The district court[3] granted summary judgment to the University, and Roe appeals. We affirm.

I.

In reviewing a summary judgment, we take all facts in the light most favorable to the nonmovant who in this case is Joan p.878 Roe. *Argenyi v. Creighton Univ.*, 703 F.3d 441, 446 (8th Cir.2013). Roe arrived at Saint Louis University to begin her freshman year of college in August 2006. She had played as a goal keeper on her high school field hockey team and was recruited by the University's intercollegiate team and received a partial scholarship. Roe has stated that she chose to attend Saint Louis University based on her favorable impressions of its athletic programs, educational opportunities, and positive environment.

Roe arrived in St. Louis in August 2006 for preseason training. She began as a second line goal keeper but hoped to move up to starter. After the season began, she injured her back, an injury she first noticed after a hockey practice in late September. Her injury was aggravated by subsequent practices and particularly by a weightlifting trial on October 26. Dr. D. Thomas Rogers, a physician who treated her after she left the University, testified by deposition that the weightlifting trial had further herniated a disc in Roe's low back.

Near the end of October Roe received disappointing midterm grades: 1 C_, 1 D, and 3 Fs. Roe's academic advisor, Peggy Dotson, believed that her low grades were partly due to the demanding field hockey schedule. Roe also experienced other difficulties. Earlier in October she had been accused of plagiarizing a speech in one of her courses. The Athletic Department's academic services coordinator, Mary Clark, contacted Roe about her midterm grades and suggested university resources which could help her improve. These potential resources included a tutor, contacts with her professors, and study arrangements. Roe met with Clark who assisted her in finding a tutor for a geography class. The Athletic Department also arranged for weekly meetings with Roe, a weekly task list from Clark, structured study hall time, and random checks on her class attendance. Meanwhile, Mary Roe had become concerned about her daughter and contacted academic advisor Peggy Dotson who provided her with names and contact information for Joan's professors.

Because of her low grades, Roe was not permitted to travel with the field hockey team to a game in Virginia the weekend of October 26. That same weekend, Roe attended a Halloween costume party on Friday, October 27 at an off campus apartment building. Three students lived in the apartment, two of whom were members of the Sigma Tau Gamma fraternity's Epilson Xi chapter. The party was not an official fraternity event, however, and was attended by other students. One guest later estimated that almost one hundred people were there while another thought there were up to two hundred.

Roe says she was raped during the Halloween party in a stairwell near the entrance to the hosts' apartment. While she is unable to remember all that happened, she later told the St. Louis police that she had been socializing with a male student whom she identified by name. He was a fraternity pledge who had been dressed in a blue Smurf costume on the night of the party. Other party attendees told the police they had seen Roe and that student dancing together; one witness described seeing them kissing in the stairwell. Both Roe and the male student admitted to drinking alcohol that night. Roe stated that she had started drinking earlier in the evening while watching a baseball game with friends in the dormitory and continued to drink at the party. The male student told the police that Roe invited him to her room while they were dancing; they then left the party and went into the nearby stairwell and began "making out." After sexual intercourse, he asked Roe if she p.879 wanted to return to the party, but she declined and he rejoined it alone.

Roe later told the police that she did not remember leaving the party. Her next memory was waking up at a friend's apartment. The friend told the police that she had seen Roe crying at the party, and Roe had explained that she had been sexually assaulted. The friend took Roe back to her apartment with the assistance of other students, and she saw blue makeup stains on Roe's clothes. Roe later told the police that her back and vagina were sore the day after the party.

Shortly after the night of the party, Roe heard that the male student with whom she had been dancing was "bragging" about "having sex with a girl in the stairwell."

On October 31 Roe sent him a Facebook message describing the Smurf costume he had worn at the party. She wanted him to be aware that she knew he was the costumed man who had raped her. In his statement to the police he claimed that he had communicated with Roe online before and after the evening of the party, all of which Roe denies.

Several days after the party Roe told one of the field hockey captains about the party and said that she had gone into a stairwell with a man dressed as a Smurf. While Roe did not remember exactly what had occurred then, she was sore afterwards. The field hockey captain was concerned and believes she advised Roe to tell their coach about the assault. She also asked "if [Roe had] contacted the police or something like that" and whether she could share her information with the other captain "so that she could help me give better advice." On November 1, the other field hockey captain reported Roe's rape to Janet Oberle, the University's assistant athletic director for NCAA (National Collegiate Athletic Association) compliance and student services.

Oberle became actively involved in trying to help Roe. She called Roe in for a meeting on November 1, the same day she heard about the rape. Before the meeting Oberle spoke with a University professor connected with athletics to seek his advice on how to communicate with Roe. During their meeting Roe told Oberle that she could not remember what had happened and she never told anyone who had assaulted her until after she left the University. Oberle advised Roe that she could contact the University's Department of Public Safety as well as the Office of Judicial Affairs which was responsible for student conduct. Oberle also told Public Safety that a student might be filing a report, but she did not contact Judicial Affairs since Roe had not told her that the man in question was a student. Oberle advised Roe to inform her parents about the rape, but Roe said she did not want Oberle to contact them. Oberle also asked Mary Clark, the academic coordinator in the Athletic Department, to contact Roe's parents about her grades. On November 2 Roe was suspended from the field hockey team due to her poor grades.

Janet Oberle, the assistant athletic director for NCAA compliance and student services, also referred Roe to Claudia Charles, the counselor for sexual assault at Student Health and Counseling Services. Roe met with Charles on November 3 and told her that she did not want to inform her parents about the rape but that she had received medical treatment after it. Roe later testified in her deposition, however, that she had not sought any such medical care while she was in St. Louis. Oberle also made her own contact with Charles to discuss how the University could support Roe, and on November 6 she spoke to Roe's parents about academic support for their daughter.

p.880 Roe's field hockey coach, Marcie Boyer, went to one of Roe's classes on November 15 to check her attendance. Although Boyer did not see her there, Roe later claimed she had been present. The professor teaching the class confirmed however that Roe had not been there. Roe has since admitted that she lied about her attendance. Due to this incident and to her unimproved academic performance, Roe was dismissed from the field hockey team. On December 15 Roe requested a medically based withdrawal from the University. The request was granted, and Roe left St. Louis and never returned to the University.

According to Roe, she did not tell her parents about the rape until after she returned home to Hawaii. On December 18 Roe told her mother that she had been raped but that she did not know the rapist's name. Her father John Roe contacted the University's Department of Public Safety and the St. Louis Police Department on December 19 to report his daughter's rape, and both began investigations. Joan Roe gave the name of the man who had raped her to the police on January 5, and her father contacted the University on January 9 with his name. John Roe also contacted a student conduct officer at the University about its adjudicative process. That office sent an incident report and hearing guidelines, but neither Roe nor her parents ever filed such a report. After being contacted by the police, the accused rapist spoke to a police detective and claimed that he had had consensual sexual intercourse with Joan Roe. No criminal charges were ever filed.

In September 2008 Roe and her parents filed this federal case against the University and unidentified defendants; an amended complaint followed in April 2009. The Roes sued the University under Title IX for deliberate indifference and disparate treatment, alleging that it had been deliberately indifferent to Joan's rape and that it was liable under a theory of disparate treatment because male athletes with health issues received better care than their female counterparts. Roe further alleged intentional misrepresentation, false promise, negligent misrepresentation, deceptive merchandising practices, and breach of contract. Roe also brought negligence claims against the University, the national fraternity, and its local chapter. Her parents were voluntarily dismissed as plaintiffs in May 2009, the month Roe turned 21.

The case was originally assigned to Judge Jean C. Hamilton who recused herself after Roe raised questions about a former law clerk who had represented the University. The case was reassigned to Judge Henry E. Autrey who denied Roe's motion for his recusal. After the University moved for summary judgment in April 2012, Roe filed a Rule 56(d) motion to extend discovery. In June 2012 Roe then submitted a "Statement and Compendium of Material Facts and Exhibits." She subsequently filed two motions for partial summary judgment, one dealing with her Title IX claims and the other with her back injury claims. On December 12, 2012 the district court denied Roe's motion to utilize a factual compendium she had created to support her motions and directed her to refile individual facts and exhibits in support of her motions as the local rules required. Roe did so and also moved for sanctions against the University for its alleged failure to produce three documents. On December 31, 2012, the district court denied Roe's 56(d) motion and granted summary judgment for the University, having previously granted summary judgment to the fraternity and its local chapter.

p.881 On her appeal Roe argues that the district court erred in granting summary judgment on her deliberate indifference claims under Title IX and on her claims for negligence, breach of contract, and misrepresentation related to her back injury. She also argues that the district court violated her due process rights and abused its discretion by declining to recuse and by denying her Rule 56(d) motion. The University responds that the district court neither erred procedurally nor substantively and that it appropriately applied the relevant court rules.

II.

Our review of a summary judgment is de novo and the record is examined "in the light most favorable to the nonmoving party." *Shrum ex rel. Kelly v. Kluck,* 249 F.3d 773, 777 (8th Cir.2001). We may affirm only if there is "no genuine dispute as to any material fact and the movant is entitled to judgment as a matter of law." Fed.R.Civ.P. 56(a). After the University submitted its statement of facts in support of its motion for summary judgment, Roe raised no objections to it under Local Rule 7-4.01(E) of the Eastern District of Missouri. That rule specifies that any memorandum opposing summary judgment must refer specifically to the "paragraph number from movant's listing of facts" with which it disagrees. The movant's facts will be admitted "unless specifically controverted." If no objections have been raised in the manner required by the local rules, a district court will not abuse its discretion by admitting the movant's facts. *Libel v. Adventure Lands of Am., Inc.,* 482 F.3d 1028, 1033 (8th Cir.2007). Roe's only response to the University's motion for summary judgment was her subsequent Rule 56(d) motion to extend the opportunity for discovery; she raised no challenges to the University's statement of facts.

A.

Roe claims that Saint Louis University was deliberately indifferent to her rape in violation of Title IX, 20 U.S.C. § 1681(a), and makes the following Title IX claims: after the University learned about her rape, it failed to inform its Title IX coordinator, her professors, or her parents about it; failed to provide subsequent academic assistance to her; and failed to begin a prompt investigation. She claims the University also exposed her to harassment and took adverse actions after the rape such as suspending her from the field hockey team and later terminating her. Roe further claims that the University exhibited a pattern of deliberate indifference to sexual assault, arguing that its sexual assault policy was inadequate and that it underreported sexual assaults.

In Title IX of the Education Amendments of 1972, 20 U.S.C. § 1681 et seq., Congress took action against discrimination on the basis of sex in any educational program that receives federal funding. The statute provides that "[n]o person in the United States shall, on the basis of sex, be excluded from participation in, be denied the benefits of, or be subjected to discrimination under any education program or activity receiving Federal financial assistance." 20 U.S.C. § 1681(a). Individuals whose Title IX rights have been violated have a private right of action. *Cannon v. Univ. of Chicago,* 441 U.S. 677, 717, 99 S.Ct. 1946, 60 L.Ed.2d 560 (1979). The Supreme Court has made it clear that sexual harassment is included within the meaning of "discrimination" under Title IX. *Gebser v. Lago Vista Indep. Sch. Dist.,* 524 U.S. 274, 281-82, 118 S.Ct. 1989, 141 L.Ed.2d 277 (1998); *see also Franklin v. Gwinnett Cnty. Pub. Sch.,* 503 U.S. 60, 75, 112 S.Ct. 1028, 117 L.Ed.2d 208 (1992).

p.882 The Supreme Court explained in *Gebser,* 524 U.S. at 290, 118 S.Ct. 1989, that Title IX damage actions which do not involve an institution's official policy require a showing that "an official who at a minimum has authority to address the alleged discrimination and to institute corrective measures on the recipient's behalf [had] actual knowledge of discrimination in the recipient's programs and fail[ed] adequately to respond." According to the Court, this failure to respond or deliberate indifference standard is in "rough parallel" to the Title IX administrative enforcement scheme, which is based on "an official decision by the recipient not to remedy the violation." *Id.; see also* 20 U.S.C. § 1682 (Title IX administrative enforcement). The Court saw "[c]omparable considerations" under Title IX to those underlying the deliberate indifference standard under § 1983. *Gebser,* 524 U.S. at 291, 118 S.Ct. 1989 (citing *Bd. of Cnty. Commis. of Bryan Cnty., Okla. v. Brown,* 520 U.S. 397, 410, 117 S.Ct. 1382, 137 L.Ed.2d 626 (1997) (deliberate indifference standard described as "stringent" and "requiring proof that [the official] disregarded a known or obvious consequence of his action")).

Educational institutions may be liable for deliberate indifference to known acts of harassment by one student against another. *Davis ex rel. LaShonda D. v. Monroe Cnty. Bd. of Educ.,* 526 U.S. 629, 643, 119 S.Ct. 1661, 143 L.Ed.2d 839 (1999). To be actionable an institution's deliberate indifference must either have caused the harassment or made students vulnerable to it. *Id.* at 644-45, 119 S.Ct. 1661. A plaintiff must show that the institution had "substantial control over both the harasser and the context in which the known harassment occurs." *Id.* at 645, 119 S.Ct. 1661. In order to avoid deliberate indifference liability an institution "must merely respond to known peer harassment in a manner that is not clearly unreasonable." *Id.* at 648-49, 119 S.Ct. 1661. The "not clearly unreasonable" standard is intended to afford flexibility to school administrators. *Id.* at 648, 119 S.Ct. 1661. The Court concluded in *Davis* that the plaintiff had presented a genuine issue of material fact on the issue of deliberate indifference by the allegation that the school board had "fail[ed] to respond in any way over a period of five months" to complaints by her and other female students. *Id.* at 649, 119 S.Ct. 1661.

Our court has previously considered deliberate indifference claims against a university based on sexual assault allegations in *Ostrander v. Duggan,* 341 F.3d 745 (8th Cir.2003). In that case, three University of Missouri students brought sexual assault complaints against fraternity members to the university's Office of Greek Life. *Id.* at 748. Administrators met with the fraternity's local advisor and wrote to its national president stating the university's expectation that the chapter would investigate the allegations and provide educational programming about sexual assault to its members. *Id.* Applying the framework developed by the Supreme Court in *Davis,* 526 U.S. 629, 119 S.Ct. 1661, and *Gebser,* 524 U.S. 274, 118 S.Ct. 1989, we held that in order to prove Title IX liability under a deliberate indifference standard, a plaintiff must show that the university was "(1) deliberately indifferent (2) to known acts of discrimination (3) which occur[red] under its control." *Ostrander,* 341 F.3d at 750 (internal quotation marks omitted) (citing *Shrum,* 249 F.3d at 782). Even if the university had controlled the location where the assault occurred in *Ostrander,* there was insufficient evidence of actual knowledge or deliberate indifference on the part of the school. *Id.* at 751.

p.883 Saint Louis University asserts that it was not deliberately indifferent to Roe and her misfortune. Oberle, the university administrator for NCAA compliance and student services, set up a meeting with Roe as soon as she learned that the student athlete had been sexually assaulted. She informed Roe about how to make a complaint and referred her to Claudia Charles, the counselor designated to deal with sexual assaults. Oberle also informed the Department of Public Safety that a student might be filing a complaint and told Charles in advance that Roe would contact her. Oberle also later conferred with Charles about how the University could support

Roe. Despite being informed of resources available to help her, Roe declined to report her rape or her assailant and told both Oberle and Charles she did not want the university to inform her parents about it. When Roe's father reported the assault on his daughter to Public Safety after she returned home to Hawaii, the university opened an investigation into it and cooperated with the St. Louis Police Department. The university denies Roe's allegations that it had an inadequate sexual assault policy and that it underreported sexual assaults.

University administrator Oberle arranged a meeting with Roe on the same day she heard about the sexual assault. Roe told Oberle that she did not remember what had happened and she did not identify the man with whom she had been involved. Oberle explained the process for reporting a rape, referred her to counseling, and also informed Public Safety that a student might be filing a sexual assault report. Oberle later contacted Roe's counselor to discuss the need to support the young woman. While Roe alleges that one of the field hockey captains had described to Oberle the costume worn by the rapist, Roe never revealed his identity to anyone at the University until after she left. Nor did she make a report to Public Safety or to Judicial Affairs while she was there. After Roe informed her parents about the rape on her return home in December, John Roe reported it to Public Safety. The university then began an investigation into the assault and cooperated with the separate investigation of the St. Louis Police Department. We conclude that the University's response to the information it had at the time in question has not been shown to exhibit deliberate indifference.

Roe overlooks her expressed desire for confidentiality while she was still on campus. The University argues that it respected her wishes by not informing her parents or professors about the sexual assault and notes the support Dotson and Clark furnished in academic advice and in finding a tutor. While Roe makes general statements about the University's lack of support, there is no evidence that her dismissal from the field hockey team was connected with the rape given her low grades and her untruthful statements about her class attendance. We conclude that the record does not contain evidence to show that the University was deliberately indifferent to student rape or to the sexual assault Roe experienced.

Roe argues that the University's failure to involve its Title IX coordinator after her rape shows its deliberate indifference to her situation. The implementing regulations require recipients of federal funding to designate a Title IX coordinator. 34 C.F.R. § 106.8(a), but the Supreme Court has cautioned that "alleged failure to comply with the [Title IX] regulations" does not establish actual notice and deliberate indifference and it has never held that "the implied private right of action under Title IX allows recovery in damages for violation of [such] administrative requirements," *Gebser,* 524 p.884 U.S. at 291-92, 118 S.Ct. 1989; *see also Sanches v. Carollton-Farmers Branch Indep. Sch. Dist.,* 647 F.3d 156, 169-70 (5th Cir.2011). In this case Roe has not explained what actions the coordinator should have been expected to take if she had made a complaint to that office or if it had been otherwise notified. On this record the noninvolvement of the Title IX coordinator has not been shown to be evidence of deliberate indifference.

Roe also argues that the district court erred by concluding that she had not shown that the rape occurred in a situation under the University's control. The district court reached that conclusion since the rape occurred during a private party in an off campus apartment. Roe argues that the University has control over its students and fraternities; she further alleges that she was potentially exposed to subsequent contact with her rapist and was harassed by the Athletic Department and other students following the rape. The National Women's Law Center argues that the University had disciplinary control over the rapist because he was a student and that universities may control certain off campus behavior due to the nature of the relationship between students and the institution.

The Supreme Court has made it clear, however, that to be liable for deliberate indifference under Title IX, a University must have had control over the situation in which the harassment or rape occurs. *Davis,* 526 U.S. at 645, 119 S.Ct. 1661; *see also Ostrander,* 341 F.3d at 750. On the facts of this case there was no evidence that the University had control over the student conduct at the off campus party. Nevertheless, this case illustrates why it would be beneficial for colleges and universities to help protect the safety of their students by developing educational programs about sexual assault and its consequences, whether or not the offensive acts occur on or off the campus.

We conclude that on this record Roe has not demonstrated a genuine issue of material fact as to whether Saint Louis University acted with deliberate indifference in respect to her rape and its aftermath. Although her sexual assault was clearly devastating to her, Roe has not shown that the University violated Title IX in its response to it or otherwise.

B.

Roe also appeals the district court's grant of summary judgment on her state law claims for negligence, misrepresentation, and breach of contract. Although she did not comply with the local rules by submitting any evidence on these claims in response to the University's summary judgment motion, Roe continues to assert them in relation to the back injury she suffered in field hockey practice which she claims was further aggravated by a weightlifting trial.

Roe first argues that the University was negligent in its treatment and supervision following her injury. Athletic Department personnel did not follow the orders of her physician, she asserts, because she was used in practices and required to participate in a "max weightlifting test" on October 26, 2006. The University first responds that Roe knowingly released any negligence claims when she signed a "Sports Medicine Authorization and Acknowledgement [sic] of Risk" form in August 2006. Roe points out that the section heading for the relevant paragraph was "Acknowledgement [sic] and Waiver for Soccer." Since the sport Roe was to play at the University was field hockey, she argues that the authorization was ambiguous and the release was not valid. To release a p.885 party from its own future negligence requires "clear, unambiguous, unmistakable, and conspicuous language." *Alack v. Vic Tanny Int'l of Mo., Inc.,* 923 S.W.2d 330, 337 (Mo.1996) (en banc).

The University argues that Roe has not shown causation or breach of any duty to conform to a standard of care. While Roe's physician testified in his deposition that allowing someone with a back injury to lift weights was below the standard of care, he admitted that he is not an athletic trainer and lacked expertise in the area. A standard of care is an objective standard of what is accepted generally in a profession, *Hickman v. Branson Ear, Nose & Throat, Inc.,* 256 S.W.3d 120, 124 (Mo.2008) (en banc), and experts from other professions are not usually qualified to testify as to it, *Brennan v. St. Louis Zoological Park,* 882 S.W.2d 271, 273 (Mo.Ct. App.1994). We conclude that Roe has not created a genuine issue of material fact because she has not presented evidence to show the University breached a duty to conform to a standard of care.

Roe also raises misrepresentation claims. Her amended complaint alleged that the University falsely represented that its athletic program was "state of the art, with proper supervision, using safe, practical exercises, techniques, and equipment" and that she would receive health care at "state of the art" health care facilities "with proper medical care and supervision" and access to "top specialists." Roe asserts that the athletic program staff and medical personnel were less experienced than promised, and that she was not provided promised academic support such as tutoring.

The University argues that Roe's misrepresentation claims would require an analysis of the quality of educational services and are thus barred by the "educational malpractice" doctrine. *See Dallas Airmotive, Inc. v. FlightSafety Int'l, Inc.,* 277 S.W.3d 696, 699-700 (Mo.Ct.App.2008) (educational malpractice claims not cognizable in Missouri "because there is no duty"). The University argues in the alternative that Roe has provided no evidence that the University failed to provide promised services and that Roe has not identified who made any misrepresentations or when and how they were made. Nor did she provide evidence of falsity, reliance, or materiality. Under Missouri law both intentional and negligent misrepresentation require proof of the element of falsity. *Colgan v. Washington Realty Co.,* 879 S.W.2d 686, 689 (Mo.Ct.App. 1994). We conclude that the district court properly granted summary judgment on Roe's misrepresentation claims because she provided no evidence that any representations made to her were actually false.

Roe also brought a breach of contract claim against the University, based in part on her signed National Letter of Intent, which stated that she had decided to enroll there and that her sport was women's field hockey, and her signed copy of the team rules. Roe's amended complaint alleged that "SLU failed to provide the academic, athletic, and holistic environment agreed to" and failed "to abide by the terms of the contract signed August 11, 2006 dictating that the most serious punishment for first-offenses was suspension from the team." She also asserts that the University was contractually obligated to pay for her medical costs related to field hockey (referencing the field hockey "media guide"), including her medical care after she left the University, and that it admitted this by paying some of these expenses.

The elements of breach of contract in Missouri are (1) a contract, (2) the parties had rights and obligations under p.886 the contract, (3) breach, and (4) damages. *Kieffer v. Icaza,* 376 S.W.3d 653, 657 (Mo. 2012) (en banc). Roe has not demonstrated a genuine issue of material fact on breach. She has not provided evidence that the University failed to provide an agreed upon environment or failed to abide by the field hockey rules. Moreover, Roe's lie about her class attendance was not her first breach of the rules, for she had previously been suspended for poor grades. Nor has Roe shown that the University breached any contractual provision requiring it to pay her medical expenses after leaving the University.

C.

Roe also appeals Judge Autrey's denial of her motion for his recusal. She alleges that he is an alumnus of Saint Louis University and its law school, has taught classes there, and has made positive comments about the school. She also asserts that Judge Autrey has common staff members with Judge Hamilton. We review recusal decisions for abuse of discretion. *United States v. Denton,* 434 F.3d 1104, 1111 (8th Cir.2006). Judges are "presumed to be impartial," and a party seeking recusal of a judge must bear the "substantial burden of proving otherwise." *Id.* (internal quotation marks omitted) (citing *Fletcher v. Conoco Pipe Line Co.,* 323 F.3d 661, 664 (8th Cir.2003)). Alumni connections are not a reasonable basis for questioning a judge's impartiality, even if alumni contribute financially or participate in educational activities. *Lunde v. Helms,* 29 F.3d 367, 370-71 (8th Cir.1994). We conclude that Roe has not shown that Judge Autrey abused his discretion by declining to recuse.

Roe further argues that the district court violated her due process rights by not considering her factual compendium which did not comport with the local rules, by denying her Rule 56(d) motion, terminating the case without a hearing, and by failing to adjudicate her motions for partial summary judgment and sanctions. While litigants have due process rights in pursuing their claims, *Logan v. Zimmerman Brush Co.,* 455 U.S. 422, 429, 102 S.Ct. 1148, 71 L.Ed.2d 265 (1982), we review their claims de novo, *United States v. Bennett,* 561 F.3d 799, 801 (8th Cir.2009) (citing *United States v. Ray,* 530 F.3d 666, 667 (8th Cir.2008)).

Roe argues that the court violated her due process rights by not considering her submitted facts, but she fails to acknowledge the local rule with which she did not comply. The district court denied her motion related to her own "compendium" of facts, ordering her to resubmit her filings as facts or exhibits in support of her motions for partial summary judgment as required by Eastern District of Missouri Local Rule 7-4.01(E). Roe never followed the court's required procedure for challenging the University's facts and her only response to its summary judgment motion was to move to extend discovery. Roe argues that the court denied her due process rights by not adjudicating her motions for partial summary judgment and for spoliation sanctions, but she failed to present her positions as required by the court rules for the orderly disposition of issues. Roe filed her partial summary judgment motions over three months after the University's summary judgment motion and moved for spoliation sanctions over eight months later (only four days before the district court issued its memorandum opinion and order granting summary judgment). We conclude that she has not shown error or abuse by the district court or violation of her due process rights.

Roe further argues that the district court abused its discretion when it denied her motion to extend discovery under p.887 Rule 56(d). A party seeking a continuance must file an affidavit "showing what specific facts further discovery might uncover." *Roark v. City of Hazen, Ark.,* 189 F.3d 758, 762 (8th Cir.1999). The district court ruled that Roe did not "present any new, significant reasons" as to why the extension motion should be granted, noting the lengthy discovery period from January 2009 through March 2010, the fact that the discovery deadline had been extended four times, and that Roe had failed to show additional discovery was necessary. *See*

Elnashar v. Speedway SuperAmerica, LLC, 484 F.3d 1046, 1054 (8th Cir.2007). We conclude that the district court did not abuse its discretion in denying Roe's motion.

III.

Joan Roe arrived at Saint Louis University looking forward to her college education and participation on the field hockey team. What followed is sad to relate: her sports injury, failing grades, ineligibility to travel with the team, her sexual assault, and her subsequent departure from the university. Nevertheless, Roe has failed to demonstrate a genuine issue of material fact on her claims that the University was deliberately indifferent to her and that it should be liable for negligence, misrepresentation, or breach of contract. Nor has she shown that the district court abused its discretion or violated her constitutional rights in its handling of her case.

For these reasons we affirm the judgment of the district court.

[1] Joan Roe is a name adopted by the plaintiff for use in this litigation.

[2] Roe also sued Sigma Tau Gamma fraternity and its local chapter but subsequently settled with them. The National Women's Law Center appears as amicus curiae in support of Roe.

[3] The Honorable Henry E. Autrey, United States District Judge for the Eastern District of Missouri.

NINTH CIRCUIT DECISIONS
Title IX

Parents for Privacy v. Barr, 949 F. 3d 1210 (9th Cir. 2020) 255

Karasek v. Regents of the University of California, 948 F. 3d 1150 (9th Cir. 2020) 283

Austin v. University of Oregon, 925 F. 3d 1133 (9th Cir. 2019) 303

Doe v. Regents of the University of California, 891 F. 3d 1147 (9th Cir. 2018) 311

US v. County of Maricopa, Arizona, 889 F. 3d 648 (9th Cir. 2018) 319

Campbell v. Hawaii Dept. of Educ., 892 F. 3d 1005 (9th Cir. 2018) 325

Stilwell v. City of Williams, 831 F. 3d 1234 (9th Cir. 2016) 343

949 F.3d 1210 (2020)

PARENTS FOR PRIVACY; Jon Golly; Kris Golly, individually and as guardians ad litem for A.G.; Nicole Lillie; Melissa Gregory, individually and as guardian ad litem for T.F.; Parents Rights in Education, an Oregon nonprofit corporation; Lindsay Golly, Plaintiffs-Appellants,

v.

William P. BARR, Attorney General; Betsy DeVos; U.S. Department of Education; United States Department of Justice; Dallas School District No. 2, Defendants-Appellees,
Basic Rights Oregon, Intervenor-Defendant-Appellee.

No. 18-35708.

United States Court of Appeals, Ninth Circuit.

Argued and Submitted July 11, 2019 Portland, Oregon.

Filed February 12, 2020.

Appeal from the United States District Court for the District of Oregon; Marco A. Hernández, District Judge, Presiding, D.C. No. CV 17-1813 HZ.

J. Ryan Adams (argued), Canby, Oregon; Herbert G. Grey, Beaverton, Oregon; for Plaintiffs-Appellants.

Dennis Fan (argued) and Marleigh D. Dover, Appellate Staff; Billy J. Williams, United States Attorney; Joseph H. Hunt, Assistant Attorney General; Civil Division, United States Department of Justice, Washington, D.C., for Defendants-Appellees William P. Barr, Betsy DeVos; U.S. Department of Education, and United States Department of Justice.

Blake H. Fry (argued) and Peter R. Mersereau, Mersereau Shannon LLP, Portland, Oregon, for Defendants-Appellees Dallas School District No. 2.

Gabriel Arkles (argued) and Shayna Medley-Warsoff, American Civil Liberties Union Foundation, New York, New York; Peter D. Hawkes and Darin M. Sands, Lane Powell PC, Portland, Oregon; Matthew W. dos Santos and Kelly Simon, ACLU Foundation of Oregon; for Intervenor-Defendant-Appellee.

Jesse Ryan Loffler, Cozen O'Connor, Pittsburgh, Pennsylvania, for Amici Curiae Transgender Students and Allies.

Anthony Todaro, Jeffrey DeGroot, and Rachael Kessler, DLA Piper LLP (US), Seattle, Washington; Fatima Goss Graves, Emily Martin, Neena Chaudhry, and Sunu P. Chandy, National Women's Law Center, Washington, D.C.; for Amicus Curiae National Women's Law Center.

Wesley R. Powell, Mary Eaton, and Patricia O. Haynes, Willkie Farr & Gallagher LLP, New York, New York; Arthur L. Coleman, Education Counsel LLC, Washington, D.C.; for Amici Curiae National PTA, GLSEN, American School Counselor Association, and National Association of School Psychologists.

Devi M. Rao, Jenner & Block LLP, Washington, D.C.; Andrew G. Sullivan, Jenner & Block LLP, Los Angeles, California; for Amici Curiae American Academy of Pediatrics, American Medical Association, American Public Health Association, and 13 Other Medical, Mental Health, and Other Health Care Organizations.

John C. Dwyer, Maureen P. Alger, Sarah R. Binning, and Emily B. Harrington, Cooley LLP, Palo Alto, California; Kyle Wong, Cooley LLP, San Francisco, California; Shannon Minter, Amy Whelan, and Asaf Orr, National Center for Lesbian Rights, San Francisco, California; Shawn Meerkamper, Transgender Law Center, Oakland, California; for Amici Curiae PFLAG Inc., Trans Youth Equality Foundation, Gender Spectrum, Gender Diversity, and Transactive Gender Project.

Alice O'Brien, Eric A. Harrington, and Gypsy M. Moore, National Education Association, Washington, D.C., for Amicus Curiae National Education Association.

Ellen F. Rosenblum, Attorney General; Benjamin Gutman, Solicitor General; Jona J. Maukonen, Assistant Attorney-In-Charge; Office of the Attorney General, Salem, Oregon; for Amicus Curiae State of Oregon.

Cynthia Cook Robertson, Pillsbury Winthrop Shaw Pittman LLP, Washington, D.C.; Tara L. Borelli, Lambda Legal Defense and Education Fund Inc., Atlanta, Georgia; Richard M. Segal and Nathaniel R. Smith, Pillsbury Winthrop Shaw Pittman LLP, San Diego, California; Robert C.K. Boyd and William C. Miller, Pillsbury Winthrop Shaw Pittman LLP, Washington, D.C.; Peter C. Renn, Lambda Legal Defense and Education Fund Inc., Los Angeles, California; for Amici Curiae School Administrators from Thirty States and the District of Columbia.

George G. Gordon, Ryan M. Moore, and Thomas J. Miller, Dechert LLP, Philadelphia, Pennsylvania; Steven M. Freeman, Kimberley Plotnik, David Barkey, and Melissa Garlick, Anti-Defamation League, New York, New York; for Amici Curiae Anti-Defamation League; Americans United for Separation of Church and State; Bend the Arc Jewish Action; Central Pacific Conference of the United Church of p.1217 Christ; Corvallis-area Lavender Women; Greater Seattle Business Association; Hadassah, The Women's Zionist Organization of America, Inc.; Human Rights Campaign; Jewish Council for Public Affairs; Jewish Federation of Greater Portland; Keshet: For LGBTQ Equality in Jewish Life; National Center for Transgender Equality; National Center for Youth Law; National Council of Jewish Women; National Queer Asian Pacific Islander Alliance; OCA — Asian Pacific American Advocates; People For the American Way Foundation; Public Counsel; South Asian Americans Leading Together; Union for Reform Judaism; and Central Conference of American Rabbis.

Before: A. WALLACE TASHIMA, SUSAN P. GRABER, and JOHN B. OWENS, Circuit Judges.

p.1215 OPINION

TASHIMA, Circuit Judge:

This case concerns whether an Oregon public school district may allow transgender students to use school bathrooms, locker rooms, and showers that match their gender identity rather than the biological sex they were assigned at birth. Plaintiffs oppose the school district's policy, asserting that it violates Title IX, as well as the constitutional rights—including the right to privacy, the parental right to direct the education and upbringing of one's children, and the right to freely exercise one's religion —of students and of parents of students in the school district. Defendants and many *amici* highlight the importance of the policy for creating a safe, non-discriminatory school environment for transgender students that avoids the detrimental physical and mental health effects that have been shown to result from transgender students' exclusion from privacy facilities that match their gender identities.

It is clear that this case touches on deeply personal issues about which many have strong feelings and beliefs. Moreover, adolescence and the bodily and mental changes it brings can be difficult for students, making bodily exposure to other students in locker rooms a potential source of anxiety—and this is particularly true for transgender students who experience gender dysphoria. School districts face the difficult task of navigating varying student (and parent) beliefs and interests in order to foster a safe and productive learning environment, free from discrimination, that accommodates the needs of all students. At the outset, we note that it is not our role to pass judgment on the school district's policy or on how the school district can best fulfill its duty as a public educational institution. We are asked only to resolve whether the school district's policy violates Title IX or Plaintiffs' constitutional rights.

In a thorough and well-reasoned opinion, the district court dismissed the federal causes of action against the school district for failure to state a claim upon which relief can be granted.[1] *Parents for Privacy v. Dallas Sch. Dist. No. 2*, 326 F. Supp. 3d 1075 (D. Or. 2018). We agree with the district court and hold that there is no Fourteenth Amendment fundamental privacy right to avoid all risk of intimate exposure to or by a transgender person who was assigned the opposite biological sex at birth. We also hold that a policy that treats all students equally does not discriminate based on sex in violation of Title IX, and that the normal use of privacy facilities does not constitute actionable sexual harassment under Title IX just because a person is transgender. We hold further that the Fourteenth Amendment does not provide a fundamental parental right to determine the bathroom policies of the public schools to which parents may send their children, either independent of the parental right to direct the upbringing and education of their children or encompassed by it. Finally, we hold that the school district's policy is rationally related to a legitimate state purpose, and does not infringe Plaintiffs' First Amendment free exercise rights because it does not target religious conduct. Accordingly, we affirm the district court's dismissal with prejudice of the action.

I.

In September 2015, a student at Dallas High School who had been born and who remained biologically female publicly identified as a boy, and he asked school officials to allow him to use the boys' bathroom and locker room.[2] Defendant-Appellee Dallas School District No. 2 (the "District") responded by creating and implementing a "Student Safety Plan" for the transgender boy ("Student A") and any other transgender student who might make a similar request in the future, in order to ensure that transgender persons like Student A could safely participate in school activities.

The Plan acknowledged Student A as a "transgender male" and permitted him to use the boys' locker room and bathroom facilities with his peers at Dallas High School.[3] The Plan also provided that, while Student A had not indicated "which bathroom he feels comfortable using," Student A could "use any of the bathrooms in the building to which he identifies sexually." In addition, to ensure Student A's safety, the Student Safety Plan provided that all staff would receive training and instruction regarding Title IX, that teachers would teach about anti-bullying and harassment, that the Physical Education ("PE") teacher would be first to enter and last to leave the locker room, and that Student A's locker would be in direct line of sight of the PE teacher in the coach's office. The Student Safety Plan also listed several "Safe Adults" with whom Student A could share any concerns.

Student A began using the boys' locker room and changing clothes "while male students were present." This caused several cisgender boys "embarrassment, humiliation, anxiety, intimidation, fear, apprehension, and stress," because they had to change clothes for their PE class and attend to their needs while someone who had been assigned the opposite sex at birth was present.[4] Although privacy stalls were available in the bathrooms, these were insufficient to alleviate the cisgender boys' fear of exposing themselves to Student A, p.1219 because the stalls had gaps through which "partially unclothed bodies" could "inadvertently" be seen. And an available single-user bathroom was often inconvenient or was considered inferior because it lacked a shower. As a consequence of their fear of exposure to Student A, some cisgender boys began using the restroom as little as possible while at school, and others risked tardiness by using distant restrooms during passing periods in order to try to find a restroom in which Student A was unlikely to be present.

When parents and other students in the Dallas community became aware of the Student Safety Plan, many opposed it publicly at successive school board meetings, in an effort to dissuade the District from implementing the policy. Some parents in the District are concerned and anxious about the prospect of their children using locker rooms or bathrooms together with a student who was assigned the opposite biological sex at birth. The Student Safety Plan also interferes with some parents' preferred moral and/or religious teaching of their children concerning modesty and nudity. In addition, several cisgender girls suffered from stress and anxiety as a result of their fear that a transgender girl student who remains biologically male would be allowed to use the girls' locker room and bathroom. Girls had the option of changing in the nurse's office, but it was on the other side of the school.

Students who opposed the Student Safety Plan attempted to circulate a petition opposing the policy, but the high school principal confiscated the petitions and ordered students to discontinue doing so or face disciplinary action. Despite the objections raised by several parents and students, the District continued to allow Student A to use the bathroom and locker room that matched the gender with which he identified.

II.

In November 2017, Plaintiffs-Appellants Parents for Privacy, Parents' Rights in Education, and several individuals (collectively, "Plaintiffs")[5] sued the District, the Oregon Department of Education, the Governor of Oregon, and various federal

officials and agencies (collectively, the "Federal Defendants"),[6] arguing that the
p.1220 Student Safety Plan violates the Constitution and numerous other laws. The
complaint alleges eight claims:

(1) violation by the Federal Defendants of the Administrative Procedure Act, 5 U.S.C. §§ 551-559;

(2) violation by the District and the Federal Defendants of the Fundamental Right to Privacy under the Fourteenth Amendment to the Constitution;

(3) violation by the District and the Federal Defendants of Parents' Fundamental Right to Direct the Education and Upbringing of Their Children under the Fourteenth Amendment;

(4) violation by the District of Title IX, 20 U.S.C. §§ 1681-1688;

(5) violation by the Federal Defendants of the Religious Freedom Restoration Act of 1993, 42 U.S.C. § 2000bb-2000bb-4;

(6) violation by the District and the Federal Defendants of the First Amendment's Guarantee of Free Exercise of Religion;

(7) violation by the District, the Governor of Oregon, and the Oregon Department of Education of Oregon's Public Accommodation Discrimination law, Or. Rev. Stat. § 659A.885; and

(8) violation by the District of Oregon's Discrimination in Education law, Or. Rev. Stat. § 659.850.

Plaintiffs sought to enjoin Defendants from enforcing the Student Safety Plan, and they sought a court order requiring the District to mandate that students use only the bathrooms, locker rooms, and showers that match their biological sex assigned at birth.

Upon the parties' stipulation, Plaintiffs' claims against Oregon Governor Kate Brown and the Oregon Department of Education were voluntarily dismissed on Eleventh Amendment grounds.[7],[8]

Thereafter the District, Basic Rights Oregon, and the Federal Defendants each moved to dismiss Plaintiffs' complaint. In a lengthy, detailed, and careful opinion, the district court granted all three motions and dismissed the case with prejudice. *Parents for Privacy*, 326 F. Supp. 3d at 1111. The court dismissed the claims against the District and Basic Rights Oregon on the merits under Federal Rule of Civil Procedure 12(b)(6), concluding that Plaintiffs had failed to state claims upon which relief could be granted because the legal theories on which Plaintiffs' claims were premised failed, and that amendment of the claims would therefore be futile. *Id.* at 1092-1110.

Separately, the court addressed the Federal Defendants' motion to dismiss Plaintiffs' claims against the Federal Defendants for lack of standing, and concluded that Plaintiffs indeed lacked Article III standing to bring their claims against the Federal Defendants. The court explained that Plaintiffs had not established causation or redressability with respect to the Federal Defendants, because the District had adopted the Student Safety Plan "in response to Student A's accommodation requests, not [the] Federal Defendants' actions," and the District would "retain[ ] the discretion to continue enforcing the Plan" p.1221 notwithstanding any relief against the Federal Defendants. *Id.* at 1087-92.

Plaintiffs appealed the district court's dismissal order, arguing that the district court erred by dismissing, for failure to state a claim under Federal Rule of Civil Procedure

12(b)(6), their Title IX and constitutional claims against the District. Plaintiffs further contend that the district court committed reversible error in failing to provide Plaintiffs an opportunity to amend their complaint and instead dismissing the case with prejudice.

III.

We have jurisdiction under 28 U.S.C. § 1291, and we review de novo the grant of a Rule 12(b)(6) motion to dismiss for failure to state a claim upon which relief may be granted. *Fields v. Palmdale Sch. Dist.*, 427 F.3d 1197, 1203 (9th Cir. 2005), *amended on denial of reh'g by* 447 F.3d 1187 (9th Cir. 2006) (per curiam). Under Rule 12(b)(6), a complaint must be dismissed when a plaintiff's allegations fail to set forth a set of facts that, if true, would entitle the complainant to relief. *Bell Atl. Corp. v. Twombly*, 550 U.S. 544, 555, 127 S.Ct. 1955, 167 L.Ed.2d 929 (2007); *see also Ashcroft v. Iqbal*, 556 U.S. 662, 679, 129 S.Ct. 1937, 173 L.Ed.2d 868 (2009) (holding that a claim must be facially plausible in order to survive a motion to dismiss). In assessing whether a plaintiff has stated a claim, we accept as true all well-pleaded factual allegations, and construe all factual inferences in the light most favorable to the plaintiff. *See Manzarek v. St. Paul Fire & Marine Ins. Co.*, 519 F.3d 1025, 1031 (9th Cir. 2008). However, we are not required to accept as true legal conclusions couched as factual allegations. *Iqbal*, 556 U.S. at 678, 129 S.Ct. 1937; *Fayer v. Vaughn*, 649 F.3d 1061, 1064 (9th Cir. 2011) (per curiam).

Dismissal of a complaint without leave to amend is improper unless it is clear, on de novo review, that the complaint could not be saved by any amendment. *See Eminence Capital, LLC v. Aspeon, Inc.*, 316 F.3d 1048, 1052 (9th Cir. 2003) (per curiam); *Lopez v. Smith*, 203 F.3d 1122, 1127 (9th Cir. 2000) (en banc). "A district court acts within its discretion to deny leave to amend when amendment would be futile...." *V.V.V. & Sons Edible Oils Ltd. v. Meenakshi Overseas, LLC*, 946 F.3d 542, 547 (9th Cir. 2019) (ellipsis in original) (quoting *Chappel v. Lab. Corp. of Am.*, 232 F.3d 719, 725 (9th Cir. 2000)).

IV.

On appeal, Plaintiffs challenge the district court's dismissal of their claims that the District violated: (1) the Fourteenth Amendment right to privacy; (2) Title IX; (3) the Fourteenth Amendment right to direct the education and upbringing of one's children; and (4) the First Amendment's Free Exercise Clause.[9] We address each claim seriatim.

A.

First, Plaintiffs challenge the district court's dismissal of their claim for violation of a fundamental right to privacy under the Fourteenth Amendment.

The Fourteenth Amendment provides that no state shall "deprive any person of life, liberty, or property, without due process of law." U.S. Const. amend. XIV, § 1. The Fourteenth Amendment's Due Process Clause "specially protects those fundamental rights and liberties which are, objectively, deeply rooted in this Nation's history and tradition, and implicit in the concept of ordered liberty, such that neither liberty nor justice would exist if they were sacrificed." *Washington v. Glucksberg,* 521 U.S. 702, 720-21, 117 S.Ct. 2258, 138 L.Ed.2d 772 (1997) (internal quotation marks and citations omitted). The Supreme Court has recognized that "one aspect of the 'liberty' protected by the Due Process Clause of the Fourteenth Amendment is 'a right of personal privacy, or a guarantee of certain areas or zones of privacy.'" *Carey v. Population Servs. Int'l,* 431 U.S. 678, 684, 97 S.Ct. 2010, 52 L.Ed.2d 675 (1977) (quoting *Roe v. Wade,* 410 U.S. 113, 152, 93 S.Ct. 705, 35 L.Ed.2d 147, (1973)). This right includes "at least two constitutionally protected privacy interests: the right to control the disclosure of sensitive information and the right to 'independence [in] making certain kinds of important decisions.'" *Fields,* 427 F.3d at 1207 (quoting *Whalen v. Roe,* 429 U.S. 589, 599-600, 97 S.Ct. 869, 51 L.Ed.2d 64 (1977); *see also Marsh v. County of San Diego,* 680 F.3d 1148, 1153 (9th Cir. 2012).)

Plaintiffs contend that the privacy protections afforded by the Fourteenth Amendment's Due Process Clause also encompass a "fundamental right to bodily privacy" that includes "a right to privacy of one's fully or partially unclothed body and the right to be free from State-compelled risk of intimate exposure of oneself to the opposite sex." Further, they assert that "[f]reedom from the risk of compelled intimate exposure to the opposite sex, especially for minors, is a fundamental right deeply rooted in this nation's history and tradition and is also implicit in the concept of ordered liberty." Because the District's Student Safety Plan allegedly infringes these rights by "requir[ing] Student Plaintiffs to risk being intimately exposed to those of the opposite biological sex ... without any compelling justification," Plaintiffs contend that the District violated their fundamental Fourteenth Amendment rights.

The district court dismissed this claim on the ground that the complaint did not allege infringement of any constitutionally protected right. It concluded that the Fourteenth Amendment does not provide high school students with a constitutional privacy right not to share restrooms or locker rooms with transgender students whose sex assigned at birth is different than theirs. *Parents for Privacy,* 326 F. Supp. 3d at 1099.

In reaching this conclusion, the district court examined the authorities on which Plaintiffs relied, but rejected those cases as inapposite because, unlike the scenario presented in this case, those cases "involve[d] egregious state-compelled intrusions into one's personal privacy," such as "government officials"—often law enforcement or correctional officers—"'viewing or touching the naked bodies of persons of the opposite sex against their will." *Id.* For example, the district court noted that *York v. Story,* 324 F.2d 450, 452 (9th Cir. 1963), the Ninth Circuit case that Plaintiffs claim provides the basis for their asserted right to bodily privacy, "involved a male police officer taking unnecessary nude photographs of a female victim in provocative positions and circulating them to other officers." *Parents for Privacy,* 326 F. Supp. 3d at 1097. Similarly, the Ninth Circuit in *Sepulveda v. Ramirez,* 967 F.2d 1413, 1415 (9th Cir. 1992), determined that a male parole officer violated a female parolee's right to bodily privacy by entering her bathroom stall over her objections and remaining in the stall while she "finished urinating, cleaned herself, and dressed." *Parents for Privacy,* 326 F. Supp. 3d at 1097. And, the district court noted, *Byrd v. Maricopa County Sheriff's Department,* 629 F.3d 1135, 1137 (9th Cir. 2011), concerned a strip search by a female cadet of a male detainee in the presence of approximately three dozen cadets and detention officers as well as other male detainees, which the Ninth Circuit determined violated the Fourth Amendment's prohibition on unreasonable searches. *Parents for Privacy,* 326 F. Supp. 3d at 1097.

Because "none of these cases support[ed] the proposition that high school students have a fundamental right not to share restrooms and locker rooms with transgender students who have a different assigned sex than theirs," the district court concluded that "Plaintiffs have failed to sufficiently allege a fundamental right to privacy cognizable under the Fourteenth Amendment."[10] *Id.* at 1096-99. It explained that "[t]o hold otherwise would sweepingly expand the right to privacy beyond what any court has recognized," in contravention of the Supreme Court's reluctance to expand the "short list" of liberty rights protected by the Due Process Clause, including "the rights to marry, to have children, to direct the education and upbringing of one's children, to marital privacy, to use contraception, to bodily integrity, and to abortion." *Id.* at 1099 (quoting *Glucksberg,* 521 U.S. at 720, 117 S.Ct. 2258). Thus, because "[t]he potential threat that a high school student might see or be seen by someone of the opposite biological sex while either are undressing or performing bodily functions in a restroom, shower, or locker room does not give rise to a constitutional violation," the district court concluded that Plaintiffs failed to state a claim for violation of the Fourteenth Amendment. *See id.*

On appeal, Plaintiffs make several ultimately unavailing arguments about why the district court erred in dismissing their privacy rights claim under the Fourteenth Amendment. First, they argue that the Ninth Circuit in *York,* 324 F.2d at 455, recognized the right to bodily privacy when it commented that "[t]he desire to shield one's unclothed figure from views of strangers, and particularly strangers of the opposite sex, is impelled by elementary self-respect and personal dignity." The problem with this argument is that *York* addressed an egregious privacy violation by police and recognized a much more specific and limited Due Process privacy right than Plaintiffs claim here. As noted, *York* involved a male police officer who coerced a female assault victim to allow him to take unnecessary nude photographs of her, which he later distributed to other officers. *See id.* at 452. In discussing the plaintiff's claim for violation of her fundamental right to privacy under the Fourteenth Amendment, we explained:

> We are not called upon to decide as an original proposition whether 'privacy,' as such, is comprehended within the 'liberty' of which one may not be deprived without due process of law, as used in the Due Process Clause of the Fourteenth Amendment. For it has already been declared by the Supreme Court that the security of one's privacy *against arbitrary intrusion by the police* is basic to a free society and is therefore 'implicit in the concept of ordered liberty,' embraced within the Due Process Clause of the Fourteenth Amendment.

Id. at 454-55 (emphasis added) (footnote omitted).

Thus, *York* recognized an established right to be free from arbitrary police intrusions upon one's privacy under the Fourth Amendment. *See id.* at 455 ("A search of one's home has been established to be an invasion of one's privacy against intrusion by the police, which, if 'unreasonable,' is arbitrary and therefore banned under the Fourth Amendment. We do not see how it can be argued that the searching of one's home deprives him of privacy, but the photographing of one's nude body, and the distribution of such photographs to strangers does not." (footnote omitted)). Thus, *York* did not recognize a more general right to be free from alleged privacy intrusions by other non-government persons, or a privacy right to avoid any risk of being exposed briefly to opposite-sex nudity by sharing locker facilities with transgender students in public schools.

Moreover, the actions that the Ninth Circuit concluded made the police's intrusion in *York* so arbitrary as to rise to the level of a violation of the plaintiff's privacy right under the Due Process Clause were far more invasive than the transgender student's actions alleged in this case. In *York,* we explained:

> [W]e [cannot] imagine a more arbitrary police intrusion upon the security of [a person's] privacy than for a male police officer to unnecessarily photograph the nude body of a female citizen who has made complaint of an assault upon her, over her protest that the photographs would show no injuries, and at a time when a female police officer could have been, but was not, called in for this purpose, and to distribute those photographs to other personnel of the police department despite the fact that such distribution of the photographs could not have aided in apprehending the person who perpetrated the assault.

Id. Here, Plaintiffs do not allege that transgender students are taking nude photographs of them or purposefully taking overt steps to invade their privacy for no legitimate reason. Thus, beyond failing to support the broad privacy right claimed by Plaintiffs, *York* is also readily distinguishable on its facts.

Next, Plaintiffs point to out-of-circuit cases to argue that the Fourteenth Amendment protects a "privacy interest in [a person's] *partially* clothed body." *See, e.g., Doe v. Luzerne County,* 660 F.3d 169, 175-76 & 176 n.5 (3d Cir. 2011). But beyond the fact that those cases are not binding, none of them directly supports Plaintiffs' argument that the Constitution affords a broad privacy right protecting against being exposed in even a partial state of undress to any person of the opposite sex, whether or not they are a government actor. For example, *Luzerne County* involved the unconsented and surreptitious filming of a female deputy sheriff by male superior officers while she was completely undressed, and the subsequent sharing of the video footage and still photos. *See id.* at 171-73, 175-78. The Third Circuit analyzed p.1225 whether the public disclosure of those files violated constitutional "protect[ions] against public disclosure [of] ... highly personal matters representing the most intimate aspects of human affairs," *id.* at 176 (second alteration in original) (quoting *Nunez v. Pachman,* 578, F.3d 228, 232 (3d Cir. 2009)), noting that "a person's right to avoid disclosure of personal matters is not absolute," *id.* at 178, because "[d]isclosure may be required if the government interest in disclosure out-weighs the individual's privacy interest," *id.* (quoting *Fraternal Order of Police, Lodge No. 5 v. City of Philadelphia,* 812 F.2d 105, 110 (3d Cir. 1987)). Thus, both the facts and the legal issue in *Luzerne* are distinguishable from the case at bench, because this case does not involve a privacy intrusion by government officers or the public disclosure of photos or video footage.[11]

Finally, Plaintiffs attempt to support their Fourteenth Amendment argument by pointing to cases suggesting that providing separate restrooms for males and females is not illegal, cases discussing Fourth Amendment violations, and cases addressing whether Title VII protects against discrimination on the basis of sexual orientation or gender identity. Those cases, however, are inapposite; none establishes a

Fourteenth Amendment right to privacy that protects against any risk of bodily exposure to a transgender student in school facilities.

In sum, Plaintiffs fail to show that the contours of the privacy right protected by the Fourteenth Amendment are so broad as to protect against the District's implementation of the Student Safety Plan.[12] This conclusion is supported by the fact that the Student Safety Plan provides alternative options and privacy protections to those who do not want to share facilities with a transgender student, even though those alternative options admittedly appear inferior and less convenient. *See Caribbean Marine Servs. Co. v. Baldrige,* 844 F.2d 668, 678 (9th Cir. 1988) (suggesting that in cases in which privacy interests must be weighed against governmental interests, inconvenience and slight discomfort that results from attempting to accommodate both interests are not enough to establish a privacy violation).

p.1226 Accordingly, we affirm the district court's dismissal with prejudice of Plaintiffs' claim for violation of privacy under the Fourteenth Amendment's Due Process Clause. *See Albright v. Oliver,* 510 U.S. 266, 271, 114 S.Ct. 807, 127 L.Ed.2d 114 (1994) (holding that the plaintiff's § 1983 claim failed where the plaintiff failed to establish that he was deprived of a substantive due process right secured by the Constitution). Because this claim is premised on the violation of an asserted right that, as a matter of law, is not protected by the Fourteenth Amendment's Due Process Clause, amendment of this claim would be futile.[13]

B.

Next, Plaintiffs contend that the district court erred in failing to recognize that the District's policy violates Title IX by turning locker rooms, showers, and multi-user restrooms into sexually harassing environments and by forcing students to forgo use of such facilities as the solution to harassment.

Title IX provides that "[n]o person in the United States shall, on the basis of sex, be excluded from participation in, be denied the benefits of, or be subjected to discrimination under any education program or activity receiving Federal financial assistance...." 20 U.S.C. § 1681(a). Plaintiffs allege that the Student Safety Plan violates Title IX because it "produces unwelcome sexual harassment and create[s] a hostile environment on the basis of sex." They allege that the Plan "needlessly subjects Student Plaintiffs to the risk that their partially or fully unclothed bodies will be exposed to students of the opposite sex and that they will be exposed to opposite-sex nudity, causing the Student Plaintiffs to experience embarrassment, humiliation, anxiety, intimidation, fear, apprehension, stress, degradation, and loss of dignity." According to Plaintiffs, "[a]llowing people to use restrooms, locker rooms or showers designated for the opposite biological sex violates privacy and creates a sexually harassing environment," in part because "[e]xposure to opposite-sex nudity creates a sexually harassing hostile environment." As a result of this allegedly harassing environment, "all Student Plaintiffs find that school has become intimidating and stressful," and some of them "are avoiding the restroom" and "are not able to concentrate as well in school."

Stating a Title IX hostile environment claim requires alleging that the school district: (1) had actual knowledge of; (2) and was deliberately indifferent to; (3)

harassment because of sex that was; (4) "so severe, pervasive, and objectively offensive that it can be said to deprive the victims of access to the educational opportunities or benefits provided by the school." *Davis ex rel. LaShonda D. v. Monroe Cty. Bd. of Educ.*, 526 U.S. 629, 650, 119 S.Ct. 1661, 143 L.Ed.2d 839 (1999); *see also Reese v. Jefferson Sch. Dist. No. 14J*, 208 F.3d 736, 738-39 (9th Cir. 2000). The district court ruled that Plaintiffs had failed to establish the third and fourth elements and, on that basis, dismissed Plaintiffs' Title IX hostile environment claim. *Parents for Privacy*, 326 F. Supp. 3d at 1104.

p.1227 The district court concluded that the alleged harassment was not discrimination *on the basis* of sex within the meaning of Title IX, because the "District's plan does not target any Student Plaintiff because of their sex." *Id.* at 1102. Rather, the Student Safety Plan applies to all students regardless of their sex, and therefore "Student Plaintiffs have not demonstrated that they are being treated any differently from other students at Dallas High School."

In addition, the district court held that Plaintiffs failed to show "that the District's Plan discriminates because of sex, or that it creates a severe, pervasive, and objectively offensive environment." *Id.* at 1104. The court explained that, in contrast to cases involving "egregious and persistent acts of sexual violence and verbal harassment," "[c]ourts have recognized that the presence of transgender people in an intimate setting does not, by itself, create a sexually harassing environment that is severe or pervasive." *Id.* at 1102; *see also id.* at 1102-04 (discussing cases). Noting Plaintiffs' failure to cite supporting authority, the district court rejected Plaintiffs' arguments that harassment was pervasive because the District's Plan is "widely applied" and that the Plan is objectively offensive because sex-segregated facilities are the well-established norm. *Id.* at 1103-04.

Again, we agree with the district court's analysis and find Plaintiffs' contrary arguments unpersuasive. First, Plaintiffs argue broadly that Title IX "unequivocally uphold[s] the right to bodily privacy" and therefore requires that facilities be segregated based on "biological" sex rather than "gender identity." To support this argument, Plaintiffs point out that the statute provides that it should not be construed to "prohibit any educational institution ... from maintaining separate living facilities for the different sexes," 20 U.S.C. § 1686, and that Title IX's implementing regulations specifically authorize providing separate but comparable "toilet, locker room, and shower facilities on the basis of sex," 34 C.F.R. § 106.33. Plaintiffs further argue that Title IX's text and its legislative history make clear that the permitted basis on which such "separate" facilities may be segregated—"sex"— refers to "biological sex" as assigned at birth, and cannot encompass gender identity.

But just because Title IX authorizes sex-segregated facilities does not mean that they are required, let alone that they must be segregated based only on biological sex and cannot accommodate gender identity. Nowhere does the statute explicitly state, or even suggest, that schools may not allow transgender students to use the facilities that are most consistent with their gender identity. That is, Title IX does not specifically make actionable a school's decision not to provide facilities segregated by "biological sex"; contrary to Plaintiffs' suggestion, the statute does not create distinct "bodily privacy rights" that may be vindicated through suit. Instead, Title IX provides recourse for discriminatory treatment "on the basis of sex." 20 U.S.C. § 1681(a). Thus, even if Plaintiffs are correct that "Congress intended to preserve distinct privacy facilities based on biological sex" and that the District chose not to do so, that fact alone is insufficient to state a legally cognizable claim under Title IX. Rather, to show that the District violated Title IX, Plaintiffs must establish that the District had actual knowledge of and was deliberately indifferent to harassment because of sex that was "so severe, pervasive, and objectively offensive that it can be said to deprive the victims of access to the educational opportunities or benefits provided by the school." *Davis,* 526 U.S. at 650, 119 S.Ct. 1661; *see also Reese,* 208 F.3d at 739.

p.1228 Plaintiffs focus on the third and fourth elements of a Title IX hostile environment claim, as did the district court, namely whether there was harassment because of sex that was so severe, pervasive, and objectively offensive that it deprived Plaintiffs of access to the educational opportunities or benefits provided by Dallas High School. First, Plaintiffs assert that the Student Safety Plan created harassment on the basis of sex "because the only way to achieve the policy's purpose of opposite-sex affirmation is to select facilities based on the sex (or gender identity) of users." But just because the Student Safety Plan implicitly addresses the topics of sex and gender by seeking to accommodate a transgender student's gender identity, or because it segregates facilities by gender identity, does not mean that the Plan harasses other students on the basis of their sex. As the district court explained, the Plan does not target students or discriminate against them on the basis of their sex; the Student Safety Plan treats all students—male and female—the same. *See Parents for Privacy,* 326 F. Supp. 3d at 1096-97.

Plaintiffs respond that the district court's conclusion that there was no harassment based on sex because the Student Safety Plan affects all students equally is "legally and logically indefensible." Plaintiffs argue that the fact that the Student Safety Plan affects both sexes does not preclude a Title IX violation, because the Plan actually harasses both sexes on the basis of their sex by allowing students assigned the opposite sex at birth to enter privacy facilities. But Plaintiffs cite no authority to support the notion that "equal harassment" against both sexes is cognizable under Title IX.

To the contrary, treating both male and female students the same suggests an absence of gender/sex animus, while Title IX is aimed at addressing discrimination based on sex or gender stereotypes. Numerous courts have ruled that a Title IX sexual harassment hostile environment claim fails where the alleged harassment is inflicted without regard to gender or sex, i.e., where there is no discrimination. *See Doe ex rel. Doe v. Boyertown Area Sch. Dist.,* 276 F. Supp. 3d 324, 394-95 (E.D. Pa. 2017) (collecting cases), *aff'd,* 897 F.3d 518 (3d Cir. 2018), *cert. denied,* ___ U.S. ___, 139 S. Ct. 2636, 204 L.Ed.2d 300 (2019). We see no reason to arrive at a different conclusion here. Plaintiffs' argument that the alleged harassment was "based on sex" because it involved opposite-sex nudity conflates the basis for the perceived harm—a distinction between biological sexes—with the basis for the alleged harassment, which, as discussed above, Plaintiffs have not shown was discriminatory or motivated by any gender animus. In sum, the district court correctly ruled that Plaintiffs failed to establish the third element of their Title IX claim. *See Parents for Privacy,* 326 F. Supp. 3d at 1102.

The district court also correctly ruled that Plaintiffs failed to establish the fourth element of their Title IX claim. *See id.* at 1104. Plaintiffs argue that they satisfy the fourth element of a hostile environment claim because the alleged harassment is both viewed subjectively as harassment by the victims and is, objectively, sufficiently severe or pervasive that a reasonable person would agree that it is harassment. However, even crediting Plaintiffs' subjective perceptions, under the totality of the circumstances, the alleged harassment is not so severe, pervasive, and objectively offensive to rise to the level of a Title IX violation. Plaintiffs do not allege that transgender students are making inappropriate comments, threatening them, deliberately flaunting nudity, or physically touching them. Rather, Plaintiffs allegedly feel harassed by the mere p.1229 presence of transgender students in locker and bathroom facilities. This cannot be enough. The use of facilities for their intended purpose, without more, does not constitute an act of harassment simply because a person is transgender. *See Cruzan v. Special Sch. Dist., # 1,* 294 F.3d 981, 984 (8th Cir. 2002) (per curiam) (concluding that a transgender woman's "merely being present in the women's ... restroom" did not constitute actionable sexual harassment of her female co-workers); *cf. Davis,* 526 U.S. at 650, 652-53, 119 S.Ct. 1661 (explaining that "peer harassment... is less likely to [violate Title IX] than is teacher-student harassment" in part because "simple acts of teasing and name-calling among school children" do not establish severe harassment, and noting that "[t]he most obvious example of student-on-student sexual harassment capable of triggering a damages claim would ... involve the overt, physical deprivation of access to school resources," for example by making effective physical threats).

Accordingly, we affirm the district court's dismissal with prejudice of Plaintiffs' Title IX hostile environment claim. Because the Student Safety Plan does not discriminate on the basis of sex, amendment would be futile.

C.

Next, Plaintiffs challenge the dismissal of their Fourteenth Amendment claim for violation of Parent Plaintiffs' fundamental rights to direct the care, education, and upbringing of their children.

As discussed above, the Fourteenth Amendment's Due Process Clause "specially protects those fundamental rights and liberties which are, objectively, deeply rooted in this Nation's history and tradition, and implicit in the concept of ordered liberty." *Glucksberg,* 521 U.S. at 720-21, 117 S.Ct. 2258 (internal quotation marks and citations omitted). The Supreme Court has held that one such fundamental liberty interest protected by the Due Process Clause is "the fundamental right of parents to make decisions concerning the care, custody, and control of their children."[14] *Troxel v. Granville,* 530 U.S. 57, 66, 120 S.Ct. 2054, 147 L.Ed.2d 49 (2000); *see also Fields,* 427 F.3d at 1204. Among other things, this right means that

> the state cannot prevent parents from choosing a specific educational program —whether it be religious instruction at a private school or instruction in a foreign language. That is, the state does not have the power to "standardize its children" or "foster a homogenous people" by completely foreclosing the opportunity of individuals and groups to choose a different path of education.

Id. at 1205 (quoting *Brown v. Hot, Sexy & Safer Prods., Inc.,* 68 F.3d 525, 533-34 (1st Cir.1995), *abrogated on other grounds by Martinez v. Cui,* 608 F.3d 54 (1st Cir. 2010)). This freedom, however, does not "encompass[ ] a fundamental constitutional right to dictate the curriculum at the public school to which [parents] have chosen to send their children." *Id.*

Parent Plaintiffs allege that the fundamental parental right to make decisions concerning the care, custody, and control of their children also encompasses the following rights: (1) "the power to direct the education and upbringing of [their] children"; (2) the right to "instill moral standards and values in their children"; (3) the "right to determine whether and when their children will have to risk being exposed to opposite sex nudity at school"; and (4) the "right to determine whether their children, while at school, will have to p.1230 risk exposing their own undressed or partially unclothed bodies to members of the opposite sex" in "intimate, vulnerable settings like restrooms, locker rooms and showers." Parent Plaintiffs claim that the District's implementation of the Student Safety Plan violates these rights, and therefore the Fourteenth Amendment, because Parent Plaintiffs "do not want their minor children to endure the risk of being exposed to the opposite sex ... nor do they want their minor children to attend to their personal, private bodily needs in the presence of members of the opposite sex." They explain that they "desire to raise their children with a respect for traditional modesty, which requires that one not undress or use the restroom in the presence of the opposite sex," and that some parents also object to the Student Safety Plan because of "sincerely-held religious beliefs."

The district court disposed of this claim on the ground that the fundamental parental right protected by the Fourteenth Amendment's Due Process Clause is narrower than Plaintiffs assert. *See Parents for Privacy,* 326 F. Supp. 3d at 1108-09. The district court reasoned that although Parent Plaintiffs have the right to choose where their children obtain an education, meaning that they have a right to remove their children from Dallas High School if they disapprove of transgender student access to facilities, binding Ninth Circuit authority makes clear that "Parent Plaintiffs' Fourteenth Amendment liberty interest in the education and upbringing of their children 'does not extend beyond the threshold of the school door.'" *Id.* at 1109 (quoting *Fields,* 427 F.3d at 1207).[15] The district court thus disagreed with Plaintiffs' unsupported proposition that parents "retain the right to prevent transgender students from sharing school facilities with their children." *Id.*

On appeal, Parent Plaintiffs argue that the district court erroneously limited their fundamental parental rights. They challenge in particular the district court's conclusion that their parental rights do not "extend beyond the threshold of the school door." Plaintiffs, relying on *Troxel,* 530 U.S. at 65-66, 120 S.Ct. 2054 (quoting *Prince v. Massachusetts,* 321 U.S. 158, 166, 64 S.Ct. 438, 88 L.Ed. 645 (1944)), note that "the custody, care, and nurture of the child reside first in the parents, whose primary function and freedom include preparation for obligations the state can neither supply nor hinder." But other than affirming that parents have a long-recognized constitutional right to "make decisions concerning the care, custody, and control of their children," *Troxel* lends no concrete support to Plaintiffs' specific argument in this case. *Id.* at 66, 120 S.Ct. 2054. *Troxel* concerned a state government's interference with a mother's decision about the amount of visitation with her daughters' paternal grandparents that was in her daughters' best interests; it did not address the extent of parents' rights to direct the policies of the public schools that their children attend.[16] *See id.* at 67-73, 120 S.Ct. 2054. Moreover, we have previously p.1231 explained that although the Supreme Court "recognized that parents' liberty interest in the custody, care, and nurture of their children resides 'first' in the parents, [it] does not reside there exclusively, nor is it 'beyond regulation [by the state] in the public interest.'" *Fields,* 427 F.3d at 1204 (second alteration in original) (quoting *Prince,* 321 U.S. at 166, 64 S.Ct. 438).

Next, Plaintiffs attempt to distinguish *Fields,* the Ninth Circuit case on which the district court relied, by pointing out that the instant case is not about curriculum, but rather "about conduct authorized by the school allowing opposite-sex students into privacy facilities." *Fields* involved conduct authorized by the school allowing a researcher to administer a survey that included questions about sexual topics. *Fields,* 427 F.3d at 1200-01. We held that although "[p]arents have a right to inform their children when and as they wish on the subject of sex," they "have no constitutional right ... to prevent a public school from providing its students with whatever information it wishes to provide, sexual or otherwise, when and as the school determines that it is appropriate to do so." *Id.* at 1206. While the purported risk of Parent Plaintiffs' children being exposed to the unclothed bodies of students who were assigned the opposite sex at birth does not involve the provision of information, as did *Fields,* it similarly involves students being exposed to things of which their parents disapprove.

In any case, in *Fields* we adopted the Sixth Circuit's view that parents not only lack a constitutional right to direct the curriculum that is taught to their children, but that they also lack constitutionally protected rights to direct school administration more generally. *See id.* at 1206 (rejecting a "curriculum exception"). Specifically, we endorsed the Sixth Circuit's explanation that:

> While parents may have a fundamental right to decide *whether* to send their child to a public school, they do not have a fundamental right generally to direct *how* a public school teaches their child. Whether it is the school curriculum, the hours of the school day, school discipline, the timing and content of examinations, the individuals hired to teach at the school, the extracurricular activities offered at the school or ... a dress code, these issues of public education are generally committed to the control of state and local authorities.

Id. (internal quotation marks omitted) (quoting *Blau v. Fort Thomas Pub. Sch. Dist.,* 401 F.3d 381, 395-96 (6th Cir. 2005)). This binding precedent thus directly supports the district court's conclusion that Parent Plaintiffs lack a fundamental right to direct Dallas High School's bathroom and locker room policy.

Plaintiffs nonetheless argue that, contrary to *Fields,* the Supreme Court has extended parental rights into the classroom. Specifically, they argue that the Supreme Court has ruled that students from Jehovah's Witness families could not be compelled to recite the Pledge of Allegiance at school.[17] *See W. Va. State Bd. of Educ. v. Barnette,* 319 U.S. 624, 642, 63 S.Ct. 1178, 87 L.Ed. 1628 (1943). But that Supreme Court decision rested on the First Amendment;[18] nowhere did the Supreme Court reference the fundamental rights of parents to direct their children's upbringing.[19] *See Barnette,* 319 U.S. at 639, 642, 63 S.Ct. 1178. Thus, Plaintiffs fail to cite any Supreme Court authority showing that parents' substantive due process rights under the Fourteenth Amendment encompass a right to direct the curriculum, administration, or policies of public schools.

Finally, perhaps recognizing the lack of supporting case law, Plaintiffs argue that the following items both "undercut[ ] the district court's unprincipled expansion of *Fields*" and support the constitutional parental rights that Plaintiffs assert: (1) that "no one would seriously suggest [that] parents lack any means to assure their students are free from physical assault, coercive threats[,] or criminal activity"; (2) that "federal law and Oregon law confer on parents the right to inspect instructional materials upon request"; (3) that Congress in 2002 "enacted a federal law that no student can be required to take a survey concerning sexual behavior or attitudes unless the school provides parents with the survey before administering the survey to students and receives consent to administer the survey"; and (4) that "many states, including Oregon, have in place laws regulating public school education that require schools to allow parents to opt their children out of certain situations concerning sexual right [sic] and sex education." However, those assertions, even if true, do not establish that the Fourteenth Amendment's Due Process Clause protects the right asserted by Plaintiffs in this case. Although state and federal statutes may expand upon constitutional protections by creating new statutory rights, statutes do not alter the protections afforded by the Constitution itself.[20]

In sum, Plaintiffs fail to cite any authority that supports their asserted fundamental p.1233 Fourteenth Amendment parental right to "determine whether and when their children will have to risk being exposed to opposite sex nudity at school" and "whether their children, while at school, will have to risk exposing their own undressed or partially unclothed bodies to members of the opposite sex" in "intimate, vulnerable settings like restrooms, locker rooms and showers." In fact, *Fields* makes clear that the fundamental right to control the upbringing of one's children does not extend so far as Plaintiffs' hypothesize. *See Fields*, 427 F.3d at 1206-07. Plaintiffs neither distinguish this precedent nor address the practical issue raised by *Fields:* that accommodating the different "personal, moral, or religious concerns of every parent" would be "impossible" for public schools, because different parents would often likely, as in this case, prefer opposite and contradictory outcomes. *Id.* at 1206. As a result, Plaintiffs' legal theory fails. Considering that Supreme Court and Ninth Circuit case law not only have not recognized the specific rights asserted by Plaintiffs, but further forecloses recognizing such rights as being encompassed by the fundamental parental rights protected by the Fourteenth Amendment's Due Process Clause, amendment of this claim would be futile.

For the foregoing reasons, we affirm the district court's dismissal with prejudice of this claim.

D.

Fourth, Plaintiffs contend that the district court erred in dismissing their claim for violation of their First Amendment free exercise rights.

The First Amendment provides that "Congress shall make no law respecting an establishment of religion, or prohibiting the free exercise thereof...." U.S. Const., amend. I. "The free exercise of religion means, first and foremost, the right to believe and profess whatever religious doctrine one desires." *Emp't Div., Dep't of Human Res. of Or. v. Smith,* 494 U.S. 872 877, 110 S.Ct. 1595, 108 L.Ed.2d 876 (1990), *superseded by statute in other contexts as stated in Holt,* 135 S. Ct. at 859-60. The Supreme Court has explained that the First Amendment "obviously excludes all 'governmental regulation of religious *beliefs* as such,'" meaning that "[t]he government may not compel affirmation of religious belief, punish the expression of religious doctrines it believes to be false, impose special disabilities on the basis of religious views or religious status, or lend its power to one or the other side in controversies over religious authority or dogma." *Id.* (citations omitted) (quoting *Sherbert v. Verner,* 374 U.S. 398, 402, 83 S.Ct. 1790, 10 L.Ed.2d 965 (1963)). The Supreme Court has also suggested that the government would interfere with the free exercise of religion impermissibly if it sought to ban the performance of or abstention from certain physical acts, but "only when [those acts] are engaged in for religious reasons, or only because of the religious belief that they display." *Id.* Nevertheless, the "freedom to act" pursuant to one's religious beliefs "cannot be" absolute; "[c]onduct remains subject to regulation for the protection of society." *Stormans, Inc. v. Selecky,* 586 F.3d 1109, 1128 (9th Cir. 2009) (citing *Cantwell v. Connecticut,* 310 U.S. 296, 303-04, 60 S.Ct. 900, 84 L.Ed. 1213 (1940)). Thus, "[t]he *Cantwell* right to freely exercise one's religion ... 'does not relieve an individual of the obligation to comply with a "valid and neutral law of general applicability on the ground that the law proscribes (or prescribes) conduct that his [or her] religion prescribes (or proscribes)."'" *Id.* at 1127 (quoting *Smith,* 494 U.S. at 879, 110 S.Ct. 1595).

Here, Plaintiffs claim that the Student Safety Plan violates their First Amendment rights to freely exercise their religion p.1234 because the Student Safety Plan forces them to be exposed to an environment in school bathrooms and locker facilities that conflicts with, and prevents them from fully practicing, their religious beliefs. Specifically, the complaint alleges that many Student Plaintiffs and some Parent Plaintiffs "have the sincere religious belief" that children "must not undress, or use the restroom, in the presence of a member of the opposite biological sex, and also that they must not be in the presence of the opposite biological sex while the opposite biological sex is undressing or using the restroom." Because the Student Safety Plan permits transgender students who were assigned the opposite biological sex at birth into their locker rooms, the Plan "prevents Student Plaintiffs from practicing the modesty that their faith requires of them, and it further interferes with Parent Plaintiffs teaching their children traditional modesty and insisting that their children practice modesty, as their faith requires." Plaintiffs further assert that, as a result, "[c]omplying with the requirements of the Student Safety Plan... places a substantial burden on the Plaintiffs' exercise of religion by requiring Plaintiffs to choose between the benefit of a free public education and violating their religious beliefs."

The district court dismissed this claim on the basis that the Student Safety Plan was neutral and generally applicable with respect to religion, noting that "neutral, generally applicable laws that incidentally burden the exercise of religion usually do not violate the Free Exercise Clause of the First Amendment" because they need only be "rationally related to a legitimate government interest." *Parents for Privacy,* 326 F. Supp. 3d at 1110 (quoting *Holt,* 135 S. Ct. at 859) (citing *Church of the Lukumi Babalu Aye, Inc. v. City of Hialeah,* 508 U.S. 520, 531, 113 S.Ct. 2217, 124 L.Ed.2d 472 (1993)). The district court rejected Plaintiffs' assertion that, because the Plan pertains specifically to Student A, the Plan is not generally applicable. *Id.* The court, citing *Lukumi,* 508 U.S. at 532-33, 113 S.Ct. 2217, explained that "Plaintiffs misunderstand the law," because neutrality and general applicability are "considered with respect to religion" rather than with respect to the person or groups to which the law most directly pertains. *Parents for Privacy,* 326 F. Supp. 3d at 1110. Because the District's Plan did not force any Plaintiff to embrace a religious belief and did not punish anyone for expressing their religious beliefs, the district court concluded that the Plan is "neutral and generally applicable with respect to religion," and therefore did not violate Plaintiffs' First Amendment rights. *Id.*

On appeal, Plaintiffs argue that the district court should have applied strict scrutiny because, contrary to the district court's conclusion, the Student Safety Plan is not neutral or generally applicable. Plaintiffs point out that the Student Safety Plan was implemented to benefit one student in particular, and they claim, without any supporting citation, that "a policy implemented for a single student is not generally applicable." Plaintiffs do not address the district court's reasoning that neutrality and general applicability are considered with respect to religion. Nor does their argument acknowledge that the Plan applies to all transgender students, not just to Student A; that is, the argument does not distinguish between an event that triggered development of a policy and the breadth of the resulting policy itself.

In assessing neutrality and general applicability, courts evaluate both "the text of the challenged law as well as the effect ... in its real operation." *Stormans, Inc. v. Wiesman,* 794 F.3d 1064, 1076 (9th Cir. 2015) (ellipsis in original) (internal quotation marks omitted). As the district court correctly explained, the two tests for p.1235 whether a law is neutral and generally applicable focus on whether a law specifically targets or singles out religion. *See Parents for Privacy,* 326 F. Supp. 3d at 1110; *Lukumi,* 508 U.S. at 532, 113 S.Ct. 2217 ("[T]he protections of the Free Exercise Clause pertain if the law at issue discriminates against some or all religious beliefs or regulates or prohibits conduct because it is undertaken for religious reasons.").

First, "if the object of a law is to infringe upon or restrict practices *because of* their religious motivation, the law is not neutral." *Selecky,* 586 F.3d at 1130 (emphasis added) (quoting *Lukumi,* 508 U.S. at 533, 113 S.Ct. 2217). For example, "[a] law lacks facial neutrality if it refers to a religious practice without a secular meaning discernable from the language or context." *Lukumi,* 508 U.S. at 533, 113 S.Ct. 2217. Even if a law is facially neutral, it may nonetheless fail the neutrality test if "[t]he record ... compels the conclusion that suppression of [a religion or religious practice] was the object of the ordinances." *Id.* at 534, 542, 113 S.Ct. 2217. Thus, in *Lukumi,* the Supreme Court concluded that an animal ordinance that in its operation effectively banned only the ritual animal sacrifice performed by practitioners of the Santeria religion, was not neutral because it accomplished a "religious gerrymander," i.e., an impermissible attempt to target religious practices through careful legislative drafting. *See id.* at 535-37, 113 S.Ct. 2217.

Here, on the other hand, Plaintiffs' complaint contains no allegation suggesting that the Student Safety Plan was adopted with the object of suppressing the exercise of religion. To the contrary, Plaintiffs allege that the District developed and implemented the Student Safety Plan in "response to the threat of [federal] enforcement action" and in "response to Student A's complaints for accommodation." Moreover, the Student Safety Plan "make[s] no reference to any religious practice, conduct, belief, or motivation." *See Wiesman,* 794 F.3d at 1076. Instead, the Plan itself states that it was "created to support a transgender male expressing the right to access the boy's locker room at Dallas High School." Plaintiffs do not counter this evidence or point to anything in the record suggesting that the Student Safety Plan was adopted with the specific purpose of infringing on Plaintiffs' religious practices or suppressing Plaintiffs' religion. Accordingly, the district court correctly concluded that the Student Safety Plan is neutral for purposes of analyzing the free exercise claim.

Second, the question of general applicability addresses whether a law treats religious observers unequally. *See Lukumi*, 508 U.S. at 542, 113 S.Ct. 2217. For example, "inequality results when a legislature decides that the governmental interests it seeks to advance are worthy of being pursued only against conduct with a religious motivation." *Id.* at 542-43, 113 S.Ct. 2217. Thus, "[a] law is not generally applicable if its prohibitions substantially underinclude non-religiously motivated conduct that might endanger the same governmental interest that the law is designed to protect." *Wiesman*, 794 F.3d at 1079 (citing *Lukumi*, 508 U.S. at 542-46, 113 S.Ct. 2217). "In other words, if a law pursues the government's interest 'only against conduct motivated by religious belief,' but fails to include in its prohibitions substantial, comparable secular conduct that would similarly threaten the government's interest, then the law is not generally applicable." *Id.* (quoting *Lukumi*, 508 U.S. at 545, 113 S.Ct. 2217). For example, in *Lukumi*, the Court concluded that the challenged ordinances were not generally applicable because they "pursue[d] the city's governmental interests only against p.1236 conduct motivated by religious belief" and "fail[ed] to prohibit nonreligious conduct that endanger[ed] these interests in a similar or greater degree than Santeria sacrifice does." *Lukumi*, 508 U.S. at 543, 545, 113 S.Ct. 2217; *see also Selecky*, 586 F.3d at 1134.

Here, the Student Safety Plan is not underinclusive, because it does not require only religious students to share a locker room with a transgender student who was assigned the opposite sex at birth, nor does the Plan require only religious teachers and staff to receive training or to teach about anti-bullying and harassment. In other words, the Student Safety Plan affects all students and staff—it does not place demands on exclusively religious persons or conduct. Plaintiffs' singular argument that the Student Safety Plan is underinclusive because it was aimed at a particular student and does not allow every student to use the facilities of their choosing regardless of biological sex or self-identified gender misses the mark because it misunderstands the applicable test. Underinclusiveness is determined with respect to the burdens on religious and non-religious conduct and the interests sought to be advanced by the policy. That the Student Safety Plan focuses on transgender students rather than allowing all students to claim a right to use whichever facility they wish regardless of gender is irrelevant because that alleged underinclusion is not related to the interests furthered by the plan, and Plaintiffs have not tied it to burdens on secular versus religious conduct. The correct inquiry here is whether, in seeking to create a safe, non-discriminatory school environment for transgender students, the Student Safety Plan selectively imposes certain conditions or restrictions only on religious conduct. Because Plaintiffs have not made any showing that the Plan does so, the district court correctly determined that the Plan is generally applicable for purposes of the free exercise analysis. *See Parents for Privacy*, 326 F. Supp. 3d at 1110.

Because the Student Safety Plan qualifies as neutral and generally applicable, it is not subject to strict scrutiny. *See Selecky*, 586 F.3d at 1129 ("[A] neutral law of general applicability will not be subject to strict scrutiny review."); *see also Smith*, 494 U.S. at 888, 110 S.Ct. 1595 ("Precisely because we are a cosmopolitan nation made up of people of almost every conceivable religious preference, and precisely because we value and protect that religious divergence, we cannot afford the luxury of deeming *presumptively invalid*, as applied to the religious objector, every regulation of conduct that does not protect an interest of the highest order." (citation and internal quotation marks omitted)).

Plaintiffs argue that strict scrutiny should nevertheless apply because this suit concerns the alleged infringement of multiple constitutional rights. Relying on *Smith*, 494 U.S. at 882, 110 S.Ct. 1595, they argue that "[w]here, as here, plaintiffs allege multiple fundamental rights arising under the First and Fourteenth Amendments (bodily privacy, parental rights and free exercise rights), hybrid rights analysis requires strict scrutiny as well." The district court rejected this argument because it had already dismissed Plaintiffs' other constitutional claims. *See Parents for Privacy*, 326 F. Supp. 3d at 1110 n.10. For the following reasons, we agree with the district court that Plaintiffs' argument—that strict scrutiny is required simply because Plaintiffs alleged multiple constitutional claims concerning fundamental rights— fails here.

The extent to which the hybrid rights exception truly exists, and what standard applies to it, is unclear. In *Smith*, the Court noted that "[t]he only decisions in which we have held that the First Amendment bars application of a neutral, generally applicable law to religiously motivated action have involved not the Free Exercise Clause alone, but the Free Exercise Clause in conjunction with other constitutional protections." *Smith*, 494 U.S. at 881, 110 S.Ct. 1595. However, *Smith* did "not present such a hybrid situation," and thus the Court did not further explain how a hybrid rights scenario should be scrutinized. *See id.* at 882, 110 S.Ct. 1595. The Ninth Circuit subsequently discussed the nature of "hybrid rights" at length, and a three-judge panel majority concluded that, "[i]n order to trigger strict scrutiny, a hybrid-rights plaintiff must show a 'fair probability'—a 'likelihood'—of success on the merits of his companion claim." *Thomas v. Anchorage Equal Rights Comm'n*, 165 F.3d 692, 706 (9th Cir.), *reh'g granted, opinion withdrawn*, 192 F.3d 1208 (9th Cir. 1999). The dissent, however, noted that "there is real doubt whether the hybrid-rights exception even exists" because "the Supreme Court itself has never explicitly held that it exists." *Id.* at 722-23 (Hawkins, J., dissenting). "[T]he paragraph in *Smith* purporting to carve out a hybrid-rights exception is dicta," "the Supreme Court in *Smith* did not announce a different test for hybrid-rights cases," and "[e]ven the cases which the Supreme Court cited as involving 'hybrid rights' did not explicitly refer to or invoke strict scrutiny or a compelling government interest test." *Id.* at 723-24. In any case, that opinion discussing the appropriate hybrid rights test in our Circuit was withdrawn upon granting rehearing en banc, and the en banc court did not address the hybrid rights issue. *See Thomas v. Anchorage Equal Rights Comm'n*, 220 F.3d 1134, 1148 (9th Cir. 2000) (en banc) (noting that "we postpone ... application of [*Smith's*] newly developed hybrid rights doctrine") (O'Scannlain, J., concurring).

Moreover, *Miller v. Reed*, the Ninth Circuit case that Plaintiffs cite as the basis for the hybrid rights exception in our Circuit, was decided after the panel opinion in *Thomas* was issued, but before the three-judge opinion was withdrawn upon granting rehearing en banc. *See Miller v. Reed*, 176 F.3d 1202 (9th Cir. 1999). Thus, no weight can be given to *Miller*'s citation to the *Thomas* panel opinion for the suggestion that the hybrid rights exception has been established in our Circuit. *See id.* at 1207 ("[W]e recently held that, to assert a hybrid-rights claim, 'a free exercise plaintiff must make out a "colorable claim" that a companion right has been violated—that is, a "fair probability" or a "likelihood," but not a certitude, of success on the merits.'" (quoting *Thomas,* 165 F.3d at 703, 707)). There is therefore no binding Ninth Circuit authority deciding the issue of whether the hybrid rights exception exists and requires strict scrutiny.

Nonetheless, we need not resolve that question now, because even if a hybrid rights exception does exist, it would not apply in this case. For the reasons discussed in the *Thomas* panel opinion, alleging multiple failing constitutional claims that do not have a likelihood of success on the merits cannot be enough to invoke a hybrid rights exception and require strict scrutiny. *See Thomas,* 165 F.3d at 703-07; *cf. id.* at 705 ("[A] plaintiff invoking *Smith*'s hybrid exception must make out a 'colorable claim' that a companion right has been infringed."); *Miller,* 176 F.3d at 1207-08 (collecting cases and noting that "[o]ther circuits have adopted ... predicates for a hybrid-rights claim" that are "similar or more stringent" than the standard adopted in *Thomas,* and holding that "a plaintiff does not allege a hybrid-rights claim entitled to strict scrutiny analysis merely by combining a free exercise claim with an utterly meritless claim of the violation of another alleged fundamental right or a claim of an alleged violation of a non-fundamental or non-existent right"). As explained earlier in this opinion, Plaintiffs have not established colorable companion p.1238 claims—they have not shown even a likelihood of success, which is why their claims were all dismissed with prejudice. Thus, even if the hybrid rights exception does exist, it would not apply to require strict scrutiny in this case. Alternatively, if the hybrid rights exception does not actually exist, then, of course, it cannot apply to this case to require strict scrutiny of Plaintiffs' purported hybrid claims. *Cf. Leebaert v. Harrington,* 332 F.3d 134, 143 (2d Cir. 2003) ("Several circuits have stated that *Smith* mandates stricter scrutiny for hybrid situations than for a free exercise claim standing alone, but, as far as we are able to tell, no circuit has yet actually applied strict scrutiny based on this theory."); *Catholic Charities of Sacramento, Inc. v. Superior Court,* 32 Cal.4th 527, 10 Cal.Rptr.3d 283, 85 P.3d 67, 88 (2004) (explaining that a rule requiring only a "colorable" and not an "ultimately meritorious" companion claim would not make sense because it would allow the hybrid exception to swallow the *Smith* rule, and noting that the California Supreme Court was "aware of no decision in which a federal court has actually relied solely on the hybrid rights theory to justify applying strict scrutiny to a free exercise claim").

In sum, whether the hybrid rights exception exists and requires at least a colorable companion claim, or whether it does not really exist at all—an issue that we do not resolve here—Plaintiffs' argument that the hybrid rights exception requires that we apply strict scrutiny to their free exercise claim fails. Because strict scrutiny does not apply, we also need not address Plaintiffs' arguments about narrow tailoring.

Instead, we review the Plan for a rational basis, which means that the Plan must be upheld if it is rationally related to a legitimate governmental purpose. *See Wiesman,* 794 F.3d at 1084; *see also Selecky,* 586 F.3d at 1127-28 ("Under the governing standard, 'a law that is neutral and of general applicability need not be justified by a compelling governmental interest even if the law has the incidental effect of burdening a particular religious practice.'" (quoting *Lukumi,* 508 U.S. at 531, 113 S.Ct. 2217)).

"Plaintiffs 'have the burden to negate every conceivable basis which might support [the Plan].'" *Wiesman,* 794 F.3d at 1084 (brackets omitted) (quoting *FCC v. Beach Commc'ns, Inc.,* 508 U.S. 307, 315, 113 S.Ct. 2096, 124 L.Ed.2d 211 (1993)). They fail to meet that burden, because they fail to negate what the record makes clear: the Student Safety Plan is rationally related to the legitimate purpose of protecting student safety and well-being, and eliminating discrimination on the basis of sex and transgender status. *Cf. New York v. Ferber,* 458 U.S. 747, 756-57, 102 S.Ct. 3348, 73 L.Ed.2d 1113 (1982) (explaining that "a State's interest in 'safeguarding the physical and psychological well-being of a minor' is 'compelling'" (quoting *Globe Newspaper Co. v. Superior Court,* 457 U.S. 596, 607, 102 S.Ct. 2613, 73 L.Ed.2d 248 (1982))); *Goehring v. Brophy,* 94 F.3d 1294, 1300 (9th Cir. 1996) (holding that a university had a compelling interest in the "health and well-being of its students").[21] Plaintiffs' argument that the Supreme Court has also recognized bodily privacy as a compelling interest is unavailing, because it does not negate the fact that the Student Safety Plan has a rational basis. Thus, we conclude that because the Student Safety Plan is neutral, generally applicable, and rationally related to a legitimate governmental purpose, the Plan does not impermissibly burden Plaintiffs' First Amendment free exercise rights. *See Wiesman,* 794 F.3d at 1085. And because Plaintiffs have not shown that any new factual allegations could alter these conclusions based on settled precedent, amendment would be futile.

For the foregoing reasons, we affirm the dismissal with prejudice of Plaintiffs' First Amendment free exercise claim.

V.

Finally, Plaintiffs argue that the district court erred in failing to allow Plaintiffs leave to replead. Although Plaintiffs correctly point out that leave to amend should be liberally granted if the complaint can be saved by amendment, Plaintiffs have not shown, either in their briefing or at oral argument, how they could amend their complaint to remedy the many legal deficiencies in their claims. Instead, Plaintiffs simply argue that their complaint, as currently alleged, is sufficient to state their claims because their claims "were not conclusory; rather, they were extensive, well-articulated statements of fact that clearly pleaded claims for relief" and "exceeded both the *Twombly* and *Iqbal* standards."

The problem with Plaintiffs' complaint, however, is not the sufficiency of their factual allegations. Rather, as we have explained above, Plaintiffs' legal theories fail. Amending the complaint will not change, for example, the extent of the rights that are protected by the Fourteenth Amendment's Due Process Clause. As a result, we affirm the district court's denial of leave to amend.[22] Further amendment would simply be a futile exercise. *See V.V.V. & Sons Edible Oils. Ltd.,* 946 F.3d at 547.

VI.

In summary, we hold that Dallas School District No. 2's carefully-crafted Student Safety Plan seeks to avoid discrimination and ensure the safety and well-being of transgender students; it does not violate Title IX or any of Plaintiffs' cognizable constitutional rights. A policy that allows transgender students to use school bathroom and locker facilities that match their self-identified gender in the same manner that cisgender students utilize those facilities does not infringe Fourteenth Amendment privacy or parental rights or First Amendment free exercise rights, nor does it create actionable sex harassment under Title IX.

Accordingly, Plaintiffs have failed to state a federal claim upon which relief can be granted. The judgment of the district court is

AFFIRMED.

[1] The district court also dismissed Plaintiffs' claims under Oregon state law, but Plaintiffs do not challenge that portion of the district court's order on appeal.

[2] For the purposes of this appeal, which is taken from the dismissal of Plaintiffs' complaint, we draw the facts from the complaint's well-pleaded factual allegations and from the exhibits attached to the complaint. *See Outdoor Media Grp., Inc. v. City of Beaumont,* 506 F.3d 895, 899-900 (9th Cir. 2007) ("When ruling on a motion to dismiss, we may 'generally consider only allegations contained in the pleadings, exhibits attached to the complaint, and matters properly subject to judicial notice.'" (quoting *Swartz v. KPMG LLP,* 476 F.3d 756, 763 (9th Cir. 2007) (per curiam))).

[3] The District also planned to spend between $200,000 and $500,000 upgrading the high school's bathrooms and locker rooms to better accommodate their use by transgender students.

[4] In the District, PE is a mandatory course for two or more years of school, and students must change into and out of clothing appropriate for PE class at the beginning and end of each PE class. Some of the cisgender boys who had PE during the same class period as Student A changed into their PE clothes as quickly as possible as a result of their anxiety that Student A might see them in a partial state of undress.

[5] The individual plaintiffs are or were students ("Student Plaintiffs") or parents of students ("Parent Plaintiffs") in the District. Specifically, Plaintiff Lindsay Golly formerly attended Dallas High School during the 2015-2016 school year while the Plan was in place. Plaintiffs Kris Golly and Jon Golly are her parents, as well as the parents of their son A.G., who at the time of filing was an eighth-grade student who would soon attend Dallas High School. Plaintiff Melissa Gregory is a parent of T.F., who at the time of filing was a student at Dallas High School.

Plaintiff Parents for Privacy is an unincorporated association whose members included, at the time of filing, current and former students and parents of current and former students in the District, as well as "other concerned members of the District community." Plaintiff Parents' Rights in Education is a nonprofit "whose mission is to protect and advocate for parents' rights to guide the education of their children."

[6] The Federal Defendants are the U.S. Department of Justice, U.S. Department of Education, Attorney General, and Secretary of Education. These defendants were involved at various times in the issuance and enforcement of a number of guidance documents that initially promoted accommodation of transgender students in public

schools, including on Title IX grounds. Subsequently, some of those guidance documents were withdrawn, and others were later superseded by contrary guidance documents. Plaintiffs asserted that, notwithstanding the withdrawal of the relevant guidance documents, the Federal Defendants, in part, caused the District to adopt the Student Safety Plan, because the guidance "has not been formally repealed, and it has continuing legal force and effect [that is] binding" upon the Dallas School District. Thus, the complaint seeks to enjoin the Federal Defendants from "taking any action" based on their previous guidance.

[7] Those two dismissed defendants later requested and were granted leave to appear as *amici*.

[8] Also, Basic Rights Oregon, a non-profit LGBTQ advocacy organization that had been involved in the development and implementation of the Student Safety Plan, moved to intervene as a defendant, which the district court granted.

[9] In their opening brief, Plaintiffs do not challenge or discuss the district court's ruling that Plaintiffs lacked Article III standing to sue Federal Defendants as a result of Plaintiffs' failure to establish causation and redressability. We therefore do not review the district court's dismissal of Plaintiffs' claims against Federal Defendants. *See Mandelbrot v. J.T. Thorpe Settlement Trust (In re J.T. Thorpe, Inc.)*, 870 F.3d 1121, 1124 (9th Cir. 2017) ("[W]e will not ordinarily consider matters on appeal that are not specifically and distinctly raised and argued in appellant's opening brief." (quoting *Int'l Union of Bricklayers & Allied Craftsman Local Union No. 20 v. Martin Jaska, Inc.*, 752 F.2d 1401, 1404 (9th Cir. 1985))).

[10] For further support for the obvious distinction between Plaintiffs' cited cases and the circumstances presented in this case, the district court pointed to several out-of-circuit cases similar to this one in which courts also rejected Plaintiffs' purported privacy interest, in favor of transgender students' access to school facilities. *Parents for Privacy*, 326 F. Supp. 3d at 1093-96; *see, e.g., Doe ex rel. Doe v. Boyertown Area Sch. Dist.*, 897 F.3d 518, 531 (3d Cir. 2018) ("[W]e decline to recognize such an expansive constitutional right to privacy —a right that would be violated by the presence of students [in restrooms or locker rooms] who do not share the same birth sex."), *cert. denied*, ___ U.S. ___, 139 S. Ct. 2636, 204 L.Ed.2d 300 (2019); *Whitaker ex rel. Whitaker v. Kenosha Unified Sch. Dist. No. 1 Bd. of Educ.*, 858 F.3d 1034, 1052 (7th Cir. 2017) ("A transgender student's presence in the restroom provides no more of a risk to other students' privacy rights than the presence of ... any other student who used the bathroom at the same time."), *cert. dismissed*, ___ U.S. ___, 138 S. Ct. 1260, 200 L.Ed.2d 415 (2018).

[11] Other cases cited by Plaintiffs are similarly inapposite. *Poe v. Leonard*, 282 F.3d 123 (2d Cir. 2002), also involved the surreptitious and unconsented filming of a female officer by a male law enforcement officer. *See id.* at 138. The court concluded that the plaintiff had stated a claim for a violation of her Fourteenth Amendment privacy rights because the officer's behavior constituted "arbitrary government action" that "shock[ed] the conscience" and was "without any reasonable justification in the service of a legitimate governmental objective." *Id.* at 139 (quoting *County of Sacramento v. Lewis*, 523 U.S. 833, 845-46, 118 S.Ct. 1708, 140 L.Ed.2d 1043 (1998)). Again, the instant case does not involve an arbitrary privacy intrusion by a law enforcement officer in the form of unconsented filming.

Similarly, *Canedy v. Boardman*, 16 F.3d 183 (7th Cir. 1994), is distinguishable because it involved a non-emergency strip search of a male inmate by two female deputies, even though other male officers were nearby and could have conducted the search. *See id.* at 184-85.

[12] As a result, Plaintiffs' argument that the District placed an unconstitutional condition on their privacy rights by implementing the Student Safety Plan also fails. If the asserted right is not protected by the Constitution, then any conditions that the District allegedly placed on the asserted right cannot be constitutionally impermissible. *See Koontz v. St. Johns River Water Mgmt. Dist.*, 570 U.S. 595, 604, 133 S.Ct. 2586, 186 L.Ed.2d 697 (2013) ("[T]he unconstitutional conditions doctrine... vindicates the Constitution's enumerated rights by preventing the government from coercing people into giving them up.").

[13] Because we agree with the district court that the right to privacy on which Plaintiffs' claim is premised is not protected by the Constitution, we do not reach the district court's further conclusions that: (1) even if the right asserted by Plaintiffs were protected by the Constitution, the presence of a transgender student in school facilities does not infringe that right, *see Parents for Privacy*, 326 F. Supp. 3d at 1100-01; and (2) policies permitting transgender access further a compelling state interest in protecting transgender students from discrimination and are narrowly tailored to satisfy strict scrutiny. *Id.*

[14] This right is commonly referred to as the *Meyer-Pierce* right because it finds its origin in two Supreme Court cases, *Meyer v. Nebraska*, 262 U.S. 390, 43 S.Ct. 625, 67 L.Ed. 1042 (1923), and *Pierce v. Society of Sisters*, 268 U.S. 510, 45 S.Ct. 571, 69 L.Ed. 1070 (1925).

[15] Although it does not affect the application of *Fields* to this case or the merits of Plaintiffs' substantive argument, it is worth noting that we deleted the phrase "do[ ] not extend beyond the threshold of the school door" from the *Fields* opinion upon denial of rehearing. *See Fields*, 427 F.3d at 1207.

[16] Similarly, Plaintiffs' reliance on *Wisconsin v. Yoder*, 406 U.S. 205, 92 S.Ct. 1526, 32 L.Ed.2d 15 (1972), in their reply brief is unavailing. In that case, the Supreme Court held that the state of Wisconsin could not compel Amish parents to send their children to formal high school up to the age of 16, because as applied to the Amish parents in that case, doing so violated the Free Exercise Clause of the First Amendment, and also interfered with "the traditional interest of parents with respect to the religious upbringing of their children." *Id.* at 214, 92 S.Ct. 1526; *see also id.* at 232-36, 92 S.Ct. 1526. *Yoder* supports the district court's recognition that parents have the right to remove their children from Dallas High School, but it does not support Plaintiffs' assertion that their parental rights go beyond that decision and extend to a right to require a particular bathroom access policy for transgender students.

[17] Plaintiffs cite *Minersville School District v. Gobitis*, 310 U.S. 586, 60 S.Ct. 1010, 84 L.Ed. 1375 (1940), for this proposition, but *Gobitis* actually held the opposite—namely, that the government could require students to salute the flag. The Supreme Court, however, overruled *Gobitis* three years later in *West Virginia State Board of Education v. Barnette*, 319 U.S. 624, 642, 63 S.Ct. 1178, 87 L.Ed. 1628 (1943). Thus, we assume that Plaintiffs actually intended to cite *Barnette*, particularly because their *Gobitis*' pincite of "642" appears in *Barnette*, but not in *Gobitis*.

[18] Similarly, *Tinker v. Des Moines Independent Community School District,* 393 U.S. 503, 89 S.Ct. 733, 21 L.Ed.2d 731 (1969), and *Shelton v. Tucker,* 364 U.S. 479, 81 S.Ct. 247, 5 L.Ed.2d 231 (1960), both of which Plaintiffs cite in their reply, also rested on the First Amendment and its protection of students' and teachers' freedoms of speech and association.

[19] Moreover, unlike the instant case, *Barnette* involved "a compulsion of students to declare a belief." *Barnette,* 319 U.S. at 631, 63 S.Ct. 1178. The Student Safety Plan does not compel a declaration of support for any particular belief. And in *Barnette,* the Court also noted that the appellees' asserted freedom not to salute the flag "does not bring them into collision with rights asserted by any other individual." *Id.* at 630, 63 S.Ct. 1178. Here, in contrast, Plaintiffs' asserted right not to be exposed to any risk of seeing in a state of undress (or being seen by) any person who was assigned the opposite sex at birth does "bring them into collision with rights asserted by ... other[s]," namely the rights of transgender students to use the locker rooms that match their gender identity and to avoid being subject to discrimination based on gender stereotypes regarding the sex assigned to them at birth. *See id.*

[20] Plaintiffs provide no citation suggesting that the statutes they cite were enacted in order to enforce existing constitutional parental rights. Rather, the opposite inference— that the statutes were enacted to create rights specifically because the Constitution does not protect such rights—may be the more reasonable one. *Cf. Holt v. Hobbs,* 574 U.S. 352, 135 S. Ct. 853, 859-60, 190 L.Ed.2d 747 (2015) ("Following our decision in *Employment Division, Department of Human Resources of Oregon v. Smith,* 494 U.S. 872, 110 S.Ct. 1595, 108 L.Ed.2d 876 (1990), Congress enacted [the Religious Freedom Restoration Act of 1993] in order to provide greater protection for religious exercise than is available under the First Amendment.").

[21] In their arguments regarding the compelling governmental interest that would be required if we were to apply strict scrutiny, Plaintiffs argue that "[t]he relevant government interest ... cannot be a general interest in prohibiting discrimination because that position has already been rejected by the Supreme Court in *Hurley v. Irish-American Gay, Lesbian & Bisexual Group of Boston,* 515 U.S. 557, 573, 115 S.Ct. 2338, 132 L.Ed.2d 487 (1995)." But *Hurley* is inapposite because that was a free speech case; the Supreme Court's suggestion in *Hurley* that a broad statutory objective of forbidding discriminatory speech in public parades would be "fatal" because "[o]ur tradition of free speech commands that a speaker who takes to the street corner to express his views in this way should be free from interference by the State based on the content of what he says" is hardly surprising or controversial. *See id.* at 578-79, 115 S.Ct. 2338. That statement in *Hurley* certainly does not preclude the District here from asserting an interest in providing an accommodating and safe school environment for transgender students and assuring that they do not suffer the stigmatizing injury of discrimination by being denied access to multi-user bathrooms that match their gender identity. And in fact, the Supreme Court has recognized repeatedly that the government has a compelling interest "of the highest order" in "eliminating discrimination and assuring its citizens equal access to publicly available goods and services." *Roberts v. U.S. Jaycees,* 468 U.S. 609, 624, 104 S.Ct. 3244, 82 L.Ed.2d 462 (1984); *see also id.* at 623, 628, 104 S.Ct. 3244 (noting that "acts of invidious discrimination in the distribution of publicly available goods, services, and other advantages cause unique evils that government has a compelling interest to

prevent," and holding that "Minnesota's compelling interest in eradicating discrimination against its female citizens justifies the impact that application of the statute to the Jaycees may have on the male members' associational freedoms").

[22] Because we affirm the dismissal with prejudice of Plaintiffs' complaint, we do not reach the district court's determination that Plaintiffs' requested relief—a court order requiring transgender students to use single-user facilities or facilities that match their biological sex—would itself violate Title IX because it "would punish transgender students for their gender nonconformity and constitute a form of [impermissible] sex-stereotyping." *Parents for Privacy*, 326 F. Supp. 3d at 1106 (citing *Whitaker ex rel. Whitaker*, 858 F.3d at 1048-50).

948 F.3d 1150 (2020)

Sofie KARASEK; Nicoletta Commins; Aryle Butler, Plaintiffs-Appellants,

v.

REGENTS OF THE UNIVERSITY OF CALIFORNIA, Defendant-Appellee.

No. 18-15841.

United States Court of Appeals, Ninth Circuit.

Argued and Submitted October 21, 2019 San Francisco, California.

Filed January 30, 2020.

Karasek v. Regents of the University of California, 948 F. 3d 1150 (9th Cir. 2020)

Appeal from the United States District Court for the Northern District of California; William Horsley Orrick, District Judge, Presiding, D.C. No. 3:15-cv-03717-v. WHO.

Alexander S. Zalkin (argued), The Zalkin Law Firm P.C., San Diego, California, for Plaintiffs-Appellants.

Hailyn J. Chen (argued) and Bradley S. Phillips, Munger Tolles & Olson LLP, Los Angeles, California; Susan M. Pelletier, Munger Tolles & Olson LLP, Washington, D.C.; for Defendant-Appellee.

Before: JAY S. BYBEE and N. RANDY SMITH, Circuit Judges, and SALVADOR MENDOZA, JR.,[*] District Judge.

p.1155 OPINION

BYBEE, Circuit Judge:

Appellants Sofie Karasek, Nicoletta Commins, and Aryle Butler were sexually p.1156 assaulted while undergraduates at the University of California, Berkeley (UC). They sued UC under Title IX of the Education Amendments of 1972 (Title IX), asserting two theories of liability. First, Appellants allege that UC violated Title IX by failing to adequately respond to their individual assaults. Second, Appellants allege that UC violated Title IX by maintaining a general policy of deliberate indifference to reports of sexual misconduct, which heightened the risk that Appellants would be assaulted. This latter theory is known as the "pre-assault claim" because it relies on events that occurred before Appellants' assaults. The district court dismissed Karasek's individual claim, Commins's individual claim, and the pre-assault claim, and it granted summary judgment to UC on Butler's individual claim. We affirm the dismissal of Karasek's and Commins's individual claims and the grant of summary judgment on Butler's individual claim. However, we vacate the dismissal of the pre-assault claim and remand for further proceedings.

I. BACKGROUND

For purposes of this appeal, we must accept as true the factual allegations in Appellants' Fourth Amended Complaint (FAC) and in documents of which the district court took judicial notice. *See United States ex rel. Lee v. Corinthian Colls.,* 655 F.3d 984, 991 (9th Cir. 2011). We remind the parties and other interested persons that the facts have not been established. *See Lacey v. Maricopa Cty.,* 693 F.3d 896, 907 (9th Cir. 2012) (en banc).

A. Karasek's Individual Claim

In February 2012, Karasek attended an overnight trip with the Cal Berkeley Democrats Club (Club). While sleeping in a bed with three other students, Karasek awoke because TH, one of the other students in the bed, was "massaging her legs, back and buttocks." This continued for thirty minutes. Karasek reported the assault to the Club president.

On February 14, 2012, the Club president informed a UC official that TH had assaulted three Club members: Karasek and two other women who had reported being assaulted to the Club president. The UC official "discouraged" the Club president from removing TH from the Club, instead suggesting she "use more informal, transformative justice models to deal with TH." After TH admitted to the Club president that he had assaulted Karasek, she asked TH to resign from his board position, but allowed him to continue attending Club events. Several months later, TH assaulted another Club member. The Club president notified UC that more women had reported that TH sexually assaulted them. The president then removed TH from the Club altogether.

On April 20, 2012, Karasek and three other women met with Denise Oldham, UC's Title IX Officer, and Hallie Hunt, the Director of the Center for Student Conduct (CSC), to formally report their assaults. Contrary to UC's Sexual Harassment Policy, Karasek was not told of the options for resolving her claim, the range of possible outcomes, the availability of interim protective measures, or that UC would not actually investigate unless Karasek submitted a written statement. One month later, Karasek learned that one of TH's other victims had submitted a written statement. She "thought it was a good idea," so she also submitted a written report to Hunt on May 15, 2012.

On May 14, 2012, Glenn DeGuzman, the Assistant Director of CSC, met with TH. TH admitted that he had "acted foolishly." No formal consequences resulted from that meeting. Instead, DeGuzman merely emailed TH the next day, asking him to p.1157 "please stay away from alcohol" and cautioning:

> If you do drink, do so responsibly. Make the decision now to not put yourself in situations to be alone with other women specifically if you are drinking. Until you can better understand what you are experiencing, it is in your best interest to not put yourself in that situation.

TH was then allowed to participate in UC's "Cal in the Capitol" program during the summer of 2012 with no restrictions.

Oldham met with TH for the first time on September 17, 2012. Several weeks later, Oldham emailed CSC, stating that she "determined that this situation could be resolved without a formal investigation by [the Title IX] office," and that "from her perspective, she considered the sexual harassment issue with TH to be resolved."

CSC then began an informal process with TH. On October 10, 2012, DeGuzman sent TH an Administrative Disposition Letter stating that TH had violated UC's Student Code of Conduct. TH could choose either to discuss this finding with DeGuzman further or to accept responsibility and submit to a number of sanctions. TH chose the former option and met with DeGuzman. Following this meeting, DeGuzman sent a second Administrative Disposition Letter. This letter, however, omitted one of the sanctions that had been included in the first letter—namely, that TH meet with a UC Health Educator to discuss "gender issues and sexual misconduct." TH accepted responsibility on October 26, 2012. As a result, the following sanctions applied: (1) disciplinary probation until TH graduated, (2) one consultation with a mental health practitioner of TH's choice, and (3) one meeting with an Alcohol and Other Drugs Counselor in UC's Social Services department.

Meanwhile, Karasek had received no communications from UC since filing her written statement in May 2012. She was not informed that Oldham opted not to formally investigate. Nor was Karasek told that her complaint against TH had been resolved informally or that TH was sanctioned. Karasek alleges that UC's failure to apprise her of the investigation or allow her to participate violated UC's Sexual Misconduct Policy and a 2011 Dear Colleague Letter issued by the Department of Education (DOE). *See* Dear Colleague Letter: Sexual Violence, Russlynn Ali, Office for Civil Rights, U.S. Dep't of Educ. (Apr. 4, 2011) [hereinafter 2011 Dear Colleague Letter or DCL].

Eventually, Karasek learned that TH would graduate from UC in December 2012. Frustrated that UC was not timely handling her complaint, Karasek met with Christine Ambrosio, the Director of Women's Resources at UC's Gender Equity Resource Center, on November 2, 2012, to voice her concerns. A couple of days later, Ambrosio emailed Karasek, saying that she had contacted CSC and was waiting for an update on the TH investigation. After Karasek sent several more emails, someone in UC's Title IX office finally responded on December 12, 2012. That email simply said that "this matter had been explored and resolved using an early resolution process outlined in our campus procedures for responding to sexual harassment complaints," and that the Title IX officer had "communicated the outcome of the resolution process to the Center for Student Conduct." The email did not describe the investigation's outcome. TH then graduated from UC. A few days later, an individual in CSC emailed Karasek, saying that TH had violated the Code of Student Conduct. Again, this email did not inform Karasek of any of the sanctions imposed. Karasek did not learn the nature of the sanctions until September 20, 2013.

p.1158 *B.* **Commins's Individual Claim**

In January 2012, Commins invited an acquaintance from the Tae Kwan Doe team, John Doe 2 (Doe 2), to her apartment. While there and without Commins's consent, Doe 2 performed oral sex on Commins, digitally penetrated her, rubbed his genitals on her face, and attempted to physically coerce her to perform oral sex on him. Commins reported the assault to UC's Tang Student Health Center the next day and to UC's Police Department on January 20, 2012. The Alameda District Attorney's Office charged Doe 2 with felony sexual assault.

On January 31, 2012, UC placed Doe 2 on interim suspension, prohibiting him from entering campus. After a hearing, UC modified the interim suspension to allow Doe 2 on campus solely to attend his classes. UC did not inform Commins of the suspension or the hearing.

Commins submitted an Incident Report Form to CSC on February 22, 2012. Several weeks later, Julio Oyola, a CSC representative, met with Commins to discuss her allegations. At this meeting, Oyola intimated that UC would not investigate until after the Berkeley Police Department finished its criminal investigation. Commins told Oyola that she was not comfortable with a delay, to no avail. UC's Dean of Students sent a letter to Doe 2 on May 11, 2012, informing him that he was again placed on interim suspension to "accommodate [his] request to postpone [UC's] hearing upon [his] charges until such time as criminal charges pending against [him] have been resolved."

Doe 2 was convicted of felony assault on October 5, 2012. UC's officials then began communicating with Doe 2 and his attorney about UC's investigation. At some point during these exchanges, a UC official told Commins that a formal hearing would be held where Commins could present evidence. No hearing was ever held. Instead, on January 21, 2013, Oldham told Commins that she had completed her investigation of Doe 2, found that he had violated UC's Policy on Sexual Harassment, and forwarded that finding to CSC.

CSC then began an informal investigation. Hunt met with Doe 2 and his attorney on February 4, 2013. Following that meeting, Hunt asked Commins if she would be comfortable with Doe 2 being suspended until she graduated. Commins said that she preferred that Doe 2 be permanently expelled, but Hunt responded that this was not possible. Commins reluctantly agreed that a suspension of her assailant was the best available option.

As a result, CSC sent Doe 2 an Administrative Disposition Letter, informing him that he had violated the Code of Student Conduct. The letter imposed the following sanctions: (1) suspension until August 31, 2015; (2) exclusion from campus and UC activities until that same date; (3) permanent disciplinary probation; (4) prohibition on contacting Commins; and (5) a reflective writing assignment. Doe 2 accepted these sanctions on March 5, 2013.

In March, Hunt emailed Commins to inform her of the outcome of CSC's investigation. This email was sent to an address that Commins had never used to communicate with UC, so Commins did not see the email. Four months later, Commins emailed Hunt, seeking an update on the investigation. Hunt promptly responded and described Doe 2's sanctions. Commins was not given an opportunity to appeal or contest these sanctions.

Nearly one year later, Commins informed Hunt that she had been accepted to UC's graduate School of Public Health and expressed concern that Doe 2 would return to campus while Commins pursued her graduate studies. Hunt confirmed that p.1159 Doe 2 planned to return to UC once his suspension ended. Commins asked UC to preclude Doe 2 from returning to campus until she graduated. UC denied that request. Doe 2 recommenced his education in August 2015. While he attended UC, he remained subject to UC's no-contact order. Commins does not allege that she saw Doe 2 again.

C. Butler's Individual Claim

During the summer of 2012, Butler worked as a research assistant to Margot Higgins, a graduate student. Higgins paid Butler directly, and Butler did not receive academic credit for her work. The research occurred in Alaska. While in Alaska, Butler lived at the Wrangell Mountains Center (WMC), a nonprofit entity unaffiliated with UC. WMC also hosted programming for the Alaska Wildlands Studies Program, where Butler's assailant, John Doe (Doe), was a part-time instructor.

Doe had a reputation for giving hugs, some of which were "longer than what felt comfortable." According to Butler, one night, while Butler was alone in WMC's common area, Doe came up behind her, trapped her against a table, put his hands down her pants, touched her inappropriately, and then left. Shortly after this incident, Butler told Higgins that "someone had done something inappropriate, had touched her inappropriately, but that she handled it." Higgins asked if it was Doe, and Butler confirmed that it was. Higgins said that she would not do anything if Butler felt like she had dealt with the situation.

Several days later, Doe approached Butler from behind, ran his fingers through her hair, and rubbed her shoulders. Doe said, "It's so nice to have such a beautiful woman around," and then left. Butler again called Higgins, told her what Doe did, and informed Higgins that the encounter made her "uncomfortable" and that she "didn't like it." Higgins told Butler that she would do whatever Butler wanted. Apparently, nothing came of this call.

A few days after that, Butler was singing while preparing dinner in WMC's kitchen. Doe came up behind her, put his hands under her shirt, and touched her breasts. As he left, Doe said, "You have such a beautiful voice." Immediately after that incident, Butler called Higgins and told her what happened. Higgins allowed Butler to stay in Higgins's cabin, which was outside of WMC's property, until Doe left. Butler did not interact with Doe again.

Butler first reported her assaults to UC on November 20, 2012, in a meeting with Ambrosio. Butler cannot recall what details they discussed, but she does know that she did not identify Doe as her assailant at that meeting. On February 28, 2013, Butler met with Oldham and Ambrosio. Butler expressed her desire to remain anonymous, fearing retaliation if she reported the assault. Ultimately, Butler told Oldham where the assaults had occurred, but did not disclose Doe's identity.

Several months later, Butler emailed Ambrosio and explained that Butler believed UC was violating federal law, state law, and UC's policies in the manner in which it was handling Butler's report. Butler and one of her friends met with Ambrosio and Oldham on April 26, 2013. At this meeting, Oldham noted that UC's policies would not apply unless Butler's assailant was UC's employee. Butler then revealed the names of the Alaska Wildlands Studies Program, WMC, Higgins, and Lynn Huntsinger, who was Higgins's faculty advisor. According to Oldham's notes, Butler asked Oldham to research the program to determine whether UC's policies would apply.

p.1160 Oldham emailed Huntsinger on May 21, 2013, asking about the Wildlands Studies Program. Huntsinger said she was not aware of that program, but after searching on the internet, she discovered that it was a California State University, Monterey Bay program. The next day, Oldham emailed Butler to ask for more details about her participation in the Wildlands Studies Program and for a copy of the contract she signed with Higgins. Before Butler responded, Oldham received an email from Leslie Arutunian, an employee with the Wildlands Studies Program. Arutunian told Oldham that the program had no connection to UC.

On May 30, 2013, Oldham emailed Butler again, notifying her that Oldham had received new information. Because of various scheduling conflicts, Butler did not meet with Oldham until August 7, 2013. Butler contends that at this meeting she identified Doe as her assailant and told Oldham that Doe was a guest lecturer at UC. Oldham showed Butler the documents Arutunian had sent and said that Arutunian was willing to speak with Butler about her assaults. Butler preferred that Oldham follow up with Arutunian instead. This was the last time Butler met with Oldham, and Oldham did not take any further steps to investigate Butler's claims.

At his deposition, Doe confirmed that he visits UC's campus "once or twice a year," and that he sporadically serves as a guest speaker. Doe estimated that he gives a guest lecture once "every year or two," and that he had been on UC's campus five or six times since the summer of 2012.

D. Pre-Assault Claim

To support Appellants' pre-assault claim, the FAC includes allegations relating to UC's history of responding to reports of sexual misconduct. The FAC describes a 2014 report prepared by the California State Auditor detailing several deficiencies in UC's handling of sexual-harassment cases between 2009 and 2013. The FAC also highlights an administrative Title IX claim filed in 2014 by thirty-one women, alleging that UC has not adequately responded to complaints of sexual assault since 1979. Appellants allege that UC resolved a majority of sexual-assault complaints with informal processes, even though Oldham publicly stated that only formal processes should be used in cases of sexual assault. And finally, the FAC alleges that UC "consciously and intentionally" chose to resolve sexual-assault reports informally to avoid its statutory duty to report cases of sexual violence to DOE. Based on these allegations, the FAC concludes that UC maintained "a policy of deliberate indifference to sexual misconduct against female students" that created a "sexually hostile environment" and heightened the risk that Appellants would be assaulted.

E. Proceedings Below

After multiple rounds of motions to dismiss, the district court dismissed all but Butler's Title IX claim. Following discovery on Butler's claim, the district court granted summary judgment to UC. The court then entered judgment in favor of UC on all claims.

Appellants timely appealed from that judgment, challenging the district court's summary-judgment order and its orders granting UC's motions to dismiss. On appeal, Appellants argue that Karasek and Commins adequately pleaded a Title IX violation based on UC's response to their reports of sexual assault, Butler established a genuine issue of material fact as to whether UC violated Title IX in its response to her report, and Appellants adequately alleged that UC's policy of indifference to sexual misconduct violated Title IX.

II. JURISDICTION AND STANDARD OF REVIEW

The district court had jurisdiction under 28 U.S.C. § 1331. We have jurisdiction under 28 U.S.C. § 1291.

We review de novo the grant of a motion to dismiss under Rule 12(b)(6) and may affirm on any ground supported by the record. *Metzler Inv. GMBH v. Corinthian Colls., Inc.,* 540 F.3d 1049, 1061 (9th Cir. 2008). This "[r]eview is limited to the complaint, materials incorporated into the complaint by reference, and matters of which the court may take judicial notice." *Id.* When considering a motion to dismiss, we accept "as true all well-pleaded allegations of fact in the complaint" and construe them in the light most favorable to the non-moving party. *Corinthian Colls.,* 655 F.3d at 991. A complaint will not survive a motion to dismiss unless it "contain[s] sufficient factual matter, accepted as true, to state a claim to relief that is plausible on its face." *Ashcroft v. Iqbal,* 556 U.S. 662, 678, 129 S.Ct. 1937, 173 L.Ed.2d 868 (2009) (internal quotation marks omitted).

We also review a grant of summary judgment de novo. *Tauscher v. Phx. Bd. of Realtors, Inc.,* 931 F.3d 959, 962 (9th Cir. 2019). A party is entitled to summary judgment "only if, taking the evidence and all reasonable inferences in the light most favorable to the non-moving party, there are no genuine issues of material fact, and the movant is entitled to judgment as a matter of law." *Id.* (citing Fed. R. Civ. P. 56(a)). "An issue of material fact is genuine if there is sufficient evidence for a reasonable jury to return a verdict for the non-moving party." *Id.* (internal quotation marks omitted). Factual determinations underlying a grant of summary judgment will not be reversed unless they are clearly erroneous. *Pyramid Techs., Inc. v. Hartford Cas. Ins. Co.,* 752 F.3d 807, 813 (9th Cir. 2014).

III. DISCUSSION

Title IX provides, "No person in the United States shall, on the basis of sex, be excluded from participation in, be denied the benefits of, or be subjected to discrimination under any education program or activity receiving Federal financial assistance." 20 U.S.C. § 1681(a). Victims of sex discrimination have a private right of action against recipients of federal education funding for alleged Title IX violations, *see Cannon v. Univ. of Chi.,* 441 U.S. 677, 709, 99 S.Ct. 1946, 60 L.Ed.2d 560 (1979), and may seek damages for those violations, *see Franklin v. Gwinnett Cty. Pub. Schs.,* 503 U.S. 60, 75-76, 112 S.Ct. 1028, 117 L.Ed.2d 208 (1992). Damages are available if the "official policy" of the funding recipient discriminates on the basis of sex. *Gebser v. Lago Vista Indep. Sch. Dist.,* 524 U.S. 274, 290, 118 S.Ct. 1989, 141 L.Ed.2d 277 (1998). In the absence of an official policy, damages are not recoverable unless "an official who at a minimum has authority to address the alleged discrimination and to institute corrective measures on the recipient's behalf has actual knowledge of discrimination in the recipient's programs and fails adequately to respond." *Id.* In other words, there must be "an official decision by the recipient not to remedy the violation." *Id.*

As already noted, Appellants assert two types of claims—individual claims and a pre-assault claim. We address the individual claims first.

A. Individual Claims

To ensure that a funding recipient is liable "only for its own misconduct," *Davis v. Monroe Cty. Bd. of Educ.*, 526 p.1162 U.S. 629, 640, 119 S.Ct. 1661, 143 L.Ed.2d 839 (1999), a plaintiff alleging a Title IX claim against a school that arises from student-on-student or faculty-on-student sexual harassment or assault must establish five elements.[1] First, the school must have "exercise[d] substantial control over both the harasser and the context in which the known harassment occur[red]." *Id.* at 645, 119 S.Ct. 1661. Second, the plaintiff must have suffered harassment "that is so severe, pervasive, and objectively offensive that it can be said to deprive the [plaintiff] of access to the educational opportunities or benefits provided by the school." *Id.* at 650, 119 S.Ct. 1661. Third, a school official with "authority to address the alleged discrimination and to institute corrective measures on the [school's] behalf" must have had "actual knowledge" of the harassment. *Reese v. Jefferson Sch. Dist. No. 14J*, 208 F.3d 736, 739 (9th Cir. 2000); *see Davis*, 526 U.S. at 650, 119 S.Ct. 1661. Fourth, the school must have acted with "deliberate indifference" to the harassment, such that the school's "response to the harassment or lack thereof [was] clearly unreasonable in light of the known circumstances." *Davis*, 526 U.S. at 648, 119 S.Ct. 1661. This is a fairly high standard— a "negligent, lazy, or careless" response will not suffice. *Oden v. N. Marianas Coll.*, 440 F.3d 1085, 1089 (9th Cir. 2006). Instead, the plaintiff must demonstrate that the school's actions amounted to "'an official decision ... not to remedy'" the discrimination. *Id.* (quoting *Gebser*, 524 U.S. at 290, 118 S.Ct. 1989) (alteration in original). And fifth, the school's deliberate indifference must have "subject[ed the plaintiff] to harassment." *Davis*, 526 U.S. at 644, 119 S.Ct. 1661. Put differently, the school must have "cause[d the plaintiff] to undergo harassment or ma[d]e [the plaintiff] liable or vulnerable to it." *Id.* at 645, 119 S.Ct. 1661 (internal quotation marks omitted).

The Supreme Court has emphasized that Title IX "does not mean that recipients can avoid liability only by purging their schools of actionable peer harassment or that administrators must engage in particular disciplinary action." *Id.* at 648, 119 S.Ct. 1661. Rather, "the recipient must merely respond ... in a manner that is not clearly unreasonable." *Id.* at 649, 119 S.Ct. 1661. Absent an unreasonable response, we cannot "second-guess[] the disciplinary decisions made by school administrators." *Id.* at 648, 119 S.Ct. 1661. And the reasonableness of the response depends on the educational setting involved —what would be unreasonable in the context of an elementary school might not be unreasonable in the context of a university. *Id.* at 649, 119 S.Ct. 1661.

The district court dismissed Karasek's and Commins's claims for failing to adequately allege the fourth element—deliberate indifference. On Butler's claim, the district court found that she failed to demonstrate the first, fourth, and fifth elements —that UC controlled Butler's assailant, acted with deliberate indifference, and caused Butler to undergo harassment. We affirm the district court's orders with respect to each of the individual claims.[2]

p.1163 **1. Karasek's individual claim**

Karasek argues that the FAC adequately alleges that UC was deliberately indifferent in four respects: (a) UC unjustifiably delayed its investigation, (b) UC violated its own policies and the DCL when responding to Karasek's report, (c) UC took no steps to prevent TH from continuing to harass Karasek, and (d) the substance of UC's response was inequitable.

a. UC's alleged delay

A school's delayed response constitutes deliberate indifference if it prejudices the plaintiff or if the delay was a "deliberate attempt to sabotage [the p]laintiff's complaint or its orderly resolution." *Oden,* 440 F.3d at 1089. In *Oden,* the plaintiff argued that a nine-month delay between the plaintiff's report of sexual assault and a formal hearing held by her college established deliberate indifference. *Id.* We rejected that argument. We noted that the college acted shortly after the plaintiff's report by providing counseling, helping her file a formal complaint, and ordering her assailant not to contact her. *See id.* Although the nine-month delay was "negligent, lazy, or careless," it did not amount to deliberate indifference, given the school's actions in the meantime. *Id.*

Here, eight and one-half months elapsed between the date when UC had actual notice of Karasek's assault and when TH accepted the sanctions UC proposed. But like the college in *Oden,* UC was not idle during those months. When the Club president told UC that TH sexually assaulted a student, UC communicated with the president to determine the best course of action. Less than one month after Karasek reported her assault to CSC, DeGuzman met with TH to discuss the charges. Oldham met with him again at the beginning of the ensuing fall semester, eventually leading to the issuance of several Administrative Disposition Letters. To be sure, the actions UC took after learning of Karasek's assault may have been less helpful than the college's actions in *Oden.* Nevertheless, UC's actions and attendant delay did not constitute a "deliberate attempt to sabotage [Karasek's] complaint or its orderly resolution." *Id.*

Karasek relies on *Williams v. Board of Regents of University System of Georgia,* 477 F.3d 1282 (11th Cir. 2007). But that case involved a level of indifference far more extreme than anything present here. In *Williams,* the University of Georgia did not hold a disciplinary hearing until eleven months after the plaintiff informed the university that she had been gang-raped by members of the basketball team. *Id.* at 1296-97. The university's police department had performed a "thorough investigation" and produced a comprehensive report within a few months of the assault that largely corroborated the plaintiff's account, but the university still took no action. *Id.* at 1296-97. By the time the disciplinary hearing was held, several of the plaintiff's assailants no longer attended the university. *Id.* at 1296. The Eleventh Circuit concluded that, in those circumstances, the university's delay was deliberately indifferent. *Id.*

Unlike the university in *Williams,* UC met with and ultimately sanctioned Karasek's assailant while he still attended school. Any delay did not prejudice Karasek. Even though UC could have acted more quickly, UC's delay did not constitute deliberate indifference.

b. UC's alleged policy violations

Ordinarily, a school's "failure to comply with [DOE] regulations ... does p.1164 not establish ... deliberate indifference." *Gebser*, 524 U.S. at 291-92, 118 S.Ct. 1989. The same is true of a school's violations of its own policies. *See Oden*, 440 F.3d at 1089 (finding no deliberate indifference even though the school's nine-month delay "contravene[d] College policy"); *see also Sanches v. Carrollton-Farmers Branch Indep. Sch. Dist.*, 647 F.3d 156, 169-70 (5th Cir. 2011) ("[J]ust because [the school official] allegedly failed to follow district policy does not mean that her actions were clearly unreasonable.").

UC's alleged conduct was inconsistent with both the DCL and its own policies. The DCL advises a school to "take immediate steps to protect" the complainant, afford the parties "an equal opportunity to present relevant witnesses and other evidence," give "periodic status updates" to both parties, and promptly notify the parties "in writing[] about the outcome of both the complaint and any appeal." 2011 Dear Colleague Letter, at 10-13.[3] Many of these provisions are reflected in UC's own policies. Further, both the DCL and UC's policies provide that a sexual-assault complaint should be resolved within sixty days. *Id.* at 12. Finally, UC's Interim Sexual Misconduct Policy requires CSC to "consult with the Complainant" before resolving a sexual-assault complaint informally via an Administrative Disposition Letter. UC followed none of these provisions.

Yet, this does not constitute deliberate indifference per se. The DCL itself states that it is applying a standard that is less exacting than the deliberate-indifference test used in "private lawsuits for monetary damages." *Id.* at 4 n.12. In other words, in DOE's view, a school could fail to abide by the DCL's provisions and yet not violate the deliberate-indifference standard. We cannot say that UC was deliberately indifferent solely by disregarding the DCL and its own policies.

To avoid this conclusion, Karasek, citing *Meritor Savings Bank, FSB v. Vinson*, 477 U.S. 57, 106 S.Ct. 2399, 91 L.Ed.2d 49 (1986), argues that the DCL is DOE's interpretation of Title IX, so we must defer to that interpretation. But *Meritor* involved a question of statutory interpretation: whether the phrase "discriminate against any individual ... because of such individual's ... sex" in Title VII encompassed a sexually hostile work environment. *See id.* at 63-67, 106 S.Ct. 2399 (quoting 42 U.S.C. § 2000e-2(a)(1)). We do not face a statutory interpretation issue. A damages remedy for Title IX violations is judicially implied, not statutorily created. The Supreme Court has crafted "a sensible remedial scheme" with "a measure of latitude... that best comports with the statute." *Gebser*, 524 U.S. at 284, 118 S.Ct. 1989. Because the DCL does not address that remedial scheme, the DCL is merely advisory and not an interpretation of Title p.1165 IX that need be afforded deference in this context under *Chevron, U.S.A., Inc. v. Natural Resources Defense Council, Inc.*, 467 U.S. 837, 104 S.Ct. 2778, 81 L.Ed.2d 694 (1984). The Supreme Court in *Davis*, not Congress, articulated the deliberate-indifference standard. All we must decide is whether UC's conduct qualifies as deliberate indifference under that standard. *Meritor* is inapposite, and the DCL does not control our inquiry here. *See Gebser*, 524 U.S. at 291-92, 118 S.Ct. 1989.

That is not to say that the DCL is entirely irrelevant to the deliberate-indifference inquiry. Although we are aware of no federal court of appeals that has addressed the impact of DOE guidance documents when analyzing deliberate indifference, many district courts have concluded that those documents may guide the analysis. *See, e.g., Doe 1 v. Baylor Univ.,* 240 F. Supp. 3d 646, 659 (W.D. Tex. 2017) ("While the Court agrees that a school's failure to comply with certain DOE guidelines generally cannot, alone, demonstrate a school's deliberate indifference, ... it also agrees with numerous courts that DOE regulations may still be consulted when assessing the appropriateness of a school's response to reports of sexual assault."); *Butters v. James Madison Univ.,* 208 F. Supp. 3d 745, 757-58 (W.D. Va. 2016) (noting that "a school's compliance or non-compliance with the DCL can be a factor that the court considers," but a violation of the DCL "would not be dispositive on the issue of deliberate indifference"); *Doe v. Forest Hills Sch. Dist.,* No. 1:13-cv-428, 2015 WL 9906260, at *10 (W.D. Mich. Mar. 31, 2015) ("Although failure to comply with Title IX guidance does not, on its own, constitute deliberate indifference, it is one consideration." (emphasis omitted)).

We agree that the DCL is useful as a persuasive document that sets forth DOE's considered views. Yet, given DOE's decision to rescind the DCL in 2017, *see supra* note 3, the DCL's persuasive force is somewhat limited. Regardless, a school's failure to follow the DCL's provisions, standing alone, will not constitute deliberate indifference. But that failing may be relevant, particularly when it reflects "an official decision ... not to remedy the [Title IX] violation." *Gebser,* 524 U.S. at 290, 118 S.Ct. 1989.

Ultimately, we conclude that UC's noncompliance with the DCL and its own policies was, at most, "negligent, lazy, [and] careless." *Oden,* 440 F.3d at 1089. Nevertheless, because UC investigated Karasek's complaint, met with her assailant shortly after she submitted her written report, and eventually imposed appropriate sanctions, UC's noncompliance did not constitute deliberate indifference to Karasek's complaint.

c. UC's alleged failure to preclude further harassment

Karasek argues that UC was deliberately indifferent by failing to preclude the possibility that TH could harass Karasek again after she reported the assault. UC could have immediately imposed interim sanctions on TH, such as barring him from campus during UC's investigation or issuing a no-contact order, particularly given that UC was aware that multiple women reported being sexually assaulted by him. Indeed, in hindsight, UC's decision to initially discourage the Club president from expelling TH from the Club is troubling. UC instead attempted to resolve the complaints against TH informally through "an early resolution process." We might have handled the situation differently, but the Supreme Court has instructed us to "refrain from second guessing the disciplinary decisions made by school administrators" unless those decisions were "clearly unreasonable." p.1166 *Davis,* 526 U.S. at 648, 119 S.Ct. 1661.

UC's decisions were not clearly unreasonable. Karasek never interacted with TH again after the assault, aside from seeing him from afar on one occasion. And there is no indication that Karasek told Oldham and Hunt that she regularly saw TH when meeting with them on April 20, 2012. As a result, UC had no reason to know that preventative measures were necessary to protect Karasek from future harassment, especially in light of the context and nature of her assault (though, as we note below, UC's lack of communication with Karasek likely prevented UC from fully understanding what preventative steps may have been necessary). UC's failure to implement protective measures did not exhibit deliberate indifference.

d. The substance of UC's response

Karasek argues that "UC's response was wholly inequitable" because UC allowed TH to participate in the "Cal in the Capitol" event and communicated with TH while ignoring Karasek. Choosing not to prohibit TH from attending "Cal in the Capitol" does not establish deliberate indifference, for "[a]n aggrieved party is not entitled to the precise remedy that he or she would prefer." *Oden,* 440 F.3d at 1089. Indeed, Karasek does not allege that she would have attended "Cal in the Capitol" but for TH's presence, so it is unclear that UC's decision not to forbid TH from attending while UC's investigation continued was clearly unreasonable. As for UC's lack of communication, this is an inexcusable omission by UC's officials. Keeping a victim of sexual assault largely in the dark about the investigation of her assailant and the ultimate sanctions imposed is not only inappropriate, but also deprives the school of information that might be crucial to its investigation. Nevertheless, despite its lack of communication, UC acted on Karasek's complaint and imposed arguably appropriate sanctions on TH. Thus, UC was not deliberately indifferent to Karasek's assault.

Because the allegations in the FAC fail to show that UC made "an official decision... not to remedy the [Title IX] violation," *Gebser,* 524 U.S. at 290, 118 S.Ct. 1989, we affirm the district court's dismissal of Karasek's individual Title IX claim.

2. Commins's individual claim

Like Karasek, Commins argues that the FAC adequately alleges deliberate indifference for several reasons: (a) UC unjustifiably delayed its investigation, (b) UC violated the DCL and its own policies, (c) UC failed to take steps to prevent Doe 2 from further harassing Commins, and (d) UC unreasonably failed to permit Commins to participate in the investigation of Doe 2.

a. UC's alleged delay

Commins argues that UC unjustifiably delayed its resolution of Commins's complaint. Thirteen months elapsed after Commins reported her assault before UC imposed final sanctions on Doe 2. This delay was partially engendered by UC's decision to stay its investigation until Doe 2's criminal charges were resolved. But UC did not sit on its hands during those months. To the contrary, within two weeks of Commins's report, UC placed Doe 2 on interim suspension, barring him from campus. Doe 2 remained on that suspension, with a slight modification allowing him to attend classes, throughout the investigation. This is unlike the University of Georgia in *Williams,* which failed to act against the assailants for eleven months. Commins's allegations thus fail to show that the thirteen-month delay prejudiced her or was a "deliberate attempt to sabotage p.1167 [her] complaint." *Oden,* 440 F.3d at 1089. UC's actions were not clearly unreasonable.

b. UC's alleged policy violations

Like Karasek, Commins argues that UC's investigation ran afoul of the DCL and UC's policies. While investigating Commins's complaint, UC acted inconsistently with all the provisions of the DCL and its own policies that we have already identified. Indeed, given the violent nature of Commins's assault, Commins likely should have been afforded the opportunity to present testimony and other evidence at a formal hearing, as the DCL recommends and UC's policies require. UC also violated its Interim Sexual Misconduct Policy's prohibition on suspending an investigation merely because of pending criminal charges against the assailant, which the DCL advises against as well. *See* 2011 Dear Colleague Letter, at 10. But for the reasons expressed above, this does not establish deliberate indifference, particularly in light of the interim suspension immediately placed on Doe 2 to protect Commins while UC's investigation was stayed.

c. UC's alleged failure to prevent further harassment

Commins asserts that UC was deliberately indifferent because "Doe 2 was not placed on interim suspension until three months" after Commins's report, and because UC "never issued a no-contact order." Both assertions are incorrect. As demonstrated by the FAC's allegations, UC placed Doe 2 on interim suspension within two weeks of Commins's report, not three months. And UC did issue a no-contact order to Doe 2 as part of the final sanctions imposed. Commins does not allege that these protective measures were ineffective. Indeed, Commins identifies no instance when she ever saw Doe 2 again after reporting her sexual assault. Thus, Commins's argument here fails to demonstrate UC's deliberate indifference.

d. UC's alleged failure to allow Commins to participate in the investigation

Finally, Commins argues that UC responded inequitably by constantly communicating with Doe 2 while failing to update Commins or provide her with an opportunity to participate in the investigation. Although UC contacted Commins several times during the investigation and discussed potential sanctions with her, we agree that UC's general lack of communication was likely a significant failing. And as noted above, the decision to resolve Commins's complaint informally without allowing Commins to testify or present evidence is troubling, given the context and nature of her assault. If she had been given that opportunity, perhaps UC would have dealt even harsher sanctions. The wisdom of UC's decision not to expel a convicted felon, or at least extend his suspension while Commins pursued graduate studies at UC, can be questioned. Despite these shortcomings, however, UC's response did not exhibit deliberate indifference. After Commins reported her assault, UC moved quickly to suspend her assailant, and UC imposed fairly stringent sanctions upon resolution of Commins's complaint. We may disagree with UC's handling of

Commins's complaint, but that does not suffice for Title IX liability. *See Oden,* 440 F.3d at 1089. We affirm the district court's dismissal of Commins's individual claim.

3. Butler's individual claim

In granting summary judgment to UC, the district court held that Butler's Title IX claim failed because UC's response was p.1168 not deliberately indifferent.[4] On appeal, Butler argues that UC was deliberately indifferent in three respects: (a) UC failed to investigate her complaint at all, (b) UC failed to take steps to prevent Doe from harassing Butler again, and (c) UC violated the DCL and its own policies.

a. UC's investigation

Butler's argument that UC failed to investigate her complaint is demonstrably false. Indeed, the district court found that this argument "misrepresents the record." After Butler reported her assault and asked Oldham to investigate, Oldham discussed the nature of the Wildlands Studies Program with a UC faculty member to determine if UC's policies would apply. That conversation led Oldham to discover that the program was affiliated with California State University, Monterey Bay, and not with UC. Oldham also emailed Leslie Arutunian, an employee with the Wildlands Studies Program, who confirmed that the program had no connection to UC. At that point, Oldham concluded that UC's policies did not apply to Butler's assault and stopped investigating. Thus, UC did in fact investigate Butler's complaint, and the extent of its investigation was not "clearly unreasonable." *See Davis,* 526 U.S. at 648, 119 S.Ct. 1661.

b. UC's alleged failure to prevent further harassment

Butler argues that UC was deliberately indifferent by failing to preclude the possibility that Doe could harass Butler again. But it is unclear what interim protective measures UC should have imposed. As the district court found, Doe "was an independent third-party with no official relationship to UC." Accordingly, UC could not directly sanction Doe, as it could if Butler's assailant had been a UC student or faculty member. And Butler never told Oldham that she feared meeting Doe on campus or that she wanted UC to issue a no-contact order. Indeed, when Butler asked for help obtaining academic accommodations, UC did so, demonstrating UC's sensitivity to Butler's requests. Finally, Butler never claims to have seen Doe again after her assault. Given the information UC knew at the time, UC's failure to immediately implement protective measures does not constitute deliberate indifference.

c. UC's alleged policy violations

Butler contends that UC violated the DCL and UC's own policies by failing to (1) "respond to Butler's complaint," (2) "act when [Butler] wanted to remain anonymous," or (3) "implement any interim measures to remediate her hostile environment on campus." We have already concluded that UC did respond to Butler's complaint and that the lack of protective measures was not clearly unreasonable. Regardless, as we explained above, UC's failure to follow the DCL's guidance or abide by the school's own policies does not establish deliberate indifference. *See supra* Section III.A.1.b. Accordingly, we affirm the grant of summary judgment to UC on Butler's individual claim.

B. Appellants' Pre-Assault Claim

In addition to their individual Title IX claims, Appellants allege that UC maintained a "policy of deliberate indifference to sexual misconduct" that "created a sexually hostile environment for [Appellants]" p.1169 and heightened the risk that Appellants would be sexually assaulted. UC argues that this pre-assault theory of Title IX liability "fails as a matter of law" because it is "contrary to ... Supreme Court precedent." The district court dismissed this claim because it found Appellants' argument that UC's "level of awareness or deficiency of response with respect to the general problem of sexual violence is enough to establish either actual knowledge or deliberate indifference for the purposes of a Title IX claim" without sufficient basis in our case law. To the district court's credit, we have never directly addressed pre-assault Title IX claims. We hold that such a claim is a cognizable theory of Title IX liability. Because we clarify the standard applicable to such claims, we vacate the district court's dismissal of Appellants' pre-assault claim and remand for further proceedings.

As explained above, a plaintiff asserting a Title IX claim based on sexual harassment committed by a faculty member or peer must demonstrate that the school had "actual knowledge" of the harassment and responded with "deliberate indifference." *See Davis*, 526 U.S. at 650, 119 S.Ct. 1661. This ensures that a school is "liable in damages under Title IX only for its own misconduct," and not that of third parties. *Id.* at 640, 119 S.Ct. 1661.

But the calculus shifts when a plaintiff alleges that a school's "official policy" violates Title IX. *See Gebser*, 524 U.S. at 290, 118 S.Ct. 1989. In that context, the school has "intentionally violate[d] the statute." *Davis*, 526 U.S. at 642, 119 S.Ct. 1661. A school need not have had actual knowledge of a specific instance of sexual misconduct or responded with deliberate indifference to that misconduct before damages liability may attach. *See Gebser*, 524 U.S. at 290, 118 S.Ct. 1989; *see also Mansourian v. Regents of Univ. of Cal.*, 602 F.3d 957, 967 (9th Cir. 2010) ("[W]here the official policy is one of deliberate indifference to a known overall risk of sexual harassment, notice of a particular harassment situation and an opportunity to cure it are not predicates for liability."). Thus, a pre-assault claim should survive a motion to dismiss if the plaintiff plausibly alleges that (1) a school maintained a policy of deliberate indifference to reports of sexual misconduct,[5] (2) which created a heightened risk of sexual harassment (3) in a context subject to the school's control, and (4) the plaintiff was harassed as a result.

We find persuasive the Tenth Circuit's decision in *Simpson v. University of Colorado Boulder*, 500 F.3d 1170 (10th Cir. 2007). There, the University of Colorado hosted talented high school football players on campus each fall. The recruits were to be shown "a good time" and "were paired with female 'Ambassadors.'" *Id.* at 1173. Some recruits were "promised an opportunity to have sex," and there was evidence that the coaching staff not only knew of this conduct, but encouraged it. *Id.* at 1173-74. The university was aware of prior complaints of sexual misconduct by recruits and had been warned by the district attorney that the university needed to supervise the recruits and implement sexual assault prevention training. *Id.* at 1173-74, 1179-84. The plaintiffs were two women who were sexually assaulted by football recruits. Asserting a pre-assault p.1170 claim, the plaintiffs argued that the university had a history of responding with deliberate indifference to reports of sexual assaults occurring in its football recruiting program. *Id.* at 1174-75, 1177. The district court granted summary judgment to the university, finding that the plaintiffs failed to establish "actual notice" and "deliberate[] indifferen[ce]." *Id.* at 1174. The Tenth Circuit reversed. It held that "when [a Title IX] violation is caused by [an] official policy," the "notice standards established... in *Gebser* and *Davis*" do not apply because, in that case, "the institution itself, rather than its employees (or students), [is] the wrongdoer." *Id.* at 1177-78. Because the "risk of ... [sexual] assault" in the football recruiting program was "obvious," the failure to remedy that risk constituted an official policy of deliberate indifference that violated Title IX. *Id.* at 1178, 1180.

UC reads *Simpson* to require that the risk of sexual harassment be a "specific problem in a specific program." Based on that understanding, UC argues that Appellants' allegations of a heightened risk of sexual harassment throughout UC's programs cannot survive.

We disagree. To be sure, *Simpson* involved a particular program. But *Simpson*'s reasoning, and the reasoning of *Gebser* and *Davis,* supports imposing Title IX liability when a school's official policy is one of deliberate indifference to sexual harassment in any context subject to the school's control. Of course, it may be easier to establish a causal link between a school's policy of deliberate indifference and the plaintiff's harassment when the heightened risk of harassment exists in a specific program. But we will not foreclose the possibility that a plaintiff could adequately allege causation even when a school's policy of deliberate indifference extends to sexual misconduct occurring across campus.

Applying the framework we have set forth, we vacate the district court's dismissal of the pre-assault claim. Allegations that UC had actual knowledge or acted with deliberate indifference to a particular incident of harassment are unnecessary to sustain this theory of liability. Instead, all Appellants need allege are facts demonstrating the four elements we have articulated above.

What the FAC does allege is troubling. The FAC describes a report issued in 2014 by the California State Auditor that details deficiencies in UC's approach to sexual-misconduct complaints. *See* CALIFORNIA STATE AUDITOR, REP. No. 2013-124, SEXUAL HARASSMENT AND SEXUAL VIOLENCE (2014). The Auditor found that, over a five-year period, UC "resolved 76 percent of Title IX complaints from students using the early resolution process" in a generally inadequate manner. *Id.* at 53. For example, UC could not "demonstrate that [it] consistently informed students of what to expect as the university investigated their complaints." *Id.* at 55. UC also failed to "provide regular updates on the status of [its] investigations to students." *Id.* at 57. It did not "consistently complete investigations in a timely manner." *Id.* at 61. And it "did not notify all student complainants of the outcome of an investigation and the subsequent disciplinary action against the accused." *Id.* at 59.

Further, the Auditor found that UC did not sufficiently educate its employees and students about preventing sexual harassment, which led to the "mishandl[ing]" of sexual-misconduct complaints and "put[] the safety of [its] students at risk." *Id.* at 15, 30.

The FAC also highlights an incongruity between UC's public statements and its handling of sexual-misconduct complaints. In February 2014, Denise Oldham—UC's p.1171 Title IX Officer—stated in an interview with the *Los Angeles Times* that she "could not imagine a situation where" using an early resolution process for cases involving sexual assault "would be appropriate." If Oldham's premise is correct—that early resolution is not an appropriate mechanism for resolving sexual-assault claims—UC's conduct during the period in question appears inexplicable. According to the FAC, of the five hundred cases of sexual misconduct reported to UC's Office for the Prevention of Harassment and Discrimination in 2012, only two were resolved through a "formal process." Similarly, of the fourteen sexual-misconduct complaints reported to UC's Center for Student Conduct in 2013, all "were resolved through the ... informal resolution process."

Finally, the FAC alleges that UC had a powerful incentive to resolve cases through an informal process. The Jeanne Clery Disclosure of Campus Security Policy and Campus Crime Statistics Act requires UC to annually publish the number of "criminal... sex offenses, forcible or nonforcible," that were "reported to campus security authorities or local police agencies" and that occurred on or around campus during the prior two years. 20 U.S.C. § 1092(f)(1)(F)(i). According to the FAC, UC "takes the position" that "it is not required to report the offense" pursuant to the Clery Act "if the matter is resolved informally." Assuming that is true (as we must, at this stage), it is plausible that choosing to resolve sexual-misconduct complaints through an early resolution process enables UC to escape these statutory disclosure requirements.

UC argues that Appellants' allegations are less probative of an official policy than the evidence mustered by the plaintiffs in *Simpson*. We agree that the allegations here are much broader than the specific problem of sexual assault in the University of Colorado's football recruiting program. But UC's argument misses the mark. We are here on a motion to dismiss. *Simpson* involved a motion for summary judgment, after the parties had conducted discovery. Thus, the question is not whether Appellants' allegations are comparable to the evidence produced in *Simpson*. Rather, the question is whether Appellants plausibly allege that UC had a policy of deliberate indifference that heightened the risk of sexual harassment on campus, resulting in the assaults Appellants experienced.

Ultimately, we leave to the district court to decide, in the first instance, whether Appellants' allegations are sufficient to survive a motion to dismiss under the principles we have set forth. We reiterate that Title IX does not require UC to purge its campus of sexual misconduct to avoid liability. *See Davis*, 526 U.S. at 648, 119 S.Ct. 1661. A university is not responsible for guaranteeing the good behavior of its students. The element of causation ensures that Title IX liability remains within proper bounds. To that end, adequately alleging a causal link between a plaintiff's harassment and a school's deliberate indifference to sexual misconduct across campus is difficult. Whether the FAC plausibly alleges such a link—or any of the four elements—is an issue for the district court to decide upon remand. And the district court retains the discretion to allow Appellants to amend their complaint if "justice so requires." Fed. R. Civ. P. 15(a)(2). In short, we vacate that portion of the district court's dismissal order addressing Appellants' pre-assault claim and remand for further proceedings.

AFFIRMED IN PART, VACATED IN PART, AND REMANDED. Each party shall bear its own costs on appeal.

[*] The Honorable Salvador Mendoza, Jr., United States District Judge for the Eastern District of Washington, sitting by designation.

[1] These five elements are in addition to the threshold requirements that the defendant be a recipient of "[f]ederal financial assistance" and that the plaintiff experienced sex discrimination. *See* 20 U.S.C. § 1681(a). Here, there is no dispute that UC receives federal funding and that Appellants' sexual assaults constituted sex discrimination. *See Davis,* 526 U.S. at 649-50, 119 S.Ct. 1661 ("[S]exual harassment is a form of discrimination for Title IX purposes....").

[2] Because we address only the fourth element, we express no opinion on the circuit split regarding the fifth element. *Compare Kollaritsch v. Mich. State Univ. Bd. of Trs.,* 944 F.3d 613 (6th Cir. 2019), *with Farmer v. Kan. State Univ.,* 918 F.3d 1094 (10th Cir. 2019).

[3] The DCL is a "good practices" or "significant guidance document," as defined by the Office of Management and Budget (OMB). *See id.* at 1 n.1. According to OMB, guidance documents may set forth an agency's "policy on ... or interpretation of a statutory or regulatory issue," but they may not "impose a legally binding requirement" that adds to existing law. Final Bulletin for Agency Good Guidance Practices, 72 Fed. Reg. 3432, 3434 (Jan. 25, 2007). DOE acknowledges that the DCL informs DOE's judgment of whether a school is "complying with [its] legal obligations," but cautions that the DCL applies the "standard for administrative enforcement of Title IX and in court cases where plaintiffs are seeking injunctive relief," and not the deliberate-indifference standard. 2011 Dear Colleague Letter, at 1 n.1, 4 n.12.

Further, we note that DOE has rescinded the DCL, albeit long after the events alleged in the FAC transpired. *See* Dear Colleague Letter, Candice Jackson, Office for Civil Rights, U.S. Dep't of Educ., at 1 (Sept. 22, 2017).

[4] The district court rejected Butler's claim for two additional, independent reasons: UC lacked control over Butler's assailant and UC did not cause Butler to experience severe and pervasive harassment. Because we affirm the district court's finding that UC was not deliberately indifferent, we do not address the district court's additional findings.

[5] We do not hold that deliberate indifference to reports of past sexual misconduct is the only form of pre-assault conduct that could result in an institution's Title IX liability. Rather, we focus on the sufficiency of such allegations because they are what the FAC articulates. We do not have occasion to consider whether other forms of pre-assault conduct could amount to an official policy of deliberate indifference that is actionable under Title IX.

925 F.3d 1133 (2019)

Brandon AUSTIN, Plaintiff-Appellant, and
Dominic Artis; Damyean Dotson, Plaintiffs,

v.

UNIVERSITY OF OREGON; Sandy Weintraub; Chicora Martin; Robin Holmes; Michael R. Gottfredson, all in their individual capacities only, Defendants-Appellees.

Dominic Artis; Damyean Dotson, Plaintiffs-Appellants, and
Brandon Austin, Plaintiff,

v.

University of Oregon; Sandy Weintraub; Chicora Martin; Robin Holmes; Michael R. Gottfredson, all in their individual capacities only, Defendants-Appellees.

Nos. 17-35559, 17-35560.

United States Court of Appeals, Ninth Circuit.

Argued and Submitted December 6, 2018 Seattle, Washington.

Filed June 4, 2019.

Austin v. University of Oregon, 925 F. 3d 1133 (9th Cir. 2019)

Appeals from the United States District Court for the District of Oregon; Michael J. McShane, District Judge, Presiding, D.C. Nos. 6:15-cv-02257-MC, 6:16-cv-00647-MC.

Alan Carl Milstein (argued), Sherman Silverstein Kohl Rose & Podolsky P.A., Moorestown, New Jersey; Marianne Dugan, Eugene, Oregon; for Plaintiff-Appellant Brandon Austin.

Brian I. Michaels (argued), Eugene, Oregon, for Plaintiffs-Appellants Dominic Artis and Damyean Dotson.

Kevin Scott Reed (argued), Office of the General Counsel, University of Oregon, Eugene, Oregon; P.K. Runkles-Pearson, Miller Nash Graham & Dunn LLP, Portland, Oregon; for Defendants-Appellees.

Before: Susan P. Graber, M. Margaret McKeown, and Morgan Christen, Circuit Judges.

OPINION

McKEOWN, Circuit Judge:

These companion cases concerning campus sexual assault raise an issue of first impression in this circuit—whether the *McDonnell Douglas*[1] evidentiary presumption applies at the pleading stage in a Title IX case. Following the Supreme Court's explanation of Title VII's pleading requirements in *Swierkiewicz v. Sorema N.A.*, 534 U.S. 506, 122 S.Ct. 992, 152 L.Ed.2d 1 (2002), we conclude that Federal Rule of Civil Procedure 8(a), not *McDonnell Douglas,* applies at the motion to dismiss stage. On this basis, we affirm the district court's dismissal of the Third Amended Complaint because, putting aside mere conclusory allegations, the complaint fails to make any claims of discrimination on the basis of sex cognizable under Title IX. We also affirm the dismissal of the remaining due process and state law claims.

BACKGROUND

Brandon Austin, Dominic Artis, and Damyean Dotson (collectively, the "student athletes") were basketball players on scholarship at the University of Oregon (the "University") in 2014. In March 2014, a female student accused the men of forcing her to engage in nonconsensual sex at an off-campus apartment. She reported the alleged sexual assault to the Eugene police department within a few days. When details of the alleged assault became public, in part because the local news published the police report in full, the campus erupted in protest. Although the Lane County District Attorney ultimately decided not to prosecute the student athletes, the University proceeded with a formal disciplinary process.

Central to this case is the University of Oregon Student Conduct Code in effect at the time, which defined "sexual misconduct" to include penetration without explicit consent. (Other types of sexual activity contemplated by the Code are not at issue here.) The Code also defined "explicit consent" as "voluntary, non-coerced and clear communication indicating a willingness to engage in a particular act," including "an affirmative verbal response or voluntary acts unmistakable in their meaning." *See* Or. Admin. R. XXX-XXX-XXXX(30), XXX-XXX-XXXX(3)(h) (2006) ("Student Conduct Code"), *available at* http://policies.uoregon. edu/vol-3-administration-student-affairs/ch-1-conduct/student-conduct-code.

The student athletes had the option to choose between two types of disciplinary hearings: a panel hearing or an administrative conference. They opted for the simpler, more streamlined administrative conference. According to the complaint and the University's Special Choice of Resolution Form, the administrative conference procedure included notice of the character p.1136 of the accusations against each student athlete, a summary description of the types of processes available, and the range of possible penalties; access to the case file; the opportunity to review and respond to the investigative report including witness interviews; representation by an advisor, including counsel; and a neutral administrator as a hearing officer. *See* Or. Admin. R. XXX-XXX-XXXX(1) (2006). The student athletes claim that the hearings deprived them of constitutionally required procedural safeguards.

The University's Director of Student Conduct & Community Standards oversaw the hearing and found the student athletes responsible for sexual misconduct because they had violated the Student Conduct Code by "engaging in penetration without explicit consent." The University suspended the student athletes for at least four years and until the female student is no longer enrolled at the University (but not longer than ten years). It also declined to renew their scholarships.

The student athletes brought this action against the University and various administrators, alleging several causes of action, including Title IX claims based on sex discrimination and due process violations. The district court dismissed the Third Amended Complaint with prejudice.

DISCUSSION

I. Rule 8(a) Pleading Standard in *Swierkiewicz*

Despite the parties' extensive briefing, we need look no further than the Supreme Court's guidance in *Swierkiewicz* to divine that Rule 8(a)[2] provides the appropriate standard for reviewing a Rule 12(b)(6) motion to dismiss under Title IX. *Swierkiewicz*, 534 U.S. at 510-11, 122 S.Ct. 992. The Sixth Circuit is in accord. *See Doe v. Baum*, 903 F.3d 575, 580-81 (6th Cir. 2018) (applying Rule 8(a) to a Title IX claim without discussing *McDonnell Douglas*).

In *Swierkiewicz*, the Supreme Court reiterated that "[t]he prima facie case under *McDonnell Douglas* . . . is an evidentiary standard, not a pleading requirement."[3] 534 U.S. at 510, 122 S.Ct. 992. Under the familiar *McDonnell Douglas* evidentiary presumption, once a plaintiff pleads a prima facie case of discrimination, the burden of proof shifts to the non-moving party to show non-discriminatory intent. *See McDonnell Douglas*, 411 U.S. at 802, 93 S.Ct. 1817. The framework "is a tool to assist plaintiffs at the summary judgment stage so that they may reach trial." *Costa v. Desert Palace, Inc.*, 299 F.3d 838, 855 (9th Cir. 2002) (en banc), *aff'd*, 539 U.S. 90, 123 S.Ct. 2148, 156 L.Ed.2d 84 (2003).

McDonnell Douglas thus sets out "the order and allocation of proof" in a Title VII case. 411 U.S. at 800, 93 S.Ct. 1817. But, the

> Court has never indicated that the requirements for establishing a prima facie case under *McDonnell Douglas* also apply to the pleading standard that plaintiffs must satisfy in order to survive a motion to dismiss. For instance, we have rejected the argument that a Title VII complaint requires greater "particularity," because this would "too narrowly constric[t] the role of the pleadings."

Swierkiewicz, 534 U.S. at 511, 122 S.Ct. 992 (alteration in original) (quoting *McDonald v. Santa Fe Trail Transp. Co.*, 427 U.S. 273, 283 n.11, 96 S.Ct. 2574, 49 L.Ed.2d 493 (1976)). The Court went on to explain that, "[c]onsequently, the ordinary rules for assessing the sufficiency of a complaint apply[:]. . . . The liberal notice pleading of Rule 8(a) is the starting point of a simplified pleading system, which was adopted to focus litigation on the merits of a claim." *Id.* at 511, 514, 122 S.Ct. 992.

Without citing *Swierkiewicz*, the Second Circuit reached the opposite result in *Doe v. Columbia University*, 831 F.3d 46, 55-56 (2d Cir. 2016), and applied the *McDonnell Douglas* presumption at the motion to dismiss stage in a Title IX case. The court did reference a previous Title VII case in which it invoked the *McDonnell Douglas* presumption at the pleading stage. *Id.* at 54-55 (analyzing *Littlejohn v. City of New York*, 795 F.3d 297, 310 (2d Cir. 2015)). In *Littlejohn*, the Second Circuit recognized that *Swierkiewicz* eliminated the possibility of a *heightened* pleading standard for Title VII claims, but then construed *Swierkiewicz* as introducing a *lower* pleading standard. *See Littlejohn*, 795 F.3d at 309 ("Reading *Swierkiewicz* on its face, it appears to have meant that a Title VII plaintiff is not required to plead facts supporting even a minimal inference of discriminatory intent."). This led the court to reason that the *McDonnell Douglas* presumption informs the application of *Ashcroft v. Iqbal*, 556 U.S. 662, 129

S.Ct. 1937, 173 L.Ed.2d 868 (2009), in Title VII cases. *See Littlejohn,* 795 F.3d at 310 ("We conclude that *Iqbal's* requirement applies to Title VII complaints of employment discrimination, but does not affect the benefit to plaintiffs pronounced in the *McDonnell Douglas* quartet."). We read the Second Circuit's application of the *McDonnell Douglas* presumption at the pleading stage as contrary to Supreme Court precedent, and we decline to embrace that approach.[4]

II. Application of Rule 8(a) to the Student Athletes' Title IX Claims

It is well established that, under Rule 8(a), a plaintiff need only provide "enough facts to state a claim to relief that is plausible on its face." *Bell Atl. Corp. v. Twombly,* 550 U.S. 544, 570, 127 S.Ct. 1955, 167 L.Ed.2d 929 (2007). All factual allegations are accepted as true, and all reasonable inferences must be drawn in favor of the plaintiff. *See Iqbal,* 556 U.S. at 678, 129 S.Ct. 1937 (noting that this standard is not a "probability requirement," but "asks for more than a sheer possibility that a defendant has acted unlawfully"). The standard provides for liberal treatment of a plaintiff's complaint at the pleading stage.

Despite three efforts to meet this pleading standard and state a Title IX claim,[5] p.1138 the student athletes failed to do so. What is missing for each theory of liability are sufficient, nonconclusory allegations plausibly linking the disciplinary action to discrimination on the basis of sex. *See Yusuf v. Vassar Coll.,* 35 F.3d 709, 715 (2d Cir. 1994) (holding that a plaintiff can allege multiple theories for his or her claim, but under any theory "wholly conclusory allegations [will not] suffice for purposes of Rule 12(b)(6)").

The student athletes advance three theories under Title IX: selective enforcement, erroneous outcome, and deliberate indifference. The essence of the selective enforcement theory is that the decision to discipline the student athletes was "grounded" in gender bias. But the student athletes fail to allege how this is so. The complaint recites such facts as the content of the University president's speech and the campus protests, but does not make any plausible link connecting these events and the University's disciplinary actions to the fact that the student athletes are male. *See Yusuf,* 35 F.3d at 715 ("[A selective enforcement] claim asserts that, regardless of the student's guilt or innocence, the severity of the penalty and/or the decision to initiate the proceeding was affected by the student's gender.").

Just saying so is not enough. A recitation of facts without plausible connection to gender is not cured by labels and conclusory statements about sex discrimination. *See Twombly,* 550 U.S. at 556, 127 S.Ct. 1955 ("[A] plaintiff's obligation to provide the grounds of his entitlement to relief requires more than labels and conclusions, and a formulaic recitation of the elements of a cause of action will not do. . . ." (internal quotations mark and alterations omitted)). *Compare Swierkiewicz,* 534 U.S. at 514, 122 S.Ct. 992 (detailing specific allegations in a discrimination case that linked a wrongful termination to age and national origin).

The student athletes also allege that, because the University disciplines male students for sexual misconduct but never female students, it is biased against men. But this allegedly disparate impact, even assuming it is true, claims too much. Significantly, the complaint does not claim that any female University students have been accused of comparable misconduct, and thus fails to allege that similarly situated students—those accused of sexual misconduct—are disciplined unequally.[6] The district court also recognized the lack of parallelism and reasoned "[s]imply because enforcement is asymmetrical does not mean that it is selectively so." We agree. Without nonconclusory allegations that the male students were treated any differently than similarly situated female students based on sex, the selective enforcement theory fails.

The erroneous outcome theory also fails because the student athletes do not articulate any basis to discern that the administration or outcomes of the disciplinary proceedings were flawed due to the student athletes' sex. *See Yusuf,* 35 F.3d at 715. Even if the outcome of the administrative conference procedure was erroneous, the complaint is missing any factual allegations that show that sex discrimination was the source of any error.

Lastly, the student athletes advance a "deliberate indifference" theory of Title IX liability, but only make passing reference to it in one line of a footnote. Without meaningful briefing on this issue, p.1139 we consider the argument waived. *See United States v. Kama,* 394 F.3d 1236, 1238 (9th Cir. 2005) ("Generally, an issue is waived when the appellant does not specifically and distinctly argue the issue in his or her opening brief.").

The district court previously dismissed the student athletes' Title IX claims with leave to amend and yet, after two efforts, they still could not allege additional facts to sufficiently plead these claims. We affirm the district court's dismissal of the Title IX claims with prejudice.

III. Claims for Violations of Due Process

The student athletes' due process claims fail because they received constitutional due process through the University's disciplinary proceedings.[7] *See Mathews v. Eldridge,* 424 U.S. 319, 335, 96 S.Ct. 893, 47 L.Ed.2d 18 (1976). Under *Mathews,* we balance three factors: (1) the private interests subjected to official action; (2) the risk of an erroneous outcome and the "probable value, if any, of additional or substitute procedural safeguards"; and (3) the governmental interest involved, including fiscal and administrative concerns. *See id.* at 334-35, 96 S.Ct. 893. Essentially, "some form of hearing is required before an individual is finally deprived of a property interest." *Id.* at 333, 96 S.Ct. 893.

We assume, without deciding, that the student athletes have property and liberty interests in their education, scholarships, and reputation as alleged in the complaint. Nonetheless, they received "the hallmarks of procedural due process": notice and a meaningful opportunity to be heard. *Ludwig v. Astrue,* 681 F.3d 1047, 1053 (9th Cir. 2012) (quoting *Guenther v. Comm'r,* 889 F.2d 882, 884 (9th Cir. 1989) (order)). Notice is not an issue here and nothing in the allegations supports a claim that the student athletes did not receive a meaningful hearing with the right to be heard. Importantly, they were represented by counsel and given a choice of a Special Administrative Conference or a Panel Hearing with a panel of students, faculty, and staff and the option to appeal. They signed a Special Choice of Resolution Form and chose the Special Administrative Conference. In doing so, they removed the possibility of expulsion and negotiated away a potential "negative notation" on their academic record, replacing it with a "notation of finding of Code violation — unspecified." Because the student athletes were represented by counsel and negotiated the scope of sanctions, they can hardly be heard to complain about the administrative hearing's procedural safeguards. Under *Mathews*, a hearing need not include every procedure possible, nor is one entitled to a hearing of one's own design. 424 U.S. at 333, 96 S.Ct. 893 ("The fundamental requirement of due process is the opportunity to be heard 'at a meaningful time and in a meaningful manner.'" (quoting *Armstrong v. Manzo*, 380 U.S. 545, 552, 85 S.Ct. 1187, 14 L.Ed.2d 62 (1965))). On these facts, the student athletes were not denied due process.

Finally, we credit the University's focus on encouraging students' personal integrity and cooperative (rather than coercive) interpersonal behavior, interest in providing an environment free of sexual misconduct, and setting up a disciplinary system that provides students an opportunity to be heard. We affirm the district court's dismissal of the due process claims. We also affirm the dismissal of the state law p.1140 claims for the reasons stated in the district court's orders dismissing the Third and Second Amended Complaints.

AFFIRMED.

[1] *McDonnell Douglas Corp. v. Green*, 411 U.S. 792, 93 S.Ct. 1817, 36 L.Ed.2d 668 (1973).

[2] Rule 8(a) provides: "[a] pleading that states a claim for relief must contain: (1) a short and plain statement of the grounds for the court's jurisdiction . . .; (2) a short and plain statement of the claim showing that the pleader is entitled to relief; and (3) a demand for the relief sought. . . ."

[3] *Swierkiewicz* was a Title VII case. We apply the principles of Title VII cases to Title IX claims. *See, e.g., Franklin v. Gwinnett Cty. Pub. Sch.*, 503 U.S. 60, 75, 112 S.Ct. 1028, 117 L.Ed.2d 208 (1992) (relying on a Title VII case to determine whether sexual harassment qualified as discrimination under Title IX); *Emeldi v. Univ. of Or.*, 698 F.3d 715, 724 (9th Cir. 2012) (applying the framework from Title VII cases to a Title IX retaliation claim).

[4] We emphasize that Rule 8(a)'s liberal pleading standard is lenient enough to allow meritorious discrimination claims to proceed while preserving the gatekeeping function of pleading standards. This opinion should in no way be interpreted as requiring a heightened pleading standard for Title IX claims.

[5] Title IX provides that "[n]o person in the United States shall, on the basis of sex, be excluded from participation in, be denied the benefits of, or be subjected to discrimination under any education program or activity receiving Federal financial assistance." 20 U.S.C. § 1681(a). Title IX applies to "all of the operations of . . . a college, university, or other postsecondary institution, or a public system of higher education." *Id.* § 1687.

[6] We agree with the district court that the only incident cited in the complaint involving an "accused" female student—threatening another student with a knife—did not constitute sexual misconduct.

[7] Because there were no due process violations, we need not reach the issue of qualified immunity.

891 F.3d 1147 (2018)

John DOE, Plaintiff-Appellee,
v.
REGENTS OF THE UNIVERSITY OF CALIFORNIA; Suzanne Perkin, in her official capacity, Defendants-Appellants.

No. 17-56110.

United States Court of Appeals, Ninth Circuit.

Argued and Submitted March 9, 2018, Pasadena, California.

Filed June 6, 2018.

Doe v. Regents of the University of California, 891 F. 3d 1147 (9th Cir. 2018)

Appeal from the United States District Court for the Central District of California; D.C. No. 2:15-cv-2478 SVW-JEM, Stephen V. Wilson, District Judge, Presiding.

Bradley S. Phillips (argued) and Hailyn J. Chen, Munger Tolles & Olson LLP, Los Angeles, California; Jonathan D. Miller and Alison M. Bernal, Nye Peabody Stirling Hale & Miller LLP, Santa Barbara, California; for Defendants-Appellants.

Scott Michael McLeod (argued) and Christopher J. Mead, Cooper White & Cooper LLP, San Francisco, California; Kimberly C. Lau (argued), Warshaw Burstein LLP, New York, New York; for Plaintiff-Appellee.

Before: A. Wallace Tashima and Jacqueline H. Nguyen, Circuit Judges, and Michael H. Simon,[*] District Judge.

ORDER AND OPINION

The request of Defendants-Appellants for publication is granted. The Memorandum filed March 27, 2018, 2018 WL 1476666, is withdrawn and replaced by the Opinion filed concurrently with this order.

Plaintiff-Appellee's petition for panel rehearing and rehearing en banc is denied as moot. Further petitions for rehearing may be filed with respect to the Opinion within the time permitted by the Rules.

OPINION

TASHIMA, Circuit Judge:

In this interlocutory appeal, The Regents of the University of California ("The Regents") and Suzanne Perkin ("Perkin"), the assistant dean of students at the University of California at Santa Barbara ("UCSB"), appeal the district court's denial of their motion to dismiss John Doe's ("Doe") second amended complaint ("SAC") on Eleventh Amendment immunity, judicial exhaustion, and *Younger* abstention grounds. We reverse.

I. BACKGROUND

The merits of Doe's lawsuit are not before us, so we recite only in brief the factual basis of his claims.[1] The procedural history of the case is more germane to the issues on appeal.

A. Doe's Suspension

Doe, a male UCSB student, sued The Regents and Perkin after he was disciplined for the sexual assault of a female UCSB student, Jane Doe ("Jane") during a trip to Lake Tahoe. Doe denies that he assaulted Jane and instead contends that the sexual encounter, which occurred in June 2014, was consensual.

On November 6, 2014, UCSB notified Doe that he had been charged with sexual assault in violation of the university's code of conduct. A week later, Doe had a meeting with Perkin, at which she read Doe a statement that Jane had written. On November 25, UCSB informed Doe that on December 11, an adjudicatory committee would hold a hearing on the assault charges. Two days before the hearing, Perkin provided Doe with an investigative report that she produced based on interviews with Doe, Jane, and other witnesses. The committee later held a second hearing, on December 19, before which Perkin completed a second investigative report. Shortly after the second hearing, the committee found Doe responsible for Jane's sexual assault and recommended the university suspend him for two quarters. In January 2015, Vice Chancellor for Student Affairs Michael Young upheld the decision and, on February 16, 2015, UCSB Chancellor Henry Yang denied Doe's appeal.

B. Complaint and First Motion to Dismiss

In April 2015, Doe filed this action against The Regents, alleging that the committee had "no basis" for its decision.[2] Doe brought a Title IX claim,[3] a claim under 42 U.S.C. § 1983 for violation of his procedural due process rights, and numerous state law claims. Doe alleged that UCSB discriminated against him because of his male sex via a "non-exhaustive list" of wrongful actions, including preventing him from presenting character evidence and disciplining him on the basis of investigative reports that "present[ed] a skewed rendition of the facts[.]" Doe also alleged, *inter alia*, that UCSB lacked jurisdiction over the Lake Tahoe trip, and that UCSB intentionally scheduled the December 19 hearing on a day when Doe's attorney was unavailable.

The Regents moved to dismiss, arguing that Doe's lawsuit was barred in its entirety because he had not petitioned for a writ of administrative mandamus under California Code of Civil Procedure § 1094.5 ("§ 1094.5 petition" or "writ petition") and had therefore not exhausted his judicial remedies. After supplemental briefing, the district court granted the motion, concluding that Doe's state law claims were barred because he had not yet filed a § 1094.5 writ petition. The court rejected The Regents' argument that Doe's § 1983 claim was also barred for failure to exhaust judicial remedies. Still, the court dismissed the § 1983 claim on Eleventh Amendment grounds and the Title IX claim for failure to state a claim.

C. First Amended Complaint and Second Motion to Dismiss

Doe filed a first amended complaint ("FAC"), which included a § 1094.5 writ petition. Doe alleged that UCSB held an unfair hearing and that its disciplinary decision was not supported by the evidence. Doe asserted Title IX and declaratory relief claims against The Regents and substituted Perkin as the sole defendant on his § 1983 due process claim.[4] Doe also added new factual allegations. For example, he alleged that UCSB exhibited gender bias against Doe as a result of "mounting pressure" from the U.S. Department of Education, Office of Civil Rights, a campus roundtable on sexual assault, campus organizations, and a University of California system-wide task force on sexual assault.

The Regents moved to dismiss under Federal Rule of Civil Procedure 12(b)(6). The court dismissed with prejudice the Title IX claim for failure to state a claim, and without prejudice the § 1983 claim as barred by the Eleventh Amendment. The court then declined to exercise supplemental jurisdiction over the § 1094.5 writ claim.

D. Second Amended Complaint and Third Motion to Dismiss

Doe then filed the SAC, in which he clarified that the § 1983 claim was alleged against Perkin in her official capacity. Doe also re-alleged the § 1094.5 writ petition. The Regents again moved to dismiss, arguing that the § 1983 claim was barred by the Eleventh Amendment and the § 1094.5 writ claim was barred for failure to exhaust judicial remedies. Before the district court ruled on The Regents' motion, Doe moved the court to reconsider its dismissal of his Title IX claim. The court granted the motion. The Regents then moved to dismiss the reinstated Title IX claim, also contending that Doe's § 1094.5 writ petition against The Regents was barred by the Eleventh Amendment. Thus, the district court had before it two motions to dismiss.

The court denied both motions. First, the court ruled that the § 1983 claim against Perkin in her official capacity did not run afoul of the Eleventh Amendment, nor was Perkin entitled to qualified or quasi-judicial immunity. Second, the court rejected The Regents' contention that the § 1094.5 petition was precluded. The court reasoned that because the SAC included the § 1094.5 writ petition, Doe had exhausted his judicial remedies. Third, the court concluded that abstention under *Younger v. Harris,* 401 U.S. 37, 91 S.Ct. 746, 27 L.Ed.2d 669 (1971), was not warranted because there were no ongoing state proceedings.

The Regents moved for reconsideration, contending that the Eleventh Amendment bars a plaintiff from bringing a state law claim, including a § 1094.5 writ petition, against The Regents in federal court. The court denied the motion. First, the court concluded that a § 1094.5 petition is a procedural mechanism that "functions as a vehicle for federal injunctive relief for Eleventh Amendment immunity purposes"; thus, the Eleventh Amendment did not bar it. Second, the court "interpret[ed]" the § 1094.5 petition against The Regents as a claim "against the University officials who have the power to effectuate any prospective injunctive relief ordered by the court[,]" and therefore concluded that it was permitted under the *Ex parte Young,* 209 U.S. 123, 28 S.Ct. 441, 52 L.Ed. 714 (1908), exception to Eleventh Amendment immunity. The Regents took an interlocutory appeal, and a motions panel of our court stayed district court proceedings.[5]

II. STANDARD OF REVIEW

A state instrumentality's Eleventh Amendment sovereign immunity and whether a plaintiff exhausted judicial remedies are both questions of law reviewed de novo. *Micomonaco v. Washington,* 45 F.3d 316, 319 (9th Cir. 1995) (sovereign immunity); *Miller v. County of Santa Cruz,* 39 F.3d 1030, 1032 (9th Cir. 1994) (exhaustion).

III. DISCUSSION

On appeal, The Regents contend that the district court should have dismissed Doe's entire complaint because the Eleventh Amendment bars the § 1094.5 writ claim and, because Doe has thus not filed a valid § 1094.5 petition, his failure to exhaust judicial remedies bars the § 1983 and Title IX claims. Alternatively, The Regents contend that the district court should at least have abstained under *Younger.* We consider The Regents' arguments *seriatim.*

A. Eleventh Amendment Immunity

We have jurisdiction over an interlocutory appeal from the denial of Eleventh Amendment immunity under the collateral order doctrine. *P.R. Aqueduct & Sewer Auth. v. Metcalf & Eddy, Inc.,* 506 U.S. 139, 147, 113 S.Ct. 684, 121 L.Ed.2d 605 (1993).

Doe, however, contends that The Regents waived the argument that Eleventh Amendment immunity bars the § 1094.5 petition. We disagree. A state's waiver of Eleventh Amendment immunity and consent to suit must be "unequivocally expressed." *Pennhurst State Sch. & Hosp. v. Halderman,* 465 U.S. 89, 99, 104 S.Ct. 900, 79 L.Ed.2d 67 (1984); *accord Actmedia, Inc. v. Stroh,* 830 F.2d 957, 963 (9th Cir. 1986) ("The test for finding waiver by a state of its eleventh-amendment immunity is 'stringent.'") (quoting *Atascadero State Hosp. v. Scanlon,* 473 U.S. 234, 241, 105 S.Ct. 3142, 87 L.Ed.2d 171 (1985)), *disapproved of on other grounds by Retail Digital Network, LLC v. Prieto,* 861 F.3d p.1153 839, 841-42 (9th Cir. 2017) (en banc). For evidence of waiver, Doe points only to The Regents' acknowledgement in a hearing on the first motion to dismiss that they had "yet to assert" Eleventh Amendment immunity. Instead, The Regents first argued that Doe's entire complaint should be dismissed for failure to exhaust judicial remedies. That was not an unequivocal waiver. We therefore consider The Regents' argument.

The Eleventh Amendment protects states and state instrumentalities, such as The Regents, from suit in federal court. *Pennhurst,* 465 U.S. at 100, 104 S.Ct. 900; *see also BV Eng'g v. Univ. of Cal., LA,* 858 F.2d 1394, 1395 (9th Cir. 1988) (affirming that the University of California is a state instrumentality protected by sovereign immunity). Under the *Ex parte Young* exception to that Eleventh Amendment bar, a party may seek prospective injunctive relief against an individual state officer in her official capacity. *Agua Caliente Band of Cahuilla Indians v. Hardin,* 223 F.3d 1041, 1045 (9th Cir. 2000). However, the *Young* exception does not apply when a suit seeks relief under state law, even if the plaintiff names an individual state official rather than a state instrumentality as the defendant. *Pennhurst,* 465 U.S. at 117, 104 S.Ct. 900.

Those Eleventh Amendment principles require dismissal of Doe's § 1094.5 writ petition, which is a state law claim. The district court erred when it determined that Doe's § 1094.5 petition was not a state law claim, but rather a "state-law procedural mechanism" and "vehicle" for Doe's federal claims. On the contrary, a § 1094.5 petition raises substantive state law claims. *Kay v. City of Rancho Palos Verdes,* 504 F.3d 803, 809 (9th Cir. 2007) ("Writs of mandate are used under California law 'for the purpose of inquiring into the validity of any final administrative order....'") (quoting Cal. Civ. Proc. Code § 1094.5(a)).

For example, the § 1094.5 writ petition permits a substantive inquiry into whether an administrative body "proceeded without, or in excess of, jurisdiction; whether there was a fair trial; and whether there was any prejudicial abuse of discretion." Cal. Civ. Proc. Code § 1094.5(b). Doe raises those same substantive § 1094.5 claims in the SAC, alleging that his suspension is invalid because UCSB did not grant him a fair hearing, exceeded its jurisdiction, and "committed a prejudicial abuse of discretion," among other allegations. California state courts have also developed a body of substantive case law around § 1094.5. *See, e.g., Doe v. Regents of the Univ. of Cal.,* 5 Cal.App.5th 1055, 210 Cal.Rptr.3d 479, 499-500 (2016); *Doe v. Univ. of S. Cal.,* 246 Cal.App.4th 221, 200 Cal.Rptr.3d 851, 866-77 (2016); *Am. Tower Corp. v. City of San Diego,* 763 F.3d 1035, 1057 (9th Cir. 2014).

In further support of this conclusion, we note that Doe requests fees pursuant to California Government Code § 800(a), which permits a plaintiff to recover attorney's fees when the court finds that a public entity acted arbitrarily and capriciously "under this code or under any other provision of *state law.*" (emphasis added). The only state law claim in the SAC is the § 1094.5 petition. Ultimately, if Doe's § 1094.5 claims were to succeed on their merits, a federal court would have to grant injunctive relief against a state instrumentality "on the basis of state law" in violation of the Eleventh Amendment. *Pennhurst,* 465 U.S. at 106, 104 S.Ct. 900. That Doe needed to bring the § 1094.5 petition to exhaust judicial remedies, as discussed in the next section, does not render it a mere procedural mechanism.

The Eleventh Amendment therefore bars Doe's § 1094.5 petition against The Regents and the district court should have dismissed it with prejudice.[6]

B. Judicial Exhaustion

The Regents contend that because Doe's § 1094.5 petition was barred from federal court, the district court also should have dismissed Doe's § 1983 and Title IX claims for failure to exhaust judicial remedies. Recognizing that we have not held that the denial of a motion to dismiss on judicial exhaustion grounds is independently appealable, The Regents ask us to exercise pendent appellate jurisdiction over that portion of the district court's order. Although Doe does not contest jurisdiction, we have an independent obligation to consider our own appellate jurisdiction. *Couch v. Telescope Inc.,* 611 F.3d 629, 632 (9th Cir. 2010).

Under the doctrine of pendent appellate jurisdiction, we may review an otherwise non-appealable ruling when it is "'inextricably intertwined' with or 'necessary to ensure meaningful review of' the order properly before us." *Meredith v. Oregon,* 321 F.3d 807, 812-13 (9th Cir. 2003) (quoting *Swint v. Chambers Cty. Comm'n,* 514 U.S. 35, 51, 115 S.Ct. 1203, 131 L.Ed.2d 60 (1995)). The first prong—on which The Regents rely—is "narrowly construed." *Id.* at 813. "[T]he legal theories... must either (a) be so intertwined that we must decide the pendent issue in order to review the claims properly raised on interlocutory appeal, or (b) resolution of the issue properly raised on interlocutory appeal necessarily resolves the pendent issue." *Cunningham v. Gates,* 229 F.3d 1271, 1285 (9th Cir. 2000) (citation omitted).

In this case, our conclusion that The Regents are entitled to Eleventh Amendment immunity-the issue properly raised on appeal-also necessarily resolves whether Doe has exhausted his judicial remedies (and means that he has not). We therefore exercise pendent appellate jurisdiction over The Regents' appeal from the district court's order denying dismissal on judicial exhaustion grounds.

We also agree with The Regents that Doe's § 1983 and Title IX claims are precluded because he has failed to exhaust judicial remedies by filing a § 1094.5 writ petition in state court.[7] Under federal common law, federal courts accord preclusive effect to state administrative proceedings that meet the fairness requirements of *United States v. Utah Construction & Mining Co.,* 384 U.S. 394, 86 S.Ct. 1545, 16 L.Ed.2d 642 (1966). *See Miller v. Cty. of Santa Cruz,* 39 F.3d at 1032-33. We evaluate the fairness of a state administrative proceeding by resort to both the underlying administrative proceeding and the available judicial review procedure. *See Olson v. Morris,* 188 F.3d 1083, 1086-87 (9th Cir. 1999). A § 1094.5 petition for a writ of administrative mandamus provides "an adequate opportunity p.1155 for de novo judicial review." *Miller,* 39 F.3d at 1033 (citing *Eilrich v. Remas,* 839 F.2d 630, 632 (9th Cir. 1988)); *see also Kenneally v. Lungren,* 967 F.2d 329, 333 (9th Cir. 1992) (holding that the § 1094.5 procedure provided the plaintiff a "meaningful opportunity" to raise constitutional claims).

Because California has adopted the *Utah Construction* standard, we give preclusive effect to a state administrative decision if the California courts would do so. *Miller,* 39 F.3d at 1032-33. In California, "[e]xhaustion of judicial remedies... is necessary to avoid giving binding 'effect to [an] administrative agency's decision[.]'" *Johnson v. City of Loma Linda,* 24 Cal.4th 61, 99 Cal.Rptr.2d 316, 5 P.3d 874, 879 (2000) (emphasis omitted) (quoting *Briggs v. City of Rolling Hills Estates,* 40 Cal.App.4th 637, 47 Cal.Rptr.2d 29, 33 (1995)). A party must exhaust judicial remedies by filing a § 1094.5 petition, the exclusive and "established process for judicial review" of an agency decision. *Id.* 99 Cal.Rptr.2d 316, 5 P.3d at 880 (citing *Westlake Cmty. Hosp. v. Superior Court,* 17 Cal.3d 465, 131 Cal.Rptr. 90, 551 P.2d 410, 421 (1976) (in bank)). UCSB's suspension of Doe is the sort of "adjudicatory, quasi-judicial decision" that is subject to the judicial exhaustion requirement. *Y.K.A. Indus., Inc. v. Redev. Agency of San Jose,* 174 Cal.App.4th 339, 94 Cal. Rptr.3d 424, 444 (2009).

It is undisputed that Doe has not filed a § 1094.5 petition in state court. Although a plaintiff is not required by statute to file a § 1094.5 petition in state court, in this case the Eleventh Amendment bars Doe from filing his writ petition in federal court. Therefore, Doe has not exhausted his judicial remedies. Because the California courts would thus accord preclusive effect to UCSB's administrative decision, we must do the same. The district court should have dismissed without prejudice[8] Doe's § 1983 and Title IX claims.[9]

...

The judgment of the district court is reversed and the case remanded to the district court with instructions to dismiss Doe's § 1094.5 writ claim with prejudice, but without prejudice to refiling in state court, and his § 1983, Title IX, and declaratory relief claims without prejudice.

REVERSED and REMANDED with directions.

[*] The Honorable Michael H. Simon, United States District Judge for the District of Oregon, sitting by designation.

[1] The factual allegations in the SAC are presumed true. *Knievel v. ESPN*, 393 F.3d 1068, 1072 (9th Cir. 2005).

[2] The initial complaint did not name Perkin as a defendant.

[3] Title IX of the Education Amendments of 1972, 20 U.S.C. §§ 1681-1688.

[4] Doe did not re-allege the other state law claims.

[5] A different motions panel denied The Regents' related petition for a writ of mandamus.

[6] The district court also erred in "interpret[ing]" the writ claim, which names only The Regents as defendant, to name Perkin. The *Ex parte Young* exception applies only when the plaintiff names an individual state official. *See S. Pac. Transp. Co. v. City of L.A.*, 922 F.2d 498, 508 (9th Cir. 1990). We have permitted plaintiffs leave to amend to conform their pleading with *Young, see Ariz. Students' Ass'n v. Ariz. Bd. of Regents*, 824 F.3d 858, 865-66 (9th Cir. 2016), but our conclusion that the § 1094.5 petition is a state law claim bars Doe from bringing the writ petition in federal court against either The Regents or Perkin and means such an amendment would be futile.

[7] Doe's contention that The Regents forfeited the exhaustion argument by not raising it in the district court, lacks merit. The Regents raised § 1094.5 judicial exhaustion in both their motion to dismiss the SAC, and their motion for reconsideration.

[8] The Regents represent that the statute of limitations on Doe's § 1094.5 writ claim has not yet run. *See Lasko v. Valley Presbyterian Hosp.*, 180 Cal.App.3d 519, 225 Cal.Rptr. 603, 606 (1986) (holding that four-year statute of limitations applies to § 1094.5 writ claims).

[9] Because we hold that the district court should have dismissed Doe's SAC in its entirety, we do not reach The Regents' argument that the district court should have abstained pursuant to *Younger*. We therefore also need not reach the threshold question of whether we would have pendant appellate jurisdiction over The Regents' appeal of that order. *See Confederated Salish v. Simonich*, 29 F.3d 1398, 1401-03 (9th Cir. 1994) (holding that an order denying dismissal on *Younger* grounds is not immediately appealable on its own).

889 F.3d 648 (2018)

UNITED STATES of America, Plaintiff-Appellee,
v.
COUNTY OF MARICOPA, ARIZONA, Defendant-Appellant, and Paul Penzone,[*] in his official capacity as Sheriff of Maricopa County, Arizona, Defendant.

No. 15-17558.

United States Court of Appeals, Ninth Circuit.

Argued and Submitted September 15, 2017 San Francisco, California.

Filed May 7, 2018.

US v. County of Maricopa, Arizona, 889 F. 3d 648 (9th Cir. 2018)

Appeal from the United States District Court for the District of Arizona, D.C. No. 2:12-cv-00981-ROS, Roslyn O. Silver, Senior District Judge, Presiding.

Richard K. Walker (argued), Walker & Peskind PLLC, Scottsdale, Arizona, for Defendant-Appellant.

Elizabeth Parr Hecker (argued) and Thomas E. Chandler, Attorneys; Gregory B. Friel, Deputy Assistant Attorney General; Civil Rights Division, United States Department of Justice, Washington, D.C.; for Plaintiff-Appellee.

Before: Ronald M. Gould, Richard C. Tallman, and Paul J. Watford, Circuit Judges.

OPINION

WATFORD, Circuit Judge:

The United States brought this action to halt racially discriminatory policing policies instituted by Joseph Arpaio, the former Sheriff of Maricopa County, Arizona. Under Arpaio's leadership, the Maricopa County Sheriff's Office (MCSO) routinely targeted Latino drivers and passengers for pretextual traffic stops aimed at detecting violations of federal immigration law. Based on that and other unlawful conduct, the United States sued Arpaio, MCSO, and the County of Maricopa under two statutes: Title VI of the Civil Rights Act of 1964, 42 U.S.C. § 2000d, and 34 U.S.C. § 12601 (formerly codified at 42 U.S.C. § 14141).[1] The district court granted summary judgment in favor of the United States on the claims relating to the unlawful traffic stops; the parties settled the remaining claims. Maricopa County is the lone appellant here. Its main contention is that it cannot be held liable for the unlawful traffic-stop policies implemented by Arpaio.

We begin with a summary of the lengthy legal proceedings involving Arpaio's unlawful policing policies. In an earlier class action lawsuit, *Melendres v. Arpaio*, a group of plaintiffs representing a class of Latino drivers and passengers sued Arpaio, MCSO, and the County of Maricopa under 42 U.S.C. § 1983 and Title VI. They alleged that execution of Arpaio's racially p.650 discriminatory traffic-stop policies violated their rights under the Fourth and Fourteenth Amendments. Following a bench trial, the district court ruled in the plaintiffs' favor and granted broad injunctive relief, which we largely upheld on appeal. *See Melendres v. Arpaio,* 695 F.3d 990 (9th Cir. 2012); *Melendres v. Arpaio,* 784 F.3d 1254 (9th Cir. 2015) (*Melendres II*).

While the *Melendres* action was proceeding, the United States filed this suit. Among other things, the United States challenged the legality of the same traffic-stop policies at issue in *Melendres.* The United States named as defendants Arpaio, in his official capacity as Sheriff of Maricopa County; MCSO; and Maricopa County. Early on, the district court dismissed MCSO from the action in light of the Arizona Court of Appeals' decision in *Braillard v. Maricopa County,* 224 Ariz. 481, 232 P.3d 1263 (Ct. App. 2010), which held that MCSO is a non-jural entity that cannot be sued in its own name. *Id.* at 1269.

Throughout the proceedings below, the County argued that it too should be dismissed as a defendant, on two different grounds. First, the County argued that when a sheriff in Arizona adopts policies relating to law-enforcement matters, such as the traffic-stop policies at issue here, he does not act as a policymaker for the county. He instead acts as a policymaker for his own office, or perhaps for the State. The County contended that, because Arpaio's policies were not policies of the County, it could not be held liable for the constitutional violations caused by execution of them. Second, the County argued that, even if Arpaio acted as a policymaker for the County, neither Title VI nor 34 U.S.C. § 12601 permits a local government to be held liable for the actions of its policymakers.

The district court rejected both of the County's arguments. The court then granted the United States' motion for summary judgment with respect to claims predicated on the traffic-stop policies found unlawful in *Melendres.* The court held that the County was barred by the doctrine of issue preclusion from relitigating the issues decided in the *Melendres* action, which by that point had reached final judgment. The County does not contest that if the *Melendres* findings are binding here, they establish violations of Title VI and § 12601.

On appeal, Maricopa County advances three arguments: (1) Arpaio did not act as a final policymaker for the County; (2) neither Title VI nor § 12601 renders the County liable for the actions of its policymakers; and (3) the County is not bound by the *Melendres* findings. We address each of these arguments in turn.

I

We have already rejected Maricopa County's first argument — that Arpaio was not a final policymaker for the County. In *Melendres v. Maricopa County,* 815 F.3d 645 (9th Cir. 2016) (*Melendres III*), we noted that "Arizona state law makes clear that Sheriff Arpaio's law-enforcement acts constitute Maricopa County policy since he 'has final policymaking authority.'" *Id.* at 650 (quoting *Flanders v. Maricopa County,* 203 Ariz. 368, 54 P.3d 837, 847 (Ct. App. 2002)). Because that determination was arguably *dicta,* we have conducted our own analysis of the issue, and we reach the same conclusion.

To determine whether Arpaio acted as a final policymaker for the County, we consult Arizona's Constitution and statutes, and the court decisions interpreting them. *See McMillian v. Monroe County*, 520 U.S. 781, 786, 117 S.Ct. 1734, 138 L.Ed.2d 1 (1997); *Weiner v. San Diego County*, 210 F.3d 1025, 1029 (9th Cir. 2000). Those p.651 sources confirm that, with respect to lawenforcement matters, sheriffs in Arizona act as final policymakers for their respective counties.

Arizona's Constitution and statutes designate sheriffs as officers of the county. The Arizona Constitution states: "There are hereby created *in and for each organized county of the state* the following officers who shall be elected by the qualified electors thereof: a sheriff, a county attorney, a recorder, a treasurer, an assessor, a superintendent of schools and at least three supervisors...." Ariz. Const. Art. 12, § 3 (emphasis added). The relevant Arizona statute explicitly states that sheriffs are "officers of the county." Ariz. Rev. Stat. § 11-401(A)(1).

Arizona statutes also empower counties to supervise and fund their respective sheriffs. The county board of supervisors may "[s]upervise the official conduct of all county officers," including the sheriff, to ensure that "the officers faithfully perform their duties." Ariz. Rev. Stat. § 11-251(1). The board may also "require any county officer to make reports under oath on any matter connected with the duties of his office," and may remove an officer who neglects or refuses to do so. Ariz. Rev. Stat. § 11-253(A). In addition, the county must pay the sheriff's expenses. Ariz. Rev. Stat. § 11-444(A); *Braillard*, 232 P.3d at 1269 n.2. As Maricopa County conceded in *Melendres*, those expenses include the costs of complying with any injunctive relief ordered against Arpaio and MCSO. *See Melendres III*, 815 F.3d at 650. A county's financial responsibility for the sheriff's unlawful actions is strong evidence that the sheriff acts on behalf of the county rather than the State. *See McMillian*, 520 U.S. at 789, 117 S.Ct. 1734; *Goldstein v. City of Long Beach*, 715 F.3d 750, 758 (9th Cir. 2013).

The limited guidance Arizona courts have provided on this topic further confirms that sheriffs act as policymakers for their respective counties. Most on point is *Flanders v. Maricopa County*, 203 Ariz. 368, 54 P.3d 837 (Ct. App. 2002), which held that then-Sheriff Arpaio acted as a final policymaker for Maricopa County with respect to jail administration. *Id.* at 847. *Flanders* relied in part on the fact that the statutory provision that specifies a sheriff's powers and duties lists "tak[ing] charge of and keep[ing] the county jail" as one of them. *Id.* (citing Ariz. Rev. Stat. § 11-441(A)(5)). That same provision also lists a wide array of law-enforcement functions that fall within the sheriff's powers and duties. Ariz. Rev. Stat. § 11-441(A)(1)-(3). Maricopa County does not explain why the Sheriff would be a final policymaker for the County with respect to jail administration but not with respect to the law-enforcement functions assigned to him in the same provision.

It is true that sheriffs in Arizona are independently elected and that a county board of supervisors does not exercise complete control over a sheriff's actions. Nonetheless, "the weight of the evidence" strongly supports the conclusion that sheriffs in Arizona act as final policymakers for their respective counties on law-enforcement matters. *See McMillian*, 520 U.S. at 793, 117 S.Ct. 1734. Because the traffic-stop policies at issue fall within the scope of a sheriff's law-enforcement duties, we conclude that Arpaio acted as a final policymaker for Maricopa County when he instituted those policies.

II

Maricopa County next argues that, even if Arpaio acted as the County's final policymaker, neither Title VI nor 34 U.S.C. § 12601 permits the County to be held liable for his acts. Whether either p.652 statute authorizes policymaker liability is an issue of first impression. We conclude, informed by precedent governing the liability of local governments under 42 U.S.C. § 1983, that both statutes authorize policymaker liability.

The concept of policymaker liability under § 1983 is well developed. Section 1983 imposes liability on any "person" who, while acting under color of law, deprives someone of a right protected by the Constitution or federal law. In *Monell v. New York City Department of Social Services,* 436 U.S. 658, 98 S.Ct. 2018, 56 L.Ed.2d 611 (1978), the Supreme Court held that the term "person" includes municipalities, which had the effect of creating liability for local governments under § 1983. *See id.* at 690, 98 S.Ct. 2018. But the Court also limited the scope of that liability. It concluded that a local government may not be held vicariously liable for the acts of its employees under the doctrine of *respondeat superior. Id.* at 691, 98 S.Ct. 2018. Instead, liability arises only if a local government's own official policy or custom caused the deprivation of federal rights. *Id.* at 694, 98 S.Ct. 2018. As the Court later explained, this "official policy" requirement is intended to ensure that a municipality's liability "is limited to acts that are, properly speaking, acts 'of the municipality' — that is, acts which the municipality has officially sanctioned or ordered." *Pembaur v. City of Cincinnati,* 475 U.S. 469, 480, 106 S.Ct. 1292, 89 L.Ed.2d 452 (1986).

Under policymaker liability, only certain employees of a local government have the power to establish official policy on the government's behalf. The government's legislative body has such power, of course, but so do officials "whose edicts or acts may fairly be said to represent official policy." *Monell,* 436 U.S. at 694, 98 S.Ct. 2018. Such officials are those who exercise "final policymaking authority for the local governmental actor concerning the action alleged to have caused the particular constitutional or statutory violation at issue." *McMillian,* 520 U.S. at 784-85, 117 S.Ct. 1734 (internal quotation marks omitted). In essence, policymaker liability helps determine when an act can properly be deemed a government's own act, such that the government may be held liable for deprivations of federal rights stemming from it.

We think this same concept of policymaker liability applies under both Title VI and § 12601. As to Title VI, the Supreme Court has held that an entity's liability is limited to the entity's own misconduct, as it is under § 1983. *See Davis ex rel. LaShonda D. v. Monroe County Board of Education,* 526 U.S. 629, 640, 119 S.Ct. 1661, 143 L.Ed.2d 839 (1999); *Gebser v. Lago Vista Independent School District,* 524 U.S. 274, 285, 118 S.Ct. 1989, 141 L.Ed.2d 277 (1998).[2] Thus, while an entity cannot be held vicariously liable on a *respondeat superior* theory, it can be held liable under Title VI if an official with power to take corrective measures is "deliberately indifferent to known acts" of discrimination. *Davis,* 526 U.S. at 641, 119 S.Ct. 1661. An entity can also be held liable for acts of discrimination that result from its own "official policy." *Gebser,* 524 U.S. at 290, 118 S.Ct. 1989; *see Mansourian v. Regents of the University of California,* 602 F.3d 957, 967 (9th Cir. 2010); *Simpson v. University of Colorado Boulder,* 500 F.3d 1170, 1177-78 (10th Cir. 2007). Because this form of "official policy" liability resembles §

1983 policymaker liability, we think the proper standard for determining which employees have the power to establish an entity's "official policy" p.653 under Title VI is the standard that governs under § 1983.

We reach the same conclusion with respect to § 12601. As relevant here, the statute provides: "It shall be unlawful for any governmental authority, or any agent thereof, or any person acting on behalf of a governmental authority, to engage in a pattern or practice of conduct by law enforcement officers ... that deprives persons of rights, privileges, or immunities secured or protected by the Constitution or laws of the United States." 34 U.S.C. § 12601(a).

Section 12601 shares important similarities with § 1983. Section 1983 was enacted to create "a broad remedy for violations of federally protected civil rights." *Monell*, 436 U.S. at 685, 98 S.Ct. 2018. Section 12601 was also enacted as a remedy for violations of federal civil rights, specifically for violations that are systematically perpetrated by local police departments. *See* Barbara E. Armacost, *Organizational Culture and Police Misconduct*, 72 Geo. Wash. L. Rev. 453, 527-28 (2004). And, like § 1983, § 12601 imposes liability on local governments. Indeed, the language of § 12601 goes even further than § 1983, making it unlawful for "any governmental authority, or any agent thereof, or any person acting on behalf of a governmental authority" to engage in the prohibited conduct. 34 U.S.C. § 12601(a).

We need not decide whether the language of § 12601 imposes liability on the basis of general agency principles, as the United States urges here. It is enough for us to conclude, as we do, that § 12601 at least imposes liability on a governmental authority whose own official policy causes it to engage in "a pattern or practice of conduct by law enforcement officers" that deprives persons of federally protected rights. *Id.* Because of the similarity between § 12601 and § 1983, we again see no reason to create a new standard for determining which officials have the power to establish a governmental authority's official policy. The same standard that governs under § 1983 applies here as well.

In short, Maricopa County is liable for violations of Title VI and § 12601 stemming from its own official policies. As discussed above, when Arpaio adopted the racially discriminatory traffic-stop policies at issue, he acted as a final policymaker for the County. Those policies were therefore the County's own, and the district court correctly held the County liable for the violations of Title VI and § 12601 caused by those policies.

III

Lastly, Maricopa County challenges the district court's application of issue preclusion, which precluded the County from relitigating the lawfulness of Arpaio's traffic-stop policies. Given the nature of the County's involvement in the *Melendres* action, we conclude that the County is bound by the adverse findings rendered in that action.

The County was originally named as a defendant in the *Melendres* action, along with then-Sheriff Arpaio and MCSO. Early in the litigation, the parties stipulated to dismissal of the County as a named defendant, without prejudice to the County's being rejoined as a defendant later in the litigation if that became necessary to afford the plaintiffs full relief. *Melendres III*, 815 F.3d at 648. In effect, the County agreed to delegate responsibility for defense of the action to Arpaio and MCSO, knowing that it could be bound by the judgment later despite its formal absence as a party.

The case proceeded to trial against Arpaio and MCSO and resulted in judgment against them. On appeal, we concluded that MCSO had been improperly named as a defendant because it could not be sued in its own name following the Arizona Court p.654 of Appeals' intervening decision in *Braillard. Melendres II*, 784 F.3d at 1260 (citing *Braillard*, 232 P.3d at 1269). Pursuant to the parties' stipulation, we ordered that the County be rejoined as a defendant in lieu of MCSO. *Id.* We later explained that we did so "[t]o assure a meaningful remedy for the plaintiffs despite MCSO's dismissal." *Melendres III*, 815 F.3d at 648. The County challenged this ruling in a petition for rehearing en banc and a petition for writ of certiorari, both of which were denied. *See id.*

Given this history, the district court properly applied issue preclusion to bar the County from relitigating the *Melendres* findings. Each of the elements of offensive non-mutual issue preclusion is satisfied: There was a full and fair opportunity to litigate the identical issues in the prior action; the issues were actually litigated in the prior action; the issues were decided in a final judgment; and the County was a party to the prior action. *See Syverson v. International Business Machines Corp.*, 472 F.3d 1072, 1078 (9th Cir. 2007). Indeed, the County contests only the last element, arguing that it was not in fact a party to *Melendres*. That is not accurate as a factual matter, because the County was originally named as a defendant in *Melendres* and is now one of the parties bound by the judgment in that action. Moreover, even though the County did not remain a party to *Melendres* throughout the litigation, it effectively agreed to be bound by the judgment in that action. Such an agreement is one of the recognized exceptions to non-party preclusion. *See Taylor v. Sturgell*, 553 U.S. 880, 893, 128 S.Ct. 2161, 171 L.Ed.2d 155 (2008).

AFFIRMED.

---

[*] Paul Penzone is the current Sheriff of Maricopa County and has, therefore, been automatically substituted for his predecessor, Joseph M. Arpaio. *See* Fed. R. Civ. P. 25(d).

[1] Title VI prohibits discrimination on the basis of "race, color, or national origin" in programs or activities that receive federal funding; § 12601 authorizes the United States to obtain declaratory and injunctive relief against any governmental authority that engages in a "pattern or practice of conduct by law enforcement officers" that deprives persons of rights protected by federal law.

[2] *Davis* and *Gebser* involved Title IX of the Education Amendments of 1972, but "the Court has interpreted Title IX consistently with Title VI." *Barnes v. Gorman*, 536 U.S. 181, 185, 122 S.Ct. 2097, 153 L.Ed.2d 230 (2002).

892 F.3d 1005 (2018)

Patricia P. CAMPBELL, Plaintiff-Appellant,

v.

State of HAWAII DEPARTMENT OF EDUCATION; Patricia Hamamoto, Superintendent of Public Schools, sued in her official capacity; Bruce Anderson, Maui Complex Area Superintendent, sued in his individual and official capacities; Susan Scofield, Principal of King Kekaulike High School, sued in her individual and official capacities; Anthony Jones, Vice Principal of King Kekaulike High School, sued in his individual and official capacities; Robyn Honda, Personnel Regional Officer, sued in her individual and official capacities; Barbara Oura, Vice Principal of King Kekaulike High School, sued in her individual and official capacities; Kurtis Saiki, Athletic Director of King Kekaulike High School, sued in his individual and official capacities, Defendants-Appellees.

No. 15-15939.

United States Court of Appeals, Ninth Circuit.

Argued and Submitted February 12, 2018, Honolulu, Hawaii.

Filed June 11, 2018.

Campbell v. Hawaii Dept. of Educ., 892 F. 3d 1005 (9th Cir. 2018)

Appeal from the United States District Court for the District of Hawaii; Derrick Kahala Watson, District Judge, Presiding, D.C. No. 1:13-cv-00083-DKW-RLP.

Daphne E. Barbree (argued), Law Office of Daphne Barbee, Honolulu, Hawaii, for Plaintiff-Appellant.

Miriam P. Loui (argued) and James E. Halvorson, Deputy Attorneys General; Douglas S. Chin, Attorney General; Department of the Attorney General, Honolulu, Hawaii; for Defendants-Appellees.

Before: Diarmuid F. O'Scannlain, Richard R. Clifton, and Sandra S. Ikuta, Circuit Judges.

OPINION

O'SCANNLAIN, Circuit Judge:

We must decide whether a high school teacher who was verbally harassed by her students has identified sufficient evidence to support claims for violations of her federal civil rights against the public school system that employed her.

I

Patricia Campbell was employed by the Hawaii Department of Education (DOE) from 2000 until she resigned in July 2009. From 2004 through 2007, Campbell taught music and band at King Kekaulike High School (KKHS) on the island of Maui. Unfortunately, Campbell's experience at KKHS was hardly pleasant. Instead, her tenure at the school was marred by numerous accusations of misconduct perpetrated against, and by, Campbell.

A

Campbell alleges that, throughout her time at KKHS, she was frequently harassed and degraded by students on the basis of her race (white) and her sex (female). She alleges that students called her a slew of offensive names, including "fucking weirdo," "cunt," "bitch," and "fucking haole."[1] According to Campbell, she was even physically threatened by one student who claimed to have a gun.

Campbell routinely reported the students' misconduct to DOE administration during the 2006-2007 school year. In response, Vice Principals Barbara Oura and Anthony Jones investigated Campbell's many complaints and imposed a variety of disciplinary measures against those students who were found to have misbehaved. The punishments ranged in severity based on both the nature of the misconduct and the student's past disciplinary history. Some students were given formal warnings or disciplinary counseling, others were placed in detention, and some were suspended from school for up to three days. Four students were even transferred out of Campbell's classes at her request. Although Campbell has no reason to doubt that these disciplinary measures took place, she claims that the school never informed her of them at the time.

B

Contemporaneously, Campbell herself was the subject of numerous complaints. During the 2006-2007 school year, Vice Principal Oura investigated complaints which the DOE had received from students, parents, and at least one other teacher, accusing Campbell of a variety of misconduct, including physical and verbal abuse of students, discrimination against students, and failure to maintain a safe classroom environment. Because the DOE determined that Campbell's presence on campus would not interfere with the investigation or present a threat to students, she was allowed to continue working during the investigation. On March 22, 2007, Oura concluded her investigation and found that Campbell had intimidated and discriminated against students, physically grabbed and verbally abused students, failed adequately to supervise students at school-sanctioned activities, and harassed a colleague. Despite Oura's findings, the DOE took no action against Campbell, who was allowed to keep her position at the school.

On May 7, 2007, Campbell reportedly stormed into the office of Vice Principal Jones as he was meeting with a student. It is not entirely clear why Campbell confronted Jones, but she allegedly yelled at Jones and others in the office and refused to leave when asked. Two days later, Jones held a counseling meeting with Campbell to discuss the incident, and he later gave Campbell a memorandum documenting that meeting. Among other things, Jones's memorandum stated that Campbell had "verbally ragged at" a security officer, and it directed Campbell not to "address adults or students on campus in a yelling or ragging manner."

Campbell took offense to the memo and in particular to Jones's use of the words "ragged" and "ragging," which she believed to be a reference to her menstrual cycle. The same day she received the memo, Campbell complained to the DOE Superintendent's office about the incident and claimed that Jones had stalked and sexually harassed her. Within a week, the DOE initiated an investigation into Campbell's allegations, which concluded roughly two months later. The investigator ultimately found that there was not enough evidence to sustain Campbell's allegations. In particular, the investigator found that Jones's use of the words "ragged" and "ragging" was not derogatory, but rather was used to mean that Campbell "railed at" or "scolded" others. No further action was taken against Jones as a result of the investigation.

C

At some point before the 2007-2008 school year, Campbell requested a transfer to teach elsewhere on Maui—specifically, to serve as the band director at Iao or Kalama Intermediate Schools or to teach kindergarten at Haiku School. Campbell alleges that she personally knew that the band teacher at Iao retired in June 2007 and that the band director at Kalama also "retired in 2007," though she does not specify when. She further alleges that she "was aware there was a kindergarten teaching position open at Haiku," but she again does not provide any further detail about when that position became open.

None of Campbell's transfer requests was granted. With respect to the band teaching position at Iao, the DOE submitted evidence indicating that Campbell's request was denied because such position was not open during the school's annual transfer period in the Spring of 2007[2] and Campbell failed to provide any information that would qualify for an emergency transfer outside the normal transfer window. Evidence in the record suggests that Campbell's requests to transfer to the other schools were also untimely, and she has not argued otherwise.

Unable to transfer, in August 2007 Campbell requested and was granted a 12-month leave of absence without pay due to work-related stress. Before the next school year, Campbell requested and was granted a second year of unpaid leave. In July 2009, as her second period of leave was coming to an end, Campbell learned that, because there were not enough students to support a full slate of music classes, she had been assigned to teach three remedial math classes and one or two music classes for the upcoming year. Campbell told Principal Susan Scofield that she wouldn't teach remedial math (a subject for which she was not certified), but Scofield insisted that Campbell would need to teach such classes in order to complete her schedule. Campbell never reported back to work after her leave expired. After being told that she would be fired if she did not p.1012 return to work, Campbell resigned. Her resignation indicated that she had left the school because of a hostile work environment, fear for her safety, and her desire not to teach remedial math.

D

On February 19, 2013, Campbell filed this suit against the DOE and various administrators (defendants collectively referred to as "the DOE"), alleging violations of her federal and state civil rights. In particular, Campbell alleged that she had been subjected to several acts of discriminatory treatment and a hostile work environment because of her race and her sex and that she had been retaliated against for complaining of harassment at the school.

The district court granted partial judgment on the pleadings to the DOE and dismissed several of Campbell's claims. The court later granted summary judgment for the DOE on Campbell's remaining claims of disparate treatment, hostile work environment, and retaliation under Title VII of the Civil Rights Act of 1964 and sex discrimination under Title IX of the Education Amendments of 1972. Campbell timely appealed but she challenges only the district court's order granting summary judgment on these four categories of claims. She does not challenge the court's earlier dismissal of her other claims.

II

We first consider Campbell's argument that the district court erred in granting summary judgment to the DOE on her Title VII disparate treatment claims.

Title VII forbids certain employers from "discriminat[ing] against any individual with respect to his compensation, terms, conditions, or privileges of employment, because of such individual's race, color, religion, sex, or national origin." 42 U.S.C. § 2000e-2(a)(1). Campbell argues that the DOE violated this provision by subjecting her to disparate treatment because of her sex and race. To prevail, Campbell must first establish a prima facie case by showing that: (1) she belongs to a protected class, (2) she was qualified for the position in question, (3) she was subject to an adverse employment action, and (4) similarly situated individuals outside her protected class were treated more favorably. *Chuang v. Univ. of Cal. Davis,* 225 F.3d 1115, 1123 (9th Cir. 2000).

If she does, the familiar *McDonnell Douglas* burden-shifting framework applies. *See id.* at 1123-24. Under such framework, if Campbell establishes a prima facie case, the burden of production shifts to the DOE to articulate a legitimate, nondiscriminatory reason for the challenged conduct. *Id.* If the DOE does so, the burden then shifts back to Campbell to show that the reason offered is pretextual. *Id.* at 1124.

The DOE concedes that Campbell can establish the first two elements of her prima facie case. The DOE argues, however, that the record does not contain sufficient evidence to establish the remaining elements of her claim. We agree.

A

For claims of disparate treatment under Title VII, an adverse employment action is one that "materially affects the compensation, terms, conditions, or privileges of employment." *Davis v. Team Elec. Co.,* 520 F.3d 1080, 1089 (9th Cir. 2008) (internal quotation marks and alterations omitted). Although Campbell argues that she suffered a number of such actions, none are availing.

p.1013 1

First, Campbell argues that the DOE committed an adverse employment action by losing her 2006 performance evaluation (in which she had been rated satisfactory in all categories). But Campbell has not identified any evidence that would show how the loss of such evaluation could have materially affected the terms or conditions of her employment. For example, there is nothing in the record to suggest that the DOE's inability to locate Campbell's performance evaluation had any bearing on the school's decision to take other actions regarding her employment. *Cf. Kortan v. Cal. Youth Auth.*, 217 F.3d 1104, 1113 (9th Cir. 2000) (employment evaluation that was not disseminated and did not lead to any changes in the employee's job responsibilities or benefits was not adverse employment action). Further, the DOE does not deny that Campbell's performance in 2006 was indeed satisfactory, and there is nothing to indicate that anyone at the DOE has attempted to portray Campbell's performance more negatively than was reflected on the evaluation.

The district court did not err in concluding that the loss of Campbell's performance evaluation was not an adverse employment action.

2

Next, and without elaboration, Campbell argues that the school's decision to "instigat[e] an investigation against" her was an adverse employment action. But, as noted above, Campbell was allowed to continue to work as normal throughout this investigation, and even though the investigator found that Campbell had committed misconduct, the DOE nonetheless took no action against her as a result. Indeed, Campbell does not identify a single aspect of her work that changed as a result of the investigation. The mere fact that the school received and investigated allegations of misconduct against Campbell—with no resulting change to the conditions of her employment—is not an adverse employment action for purposes of her disparate treatment claim.[3]

3

Campbell next argues that the DOE's denial of her request to transfer to another school was an adverse employment action. Adverse employment actions may include not only actions an employer affirmatively takes against an employee (e.g., firing or demoting the employee) but also situations in which the employer denies an employee a material employment benefit or opportunity that was otherwise available to her. *See, e.g., Breiner v. Nev. Dep't of Corr.*, 610 F.3d 1202, 1208 (9th Cir. 2010) ("[T]he denial of a single promotion opportunity ... is actionable under Title VII."); *Chuang*, 225 F.3d at 1124-25 (denial of promotion to tenured position that had been promised to a professor was adverse employment action). The record, however, does not support the conclusion that Campbell was ever denied a transfer opportunity that her job actually promised.

Campbell concedes that the DOE provided formal rules for how tenured teachers like she could request a transfer to a different school. Yet the record contains no evidence that Campbell ever requested a transfer through such procedures. Indeed, as outlined above, the record contains unrebutted p.1014 evidence that Campbell had *not* gone through the proper transfer procedures and had failed to request any transfer during the applicable transfer window from February 28, 2007, through May 8, 2007. Campbell herself stated that she did not request a transfer until July 2007, well past the deadline. Moreover, Campbell has not identified evidence that would contradict the testimony of the DOE's personnel officer that Campbell failed to support a case for an emergency transfer that could be granted outside the normal procedures. There is no indication that the DOE had any other policy or practice that would have allowed for consideration of untimely and non-emergency transfer requests like hers. *Cf. Chuang,* 225 F.3d at 1124-25 (denial of tenure to professor who failed to submit formal application was adverse action because school had granted tenure in similar circumstances to other professors).

In short, the record cannot support the conclusion that Campbell ever availed herself of the established channels through which she might have been able to receive a transfer. The failure to give Campbell what would essentially have been a gratuitous accommodation was not an adverse employment action.

4

Campbell also complains that, unlike some male teachers who were put on paid administrative leave while the school investigated complaints against them, she was never given leave with pay. It is not clear whether Campbell means to argue that the DOE committed an adverse employment action by failing to place her on paid leave during its investigation into the complaints against her, or that the DOE committed such an action by failing to pay her during her two years of voluntary leave. Regardless, both arguments are meritless.

To the extent that Campbell complains that she was not involuntarily placed on paid administrative leave during the school's investigation of her, she is essentially complaining that the DOE chose *not* to alter the terms and conditions of her employment. By not placing Campbell on leave, the DOE instead allowed her to continue working just as she had before, with no changes in her duties or the conditions of her work. This decision to retain the status quo is quite obviously not an adverse employment action.

If Campbell means to argue that she should have been paid during her two years of voluntary leave, she has completely failed to support the notion that the DOE had any policy or practice that would allow teachers to volunteer for extended periods of paid leave. The fact that other teachers might have been paid when they were *forced* by the DOE to take administrative leave is beside the point. The DOE never placed Campbell on leave, nor did it do anything to prevent her from continuing to work in her job if she so chose. Campbell voluntarily applied for two consecutive years of unpaid leave, and the school simply granted her requests. Granting a teacher's own request to take two years off of work can hardly be said to be an adverse employment action.

5

Campbell next argues that the DOE committed an adverse employment action when it assigned her to teach remedial math classes (in addition to some music classes) upon her anticipated return to teaching in 2009. Campbell argues that because she was not certified to teach math, she should have been given either additional music classes or French classes, for which she is actually certified.

First, the record contains no evidence that the classes Campbell preferred to teach were even available during the 2009-2010 p.1015 school year. Indeed, Principal Scofield testified that there were *not* enough music classes to fill Campbell's schedule. Second, Campbell has not identified any evidence that would suggest the school had a policy or practice that promised teachers they would only be assigned to classes within certification areas. Again, Principal Scofield provided unrebutted testimony to the contrary, stating that "[a]ny other full time teacher without a complete complement of classes ... for the 2009-2010 school year also would have been assigned to teach classes outside of his/her certification area(s)." Indeed, Campbell herself admitted that another band teacher at the school—Mr. Ota, who had replaced her during her leave of absence—had also been assigned to teach a subject for which he was not certified (Japanese).

Because there were not enough music classes, and because Campbell had specifically requested not to teach dance anymore, Campbell needed additional classes to fill her schedule. It so happens that the classes the school found available for her were in remedial math. There is nothing in the record to suggest that such assignment was unusual or, more to the point, that it materially altered any term or condition of Campbell's employment at the school. Such assignment was not an adverse employment action.

6

Finally, Campbell argues that the DOE's failure to respond adequately to her complaints of offensive student conduct was also an adverse employment action. The record simply does not support such assertion. As explained below, there is no genuine dispute that the DOE *did* respond adequately to Campbell's complaints by taking prompt action that was reasonably calculated to end the harassment she alleged. *See infra* Part III.A. The DOE's thorough action in response to Campbell's complaints did not adversely affect the terms or conditions of her employment.[4]

B

Moreover, even if the various alleged actions *could* be adverse employment actions, the record is devoid of evidence that any similarly situated employees of a different race or sex were treated more favorably than Campbell was. To satisfy such element, Campbell must identify employees outside her race and sex who were similarly situated to her "in all material respects" but who were given preferential treatment; they must "have similar jobs and display similar conduct." *Nicholson v. Hyannis Air*

Serv., Inc., 580 F.3d 1116, 1125 (9th Cir. 2009) (internal quotation marks and emphasis omitted).

For many of Campbell's claims, she has not identified even a single employee for comparison. For example, Campbell has not identified any other employees whose untimely transfer requests were granted, who were accused of misconduct but were not investigated by the DOE, or whose complaints of student harassment were handled any differently than her own. Indeed, Campbell has identified only a handful of individuals who seem to have any relevance to her case at all.

First, she claims that some male teachers were placed on paid administrative leave as the DOE investigated allegations of misconduct against them. But, even assuming that these men were similarly situated to Campbell in all material respects (which she has hardly attempted to show), we have no reason to conclude that they were treated any more favorably than she was. As mentioned, during Campbell's investigation, she was allowed to *continue working* without restriction; it cannot be said that being forced to take involuntary (even paid) leave is somehow preferable to that. Indeed, we have held that, at least for purposes of a First-Amendment retaliation claim, being placed on involuntary paid leave can *itself* be an adverse employment action. *See Dahlia v. Rodriguez,* 735 F.3d 1060, 1078 (9th Cir. 2013) (en banc). Even if Campbell is right that she was treated differently than these men solely because of her sex or her race, she has shown only that she was treated *better* on that account.

Second, Campbell has argued that her replacement, Mr. Ota, was not required to teach remedial math but instead taught Japanese, a course for which he was not certified. But Campbell has failed to show that she and Mr. Ota were similar in all material respects. There is no indication, for example, what other classes he taught, how full his schedule was, the relative availability of other teachers to fill in for the various classes at issue, or indeed whether he even wanted to teach Japanese or was simply assigned it out of necessity. Moreover, her comparison actually undercuts her claim of disparate treatment, as it shows that other teachers were also assigned to teach classes for which they were not certified.

Campbell has also argued that Mr. Ota was generally treated more favorably than she was and was allowed certain liberties she was not. But even if that is true, Campbell has not identified evidence that would show he was treated more favorably in the specific situations relevant to her claims. The record is completely devoid of any indication, for example, that Mr. Ota filed transfer requests that were handled differently, that the school declined to investigate allegations of misconduct against him, or that he was granted extended periods of paid leave. The general comparison, therefore, is beside the point.

C

In sum, Campbell has failed to identify any evidence showing that she suffered an adverse employment action and the record is almost completely silent as to whether the treatment Campbell experienced was shared by others in materially similar circumstances. The district court did not err in holding that, on the basis of such record, Campbell cannot establish a prima facie claim for disparate treatment.

III

Campbell also argues that the DOE violated Title VII by creating a hostile work environment that adversely affected the terms or conditions of her employment. To establish a prima facie case, Campbell must be able to show that, because of her race or sex, she was subjected to unwelcome conduct that was "sufficiently severe or pervasive to alter the conditions of [her] employment and create an abusive working environment." *Fuller v. Idaho Dep't of Corr.,* 865 F.3d 1154, 1161 p.1017 (9th Cir. 2017) (internal quotation marks omitted). The work environment must be both subjectively and objectively perceived as abusive. *Id.* We consider all circumstances, with a particular focus on issues such as the frequency and severity of the conduct, whether the conduct was physically threatening or humiliating, and the extent to which it unreasonably interfered with Campbell's work performance. *Id.* She must also be able to show that the DOE itself is "liable for the harassment that caused the hostile environment to exist." *Freitag v. Ayers,* 468 F.3d 528, 539 (9th Cir. 2006).

A

Campbell primarily argues that her work environment was made hostile by the derogatory comments she received from students. First, we observe that most of the complaints Campbell referred to the school were about issues unrelated to her harassment claims—for example, class cutting or general insubordination. Campbell did also submit several referrals for offensive comments that were, by their very terms, based on Campbell's race or sex, some of which were severe. But the students were not Campbell's employers. Thus, even if comments like the students' are sufficient to create a hostile work environment, the DOE may be held liable for the students' harassing conduct only to the extent that it failed reasonably to respond to the conduct or to the extent that it ratified or acquiesced in it. *See id.* at 538; *Folkerson v. Circus Circus Enters., Inc.,* 107 F.3d 754, 755-56 (9th Cir. 1997). That is, the DOE may be held to account for the students' actions only if, after learning of the harassment, it failed to take prompt corrective measures that were "reasonably calculated to end the harassment." *Freitag,* 468 F.3d at 539-40 (internal quotation marks omitted).

The record contains unrebutted evidence that, once it learned of the students' alleged harassment of Campbell, the DOE did quite a lot in response. Campbell does not deny that vice principals promptly investigated all incidents of student misconduct she reported or that the school took corrective action where her complaints were substantiated. As we have related, those actions varied from issuing warnings to some students, to placing others in detention, suspending them, and even transferring some out of Campbell's classes. A few of Campbell's complaints were found after investigation to be unsubstantiated and thus resulted in no discipline for the students. But Campbell has not argued (and we see no evidence that would show) that the DOE's findings on such complaints were unfounded or that the process that led to them was inadequate. *Cf. Swenson v. Potter,* 271 F.3d 1184, 1196-97 (9th Cir. 2001) (employer may reasonably decline to discipline alleged harasser if, after conducting a fair investigation, it does not "find what [the employer] consider[s] to be sufficient evidence of harassment"). In other words, there can be no dispute at this point that the DOE promptly evaluated and responded to each of Campbell's complaints.[5]

Campbell does not seriously grapple with the reasonableness of the many measures p.1018 the DOE undertook. Instead, her chief complaint seems to be that the DOE was unable to put a complete stop to the harassment immediately, and that students continued to harass her even after she complained to the school. As a factual matter, Campbell seems to overstate her case. Our record reflects very little recurrent harassment by students after they were disciplined for similar conduct. During the 2006-2007 school year, hardly any students were even referred by Campbell for harassing her more than once, let alone found to have done so. Moreover, of the many referrals filed by Campbell during the school year, only four were for harassment that occurred sometime after December 2006—three from the same date in May 2007. As conceded at oral argument, at most two of these referrals related to students who had been disciplined for similar conduct before. And the record does not reflect that any of the students later harassed Campbell again. In other words, the evidence in the record suggests that the school's disciplinary process was quite effective at stopping students from repeatedly harassing Campbell over the course of the year.

More fundamentally, our law does not require an employer to be immediately and perfectly effective in preventing all future harassment by a third party. Again, the question is one of negligence: Did the employer take steps that were *reasonably calculated* to end the harassment of which it was aware? *Freitag*, 468 F.3d at 538-40; *Swenson*, 271 F.3d at 1191-92, 1196; *see also Saxton v. Am. Tel. & Tel. Co.*, 10 F.3d 526, 536 (7th Cir. 1993) ("No doubt ... AT & T could have done more to remedy the adverse effects of Richardson's conduct. But Title VII requires only that the employer take steps reasonably likely to stop the harassment."). Although the issue of whether the employer's actions successfully ended the harassment will be relevant to the question of whether those actions were reasonable, *see Freitag*, 468 F.3d at 540, our inquiry cannot be purely retrospective. That a corrective action did not actually end the harassment does not necessarily mean that, at the time the employer chose such course of action, it was *unreasonable to expect* that it would. We can evaluate the reasonableness of an employer's corrective measures only from the perspective of what the employer knew or should have known at the time it acted.

Thus, we have recognized that an employer must be permitted to respond incrementally to allegations of harassment by a third party. As an initial matter, the employer must learn what actually happened. Indeed, "[t]he most significant immediate measure an employer can take in response to a sexual harassment complaint is to launch a prompt investigation to determine whether the complaint is justified." *Swenson*, 271 F.3d at 1193. That is exactly what the DOE did here. Such an investigation, itself, "is a warning, not by words but by action" that puts all parties "on notice that [the employer] takes such allegations seriously and will not tolerate harassment in the workplace." *Id.* Even where a complaint is found to be true, sometimes counseling or formally warning the perpetrator may be a sufficient response if the circumstances suggest that such action is reasonably expected to end the problem. *See Star v. West*, 237 F.3d 1036, 1039 (9th Cir. 2001); *Intlekofer v. Turnage*, 973 F.2d 773, 780, 783, 786 (9th Cir. 1992). Of course, if the harassment continues, then the employer may need to escalate to more aggressive disciplinary measures as less severe measures prove inadequate. *See Intlekofer,* 973 F.2d at 780, 783; *see also Baldwin v. Blue Cross/Blue Shield of Ala.,* 480 F.3d 1287, 1306 (11th Cir. 2007) ("This is not a case where the employer's first remedy proved inadequate, p.1019 and it failed to take further corrective action to correct the problem."). That is, the employer cannot unreasonably fail to follow through on its warnings or repeatedly resort to corrective measures that have proven ineffective.

The record in our case does not support a conclusion that the DOE effectively turned a blind eye to the students' misconduct or that it undertook only disciplinary measures that were unlikely to resonate with the students. The school did exactly what we have held it may do: it responded to the circumstances of student misconduct by investigating each incident and then by imposing corrective measures it deemed to be reasonably tailored to the incident at hand, including by increasing punishments as needed. This is simply not a case where the employer ignored, downplayed, or gave only superficial lip service to complaints that its employees were being harassed while on the job. *See, e.g., Freitag,* 468 F.3d at 533-35, 539-40 (prison could be held liable for repeated harassment of prison guard by inmates, where prison officials ignored and failed to act on multiple complaints of such harassment).

Finally, we must keep in mind that the DOE was dealing with the misbehavior of adolescent students. In this setting, DOE administrators imposed a variety of the quintessential disciplinary measures at their disposal, and to great effect. Campbell's suggestion that the DOE's response should have been even more severe and exacting—that it should have done everything in its means immediately and permanently to end all student harassment once it started—would be essentially impossible to satisfy, unless Campbell means to suggest that Title VII requires a school to behave in the most draconian way possible, perhaps by expelling any student who ever harasses a teacher. While such action may be appropriate in some situations, this is not what the law requires in all circumstances. *See, e.g., Lucero v. Nettle Creek Sch. Corp.,* 566 F.3d 720, 732 (7th Cir. 2009) (school acted reasonably by suspending students who harassed teacher); *Salvadori v. Franklin Sch. Dist.,* 293 F.3d 989, 997 (7th Cir. 2002) (school responded reasonably to complaints of harassment in hallways by posting hall monitors to find and discipline responsible students).

B

Aside from the student conduct that forms the core of her hostile work environment claim, Campbell alleges only two isolated incidents of harassment committed by school officials themselves, both relating to Vice Principal Jones.

1

First, Campbell argues that Jones created a hostile work environment when he chided Campbell for "ragging" at students and staff. A memorandum formally reprimanding Campbell for these actions stated that she "verbally ragged" a security officer and students, and it instructed her not to address people on campus "in a yelling or ragging manner."

Campbell argues that Jones's use of the phrase "ragging" or to "rag" on or at someone was sexually motivated and offensive. Namely, she contends that these comments are tantamount to the phrase "on the rag"—a phrase both sides concede can be a crass and insulting way to refer to a woman's menstrual cycle. She argues that a reasonable jury could therefore conclude that Jones's use of such language created a sexually hostile work environment. We disagree.

First, Campbell's argument entirely disregards the difference between the well-known phrase to "rag" or "rag on" something and the potentially offensive phrase "on the rag." As both the DOE's investigator and the district court found, the distinction is critical. The phrase to "rag" something is not at all offensive; it simply means "rail at" and "scold" or "torment" and "tease." Rag, *Merriam-Webster Dictionary*, https://www.merriam-webster.com/dictionary/rag (last visited May 29, 2018); *accord* Rag, *Oxford English Dictionary*, http://www.oed.com/view/Entry/157425 (last visited May 29, 2018). *Webster's* gives a perfectly benign example: "[S]everal readers called in to *rag* the editor for his paper's repeated grammatical lapses." Rag, *Merriam-Webster Dictionary*, https://www.merriam-webster.com/dictionary/rag (last visited May 29, 2018). Campbell points to nothing that would contradict this well understood meaning of to "rag" or "rag on" something. Instead, she conflates the phrases, repeatedly citing sources that recognize the offensive nature of specifically saying that a woman is "on the rag," but which say nothing of the phrases Jones actually used.

Second, even if Jones's one-time comments could somehow be construed as a veiled reference to Campbell's menstrual cycle, those isolated comments would not alone support a claim for a hostile work environment. *See, e.g., EEOC v. Prospect Airport Servs., Inc.*, 621 F.3d 991, 998 (9th Cir. 2010) ("A violation is not established merely by evidence showing sporadic use of abusive language, gender-related jokes, and occasional teasing." (internal quotation marks omitted)); *Dominguez-Curry v. Nev. Transp. Dep't*, 424 F.3d 1027, 1034 (9th Cir. 2005) ("Simple teasing, offhand comments, and isolated incidents (unless extremely serious) will not amount to discriminatory changes in the terms and conditions of employment." (internal quotation marks omitted)); *Kortan*, 217 F.3d at 1110 (rejecting hostile work environment claim where offensive comments were "mainly made in a flurry" on one day). As soon as Campbell complained about Jones's comments, the school investigated and found the incident to warrant no further punishment. Such isolated comments were not part of a larger series of ongoing harassment that Campbell suffered; there is no suggestion that Jones had ever made such comments to her before or that he ever did again.

2

Second—and largely in passing—Campbell argues that Jones contributed to a hostile working environment by allegedly referring over the school's loudspeaker to female students who dressed as "hoochi mammas" and commenting at a faculty meeting that the students needed to "cover up their business." Certainly, these alleged remarks are gender-specific and potentially offensive. But, once again, such passing comments cannot support Campbell's claim for a hostile work environment, especially as they were not directed at Campbell or even at female employees in general. *Cf. Kortan,* 217 F.3d at 1110 (suggesting that comments directed at people other than the plaintiff are less severe). Indeed, it is not clear whether Campbell even heard Jones make such remarks herself; the only reference to them in our record is from the testimony of another school employee. And Campbell certainly has not found evidence to show that these alleged remarks about student attire were anything more than isolated incidents.

In sum, alone or in combination, the few isolated and relatively mild comments that Campbell alleges Jones made in reference to her or to female students are not sufficient to show a severe and pervasive environment that altered the terms or conditions of Campbell's employment. *See Prospect Airport Servs.,* 621 F.3d at 998-99; *Dominguez-Curry,* 424 F.3d at p.1021 1034. Because Campbell has not identified any other allegedly harassing conduct that can be attributed to the DOE, the district court did not err in granting summary judgment to the DOE on Campbell's hostile work environment claims.[6]

IV

Next, Campbell argues that the DOE violated Title VII's anti-retaliation provisions by taking action against her because she voiced complaints of harassment at the school. Title VII prohibits employers from "discriminat[ing] against" an employee "because he has opposed any practice" prohibited under Title VII. 42 U.S.C. § 2000e-3(a). To establish a prima face claim of retaliation, Campbell must be able to show that she suffered an adverse employment action because she engaged in activity protected by the statute. *See Davis,* 520 F.3d at 1093-94. Once again, if she can establish a prima facie case, then the *McDonnell Douglas* framework applies, shifting the burden to the DOE to show a non-retaliatory justification for the challenged action, and then back to Campbell to show that the proffered justification is pretextual. *Id.* at 1088-89, 1094-95.

A

The DOE argues that, once again, Campbell cannot establish even a prima facie case because the record does not support a finding that she suffered any adverse employment action.[7] And Campbell indeed relies on the same alleged adverse actions discussed above to support her retaliation claims. But, even though such actions are insufficient to sustain a prima facie case of disparate treatment, Title VII retaliation claims may be brought against a much broader range of employer conduct than substantive claims of discrimination. *See Burlington N. & Santa Fe Ry. Co. v. White,* 548 U.S. 53, 67-68, 126 S.Ct. 2405, 165 L.Ed.2d 345 (2006). Namely, a Title VII retaliation claim need not be supported by an adverse action that materially altered the terms or conditions of the plaintiff's employment; instead an allegedly retaliatory action is subject to challenge so long as the plaintiff can show that "a reasonable employee would have found the challenged action materially adverse, which in this context means it well might have dissuaded a reasonable worker from making or supporting a charge of discrimination." *Id.* at 68, 126 S.Ct. 2405 (internal quotation marks omitted). Thus, even though the DOE's alleged actions cannot support

Campbell's claims of disparate treatment, the same is not necessarily true for her retaliation claims.

To be sure, even under this broader standard, most of the alleged adverse actions cannot support a prima facie case of retaliation. For the same reasons discussed above, Campbell has simply failed to identify any evidence in the record that would support her assertions that she was denied an appropriately submitted request to transfer to a vacant position at another school or that she was denied an opportunity to receive paid administrative leave. Likewise, even if the school did lose its copy of Campbell's satisfactory 2006 performance evaluation, Campbell has not p.1022 pointed to any evidence to support the notion that such loss, standing alone, is the type of "material adversity" that would reasonably chill a teacher from exercising her protected rights in the future. *See id.* (emphasis omitted).

But two potential adverse employment actions remain: (1) the DOE's investigation into Campbell's alleged misconduct and (2) Campbell's assignment to teach remedial math for the 2009-2010 school year. We have previously indicated that merely investigating an employee—regardless of the outcome of that investigation—likely can support a claim for Title VII retaliation. *See Lakeside-Scott,* 556 F.3d at 803 n.7; *Poland,* 494 F.3d at 1180. And a generous reading of Campbell's allegations might suggest that Principal Scofield intentionally assigned Campbell to teach a subject that she knew Campbell disliked. Even if such assignment did not alter the terms or conditions of Campbell's employment, arguably such intentionally unfavorable assignments could be expected to dissuade other teachers form voicing complaints in the future.

We assume *arguendo* that either of these two allegations could support Campbell's prima facie case for retaliation. Even if so, Campbell's claims fail at the remaining steps of our *McDonnell Douglas* inquiry.

B

Once Campbell establishes a prima facie case for retaliation, the burden shifts to the DOE to produce evidence showing that the challenged actions were done for non-retaliatory purposes. Thus, assuming that Campbell can establish a prima facie claim based on the school's decision to investigate her and her assignment to teach remedial math, the DOE must show that both actions were, in fact, supported by neutral reasons. If it does, the burden then shifts back to Campbell to point to evidence that may show the DOE's asserted rationale to be mere pretext.

1

Based on the evidence in the record, the DOE has clearly met its burden of supplying evidence of neutral, non-retaliatory reasons for its actions. First, the DOE has provided unrebutted evidence that it investigated Campbell specifically because it received multiple allegations of misconduct against her from parents, students, and staff. There is no dispute that the DOE is permitted—indeed, required—to investigate when it receives credible allegations of teacher misconduct and in particular to ensure the wellbeing of its students.

Second, Principal Scofield testified that she assigned Campbell to teach remedial math because there were not enough music classes available to fill a teaching schedule. She testified that this was in keeping with her standard practice for ensuring teachers had full-time schedules when there were not enough courses in their certified areas, and that any other teacher in Campbell's position would have received a similar assignment.

2

Campbell has not pointed to evidence that would carry her burden of showing that the school's neutral justifications for its actions were pretextual. Campbell may do so either "directly by persuading the court that a [retaliatory] reason more likely motivated the employer or indirectly by showing that the employer's proffered explanation is unworthy of credence." *Davis,* 520 F.3d at 1089 (internal quotation marks omitted). She has not identified evidence that could be sufficient to do either.

p.1023 First, Campbell has essentially not responded to the DOE's assertion that it had to investigate, and could not ignore, the credible allegations of misconduct against her. Campbell certainly does not dispute that students, parents, and coworkers had levied such accusations against her—accusations which, it turns out, were found largely to be true. And she has not pointed to evidence that would show that other DOE employees were let off the hook when similar allegations had been raised. Indeed, the record shows that at least Vice Principal Jones was similarly investigated when Campbell herself accused him of harassment. Elsewhere, Campbell refers to the DOE's investigation of other teachers who were accused of misconduct, with no suggestion that such teachers had similarly engaged in protected activity under Title VII. In short, Campbell has pointed to no evidence at all to dispute, let alone to refute, the school's neutral justification for its decision to investigate her.

Second, Campbell does not dispute that there were not enough band and music classes available to fill her schedule during the 2009-2010 school year, nor that she was required to teach six classes as a full-time teacher, nor that it was common for the school to assign teachers to classes outside their core areas when necessary. Instead, Campbell's only argument that the DOE's justification for assigning her to teach remedial math was pretextual seems to be that Mr. Ota was allowed to teach Japanese as an additional subject, though she was not allowed to teach French. However, Campbell has identified no evidence that there were indeed French classes available to be taught during the 2009-2010 school year. Nor has she given any reason to believe that Mr. Ota preferred to teach Japanese over other subjects that might have been available, like remedial math. And, of course, Campbell's recognition that Mr. Ota was also assigned to teach a class outside his core area seems to undermine—not support—her claim of pretext. The simple fact that Mr. Ota was not also assigned to the specific class that Campbell apparently disliked is not enough to show that the school was more likely motivated by retaliatory animus than by its stated legitimate reasons for assigning such class to Campbell.

Campbell has failed to raise a triable issue regarding her retaliation claim.

V

Finally, Campbell argues that the DOE's conduct violated Title IX's command that no person "shall, on the basis of sex, be excluded from participation in, be denied the benefits of, or be subjected to discrimination under any education program or activity receiving Federal financial assistance." 20 U.S.C. § 1681(a). Campbell claims that the DOE violated this provision both by directly and intentionally discriminating against her in the ways described above, and by acting with deliberate indifference to the sexual harassment she endured from students and from Vice Principal Jones.

A

Campbell's Title IX claims for intentional sex discrimination mirror those she raised under Title VII. Indeed, federal courts generally evaluate employment discrimination claims brought under both statutes identically, and the parties concede that the same analysis should apply to both here. *See Weinstock v. Columbia Univ.,* 224 F.3d 33, 42 n.1 (2d Cir. 2000); *Johnson v. Baptist Med. Ctr.,* 97 F.3d 1070, 1072 (8th Cir. 1996); *see also Wolfe v. Fayetteville, Ark. Sch. Dist.,* 648 F.3d 860, 865 n.4 (8th Cir. 2011) (collecting Title IX cases applying guidance from Title VII standards); *Oona R.S. v. McCaffrey,* 143 p.1024 F.3d 473, 476-78 (9th Cir. 1998) (discussing applicability of Title VII standards to Title IX claims). Thus, for the same reasons expressed above, the district court did not err in granting summary judgment to the DOE on Campbell's Title IX discrimination claims.

B

Likewise, Campbell's claim that the DOE acted with deliberate indifference to the sexual harassment she endured from students and from Vice Principal Jones essentially just repeats her Title VII claim that the DOE fostered a hostile work environment by failing reasonably to respond to Campbell's complaints of harassment. Indeed, under Title IX the DOE may be held liable for its deliberate indifference to the harassment Campbell allegedly endured only if its response to such harassment was "clearly unreasonable." *Oden v. N. Marianas Coll.,* 440 F.3d 1085, 1089 (9th Cir. 2006) (internal quotation marks omitted). Because it cannot be doubted that the school's thorough response to Campbell's complaints of student harassment was reasonably calculated to end the problem, the DOE cannot be said to have been deliberately indifferent to the situation. Likewise, we see no basis in the record to support a conclusion that the DOE acted with deliberate indifference to Campbell's complaints about harassment from Vice Principal Jones. Just as was the case with Campbell's complaints of student misconduct, the DOE immediately conducted an investigation into her allegations against Jones. That investigation ultimately determined that Jones had not engaged in misconduct. Campbell does not contend that the process that led to this conclusion was somehow inadequate. And Campbell does not assert that Jones thereafter did anything else to harass her. In sum, Campbell has not pointed to anything in the record that would show the school's handling of her complaints against Jones was clearly unreasonable.

The district court did not err in concluding that Campbell's Title IX claims fail for essentially the same reasons that her Title VII claims do.

VI

The judgment of the district court is AFFIRMED.

---

[1] "Haole," as previously described by our court, is "a Hawaiian term, sometimes used derogatorily, referring to persons of the Caucasian race." *B.K.B. v. Maui Police Dep't*, 276 F.3d 1091, 1095 n.2 (9th Cir. 2002).

[2] The transfer period ran from February 28, 2007, through May 8, 2007, and the position did not become vacant until the band teacher retired on July 31, 2007.

[3] As addressed below, merely investigating an employee might be a sufficient adverse employment action for purposes of a Title VII *retaliation* claim. *See Lakeside-Scott v. Multnomah County*, 556 F.3d 797, 803 n.7 (9th Cir. 2009); *Poland v. Chertoff*, 494 F.3d 1174, 1180 (9th Cir. 2007).

[4] Campbell appears to have abandoned on appeal two additional adverse employment actions that she argued before the district court: (1) that she was assigned an "excessive" class schedule in 2006 and (2) that she was denied the opportunity to lead the band at its performance at a state championship football game. Regardless, both arguments would fail.

First, there is no actual evidence that Campbell was given an especially burdensome class schedule. In 2006, she was assigned to teach five subjects and a total of six classes; Principal Scofield provided unrebutted testimony that such a schedule constitutes a "regular teaching line of classes."

Second, even assuming Campbell was not allowed to lead the band at the championship football game, she has failed to show how her inability to work at a single extracurricular activity somehow materially altered the terms or conditions of her employment.

[5] At most, Campbell suggests that she does not know whether appropriate procedures were followed in all cases, because the school failed to notify her at the time of any disciplinary measures it took against the students. First, there is evidence in the record that such that such information *was* available to Campbell in the school's computer database or upon request. Second, at this stage, the critical point is that Campbell has failed to discover any evidence at all to contradict the DOE's testimony that the school did indeed follow such procedures in response to all of Campbell's complaints.

[6] For these same reasons, we reject Campbell's suggestion that her resignation was "not voluntary" and that in effect she was constructively discharged. Because Campbell does not raise a genuine issue of material fact regarding the hostile work environment claim, she likewise fails to raise a genuine issue of material fact on constructive discharge. *See Brooks v. City of San Mateo*, 229 F.3d 917, 930 (9th Cir. 2000).

[7] The DOE does not dispute that Campbell may be able to establish the other elements of a prima facie case.

831 F.3d 1234 (2016)

Ronnie D. STILWELL; Courtney Stilwell, husband and wife, Plaintiffs-Appellants,

v.

CITY OF WILLIAMS, an Arizona Municipal Corporation; Joseph Duffy, Interim City Manager of the City of Williams; Lyda Duffy, husband and wife; Raymond Glenn Cornwell, former Public Works Director of the City of Williams; Elsie Cornwell, husband and wife; Billy Pruitt; Bessie Pruitt, husband and wife; Tracy Fuller; Kathy Fuller, husband and wife, Defendants-Appellees.

No. 14-15540.

United States Court of Appeals, Ninth Circuit.

Argued and Submitted March 14, 2016 San Francisco, California.

Filed August 5, 2016.

Stilwell v. City of Williams, 831 F. 3d 1234 (9th Cir. 2016)

p.1237 Appeal from the United States District Court for the District of Arizona, D.C. No. 3:12-cv-08053-HRH, H. Russel Holland, District Judge, Presiding.

Charles Anthony Shaw (argued), Law Offices of Charles Anthony Shaw, PLLC, Prescott, Arizona, for Plaintiffs-Appellants.

Kenneth H. Brendel (argued), Mangum, Wall, Stoops & Warden, PLLC, Flagstaff, Arizona, for Defendants-Appellees.

Before: FERDINAND F. FERNANDEZ, RONALD M. GOULD, and MICHELLE T. FRIEDLAND, Circuit Judges.

Dissent by Judge FERNANDEZ

p.1238 OPINION

FRIEDLAND, Circuit Judge:

Plaintiff-Appellant Ronnie Stilwell sued his city employer for retaliation, alleging that he was fired for planning to testify against the City in a lawsuit relating to age discrimination. Stilwell asserted that his termination violated both the First Amendment and the retaliation provision of the Age Discrimination in Employment Act ("ADEA"), 29 U.S.C. § 623(d). The question we must answer is whether the retaliation provision of the ADEA precludes a plaintiff such as Stilwell from bringing a First Amendment retaliation claim under 42 U.S.C. § 1983. We hold that it does not.

I.

Stilwell became Superintendent of the Water Department of the City of Williams, Arizona (the "City"), in 1991, and he served in that position until his termination in

January 2011. It is the events surrounding his termination that gave rise to the instant lawsuit.[1] Those events began when Stilwell became aware of a lawsuit against the City filed by Carolyn Smith, the City's former Human Resources Director (the "*Smith* suit"). Smith alleged that the City retaliated against her in violation of the retaliation provision of the ADEA, after she complained about age discrimination against a different city employee, Glen Cornwell. In August 2009, Stilwell signed a sworn statement that supported Smith's ADEA retaliation claim, and agreed to testify in Smith's lawsuit. Later that month, a formal disclosure regarding Stilwell's involvement as a witness was served upon the City as well as on then-Assistant City Manager Joe Duffy.

Stilwell alleges that following this agreement to testify, Duffy took numerous negative actions towards him that constituted retaliation. Between August and December 2009, Duffy sent Stilwell emails with negative comments, including emails attacking his job performance. In December 2009, Duffy became Interim City Manager and met with Stilwell to discourage him from testifying in the *Smith* suit.

In June 2010, the judge in the *Smith* suit denied a motion from the City Attorney to prevent Stilwell's testimony. Duffy then had another meeting with Stilwell, in which Duffy stated that he wanted Stilwell to find a way out of testifying.

In September 2010, at a meeting with another city department head, the issue of Stilwell's anticipated testimony for the *Smith* suit arose again. Stilwell explained that he would tell the truth if he was called to the stand, including by describing how Duffy had retaliated against Smith. Duffy and Stilwell subsequently had another confrontation in which Duffy expressed displeasure about Stilwell's agreeing to testify. Following that confrontation, Duffy began to express additional concerns about Stilwell's job performance.

In October 2010, Duffy continued to find problems with Stilwell's job performance, including criticizing Stilwell's handling of a situation in which the City's water turned brown. Duffy also sent the City Council a memo accusing Stilwell of neglecting security concerns at the City's water plant. Stilwell asserted that these issues were not his fault.

In December 2010, Stilwell was placed on paid administrative leave, pending an investigation into Duffy's allegations. In January 2011, the City terminated Stilwell's employment based on the results of that investigation.

p.1239 Stilwell sued the City and Duffy, among others, in the United States District Court for the District of Arizona. The suit asserted sixteen claims, including retaliation in violation of the ADEA and the First Amendment.[2] Stilwell moved for partial summary judgment, and Defendants cross-moved for summary judgment as to all claims. The district court granted Defendants' motion, and Stilwell appealed the rulings on eight claims.[3]

II.

The district court granted summary judgment in favor of Defendants on Stilwell's § 1983 First Amendment claim on the sole ground that the retaliation provision of the ADEA, 29 U.S.C. § 623(d), precluded a § 1983 First Amendment retaliation claim such as Stilwell's. We review the district court's decision *de novo*. *In re Oracle Corp. Sec.*

Litig., 627 F.3d 376, 387 (9th Cir. 2010). Applying the framework set forth in *Fitzgerald v. Barnstable School Committee,* 555 U.S. 246, 129 S.Ct. 788, 172 L.Ed.2d 582 (2009), for determining the preclusive effect of a statute on § 1983 actions to remedy constitutional violations, we hold that Stilwell's § 1983 First Amendment lawsuit is not precluded.

A.

As a threshold matter, before turning to the preclusion question, we reject the City's argument that Stilwell's speech was not "speech as a citizen on a matter of public concern" and so fell outside the First Amendment's protections. *Lane v. Franks,* ___ U.S. ___, 134 S.Ct. 2369, 2378, 189 L.Ed.2d 312 (2014). Stilwell's sworn statement and imminent testimony were "outside the scope of his ordinary job duties," which means that he was engaged in "speech as a citizen for First Amendment purposes." *Id.* (explaining that an employee's testimony in response to a subpoena about his employer's practices was "outside the scope of his ordinary job duties" and thus "speech as a citizen"). And Stilwell's sworn statement and planned testimony about the City's retaliatory conduct were on a matter of public concern. *See Alpha Energy Savers, Inc. v. Hansen,* 381 F.3d 917, 927 (9th Cir. 2004) ("[W]e hold that a public employee's testimony addresses a matter of public concern if it contributes in some way to the resolution of a judicial or administrative proceeding in which discrimination or other significant government misconduct is at issue.").

Moreover, contrary to the City's argument, the fact that Stilwell had submitted only an affidavit and did not ultimately testify in court does not foreclose First Amendment protection. In *Alpha Energy Savers,* we held that although the plaintiff, a city contractor, never actually testified in a former associate's federal discrimination lawsuit because the suit settled, the conduct that occurred prior to the settlement was protected under the First Amendment. 381 F.3d at 922, 923-24. That conduct included "not only the affidavit that [the contractor] filed on [the associate's] behalf and his testimony at [the associate's] grievance hearing but also [the contractor's] agreement to be listed as a witness in the judicial proceedings." *Id.* at 923-24. Similarly, Stilwell's sworn statement on a matter of public concern and his express plan to testify in court along the same lines, fall within the purview of the First Amendment. *Cf. Heffernan v. City of Paterson, N.J.,* ___ U.S. ___, 136 S.Ct. p.1240 1412, 1418, 194 L.Ed.2d 508 (2016) (holding that whether the protected speech was actually engaged in by the employee is not determinative because it is the perception of the employer as to whether that protected activity occurred that matters to a First Amendment retaliation claim).

B.

Congress enacted the ADEA in order to "to promote employment of older persons based on their ability rather than age; to prohibit arbitrary age discrimination in employment; [and] to help employers and workers find ways of meeting problems arising from the impact of age on employment." 29 U.S.C. § 621(b). Although nearly all of the ADEA focuses on direct age discrimination, it contains a retaliation provision as well:

It shall be unlawful for an employer to discriminate against any of his employees or applicants for employment, for an employment agency to discriminate against any individual, or for a labor organization to discriminate against any member thereof or applicant for membership, because such individual, member or applicant for membership has opposed any practice made unlawful by this section, or because such individual, member or applicant for membership has made a charge, testified, assisted, or participated in any manner in an investigation, proceeding, or litigation under this chapter.

29 U.S.C.A. § 623(d).

Section 1983, in contrast, is not itself a source of substantive rights, but is a mechanism for vindicating federal statutory or constitutional rights. *Baker v. McCollan*, 443 U.S. 137, 144 n.3, 99 S.Ct. 2689, 61 L.Ed.2d 433 (1979). Specifically, § 1983 provides that "[e]very person who, under color of [State law] ... subjects, or causes to be subjected, any citizen of the United States or other person within the jurisdiction thereof to the deprivation of any rights, privileges, or immunities secured by the Constitution and laws, shall be liable to the party injured." 42 U.S.C. § 1983.

Despite § 1983's broad wording, that section's availability as a remedy for violations of federal statutory or constitutional rights may be foreclosed in the event that Congress enacts a statutory scheme indicating an intent to preclude § 1983 suits. In a line of cases beginning with *Middlesex County Sewerage Authority v. National Sea Clammers Association*, 453 U.S. 1, 101 S.Ct. 2615, 69 L.Ed.2d 435 (1981), the Supreme Court has set forth principles for determining when a § 1983 cause of action is precluded. Because this line of cases, and particularly *Fitzgerald*, 555 U.S. 246, 129 S.Ct. 788, the most recent of them, provides the framework for our analysis here, we describe the cases in some detail.

In *Sea Clammers,* the Court addressed whether the Federal Water Pollution Control Act and the Marine Protection, Research, and Sanctuaries Act precluded § 1983 suits to remedy violations of those Acts. To divine Congress's intent, the Court examined "the remedial devices provided in [each] particular Act," to determine if they were "sufficiently comprehensive" to indicate a "congressional intent to preclude the remedy of suits under § 1983." *Sea Clammers,* 453 U.S. at 20, 101 S.Ct. 2615. The Court observed the "unusually elaborate enforcement provisions" in each Act — which provided for civil as well as criminal penalties that could be assessed by the Environmental Protection Agency, and included citizen suit provisions that required private plaintiffs to "comply with specified procedures" before filing in court. *Id.* at 13-14, 101 S.Ct. 2615. The Court held that these comprehensive remedial provisions demonstrated that p.1241 Congress intended to preclude § 1983 lawsuits to remedy a violation of the statutory rights created in those same Acts. Thus, the Court held that a plaintiff could not bring a § 1983 suit to remedy a violation of either the Federal Water Pollution Control Act or the Marine Protection, Research, and Sanctuaries Act.

In *Smith v. Robinson,* 468 U.S. 992, 1013, 104 S.Ct. 3457, 82 L.Ed.2d 746 (1984), *superseded on other grounds by* Handicapped Children's Protection Act, Pub. L. No. 99-372, § 2, 100 Stat. 796 (1986) (codified at 20 U.S.C. § 1415(1)), the Supreme Court considered a related, but distinct question — whether a statute precluded a § 1983 suit to enforce a constitutional right. In *Smith,* the Court examined whether the Education of the Handicapped Act (the "EHA") precluded § 1983 suits alleging

Fourteenth Amendment equal protection violations based on disability discrimination in education. 468 U.S. at 1013, 104 S.Ct. 3457.[4] In holding that such suits were precluded, the Court first explained that constitutional equal protection rights and the rights protected by the EHA were essentially coextensive. *See id.* at 1009, 104 S.Ct. 3457. Such congruence was unsurprising given that the EHA was enacted as a response to a series of court cases that established the "right to an equal education opportunity for handicapped children," *id.* at 1010, 104 S.Ct. 3457, and that "Congress perceived the EHA as the most effective vehicle for protecting the constitutional right of a handicapped child to a public education" recognized in those cases. *Id.* at 1013, 104 S.Ct. 3457. Indeed, the Senate Report on the EHA described the statute as having "incorporated the major principles of th[ose] right to education cases." *Bd. of Educ. of Hendrick Hudson Cent. Sch. Dist. v. Rowley*, 458 U.S. 176, 194 n.18, 102 S.Ct. 3034, 73 L.Ed.2d 690 (1982). After concluding that the statutory and constitutional claims were "virtually identical," *Smith*, 468 U.S. at 1009, 104 S.Ct. 3457, the Supreme Court turned to the EHA's remedial scheme, explaining that "the Act establishes an elaborate procedural mechanism to protect the rights of handicapped children," that "begins on the local level and includes ongoing parental involvement, detailed procedural safeguards, and a right to judicial review." *Id.* at 1010-11, 104 S.Ct. 3457. Ultimately, the Court held that "[a]llowing a plaintiff to circumvent the EHA administrative remedies" through a § 1983 action "would be inconsistent with Congress' carefully tailored scheme," *id.* at 1012, 104 S.Ct. 3457, and that because Congress gave no indication in the EHA's legislative history that it intended to allow such § 1983 suits, the alternative § 1983 remedy was precluded.

The Supreme Court again confronted the question of preclusion of § 1983 actions in *City of Rancho Palos Verdes, California v. Abrams*, 544 U.S. 113, 127, 125 S.Ct. 1453, 161 L.Ed.2d 316 (2005). The Court there asked whether the Telecommunications Act of 1996 precluded § 1983 suits alleging violations of that Act — a question of enforcement of a statutory right akin to that in *Sea Clammers*. To answer that question, the Court contrasted *Sea Clammers* and *Smith* with other cases that had held § 1983 actions to be available to enforce federal statutes that "*did not* provide a private judicial remedy (or, in most of the cases, even a private administrative remedy) for the rights violated." 544 U.S. at 121, 125 S.Ct. 1453 (citing *Livadas v. Bradshaw*, 512 U.S. 107, 133-34, 114 S.Ct. 2068, 129 L.Ed.2d 93 (1994) and *Golden State Transit Corp. v. City of Los Angeles*, 493 U.S. 103, 108-09, 110 S.Ct. 444, 107 L.Ed.2d 420 (1989), among other cases).[5] Because the Telecommunications Act created a private right of action — and, particularly, a limited one with a 30-day statute of limitations and no provision for attorney fees or costs — the Court held that allowing § 1983 suits that would not have those limitations "would distort the scheme of expedited judicial review and limited remedies created by [the Act]." *Id.* at 127, 125 S.Ct. 1453. The Act thus "precluded resort to § 1983." *Id.*

Most recently, in *Fitzgerald v. Barnstable School Committee*, 555 U.S. 246, 129 S.Ct. 788, 172 L.Ed.2d 582 (2009), the Supreme Court considered again, as it had in *Smith*, whether a statute precluded use of § 1983 to remedy an alleged constitutional violation. Specifically, the Court evaluated whether Title IX, which prohibits gender discrimination in educational programs receiving Federal financial assistance, 20 U.S.C. § 1681(a), was "meant to be an exclusive mechanism for addressing gender discrimination in schools," or whether plaintiffs alleging gender discrimination could also bring equal protection claims under § 1983. 555 U.S. at 258, 129 S.Ct. 788. Looking to *Sea Clammers, Smith,* and *Rancho Palos Verdes* as guiding precedent, the Court emphasized that those "cases establish that 'the crucial consideration is what Congress intended.'" *Fitzgerald,* 555 U.S. at 252, 129 S.Ct. 788 (alteration omitted) (quoting *Smith,* 468 U.S. at 1012, 104 S.Ct. 3457).

The Court then summarized different approaches for determining Congress's intent with respect to preclusion of § 1983 suits, depending on whether the § 1983 suits would enforce statutory or constitutional rights. "In those cases in which the § 1983 claim is based on a *statutory right,* 'evidence of such congressional intent [to preclude the § 1983 remedy] may be found directly in the statute creating the right, or inferred from the statute's creation of a comprehensive enforcement scheme that is incompatible with individual enforcement under § 1983.'" *Id.* (quoting *Rancho Palos Verdes,* 544 U.S. at 120, 125 S.Ct. 1453 (emphasis added)). With respect to constitutional claims, however, the Court explained:

> p.1243 In cases in which the § 1983 claim alleges a *constitutional violation,* lack of congressional intent may be inferred from a comparison of the rights and protections of the statute and those existing under the Constitution. Where the contours of such rights and protections diverge in significant ways, it is not likely that Congress intended to displace § 1983 suits enforcing constitutional rights. Our conclusions regarding congressional intent can be confirmed by a statute's context.

Id. at 252-53, 129 S.Ct. 788 (emphasis added).

After setting forth these inquiries, the Court first observed that, in contrast to the statutes at issue in *Sea Clammers, Smith,* and *Rancho Palos Verdes,* "Title IX has no administrative exhaustion requirement and no notice provisions." *Id.* at 255, 129 S.Ct. 788. Rather, Title IX's implied right of action allows plaintiffs to "file directly in court," and to "obtain the full range of remedies." *Id.* The Court stated that, "[a]s a result, parallel and concurrent § 1983 claims will neither circumvent required procedures, nor allow access to new remedies." *Id.* at 255-56, 129 S.Ct. 788.

The Court then compared the "substantive rights and protections" provided by Title IX to those afforded under § 1983 suits to remedy violations of the Equal Protection Clause. The Court examined the mismatch in which entities may be sued and which entities are exempted, *id.* at 256-57, 129 S.Ct. 788, the differences in what conduct is prohibited, *id.* at 257, 129 S.Ct. 788, and the disparate standards of liability and burdens of proof required to prevail under each provision, *id.* at 257-58, 129 S.Ct. 788. With respect to which entities may be sued under Title IX and § 1983 equal protection causes of action, respectively, the Court explained that "Title IX reaches institutions and programs that receive federal funds, which may include nonpublic institutions," but does not "authoriz[e] suit against school officials, teachers, and other individuals." 555 U.S. at 257, 129 S.Ct. 788 (citations omitted). In contrast, "[t]he Equal Protection Clause reaches only state actors, [and] § 1983 equal protection claims may be brought against individuals as well as municipalities and certain other state entities." *Id.*

In its comparison of the "substantive rights and protections," the Court also underscored the differences between the types of conduct prohibited under each of the schemes. The Court explained that "Title IX exempts elementary and secondary schools from its prohibition against discrimination in admissions, § 1681(a)(1); it exempts military service schools and traditionally single-sex public colleges from all of its provisions, §§ 1681(a)(4)-(5)." *Fitzgerald,* 555 U.S. at 257, 129 S.Ct. 788. But, the Court noted, some of what is exempted under Title IX "may form the basis of equal protection claims" for gender discrimination under § 1983. *Id.*

Finally, the Court observed that "[e]ven where particular activities and particular defendants are subject to both Title IX and the Equal Protection Clause, the standards for establishing liability may not be wholly congruent." *Id.* at 257, 129 S.Ct. 788. It explained that "a Title IX plaintiff can establish school district liability by showing that a single school administrator with authority to take corrective action responded to harassment with deliberate indifference," whereas "[a] plaintiff stating a similar claim via § 1983 for violation of the Equal Protection Clause by a school district or other municipal entity must show that the harassment was the result of municipal custom, policy, or practice." *Id.* at 257-58, 129 S.Ct. 788 (citing *Monell v. N.Y. City Dept. of Soc. Servs.,* 436 U.S. p.1244 658, 694, 98 S.Ct. 2018, 56 L.Ed.2d 611 (1978)).

The Court concluded that "[i]n light of the divergent coverage of Title IX and the Equal Protection Clause, as well as the absence of a comprehensive remedial scheme comparable to those at issue in *Sea Clammers, Smith,* and *Rancho Palos Verdes,* ... Title IX was not meant to be an exclusive mechanism for addressing gender discrimination in schools." *Fitzgerald,* 555 U.S. at 258, 129 S.Ct. 788. Because Title IX was not intended as a "substitute for § 1983 suits as a means of enforcing constitutional rights," the Court held "that § 1983 suits based on the Equal Protection Clause remain available to plaintiffs alleging unconstitutional gender discrimination in schools." *Id.*

The Supreme Court then reasoned that its "conclusion [was] consistent with Title IX's context and history." *Id.* The Court explained that "Congress modeled Title IX after Title VI of the Civil Rights Act of 1964," and "[a]t the time of Title IX's enactment ... Title VI was routinely interpreted to allow for parallel and concurrent § 1983 claims." *Id.* Given "the absence of any contrary evidence, it follows that Congress intended Title IX to be interpreted similarly to allow for parallel and concurrent § 1983 claims." *Id.* at 259, 129 S.Ct. 788. The Court noted that "the relevant question is not whether Congress envisioned that the two types of claims would proceed together in addressing gender discrimination in schools; it is whether Congress affirmatively intended to preclude this result," *id.* at 259 n.2, 129 S.Ct. 788, and the Court found no such intent reflected in the legislative history, *id.* at 259, 129 S.Ct. 788.

The *Sea Clammers* line of cases teaches that when Congress creates a right by enacting a statute but at the same time limits enforcement of that right through a specific remedial scheme that is narrower than § 1983, a § 1983 remedy is precluded. This makes sense because the limits on enforcement of the right were part and parcel to its creation. When a right is created by the Constitution, however, and a statute merely recognizes it or adds enforcement options, the analysis differs. *Fitzgerald* teaches that, in that situation, if the statute's rights and protections diverge in "significant ways" from those provided by the Constitution, a § 1983 remedy is not precluded. 555 U.S. at 252-53, 129 S.Ct. 788.

C.

Following *Fitzgerald*, to determine whether the ADEA's retaliation provision precludes § 1983 First Amendment retaliation suits, we must determine whether the "contours of such rights and protections" provided by the two "diverge in significant ways." *Fitzgerald*, 555 U.S. at 252-53, 129 S.Ct. 788. The ADEA provides an express private right of action, which weighs in favor of finding preclusion under *Sea Clammers* and its progeny. But the disparities between the rights and protections of the ADEA's retaliation provision and the First Amendment as enforced through § 1983 — including differences in who may sue and be sued, the standards for liability, and the damages available — which make the ADEA's protections narrower than the First Amendment's in some important respects, cause us to conclude that Congress did not intend to preclude § 1983 First Amendment retaliation suits.

1.

The ADEA provides both an express private right of action, *see Kimel v. Fla. Bd. of Regents*, 528 U.S. 62, 67, 120 S.Ct. 631, 145 L.Ed.2d 522 (2000), and an administrative exhaustion requirement to file a p.1245 complaint with the EEOC. 29 U.S.C. § 626(c)-(d).

If we were evaluating the preclusion of § 1983 suits as a mechanism to enforce a *statutory* right created by the ADEA, the detailed nature of its remedial scheme might be dispositive. But, under *Fitzgerald*, it is not. *Fitzgerald* instructed that, "[i]n cases in which the § 1983 claim alleges a constitutional violation," the presence of significant differences in the "rights and protections" offered by the Constitution and the statute in question make it unlikely "that Congress intended to displace § 1983 suits enforcing constitutional rights" by enacting the statute. 555 U.S. at 252-53, 129 S.Ct. 788.[6] Accordingly, the Supreme Court in *Fitzgerald* looked not only to whether Title IX had an express cause of action; it also engaged in a detailed comparison of Title IX's implied right of action and § 1983 equal protection claims. Following this guidance from *Fitzgerald*, we turn to comparing the substantive rights and protections afforded by the ADEA's retaliation provision and those provided under the First Amendment, as enforced through § 1983.

2.

a.

Like the disparities identified in *Fitzgerald*, our examination of the ADEA's retaliation provision and First Amendment retaliation claims brought under § 1983 reveals differences in who may sue and be sued. First, the ADEA does not allow for suit against individuals, whereas § 1983 does. *See Miller v. Maxwell's Int'l, Inc.*, 991 F.2d 583, 587-88 (9th Cir. 1993) (holding that individual defendants cannot be held liable for damages under the ADEA); *Hafer v. Melo*, 502 U.S. 21, 31, 112 S.Ct. 358, 116 L.Ed.2d 301 (1991) ("We hold that state officials, sued in their individual capacities, are 'persons' within the meaning of § 1983."); *see also Levin v. Madigan*, 692 F.3d 607,

621 (7th Cir. 2012) ("In contrast [to an ADEA plaintiff], a § 1983 plaintiff may file suit against an individual, so long as that individual caused or participated in the alleged deprivation of the plaintiff's constitutional rights." (citation omitted)).

Second, state employees, in practice, cannot sue under the ADEA but can sue under § 1983. In *Kimel,* the Supreme Court held that "in the ADEA, Congress did not validly abrogate the States' sovereign immunity to suits by private individuals," and thus, state employers could not be sued by state employees under the ADEA. 528 U.S. at 91, 120 S.Ct. 631. This holding, combined with the fact that the ADEA does not allow suits against individuals (and thus does not allow suits against state officials or supervisors), means that state employees may not bring claims under the ADEA. *See Ahlmeyer v. Nev. Sys. of Higher Educ.,* 555 F.3d 1051, 1060 (9th Cir. 2009) (explaining that "[i]f the ADEA is the exclusive remedy for age discrimination in the workplace, then plaintiffs are left without a federal forum for age discrimination claims against state actors."). Although § 1983 likewise did not abrogate States' Eleventh Amendment immunity and therefore does not allow suits against States themselves or individuals in their official capacities, *Will v. Mich. Dep't of State Police,* 491 U.S. 58, 71, 109 S.Ct. 2304, 105 L.Ed.2d 45 (1989), § 1983 does provide a remedy to state employees by allowing suits against state officials in p.1246 their individual capacities, *see Hafer,* 502 U.S. at 31, 112 S.Ct. 358.

Third, the ADEA is generally applicable to private and public (but not state) employers with twenty or more employees. 29 U.S.C. § 630(b) (defining "employer").[7] In contrast, § 1983 is generally inapplicable to private employers.[8] *See Am. Mfrs. Mut. Ins. Co. v. Sullivan,* 526 U.S. 40, 49-50, 119 S.Ct. 977, 143 L.Ed.2d 130 (1999) ("[T]he under-color-of-state-law element of § 1983 excludes from its reach 'merely private conduct, no matter how discriminatory or wrongful.'" (quoting *Blum v. Yaretsky,* 457 U.S. 991, 1002, 102 S.Ct. 2777, 73 L.Ed.2d 534 (1982))).

Finally, the Supreme Court has held that independent contractors may sue under § 1983 for First Amendment retaliation. *Bd. of Cty. Comm'rs, Wabaunsee Cty., Kan. v. Umbehr,* 518 U.S. 668, 686, 116 S.Ct. 2342, 135 L.Ed.2d 843 (1996) ("[W]e recognize the right of independent government contractors not to be terminated for exercising their First Amendment rights."). In contrast, "[a] claimant under ... the ADEA must establish himself as an 'employee,'" thus excluding independent contractors. *Barnhart v. N.Y. Life Ins. Co.,* 141 F.3d 1310, 1312 (9th Cir. 1998).

b.

Also similar to the differences identified in *Fitzgerald,* there is a difference between ADEA retaliation suits and § 1983 First Amendment retaliation suits in how liability is established under each. *See Fitzgerald,* 555 U.S. at 257, 129 S.Ct. 788 (examining different standards of liability for Title IX and § 1983 claims).

First, an ADEA plaintiff bears a greater burden of proof as to causation than a plaintiff bringing a First Amendment retaliation claim. Once the plaintiff bringing a First Amendment retaliation claim via § 1983 has demonstrated that the protected conduct was a "motivating factor" in the retaliatory action, "the burden shifts to the government to show that it 'would have taken the same action even in the absence of the protected conduct.'" *O'Brien v. Welty,* 818 F.3d 920, 932 (9th Cir. 2016) (quoting

Pinard v. Clatskanie Sch. Dist. 6J, 467 F.3d 755, 770 (9th Cir. 2006)); *see also Thomas v. County of Riverside,* 763 F.3d 1167, 1169 (9th Cir. 2014) (per curiam) (explaining that First Amendment retaliation cases are governed by *Mt. Healthy City School District Board of Education v. Doyle,* 429 U.S. 274, 97 S.Ct. 568, 50 L.Ed.2d 471 (1977), under which, once a plaintiff makes a showing that protected speech was a substantial or motivating factor in the employer's taking a non-trivial adverse employment action, a defendant can escape liability only by meeting the burden of proving by a preponderance of the evidence that it would have reached the same decision even absent the plaintiff's protected speech).

In contrast, in *University of Texas Southwestern Medical Center v. Nassar,* ___ U.S. ___, 133 S.Ct. 2517, 186 L.Ed.2d 503 (2013), the Supreme Court outlined a different framework in the context of Title VII retaliation claims — which is relevant to ADEA retaliation claims because we have long considered the ADEA retaliation provision to be the "equivalent of the anti-retaliation provision of Title VII," *O'Day v. McDonnell Douglas Helicopter Co.,* 79 F.3d 756, 763 (9th Cir. 1996). In *Nassar,* the Court held that a plaintiff alleging retaliation under Title VII must prove "that the unlawful retaliation would not have occurred in the absence of the alleged wrongful action or actions of the employer." 133 S.Ct. at 2533. The Court explained that this burden on the plaintiff to "establish that his or her protected activity was a but-for cause of the alleged adverse action by the employer" is "more demanding than the motivating-factor standard." *Id.* at 2534.

Second, exactly as in *Fitzgerald,* 555 U.S. at 257, 129 S.Ct. 788, there is a difference in the requirements for establishing liability between the ADEA retaliation clause and § 1983 when the defendant is a municipality. Under § 1983, "municipalities [may not] be held liable unless action pursuant to official municipal policy of some nature caused a constitutional tort." *Monell v. Dep't of Soc. Servs. of City of N.Y.,* 436 U.S. 658, 691, 98 S.Ct. 2018, 56 L.Ed.2d 611 (1978). In contrast, no such requirement exists for ADEA claims brought against municipalities. *See Hill v. Borough of Kutztown,* 455 F.3d 225, 245, 247 (3d Cir. 2006) (explaining that "a municipality may be held liable for the conduct of an individual employee or officer only when that conduct implements an official policy or practice" in § 1983 actions, but that "a plaintiff may bring an ADEA claim against a political subdivision of a state based on the actions of its employee(s)" (footnotes omitted)); *see also Spengler v. Worthington Cylinders,* 615 F.3d 481, 491 (6th Cir. 2010) (explaining in the context of an ADEA retaliation claim that "[a]n employer will be strictly liable for a supervisor's proven discrimination where such discrimination results in an adverse employment action").

c.

Finally, the remedies available to those individuals bringing suit under the ADEA's retaliation provision and § 1983 are different. For example, ADEA plaintiffs may recover lost wages and liquidated damages from employers but may not recover damages for emotional pain and suffering. *See C.I.R. v. Schleier,* 515 U.S. 323, 326, 115 S.Ct. 2159, 132 L.Ed.2d 294 (1995) ("[T]he Courts of Appeals have unanimously held, and respondent does not contest, that the ADEA does not permit a separate recovery of compensatory damages for pain and suffering or emotional distress."). In contrast, the Supreme Court has explained that "compensatory damages [in § 1983 suits] may include not only out-of-pocket loss and other monetary harms, but also such injuries as 'impairment of reputation..., personal humiliation, and mental anguish and suffering.'" *Memphis Cmty. Sch. Dist. v. Stachura,* 477 U.S. 299, 307, 106 S.Ct. 2537, 91 L.Ed.2d 249 (1986) (second alteration in original) (quoting *Gertz v. Robert Welch, Inc.,* 418 U.S. 323, 350, 94 S.Ct. 2997, 41 L.Ed.2d 789 (1974)).

3.

These distinctions demonstrate that the ADEA's retaliation protections diverge significantly from those available under § 1983 First Amendment lawsuits.[9] Most significantly in our view, the ADEA's retaliation provision provides less protection to an alleged victim of retaliation than does the First Amendment in several important ways — the ADEA's protections exclude independent contractors and state employees, do not allow for suit against individuals, require plaintiffs to bear a heavier burden of proof as to causation, p.1248 and exclude certain types of remedies like damages for mental suffering. And although the ADEA affords greater protection to some individuals that would not normally be covered by § 1983 because it subjects private employers to suits and it does not require proof of a municipal policy for those suing municipalities, this does not negate the fact that the ADEA provides less protection in the important ways discussed above.

If we were evaluating a purely statutory right, as in *Sea Clammers* or *Rancho Palos Verdes,* the fact that some aspects of the ADEA's protections are narrower would suggest preclusion. That is because, if a statute creating a right also creates a mechanism for enforcement that is more limited than § 1983, we assume Congress intended those limits to apply to that right. *See Rancho Palos Verdes,* 544 U.S. at 121, 125 S.Ct. 1453 ("[T]he existence of a more restrictive private remedy for statutory violations has been the dividing line between those cases in which we have held that an action would lie under § 1983 and those in which we have held that it would not.").

When considering "substantial" constitutional rights, however, we are "[m]indful that we should 'not lightly conclude that Congress intended to preclude reliance on § 1983 as a remedy.'" *Fitzgerald,* 555 U.S. at 256, 129 S.Ct. 788 (quoting *Smith,* 468 U.S. at 1012, 104 S.Ct. 3457). Thus, if there are differences in the protections offered by the statute as compared to those provided by the Constitution, particularly if the protections granted by the statute are narrower, we will not hold § 1983 suits to be precluded unless Congress manifested an intent to preclude. *See id.* at 259 n.2, 129 S.Ct. 788 (explaining that the relevant inquiry is not whether "Congress envisioned that the two types of claims would proceed together," but whether "Congress *affirmatively intended* to preclude," § 1983 suits to vindicate constitutional rights) (emphasis added). Here, as in *Fitzgerald,* the disparities — in particular those that demonstrate the ADEA's protections are narrower than those guaranteed by the Constitution — are sufficient to cause us to conclude that, unless Congress manifested a clear intent to do so, § 1983 First Amendment retaliation suits are not precluded. And there is no express statement of preclusion in the text of the ADEA that would cause us to conclude that Congress did in fact affirmatively intend to preclude § 1983 First Amendment retaliation suits relating to speech about age discrimination.

D.

The Senate and House Reports on the ADEA also offer no reason to believe that Congress intended through the ADEA to preclude § 1983 First Amendment retaliation claims related to allegations of age discrimination. "Speech by citizens on matters of public concern lies at the heart of the First Amendment, which 'was fashioned to assure unfettered interchange of ideas for the bringing about of political and social changes desired by the people.'" *Lane v. Franks,* ___ U.S. ___, 134 S.Ct. 2369, 2377, 189 L.Ed.2d 312 (2014) (quoting *Roth v. United States,* 354 U.S. 476, 484, 77 S.Ct. 1304, 1 L.Ed.2d 1498 (1957)). Given the importance of speech in our democracy, it seems unlikely that Congress would narrow First Amendment protections without serious consideration. At a minimum, we would expect to find some discussion of such a significant change in the official Reports on the ADEA. Yet we find nothing in those Reports suggesting that Congress even considered preclusion of First Amendment claims, let alone intended such a result.[10]

p.1249 Unlike in *Smith* where the legislative history made clear that the EHA was specifically designed to "protect[] the constitutional right of a handicapped child to a public education," *Smith,* 468 U.S. at 1013, 104 S.Ct. 3457, the Senate Committee Report accompanying the original ADEA legislation says nothing about the purpose of the retaliation provision, and it never mentions the First Amendment. With respect to the retaliation provision, the full statement in the "section by section" analysis portion of the Report provides:

> [This subsection] makes it unlawful for employers, employment agencies and labor unions to discriminate against a person because he has opposed a practice made unlawful by this act, or because he has made a charge, testified, or assisted or participated in any manner in an investigation, proceeding, or litigation under this act.

S. Rep. No. 90-723, at 8 (1967). This statement is essentially a recitation of the language of the retaliation provision and sheds no additional light on its purpose.

The House Report accompanying the original legislation is similarly devoid of any indication that Congress considered the preclusive effect of the retaliation provision of the ADEA on § 1983 First Amendment retaliation claims. *See* H.R. Rep. No. 90-805, at 9 (1967). The House Report offered essentially the same recitation of the statutory language as the Senate Report, with no additional analysis that would shed light upon Congress's intent. *Id.* ("[This subsection] makes it unlawful for employers, employment agencies and labor unions to discriminate against a person because he has opposed a practice made unlawful by this act, or because he has made a charge, testified, or assisted or participated in any manner in an investigation, proceeding, or litigation under this act.").[11]

E.

The result that the retaliation provision of the ADEA does not preclude § 1983 First Amendment retaliation suits makes sense in light of the heightened level of protection that the Constitution affords First Amendment rights. Rights subject to heightened scrutiny are much more likely to be the basis of a successful constitutional claim than are those subject to rational basis review. *See, e.g., Kimel v. Fla. Bd. of Regents,*

528 U.S. 62, 84, 120 S.Ct. 631, 145 L.Ed.2d 522 (2000) (explaining the greater difficulty in prevailing on an equal protection claim subject to rational basis review than on one subject to heightened scrutiny).

When a statute creates a cause of action to enforce a right that would only be subject to rational basis review under the Constitution, it is very unlikely as a practical matter that the statute will provide p.1250 less protection than the Constitution. For example, as the Supreme Court explained in *Kimel,* "[t]he [ADEA], through its broad restriction on the use of age as a discriminating factor, prohibits substantially more state employment decisions and practices than would likely be held unconstitutional under the applicable equal protection, rational basis standard." *Id.* at 86, 120 S.Ct. 631. As a consequence, we look to such a statute for the substance of the right, just as we do with a right created entirely by statute. And as with situations in which the right is entirely created by statute, *see Rancho Palos Verdes,* 544 U.S. at 121, 125 S.Ct. 1453, if Congress has also limited enforcement through the provisions in the statute, those limits indicate an intent to preclude recourse to § 1983 as a remedy.

In contrast, where a constitutional right is protected by heightened scrutiny, neither the substance nor the enforcement of the right will typically depend on any statute further defining the right. We do not assume that when a statute merely touches upon conduct that would violate the Constitution, the statute precludes the enforcement of that constitutional right unless there is a clear indication of Congressional intent that it do so. *See Fitzgerald,* 555 U.S. at 256, 259 n.2, 129 S.Ct. 788 (declining to preclude § 1983 suits alleging constitutional equal protection claims for gender discrimination in the absence of an indication that Congress affirmatively intended such preclusion).

Consistent with this, courts have allowed § 1983 constitutional claims and statutory claims to coexist when the constitutional claim gets heightened scrutiny, but not when the constitutional claim gets rational basis review. For instance, in *Fitzgerald,* as discussed above, the Supreme Court held that Title IX does not preclude § 1983 suits alleging equal protection violations based on gender discrimination, 555 U.S. at 258, 129 S.Ct. 788, which are subject to heightened scrutiny, *J.E.B. v. Alabama ex rel. T.B.,* 511 U.S. 127, 135, 114 S.Ct. 1419, 128 L.Ed.2d 89 (1994). Similarly, we have explained that Title VII of the Civil Rights Act of 1964, which prohibits employers from discriminating on the basis of "race, color, religion, sex, or national origin," 42 U.S.C. § 2000e-2, does not preclude suits under § 1983 alleging constitutional equal protection violations for discrimination on the basis of race or sex, both of which receive heightened scrutiny under the Equal Protection Clause. *Ahlmeyer v. Nev. Sys. of Higher Educ.,* 555 F.3d 1051, 1058 (9th Cir. 2009) (explaining that Title VII does not deprive plaintiffs of other avenues for asserting claims of race and sex discrimination) (citing *Johnson v. Ry. Express Agency, Inc.,* 421 U.S. 454, 459, 95 S.Ct. 1716, 44 L.Ed.2d 295 (1975)); *City of Cleburne, Tex. v. Cleburne Living Ctr.,* 473 U.S. 432, 440, 105 S.Ct. 3249, 87 L.Ed.2d 313 (1985) (explaining that classifications based on race, alienage, national origin, and gender all receive heightened scrutiny).

In contrast, in *Smith,* the Supreme Court held that the EHA precluded § 1983 equal protection claims regarding disability discrimination in education. *Smith,* 468 U.S. at 1009, 104 S.Ct. 3457. Disability, like age, is subject to rational basis review, not heightened scrutiny, under the Equal Protection Clause. *See City of Cleburne,* 473 U.S. at 446, 105 S.Ct. 3249.

It is well established that First Amendment claims like Stilwell's, that allege retaliation following speech on a matter of public concern, are reviewed with heightened scrutiny. *Lane v. Franks,* ___ U.S. ___, 134 S.Ct. 2369, 2381, 189 L.Ed.2d 312 (2014) (explaining that "a stronger showing [than legitimate government interests] may be necessary if the employee's speech ... involve[s] matters p.1251 of public concern" (last alteration in original) (quoting *Connick v. Myers,* 461 U.S. 138, 151-52, 103 S.Ct. 1684, 75 L.Ed.2d 708 (1983))). Our holding today that § 1983 suits alleging retaliation in violation of the First Amendment are not precluded by the ADEA's retaliation provision is thus consistent with the tendency of courts to conclude that there is a lack of preclusion when the right to be enforced is subject to heightened scrutiny.

F.

Contrary to Defendants' argument, a different result is not required by our prior decision in *Ahlmeyer v. Nevada System of Higher Education,* 555 F.3d 1051, 1054 (9th Cir. 2009), which held that the ADEA precludes § 1983 suits to remedy equal protection violations based on age discrimination.

In *Ahlmeyer,* we compared § 1983 equal protection claims based on age discrimination in employment to such claims under the ADEA and determined that "the ADEA provides broader protection than the Constitution," so "a plaintiff has 'nothing substantive to gain' by ... asserting a § 1983 claim" in addition to an ADEA claim. *Id.* at 1058 (quoting *Williams v. Wendler,* 530 F.3d 584, 586 (7th Cir. 2008)). In light of the ADEA's greater protections, we held that its discrimination provisions are sufficiently comprehensive to preclude § 1983 equal protection claims.[12]

Ahlmeyer's holding was motivated at least in part by the fact that classifications based on age are subject to rational basis review. *Ahlmeyer* relied heavily on *Zombro v. Baltimore City Police Department,* 868 F.2d 1364, 1366 (4th Cir. 1989), a pre-*Fitzgerald* case holding that § 1983 suits alleging age discrimination were precluded by the ADEA in part because of this level-of-scrutiny characteristic. *See Ahlmeyer,* 555 F.3d at 1057. *Zombro* had emphasized that "the equal protection clause does not recognize a 'class defined as the aged' to be a suspect class in need of special protection in which alleged discrimination is subject to 'strict judicial scrutiny,'" 868 F.2d at 1370 (quoting *Mass. Bd. of Ret. v. Murgia,* 427 U.S. 307, 313-14, 96 S.Ct. 2562, 49 L.Ed.2d 520 (1976) (per curiam)), and that this differentiated age discrimination claims from "§ 1983 actions predicated on race, sex, or religious discrimination or an infringement of specific First Amendment rights." *Id.* at 1370. *Ahlmeyer* itself also noted that, unlike "claims of discrimination based on race or sex [that] are entitled to heightened scrutiny, age discrimination claims under the Constitution are subject to rational basis scrutiny." *Ahlmeyer,* 555 F.3d at 1059 n.8. Thus, a plaintiff "has little to gain by circumventing the ADEA, which affords more protection in the area of age discrimination than does the federal Constitution." *Id.*

Because the ADEA's retaliation provision is critically different from the ADEA's p.1252 discrimination provision at issue in *Ahlmeyer,* that opinion is not controlling here. As explained above, the ADEA's retaliation protections are narrower than the First Amendment's in some important respects, whereas the ADEA discrimination provision provides more protection against age discrimination than does the Equal

Protection Clause. *Cf. Kimel,* 528 U.S. at 86, 120 S.Ct. 631 ("Judged against the backdrop of our equal protection jurisprudence, it is clear that the ADEA is 'so out of proportion to a supposed remedial or preventive object that it cannot be understood as responsive to, or designed to prevent, unconstitutional behavior.'" (quoting *City of Boerne v. Flores,* 521 U.S. 507, 532, 117 S.Ct. 2157, 138 L.Ed.2d 624 (1997))).

Given the substantial difference between the level of scrutiny afforded age discrimination equal protection claims and First Amendment retaliation claims, we cannot assume that Congress intended the ADEA to affect the availability of § 1983 claims in the same manner in both subject areas.

III.

For the foregoing reasons, we REVERSE and REMAND for proceedings consistent with this opinion.

FERNANDEZ, Circuit Judge, dissenting:

I respectfully dissent.

Our quest here is not to search for or to explicate constitutional principles; it is to search for congressional intent. That is to say, Congress can set up a statutory scheme wherein it demonstrates its intent to have that scheme, not 42 U.S.C. § 1983, apply to claims for enforcement of rights under the statute. *See, e.g., Fitzgerald v. Barnstable Sch. Comm.,* 555 U.S. 246, 252-54, 129 S.Ct. 788, 793-94, 172 L.Ed.2d 582 (2009); *Middlesex Cty. Sewerage Auth. v. Nat'l Sea Clammers Ass'n,* 453 U.S. 1, 13, 20-21, 101 S.Ct. 2615, 2622-23, 2626-27, 69 L.Ed.2d 435 (1981). Here our task is to determine whether Congress intended to make the ADEA[1] exclusive in that sense.

We have already said that Congress did just that. Specifically, we have held that "the ADEA precludes the assertion of age discrimination in employment claims, even those seeking to vindicate constitutional rights, under § 1983." *Ahlmeyer v. Nev. Sys. of Higher Educ.,* 555 F.3d 1051, 1057 (9th Cir. 2009). In that case, lest there be any doubt, we went on to conclude that: "the ADEA is the exclusive remedy for claims of age discrimination in employment, even those claims with their source in the Constitution." *Id.* at 1060-61. In *Ahlmeyer,* we were dealing with the claim of an older employee that her employer had discriminated against her on account of her age. *Id.* at 1054; *see also* 29 U.S.C. § 623(a)(1). The majority says that this case differs from *Ahlmeyer* because what is involved here is a claim of retaliation.[2] *See* 29 U.S.C. § 623(d). In effect, the majority says that Congress has had two different intents regarding the ADEA.

The first of those relates to individuals whose need for protection formed the mainspring of the ADEA — employees discriminated against on account of their age. *See id.* § 621; *see also id.* § 623(a)-(c). The second, somewhat more collateral, intention was designed to more fully protect the older employees for whom the ADEA was created. It relates to individuals who are retaliated against, not necessarily because p.1253 of their own ages, but because they have "opposed any practice made unlawful" by the ADEA. *Id.* § 623(d).

While the majority's opinion is quite persuasively written, I am not quite persuaded because I do not believe that in creating this relatively simple piece of legislation Congress held two very different intentions regarding the ADEA. Those for whom the ADEA was primarily designed had to rely upon ADEA remedies alone, but those who were protected in order to assure that the protection of those in the first group would be more effective did not have their remedies so limited. The latter could spell out a § 1983 claim also. Nothing Congress *said* makes that so,[3] and I am unable to conclude that Congress contemporaneously held separate intentions when enacting and amending this fairly uncomplicated piece of legislation.

Again, it is congressional intent that we must seek, and even if we ignore the broad and encompassing language of *Ahlmeyer,* I cannot say that Congress held those two separate intents. In short, I believe that in deciding this case we are bound by *Ahlmeyer.*

Thus, I must respectfully dissent.

[1] Because this case comes to us on appeal from a grant of summary judgment to Defendants, "[w]e view the facts in the light most favorable to Stilwell, the non-moving party." *Stilwell v. Smith & Nephew, Inc.,* 482 F.3d 1187, 1193 (9th Cir. 2007).

[2] Stilwell sued along with his wife. Because the Complaint does not allege any claims individual to Stilwell's wife, we have referred to the claims as Stilwell's claims.

[3] Stilwell's appellate arguments relating to claims other than his § 1983 First Amendment retaliation claim are addressed in a concurrently-filed memorandum disposition.

[4] In *City of Rancho Palos Verdes, California v. Abrams,* 544 U.S. 113, 125 S.Ct. 1453, 161 L.Ed.2d 316 (2005), the Court appears to have mischaracterized *Smith* as involving the question of whether § 1983 suits could enforce statutory rights. *Compare Rancho Palos Verdes,* 544 U.S. at 121, 125 S.Ct. 1453 ("We have found § 1983 unavailable to remedy violations of federal statutory rights in two cases: *Sea Clammers* and *Smith.*"), *with Smith,* 468 U.S. at 1008-09, 104 S.Ct. 3457 ("As petitioners emphasize, their § 1983 claims were not based on alleged violations of the EHA, but on independent claims of constitutional deprivations." (footnote omitted)).

[5] In *Gonzaga University v. Doe,* 536 U.S. 273, 281-83, 122 S.Ct. 2268, 153 L.Ed.2d 309 (2002), the Supreme Court made it much more difficult to infer privately enforceable rights in federal statutes that lack private rights of action. This decision had the effect of cabining the line of cases that had held § 1983 actions to be available to enforce such statutes. Post-*Gonzaga,* "'[t]he question whether Congress ... intended to create a private right of action [is] definitively answered in the negative' where a 'statute by its terms grants no private rights to any identifiable class.'" *Id.* at 283-84, 122 S.Ct. 2268 (alterations in original) (quoting *Touche Ross & Co. v. Redington,* 442 U.S. 560, 576, 99 S.Ct. 2479, 61 L.Ed.2d 82 (1979)); *see Sanchez v. Johnson,* 416 F.3d 1051, 1057 (9th Cir. 2005) (explaining that *Gonzaga* clarified that it is only "Congress's use of explicit, individually focused, rights-creating language that reveals

congressional intent to create an individually enforceable right in a spending statute"). And, where there was no private right to enforce, there could be no § 1983 action to enforce it. *See Sanchez,* 416 F.3d at 1062 ("After *Gonzaga,* ... a plaintiff seeking redress under § 1983 must assert the violation of an individually enforceable *right* conferred specifically upon him, not merely a violation of federal law or the denial of a *benefit* or *interest,* no matter how unambiguously conferred.").

[6] Of course, because *Fitzgerald* was discussing a statute that lacked an express private right of action, the Supreme Court was not confronted with the question of how important the comprehensiveness of the remedial scheme is vis-à-vis the significant divergence of "the contours of ... rights and protections." 555 U.S. at 252-53, 129 S.Ct. 788. Nor did it attempt to answer that question.

[7] The 1974 Amendments to the ADEA extended the protections of the ADEA to federal employees. *Bunch v. United States,* 548 F.2d 336, 338 (9th Cir. 1977); 29 U.S.C. § 633a (setting forth ADEA requirements for federal employers).

[8] In certain circumstances a private employer could be considered a state actor. In such circumstances, an employee plaintiff could sue such an employer under § 1983 as well as under the ADEA. *See Dennis v. Sparks,* 449 U.S. 24, 27-28, 101 S.Ct. 183, 66 L.Ed.2d 185 (1980).

[9] The list of differences between ADEA retaliation actions and § 1983 First Amendment retaliation actions discussed herein is not necessarily exhaustive.

[10] We "rel[y] on official committee reports when considering legislative history." *Hertzberg v. Dignity Partners, Inc.,* 191 F.3d 1076, 1082 (9th Cir. 1999). The parties have not pointed us to any other legislative history, beyond the Committee Reports, describing the purpose or intent of the retaliation provision of the ADEA.

[11] This lack of comment on the retaliation provision's relationship to the First Amendment is unsurprising because as originally enacted, the ADEA did not apply to states or the federal government. *See Kimel v. Florida Bd. of Regents,* 528 U.S. 62, 68, 120 S.Ct. 631, 145 L.Ed.2d 522 (2000) ("In 1974, in a statute consisting primarily of amendments to the FLSA, Congress extended application of the ADEA's substantive requirements to the States."). The focus of the Reports accompanying those amendments was on the expansion of coverage, and there is no indication that Congress reconsidered the retaliation provision in light of the expansion of coverage. *See* S. Rep. No. 93-690, at 55-56 (1974) (discussing the amendments to the definition of employer to expand coverage, but not mentioning the retaliation provision); H.R. Rep. No. 93-913, at 40-41 (1974) (same).

[12] There is a circuit split on this issue. *Compare, e.g., Hildebrand v. Allegheny County,* 757 F.3d 99 (3d Cir. 2014) (holding that because the ADEA provides more expansive protection against age discrimination than the Equal Protection Clause, the ADEA precludes § 1983 suits alleging equal protection violations based on age discrimination in employment), *cert. denied,* ___ U.S. ___, 135 S.Ct. 1398, 191 L.Ed.2d 359 (2015), *with Levin v. Madigan,* 692 F.3d 607, 617 (7th Cir. 2012) (holding that "[a]lthough the ADEA enacts a comprehensive statutory scheme for enforcement of its own statutory rights, akin to *Sea Clammers* and *Rancho Palos Verdes,* ... it does not preclude a § 1983 claim for constitutional rights" because of "the ADEA's lack of legislative history or statutory language precluding constitutional claims, and the

divergent rights and protections afforded by the ADEA as compared to a § 1983 equal protection claim" (citing *Fitzgerald,* 555 U.S. at 252-53, 129 S.Ct. 788)).

[1] Age Discrimination in Employment Act, 29 U.S.C. §§ 621-634.

[2] *Ahlmeyer* did not draw that distinction. Of course, it is not at all unusual for those who make claims of discrimination to make claims of retaliation also. In fact, at the trial court level that happened in *Ahlmeyer* itself. *See Ahlmeyer,* 555 F.3d at 1054 n.1.

[3] Indeed, the majority explains that the legislative history helps not at all.

TENTH CIRCUIT DECISIONS
Title IX

Doe v. University of Denver, 952 F. 3d 1182 (10th Cir. 2020) 363
Farmer v. Kansas State University, 918 F. 3d 1094 (10th Cir. 2019) 383
Ross v. University of Tulsa, 859 F. 3d 1280 (10th Cir. 2017) 397
Hiatt v. Colorado Seminary, 858 F. 3d 1307 (10th Cir. 2017) 413
Levy v. Kansas Dept. of Social & Rehab. Services, 789 F. 3d 1164 (10th Cir. 2015) 431
Varnell v. Dora Consol. School Dist., 756 F. 3d 1208 (10th Cir. 2014) 441

952 F.3d 1182 (2020)

John DOE, Plaintiff-Appellant,

v.

UNIVERSITY OF DENVER; University of Denver Board of Trustees; Rebecca Chopp, individually and as agent for University of Denver; Kristin Olson, individually and as agent for University of Denver; Jean McAllister, individually and as agent for University of Denver; Kathryne Grove, individually and as agent for University of Denver; Eric Butler, individually and as agent for University of Denver, Defendants-Appellees.

No. 18-1162.

United States Court of Appeals, Tenth Circuit.

FILED March 9, 2020.

Doe v. University of Denver, 952 F. 3d 1182 (10th Cir. 2020)

Appeal from the United States District Court for the District of Colorado; (D.C. No. 1:16-CV-00152-PAB-STV).

Philip A. Byler of Nesenoff & Miltenberg, LLP, New York, New York (Andrew T. Miltenberg, Stuart Bernstein, Tara J. Davis, and Jeffrey Berkowitz of Nesenoff & Miltenberg, LLP, New York, New York, and Michael J. Mirabella and Patricia Mellen of Michael J. Mirabella, P.C., Denver, Colorado, with him on the briefs), for Plaintiff-Appellant.

Jim Goh (E. Rayner Mangum with him on the brief), Constangy, Brooks, Smith & Prophete, LLP, Denver, Colorado, for Defendants - Appellees.

Before BACHARACH, McKAY, and CARSON, Circuit Judges.

Judge BACHARACH joins the opinion except for footnote 18.

McKAY, Circuit Judge.

This appeal involves the fairness of sexual-misconduct disciplinary proceedings at colleges and universities. In the district court, Plaintiff John Doe asserted that the disciplinary proceeding brought against him by Defendants, the University of Denver ("DU") along with several of its employees, violated his rights under the Fourteenth Amendment's Due Process Clause and under Title IX. The court granted summary judgment to Defendants on the Fourteenth Amendment claim because Plaintiff had failed to show that DU was a state actor. The court also granted Defendants summary judgment on the Title IX claim, concluding that Plaintiff had adduced insufficient evidence of gender bias.[1]

I. Fourteenth Amendment Due Process Claim

We turn first to Plaintiff's due process claim. DU is a private school, and thus its actions are not normally subject to constitutional due process requirements. *See Brentwood Acad. v. Tenn. Secondary Sch. Athletic Ass'n*, 531 U.S. 288, 295, 121 S.Ct. 924, 148 L.Ed.2d 807 (2001) ("[S]tate action [is] subject to Fourteenth Amendment scrutiny[,] and private conduct (however exceptionable) ... is not."); *Browns v. Mitchell*,

409 F.2d 593, 594 (10th Cir. 1969) ("It is axiomatic that the due process provisions of the Fourteenth Amendment proscribe state action only and do not reach acts of private persons unless they are acting under color of state law." (internal quotation marks omitted)). As Plaintiff's briefing suggests, his claim is cognizable only if DU may be deemed a state actor for purposes of constitutional due process. *See Brentwood Acad.,* 531 U.S. at 296, 121 S.Ct. 924 (outlining tests used to determine whether state action should be attributed to nominally private entities). Thus, at summary judgment, Plaintiff had the burden to produce evidence demonstrating that DU should be deemed a state actor. *See Gallagher v. Neil Young Freedom Concert,* 49 F.3d 1442, 1450, 1455-56 (10th Cir. 1995) (affirming summary judgment in favor of defendants in part because plaintiffs failed to produce evidence to satisfy state-action tests).

p.1187 There are two constitutional sources of due process rights, the Fifth Amendment and the Fourteenth Amendment. Plaintiffs pursuing procedural due process claims based on actions by the federal government must proceed under the Fifth Amendment, while plaintiffs bringing such claims based on actions by state governments must proceed under the Fourteenth Amendment. *See Koessel v. Sublette Cty. Sheriff's Dep't,* 717 F.3d 736, 748 n.2 (10th Cir. 2013).

Plaintiff has eschewed any reliance on the Fifth Amendment. Plaintiff expressly relied only on the Fourteenth Amendment in his complaint and district court briefing, and he continues to do so on appeal even in the face of both the district court's suggestion and DU's assertion that the Fourteenth Amendment is inapposite for a due process claim based exclusively on the federal government's activities. (*See* Appellant's Opening Br. at 53-54 (arguing that, although the district court suggested "federal government activity is irrelevant to the 14th Amendment[,] ... the 14th Amendment ... appl[ies]").) Plaintiff is the master of his complaint. *See Bledsoe v. Vanderbilt,* 934 F.3d 1112, 1119 (10th Cir. 2019). We are satisfied that Plaintiff intended to bring this claim under the Fourteenth Amendment, and that is how we will assess it. *See In re Storer,* 58 F.3d 1125, 1129 & n.6 (6th Cir. 1995) (declining to assess claims under Fourteenth Amendment Due Process Clause where plaintiffs clearly intended to rely only on Fifth Amendment Due Process Clause).[2]

In support of his claim that DU was a state actor, Plaintiff relied solely on evidence of the federal government's involvement in DU's affairs. Specifically, p.1188 Plaintiff pointed to (1) DU's compliance with guidance from the Department of Education's Office for Civil Rights regarding Title IX's requirements that was contained in a 2011 Dear Colleague Letter ("DCL"),[3] which, Plaintiff asserts, pressured DU to amend its policies in ways that were biased against male students accused of sexual misconduct; and (2) the threatened loss of federal funding if DU failed to conform to the DCL's guidance. We have previously held, however, that evidence regarding the *federal* government's involvement with a private school or its decision to discipline students has no bearing on whether the school is a state actor under the Fourteenth Amendment, which is concerned only with the actions of *state* governments. *See Browns,* 409 F.2d at 595 ("Inasmuch as ... 42 U.S.C. § 1983[[4]] is concerned only with state action and does not concern itself with federal action[,] we lay to one side as entirely irrelevant any evidence concerning the participation of the federal government in the affairs of the University. And so it is state action with which we are here concerned and more particularly... whether the State of Colorado ... [should be viewed as involved in] the challenged disciplinary proceeding." (citation and quotation marks omitted)).[5] Thus, Plaintiff failed to adduce any relevant evidence to show that DU is a state actor for purposes of his Fourteenth Amendment claim.

In sum, although we agree with the district court that Plaintiff failed to demonstrate that DU was a state actor for purposes of his Fourteenth Amendment due process claim, we reach this conclusion on somewhat different grounds, namely that Plaintiff failed to adduce any evidence of a *state's* involvement in the disciplinary proceeding he challenges. *See Richison v. Ernest Grp., Inc.,* 634 F.3d 1123, 1130 (10th Cir. 2011) ("[W]e may affirm on any basis supported by the record...."). Accordingly, we will affirm the court's decision to grant Defendants summary judgment on the due process claim.

II. Title IX Claim

We now turn to Plaintiff's Title IX claim, which requires some background. Plaintiff is a male who enrolled as a freshman at DU in 2014. In October 2014, Plaintiff had a sexual encounter with Jane Doe, a female freshman, in his dorm room. Six months later, in April 2015, Jane's boyfriend reported the encounter as an alleged sexual assault to a DU resident director. The resident director then spoke with Jane, who repeated the allegations and later filed with DU's Office of Equal Opportunity a complaint of non-consensual sexual contact.

Under DU's policies, a student's non-consensual sexual contact with another is a policy violation. Prohibited sexual contact p.1189 includes contact by "coercion," which the policy defines as "unreasonable and persistent pressure to compel another individual to initiate or continue sexual activity against an individual's will," such as "continued pressure" after "someone makes clear that they do not want to engage in sexual contact." (Appellant's App. at A139.)

Two of the named Defendants, Kathryne Grove, OEO's director, and Eric Butler, an OEO investigator, investigated Jane's allegations. The investigators separately interviewed Plaintiff and Jane twice in May and June 2015, allowing each of them to offer corrections to their own summary statements, which the investigators had drafted for them based on their respective interviews, and allowing Plaintiff to submit a list of witnesses for the investigators to interview. The investigators also interviewed other witnesses—Plaintiff's roommate, a mutual acquaintance who was present in the dorm room before the encounter took place, Jane's boyfriend, and the resident director who first received the allegations. In late June, the investigators issued a preliminary report to Plaintiff and Jane, allowing them to offer any further corrections to their own statements. The preliminary report, which did not make any findings or conclusions, offered Plaintiff the first opportunity to see Jane's allegations against him.

In mid-July 2015, the investigators issued their final report, which depicted a he-said-she-said situation. After summarizing witness interviews, the investigators "f[ound] it more likely than not that [Plaintiff]'s actions ... resulted in non-consensual sexual contact with [Jane] by means of coercion in violation of [DU's] policies." (Appellant's App. at A159.) No hearing was held. Pursuant to its procedures, DU convened an outcome council to review the case and determine a sanction. The outcome council decided to permanently dismiss Plaintiff from DU. Plaintiff submitted an internal appeal challenging the investigation process, but it was denied.

In his complaint, Plaintiff claimed the disciplinary proceedings DU subjected him to violated Title IX. The district court granted Defendants summary judgment on the claim, concluding Plaintiff had failed to adduce evidence showing DU's actions were motivated by gender bias.

"We review the district court's summary-judgment order de novo, applying the same standard that the district court is to apply." *Singh v. Cordle,* 936 F.3d 1022, 1037 (10th Cir. 2019). "Summary judgment is appropriate 'if the movant shows that there is no genuine dispute as to any material fact and the movant is entitled to judgment as a matter of law.'" *Evans v. Sandy City,* 944 F.3d 847, 852 (10th Cir. 2019) (quoting Fed. R. Civ. P. 56(a)). "A fact is material if, under the governing law, it could have an effect on the outcome of the lawsuit. A dispute over a material fact is genuine if a rational jury could find in favor of the nonmoving party on the evidence presented." *Jones v. Norton,* 809 F.3d 564, 573 (10th Cir. 2015) (internal quotation marks omitted). "In reviewing a motion for summary judgment, we review the facts and all reasonable inferences those facts support[] in the light most favorable to the nonmoving party." *Evans,* 944 F.3d at 852 (internal quotation marks omitted).

Title IX provides that "[n]o person in the United States shall, on the basis of [gender], be excluded from participation in, be denied the benefits of, or be subjected to discrimination under any education program or activity receiving Federal financial assistance." 20 U.S.C. § 1681(a). Title IX is "enforceable through an implied private right of action." *Gebser v. Lago Vista Indep. Sch. Dist.,* 524 U.S. 274, 281, 118 S.Ct. 1989, 141 L.Ed.2d 277 (1998); *see also Jackson v. Birmingham Bd. of Educ.,* 544 U.S. 167, 183, 125 S.Ct. p.1190 1497, 161 L.Ed.2d 361 (2005) (explaining the Supreme Court "ha[s] consistently interpreted Title IX's private cause of action broadly to encompass diverse forms of intentional [gender] discrimination"). Generally, to succeed on a claim under Title IX, "a plaintiff must show: (1) that he or she was excluded from participation in, denied the benefits of, or subjected to discrimination in an educational program; (2) that the program receives federal assistance; and (3) that the exclusion from the program was on the basis of [gender]." *Seamons v. Snow,* 84 F.3d 1226, 1232 (10th Cir. 1996). Here, there is no dispute that DU offers an educational program receiving federal assistance or that Plaintiff was excluded from participating in that program. Thus, the only issue is whether Plaintiff adduced sufficient evidence to raise a genuine dispute that he was excluded from DU on the basis of gender.

The district court concluded that Plaintiff had failed to adduce sufficient evidence to raise a genuine dispute that gender was a motivating factor in DU's decision to expel him. The court recounted the litany of evidentiary arguments Plaintiff raised in opposition to summary judgment but in the end concluded that most of Plaintiff's evidence was aimed at demonstrating that DU was biased in favor of sexual-misconduct complainants and against sexual-misconduct respondents. In the court's view, assuming Plaintiff had created a genuine dispute that DU's process is biased against respondents, it was not reasonable to infer from this, without additional evidence, that DU's process is biased against males. The court found the remainder of Plaintiff's evidence similarly unavailing, concluding that none of it raised a genuine dispute that DU's decision was motivated by gender bias.

On appeal, Plaintiff argues that the district court erred both in refusing to consider all of the evidence he presented and in concluding that his evidence was insufficient to support an inference that DU's decision to expel him was motivated by gender bias. We consider these arguments in turn.

A. Exclusion of Evidence

In support of his opposition to summary judgment, Plaintiff submitted the expert report of law professor Aya Gruber. In her report, Prof. Gruber opines that Plaintiff's disciplinary proceeding was marked by numerous deficiencies that give rise to an appearance of bias based on gender stereotypes. The court declined to consider Prof. Gruber's report in its assessment of Plaintiff's Title IX claim for two reasons. First, the court pointed out that Plaintiff cited the report in his opposition only three times, and never in support of his Title IX claim. Second, although the court acknowledged that the report highlights alleged deficiencies in the disciplinary proceedings against Plaintiff, the court concluded the report was not material to the question before it—whether DU's decisions were motivated by gender bias. On appeal, Plaintiff argues the court erred by failing to consider Prof. Gruber's report in support of his Title IX claim.[6] He contends the court should have considered the report because it directly addresses the issue the district court said it did not, namely whether gender bias was a motivating factor in DU's decision to expel him.

p.1191 "We review a district court's decisions excluding evidence at the summary judgment stage only for an abuse of discretion." *LifeWise Master Funding v. Telebank*, 374 F.3d 917, 927 (10th Cir. 2004). "Under this standard, we will not disturb the district court's decision unless we have a definite and firm conviction that the lower court made a clear error of judgment or exceeded the bounds of permissible choice in the circumstances." *Id.* (internal quotation marks omitted). Under Rule 56, "[a] party asserting that a fact... is genuinely disputed must support the assertion by ... citing to particular parts of materials in the record." Fed. R. Civ. P. 56 (c)(1). Where a report or other material is "made part of the record" but the party "fail[s] to cite to the 'particular parts' of the record that support[] [a particular] argument," the district court is "under no obligation to parse through the record to find the uncited materials." *Unal v. Los Alamos Pub. Sch.*, 638 F. App'x 729, 742 (10th Cir. 2016); *see also Cross v. Home Depot*, 390 F.3d 1283, 1290 (10th Cir. 2004) ("[I]t is the responding party's burden to ensure that the factual dispute is portrayed with particularity, without depending on the trial court to conduct its own search of the record." (ellipsis and internal quotation marks omitted)); *Mitchell v. City of Moore*, 218 F.3d 1190, 1199 (10th Cir. 2000) ("The district court was not obligated to comb the record in order to make [the non-movant]'s arguments for him.").

The district court did not abuse its discretion in declining to consider Prof. Gruber's report for purposes of the Title IX claim. Even assuming the court misapprehended the contents of Prof. Gruber's report, the court properly declined to consider it in addressing the Title IX claim because Plaintiff failed to cite the report in his summary-judgment arguments regarding that claim. Instead, he only cited the report (1) in his statement of facts to dispute DU's assertion that its investigators understood the preponderance-of-the-evidence standard and (2) in his arguments regarding his state-law claims to assert, based on the investigators' allegedly one-sided credibility assessments, that there remained a genuine dispute whether the investigation was thorough, impartial, and fair enough to satisfy DU's contractual obligations. Plaintiff neither cited the report nor discussed the investigators' understanding of the preponderance standard or their credibility assessments in his arguments regarding his Title IX claim. In other words, Plaintiff did not meet his burden to cite the particular part of the record he now claims should have been considered to support his Title IX argument. *See Unal,* 638 F. App'x at 742. Under these circumstances, we cannot fault the district court for declining to parse through the record in order to conjure up arguments from the record that Plaintiff might have made on his own, and its decision to refrain from doing so was no abuse of discretion.[7]

p.1192 B. Evidence of gender bias

On appeal, Plaintiff argues that several categories of evidence he adduced in the district court were sufficient to create a genuine dispute regarding whether gender was a motivating factor in the proceeding DU brought against him. We evaluate each category in turn.

First, as other plaintiffs have in recent years, Plaintiff sets the stage for his Title IX claim by shining a spotlight on the 2011 Dear Colleague Letter, which "ushered in a more rigorous approach to sexual misconduct allegations," *Doe v. Purdue Univ.,* 928 F.3d 652, 668 (7th Cir. 2019); *accord Menaker v. Hofstra Univ.,* 935 F.3d 20, 26 (2d Cir. 2019), by providing guidance to schools receiving federal funding regarding Title IX's requirements as they relate to sexual assault. Moreover, Plaintiff presents evidence specific to DU's response to the DCL, which included "engag[ing] national experts" to "evaluat[e] its processes"; "[c]reat[ing] a team of administrators to address concerns"; establishing positions for a Title IX coordinator and a second Title IX investigator at the school; altering its investigative model; engaging in several sexual-assault awareness campaigns on campus; and "review[ing and] revis[ing]" its "support and resources for victims," methods of "handl[ing] expressions of concern," and "prevention efforts." (Appellant's App. at A507.) Plaintiff further presents evidence that DU's training materials warned employees that they "need to take [compliance with Title IX] very seriously" because it "is the focus of OCR right now," emphasizing that (1) the Department of Education could "cut off federal funding/initiate proceedings to do so"; (2) OCR could commence "compliance review," which "is very time consuming, creates extremely negative publicity for the school, and is very thorough"; and (3) "individual employees" could be "personally sued in a civil lawsuit by student[s]" if they failed to comply with Title IX or "possibly ... be held personally liable" if they were "aware of sexual harassment of student[s] and show[ed] 'deliberate indifference'" to it. (*Id.* at A510-11.) Plaintiff then contends that the DCL and the pressure DU felt to comply with its guidance give rise to an inference of gender bias.

The majority of other courts to have considered this issue have concluded that, although evidence of the DCL and external pressure placed on the school to conform with its guidance may provide the plaintiff with "a story about why [the school] might have been motivated to discriminate against males accused of sexual assault," such evidence is insufficient in itself to support any inference that the school's actions in a particular case were motivated at least in part by gender bias. *Purdue Univ.,* 928 F.3d at 669; *see also, e.g., Doe v. Baum,* 903 F.3d 575, 586 (6th Cir. 2018) ("Of course, all of this external pressure alone is not enough to state a claim that the university acted with bias in this particular case. Rather, it provides a backdrop that, when combined with other circumstantial evidence of bias in Doe's specific proceeding, gives rise to a plausible claim."). We agree. The DCL is gender-neutral on its face, *see Neal v. Colo. State Univ.,* No. 16-cv-873-RM-CBS, 2017 WL 633045, at *11 (D. Colo. Feb. 16, 2017), and evidence that a school felt pressured p.1193 to conform with its guidance cannot alone satisfy Title IX's fundamental requirement that the challenged action be "on the basis of [gender]," 20 U.S.C. § 1681(a). Thus, Plaintiff's evidence of the DCL and the pressure DU felt to comply with its guidance cannot support his summary judgment burden unless combined with a "particularized 'something more,'" *Doe v. Columbia Coll. Chi.,* 933 F.3d 849, 856 (7th Cir. 2019), that would indicate that DU's decision in his particular case was based on his gender. And, as explained below, we conclude that Plaintiff has not made this particularized showing here.

Second, Plaintiff points to statistical evidence showing an overwhelming disparity in the gender makeup of sexual-assault complainants and sexual-assault respondents at DU. Specifically, between 2011 and 2016, nearly all complainants (35 out of 36) were female, and all respondents (36 out of 36) were either listed as male or could be presumed to be male based on the nature of the complaint. Plaintiff does not explain how this disparity amounts to gender bias on the part of DU, except to say that DU should have expected that its implementation of the DCL's guidance would disproportionately affect men because the DCL was intended to address a perceived epidemic of male sexual assault against women. But, on its face, the DCL says no such thing, and Plaintiff points to no evidence suggesting that DU changed its policies in light of this statistical disparity or in order to combat sexual assault perpetrated specifically by men against women. At best, then, the statistical disparity can only create a genuine dispute to the extent it generates a reasonable inference that DU's decision to expel Plaintiff was motivated by considerations of gender. Plaintiff's argument thus reduces down to an inferential proposition: a factfinder can reasonably infer from the fact that sexual-assault respondents are overwhelmingly male that a school's decision to initiate proceedings against respondents is motivated by the fact that they are male.

Assessing what inferences may reasonably be drawn from the statistical disparity in the gender makeup of sexual-assault complainants and respondents is one of the more perplexing aspects of addressing Title IX challenges to sexual-misconduct disciplinary proceedings.[8] *See Doe v. Univ. of Colo. ex rel. Bd. of Regents of Univ. of Colo.,* 255 F. Supp. 3d 1064, 1075-76 (D. Colo. 2017) (cautioning against accepting or rejecting inferences in similar context without reflection). The courts that have engaged in this analysis have generally concluded that statistical disparities in the gender makeup of complainants and p.1194 respondents can readily be explained by "an array of alternative" nondiscriminatory possibilities, potentially "reflect[ing], for example, that male students on average... committed more serious assaults," that sexual-assault victims are likelier to be women, or that female victims are likelier than male victims to report sexual assaults. *Haidak v. Univ. of Mass.-Amherst,* 933 F.3d 56, 75 (1st Cir. 2019); *see also Doe v. Trs. of Bos. Coll.,* 892 F.3d 67, 92 (1st Cir. 2018); *Doe v. Cummins,* 662 F. App'x 437, 453-54 (6th Cir. 2016); *Doe v. Univ. of Cincinnati,* 173 F. Supp. 3d 586, 607-08 (S.D. Ohio 2016). When the statistical evidence does nothing to eliminate these obvious, alternative explanations for the disparity, an inference that the disparity arises from gender bias on the part of the school is not reasonable. *See Haidak,* 933 F.3d at 75; *Bos. Coll.,* 892 F.3d at 92; *Cummins,* 662 F. App'x at 453-54; *Univ. of Cincinnati,* 173 F. Supp. 3d at 607-08.

We agree with this analysis. A factfinder could not reasonably infer from bare evidence of statistical disparity in the gender makeup of sexual-assault complainants and respondents that the school's decision to initiate proceedings against respondents is motivated by their gender. This is so because, at least in the discrimination context, the extent to which a discriminatory motive may be reasonably inferred from evidence of statistical disparity often depends on the evidence's ability to eliminate obvious nondiscriminatory explanations for the disparity. *See Luster v. Vilsack,* 667 F.3d 1089, 1094 (10th Cir. 2011) ("In order to be probative of discrimination, statistical evidence must eliminate nondiscriminatory explanations for the disparity." (internal quotation marks omitted)); *Turner v. Pub. Serv. Co. of Colo.,* 563 F.3d 1136, 1147 (10th Cir. 2009) ("In order for statistical evidence to create an inference of discrimination, the statistics must show a significant disparity and eliminate nondiscriminatory explanations for the disparity." (brackets omitted)) (quoting *Fallis v. Kerr-McGee Corp.,* 944 F.2d 743, 746 (10th Cir. 1991)); *Schulte v. Potter,* 218 F. App'x 703, 714 (10th Cir. 2007) (explaining that, where evidence "wholly fail[s] to eliminate non-discriminatory explanations for" disparate treatment, "[i]t would be unreasonable to draw an inference of" intentional discrimination (internal quotation marks omitted)).

This principle is especially applicable here. In employment discrimination cases, the nondiscriminatory explanations for statistical disparity that prevent an inference of discriminatory intent often involve the employer's own hiring or promotion criteria. *See, e.g., Turner,* 563 F.3d at 1148. One might suspect that the principle requiring a plaintiff to negate nondiscriminatory explanations of statistical disparity would be at its weakest where the defendant controls the putative nondiscriminatory causes of disparate treatment. In Title IX challenges to sexual-misconduct proceedings, however, the putative nondiscriminatory causes of disparity—the gender makeup of sexual-assault perpetrators, victims, and reporters—are almost completely beyond the control of the school. *See Univ. of Colo.,* 255 F. Supp. 3d at 1078 ("[T]he University is not responsible for the gender makeup of those who are accused *by other students* of sexual misconduct." (internal quotation marks omitted)); *accord Cummins,* 662 F. App'x at 454. We think then that the principle would be at its strongest in this context.[9]

p.1195 Here, Plaintiff's statistical evidence does not create a reasonable inference that DU's decisions regarding the initiation of sexual-misconduct proceedings were motivated by considerations of gender. His statistical evidence does nothing to eliminate the nondiscriminatory explanations for the disparity identified above, and thus it would be unreasonable for a factfinder to infer from the statistical disparity alone that DU decides to initiate proceedings against respondents based on their gender. Something more is needed to show the disparity results from gender bias rather than nondiscriminatory, exogenous factors—something like an affidavit from a knowledgeable person stating the school exhibits a pattern of prosecuting complaints against male but not female students, *see Doe v. Miami Univ.*, 882 F.3d 579, 593 (6th Cir. 2018), or a statement from school officials touting such statistics in response to public criticism of the school's previous handling of female students' sexual-assault allegations, *see Doe v. Geo. Wash. Univ.*, 366 F. Supp. 3d 1, 12-13 (D.D.C. 2018). Plaintiff points to no additional evidence of this kind.

Third, Plaintiff points to evidence of DU's alleged bias against respondents in sexual-misconduct proceedings. Specifically, Plaintiff presented evidence that DU's training materials[10] referred to sexual-misconduct complainants as "survivors" and directed staff to "[e]mpower the survivor" and "[c]ommunicate that you believe the survivor." (Appellant's App. at A519.)[11] Plaintiff also presented evidence that, when the investigation against him began, DU provided a list of resources to him and Jane to help them navigate the Title IX process. Plaintiff asserts these resources were complainant-specific and thus supported the needs of complainants but not respondents. For instance, Ms. Grove testified at her deposition that one resource on the list, the Center for Advocacy and Prevention and Empowerment, did not "support men who were accused of sexual assault." (*Id.* at A351.) Of course, as the district court noted, there is no evidence in the record that CAPE would support women accused of sexual assault either, and Ms. Grove testified that other resources on the list would provide support to men accused of sexual assault. p.1196 Additional testimony from Ms. McAllister that Plaintiff himself points to—that she would like to develop named support programs for respondents in the same way DU has developed named support programs for complainants—highlights that Plaintiff's argument is based on the relative disparity between resources for complainants and resources for respondents.

Whether factfinders may reasonably infer anti-male bias from evidence of a school's anti-respondent bias is another thorny issue that often arises in Title IX challenges to sexual-misconduct disciplinary proceedings. *See Norris v. Univ. of Colo.*, 362 F. Supp. 3d 1001, 1014-15 (D. Colo. 2019); *Univ. of Colo.*, 255 F. Supp. 3d at 1075-76. Most courts to have addressed the issue have concluded that evidence of a school's anti-respondent bias does not create a reasonable inference of anti-male bias. *See Cummins*, 662 F. App'x at 453; *Doe v. Rider Univ.*, No. 3:16-cv-4882-BRM-DEA, 2018 WL 466225, at *10 (D.N.J. Jan. 17, 2018); *Doe v. Colgate Univ.*, No. 5:15-cv-1069 (LEK/DEP), 2017 WL 4990629, at *11 (N.D.N.Y Oct. 31, 2017); *Doe v. Columbia Coll. Chi.*, 299 F. Supp. 3d 939, 956-57 (N.D. Ill. 2017); *Ruff v. Bd. of Regents of Univ. of N.M.*, 272 F. Supp. 3d 1289, 1302 (D.N.M. 2017); *Univ. of Colo.*, 255 F. Supp. 3d at 1079; *Doe v. Univ. of St. Thomas*, 240 F. Supp. 3d 984, 991 (D. Minn. 2017); *Doe v. Univ. of Mass.*, No. 14-30143-MGM, 2015 WL 4306521, at *8 (D. Mass. July 14, 2015); *Haley v. Va. Commonwealth Univ.*, 948 F. Supp. 573, 579 (E.D. Va. 1996). They reason that evidence of a school's anti-respondent bias does not permit a reasonable inference of an anti-male bias because both males and females can be respondents. *See, e.g., Cummins*, 662 F. App'x at 453 ("[A] disciplinary system that is biased in favor of alleged victims and against those accused of misconduct ... does not equate to gender bias because sexual-assault victims can be both male and female.").

We agree. We have relied on the same rationale in the employment discrimination context and have held that, on its own, evidence of an employer's discriminatory treatment of a group to which both genders can belong does not give rise to an inference of gender discrimination. *See Adamson v. Multi Cmty. Diversified Servs., Inc.*,

514 F.3d 1136, 1148-49 (10th Cir. 2008) ("'Familial status' is not a classification based on [gender] any more than is being a 'sibling' or 'relative' generally. It is, by definition, gender neutral.... Assertions that an employer discriminated against an individual on the basis of his or her 'familial status' alone state no cognizable cause of action under Title VII.").[12] The reasoning applies equally well in the Title IX context. *See Gossett v. Oklahoma ex rel. Bd. of Regents for Langston Univ.*, 245 F.3d 1172, 1176 (10th Cir. 2001) ("Courts have generally assessed Title IX discrimination claims under the same legal analysis as Title VII claims."). Classification as a sexual-misconduct respondent is not a classification based on gender. It is p.1197 gender-neutral because both men and women can be respondents. Accordingly, by itself, evidence of a school's anti-respondent bias does not permit a reasonable inference of discrimination based on gender.

Here, Plaintiff's evidence demonstrates at most that DU had an anti-respondent or pro-complainant bias, which is insufficient to create an inference of anti-male bias. A number of courts have determined that references to complainants as "victims" or "survivors" or language suggesting a pro-victim viewpoint exhibits at most a bias in favor of complainants *qua* complainants and against respondents *qua* respondents. *See Bos. Coll.*, 892 F.3d at 92; *Doe v. Quinnipiac Univ.*, 404 F. Supp. 3d 643, 661 n.6 (D. Conn. 2019); *Rider Univ.*, 2018 WL 466225, at *10; *Colgate Univ.*, 2017 WL 4990629, at *14-15; *Columbia Coll. Chi.*, 299 F. Supp. 3d at 955. Plaintiff's reliance on similar pro-victim language in DU's training materials at most demonstrates an anti-respondent bias. Likewise, the relative lack of support resources DU offers to respondents compared to the resources it offers complainants demonstrates at most a bias against respondents. However, this evidence of anti-respondent bias does not raise an inference of discrimination based on gender.[13]

Fourth, Plaintiff argues the investigators exhibited bias by finding Plaintiff responsible for non-consensual sexual contact despite evidence supporting his version of the events. In Plaintiff's view, the evidence before the investigators so clearly favored a finding that Plaintiff's and Jane's sexual encounter was consensual that the investigators' finding to the contrary creates an inference of bias in their decision.

For support, Plaintiff relies on *Doe v. Columbia University*, 831 F.3d 46 (2d Cir. 2016). In *Columbia University*, the Second Circuit reviewed an order dismissing a complaint pursuant to Fed. R. Civ. P. 12(b)(6). According to the allegations in the complaint, the student complainant was "an altogether willing participant" in the underlying sexual encounter; "'no evidence was presented'" to the school's tribunal to support the complainant's claim that sexual activity was coerced; and the tribunal "chose to accept [the complainant's] unsupported accusatory version" of events and "declined even to explore the testimony of [the] [p]laintiff's witnesses." *Columbia Univ.*, 831 F.3d at 57. These allegations, which the court was obligated to "accept in the light most favorable to [the] [p]laintiff," gave "plausible support to the proposition that the [tribunal's members] were motivated by bias" because, "[w]hen the evidence substantially favors one party's version of a disputed matter, but an evaluator forms a conclusion in favor of the other side (without an apparent reason based in the evidence), it is plausible to infer ... that the evaluator has been influenced by bias." *Id.*

Columbia University does not aid Plaintiff's cause. We assume, without deciding, that the chief proposition from *Columbia University* Plaintiff relies on—that an inference of bias arises when an evaluator's decision in favor of one side lacks an apparent, evidence-based reason, and the evidence p.1198 substantially favors the other side— is correct. But that proposition has no application here. Simply put, DU's investigators were not faced with a situation in which the evidence substantially favored Plaintiff. Unlike in *Columbia University,* there was evidence presented in favor of Jane's claim that the sexual encounter was not consensual, and it cannot be said that the investigators lacked an evidence-based reason for reaching their decision. Thus, it would not be plausible or reasonable to infer merely from the investigators' weighing of the evidence that they were biased.

Further, even if we agreed with Plaintiff that the evidence before the investigators was so one-sided in Plaintiff's favor that their decision in favor of Jane could reasonably give rise to an inference of bias, this would still fall short of demonstrating bias based on gender. *Columbia University* itself acknowledges that an evaluator's decision at odds with the great weight of evidence "support[s] [an] inference of bias" but "not necessarily" a "bias on account of [gender]." *Id.* The Second Circuit instead concluded that additional allegations in the complaint gave "ample plausible support to a bias with respect to [gender]," namely "substantial criticism" from "the student body and in the public media, accusing the [school] of not taking seriously complaints of *female* students alleging sexual assault by *male* students" as well as an allegation that the school "was cognizant of, and sensitive to, these criticisms." *Id.* (emphasis added). Thus, in our view, the allegations at issue in *Columbia University* reflect gender-biased public pressure accompanied by procedural irregularity in the proceeding at issue. Here, however, Plaintiff has adduced only evidence of gender-neutral public pressure. So, even if we were to accept the inference of bias he presses, he has failed to adduce the additional evidence needed to demonstrate bias *on account of gender.*[14]

Fifth, Plaintiff argues that the severity of the sanction he received—expulsion— resulted from DU's anti-male bias. Under DU's policies, the outcome council is to consider a number of factors to determine an appropriate sanction for a student found responsible for violating DU's sexual-misconduct policy, including (1) the "nature and severity of the act," (2) the "number of complainants," (3) the "prior student conduct history of the respondent," (4) the outcome council's "assessment of the effect... the act or policy violation has on the complainant, community[,] and University environment," and (5) the "complainant['s] and community['s] safety." (Appellant's App. at A153 (capitalization standardized).) Plaintiff also elicited deposition testimony from Defendant Kristin Olson, a member of DU's outcome council in Plaintiff's proceeding, that, in her experience, the respondent was expelled in every case where investigators found non-consensual sexual conduct involving penetration. Plaintiff also points to DU's records confirming that, for the 14 non-consensual sexual contact cases between 2013 and 2016 that resulted in dismissal or rescission of an admission offer, each case involved a female complainant, a male respondent, and allegations of penetration.

Plaintiff contends that DU, in derogation of its own policies, expels males found responsible for non-consensual sexual contact involving penetration regardless of the circumstances. For instance, in his case, Plaintiff points out that several of the factors the outcome council was required to consider weighed in his favor: the allegations did not involve physical violence or p.1199 lead to a criminal investigation; only one complainant accused him of misconduct; he had no prior record of student conduct issues; and the facts that Plaintiff and Jane met socially after the incident and that DU did not impose an interim suspension on him after the complaint was filed suggest he posed no threat to Jane's or the community's safety. He argues that the outcome council simply ignored these factors and imposed expulsion without considering them. The severity of the sanction, Plaintiff asserts, gives rise to an inference of bias on account of gender, as it reflects a belief that males need to be sanctioned severely for sexual misconduct.

A factfinder could not reasonably infer from this evidence that the severity of the sanction DU imposed was motivated by Plaintiff's gender. First, Plaintiff ignores the fact that DU's policies, in addition to laying out factors for the outcome council to consider, also expressly state that, "[i]n general[,] violations of the non-consensual sexual contact provision" of the policy "typically result in a dismissal." (*Id.* at A154.) Moreover, much of Plaintiff's argument again relies to some degree on evidence of a statistical disparity between the numbers of men and women expelled from DU for engaging in non-consensual sexual contact involving penetration. However, for evidence of this nature to raise an inference of gender bias, it must eliminate obvious, nondiscriminatory explanations for the disparity. Again, Plaintiff has not eliminated the obvious, nondiscriminatory explanation that DU, as expressed in its own policy, has legitimate interests in expelling students—regardless of their gender—who engage in non-consensual sexual contact, and, though not expressed in its policies, DU might have even greater interests in doing so when that contact involves penetration. In short, something more is needed to show that the cited expulsions resulted from the fact the respondents were male rather than the fact they were found responsible for sexual misconduct, but Plaintiff has failed to adduce it.

To the extent Plaintiff contends that the outcome council ignored the factors it was required to consider in his proceeding, that contention is not borne out by the record. Plaintiff points to no evidence showing that the outcome council failed to consider the factors. In fact, the only evidence in the record on this point—Ms. Olson's deposition testimony—strongly suggests the outcome council did consider those factors when contemplating the sanction it would impose on Plaintiff. Her testimony also strongly suggests the out-come council concluded that the nature and severity of the contact (non-consensual penetration) and the threat Plaintiff posed to the community (as he did not consider himself responsible and was thus unlikely to rehabilitate) outweighed any of the factors that might be in his favor. The out-come council's letter to Plaintiff notifying him of its decision specifically referenced these two factors, explaining that its decision to expel him was "due to the nature and severity of [Plaintiff]'s actions and in an effort to protect the community." (Appellant's App. at A163.) We have no call to review the outcome council's consideration of these sanctioning factors, for, where the evidence regarding sanctioning factors is not clearly one-sided, the mere fact that Plaintiff or this court might have considered the factors differently or imposed a less severe sanction does not create a reasonable inference of bias, let alone bias based on gender. *See Doe v. Colgate Univ.*, 760 F. App'x 22, 33 (2d Cir. 2019); *cf. Davis ex rel. LaShonda D. v. Monroe Cty. Bd. of Educ.*, 526 U.S. 629, 648, 119 S.Ct. 1661, 143 L.Ed.2d 839 (1999) ("[C]ourts should refrain from second-guessing the disciplinary decisions made by school administrators.").

p.1200 Further, even if we agreed that DU's pattern of sanctions exhibited some bias against students who, like Plaintiff, are found responsible for non-consensual sexual contact involving penetration, this would not amount to a bias *on account of gender*. This is so because both men and women can engage in non-consensual sexual contact, and, for both men and women, that contact can involve penetration.[15] As we have explained above, evidence of a school's discriminatory treatment of a group that can include both men and women does not create a reasonable inference of gender discrimination. *See Adamson*, 514 F.3d at 1148-49. DU's treatment of students found responsible for non-consensual sexual contact involving penetration is gender-neutral because both men and women can be included in that group. Thus, DU's alleged bias against that group does not permit a reasonable inference of bias based on gender.

Sixth, Plaintiff argues that DU encouraged the filing of sexual-misconduct complaints specifically against males. For support, Plaintiff cites his own deposition testimony in which he stated that DU placed "numerous posters all around the school" to encourage the reporting of sexual misconduct and recalled seeing one "poster that said [']if you regret it, it was rape.[']" (Appellant's App. at A425-26.) In Plaintiff's view, this kind of encouragement was intended to increase the number of sexual-misconduct complaints in a way that targeted males.

To the extent Plaintiff contends that an inference of anti-male bias arises from DU's attempts to encourage sexual-misconduct reporting generally, we find any such argument unpersuasive. At most, encouragement of this nature might possibly be construed as exhibiting a bias against potential respondents because it increases the likelihood that potential respondents will be subjected to investigation and possibly sanctioned if found responsible. But both men and women can be potential respondents, and therefore any bias against them would not be bias on account of gender.

As for the specific poster Plaintiff recalls, the poster's language—"if you regret it, it was rape"—viewed in Plaintiff's favor, can reasonably be interpreted to encourage the reporting of sexual misconduct committed specifically by men against women. Although in modern usage "rape" can refer generally to "forced, non-consenting, or illegal sexual intercourse with another person" or "sexual violation or assault," regardless of the gender of the perpetrator or victim,[16] the term "[o]riginally" and still "chiefly" can refer to "the act or crime, *committed by a man,* of forcing a *woman* to have sexual intercourse with him against her will." *Rape,* Oxford English Dictionary (3d ed. 2008) (emphasis added). Thus, viewed in Plaintiff's favor, the poster could be understood to have been directed at women who had sexual encounters with men, and it encouraged them to view and report encounters with men they regretted as instances of sexual misconduct by equating regret, which typically is not viewed as an indication of misconduct, with rape, perhaps the most serious form of misconduct.

Even viewed in Plaintiff's favor, however, the poster does not create a genuine dispute that DU was motivated by considerations of gender in Plaintiff's proceeding. For one thing, there is no evidence suggesting that the poster Plaintiff recalls was sponsored or approved by DU or that its p.1201 message otherwise can be attributed to DU generally or to any of the decisionmakers in his proceeding specifically.[17] *See Hysten v. Burlington N. Santa Fe Ry. Co.,* 415 F. App'x 897, 911 (10th Cir. 2011) ("[E]vidence of discrimination in the decision-making process must be distinguished from 'stray remarks in the workplace, statements by nondecisionmakers, or statements by decisionmakers unrelated to the decisional process.'" (quoting *Clearwater v. Indep. Sch. Dist. No. 166,* 231 F.3d 1122, 1126 (8th Cir. 2000))). Thus, the poster's connection to DU's motivations in pursuing sexual-misconduct allegations generally, not to mention its motivations in regard to Plaintiff's proceeding particularly, is tenuous at best. And, even if the poster could be attributed somehow to DU or the decisionmakers at issue, it amounts to nothing more than "an isolated and ambiguous comment" that "is generally considered too abstract to support an inference of discrimination." *Adamson,* 514 F.3d at 1151. Beyond this, we think a single reference in Plaintiff's own deposition testimony to an ambiguously-worded poster with nothing connecting it to DU, the relevant decisionmakers, or Plaintiff's proceeding amounts to nothing more than a scintilla of evidence that is insufficient to withstand summary judgment. *See Turner,* 563 F.3d at 1142.

In sum, we conclude the district court did not err in determining that Plaintiff failed to adduce sufficient evidence to create a genuine dispute that DU was motivated by considerations of gender in the proceeding it brought against him. The only potential evidence of bias on account of gender Plaintiff presented was his recollection of the if-you-regret-it-it-was-rape poster, which is simply too thin a nail to hang a claim of gender bias on. Aside from the poster, Plaintiff's evidence demonstrates, at most, only that (1) as is almost certainly the case at nearly every school, the overwhelming majority of sexual-misconduct respondents are men, and (2) DU's policies and procedures exhibit an anti-respondent bias. As we have explained, neither the statistical disparity in the gender makeup of respondents nor evidence of an anti-respondent bias can create a reasonable inference of bias on account of gender.

We are not unmindful that the combination of this statistical disparity and overt anti-respondent bias—a combination not unlikely to recur with some frequency at other schools—raises palpable concerns that schools might be making a distinction without a real difference and that stereotypes and prejudices against a class protected by Title IX (males) are beginning to infect the enforcement of sexual-misconduct policies under the auspices of presumptions regarding an unprotected class (respondents). *See generally Univ. of Colo.,* 255 F. Supp. 3d at 1075-76.[18] Nevertheless, these concerns do not alter the obligation of a Title IX plaintiff opposing summary judgment to adduce evidence from which a reasonable factfinder could infer that the school's proceeding was motivated by considerations of gender. We will therefore affirm the grant of summary judgment to Defendants.

* * *

We AFFIRM the district court's summary judgment order dismissing with prejudice Plaintiff's Fourteenth Amendment Due Process and Title IX claims and dismissing without prejudice his state-law claims and his claim for declaratory relief.[19]

[1] Plaintiff's complaint also asserted several state-law claims and sought declaratory relief. After disposing of the substantive federal-law claims, the court declined to retain jurisdiction over the state-law claims, dismissed them and the request for declaratory relief without prejudice, and closed the case.

[2] Plaintiffs might fail to reference the correct constitutional amendment through mere inadvertence. Or, they might do so simply because they mistakenly believe they need only show that a defendant's actions should be attributed to government in the generic sense, without distinguishing between federal and state government. So, we have sometimes winked at a plaintiff's reliance on the incorrect amendment as an inconsequential mistake when the error appears to be the product of inadvertence and where the distinction would be immaterial to the analysis, *see Ward v. Anderson*, 494 F.3d 929, 932 n.3 (10th Cir. 2007); *see also Greene v. Impson*, 530 F. App'x 777, 779 n.3 (10th Cir. 2013); *Sawyer v. Burke*, 504 F. App'x 671, 673-74 (10th Cir. 2012), and district courts within this circuit have done the same, *see Sigg. v. Dist. Ct.*, No. 06-2436-KHV, 2007 WL 913926, at *5 n.9 (D. Kan. Mar. 23, 2007); *Thunder v. Gunja*, No. Civ.A03CV01575REBOES, 2005 WL 2141068, at *9 (D. Colo. Aug. 11, 2005), *adopted by* 2005 WL 2372816 (D. Colo. Sept. 27, 2005). Other courts of appeal have done so as well. *See Kell v. Smith*, 743 F. App'x 292, 295-96 (11th Cir. 2018); *Martial-Emanuel v. Holder*, 523 F. App'x 345, 349 n.1 (6th Cir. 2013); *Collins v. Univ. of N.H.*, 664 F.3d 8, 12 n.1 (1st Cir. 2011); *High v. Angleone*, 168 F.3d 499 (table), 1999 WL 97353, at *3 (9th Cir. 1999); *Bieregu v. Reno*, 59 F.3d 1445, 1454 (3d Cir. 1995), *abrogated on other grounds by Lewis v. Casey*, 518 U.S. 343, 116 S.Ct. 2174, 135 L.Ed.2d 606 (1996), *as recognized by Oliver v. Fauver*, 118 F.3d 175, 178 (3d Cir. 1997); *United States v. Couch*, 896 F.2d 78, 79-83 & n.2 (5th Cir. 1990). And, of course, excusing a mistaken reference to the wrong amendment is especially appropriate when, unlike here, the plaintiff is proceeding pro se and cannot be expected to identify the specific legal source of his claim with the precision of a trained lawyer. *See Firstenberg v. City of Santa Fe*, 696 F.3d 1018, 1024 (10th Cir. 2012). However, the error might also be the result of a calculated decision. For instance, plaintiffs might avoid reliance on the Fifth Amendment due to the limitations on such claims. *See generally Big Cats of Serenity Springs, Inc. v. Rhodes*, 843 F.3d 853, 858-64 (10th Cir. 2016); *Peoples v. CCA Detention Ctrs.*, 422 F.3d 1090, 1096-1108 (10th Cir. 2005).

Here, we cannot construe Plaintiff's claim as if brought under the Fifth Amendment. Plaintiff is represented by capable attorneys, and his choice to eschew reliance on the Fifth Amendment cannot be chalked up to mere inadvertence.

[3] As explained below, the DCL "ushered in a more rigorous approach to campus sexual misconduct allegations" by providing guidance that encouraged schools to take tougher stances on students accused of sexual misconduct. *Doe v. Purdue Univ.*, 928 F.3d 652, 668 (7th Cir. 2019). By informing schools that funding depended on compliance with OCR's guidance, the DCL was viewed as pressuring schools to adhere to its guidance or else lose federal funding. *See id.* at 668-69.

[4] For purposes of determining whether a private entity may be held liable as a state actor, the state-action requirement of the Fourteenth Amendment and the

under-color-of-state-law requirement of § 1983 are identical. *See Neil Young Freedom Concert*, 49 F.3d at 1446-47.

[5] Other circuits have readily employed this same principle without hesitation. *See Musso v. Suriano*, 586 F.2d 59, 61 n.4 (7th Cir. 1978); *Berrios v. Int'l Am. Univ.*, 535 F.2d 1330, 1332 n.5 (1st Cir. 1976); *Weise v. Syracuse Univ.*, 522 F.2d 397, 404 (2d Cir. 1975); *Blackburn v. Fisk Univ.*, 443 F.2d 121, 123 (6th Cir. 1971).

[6] After filing their motion for summary judgment, Defendants filed a motion to exclude Prof. Gruber's expert testimony pursuant to Fed. R. Evid. 702. Because the district court concluded it would not consider Prof. Gruber's report on other grounds, the court declined to resolve DU's motion to exclude her expert testimony under Rule 702 and denied the motion as moot. On appeal, some of Plaintiff's argument is directed at showing that Prof. Gruber was qualified and that her testimony should have been admitted under Rule 702. Because the district court never decided those issues, we do not address them.

[7] On appeal, Defendants assert that Plaintiff adduced no direct evidence of gender bias and that, even if we concluded the district court erred by refusing to consider Prof. Gruber's report, we should nonetheless affirm the dismissal of the Title IX claim because a party opposing summary judgment cannot rely solely on an expert report to create a genuine dispute on a material issue. This argument is debatable. *See KSR Int'l Co. v. Teleflex Inc.*, 550 U.S. 398, 427, 127 S.Ct. 1727, 167 L.Ed.2d 705 (2007) (explaining that "expert testimony ... may resolve or keep open certain questions of fact" at summary-judgment stage); *Talkington v. Atria Reclamelucifers Fabrieken BV*, 152 F.3d 254, 264 (4th Cir. 1998) (concluding that expert testimony on causation element, standing alone, is sufficient to support jury verdict). Defendants also argue that Prof. Gruber's report is unsworn and is thus not competent summary judgment evidence. This argument is likewise debatable. Prof. Gruber signed and dated her report and later signed and dated a declaration, sworn under penalty of perjury, stating that the report, which she attached, was a true and correct copy. These actions might satisfy the requirements of 28 U.S.C. § 1746, which would render Prof. Gruber's report competent for summary judgment purposes. *See* Fed. R. Civ. P. 56(c)(4) advisory committee's notes to 2010 Amendments. Ultimately, however, we decline to address these arguments because we conclude the district court properly refused to consider Prof. Gruber's report, regardless of whether it was competent summary judgment evidence.

[8] Under similar anti-discrimination statutes, statistical disparities of this nature are often used to prove a disparate-impact theory of liability, which does not require proof of intentional discrimination. Some courts of appeals, however, have held or suggested that a disparate-impact theory of liability is not cognizable under Title IX. *See Fort v. Dallas Indep. Sch. Dist.*, 82 F.3d 414 (table), 1996 WL 167072 at *3 n.3 (5th Cir. 1996) (noting circuit split). Although noting that "there has been some question whether Title IX prohibits disparate impact discrimination," we have suggested that a Title IX disparate-impact claim might be viable, *Mabry v. State Bd. of Cmty. Colls. & Occupational Educ.*, 813 F.2d 311, 316 n.6, 318 (10th Cir. 1987), but we have never directly addressed the issue. This appeal does not present an occasion to do so, as Plaintiff disclaims any reliance on a disparate-impact theory of liability. But, aside from proving disparate impact, "proper evidence of a statistical disparity may [also] generate an inference of intentional discrimination" if it "'tend[s] to show that there

was a causal connection between the outcome of the disciplinary proceedings and gender bias.'" *Haidak v. Univ. of Mass.-Amherst,* 933 F.3d 56, 75 (1st Cir. 2019) (brackets omitted) (quoting *Doe v. Trs. of Bos. Coll.,* 892 F.3d 67, 91 (1st Cir. 2018)).

[9] Further, statistical disparity by itself does little to inform the factfinder of whether the school was motivated by gender with respect to the particular proceeding brought against the plaintiff. *See Haidak,* 933 F.3d at 75 ("Even if one could infer from the data that another decision maker issued higher penalties based on [gender], that inference says little about whether the decision maker in this case brought to bear any bias on the basis of [gender]."); *Turner,* 563 F.3d at 1147 ("Turner's statistic regarding the gender imbalance of the ... workforce ... does not, without additional evidence, suggest that Turner herself experienced discrimination. The numbers fail to provide any information regarding whether the decision not to hire Turner, and that decision alone, involved discrimination on the basis of [gender]." (internal quotation marks omitted)).

[10] Plaintiff also points to Prof. Gruber's report, which asserts that the training received by the two investigators assigned to Plaintiff's case, Mr. Butler and Ms. Grove, was suffused with stereotypical assumptions about men and women, leading them to investigate Jane's allegations in a gender-biased way. We have already concluded that the district court did not err by declining to consider Prof. Gruber's report for purposes of Plaintiff's Title IX claim. We do not consider the report here either.

[11] In this same vein, Plaintiff points out that DU's Title IX Coordinator, Defendant Jean McAllister, referred to complainants as "victims" and "survivors" during her deposition and acknowledged approaching interviews of complainants with the belief that they are "survivor[s]" and that their "report[s] [are] legitimate." (Appellant's App. at A431-32.) Citing *Mallory v. Ohio Univ.,* 76 F. App'x 634, 640 (6th Cir. 2003), the district court concluded that any indication that Ms. McAllister had a bias against males was irrelevant because Plaintiff had failed to raise a genuine dispute that Ms. McAllister, who began her position with DU as the proceeding against Plaintiff neared its end, had any meaningful involvement in the proceeding. Plaintiff does not contest this conclusion on appeal, so his argument regarding Ms. McAllister's bias is waived. *See Talley v. Time, Inc.,* 923 F.3d 878, 906 n.28 (10th Cir. 2019).

[12] Other courts have also employed this rationale in employment discrimination cases involving employer policies that might be understood to discriminate against a group that may include both men and women, such as employees who suffer from infertility or employees who are new parents. *See, e.g., Saks v. Franklin Covey Co.,* 316 F.3d 337, 347 (2d Cir. 2003) ("Because male and female employees... are equally disadvantaged by the [policy], we conclude that the Plan does not discriminate on the basis of [gender]."); *Piantanida v. Wyman Ctr., Inc.,* 116 F.3d 340, 342 (8th Cir. 1997) (explaining that "[a]n employer's discrimination... based on a gender-neutral status potentially possessible by all employees, including men and women," is not cognizable); *cf. Hall v. Nalco Co.,* 534 F.3d 644, 646-49 (7th Cir. 2008) (implying that policy affecting group that includes both male and female employees is not cognizable).

[13] Plaintiff's only response to this analysis has been to argue that his evidence of DU's anti-respondent bias amounts to evidence of an anti-male bias because the

statistical evidence shows that respondents are overwhelmingly male. But we have already determined that Plaintiff's statistical evidence is insufficient because it fails to eliminate non-gender-based explanations for the disparity. Indeed, other courts have viewed a school's bias in favor of complainants as one of the legitimate, non-gender-based explanations for the disparity that bare statistical evidence fails to eliminate. *See, e.g., Univ. of Colo.,* 255 F. Supp. 3d at 1079.

[14] Plaintiff again resorts to Prof. Gruber's report to argue that the investigation was pockmarked by procedural deficiencies that disfavored Plaintiff. We again do not consider Prof. Gruber's report.

[15] Ms. Olson's deposition testimony makes clear that DU considers penetration to include oral, anal, or vaginal penetration with a penis, digit, or foreign object.

[16] *See also Rape,* American Heritage Dictionary of the English Language (5th ed. 2011) (defining the term without reference to the gender of either perpetrator or victim).

[17] In other contexts, when a plaintiff's claim hinges to some degree on a message contained in a poster, flyer, or the like, courts have often looked for indications that the message can be attributed to the defendant. *See, e.g., Child Evangelism Fellowship of N.J., Inc. v. Stafford Twp. Sch. Dist.,* 386 F.3d 514, 525 (3d Cir. 2004); *Munoz-Feliciano v. Monroe-Woodbury Cent. Sch. Dist.,* No. 13-CV-4340 (CS), 2015 WL 1379702, at *5 (S.D.N.Y Mar. 25, 2015); *DeCarolis v. Presbyterian Med. Ctr.,* No. 11-cv-1422, 2012 WL 12860872, at *6 (E.D. Pa. Aug. 20, 2012); *Chachas v. City of Ely,* 615 F. Supp. 2d 1193, 1209 (D. Nev. 2009). And in the context of challenges to sexual-misconduct disciplinary proceedings, courts have emphasized that circumstantial evidence of gender bias on the part of nondecisionmakers is largely irrelevant. *See, e.g., Haidak,* 933 F.3d at 75. We have made the same point in employment discrimination cases. *See, e.g., Turner,* 563 F.3d at 1147.

[18] This concern is only heightened when there is not only evidence that the school exhibits an anti-respondent bias generally but also colorable evidence that the school employed that bias in the sexual-misconduct proceeding at issue. Here, for instance, there is colorable evidence that the investigators:

• refused to follow leads that were potentially exculpatory;

• disbelieved Plaintiff from the outset due to the "innate motive" respondents have to lie about wrongdoing (Suppl. App. at 61), while failing to consider obvious motives Jane might have to lie about the extent to which she initiated or invited the sexual encounter with Plaintiff, such as her new boyfriend's insistence that she report the incident as well as his presence at her initial reporting and subsequent interviews;

• selectively determined which post-encounter evidence they would consider relevant (*e.g.,* considering Jane's allegation that Plaintiff offered her Aderall after the encounter in assessing Plaintiff's credibility but not considering Jane's inconsistent statements on whether the two saw each other after the encounter in assessing her credibility);

• allowed Jane's boyfriend to act both as Jane's support person who was present at her interviews and as a fact witness who provided information in the proceeding to corroborate Jane's story and to impeach the testimony of witnesses who contradicted her story, in violation of DU's policies;

- selectively viewed Jane as "heavily intoxicated," implicitly rejecting Plaintiff's and his roommate's statements that Jane exhibited no indication of intoxication in order to support a finding that Plaintiff coerced Jane into sex (Suppl. App. at 58) but then accepting Plaintiff's and his roommate's statement in order to find that Jane's intoxication had little effect on her ability to accurately recollect the encounter that night;
- faulted Plaintiff for making corrections to his summary statement and used it to attack his credibility, despite expressly inviting Plaintiff to make such corrections and apparently violating DU's informal policy allowing interviewees to correct summary statements in order to accurately reflect their testimony;
- emphasized inconsistencies in Plaintiff's and his roommate's story while disregarding numerous inconsistencies in the versions of the story told by Jane and her friend;
- suggested Plaintiff's failure to recollect details was indicative of deception and guilt while suggesting Jane's failure to recollect details was the result of intoxication;
- viewed Plaintiff's roommate's statements corroborating Plaintiff's story as tainted by Plaintiff's and his roommate's prior conferral regarding the events of that night, while not applying this same logic to the statements of Jane's friend who corroborated Jane's story, even though Jane called her friend specifically to relate to him "her portrayal of the night" and to tell him "that it was rape" (Appellant's App. at A229);
- attacked Plaintiff's and his roommate's credibility on the grounds they seemed overly eager to offer consistent denials of any on-campus alcohol use, without applying the same logic to the vague and inconsistent stories provided by Jane and her friend regarding their own on-campus alcohol use, even though DU offers amnesty to complainants who admit to on-campus drug and alcohol use, but not to respondents.

A few procedural irregularities in this vein are not necessarily uncommon or even all that troubling. After all, sexual-misconduct investigations and proceedings will not be perfect. But an accumulation of irregularities all disfavoring the respondent becomes deeply troubling because benign, stochastic explanations for the errors become implausible. Instead, it looks more like a railroading. Patterns of procedural irregularities like this become even more troubling when, as in the case of DU's investigative model, the investigators committing such errors are also the finders of fact on the ultimate issue of whether the alleged sexual misconduct occurred. Indeed, permitting, or even encouraging, an investigator who also acts as inquisitor, judge, and jury to harbor an anti-respondent bias is repugnant to basic notions of due process and substantial justice. However, as deeply troubling as this kind of bias may be, it is simply not proscribed by Title IX, which only prohibits discrimination "on the basis of [gender]." 20 U.S.C. § 1681(a).

[19] Plaintiff argues that the district court should have retained supplemental jurisdiction over his state-law claims because it erred in dismissing his federal-law claims. Because we conclude that the court properly dismissed the federal-law claims, we see no error in the court's decision to decline supplemental jurisdiction over the state-law claims.

918 F.3d 1094 (2019)

Tessa FARMER, Plaintiff-Appellee,
v.
KANSAS STATE UNIVERSITY, Defendant-Appellant.
Sara Weckhorst, Plaintiff-Appellee,
v.
Kansas State University, Defendant-Appellant.

No. 17-3207, No. 17-3208.

United States Court of Appeals, Tenth Circuit.

FILED March 18, 2019.

Farmer v. Kansas State University, 918 F. 3d 1094 (10th Cir. 2019)

Appeals from the United States District Court for the District of Kansas; (D.C. Nos. 2:16-CV-02255-JAR-GEBand 2:16-CV-02256-JAR-GEB).

Derek T. Teeter (Allan V. Hallquist and Michael T. Raupp, with him on the briefs), Husch Blackwell LLP, Kansas City, Missouri, for Defendant-Appellant.

Jonathon D. Fazzola (Dustin L. Van Dyk, Gary D. White, Jr., and Meaghan M. Girard, Palmer, Leatherman, White, Girard & Van Dyk, LLP, Topeka, Kansas, and Douglas E. Fierberg, The Fierberg National Law Group, PLLC, Traverse City, Michigan, with him on the brief), The Fierberg National Law Group, PLLC, Traverse City, Michigan, for Plaintiffs-Appellees.

Emily Martin and Neena Chaudhry, National Women's Law Center, Washington, D.C.; Sunu Chandy and Alexandra Brodsky, of counsel; and Seanna R. Brown, Maximillian S. Shifrin and Tiffany A. Miao, Baker & Hostetler, LLP, New York, New York, on the brief for Amici Curiae.

Before MATHESON, EBEL, and EID, Circuit Judges.

EBEL, Circuit Judge.

Congress, through Title IX, bans discrimination on the basis of sex in education programs receiving federal funding. Plaintiffs, two students at Kansas State University ("KSU"), allege that KSU, a recipient of federal educational funds, violated Title IX by being deliberately indifferent to reports it received of student-on-student sexual harassment which, in this case, involved rape. Often Title IX plaintiffs allege that a funding recipient's deliberate indifference to prior reports of rape caused the plaintiff subsequently to be raped or assaulted. But that is not the claim Plaintiffs assert here. Instead, they allege that KSU violated Title IX's ban against sex discrimination by being deliberately indifferent after Plaintiffs reported to KSU that other students had raped them, and that deliberate indifference caused Plaintiffs subsequently to be deprived of educational benefits that were available to other students. At the procedural posture presented by these interlocutory appeals, which address the denial of KSU's motions to dismiss, we accept as true Plaintiffs' factual allegations indicating that KSU was deliberately indifferent to their rape reports. That is not being challenged in these appeals. Accepting, then, that KSU was deliberately indifferent, the narrow legal question presented here involves the element of causation: what harm must Plaintiffs allege that KSU's deliberate indifference caused them?

KSU contends that, in order to state a Title IX claim, Plaintiffs must allege that the university's deliberate indifference caused each of them to undergo further incidents of actual harassment by other students. Plaintiffs assert, instead, that they state a viable Title IX claim by alleging that KSU's deliberate indifference to their reports of rape caused them to be vulnerable to further harassment, which in turn deprived them of the educational opportunities that KSU offers its students.

The Supreme Court has already answered the legal question presented here, ruling, as Plaintiffs allege, that a funding recipient's "deliberate indifference must, at a minimum, cause students to undergo harassment or make them liable or vulnerable to it." Davis ex rel. LaShonda D. v. Monroe Cty. Bd. of Educ., 526 U.S. 629, 644-45, 119 S.Ct. 1661, 143 L.Ed.2d 839 (1999) (alterations, internal quotation marks omitted) (emphasis added).

We conclude that, in this case, Plaintiffs have sufficiently alleged that KSU's deliberate indifference made each of them "vulnerable to" sexual harassment by allowing their student-assailants—unchecked and without the school investigating—to continue attending KSU along with Plaintiffs. This, as Plaintiffs adequately allege, caused them to withdraw from participating in the educational opportunities offered by KSU. Having jurisdiction under 28 U.S.C. § 1292(b), therefore, we AFFIRM the district court's decision to deny KSU's Fed. R. Civ. P. 12(b)(6) motions to dismiss Plaintiffs' Title IX claims. Our ruling, of course, does not address the merits of the issues in this case which must await further factual development.

I. OVERVIEW OF TITLE IX

We begin with a quick overview of Title IX, 20 U.S.C. §§ 1681-88. With exceptions not relevant here, Title IX provides that

> [n]o person in the United States shall, on the basis of sex, be excluded from participation in, be denied the benefits of, or be subjected to discrimination under any education program or activity receiving Federal financial assistance....

Id. § 1681(a). Congress enacted Title IX under its spending power, "conditioning an offer of federal funding on a promise by the recipient not to discriminate, in what amounts essentially to a contract between the Government and the recipient of funds." Gebser v. Lago Vista Indep. Sch. Dist., 524 U.S. 274, 286, 118 S.Ct. 1989, 141 L.Ed.2d 277 (1998). In enacting Title IX, Congress sought both "to avoid the use of federal resources to support discriminatory practices" and "to provide individual citizens effective protection against those practices." Cannon v. Univ. of Chicago, 441 U.S. 677, 704, 99 S.Ct. 1946, 60 L.Ed.2d 560 (1979).

Title IX is enforceable, not only by federal administrative agencies, but also through private causes of action, like the cases at issue here, brought by victims of prohibited sex discrimination against the federal funding recipient. See Jackson v. Birmingham Bd. of Educ., 544 U.S. 167, 173, 125 S.Ct. 1497, 161 L.Ed.2d 361 (2005). A funding recipient, however, "may be liable in damages under Title IX only for its own misconduct." Davis, 526 U.S. at 640, 119 S.Ct. 1661. "The recipient itself must 'exclud[e] [persons] from participation in, ... den[y] [persons] the benefits of, or ...

subjec[t] [persons] to discrimination under' its 'program[s] or activit[ies]' in order to be liable under Title IX." Id. at 640-41, 119 S.Ct. 1661 (quoting 20 U.S.C. § 1681(a)) (alterations added in Davis); see also id. at 640-43, 119 S.Ct. 1661.

That point is critical in this case because, although the sex discrimination that Title IX prohibits can include sexual harassment, see id. at 649-53, 119 S.Ct. 1661, the sexual harassment—rapes—alleged here were committed, not by the recipient KSU, but by KSU students. In such a situation, the funding recipient can only be liable for its own deliberately indifferent response to known sexual harassment by students against other students. See Gebser, 524 U.S. at 291, 118 S.Ct. 1989; Davis, 526 U.S. at 640-43, 119 S.Ct. 1661. Critically, "a recipient's deliberate indifference to one student's sexual harassment of another ... constitute[s] intentional discrimination on the basis of sex" prohibited by Title IX. Jackson, 544 U.S. at 182, 125 S.Ct. 1497 (citing Davis, 526 U.S. at 650, 119 S.Ct. 1661).

Here, Plaintiffs base their Title IX claims on KSU's deliberate indifference after Plaintiffs reported to KSU that other students had raped them. We accept as true the allegation that KSU responded with deliberate indifference to Plaintiffs' reports of rape. Plaintiffs then allege that KSU's deliberate indifference caused them to have to continue attending KSU with the student-rapists potentially emboldened by the indifference expressed by KSU which, in turn, caused Plaintiffs to withdraw from participating in educational opportunities that KSU offers and prevented them from using available KSU resources for fear of encountering the unchecked student-rapists and other students who knew of the rapes. It is in this way that Plaintiffs allege that KSU has excluded p.1099 them "from participation in, den[ied] [them] the benefits of, or subject[ed] [them] to discrimination under its programs or activities." Davis, 526 U.S. at 640-41, 119 S.Ct. 1661 (internal quotation marks, alterations omitted) (quoting 20 U.S.C. § 1681(a)).

Although Plaintiffs allege that KSU's response to their reports of rape was so deficient as to amount to deliberate indifference, we note that Title IX does not require a funding recipient to acquiesce in the particular remedial action a victim seeks. Nor does Title IX prescribe any particular mandatory remedial action. Davis

> stress[ed] that [the Court's] conclusion... —that recipients may be liable for their deliberate indifference to known acts of peer sexual harassment—does not mean that recipients can avoid liability only by purging their schools of actionable peer harassment or that administrators must engage in particular disciplinary action. ...
>
> ... [T]he recipient must merely respond to known peer harassment in a manner that is not clearly unreasonable.

Id. at 648-49, 119 S.Ct. 1661 (citations omitted).

II. BACKGROUND

With these general Title IX principles in mind, we consider Plaintiffs' specific factual allegations against KSU, accepted as true and viewed in the light most favorable to Plaintiffs. See Straub v. BNSF Ry. Co., 909 F.3d 1280, 1287 (10th Cir. 2018).

A. Plaintiff Tessa Farmer

Plaintiff Farmer alleged the following: In March 2015, she went to a fraternity party and became very drunk. A designated driver took Farmer back to her dorm room. At 2:00 a.m., Farmer received a Facebook message from T.R., another KSU student who Farmer knew from high school. T.R. invited Farmer to the fraternity house where the party was continuing, offering to pick up Farmer and drive her there. Farmer agreed. T.R. drove to Farmer's dorm, picked her up and took her to his room at the fraternity house, where the two had sex. T.R. then left the room, telling Farmer he was going to start his car, presumably to take her back to her dorm room. After T.R. left, C.M., another KSU student who was a stranger to Farmer and who had been hiding in the closet while T.R. and Farmer had sex, emerged from the closet and raped Farmer. When T.R. returned to the room, he was not surprised by C.M.'s presence or by Farmer's being upset and sobbing.

Farmer reported to the Riley County Police Department that C.M. had raped her. She also reported the rape to the director of the KSU Center for Advocacy, Response and Education ("CARE"). The CARE director told Farmer that, although she could report the rape to the KSU Interfraternity Council ("IFC"), the IFC would not investigate the rape but would only investigate the fraternity chapter more generally. Farmer, nevertheless, filed a complaint with the IFC; three months later the IFC responded to Farmer that the fraternity chapter as a whole had not violated any IFC policies.

Farmer later learned that, contrary to what KSU's CARE director had told her, there might be other avenues through which Farmer could complain to KSU about the rape. In August 2015, Farmer filed a complaint with KSU's Office of Institutional Equity, alleging C.M. had violated KSU's sexual misconduct policy. Farmer was told, however, that that policy did not cover fraternity houses.

Farmer, living in fear that she would run into her attacker, missed classes, p.1100 struggled in school, secluded herself from friends, withdrew from KSU activities in which she had previously taken a leadership role, fell into a deep depression, slept excessively, and engaged in self-destructive behaviors such as excessive drinking and slitting her wrist. Farmer alleges that,

> [b]y refusing to investigate off-campus sexual assaults at fraternities and fraternity events, like those [she] endured, K-State makes students like Tessa [Farmer] more vulnerable to rape because it sends a message to fraternity members that students can rape other students with no fear of school disciplinary action. K-State's practice ignores the reality that many off-campus sexual assaults adversely impact the on-campus educational environment for victims, just as it did Tessa's.

(Aplt. App. 25 ¶ 73.)

B. Plaintiff Sara Weckhorst

Plaintiff Weckhorst alleged that, in April 2014, she attended a fraternity event at Pillsbury Crossing, "a frequent K-State party location not far from campus." (Id. 620 ¶ 13.) There, Weckhorst "consum[ed] a large amount of alcohol and blacked out" while speaking with J.F., another KSU student who was one of the fraternity's designated drivers. (Id.) J.F. took the passed-out Weckhorst to his truck and raped her in front of approximately fifteen other students, some of whom took video and photographs of the rape which they later posted on social media. J.F. then drove Weckhorst to the fraternity house. On the way, he again sexually assaulted her. At the fraternity house, "J.F. took Sara to the 'sleep room,' lined with beds, and raped her again. When he was finished, J.F. left her there, naked and passed out, and joined other fraternity members in partying downstairs." (Id. ¶ 15.) Several hours later, Weckhorst awoke to find another student and fraternity member, J.G., raping her. Weckhorst "made her way out of the bed and to a nearby patio," but J.G. followed and raped Weckhorst again. (Id. 621 ¶ 16.)

Weckhorst sought help at the KSU Women's Center and the Manhattan, Kansas, Rape Crisis Center. The director of the Women's Center helped Weckhorst file a complaint with the KSU Affirmative Action Office. As a result, a KSU investigator interviewed Weckhorst but told her that KSU "would do nothing about the rapes or the two student-assailants because the rapes occurred off-campus." (Id. 622 ¶ 22.) Weckhorst then reported the rapes to the Riley County Police. In the meantime, the director of the KSU Women's Center called the two perpetrators and told them Weckhorst had filed charges against them, which according to the allegations tipped off "the student-assailants and g[ave] them an opportunity to coordinate their stories," in addition to invading Weckhorst's privacy rights, exposing her to potential retaliation, compromising her safety, and placing her in fear. (Id. 624-25 ¶ 33.)

Weckhorst later met with two associate deans for student life at KSU. They reiterated that KSU would do nothing because the rapes occurred off campus. But the deans encouraged Weckhorst to file a complaint about the presence of alcohol at the fraternity party. She did so anonymously and, as a result, KSU's Interfraternity Council ("IFC") suspended the fraternity's charter.

Weckhorst and her parents continued to ask KSU to investigate the rapes, but KSU refused. Without permission, one of the associate deans took language from an email received from Weckhorst and filed it as a complaint with KSU's Office of Greek Affairs and the IFC. This action "released Sara's highly sensitive, private information, including her full name and a detailed p.1101 description of the multiple rapes, to student peers on the IFC board without any chance of this action benefitting Sara" because the Office of Greek Affairs "did not have jurisdiction to punish the student-assailants, only the fraternity." (Id. 629 ¶ 48.) Because of this unauthorized release of information, Weckhorst "has since lived day-to-day not knowing who she might encounter who knows the details about the nightmare she endured." (Id. 630 ¶ 48.)[1]

Moreover, because the alleged perpetrators remained on campus, Weckhorst alleges she

> is always afraid, apprehensive, and hyper-alert, on-campus and off. Every man who passes her on the sidewalk terrifies her. At least once a day on-campus, Sara is overcome by panic, anxious that any passing man could be one of the student-assailants. She is constantly on the lookout for J.F. Recently, walking to the K-State library she passed a man who turned toward her. She jumped, screamed, and began to cry. Sara only uses campus resources like the library when she is

joined by friends or her Chi Omega sorority sisters, and otherwise stayed home to avoid being alone in a campus setting.

(Id. 637 ¶ 77.) Weckhorst's grades "plummeted" and she lost her academic scholarship. (Id. 638 ¶ 79.) She "has exhibited symptoms of post-traumatic stress disorder," has nightmares, has distanced herself from family and friends, and "has decreased her involvement in her sorority and philanthropy and has turned down leadership opportunities." (Id. 637 ¶ 78, 638 ¶ 80.) Although she "wants to continue her K-State education, ... doing so means facing emboldened student-assailants who know K-State will protect them and not the victim of their attacks." (Id. 637 ¶ 75.) Similar, to Plaintiff Farmer, Plaintiff Weckhorst alleges that,

> [b]y refusing to investigate off-campus sexual assaults at fraternities and fraternity events, like those Sara [Weckhorst] endured, K-State makes students, like Sara, more vulnerable to rape because it sends a message to fraternity members that students can rape other students with no fear of school disciplinary action. K-State's practice ignores the reality that many off-campus sexual assaults adversely impact the on-campus educational environment for victims, just as it did Sara's.

(Id. 638-39 ¶ 83.)

C. These cases

Each Plaintiff separately sued KSU, asserting claims under Title IX and state law. In each case, KSU moved under Fed. R. Civ. P. 12(b)(6) to dismiss all claims. The district court denied KSU's motions to dismiss the Title IX claims; that is the matter now before us on appeal.[2]

The district court held that each Plaintiff had sufficiently alleged an actionable Title IX violation. In reaching that conclusion, the district court, citing Davis, 526 U.S. 629, 119 S.Ct. 1661, 143 L.Ed.2d 839, and Rost ex rel. K.C. v. Steamboat Springs RE-2 School District, 511 F.3d 1114, 1119 (10th Cir. 2008), began by noting that, to p.1102 state a Title IX claim, Plaintiffs had to allege sex discrimination that occurred within a KSU educational program or activity; KSU had actual knowledge of, but was deliberately indifferent to, sexual harassment that was so severe, pervasive and objectively offensive that it deprived Plaintiffs of access to the educational benefits or opportunities provided by KSU; and that KSU's deliberate indifference caused each Plaintiff, at a minimum, to undergo harassment or made her liable or vulnerable to it. In its motions to dismiss, KSU argued, among other things, that Plaintiffs had failed to allege that any deliberate indifference by KSU had caused harm to Plaintiffs that is actionable under Title IX. The district court rejected that argument and declined to dismiss Plaintiffs' Title IX claims.

At KSU's request, the district court invoked 28 U.S.C. § 1292(b) and

> certifie[d] its ... Memorandum and Order... for interlocutory appeal for determination of the following controlling questions of law: (1) whether Plaintiff was required to allege, as a distinct element of her Title IX claim, that KSU's deliberate indifference caused her to suffer actual further harassment, rather than alleging that Defendant's post-assault deliberate indifference made her 'liable or vulnerable to' harassment; and (2) if Plaintiff is required to plead actual

further harassment, whether her allegations of deprivation of access to educational opportunities satisfy this pleading requirement.

(Aplt. App. 606; see also id. 1247.) The Tenth Circuit, then, permitted KSU to pursue these interlocutory appeals presenting these certified questions, see 28 U.S.C. § 1292(b), and ordered these appeals consolidated.[3]

III. STANDARD OF REVIEW

This court reviews de novo the district court's rulings on KSU's Fed. R. Civ. P. 12(b)(6) motions to dismiss, accepting as true all well pled facts and viewing those facts in the light most favorable to Plaintiffs. See Straub, 909 F.3d at 1287. "To withstand a motion to dismiss, a complaint must contain enough allegations of fact 'to state a claim that is plausible on its face.'" Id. (quoting Bell Atl. Corp. v. Twombly, 550 U.S. 544, 570, 127 S.Ct. 1955, 167 L.Ed.2d 929 (2007)).

IV. LEGAL DISCUSSION

Accepting, for the purpose of these interlocutory appeals, that Plaintiffs' factual allegations charge that KSU was deliberately indifferent to their reports that they had been raped, the narrow question we consider is whether each "Plaintiff was required to allege, as a distinct element of her Title IX claim, that KSU's deliberate indifference caused her to suffer actual further harassment, rather than alleging that Defendant's post-assault deliberate indifference made her '... vulnerable to' harassment." (Aplt. App. 606.) KSU asserts that each Plaintiff must allege, as an element of her Title IX claim, that KSU's deliberate indifference caused her to be subjected to actual further harassment by a student. Plaintiffs, instead, contend that it is sufficient for them to allege that KSU's deliberate indifference made them "vulnerable to" harassment. As explained below, Plaintiffs have the more persuasive p.1103 argument and we, therefore, affirm the district court's decision.

A. It is sufficient for Plaintiffs to allege that KSU's deliberate indifference made them "vulnerable to" sexual harassment. Title IX does not require a subsequent sexual assault before a plaintiff can sue.

The Supreme Court, in Davis, has already answered the legal question presented here. To explain, we begin with the statutory language. Title IX provides:

[n]o person in the United States shall, on the basis of sex, be excluded from participation in, be denied the benefits of, or be subjected to discrimination under any education program or activity receiving Federal financial assistance....

20 U.S.C. § 1681(a) (emphasis added). In applying Title IX's language—"[n]o person... shall, on the basis of sex, ... be subjected to discrimination ..."—to a case involving student-on-student harassment, the Supreme Court ruled:

If a funding recipient does not engage in harassment directly, it may not be liable for damages unless its deliberate indifference "subject[s]" its students to harassment. That is, the deliberate indifference must, at a minimum, "cause [students] to undergo" harassment or "make them liable or vulnerable" to it.

Random House Dictionary of the English Language 1415 (1966) (defining "subject" as "to cause to undergo the action of something specified; expose" or "to make liable or vulnerable; lay open; expose"); Webster's Third New International Dictionary 2275 (1961) (defining "subject" as "to cause to undergo or submit to: make submit to a particular action or effect: EXPOSE").

Davis, 526 U.S. at 644-45, 119 S.Ct. 1661 (emphasis added).

Davis, then, clearly indicates that Plaintiffs can state a viable Title IX claim by alleging alternatively either that KSU's deliberate indifference to their reports of rape caused Plaintiffs "'to undergo' harassment or 'ma[d]e them liable or vulnerable' to it." 526 U.S. at 645, 119 S.Ct. 1661 (emphasis added); see Fitzgerald v. Barnstable Sch. Comm., 504 F.3d 165, 172 (1st Cir. 2007) (citing Davis and stating that "to 'subject' a student to harassment, the institution's deliberate indifference must, at a minimum, have caused the student to undergo harassment, made her more vulnerable to it, or made her more likely to experience it"), rev'd on other grounds, 555 U.S. 246, 129 S.Ct. 788, 172 L.Ed.2d 582 (2009); id. at 172 (stating that Davis's language, "mak[ing] them liable or vulnerable to" harassment, "sweeps" broader than requiring further actual harassment to have occurred); Hernandez v. Baylor Univ., 274 F.Supp.3d 602, 613 (W.D. Tex. 2017) (citing Davis and stating that "the Supreme Court has made clear that to 'subject' a student to harassment a school need only make the student vulnerable to that harassment"; further stating that a recipient's actionable "discriminatory harm can include the harm faced by student-victims who are rendered vulnerable to future harassment and either leave school or remain at school and endure an educational environment that constantly exposes them to a potential encounter with their harasser or assailant"; elaborating that the required harm could include "forcing the student to change his or her study habits ... or lowering the student's grades"); see also, e.g., Joyce v. Wright State Univ., No. 3:17-cv-387, 2018 WL 3009105, at *8 (S.D. Ohio June 15, 2018); Karasek v. Regents of Univ. of Calif., No. 15-cv-03717-WHO, 2015 WL 8527338, at *12-*13 (N.D. Cal. Dec. 11, 2015) (unreported) (citing cases); Takla v. Regents of Univ. of Calif., No. 2:15-cv-04418-CAS(), 2015 WL 6755190, at *4-*5 (C.D. Cal. Nov. 2, 2015) (unreported); Kelly v. Yale Univ., No. Civ.A 3:01-CV-1591, 2003 WL 1563424, at *4-*5 (D. Conn. Mar. 26, 2003) (unreported). To underscore that a Title IX plaintiff is not required to allege that she suffered actual additional incidents of sexual harassment, the Supreme Court in Davis referred to the Random House Dictionary definition of "subject" to include, "to make liable ...; lay open; expose." Davis, 526 U.S. at 645, 119 S.Ct. 1661.

KSU's contrary argument, that Plaintiffs must allege (and eventually prove) that KSU's deliberate indifference to their reports of rape caused each Plaintiff to endure further actual incidents of sexual harassment simply ignores Davis's clear alternative language recognizing that a funding recipient's "deliberate indifference must, at a minimum, 'cause students to undergo' harassment or make them 'liable or vulnerable to'" sexual harassment, 526 U.S. at 645, 119 S.Ct. 1661 (emphasis added). We must give effect to each part of that sentence.

Doing so is consistent with Title IX's objectives, which include protecting individual students against discriminatory practices, Cannon, 441 U.S. at 704, 99 S.Ct. 1946.

The alternative offered by the University —i.e., that a student must be harassed or assaulted a second time before the school's clearly unreasonable response to the initial incident becomes actionable, irrespective of the deficiency of the school's response, the impact on the student, and the other circumstances of the case—runs counter to the goals of Title IX and is not convincing.

Karasek, 2015 WL 8527338, at *12.

Once a funding recipient, like KSU, has actual knowledge of sexual harassment that is severe, pervasive and objectively offensive enough to deprive a student of access to the educational benefits and resources the recipient offers,[4] see Davis, 526 U.S. at 633, 650-51, 119 S.Ct. 1661, the recipient cannot, acting with deliberate indifference, turn a blind eye to that harassment. See id. at 641, 119 S.Ct. 1661 (indicating that funding recipient can be liable under Title IX for "remain[ing] idle in the face of known student-on-student harassment"). Critically, then, KSU's alleged liability stems directly from its own conduct, its own deliberate indifference to known student-on-student sexual harassment occurring in its programs and activities that is sufficiently severe, pervasive, and objectively offensive enough to deprive a student of access to the educational opportunities the recipient provides. See Davis, 526 U.S. at 633, 119 S.Ct. 1661. KSU is wrong to contend that, by holding it liable for its own deliberate indifference to the serious rape charges, we are requiring the university to remediate the harm caused by the student rapists rather than KSU itself.

We conclude, then, that Plaintiffs can state a viable Title IX claim for student-on-student harassment by alleging that the funding recipient's deliberate indifference caused them to be "vulnerable to" further harassment without requiring an allegation of subsequent actual sexual harassment.

B. Plaintiffs have adequately pled that KSU made them "vulnerable to" harassment

Plaintiffs sufficiently pled that KSU's deliberate indifference to their reports of rape made them vulnerable to harassment by alleging that the fear of running into their student-rapists caused them, among other things, to struggle in school, lose a scholarship, withdraw from activities KSU offers its students, and avoid going anywhere on campus without being accompanied by friends or sorority sisters. See Joyce, 2018 WL 3009105, at *7-*8 (S.D. Ohio) (declining to dismiss Title IX claim based on funding recipient university's failure to enforce restraining order prohibiting assailant from being on campus because "it could be said that [university's] alleged failure to enforce the expulsion order made [plaintiff] Joyce 'vulnerable' to additional incidents of sexual assault and sexual harassment by [the perpetrator], even though she never actually encountered him on campus"); Kelly, 2003 WL 1563424, at *4-*5 (D. Conn.) (holding Title IX plaintiff sufficiently alleged that funding recipient's deliberate indifference to her reported rape—by ignoring her "requested academic and residential accommodations after the assault" and her reported "discomfort and fear that she would feel if she encountered" the alleged assailant—made her "liable or vulnerable" to her assailant's harassment, even though no further actual harassment occurred because victim left her dorm and her classes); see also Doe ex rel. Doe v. Coventry Bd. of Educ., 630 F.Supp.2d 226, 233 (D. Conn. 2009) (stating that a reasonable jury could find that funding recipient forcing high school victim of sexual assault to attend school with her assailant amounted to sufficiently severe harassment to deprive victim of access to educational opportunities, based on "potential interactions" between victim and the student harasser); Doe ex rel. Doe v. Derby Bd. of Educ., 451 F.Supp.2d 438, 440, 444-45 (D. Conn. 2006) (holding, in case where junior high student reported that senior high student raped her and where funding recipient housed both junior and senior high schools in same building, funding recipient could be liable under Title IX for its post-assault deliberate indifference which "constantly exposed" the plaintiff "to the possibility of an encounter with" the perpetrator, even if there was no evidence that the perpetrator actually harassed the victim after she reported rape).

Plaintiffs' allegations are quite specific and reasonable under the circumstances. Plaintiffs allege more than a general fear of running into their assailants. They allege that their fears have forced them to take very specific actions that deprived them of the educational opportunities offered to other students. In addition, they have alleged a pervasive atmosphere of fear at KSU of sexual assault caused by KSU's inadequate action in these cases. A Title IX plaintiff's alleged fear of encountering her attacker must be objectively reasonable, but under the horrific circumstances alleged here Plaintiffs have adequately alleged that KSU's deliberate indifference to their rape reports reasonably deprived them of educational opportunities available to other students at KSU. See Williams v. Bd. of Regents of Univ. Sys. of Ga., 477 F.3d 1282, 1297 (11th Cir. 2007) (stating that student rape victim's decision to withdraw from school was "reasonable and expected" "[i]n light of the harrowing ordeal" she endured). Future cases will undoubtedly be asked to draw lines on when a victim's fear of further sexual harassment is sufficient to deprive that student of educational opportunities that the educational institution offers to others, but we have no hesitation in concluding that the allegations in these complaints are sufficient to survive a motion to dismiss, where all inferences are drawn in favor of Plaintiffs.

p.1106 C. KSU's arguments to the contrary are unavailing

We now briefly address KSU's contrary arguments. KSU latches on to a number of cases invoking the phrases "further discrimination" or "further sexual harassment."

1. Rost ex rel. K.C. v. Steamboat Springs RE-2 School District, 511 F.3d 1114 (10th Cir. 2008), and Escue v. Northern Oklahoma College, 450 F.3d 1146 (10th Cir. 2006)

The primary cases on which KSU relies are the Tenth Circuit's decisions in Rost ex rel. K.C. v. Steamboat Springs RE-2 School District, 511 F.3d 1114 (10th Cir. 2008), and Escue v. Northern Oklahoma College, 450 F.3d 1146 (10th Cir. 2006). As detailed below, Rost and Escue were decided at the summary judgment stage of litigation, rather than at the pleading stage. In each case, the Tenth Circuit upheld the district court's summary judgment determination that the Title IX plaintiff had failed to present sufficient evidence for a reasonable jury to find that the funding recipient was deliberately indifferent. In making that determination, the Tenth Circuit pointed to evidence that the sexual harassment stopped after the funding recipient took action. Thus, although both cases did look at whether there had been continuing sexual harassment after the recipient took remedial action, they did so for the purpose of illuminating whether the funding recipient had been clearly unreasonable. Neither case had occasion to address the question at issue here, what injury does the funding recipient's deliberate indifference have to cause a plaintiff to be actionable under Title IX. Neither case held that a Title IX plaintiff was required to allege subsequent actual incidents of sexual harassment had occurred following the school's inadequate response to the victim's complaint.

In our cases, by contrast, because they come to us on an interlocutory appeal on the pleadings, all parties have to accept, and do accept, that KSU was deliberately indifferent in failing to take remedial actions. Thus, the issue presented in Rost and Escue—whether the educational institution was deliberately indifferent—is not before us. Instead, here KSU is seeking to add a new pleading burden to a Title IX claimant, which is that, even accepting that KSU was deliberately indifferent, a Title IX plaintiff must further allege as an element of her case that subsequent discrete acts of sexual harassment directed at her followed the funding recipient's deliberately indifferent response to her complaints.

Plaintiffs, instead, argue—and we have agreed—that once they show that the funding recipient was deliberately indifferent to their complaints of peer sexual harassment, they can show the requisite harm caused by that deliberate indifference by alleging and proving that the prior sexual assaults were so grievous and the likelihood of continuing to encounter the sexual predators on campus so credible that KSU's inaction by itself deprived them of the "benefits ... under any education program ... receiving Federal financial assistance." Rost, 511 F.3d at 1119. In short, they allege that KSU created such an adverse environment for learning for them by its dismissive treatment of their complaints of rape that it was that environment that reasonably prevented them from accessing the educational opportunities available to other students. That issue was not presented in nor resolved by either Rost or Escue.

In Escue, a college student alleged that her professor sexually harassed her. 450 F.3d at 1149. Once the student reported the harassment to the school, the school acted to prevent further contact between the student and the professor, including immediately transferring the student out of the offending professor's class, confronting the professor about his behavior, and eventually non-renewing him. Id. at 1150. This court determined that the school's actions (which are dramatically different from essentially no action taken here by KSU) were sufficient to rebut the plaintiff's allegation that the University had been deliberately indifferent. Id. at 1154-56. In reaching that conclusion on the deliberate indifference issue, the Tenth Circuit noted that, "Ms. Escue [the student] does not allege that further sexual harassment occurred as a result of [the school's] deliberate indifference." Id. at 1155. That determination was made in the context of illuminating the adequacy of the university's actions. Nothing in that opinion held or even suggested that a complaining student would have to show subsequent offending conduct as a causation element in order to prevail even after the funding recipient had been found to have been deliberately indifferent.

In Rost, a special education student alleged that several of her male high school classmates coerced her into performing sexual acts with them. 511 F.3d at 1117. Rost upheld summary judgment for the recipient school district because there was no evidence that the school district's response —"immediately contact[ing] law enforcement officials, cooperat[ing] fully in the investigation, and ke[eping] informed of the investigation"—was so unreasonable as to amount to deliberate indifference. Id. at 1121. It was in that context that Rost noted that the student-victim's mother "does not contend that further sexual harassment occurred as a result of the district's deliberate indifference after [the student-victim's] disclosure" of the ongoing sexual harassment to the school district. Id. at 1123-24. In fact, there was no opportunity for further harassment there because the victim's mother withdrew the victim from the school and "[t]here [wa]s no evidence in the record that Ms. Rost was willing to work with school officials and allow K.C. to return to school under some accommodation." Id. at 1124. Still, we noted that, "[i]f K.C. had expressed interest in returning to the school and school officials had not provided a safe educational environment, then she would likely have a Title IX claim." Id. That is, of course, essentially the issue that is presented in our case.

Admittedly, in the course of concluding that the school district was not deliberately indifferent, Rost mentions causation. Id. at 1123. But causation was not listed as one of the issues in that case. Moreover, Rost certainly did not hold that a Title IX plaintiff had to prove an actual subsequent sexual assault or harassment in order to state a viable Title IX claim. If anything, Rost's closing hypothetical suggests that, had the victim returned to school and had the district had been deliberately indifferent, causing an unsafe school environment, that would "likely" be enough to state a Title IX claim against the district. Id. at 1124.

It is not surprising, in addressing the question of whether the educational funding recipient had been "deliberately indifferent," that courts might look to see whether the offending action continued thereafter. However, consulting subsequent behavior as an evidentiary aid in determining if the school's action taken had been deliberately indifferent is a wholly different thing than requiring a continuation of the offending behavior as a separate element of causation before a Title IX claim may be maintained.

2. Out-of-circuit cases

KSU also cites to a group of out-of-circuit cases that it believes supports its position. Most relevant is the Eleventh Circuit's decision in Williams v. Board of Regents of University System of Georgia, 477 F.3d 1282 (11th Cir. 2007), a case cited by both parties. In that case, Plaintiff Williams alleged that the funding recipients at issue there—the University of Georgia and its athletic association, id. at 1294—were deliberately indifferent, id. at 1288-90.[5] The Eleventh Circuit did say "that a Title IX plaintiff at a motion to dismiss stage must allege that the Title IX recipient's deliberate indifference to the initial discrimination subjected the plaintiff to further discrimination." Id. at 1296 (emphasis added). Importantly, however, Williams defined "further discrimination" not to require further overt acts of assault or abuse. Instead, the Eleventh Circuit recognized that injuries similar to those Plaintiffs allege here would satisfy its "further harassment" requirement. Williams explained that "further discrimination" included "effectively denying Williams an opportunity to continue to attend" the University of Georgia by delaying any action against the student-rapists for months and by failing "to take any precautions that would prevent future attacks" by the student-rapists themselves or other "like-minded" students by, for example, removing the alleged student-rapists from student housing or suspending them, or by "implementing a more protective sexual harassment policy to deal with future incidents," id. at 1296-97; see also, e.g., Hernandez, 274 F.Supp.3d at 613 (W.D. Tex.) (holding that, "[w]hile allegations of further assault or harassment are necessary for a claim under Title IX," that requirement can be met by allegations of "harm faced by student-victims who are rendered vulnerable to future harassment and either leave school or remain at school and endure an educational environment that constantly exposes them to a potential encounter with their harasser or assailant" (emphasis added)); Kinsman v. Fla. State Univ. Bd. of Trs., No. 4:15cv235, 2015 WL 11110848, at *4 (N.D. Fla. Aug. 12, 2015) (unreported) (applying Williams to require allegations that the funding recipient's deliberate indifference caused "further discrimination," but holding such "further discrimination" can include the hostile environment created by "the possibility of further encounters between a rape victim and her attacker," which can "deprive the victim of access to educational opportunities provided by a university" (internal quotation marks omitted)).

KSU further cites decisions from other circuits that it argues require a showing of "further harassment" or "further discrimination." But those cases are easily distinguishable. See K.T. v. Culver-Stockton College, 865 F.3d 1054, 1058 (8th Cir. 2017) (addressing situation where there was no opportunity for further harassment because the victim did not attend the school); Reese v. Jefferson School District No. 14J, 208 F.3d 736, 738, 740 (9th Cir. 2000) (addressing situation where there was no opportunity for further harassment because students involved were graduating.)

In conclusion, the out-of-circuit cases that KSU cites are not only not binding on us but are also either distinguishable or they end up ultimately supporting the conclusion we reach here. To the extent that ambiguous dicta can be found in any of them, they certainly cannot p.1109 affect the binding guidance that we get from the Supreme Court in Davis, 526 U.S. at 644-45, 119 S.Ct. 1661.[6]

V. CONCLUSION

Plaintiffs alleged that they reported to KSU that other KSU students had raped them. We must assume for purposes of these interlocutory appeals that KSU was deliberately indifferent in responding to Plaintiffs' rape reports by failing to take any reasonable action to address and remedy those matters. The Supreme Court, in Davis, held that, to be actionable, a federal education funding recipient's deliberate indifference to reports of student-on-student sexual harassment—here, rape— "must, at a minimum, cause students to undergo harassment or make them liable or vulnerable to it." 526 U.S. at 644-45, 119 S.Ct. 1661 (internal quotation marks, alterations omitted) (emphasis added). We conclude, therefore, that a Title IX plaintiff must allege, at a minimum, that the funding recipient's deliberate indifference caused her to be vulnerable to further harassment. Plaintiffs have met that pleading requirement here by alleging, among other things, that KSU's deliberate indifference caused them objectively to fear encountering their unchecked assailants on campus, which in turn caused Plaintiffs to stop participating in the educational opportunities KSU offered its students. We, therefore, AFFIRM the district court's decision to deny KSU's motions to dismiss Plaintiffs' Title IX claims.

[1] Although Weckhorst alleges that KSU was deliberately indifferent because it did very little in response to her reports of rape, she also alleges that some of KSU's alleged actions affirmatively caused her additional harm. For example, Weckhorst alleged that KSU informed the student-rapists that Weckhorst had gone to the police and KSU, without permission, and had released confidential information about Weckhorst and the rapes to fellow students.

[2] The district court dismissed the state-law claims. Those claims are not before us in these interlocutory appeals.

[3] In light of the narrow issues presented by these interlocutory appeals pursued under § 1292(b), we have no occasion here to address KSU's contention that the sexual harassment of which Plaintiffs complain did not occur within a KSU program or activity and, thus, KSU is not responsible for student-on-student sexual harassment occurring off campus at fraternity parties or in fraternity houses.

[4] No one asserts that the sexual harassment alleged in these cases is not sufficiently extreme.

[5] KSU asserts that Williams is a pre-assault deliberate indifference case. In fact, the plaintiff in Williams asserted claims alleging the funding recipients were deliberately indifferent both before and after she was sexually assaulted. See 477 F.3d at 1288-90, 1296-97.

[6] KSU finally asserts that Plaintiffs lack Article III standing to assert their claims. KSU did not raise this argument below and the district court did not certify this question for interlocutory appeal. We address the argument briefly because Article III standing implicates our jurisdiction. However, Plaintiffs have adequately alleged their standing under Article III, which "requires allegations—and, eventually, proof—that the plaintiff personally suffered a concrete and particularized injury in connection with the conduct about which [s]he complains." Trump v. Hawaii, ___ U.S. ___, 138 S.Ct. 2392, 2416, 201 L.Ed.2d 775 (2018) (internal quotation marks, alteration omitted). Plaintiffs have alleged that the conduct of which they complain caused them a concrete and particularized injury by depriving them of access to the educational resources and opportunities KSU offers its students.

859 F.3d 1280 (2017)

Abigail ROSS, Plaintiff-Appellant,

v.

UNIVERSITY OF TULSA, Defendant-Appellee.

Equal Rights Advocates; SurvJustice Inc., Amici Curiae.

No. 16-5053.

United States Court of Appeals, Tenth Circuit.

June 20, 2017.

Ross v. University of Tulsa, 859 F. 3d 1280 (10th Cir. 2017)

p.1282 Appeal from the United States District Court for the Northern District of Oklahoma; (D.C. No. 4:14-CV-00484-TCK-PJC).

John Clune, Hutchinson Black and Cook, LLC, Boulder, Colorado (Lauren E. Groth, Hutchinson Black and Cook, LLC, Boulder, Colorado, J. Spencer Bryan, and Steven J. Terrill, Bryan & Terrill Law, PLLC, Tulsa, Oklahoma, with him on the briefs), for Plaintiff-Appellant Abigail Ross.

John David Lackey, Paul & Lackey, P.C., Tulsa, Oklahoma, for Defendant-Appellee University of Tulsa.

Rebecca Peterson-Fisher, Equal Rights Advocates, San Francisco, California, filed a brief for Amici Curiae Equal Rights Advocates and SurvJustice Inc.

Before KELLY, EBEL, and BACHARACH, Circuit Judges.

BACHARACH, Circuit Judge.

The plaintiff (Ms. Abigail Ross) was allegedly raped by a fellow student at the University of Tulsa (Mr. Patrick Swilling). The alleged rape led Ms. Ross to sue the university for money damages under Title IX of the Education Amendments Act of 1972. Under Title IX, universities that receive federal financial assistance cannot discriminate on the basis of gender. *See* 20 U.S.C. § 1681(a). Such discrimination occurs when a university obtains notice of sexual harassment and responds with deliberate indifference. *See Gebser v. Lago Vista Indep. Sch. Dist.*, 524 U.S. 274, 290, 118 S.Ct. 1989, 141 L.Ed.2d 277 (1998).

In this case, Ms. Ross presents distinct theories of the university's deliberate indifference.

The first theory involves what happened before the alleged rape: that the university acted with deliberate indifference by failing in 2012 to adequately investigate reports that Mr. Swilling had raped another student (J.M.).

The second theory involves what happened after the alleged rape of Ms. Ross. After Ms. Ross reported the rape, the university conducted a student-conduct hearing. The purpose was to determine whether Mr. Swilling had violated university policy by raping Ms. Ross. By the time of the hearing, university officials had learned of prior reports of sexual harassment committed by Mr. Swilling. But these reports were excluded at the hearing. Ms. Ross alleges that exclusion of these reports constituted deliberate indifference on the part of the university.

p.1283 The University of Tulsa obtained summary judgment on both theories, and Ms. Ross appeals. On the first theory, the dis-positive issue is whether a fact-finder could reasonably infer that an appropriate person at the university had actual notice of a substantial danger to others. On the second theory, we must determine whether a reasonable fact-finder could characterize exclusion of the prior reports as deliberate indifference.

We conclude that both theories fail as a matter of law. On the first theory, campus-security officers were the only university employees who knew about reports that J.M. had been raped. Based on Ms. Ross's arguments, a reasonable fact-finder could not infer that campus-security officers were appropriate persons for purposes of Title IX. And on the second theory, there is no evidence of deliberate indifference by the University of Tulsa. The university excluded prior reports of sexual harassment based on a reasonable application of university policy. Thus, we affirm the award of summary judgment to the university.

I. Standard of Review

In considering the award of summary judgment, we engage in de novo review. *Koch v. City of Del City*, 660 F.3d 1228, 1237 (10th Cir. 2011). This review requires us to view the summary-judgment evidence in the light most favorable to Ms. Ross, resolving all factual disputes and drawing all reasonable inferences in her favor. *Estate of Booker v. Gomez*, 745 F.3d 405, 411 (10th Cir. 2014). Summary judgment is appropriate only if the University of Tulsa shows that (1) there are no genuine issues of material fact and (2) the University of Tulsa is entitled to judgment as a matter of law. *Koch*, 660 F.3d at 1238.

II. The Elements of Ms. Ross's Claim

For both theories, Ms. Ross must satisfy four elements:
1. The University of Tulsa had actual notice of a substantial risk that Mr. Swilling would commit an act of sexual harassment (such as sexual violence) against a student.
2. The University of Tulsa was deliberately indifferent to that risk.
3. The sexual harassment was severe, pervasive, and objectively offensive.
4. The sexual harassment deprived Ms. Ross of access to the university's educational benefits or opportunities.

See Murrell v. Sch. Dist. No. 1, 186 F.3d 1238, 1246 (10th Cir. 1999). The University of Tulsa challenges only the first and second elements.

On the first element, the University of Tulsa could obtain notice only through an appropriate person. *Gebser v. Lago Vista Indep. Sch. Dist.*, 524 U.S. 274, 290, 118 S.Ct. 1989, 141 L.Ed.2d 277 (1998). An appropriate person "is, at a minimum, an official of the [university] with authority to take corrective action [on behalf of the university] to end the discrimination." *Id.*

On the second element, a university is "deemed 'deliberately indifferent' to acts of student-on-student harassment only where the [university's] response to the harassment or lack thereof is clearly unreasonable in light of the known circumstances." *Davis ex rel. LaShonda D. v. Monroe Cty. Bd. of Educ.,* 526 U.S. 629, 648, 119 S.Ct. 1661, 143 L.Ed.2d 839 (1999).

III. Ms. Ross's First Theory (Prior to the Alleged Rape of Ms. Ross)

Ms. Ross's first theory involves what happened before her alleged rape: According to Ms. Ross, the University of Tulsa failed to adequately investigate two reports in 2012 that Mr. Swilling had raped p.1284 J.M.[1] For this theory, Ms. Ross points to evidence that in 2012, two football players had reported a rape of J.M. to campus security and J.M. then confirmed the rape. But at J.M.'s behest, campus-security officers dropped the matter. Ms. Ross contends that dropping the matter left Mr. Swilling free to sexually assault others at the university.

Like the district court, we reject this theory as a matter of law. But our reasoning differs from the district court's.

In the district court's view, a fact-finder could reasonably conclude that two high-ranking campus-security officers were appropriate persons. But the district court held that (1) J.M.'s report was too vague to provide notice and (2) even if J.M.'s report had provided such notice, the University of Tulsa's response would not have been clearly unreasonable. To support the second holding, the district court observed that

- J.M. had declined to press criminal charges against Mr. Swilling or file a student-conduct complaint and
- J.M. had indicated that she did not want disruption in her life prior to her upcoming graduation.

Thus, the court reasoned, it was not clearly unreasonable for the university to drop the matter.

We take a different view. Viewing the evidence in the light most favorable to Ms. Ross, a fact-finder could justifiably infer that campus-security officers had learned of the reported rape. That knowledge could reasonably suggest that dropping the investigation was clearly unreasonable, leaving a potential predator free to sexually assault others at the university. But based on Ms. Ross's arguments, a reasonable fact-finder could not conclude that the campus-security officers had authority to take corrective action. In the absence of such authority, Ms. Ross's first theory fails as a matter of law.

A. The reports by the football players and J.M. could have provided campus-security officers with actual notice.

The threshold inquiry is whether the campus-security officers obtained actual notice in 2012 of a substantial risk to individuals on campus. In our view, a reasonable fact-finder could infer such notice.

"'[A]ctual notice requires more than a simple report of inappropriate conduct...
.'" *Escue v. N. Okla. Coll.,* 450 F.3d 1146, 1154 (10th Cir. 2006) (quoting *Doe v. Sch. Admin. Dist. No. 19,* 66 F.Supp.2d 57, 63 (D. Me. 1999)). Here, however, the reports provided far more. In our view, these reports could have led a fact-finder to reasonably infer actual notice on the part of campus-security officials.

1. A reasonable fact-finder could infer that J.M. had characterized her sexual encounter as a rape.

In 2012, two football players called campus security and reported that their friend, J.M., had been raped in her campus apartment by Mr. Swilling. The football players explained that they had learned of the rape from J.M.'s roommate. According to the football players, the roommate had overheard the rape.

Following this report, J.M. spoke with campus-security officers. The parties disagree p.1285 over what J.M. shared with campus security. According to Ms. Ross, J.M. confirmed that she had been raped the prior night; according to the University of Tulsa, J.M. stated that the sexual encounter had been consensual. Ms. Ross's position is supported by at least three evidentiary items.

The first is a recorded conversation in 2014 between J.M. and a campus-security officer, Sergeant Zach Livingston. During this conversation, J.M. acknowledged that (1) Mr. Swilling had sexually assaulted her in 2012 and (2) she had reported the assault shortly thereafter to campus-security officers. The conversation included this exchange:

> Sergeant Livingston: I'm just trying to figure out because when, you know, everything that we've discovered about it has said that when you came in that you said it was a consensual deal.
>
> J.M.: No.

Appellant's App'x, vol. V at 1201, 3:16-3:28 (Plaintiff's Response to Defendant's Partial Motion for Summary Judgment, Exhibit 12).[2]

The second evidentiary item is a recorded conversation between J.M. and an investigator from the Tulsa County District Attorney's Office. During this conversation, J.M. said that in 2012, she had told campus-security officers: "Patrick [Swilling] had taken advantage of me," "it was not with my ... acknowledgement," and "I just don't want to even think about it anymore." Appellant's App'x, vol. V at 1202, 39:02-39:47 (Plaintiff's Response to Defendant's Partial Motion for Summary Judgment, Exhibit 13). J.M. also indicated that she had explained her preference not to pursue the matter with Mr. Swilling because

- she had only one semester remaining before graduation,
- she did not want her private life to be publicized, and
- Mr. Swilling's father was a powerful figure who had played professional football.

J.M. added that the campus-security officers had agreed that Mr. Swilling's father was a prominent figure.

The third evidentiary item is a recorded conversation between a former campus-security officer and a Tulsa police detective. The detective stated: "[T]he other thing was that [J.M.] said that you guys knew ... that ... when she filled out [a written report] that ... she put in there that she was raped." Appellant's App'x, vol. V at 1203, 13:43-13:54 (Plaintiff's Response to Defendant's Partial Motion for Summary Judgment, Exhibit 14).[3]

The University of Tulsa points to contrary accounts from current and former campus-security officers. According to these accounts, J.M. reported in 2012 that the sexual activity had been consensual. Although a fact-finder could reasonably p.1286 credit these accounts, we must resolve this factual dispute favorably to Ms. Ross. *See* Part I, above. Doing so, we conclude that a fact-finder could reasonably determine that J.M. had told campus security in 2012 that she was raped by Mr. Swilling.

2. The fact-finder could reasonably infer that the reports by J.M. and the football players had been sufficiently specific to supply actual notice.

In our view, the fact-finder could justifiably infer that (1) J.M.'s report was sufficiently detailed and (2) the reports by the football players added specificity to J.M.'s report. The district court reached a different conclusion, concluding for four reasons that J.M.'s report was too vague to provide actual notice. We disagree with the court's reasoning.

First, the district court noted that J.M. had been reluctant to speak with campus security in 2012. But J.M.'s reluctance need not mean that her report was vague.

Second, the district court noted that J.M. had not used the words "rape" or "assault" when talking to campus-security officers. This observation is immaterial, for J.M. denied telling campus-security officers that the sexual encounter had been consensual. *See* Part III(A)(1), above. Thus, a fact-finder could justifiably conclude that J.M. had described a rape. *See Ferris v. Delta Air Lines, Inc.,* 277 F.3d 128, 132, 136-37 (2d Cir. 2001) (accepting for purposes of summary judgment that a woman had reported a rape to her employer even though the woman had not used the word "rape"). In addition, the football players added clarity, stating that J.M. had been raped by Mr. Swilling.

Third, the district court stated that J.M. had not provided campus security with "facts or details." *Ross v. Univ. of Tulsa,* 180 F.Supp.3d 951, 968 (N.D. Okla. 2016). But, from the reports by J.M. and the football players, the campus-security officers could ascertain "the basic facts, the who, what, when, and where." *See United States v. Fusaro,* 708 F.2d 17, 25 (1st Cir. 1983). For example, a fact-finder could justifiably conclude that the campus-security officers had known

- who was reportedly involved (J.M. and Mr. Swilling),
- what reportedly happened (Mr. Swilling raped J.M.),
- when the rape reportedly occurred (the prior evening), and
- where the rape reportedly occurred (in J.M.'s campus apartment).

A fact-finder could justifiably conclude that these basic facts provided campus-security officers with actual notice.

The University of Tulsa appears to argue that greater specificity is required when the alleged harasser was a student rather than a teacher. But, even if this were true, the reports here were sufficiently specific to provide actual notice to the university.

Fourth, the district court asserted that J.M. had not accused Mr. Swilling of any specific misconduct. But, as discussed above, a fact-finder could justifiably conclude that J.M. had reported a rape. *See* Part III(A)(1), above.[4]

p.1287 Rejecting the district court's four rationales, we conclude that the fact-finder could reasonably view the reports by J.M. and the football players as sufficiently specific to constitute actual notice to campus-security officers.

* * *

A fact-finder could reasonably conclude that J.M. had reported a rape in 2012. Of course, the fact-finder might also reach the opposite conclusion. But at this stage of the proceedings, we must resolve this factual dispute favorably to Ms. Ross. *See* Part I, above. Based on the reports by J.M. and the football players, the fact-finder could justifiably conclude that campus-security officers had actual notice of a substantial danger posed by Mr. Swilling's presence at the university.[5]

B. The fact-finder could justifiably conclude that campus-security officers had acted with deliberate indifference.

A university is "deemed 'deliberately indifferent' to acts of student-on-student harassment only where the [university's] response to the harassment or lack thereof is clearly unreasonable in light of the known circumstances." *Davis ex rel. LaShonda D. v. Monroe Cty. Bd. of Educ.*, 526 U.S. 629, 648, 119 S.Ct. 1661, 143 L.Ed.2d 839 (1999). The resulting issue is whether a fact-finder could justifiably conclude that campus-security officers had acted in a clearly unreasonable manner.

Viewing the summary-judgment evidence in the light most favorable to Ms. Ross, the fact-finder could reasonably conclude that campus-security officers had acted in a clearly unreasonable manner when dropping the investigation. Thus, the fact-finder could reasonably conclude that campus-security officers had been deliberately indifferent.

Ms. Ross does not dispute that in 2012, J.M.

- declined to press criminal charges against Mr. Swilling or to file a student-conduct complaint and
- indicated that she did not want disruption in her life prior to graduation.

The district court focused on these facts, reasoning that further investigation of Mr. Swilling would have disrupted J.M.'s life. Thus, the district court concluded that campus-security officers had not acted with deliberate indifference when dropping the investigation.

But the fact-finder could reasonably conclude that campus-security officers had known that further investigation was necessary p.1288 to gauge the significance of Mr. Swilling's danger to others. One campus-security officer acknowledged that investigation is necessary to avert a threat to other students regardless of whether an alleged victim has chosen to cooperate:

Q. Okay. Why would you retain or even begin an investigation when the alleged victim doesn't appear to want to make a report?

A. Whether or not the victim was interested in making a report or not, it was still a reportable offense. And the university had a duty to investigate and determine if that offense had been committed and report accordingly if it was found that it had been, with or without the victim cooperation.

Q. You would agree that merely because somebody does not want to report something, doesn't mean the alleged perpetrator is not still a threat to other students?

A. Correct. Most generally failure of victim cooperation is likely in sexual related offenses. And it could be for a number of — you know, fear, embarrassment or other reasons for them not to cooperate. However, as a law enforcement officer there is still a duty to investigate the crime.

Appellant's App'x, vol. VI at 1222-23. Similarly, guidance from the Office for Civil Rights states that universities should investigate even when an alleged victim fails to report sexual harassment or to cooperate in the investigation:

> Once a school has notice of possible sexual harassment of students ... it should take immediate and appropriate steps to investigate or otherwise determine what occurred and take prompt and effective steps reasonably calculated to end any harassment, eliminate a hostile environment if one has been created, and prevent harassment from occurring again. These steps are the school's responsibility whether or not the student who was harassed makes a complaint or otherwise asks the school to take action.

Office for Civil Rights Guidance at 15. Perhaps for this reason, University of Tulsa Dean Yolanda Taylor acknowledged that the university would have incurred an obligation to investigate even if the complaining individual had declined to participate. In these circumstances, a fact-finder could justifiably conclude that

- the presence of a rapist on the university campus would pose a substantial risk to others and
- campus-security officers had acted in a clearly unreasonable manner when dropping the investigation.[6]

But this does not mean that we can impute deliberate indifference to the university itself. Until Ms. Ross reported the rape, the only university employees that knew of J.M.'s alleged rape were campus-security officers. The resulting issue is whether these officers were appropriate persons under Title IX.

C. Based on Ms. Ross's arguments, a reasonable fact-finder could not conclude that the University of Tulsa's campus-security officers were appropriate persons.

To trigger Title IX liability, a university must have actual notice through an appropriate person. *Escue v. N. Okla. Coll.*, 450 F.3d 1146, 1152 (10th Cir. 2006). An appropriate person "is, at a minimum, an official of the [university] with authority to take corrective action [on behalf of the university] p.1289 to end the discrimination." *Gebser v. Lago Vista Indep. Sch. Dist.*, 524 U.S. 274, 290, 118 S.Ct. 1989, 141 L.Ed.2d 277 (1998); *see* Part II, above.

A fact-finder could reasonably conclude that campus-security officers had learned in 2012 that J.M. was complaining of a rape rather than describing a consensual sexual encounter. But there is nothing to suggest that this information went beyond campus-security officers. Therefore, we must consider whether Ms. Ross's arguments could reasonably support characterization of campus-security officers as appropriate persons.

In district court, Ms. Ross argued that all campus-security officers were appropriate persons. The district court did not go this far. Instead, the court concluded only that a reasonable fact-finder could regard two high-ranking campus-security officers as appropriate persons: Security Director Joe Timmons and Patrol Captain Paul Downe. For this conclusion, the district court gave three reasons. On appeal, Ms.

Ross defends the district court's conclusion and argues that the court's reasoning would support characterization of all campus-security officers as appropriate persons.

In our view, Ms. Ross has not justified treatment of all campus-security officers as appropriate persons. Thus, Ms. Ross cannot avoid summary judgment on her theory regarding the university's response to the reports by the football players and J.M.

1. The District Court's First Reason

The district court's first reason was that the University of Tulsa had designated campus security as a proper recipient of sexual-harassment reports. Based on this designation, the district court compared the role of campus-security officers to the role that teachers had in *Montgomery v. Independent School District No. 709*, 109 F.Supp.2d 1081 (D. Minn. 2000). The *Montgomery* court explained that

> the School District's sexual harassment policy imposes upon teachers a duty to convey reports of sexual harassment to the school principals. It is therefore clear that teachers had the authority to take at least this minimal corrective measure which, if effectively carried out, would impart knowledge of the harassment to higher School District officials with even greater authority to act.

Id. at 1099. Factually, our case bears some resemblance to *Montgomery*. Legally, however, the Supreme Court in *Gebser* has rejected use of vicarious liability and agency principles as grounds for liability under Title IX. In our view, *Gebser* requires us to reject the district court's first reason.

Analogizing her circumstances to those in *Montgomery*, Ms. Ross notes that university policy required campus-security officers to automatically report sexual assaults to the Office of Student Affairs. For this argument, Ms. Ross interprets the Supreme Court's opinion in *Gebser v. Lago Vista Independent School District*, 524 U.S. 274, 118 S.Ct. 1989, 141 L.Ed.2d 277 (1998). There the Supreme Court explained that an appropriate person "is, at a minimum, an official of the [university] with authority to take corrective action [on behalf of the university] to end the discrimination." 524 U.S. at 290, 118 S.Ct. 1989; *see* Parts II, III(C), above. In Ms. Ross's view, campus security's role in receiving and forwarding complaints means that campus-security officers "institute corrective measures" for the University of Tulsa. *Gebser*, 524 U.S. at 290, 118 S.Ct. 1989. Essentially, Ms. Ross reads *Gebser* as holding that anyone who participates in the initiation of a corrective process is an "appropriate person."

The district court's reasoning and Ms. Ross's argument would stretch the Supreme Court's opinion in *Gebser*. *Gebser* p.1290 provides that if campus-security officers cannot themselves take corrective action, they would not be considered appropriate persons. *See* Part II, above. And merely passing on a report of sexual harassment to someone authorized to take corrective action is not itself corrective action. *See Plamp v. Mitchell Sch. Dist. No. 17-2*, 565 F.3d 450, 459 (8th Cir. 2009) (holding that specified school personnel are authorized to report potentially discriminatory conduct, "[b]ut that authority does not amount to an authority to take a corrective measure or institute remedial action within the meaning of Title IX"); *Rosa H. v. San Elizario Indep. Sch. Dist.*, 106 F.3d 648, 660-61 (5th Cir. 1997) (indicating that notice of harassment by employees who lack authority, beyond reporting the misconduct to other employees, is insufficient to trigger a school's liability under Title IX).

To decide otherwise would turn the deliberate-indifference standard into vicarious liability. For example, consider a school where every employee receiving a report of sexual harassment must convey the report to the principal. If one employee fails to convey a report to the principal, that failure could be attributed to the school as a whole. This type of vicarious liability is precisely what the Supreme Court sought to avoid through the deliberate-indifference standard. *See Gebser,* 524 U.S. at 287-90, 118 S.Ct. 1989 (rejecting the application of vicarious liability and agency principles as grounds for triggering liability under Title IX); *see also Davis v. Monroe Cty. Bd. of Educ.,* 526 U.S. 629, 642, 119 S.Ct. 1661, 143 L.Ed.2d 839 (1999) (stating that in *Gebser,* the Supreme Court "rejected the use of agency principles to impute liability to the district for the misconduct of its teachers").

Ms. Ross's contrary interpretation of *Gebser* would create Title IX liability for clerical errors by ministerial personnel who lack any discretionary authority to take corrective measures. For example, consider the assistant for a Dean of Students who is tasked with adjudicating student-conduct complaints. Under Ms. Ross's interpretation, this assistant would be considered an appropriate person simply for receiving and forwarding reports to the Dean of Students. The clerical act of receiving and forwarding a report may ultimately lead the Dean of Students to take corrective action, but is not itself corrective action. Nothing in *Gebser* would suggest liability for a university based solely on the assistant's loss of a report or failure to forward it to the Dean of Students. *See, e.g., Hill v. Cundiff,* 797 F.3d 948, 971 (11th Cir. 2015) (holding that a teacher's aide was not an "appropriate person" for purposes of Title IX).

Under *Gebser,* we reject the district court's first reason for treating campus-security officers as appropriate persons.

2. The District Court's Second Reason

The district court's second reason focused on campus security's investigative role. For example, the district court observed that campus-security officers "work[ ] directly with [the Office of Student Affairs] to investigate ... instances of campus violence...." *Ross v. Univ. of Tulsa,* 180 F.Supp.3d 951, 967 (N.D. Okla. 2016).[7] On appeal, Ms. Ross similarly asserts p.1291 that campus-security officers' investigative role makes the officers appropriate persons for purposes of Title IX.

It is not clear what Ms. Ross is arguing. She might be arguing that campus-security officers are appropriate persons because investigations are necessary for the university to start its corrective process. This potential argument would assume that anyone participating in the initiation of a corrective process is an "appropriate person." But this assumption would entail the sort of vicarious liability that the Supreme Court tried to avoid in *Gebser. See* Part III(C)(1), above.

If Ms. Ross is instead characterizing the investigation itself as a form of corrective action, the argument would also fail. Perhaps investigation is a form of corrective action; perhaps not. The answer is not self-evident and we need not resolve this question today, for Ms. Ross has not explained or supported characterization of an investigation as a form of corrective action. To the extent that she is taking this position, her argument is perfunctory and therefore waived. *See Hill v. Kemp,* 478 F.3d 1236, 1255 n.21 (10th Cir. 2007) (declining to consider an argument raised in a "perfunctory manner"). We therefore reject the district court's second reason for treating campus-security officers as appropriate persons.

3. The District Court's Third Reason

The district court's third reason involved the university's designation of campus-security officers as appropriate persons. The court reasoned that this designation created an expectation among students:

> Third, [the university's] Sexual Violence Policy and other surrounding facts could be viewed as creating an equitable expectation in students (and their parents) that a report to [the university's campus-security officers] triggers any and all of [the university's] "corrective processes." Adopting [the university's] argument would allow it to designate [the university's campus-security officers] as an entity to receive sexual violence complaints in its own Title IX policies, fail to ensure that such entity delivers reports to the school's Title IX coordinators, and effectively shield itself from Title IX civil liability. The Court does not read *Gebser* to require this result. Therefore, a jury could find the 2012 Report to [the university's campus-security officers] was made to an "appropriate person."

Ross v. Univ. of Tulsa, 180 F.Supp.3d 951, 967 (N.D. Okla. 2016). In her reply brief, Ms. Ross supports this rationale:

> As is clear, the district court recognized that it would circumvent the purpose of Title IX if [the university] were permitted to designate its law enforcement officers as appropriate persons in its own Title IX policies, then avoid liability by merely suggesting otherwise in summary judgment briefing. This would render Title IX law on "appropriate person" utterly meaningless. Accordingly, the district court's ruling on this issue should be affirmed.[8]

Appellant's Reply Br. at 13.

We reject this argument. To the extent that university policy indicates that campus-security officers would begin the university's p.1292 "corrective processes," that fact would not justify treating the officers as appropriate persons for purposes of Title IX. *See* Part III(C)(1), above.

Ms. Ross adds that university policy designated campus security as "appropriate persons." But university policy does not expressly designate campus security as appropriate persons.

As a result, we reject the district court's third reason for treating campus-security officers as appropriate persons.

* * *

Ms. Ross's summary-judgment evidence indicates that campus-security officers learned in 2012 that J.M. was reporting a rape committed by Mr. Swilling. But Ms. Ross has not justified treatment of campus-security officers as appropriate persons for purposes of Title IX. Thus, Ms. Ross's first theory fails as a matter of law.[9]

IV. Ms. Ross's Second Theory (After the Alleged Rape of Ms. Ross)

Ms. Ross also presents a second theory: that the University of Tulsa responded to her report in a way that was clearly unreasonable. This theory is based on an evidentiary rule that the University of Tulsa allegedly uses for student-conduct hearings: Evidence of the student's prior misconduct may be considered only if there had been an earlier finding of responsibility. Ms. Ross alleges improper reliance on this rule to exclude evidence of Mr. Swilling's prior misconduct.[10]

A. The Absence of a Prior Finding of Responsibility

When the university conducted the hearing on Ms. Ross's complaint, Mr. Swilling had not been found responsible for any acts of sexual harassment. As a result, the hearing officer did not consider reports of Mr. Swilling's other acts of sexual misconduct. In her opening brief, Ms. Ross attributed the absence of a finding of responsibility to the University of Tulsa's failure to properly investigate Mr. Swilling's past acts of sexual harassment. This theory fails as a matter of law.

Ms. Ross's theory is subject to the same deliberate-indifference standard set out in *Davis ex rel. LaShonda D. v. Monroe County Board of Education:* A university is "deemed 'deliberately indifferent' to acts of student-on-student harassment only when the recipient's response to the harassment or lack thereof is clearly unreasonable p.1293 in light of the known circumstances." 526 U.S. 629, 648, 119 S.Ct. 1661, 143 L.Ed.2d 839 (1999); *see* Part II, above.

As a threshold matter, it is not clearly unreasonable for the University of Tulsa to apply its alleged evidentiary rule. We base this conclusion on guidance from the U.S. Department of Education's Office for Civil Rights.

This guidance indicates that it "may be helpful" for schools to consider evidence of prior acts of sexual harassment when there has been a finding of responsibility:

> If there is a dispute about whether harassment occurred or whether it was welcome ... [,] [t]he following types of information may be helpful in resolving the dispute:
>
> . . . .
>
> • Evidence that the alleged harasser has been found to have harassed others may support the credibility of the student claiming the harassment....

Office for Civil Rights Guidance at 9. This guidance does not recommend use of prior reports in the absence of a finding of responsibility. Thus, the University of Tulsa's alleged evidentiary rule conforms to this guidance.

Ms. Ross does not argue that the use of this rule was inherently unreasonable.[11] Rather, she argues that using this rule at the hearing was clearly unreasonable because the University of Tulsa had failed to properly investigate Mr. Swilling's past acts.

This argument fails because further investigation, standing alone, would not have permitted consideration of Mr. Swilling's alleged acts of sexual harassment in the past. The summary-judgment record contains unrebutted evidence that university policy would permit consideration of these alleged acts only if there had been a separate hearing, trial, or similar proceeding that had resulted in a finding of responsibility on the part of Mr. Swilling.

In her reply brief, Ms. Ross shifted her argument, contending that the university should also have adjudicated Mr. Swilling's responsibility for other alleged acts of sexual harassment prior to adjudicating his responsibility for the alleged rape of Ms. Ross. This argument is waived, for it did not appear in the opening brief. *State Farm Fire & Cas. Co. v. Mhoon,* 31 F.3d 979, 984 n.7 (10th Cir. 1994) ("[A]ppellant failed to raise this issue in his opening brief and, hence, has waived the point.").

The argument also fails as a matter of law. Prior to Ms. Ross's report, the only university officers that knew about the incident with J.M. were campus-security officers. And the two other reports about Mr. Swilling were unknown even to campus-security officers prior to Ms. Ross's report. By the time others at the university learned of the incident involving J.M., she had already left the university and p.1294 indicated that she did not want to participate in a student-conduct hearing. Similarly, a second alleged victim had refused to file a complaint or to speak with anyone at the university about the incident. And a third alleged victim had never even attended the University of Tulsa.

In addition, summary-judgment evidence indicates that

- when an alleged victim refuses to participate in a hearing, it can become more difficult for the school to find the alleged aggressor responsible for misconduct and
- university policy prevents hearings from taking place when the victim refuses to even give a statement to the university.

And there is no evidence that Ms. Ross had asked the University of Tulsa to adjudicate responsibility for the other alleged acts prior to the hearing on her own student-conduct complaint.

In our view, the university did not act in a way that was clearly unreasonable by failing to sua sponte adjudicate Mr. Swilling's responsibility for the prior reports of sexual harassment.

B. The Alleged Failure to Consider Guidance from the Office for Civil Rights

Ms. Ross does not argue that any of the university's policies are inherently unreasonable, but the amici do. They argue that the district court erred by failing to consider applicable federal guidance in determining the validity of the university's evidentiary rule. In the amici's view, "the exclusion of evidence of prior sexual violence in student disciplinary hearings 'could lead to a "target rapist" on a college campus being repeatedly accused but repeatedly cleared despite a pattern of the same conduct.'" Amici Br. at 16 (quoting *Ross v. Univ. of Tulsa,* 180 F.Supp.3d 951, 972 (N.D. Okla. 2016)). In the view of the amici, this result would be absurd. But the university's application of its rule conforms to the federal guidance. *See* Part IV(A), above. Thus, it was not absurd for the University of Tulsa to apply its evidentiary rule.

C. The District Court's Alleged Reliance on the Defense of Good-Faith Reliance on Counsel

Ms. Ross argues that the district court erred in crediting the defense of good-faith reliance on counsel. According to Ms. Ross, the University of Tulsa "neither asserted this defense in its summary judgment briefing nor offered any evidence necessary to meet its burden of proving the defense." Appellant's Reply Br. at 19. For the sake of argument, we may assume that (1) the district court drew this conclusion and (2) this conclusion was erroneous. But these assumptions would not affect the outcome, for the University of Tulsa would prevail as a matter of law even without a defense involving good-faith reliance on counsel.

D. The Actions of the University's Outside Counsel

At oral argument, Ms. Ross also contended that the university's outside counsel was an appropriate person for purposes of Title IX. This contention was presented for the first time at oral argument, which was too late. *See Lebahn v. Nat'l Farmers Union Uniform Pension Plan,* 828 F.3d 1180, 1188 n.8 (10th Cir. 2016) (stating that arguments made for the first time at oral argument are waived). Therefore, we decline to consider this argument.

* * *

We conclude that a reasonable fact-finder could not find that the University of Tulsa had responded to Ms. Ross's report in a way that was clearly unreasonable. p.1295 Thus, Ms. Ross's second theory fails as a matter of law.

V. Disposition

The district court awarded summary judgment to the University of Tulsa. We affirm, rejecting Ms. Ross's two theories.

On the first theory, Ms. Ross is correct that a fact-finder could reasonably conclude that (1) the reports about J.M. had put campus-security officers on notice of a rape and (2) the campus-security officers acted with deliberate indifference by dropping their investigation into the reported rape of J.M. But based on Ms. Ross's arguments, the fact-finder could not reasonably conclude that campus-security officers were appropriate persons. Thus, Ms. Ross's first theory fails as a matter of law.

Ms. Ross's second theory also fails, for it was not clearly unreasonable for the university to apply its policy excluding evidence of other sexual harassment in the absence of a prior finding of responsibility.

Affirmed.

---

[1] Courts are split on whether notice can consist of prior reports. *See Rost ex rel. K.C. v. Steamboat Springs RE-2 Sch. Dist.,* 511 F.3d 1114, 1119 (10th Cir. 2008); *Escue*

v. N. Okla. Coll., 450 F.3d 1146, 1153 (10th Cir. 2006). But we need not weigh in on this split, as the university does not deny that notice can theoretically consist of prior reports of sexual harassment. For the sake of argument, we assume that prior reports can be sufficient. Even with that assumption, Ms. Ross's first theory would fail as a matter of law.

[2] The record of this interview, like others cited in this opinion, is available only as an audio recording. Our citations for the audio recordings provide the page numbers where the recordings are indexed and the time stamps of the relevant material. The parentheticals provide the titles of the exhibits as given in the table of contents to the appendix.

[3] Some summary-judgment evidence indicates that campus-security officers destroyed J.M.'s written statement. In light of this potential destruction of evidence, Ms. Ross argues that "it was inappropriate for the district court to have credited [the University of Tulsa] with [J.M.]'s report being too 'vague' to require further action when the precise content of that complaint is no longer available due to [the University of Tulsa's] own destruction." Appellant's Opening Br. at 34. We need not address this argument because the district court's vagueness analysis was otherwise flawed. *See* Part III(A)(2), below.

[4] The two amici curiae argue that the district court's analysis is also flawed because under § 1983, "an official cannot escape a finding of deliberate indifference where the evidence shows that he 'refused to verify underlying facts that he strongly suspected to be true, or declined to confirm inferences of risk that he strongly suspected to exist.'" Amici Br. at 14 (quoting *Mata v. Saiz*, 427 F.3d 745, 752 (10th Cir. 2005)). Because we have elsewhere determined that the district court's analysis was erroneous for other reasons, we need not address the amici's argument.

[5] In discussing the existence of actual notice, the University of Tulsa apparently contends that the university lacked substantial control over the context for the alleged rapes of J.M. and Ms. Ross.

The apparent contention about J.M.'s rape appears irrelevant because J.M. has not sued.

For the alleged rape of Ms. Ross, the university could incur liability only by exercising "substantial control over ... the context in which the [alleged rape] occur[red]." *Davis ex rel. LaShonda D. v. Monroe Cty. Bd. of Educ.*, 526 U.S. 629, 645, 119 S.Ct. 1661, 143 L.Ed.2d 839 (1999). Ms. Ross's alleged rape occurred in a private apartment on campus.

The fact-finder could reasonably infer university control over a rape in the apartment. For example, the summary-judgment evidence indicates that the university exerts disciplinary authority over students for misconduct that occurs in private apartments on campus. In addition, if Mr. Swilling had been found responsible in 2012 for raping J.M., the university could have expelled him and barred him from the campus. By barring Mr. Swilling from the campus, the university could potentially have prevented him from sexually harassing students on campus. In these circumstances, a fact-finder could reasonably conclude that the university had retained substantial control over the context for Ms. Ross's alleged rape.

[6] Ms. Ross and the amici also present other arguments, contending that the university acted with deliberate indifference in (1) failing to provide J.M. with all

necessary information and accommodations and (2) disregarding the university's own policies, past practices, and legal obligations. We need not address these arguments.

[7] The district court also stated that campus security works with the Office of Student Affairs to "combat campus violence and properly report instances of campus violence to the federal government." *Ross,* 180 F.Supp.3d at 967. But aside from conducting investigations, Ms. Ross has not

- explained how campus-security officers combat campus violence or
- argued that reporting instances of campus violence to the federal government would constitute corrective action.

[8] In her reply brief, Ms. Ross alleged that "Dean [of Students Yolanda] Taylor [has] explained that a report to [campus security] is the equivalent of a report to the Title IX coordinator." Appellant's Reply Br. at 12 (citing Appellant's App'x, vol. V at 984). But the cited material — a deposition of Dean Taylor — does not support this allegation. In this deposition, Ms. Taylor was asked to "list out the different people that might interact with somebody who has reported sexual violence." Appellant's App'x, vol. V at 983. She complied by listing the Title IX coordinator and various deputy coordinators. Dean Taylor was then asked whether there was "[a]nybody else besides those coordinators and yourself? ... What about campus security?" *Id.* at 948. She responded: "I'm sorry, and campus security of course." *Id.* Dean Taylor was simply stating that campus-security officers "might interact with somebody who has reported sexual violence." *See* Appellant's App'x, vol. V at 983-84. She was not characterizing a report to campus security as the equivalent of a report to the Title IX coordinator.

[9] At oral argument, the panel asked the University of Tulsa (1) whether campus-security officers had the power to arrest and (2) if so, whether that power would make these officers appropriate persons. But Ms. Ross did not rely on the arrest power in district court or in her appellate briefs. Thus, we need not decide whether the possible power to arrest would make campus-security officers appropriate persons.

More generally, we caution that our holding today is limited to the evidence and arguments before us. As a result, our holding does not foreclose consideration of campus-security officers as appropriate persons. See *Murrell v. Sch. Dist. No. 1,* 186 F.3d 1238, 1247 (10th Cir. 1999) (declining "simply to name job titles that would or would not" constitute appropriate persons and explaining that "[b]ecause officials' roles vary among school districts, deciding who [is an appropriate person] for the purposes of Title IX liability is necessarily a fact-based inquiry"). Faced with different evidence or arguments, a court might characterize campus-security officers as appropriate persons.

[10] At oral argument, Ms. Ross appeared to contend that this evidentiary rule had not been applied in the hearing. Instead, she contended that the university had imposed a blanket ban on all evidence of prior sexual history. This argument is waived because it was presented for the first time at oral argument. *See Lebahn v. Nat'l Farmers Union Uniform Pension Plan,* 828 F.3d 1180, 1188 n.8 (10th Cir. 2016) (stating that arguments made for the first time at oral argument are waived). Thus, we need not consider this contention.

[11] Ms. Ross argues that the university's dean of students acknowledged that use of this evidentiary rule had been unreasonable. Appellant's Opening Br. at 42 n.7 ("[Dean Taylor] has since acknowledged that she knew the school was acting unreasonably in failing to consider the prior accusations of sexual assault against Mr. Swilling."). This characterization is inaccurate. Dean Taylor was asked about using past sexual-harassment allegations in a conduct hearing; she responded that she would "like to be able to use all of the information," but understood from counsel that she could not do that. Appellant's App'x, vol. V at 1090. Dean Taylor did not say or imply that she regarded exclusion of the prior allegations as "unreasonable."

Similarly, Ms. Ross argues that Dean Taylor "acknowledged that had she been permitted to consider all four sexual misconduct allegations against Swilling, the outcome would have been different." Appellant's Opening Br. at 3. But Ms. Ross elsewhere acknowledges that Dean Taylor corrected this testimony with an erratum, "chang[ing] 'would' to 'could.'" Appellant's Opening Br. at 42 n.7. But even if Dean Taylor believed that the outcome would have been different, exclusion of the evidence would not have been clearly unreasonable.

858 F.3d 1307 (2017)

Tawny HIATT, Plaintiff-Appellant,

v.

COLORADO SEMINARY, a Colorado nonprofit corporation; Alan Kent; Jacaranda Palmateer, Defendants-Appellees.

No. 16-1159.

United States Court of Appeals, Tenth Circuit.

FILED June 2, 2017.

Hiatt v. Colorado Seminary, 858 F. 3d 1307 (10th Cir. 2017)

p.1309 Appeal from the United States District Court for the District of Colorado; (D.C. No. 1:15-CV-00192-RBJ).

Charlotte N. Sweeney (Ariel B. DeFazio, with her on the briefs), Sweeney & Bechtold, LLC, Denver, Colorado, appearing for Appellant.

Jim Goh (Heidi K. Wilbur, with him on the brief), Constangy, Brooks, Smith & Prophete, LLP, Denver, Colorado, appearing for Appellees.

Before HARTZ, MATHESON, and PHILLIPS, Circuit Judges.

p.1310 MATHESON, Circuit Judge.

Dr. Tawny Hiatt appeals from the district court's grant of summary judgment to her former employer, Colorado Seminary, and her former supervisors, Dr. Alan Kent and Dr. Jacaranda Palmateer, on her Title VII and Title IX discrimination and retaliation claims. Exercising jurisdiction under 28 U.S.C. § 1291, we affirm.

I. BACKGROUND

A. Factual Background

The following facts are presented in the light most favorable to Dr. Hiatt, the non-moving party on summary judgment. *See Twigg v. Hawker Beechcraft Corp.*, 659 F.3d 987, 997 (10th Cir. 2011).[1]

Colorado Seminary owns and operates the University of Denver ("DU"), including DU's Health and Counseling Center ("HCC"), which provides wellness services such as counseling to DU's student body. In November 2011, DU hired Dr. Hiatt to be a Staff Psychologist and the Training Director at the HCC.

The following recounts Dr. Hiatt's employment at DU from November 2011 until her resignation in June 2014.[2]

1. Dr. Hiatt's Position as Training Director and Her Supervisory Duties

As Training Director, Dr. Hiatt was responsible for supervising psychology students seeking their professional licensure. Supervisees included both pre-doctoral interns and post-doctoral fellows.[3] Dr. Hiatt was, in turn, supervised by Dr. Kent, the Executive Director of the HCC, and Dr. Palmateer, the HHC's Director of Counseling Services. Apart from her work at DU, Dr. Hiatt also maintained a private practice, which DU permitted so long as her job at DU remained her first priority.

From November 2011 to August 2012, Dr. Hiatt supervised four interns, including Dr. Emily Fogle, from DU's Graduate School of Professional Psychology ("GSPP") Internship Consortium. After the academic term, the interns provided positive reviews of Dr. Hiatt's supervision.

When Dr. Fogle returned to the HCC as a post-doctoral fellow, she requested that Dr. Hiatt supervise her during the 2012-2013 academic year. They started their supervisory relationship in the fall of 2012. Soon thereafter, Dr. Fogle suggested to Dr. Abby Coven, her former GSPP classmate, that she hire Dr. Hiatt to supervise her work in a private practice unaffiliated with DU. Dr. Coven did so.

p.1311 In December 2012, Dr. Hiatt and Dr. Coven developed romantic feelings for one another. On January 3, 2013, Dr. Hiatt ended her supervision of Dr. Coven's work in private practice. They continued their personal relationship.

On January 1, 2013 — before anyone at DU knew about Dr. Hiatt's relationship with Dr. Coven — Dr. Hiatt was promoted to Assistant Director of Counseling Services/Training Director. In this role, Dr. Hiatt continued to supervise students, including Dr. Fogle as a post-doctoral fellow and a group of HCC interns — Dave Shanley, Kim Mathewson, Alexis Wilbert, and Christine DeVore.

2. Revelation of the Relationship

On January 28, 2013, Dr. Coven told Dr. Fogle about her romantic relationship with Dr. Hiatt. Dr. Fogle told Dr. Palmateer about the relationship and that she had seen text messages showing it had started before Dr. Hiatt ended her supervision of Dr. Coven. Dr. Hiatt disputes that any such messages occurred.

Dr. Fogle also told Dr. Hiatt's four intern supervisees about the relationship. Dr. Fogle then expressed her concerns about the relationship to Dr. Hiatt. Dr. Hiatt offered to stop supervising Dr. Fogle, but Dr. Fogle declined.

Dr. Kent and Dr. Palmateer decided to hold an "open meeting" on February 19, 2013, with Dr. Hiatt and her supervisees so the supervisees could air any concerns. During the meeting, Dr. Hiatt apologized for disappointing the supervisees and explained how her supervision of Dr. Coven was different from that of an intern.

3. Post-Meeting Events

After the meeting, four relevant events happened.

First, Dr. Fogle, Dr. Mathewson, and Dr. Shanley elected to end supervision with Dr. Hiatt. Dr. Wilbert and Dr. DeVore, along with Dr. Hiatt's four graduate student supervisees, continued their supervision with Dr. Hiatt.

Second, Dr. Kent met with Dr. Fogle after the meeting. Dr. Fogle reported that supervision with Dr. Hiatt was like therapy. Dr. Fogle explained that Dr. Hiatt "had [her] sobbing in her office," and that Dr. Hiatt "made [her] feel vulnerable." *Id.*[4] According to Dr. Hiatt's own deposition testimony, supervisees called the experience of crying or breaking down during supervision with her as "being Tawny-ed." *Id.* at 166.

Third, Dr. Kent sought ethics guidance from DU administrators, psychologists unaffiliated with DU, and the American Psychological Association ("APA") about Dr. Hiatt's relationship relative to her work. Based on those conversations, Dr. Kent determined Dr. Hiatt was in an "ethical grey area." *Id.* at 66 ¶ 13. The asserted grey area arose from two rules in the APA's Code of Conduct: one prohibiting a psychologist from having sexual relationships with supervisees,[5] and another prohibiting a psychologist from having a personal relationship with someone closely connected to someone with whom the psychologist has a professional relationship.[6]

Fourth, Dr. Kent talked frequently with Dr. Hiatt about these matters. According to Dr. Kent, Dr. Hiatt failed to acknowledge that the way she handled her relationship at work had detrimental effects on her supervisees. Further, rather than take personal responsibility for the supervisees' reactions, Dr. Hiatt blamed the supervisees' pathologies as causing their strong reactions, including their decisions to stop supervision with her. Dr. Kent also said Dr. Hiatt showed no awareness of how her supervisory style affected them. Apart from ethical concerns, Dr. Kent determined that Dr. Hiatt's conduct showed "a serious lack of judgment given her position as a role model for the trainees." *Id.* at 66 ¶ 13.

4. The Demotion Decision

On February 22, 2013, Dr. Hiatt met with Dr. Kent and Dr. Palmateer. Dr. Kent presented Dr. Hiatt with three options: (1) resign; (2) be demoted and undergo six months of outside counseling about her supervisory style; or (3) remain in her position and allow Human Resources ("HR") to handle the matter.

Dr. Kent and Dr. Palmateer explained they were presenting these options because: (1) a "majority" of trainees refused to be supervised by Dr. Hiatt and she had lost "credibility and authority in their view"; (2) her conduct posed a "grey ethical issue," and a Training Director needed to display "exemplary ethics, boundaries, and professionalism"; and (3) her "approach to therapy and supervision requires a strict adherence to boundaries which weren't demonstrated in this situation" and her response to the students' reactions showed a "lack of personal responsibility." *Id.* at 450.

On February 27, 2013, before Dr. Hiatt chose an option, her attorney sent DU a letter claiming DU's request for Dr. Hiatt to leave her position as Training Director amounted to sex discrimination.

On March 4, 2013, Dr. Hiatt accepted the second option — demotion. In her new position as Staff Psychologist/Outreach Coordinator, Dr. Hiatt was paid $58,000 — a $2,000 reduction in pay from her previous position.

5. Period of Demotion

As a condition of her demotion, Dr. Hiatt met with Dr. Shirley Asher, an out-side consultant. Based on her sessions with Dr. Hiatt, Dr. Asher opined that Dr. Hiatt "likely could return" to a supervisory role, but also noted that she was not likely to change her supervisory style. *Id.* at 526.

During this time, Dr. Palmateer gave Dr. Hiatt a performance review that criticized her for taking paid time off in a manner that made her unavailable to her clients. Dr. Hiatt nonetheless received a raise of $500, which Dr. Hiatt calls "negligible." Aplt. Br. at 16.

In August 2013, Dr. Kent and Dr. Palmateer reassessed whether Dr. Hiatt should return to supervision. Based on Dr. Asher's input, some supervisees' negative feedback in their exit interviews about Dr. Hiatt's supervision style, and Dr. Kent's and Dr. Palmateer's own observations, they determined that Dr. Hiatt should not return to supervision at that time. They shared with Dr. Hiatt the supervisees' "perception that she intentionally breaks them down to the point of tears, is intrusive in their personal issues, blurs the boundaries of supervision and therapy, and then holds herself up as the rescuer." App. at 109. They also shared their own concerns that she had behaved unprofessionally in staff interviews, had unclear boundaries when supervising, and continued to focus on the supervisees' psychopathologies as explaining why they were upset about the way she handled the relationship at work, rather than acknowledging her contribution to their concerns.

In September 2013, Dr. Hiatt filed an internal grievance with DU's HR department requesting, among other things, that DU restore Dr. Hiatt to her position as Training Director. In the same month, she filed an internal Equal Employment Opportunity ("EEO") complaint with DU alleging sex discrimination, as well as retaliation.

In a September 26, 2013 response to her internal EEO complaint, Dr. Kent and Dr. Palmateer further detailed their reasons for demoting Dr. Hiatt and not returning her to a supervisory position. They explained that, because Dr. Asher stated Dr. Hiatt would not likely change her supervisory style, they did not reinstate Dr. Hiatt's supervisory duties.

Their response also reported that "several" supervisees in their exit interviews described "troubling interactions" with Dr. Hiatt — such as denigrating other HCC staff members, "sham[ing]" the supervisees and then trying to "rescue" them, and insisting that a supervisee give her a hug during a supervisory session. App. at 526-27. Those examples led Dr. Kent and Dr. Palmateer to believe Dr. Hiatt had "very poor boundaries which create[d] a hostile training environment." *Id.* at 527. The response also highlighted that Dr. Hiatt continued to blame the supervisees and their associated "pathologies" for the upheaval at the HCC, and that she failed to demonstrate awareness of how she contributed to the situation or how her supervisory style negatively affected the supervisees.

Dr. Kent and Dr. Palmateer explained in summary:

> While Dr. Hiatt's romantic relationship with her supervisee was not the reason for her removal from supervisory duties, it was the catalyst for a series of complaints which le[d] to a comprehensive review of her supervisory approach and her performance as Training Director. After the majority of trainees refused to be supervised by Dr. Hiatt, we had no option but to reevaluate her role. After several meetings with Dr. Hiatt and extensive conversations with the trainees, many concerning and disturbing behaviors about Dr. Hiatt's supervisory style

were revealed. We determined that it was in the best interest of the trainees, the University, and the [HCC] to find a more suitable Training Director.

Id. at 528.

In an October 2013 email to Dr. Hiatt, DU set forth criteria for Dr. Hiatt to eventually resume supervision, including having "better awareness about the power she holds" and "demonstrating appropriate professional boundaries in all contexts." App. at 546.

On October 30, 2013, following an investigation, DU denied Dr. Hiatt's internal EEO complaint.

6. Medical Leave and EEOC Charge

From November 15, 2013, to February 2, 2014, Dr. Hiatt took a medical leave of absence because the work environment at DU was causing her problems such as panic attacks.

p.1314 On December 23, 2013, while on medical leave from DU, Dr. Hiatt filed a charge with the U.S. Equal Employment Opportunity Commission ("EEOC") alleging sex discrimination and retaliation.

7. Return to Work

In February 2014, Dr. Hiatt returned to work at DU. Upon her return, Dr. Palmateer increased Dr. Hiatt's weekly clinical hours from 22 to 24 hours. She also required Dr. Hiatt to provide a doctor's note to justify non-Family Medical Leave Act ("FMLA") sick leave, obtain permission before "blocking her schedule" (i.e., make certain blocks of time in her calendar unavailable for clinical appointments), and make up for missed clinical time. Dr. Hiatt asserts that no other HCC clinical staff member faced similar requirements.

Dr. Hiatt requested several "accommodations" on her return, including that she work no longer than eight-hour days and that DU provide dictation software to help her timely draft case notes. DU denied the request for dictation software, and it is not clear whether it approved the eight-hour request.

On April 23, 2014, Dr. Kent and Dr. Palmateer criticized Dr. Hiatt for absenteeism and late case notes. Dr. Kent also told Dr. Hiatt that if she wanted to keep her personnel matters private, as she had requested, she should not tell people that she was "suing the university" (presumably referring to her EEOC charge). App. at 204 ¶ 49. In April and May 2014, Dr. Kent drove by Dr. Hiatt's private practice. Dr. Kent maintains that he did so on his way to dog day care. Dr. Hiatt asserts that he was checking to see if she was there during times she was supposed to be at DU.

On May 30, 2014, Dr. Hiatt submitted a letter of resignation, in which she complained of retaliation for filing her internal EEO and EEOC complaints. She stopped working at DU four weeks later.

B. Procedural Background

On January 28, 2015, Dr. Hiatt filed this lawsuit in the United States District Court for the District of Colorado. Her amended complaint, the operative one here, brought federal claims for sex discrimination under both Title VII of the Civil Rights Act of 1964 and Title IX of the Education Amendments Act of 1972, and for retaliation for engaging in protected opposition to unlawful discrimination under both Title VII and Title IX. The amended complaint also alleged several state law claims, including for wrongful discharge in violation of public policy and intentional infliction of emotional distress.

On January 11, 2016, Defendants Colorado Seminary, Dr. Kent, and Dr. Palmateer filed a motion for summary judgment, which the district court granted on April 5, 2016. The court held Dr. Hiatt had failed to state a prima facie case for her sex discrimination claims under the *McDonnell Douglas* burden-shifting framework described below. The court reasoned that Dr. Hiatt had failed to show she was treated less favorably than similarly situated employees not in her protected class, which the court believed was "required" for Dr. Hiatt to state a prima facie case of sex discrimination. App. at 659-60.

On the retaliation claims, the court reasoned that, even if she could state a prima facie case, the claims failed because she did not show DU's reasons for any adverse employment actions were pretextual for retaliation.

Having rejected the federal claims, the court declined to exercise supplemental jurisdiction over the remaining state law claims. This appeal followed.

p.1315 II. DISCUSSION

Our review focuses on DU's reasons for the alleged adverse employment actions regarding Dr. Hiatt and whether those reasons were pretextual. As so limited, we have no reason to resolve whether Dr. Hiatt handled her personal relationship with Dr. Coven in accordance with her professional responsibilities. We consider only whether the reasons DU gave for Dr. Hiatt's demotion and maintaining her non-supervisory role were (1) legitimate, non-discriminatory, and nonretaliatory, and (2) not pretextual.

We affirm all claims on appeal on the same basis: Dr. Hiatt is unable to show that DU's reasons for any alleged adverse employment actions were pretextual for discrimination or retaliation.[7]

A. Standard of Review

"We review a district court's grant of summary judgment de novo, applying the same legal standard as the district court." *Twigg*, 659 F.3d at 997. "The court shall grant summary judgment if the movant shows that there is no genuine dispute as to any material fact and the movant is entitled to judgment as a matter of law." Fed. R. Civ. P. 56(a). "In applying this standard, we view the evidence and the reasonable inferences to be drawn from the evidence in the light most favorable to the nonmoving party." *Twigg*, 659 F.3d at 997.

B. Legal Standards

1. Title VII and Title IX

Title VII of the Civil Rights Act of 1964 prohibits employers from discriminating against an individual "because of such individual's... sex." 42 U.S.C. § 2000e-2(a)(1). Title VII also prohibits employers from retaliating against employees who have opposed an unlawful employment practice such as sex discrimination. *Id.* § 2000e-3(a).

Title IX of the Education Amendments Act of 1972 provides similar protections. It prohibits discrimination "on the basis of sex" in educational programs or activities receiving federal funding. 20 U.S.C. § 1681(a). This includes a prohibition on employment discrimination in federally funded educational programs. *N. Haven Bd. of Educ. v. Bell*, 456 U.S. 512, 535-36, 102 S.Ct. 1912, 72 L.Ed.2d 299 (1982). Title IX also prohibits retaliation against individuals because they have complained of sex discrimination. *Jackson v. Birmingham Bd. of Educ.*, 544 U.S. 167, 183, 125 S.Ct. 1497, 161 L.Ed.2d 361 (2005) (interpreting Title IX as creating a private right of action for such a claim).

2. Burden-Shifting Framework

In district court, Dr. Hiatt relied on indirect evidence to oppose summary judgment on her discrimination and retaliation claims. This approach uses the burden-shifting framework from *McDonnell Douglas Corp. v. Green*, 411 U.S. 792, 802-05, 93 S.Ct. 1817, 36 L.Ed.2d 668 (1973).[8]

p.1316 Under *McDonnell Douglas*, a plaintiff must first establish a prima facie case for discrimination or retaliation by showing an employer took adverse employment action against the plaintiff based on the plaintiff's sex or protected activity. *Bird*, 832 F.3d at 1200 (sex discrimination claim); *Fye*, 516 F.3d at 1225 (retaliation claim). The burden then shifts to the employer "to articulate a legitimate, nondiscriminatory [or nonretaliatory] reason for the adverse action." *Bird*, 832 F.3d at 1200. If the employer satisfies this burden, "then summary judgment is warranted unless [the plaintiff] can show there is a genuine issue of material fact as to whether the proffered reason[] [is] pretextual." *Id.* (quotations omitted).

We provide further background on two parts of the burden-shifting framework, adverse employment actions and pretext.

3. Adverse Employment Action

For discrimination claims, "[a]n adverse employment action is a significant change in employment status, such as hiring, firing, failing to promote, reassignment with significantly different responsibilities, or a decision causing a significant change in benefits." *Daniels v. United Parcel Serv., Inc.*, 701 F.3d 620, 635 (10th Cir. 2012) (emphasis and quotations omitted). "[A] mere inconvenience or an alteration of job responsibilities" does not qualify as an adverse action. *Piercy v. Maketa*, 480 F.3d 1192, 1203 (10th Cir. 2007) (quotations omitted).

For retaliation claims, "a plaintiff must show that a reasonable employee would have found the challenged action materially adverse, which in this context means it well might have dissuaded a reasonable worker from making or supporting a charge of discrimination." *Burlington N. & Santa Fe Ry. Co. v. White,* 548 U.S. 53, 68, 126 S.Ct. 2405, 165 L.Ed.2d 345 (2006) (quotations omitted). The action must be materially adverse "to separate significant from trivial harms," such as "petty slights, minor annoyances, and simple lack of good manners...." *Id.*

4. Pretext

"[A] plaintiff can establish pretext by showing the defendant's proffered nondiscriminatory [and/or nonretaliatory] explanations for its actions are so incoherent, weak, inconsistent, or contradictory that a rational factfinder could conclude they are unworthy of belief." *Johnson v. Weld Cty., Colo.,* 594 F.3d 1202, 1211 (10th Cir. 2010) (brackets and quotations omitted). "Evidence that the employer should not have made the [adverse employment] decision — for example, that the employer was mistaken or used poor business judgment — is not sufficient to show that the employer's explanation is unworthy of credibility." *Swackhammer v. Sprint/United Mgmt. Co.,* 493 F.3d 1160, 1169-70 (10th Cir. 2007). "The relevant inquiry is not whether the employer's proffered reasons were wise, fair or correct, but whether it honestly believed those reasons and acted in good faith upon those beliefs." *Id.* (quotations omitted).

C. Analysis

We assume without deciding that Dr. Hiatt could make a prima facie *McDonnell Douglas* showing of sex discrimination and retaliation under Title VII and Title IX. But her claims cannot survive summary judgment because she has failed to show DU's proffered reasons for taking any adverse employment actions were pretextual. Because all of Dr. Hiatt's federal claims require a showing of pretext, and because she relies on the same evidence and arguments to show pretext,[9] we resolve all of her claims on this ground.[10]

We first identify Dr. Hiatt's alleged adverse employment actions. We then explain why Dr. Hiatt has not met her burden to show that DU's reasons for those actions were pretextual.

1. Adverse Employment Actions

In her opening brief on appeal, Dr. Hiatt identifies four adverse employment actions: (1) her demotion from Training Director to Outreach Coordinator in February 2013; (2) DU's failure to reinstate her supervisory duties in August 2013; (3) her "constructive discharge" in May 2014; and (4) DU's differential treatment of her in the period leading up to her resignation in May 2014.[11] At oral argument, Dr. Hiatt's counsel stated that the first three actions pertain to the discrimination claims, and the fourth is relevant to the retaliation claims. But she did not make such a distinction in her opening brief. Construing her arguments generously, we consider whether the following actions qualify as adverse employment actions for either the discrimination or retaliation claims.

a. The Demotion and Failure to Reinstate Supervisory Duties

A reasonable person in Dr. Hiatt's position would view her demotion to Outreach Coordinator, coupled with a salary decrease of $2,000, as an adverse employment action. *See Burlington,* 548 U.S. at 71, 126 S.Ct. 2405 ("Whether a particular reassignment is materially adverse depends upon the circumstances of the particular case, and should be judged from the perspective of a reasonable person in the plaintiff's position, considering all the circumstances." (quotations omitted)). DU's later decision not to reinstate her supervisory duties was closely related to her demotion. We analyze it as a separate adverse action below.

p.1318 b. Constructive Discharge

Dr. Hiatt was not constructively discharged, so there was no adverse employment action on this basis.

"[C]onstructive discharge occurs when the employer by its illegal discriminatory acts has made working conditions so difficult that a reasonable person in the employee's position would feel compelled to resign." *Bennett v. Windstream Commc'ns, Inc.,* 792 F.3d 1261, 1269 (10th Cir. 2015) (quotations omitted). "To establish constructive discharge, a plaintiff must show that she had no other choice but to quit." *Id.* (quotations omitted).

The record shows Dr. Hiatt cannot meet those standards. Although she may have subjectively believed that DU left her with "no other choice but to quit," her "subjective views of the situation are irrelevant," and she must instead show "[t]he conditions of employment [were] objectively intolerable." *Id.* (quotations omitted). The working conditions she describes — such as being required to work two extra hours per week, turn in timely case notes, and justify non-FMLA sick time — do not amount to an objectively intolerable working environment. *See Sandoval v. City of Boulder, Colo.,* 388 F.3d 1312, 1325-26 (10th Cir. 2004) (finding no constructive discharge when the plaintiff was humiliated due to an investigation into her management practices and reassigned to another position whose conditions were not objectively intolerable); *Sanchez v. Denver Pub. Schs.,* 164 F.3d 527, 533-34 (10th Cir. 1998) (finding no constructive discharge when the plaintiff was the "only teacher required to bring a doctor's note when she was sick," and was reprimanded for walking out of a meeting because the work environment, "while unpleasant," was not objectively intolerable).

We thus do not address Dr. Hiatt's alleged constructive discharge in our pretext analysis.

c. Differential Treatment

Dr. Hiatt asserts DU treated her differently from other HCC staff. Although she cites differential treatment as evidence of pretext in her opening brief, she changed her position at oral argument and claimed that differential treatment was a separate adverse action. Either way, Dr. Hiatt has not pointed to any similarly situated employees to show differential treatment.

A plaintiff can show differential treatment by providing evidence the employer treated the plaintiff differently from other similarly situated employees. *See Kendrick v. Penske Transp. Servs., Inc.,* 220 F.3d 1220, 1232 (10th Cir. 2000). An employee is similarly situated to the plaintiff if the employee shares the same supervisor, is subject to the same standards governing performance evaluation and discipline, and has similar relevant employment circumstances, such as work history. *Id.*

Dr. Hiatt has failed to identify any other similarly situated employees who allegedly received differential treatment. She suggests Ross Artwohl and Kimberly Mercer as relevant comparators because, like she did, they reported to Dr. Palmateer. But having a common supervisor, alone, is insufficient, and she mentions no other factors to support comparability. *See id.* at 1232.

Dr. Hiatt also proposes Dr. Fogle and Dr. Mathewson because Dr. Palmateer supervised them and the same professional standards applied to them as to Dr. Hiatt. But because Dr. Hiatt supervised these two individuals, they were not in positions comparable to Dr. Hiatt.

p.1319 * * * *

For the foregoing reasons, the only actions that qualify as adverse employment actions against Dr. Hiatt were (1) the demotion and (2) the failure to reinstate her supervisory duties.

2. Legitimate Reasons and Pretext

We now apply the second and third steps of the *McDonnell Douglas* framework and address (1) whether DU's reasons for the alleged adverse actions were legitimate, nondiscriminatory, and nonretaliatory; and, if so, (2) whether those reasons were pretextual. We conclude that DU's reasons were legitimate and that Dr. Hiatt has not met her burden to show the reasons were pretextual.

a. The demotion

i. Legitimate, nondiscriminatory, and nonretaliatory reasons

DU's reasons for demoting Dr. Hiatt fall into three categories: (1) the "upheaval among her students," including at least three out of five supervisees discontinuing supervision with her; (2) the "ethically grey" manner in how she handled her relationship with Dr. Coven relative to her professional responsibilities; and (3) her therapy-based supervisory style and failure to take personal responsibility for the supervisees' reactions to how she handled her relationship relative to her work. *See* Aplee. Br. at 29-32.

DU's proffered reasons satisfy its burden to articulate legitimate, nondiscriminatory, and nonretaliatory reasons for the demotion. *See Williams v.*

FedEx Corp. Servs., 849 F.3d 889, 900 (10th Cir. 2017). Dr. Hiatt does not challenge that determination.

We therefore next assess whether those reasons were pretextual for discrimination or retaliation. *See Lobato v. N.M. Env't Dep't,* 733 F.3d 1283, 1289 (10th Cir. 2013) ("The parties do not dispute the first two steps in the *McDonnell Douglas* framework. Our analysis thus turns on the third step — pretext."); *see also Foster v. Mountain Coal Co.,* 830 F.3d 1178, 1194 (10th Cir. 2016) (adopting the same approach).

ii. Pretext

Dr. Hiatt has not satisfied her burden of showing DU's reasons for demoting her were pretextual for discrimination or retaliation. The record instead supports that DU "honestly believed" its proffered reasons and "acted in good faith upon those beliefs." *Swackhammer,* 493 F.3d at 1169-70 (quotations omitted). We begin with general considerations as to why DU's reasons were not pretextual and then analyze DU's specific reasons.

1) General considerations

Two general considerations — consistency and timing — support that DU's reasons were not pretextual.

a) Consistency

When Dr. Kent and Dr. Palmateer met with Dr. Hiatt on February 22, 2013, and presented the three options to her, the reasons they stated then are the same reasons that DU provides in this litigation. The consistency of their explanations cuts against a finding of pretext. *See Johnson,* 594 F.3d at 1211 (providing that inconsistent rationales may show pretext); *Plotke v. White,* 405 F.3d 1092, 1102-03 (10th Cir. 2005) (providing that new rationales not given at the time of the adverse action may show pretext).

First, in the meeting, Dr. Kent and Dr. Palmateer explained to Dr. Hiatt that a "majority" of trainees refused to be supervised by her. App. at 450. This aligns with the rationale DU has presented in this case regarding the "upheaval" among the students, including at least three out of five supervisees' ending their supervision with Dr. Hiatt. Aplee. Br. at 29, 31-32.

Second, Dr. Hiatt was told in the meeting that her conduct posed a "grey ethical issue" and that a Training Director needed to "display exemplary ethics, boundaries, and professionalism." App. at 450. DU's second rationale in this litigation similarly posits that Dr. Hiatt lacked judgment in the way she handled her relationship with Dr. Coven relative to her professional responsibilities. DU also points to the steps leading to its determination that she had entered ethical grey territory. *See* Aplee. Br. at 29, 32.

Third, Dr. Kent and Dr. Palmateer explained during the meeting that Dr. Hiatt's "approach to therapy and supervision requires a strict adherence to boundaries which weren't demonstrated in this situation" and that her response to the students' upheaval showed a "lack of personal responsibility." App. at 450. In this case, DU has proffered a parallel rationale that Dr. Hiatt lacked boundaries in supervision and failed to take personal responsibility for the students' reactions. Aplee. Br. at 30-33.

The consistency over time of DU's reasons for demoting Dr. Hiatt supports the conclusion that DU's reasons for demoting Dr. Hiatt were not pretextual.

b) Timing

The timing of when DU first provided its reasons for Dr. Hiatt's demotion further undermines a finding of pretext for her retaliation claim. Dr. Kent and Dr. Palmateer initially gave Dr. Hiatt the reasons for her demotion in their February 22, 2013 meeting. But her first protected activity opposing discrimination — a necessary element for her retaliation claim — occurred on February 27, 2013, when her lawyer sent DU a letter making allegations of discrimination. This timing undercuts Dr. Hiatt's argument that DU's reasons for the demotion decision were pretextual. DU could not retaliate for Dr. Hiatt's protected activity until she had engaged in such activity. *See Kilcrease v. Domenico Transp. Co.*, 828 F.3d 1214, 1225-26 (10th Cir. 2016) (providing that to show retaliation, a plaintiff must show an "adverse action by an employer either after or contemporaneous with the employee's protected action" and holding that the plaintiff could not show that element because the employer had made the adverse employment decision before learning about the plaintiff's protected activity); *Kenfield v. Colo. Dep't of Pub. Health & Env't*, 557 Fed.Appx. 728, 733 (10th Cir. 2014) (unpublished) ("By its very nature, retaliatory conduct must come *after* the protected activity.").[12]

2) Specific reasons

DU's specific reasons for the demotion also withstand Dr. Hiatt's arguments.

First, the record supports that DU honestly and in good faith believed the "upheaval among her supervisees" rendered Dr. Hiatt unable to continue as Training Director. Aplee. Br. at 29. Three of Dr. Hiatt's supervisees elected to end supervision with her — three out of nine according to Dr. Hiatt and three out of five according to DU. Regardless, three supervisees electing to discontinue supervision with Dr. Hiatt validated DU's concerns that she could not continue in a supervisory role.

Second, on appeal, Dr. Hiatt disputes DU's determination that her relationship with Dr. Coven placed her in an ethical grey area. But whether or not DU's "ethical greyness" assessment was valid, its investigation into the ethics of Dr. Hiatt's conduct shows its assessment was not a pretextual reason for her demotion.

Dr. Kent and Dr. Palmateer listened to Dr. Hiatt's and Dr. Fogle's accounts. Dr. Hiatt told them her supervisory relationship with Dr. Coven ended before a romantic one began. Dr. Fogle told them the romance started before the supervision ended. Dr. Kent presented both Dr. Hiatt's and Dr. Fogle's timelines of events to Dr. Philinda Hutchings — the Dean of the Midwestern School of Professional Psychology — and Dr. Bill Bracker — the former Director of the Nova Southeastern University Consortium Internship. Both Dr. Hutchings and Dr. Bracker concluded Dr. Hiatt's relationship was a "clear" ethical breach. App. at 447. In addition, Dr.

Kent called the APA ethics office, which advised that "given the alleged timing, [the relationship] could be seen as a gray area or it could be a violation." App. at 447-48.

Dr. Hiatt argues that DU improperly relied on Dr. Fogle's timeline, but an "[e]mployer may defeat the inference that an employment decision was a product of reliance on a biased subordinate by simply asking an employee for [her] version of events, and not relying exclusively on the say-so of the biased subordinate." *Smothers v. Solvay Chems., Inc.*, 740 F.3d 530, 543 (10th Cir. 2014) (quoting *EEOC v. BCI Coca-Cola Bottling Co. of L.A.*, 450 F.3d 476, 488 (10th Cir. 2006) (brackets and quotations omitted). Consistent with *Smothers*, DU gave Dr. Hiatt multiple opportunities to explain her version of events.

In sum, DU's investigation into Dr. Hiatt's relationship as it related to her professional responsibilities was substantial and bore no marks of unfairness. Its determination that Dr. Hiatt had entered ethical grey territory as a result of that investigation — even if mistaken — does not suggest pretext. *See Piercy*, 480 F.3d at 1202 ("If the employer's stated reasons were held in good faith at the time of the discharge, even if they later prove to be untrue, we cannot conclude they were a subterfuge for discrimination or, likewise, retaliation.").

Third, DU administrators believed the demotion decision was justified because Dr. Hiatt lacked boundaries in supervision and failed to take personal responsibility for her supervisees' reactions. Dr. Kent's meeting notes documented how Dr. Hiatt blamed her supervisees' pathologies for the upheaval. The revelation of Dr. Hiatt's relationship with Dr. Coven had the unexpected effect of shedding light on Dr. Hiatt's approach to supervision. During Dr. Kent's discussion with Dr. Fogle after the "open meeting," Dr. Fogle described Dr. Hiatt's therapeutic supervisory style as sometimes causing Dr. Fogle to cry and feel vulnerable. Dr. Hiatt does not challenge Dr. Fogle's description of her therapy style. Indeed, Dr. Hiatt admitted in her deposition that supervisees even had a name for it — getting "Tawny-ed." App. at 166. Before Dr. Fogle's meeting with Dr. Kent, Dr. Shanley also had complained about Dr. Hiatt's approach, stating it made him feel "uncomfortable" and was "intrusive." App. at 178. This information reinforced DU's belief that Dr. Hiatt lacked proper boundaries when supervising.[13]

* * * *

p.1322 Dr. Hiatt has not shown that DU's reasons for removing her from her position as Training Director and demoting her to Outreach Coordinator were dishonest or made in bad faith, *Swackhammer*, 493 F.3d at 1169-70, or were "so incoherent, weak, inconsistent, or contradictory that a rational factfinder could conclude they are unworthy of belief," *Johnson*, 594 F.3d at 1211 (brackets and quotations omitted). She has thus not met her burden to show pretext to survive summary judgment on her discrimination or retaliation claims.

b. Failure to Reinstate

Dr. Hiatt also challenged DU's decision not to reinstate her supervisory duties, arguing that Dr. Asher recommended she return to supervision.

i. Legitimate, nondiscriminatory, and nonretaliatory reasons

DU disputes that Dr. Asher had made such a recommendation, but even if she did, DU contends it could reasonably disagree with Dr. Asher's assessment and that her recommendation was just one factor in making its decision. According to DU, other factors included the supervisees' negative feedback about Dr. Hiatt, Dr. Kent's and Dr. Palmateer's observations of Dr. Hiatt's job performance, and their view that Dr. Hiatt continued to blame the interns for her demotion and failed to acknowledge her role in contributing to their reactions.

Once again, Dr. Hiatt does not contest these were legitimate, nondiscriminatory, and nonretaliatory reasons. We agree and turn to whether they were pretextual for discrimination or retaliation. *See Lobato*, 733 F.3d at 1289; *Foster*, 830 F.3d at 1194.

ii. Pretext

Dr. Hiatt has not met her burden to show that DU's reasons for not reinstating her supervisory duties were pretextual for discrimination or retaliation.

1) General Considerations

Like its demotion decision, DU consistently provided the same reasons for not returning Dr. Hiatt to a supervisory position in (1) the August 2013 meeting with Dr. Hiatt explaining the decision, (2) the September 2013 response to Dr. Hiatt's internal EEO complaint, and (3) this litigation. The consistency of DU's responses from the time of the employment action to now supports that DU's reasons were not pretextual. *See Plotke*, 405 F.3d at 1102-03; *Johnson*, 594 F.3d at 1211.

2) Specific Reasons

Dr. Hiatt presents two main pretext arguments: (1) DU did not follow Dr. Asher's recommendation to reinstate her supervisory duties, and (2) DU imposed subjective standards to measure whether she could return to supervision. Neither shows pretext.

First, DU acted honestly and in good faith in not accepting Dr. Asher's recommendation. In Dr. Kent's view, Dr. Asher's recommendation was equivocal. Even assuming Dr. Asher firmly endorsed Dr. Hiatt's return to supervision, we agree with the district court that DU could reasonably disagree with her recommendation. And if DU exercised poor judgment, that is not enough to show pretext. *See Swackhammer*, 493 F.3d at 1169-70 (providing that an employer's mistake or use of poor business judgment is insufficient to show pretext).

DU had several legitimate reasons to disagree with Dr. Asher's recommendation. In their September 26, 2013 response to Dr. Hiatt's internal EEO complaint, Dr. Kent and Dr. Palmateer noted that Dr. Asher's recommendation came with the caveat p.1323 that Dr. Hiatt was not likely to change her supervision style if she resumed her supervisory duties. In the six months after Dr. Hiatt was demoted, DU discovered additional cause for concern about her supervision style. In their exit interviews after she was demoted, several supervisees described "troubling interactions" with Dr. Hiatt during supervision that gave DU further reason to believe Dr. Hiatt had "very poor boundaries." App. at 526-27.

Dr. Kent and Dr. Palmateer also noted in their response to Dr. Hiatt's internal EEO complaint that Dr. Hiatt had not demonstrated any awareness of how her supervisory style negatively affected the supervisees. Their response documented that, in her meetings with Dr. Asher, Dr. Hiatt continued to blame the supervisees' pathologies as causing the upheaval in the winter of 2013 rather than acknowledging her own contribution.

In sum, DU gave several reasons to disregard Dr. Asher's recommendation. Dr. Hiatt has not provided evidence to show that a reasonable factfinder could find those reasons unworthy of belief. *See Swackhammer,* 493 F.3d at 1169-70

Second, Dr. Hiatt tried to show pretext in district court by pointing to DU's use of "subjective criteria" to measure whether Dr. Hiatt could resume her supervisory duties. She pointed to the October 2013 email from Associate Provost for Student Life Patricia Helton, which called on Dr. Hiatt to have "better awareness about the power she holds" and "demonstrate[] appropriate professional boundaries in all contexts" before she could resume supervision. App. at 546.

Dr. Hiatt did not adequately explain in district court or here how the email instructions were subjective. But even if they were, the criteria do not signal pretext. Nothing in the email or elsewhere suggests DU implemented these criteria dishonestly or in bad faith. Instead, the criteria show DU was trying to create a path for Dr. Hiatt to resume supervision. The email even expressed DU's hope that Dr. Hiatt eventually would return to supervision.

Dr. Hiatt has not shown DU's reasons for refusing to reinstate her supervisory duties were pretextual for retaliation or discrimination.

* * * *

Dr. Hiatt has not satisfied her burden of showing DU's reasons for demoting her or failing to reinstate her supervisory duties were pretextual for discrimination or retaliation. DU's proffered reasons were not so "incoherent, weak, inconsistent, or contradictory" as to be unworthy of belief by a reasonable factfinder. *See Johnson,* 594 F.3d at 1211. At most, Dr. Hiatt's evidence may support that DU may have made mistaken employment decisions. But arguments questioning the soundness of DU's decisions are insufficient to show DU acted dishonestly or in bad faith. *See Swackhammer,* 493 F.3d at 1169-70. Dr. Hiatt cannot, therefore, create a triable issue that DU's reasons for any adverse employment actions were pretextual for sex discrimination or retaliation.

III. CONCLUSION

We affirm the district court's grant of summary judgment on Dr. Hiatt's Title VII and Title IX discrimination and retaliation claims.

[1] The parties have made our presentation of the facts challenging as they frequently cite briefs to support factual assertions rather than evidence in the record. We have endeavored to rely on record evidence, such as deposition testimony or meeting notes, rather than the parties' district court briefing.

[2] Dr. Hiatt alleges her resignation amounted to a constructive discharge. We discuss this assertion below.

[3] We refer to the supervisees as "doctors," even if they were not doctors at the time of these events, where there is record support for their since becoming doctors.

[4] The record shows another supervisee had expressed similar concerns about Dr. Hiatt's supervisory style before the February 13, 2013 meeting. *See* App. at 178 (Dr. Kent's deposition relaying that Dr. Shanley had felt, "shortly after beginning therapy supervision with her," that Dr. Hiatt's supervisory style was "uncomfortable and intrusive").

[5] APA Rule 7.07 states "[p]sychologists do not engage in sexual relationships with students or supervisees who are in their department, agency, or training center or over whom psychologists have or are likely to have evaluative authority." App. at 189.

[6] APA Rule 3.05 states a psychologist should refrain from entering a "multiple relationship" — defined as having a relationship with someone closely associated with a person with whom the psychologist has a professional relationship — if the multiple relationship "could reasonably be expected to impair the psychologist's objectivity, competence, or effectiveness in performing his or her functions as a psychologist, or otherwise risks exploitation or harm to the person with whom the professional relationship exists." App. at 188.

[7] We affirm on the retaliation claims on the same ground the district court relied on — lack of pretext. We affirm on the discrimination claims for lack of pretext — an alternative ground from the district court.

[8] The *McDonnell Douglas* framework applies both to the Title IX and Title VII sex discrimination claims. *See Bird v. W. Valley City*, 832 F.3d 1188, 1200 (10th Cir. 2016) (Title VII sex discrimination claim); *Gossett v. Okla. ex rel. Bd. of Regents for Langston Univ.*, 245 F.3d 1172, 1176 (10th Cir. 2001) ("Courts have generally assessed Title IX discrimination claims under the same legal analysis as Title VII claims.").

McDonnell Douglas applies to Title VII retaliation claims. *Fye v. Okla. Corp. Comm'n*, 516 F.3d 1217, 1225 (10th Cir. 2008). We also have applied the framework to Title IX retaliation claims, albeit not in a published case. *See, e.g., Berry v. Mission Grp. Kan., Inc.*, 463 Fed.Appx. 759, 766 n.7 (10th Cir. 2012) (unpublished). We apply the *McDonnell Douglas* framework here, as we have stated that Title VII is "the most appropriate analogue when defining Title IX's substantive standards." *Roberts v. Colo. State Bd. of Agric.*, 998 F.2d 824, 832 (10th Cir. 1993).

[9] At oral argument, Dr. Hiatt's counsel stated that the "vast majority" of her pretext arguments were the same for both the discrimination and retaliation claims, but that "some" of them were different. Oral Arg. at 12:00-13:26. She failed, however, to identify then or in her briefing any pretext arguments that are different for any of her claims. *Id.*

[10] We have previously affirmed a grant of summary judgment on the basis of failure to show pretext after assuming without deciding that an employee has stated

a prima facie case. *See, e.g., Bird,* 832 F.3d at 1201 (analyzing pretext after "assum[ing] without deciding that [plaintiff-appellant] ... has established a prima facie case showing that she was terminated because she is a woman."); *Etsitty v. Utah Transit Auth.,* 502 F.3d 1215, 1224 (10th Cir. 2007) ("Assuming [the plaintiff-appellant] has established a prima facie case ... of gender stereotyping, the burden then shifts to [the defendant-appellee] to articulate a legitimate, nondiscriminatory reason for [the plaintiff's] termination.").

[11] At oral argument, Dr. Hiatt's counsel cited an exhibit to her opposition to summary judgment in district court, in which she listed several adverse employment actions relevant to her retaliation claims. To the extent the list contains any actions not raised in her opening brief, we decline to consider them. *See EEOC v. TriCore Reference Labs.,* 849 F.3d 929, 941 (10th Cir. 2017) (declining to consider arguments raised for the first time at oral argument not raised in an opening brief).

Also at oral argument, Dr. Hiatt's counsel argued that DU's failure to respond appropriately to the supervisees' reactions to her relationship was an adverse action. Oral Arg. at 9:41-11:11. But because Dr. Hiatt did not identify this issue as a separate adverse action in her opening brief on appeal, we do not address it. *See TriCore Reference Labs.,* 849 F.3d at 941.

[12] Although unpublished and not precedential, we cite this decision for its persuasive value. *See* 10th Cir. R. 32.1(A).

[13] Dr. Hiatt points to her supervisees' positive reviews of her supervision before they learned about her relationship with Dr. Coven as undermining any later criticism that she lacked boundaries in supervision. But those reviews were not anonymous. Dr. Hiatt has not presented facts that would discredit DU's belief.

789 F.3d 1164 (2015)

**Paul LEVY, Plaintiff-Appellant,
Brenda Umholtz; Tina Bruce, Plaintiffs,**

v.

**KANSAS DEPARTMENT OF SOCIAL AND REHABILITATION
SERVICES, Defendant-Appellee.**

No. 14-3061.

United States Court of Appeals, Tenth Circuit.

June 16, 2015.

Levy v. Kansas Dept. of Social & Rehab. Services, 789 F. 3d 1164 (10th Cir. 2015)

p.1166 Alan V. Johnson of Sloan, Eisenbarth, Glassman, McEntire & Jarboe, L.L.C., Topeka, KS, for Plaintiff-Appellant.

Gregory A. Lee, (Jenna R. Seematter, with him on the brief), of Cooper & Lee, LLC, Topeka, KS, for Defendant-Appellee.

Before BRISCOE, Chief Judge, MURPHY and GORSUCH, Circuit Judges.

BRISCOE, Chief Judge.

Paul Levy alleges that he was constructively discharged from the Kansas Department of Social and Rehabilitation Services (SRS) in retaliation for advocating for better accommodation for a disabled co-worker. He filed retaliation claims against SRS under the Americans with Disabilities Act (ADA) and the Rehabilitation Act. The district court granted summary judgment to SRS on both claims, concluding that SRS was entitled to sovereign immunity on Levy's ADA claim and that Levy's Rehabilitation Act claim was barred by the statute of limitations. Levy appeals from that decision. Exercising jurisdiction pursuant to 28 U.S.C. § 1291, we affirm the district court's dismissal of his claims.

I

A. Factual background

Paul Levy was hired as a rehabilitation counselor in the Wichita office of SRS in 2001. In December 2008, Levy agreed to serve as a counselor for a coworker in his office, Tina Bruce, who had requested a vocational assessment to determine whether her disability (blindness) was being fully accommodated. Levy ordered the assessment from a contractor, Brenda Umholtz, who had done extensive work for both Levy and Bruce at SRS. Umholtz's report stated that Bruce was not receiving adequate accommodation for her blindness and could not compete on an "'equal-playing field' as her ... counterparts even within her office." App. at 73. The report also noted that Bruce was "protected by A.D.A. laws regarding accommodations that dictate that she cannot be fairly evaluated until such accommodations are consistently available, in working order during her entire work hours." *Id.*

On February 20, 2009, SRS department director Michael Donnelly sent Levy a letter proposing Levy's termination. The stated reason for Levy's termination was a violation of the department's conflict of interest policies. Donnelly stated that Umholtz's report contained "numerous sweeping legal opinions and inflammatory statements" that made the conflicts of interest between Levy, Bruce, and Umholtz apparent. *Id.* at 110. Donnelly's letter also contained several other instances of allegedly inappropriate conduct by Levy during the course of his employment. Levy was given the opportunity to appear in person to respond to the allegations on February 24, 2009.

Levy stated in interrogatories that he met with Donnelly on February 12, 2009, prior to receiving the termination letter. Levy stated that he told Donnelly at the meeting that other counselors in the division had served as counselors for co-workers without being punished. He also noted that he informed his supervisor about opening Bruce's case in January 2009 — "prior to any substantial services being delivered" — and that he transferred Bruce's case to his supervisor immediately when asked to do so. *Id.* at 140, 143. Levy stated that prior to the February 24th meeting, he asked whether it would be possible for him to resign instead of being terminated. However, Levy said that he did not officially resign until February 25, 2009, after it became clear in his February 24th meeting that Donnelly was planning to terminate him regardless of what he said at the meeting.

p.1167 B. Procedural background

Umholtz filed suit against SRS on February 11, 2011. Levy joined the suit on March 2, 2011, and Bruce joined shortly thereafter. In the Second Amended Complaint, Levy alleged that SRS had retaliated against him in violation of the ADA. Levy requested reinstatement, compensatory damages in excess of $100,000, and attorneys' fees and other litigation expenses. The plaintiffs later amended their complaint to add Rehabilitation Act claims for Bruce and Levy, and SRS agreed not to oppose the amendment in exchange for the plaintiffs' agreement that SRS had not waived its sovereign immunity defense.

On March 23, 2012, SRS filed for summary judgment on all of Levy's claims. Among other arguments, SRS contended that Levy's ADA claim was barred by the Eleventh Amendment because the Supreme Court had determined in *Board of Trustees of the University of Alabama v. Garrett,* 531 U.S. 356, 121 S.Ct. 955, 148 L.Ed.2d 866 (2001), that Congress had not constitutionally abrogated a state's immunity from employment discrimination suits under Title I of the ADA. Although retaliation claims fall under Title V of the ADA, SRS argued that a retaliation claim based on alleged Title I discrimination rendered it subject to the *Garrett* decision.

SRS also argued that Levy's Rehabilitation Act claim was barred by the statute of limitations. Congress did not specify a federal statute of limitations for the Rehabilitation Act, but SRS noted that this circuit concluded that Rehabilitation Act claims resemble § 1983 claims and that both types of claims can best be analogized to claims for injury to personal rights, for which Kansas imposes a two-year statute of limitations. *See Baker v. Bd. of Regents of Kan.,* 991 F.2d 628, 630-32 (10th Cir. 1993) (citing *Wilson v. Garcia,* 471 U.S. 261, 276-77, 105 S.Ct. 1938, 85 L.Ed.2d 254 (1985), which affirmed the Tenth Circuit's characterization of § 1983 claims as similar to personal injury claims for the purpose of applying an appropriate state statute of limitations). Because Levy resigned or was terminated in February 2009 and did not join Umholtz's suit until March 2011, SRS contended that his claims were time-barred. Levy argued in response that SRS waived its Eleventh Amendment immunity for ADA claims by accepting federal funds, and that Rehabilitation Act claims are more appropriately categorized as statutorily created rights governed by Kansas's three-year statute of limitations.

The district court ruled that SRS was entitled to summary judgment on Levy's ADA claim because the claim against SRS was barred by sovereign immunity. Specifically, the district court concluded that SRS did not waive its sovereign immunity for ADA claims through a waiver provision in the Rehabilitation Act enacted four years prior to the ADA. That provision required states who accept federal funds to waive their sovereign immunity for claims under the Rehabilitation Act, Title IX of the Education Amendments Act of 1972, the Age Discrimination Act of 1975, Title VI of the Civil Rights Act of 1964 "or the provisions of any other Federal statute prohibiting discrimination by recipients of Federal financial assistance." 42 U.S.C. § 2000d-7(a)(1). The district court noted that the Supreme Court's ruling in *Garrett* only discussed whether Congress had validly abrogated state sovereign immunity under Title I of the ADA (and by implication, Title I-based claims under Title V) and not whether a state had waived its immunity. Nonetheless, the district court concluded that the waiver provision in the Rehabilitation Act was not sufficient to meet the "stringent" test for whether a state, by accepting federal funds, has made a clear and voluntary waiver of its sovereign immunity for ADA claims.

p.1168 The district court also concluded that Levy's claims under the Rehabilitation Act were untimely because this court's precedent analogizes Rehabilitation Act claims to claims for injury to personal rights under Kansas law and applies the state's two-year statute of limitations. *See Baker*, 991 F.2d at 631-32. It is undisputed that Levy filed his claim more than two years after being discharged. The district court declined to rule on SRS's other arguments.

II

A. Subject matter jurisdiction

The district court had jurisdiction over this case pursuant to 28 U.S.C. § 1331. Although SRS does not challenge the court's subject-matter jurisdiction on appeal, there was initially some debate as to whether it was appropriate to permit Levy and Bruce to add Rehabilitation Act claims when their initial claims under the ADA were ultimately barred by sovereign immunity. The district court noted that sovereign immunity is often equated with a lack of subject-matter jurisdiction, but "the equation is more of an approximation" because sovereign immunity can be waived, and courts are not required to raise the issue sua sponte. App. at 157-58 (citing *Wisconsin Dep't of Corr. v. Schacht*, 524 U.S. 381, 389, 118 S.Ct. 2047, 141 L.Ed.2d 364 (1998)). Because SRS did not "effectively raise" its immunity until its motion for summary judgment, which was filed *after* the district court had already permitted Levy and Bruce to add their Rehabilitation Act claims, the district court concluded that it had subject-matter jurisdiction. *Id.* at 158 (citing *Harris v. Owens,* 264 F.3d 1282, 1288 (10th Cir.2001) ("Once *effectively raised,* the Eleventh Amendment becomes a limitation on our subject-matter jurisdiction") (emphasis added)).

Such a conclusion is consistent with how other courts view the interplay between amendments to complaints and the assertion of a sovereign immunity defense. *Cf. Mills v. State of Me.,* 118 F.3d 37, 53 (1st Cir.1997) (denying a party the right to amend its complaint on appeal to create subject-matter jurisdiction in a sovereign immunity case, but noting the plaintiff "had an opportunity to seek to amend its pleadings in the district court"); *Oliver Sch., Inc. v. Foley,* 930 F.2d 248, 252 (2d Cir.1991) ("We take issue, however, both with the court's refusal to construe the complaint as asserting claims against the individual defendants in their personal capacities and with its refusal to allow Oliver to amend the complaint to assert such claims unequivocally."). We agree with the district court that Levy and Bruce successfully added Rehabilitation Act claims to their complaint prior to SRS raising a sovereign immunity defense.

B. Standard of review

"We review the grant of summary judgment de novo applying the same standard as the district court." *Adler v. Wal-Mart Stores, Inc.,* 144 F.3d 664, 670 (10th Cir. 1998). "Summary judgment is proper if the movant demonstrates that there is 'no genuine issue as to any material fact' and that it is 'entitled to a judgment as a matter of law.'" *Id.* (quoting Fed.R.Civ.P. 56(c)).

C. ADA claim and sovereign immunity

Generally, states and their agencies are protected from suit by sovereign immunity, as guaranteed by the Eleventh Amendment. "The ultimate guarantee of the Eleventh Amendment is that nonconsenting States may not be sued by private individuals in federal court." *Bd. of Trs. of Univ. of Ala. v. Garrett,* 531 U.S. 356, 363, 121 S.Ct. 955, 148 L.Ed.2d 866 (2001). However, there are three exceptions to the Eleventh Amendment's guarantee of sovereign immunity to states:

> First, a state may consent to suit in federal court. Second, Congress may abrogate a state's sovereign immunity by appropriate legislation when it acts under Section 5 of the Fourteenth Amendment. Finally, under *Ex parte Young,* 209 U.S. 123, 28 S.Ct. 441, 52 L.Ed. 714 (1908), a plaintiff may bring suit against individual state officers acting in their official capacities if the complaint alleges an ongoing violation of federal law and the plaintiff seeks prospective relief.

Muscogee (Creek) Nation v. Pruitt, 669 F.3d 1159, 1166 (10th Cir.2012) (internal citations omitted and altered).

In *Garrett,* the Supreme Court held that Congress did not validly abrogate sovereign immunity for employment discrimination claims made against states under Title I of the ADA. 531 U.S. at 374, 121 S.Ct. 955. However, the Supreme Court later concluded that states can be sued on claims of discrimination in the provision of public services under Title II of the ADA when states actually violate the Fourteenth Amendment or when such services implicate fundamental constitutional rights. *See*

United States v. Georgia, 546 U.S. 151, 159, 126 S.Ct. 877, 163 L.Ed.2d 650 (2006); *Tennessee v. Lane,* 541 U.S. 509, 533 n. 20, 124 S.Ct. 1978, 158 L.Ed.2d 820 (2004). The Court has not ruled on whether Congress abrogated sovereign immunity for retaliation claims under Title V of the ADA, but many courts have distinguished between retaliation claims that stem from Title I employment discrimination and Title II discrimination in the provision of public services. *See, e.g., Demshki v. Monteith,* 255 F.3d 986, 988 (9th Cir.2001) ("We ... conclude that the Court's holding necessarily applies to claims brought under Title V of the ADA, at least where ... the claims are predicated on alleged violations of Title I."); *Collazo-Rosado v. Univ. of Puerto Rico,* 775 F.Supp.2d 376, 386-87 (D.P.R.2011); *Chiesa v. N.Y. State Dep't of Labor,* 638 F.Supp.2d 316, 323 (N.D.N.Y.2009); *Sarkissian v. W. Va. Univ. Bd. of Governors,* No. CIV. A. 1:05CV144, 2007 WL 1308978, at *8 (N.D.W.Va. May 3, 2007) (concluding that the discharge of a medical resident fell under Title II because it is "more akin to a program of higher education than an employment position"); *Cisneros v. Colorado,* No. CIV.A.03CV02122WDMCB, 2005 WL 1719755, at *6 (D.Colo. July 22, 2005); *Shabazz v. Texas Youth Comm'n,* 300 F.Supp.2d 467, 472-73 (N.D.Tex.2003).

However, Levy does not argue that Congress abrogated state sovereign immunity for employment discrimination-based retaliation claims under the ADA. Rather, Levy's primary argument on appeal is that SRS has *waived* its sovereign immunity by accepting federal funds. In particular, he argues that the waiver provisions of the Rehabilitation Act, which we have upheld as valid, similarly apply to the ADA because the Rehabilitation Act and ADA are closely linked. Aplt. Br. at 9-11 (citing *Robinson v. Kansas,* 295 F.3d 1183, 1189-90 (10th Cir.2002)). The Rehabilitation Act's waiver provision, enacted pursuant to Congress's Spending Clause power, states:

> A State shall not be immune under the Eleventh Amendment of the Constitution of the United States from suit in Federal court for a violation of section 504 of the Rehabilitation Act of 1973 [29 U.S.C. § 794], title IX of the Education Amendments of 1972 [20 U.S.C. § 1681 et seq.], the Age Discrimination Act of 1975 [42 U.S.C. § 6101 et seq.], title VI of the Civil Rights Act of 1964 [42 U.S.C. § 2000d et seq.], or the provisions of any other Federal statute prohibiting discrimination by recipients of Federal financial assistance.

42 U.S.C. § 2000d-7(a)(1).

Levy argues that "[t]he waiver provision in § 2000d-7 likewise applies to a retaliation claim under § 12203(a) of the ADA because § 12203 is expressly incorporated into section 504 of the Rehabilitation Act." Aplt. Br. at 11. Section 504 reads:

> The standards used to determine whether this section has been violated in a complaint alleging employment discrimination under this section shall be the standards applied under title I of the Americans with Disabilities Act of 1990 (42 U.S.C. § 12111 et seq.) and the provisions of sections 501 through 504, and 510, [1] of the Americans with Disabilities Act of 1990 (42 U.S.C. §§ 12201-12204 and 12210), as such sections relate to employment.

29 U.S.C. § 794(d). Levy is correct that the Rehabilitation Act and the ADA are closely linked, and that the ADA was intended to build on the Rehabilitation Act. *See* Charles R. Richery, 1 Manual on Employment Discrimination § 6:1 (updated February 2015). However, the close relationship between the two statutes is not sufficient to conclude that the Rehabilitation Act's waiver provisions apply by

implication to the ADA. Section 504 of the Rehabilitation Act applies the same standards as a retaliation claim under § 12203(a) of the ADA to determine whether a violation exists, but the statutes were enacted for slightly different purposes and under wholly different provisions of the Constitution. *See Shotz v. City of Plantation, Fla.,* 344 F.3d 1161, 1174-75 (11th Cir.2003) (noting that the ADA was enacted pursuant to the Fourteenth Amendment and the Rehabilitation Act was enacted pursuant to the Spending Clause).

The "test for determining whether a State has waived its immunity from federal-court jurisdiction is a stringent one." *Atascadero State Hosp. v. Scanlon,* 473 U.S. 234, 241, 105 S.Ct. 3142, 87 L.Ed.2d 171 (1985). "Generally, we will find a waiver either if the State voluntarily invokes our jurisdiction, or else if the State makes a 'clear declaration' that it intends to submit itself to our jurisdiction." *Coll. Sav. Bank v. Fla. Prepaid Postsecondary Educ. Expense Bd.,* 527 U.S. 666, 675-76, 119 S.Ct. 2219, 144 L.Ed.2d 605 (1999) (internal citations and quotation marks omitted). "In deciding whether a State has waived its constitutional protection under the Eleventh Amendment, we will find waiver only where stated 'by the most express language or by such overwhelming implications from the text as (will) leave no room for any other reasonable construction.'" *Edelman v. Jordan,* 415 U.S. 651, 673, 94 S.Ct. 1347, 39 L.Ed.2d 662 (1974) (citing *Murray v. Wilson Distilling Co.,* 213 U.S. 151, 171, 29 S.Ct. 458, 53 L.Ed. 742 (1909)).

Although Levy's argument is novel, we must reject it and agree with the Supreme Court when it stated that Congress "does not ... hide elephants in mouseholes." *Whitman v. Am. Trucking Ass'ns,* 531 U.S. 457, 468, 121 S.Ct. 903, 149 L.Ed.2d 1 (2001). The same logic that the Court applied in *Whitman* with regard to changes in the Clean Air Act's regulatory scheme applies with equal force to the Eleventh Amendment waiver issue in this case. For a waiver of sovereign immunity to be "knowing and voluntary," it cannot be hidden in another statute and only applied to the ADA through implication. At best, there may be an argument that the ADA falls into the residual clause of the Rehabilitation Act's waiver for violations of "the provisions of any other Federal statute prohibiting discrimination by recipients of Federal financial assistance." 42 U.S.C. § 2000d-7. *Cf. Sossamon v. Texas,* 563 U.S. 277, 131 S.Ct. 1651, 1662, 179 L.Ed.2d 700 (2011) (analyzing whether the Religious Land Use and Institutionalized Persons Act qualified as a "statute prohibiting discrimination" under the assumption that p.1171 "a residual clause like the one in [42 U.S.C. § 2000d-7] could constitute an unequivocal textual waiver"). However, as other courts have noted, the ADA has a much broader focus than discrimination by recipients of federal financial assistance. *See, e.g., Panzardi-Santiago v. Univ. of Puerto Rico,* 200 F.Supp.2d 1, 9 (D.P.R.2002) ("Panzardi does not direct the Court to any language in the ADA that represents an unequivocal indication by Congress that states in accepting funds, in general from the federal government, do so on condition that they have knowingly waived their Eleventh Amendment protection."). Indeed, the expansion of liability is one of the primary differences between the ADA and Rehabilitation Act. *See, e.g., Schrader v. Fred A. Ray, M.D., P.C.,* 296 F.3d 968, 974 (10th Cir.2002) ("Unlike the blanket involuntary coverage of the ADA, however, the Rehabilitation Act's coverage extends only to entities that choose to receive federal assistance."); *Zimmerman v. Or. Dep't of Justice,* 170 F.3d 1169, 1180 (9th Cir.1999) ("Unlike the Rehabilitation Act, Title II applies to all public entities, whether or not they receive federal financial assistance. Thus, in some respects, it is true that Congress broadened the provisions of the Rehabilitation Act in Title II.").

Moreover, no court has concluded that the Rehabilitation Act's waiver provisions apply to the ADA. *See Fields v. Dep't of Pub. Safety,* 911 F.Supp.2d 373, 379 (M.D.La.2012); *Swart v. Colo. Dep't of Corr.,* No. CIV.A. 07-CV-02718LT, 2009 WL 230699, at *2 (D.Colo. Jan. 30, 2009) ("Not surprisingly, Plaintiff has cited no authority for the proposition that [the waiver] provision of the Rehabilitation Act is applicable to claims under the ADA or that it overrides the clear holding of *Garrett* that states are immune to ADA claims for money damages by employees."); *Dansby-Giles v. Jackson State Univ.,* 638 F.Supp.2d 698, 700-01 (S.D.Miss.2009); *Gary v. Ga. Dep't of Human Res.,* 323 F.Supp.2d 1368, 1372 (M.D.Ga.2004) ("The acceptance of federal funds does not constitute a state's waiver of Eleventh Amendment immunity for alleged violations of Title I of the ADA."); *Sanders ex rel. Rayl v. Kan. Dep't of Soc. & Rehab. Servs.,* 317 F.Supp.2d 1233, 1242 & n. 2 (D.Kan.2004) (concluding that the Rehabilitation Act's waiver applies solely to § 504 claims and not ADA or § 1983 claims).

Lastly, the district court noted that the ADA was passed *after* the Rehabilitation Act's waiver provisions. Congress could have included a similar waiver provision in the ADA or added the ADA to the list of nondiscrimination statutes in the Rehabilitation Act's waiver provisions, but it did not. 42 U.S.C. § 2000d-7(a)(1). In the absence of clear evidence that Congress intended for states to waive their immunity under the ADA by accepting federal funds,[1] we will not stretch the language of the Rehabilitation Act to conclude that SRS has made a clear and voluntary waiver of its sovereign immunity for ADA claims. *Cf. Schrader,* 296 F.3d at 974 (concluding that the 1992 addition of § 794(d) to the Rehabilitation Act did not limit the definition of employer under the Act to the definition provided under the ADA because "[h]ad this been the intent of Congress, it surely would have been explicit on this significant change").

D. Statute of limitations for Rehabilitation Act claims in Kansas

For federal causes of action created prior to 1990 for which "Congress has not established a time limitation for a federal cause of action, the settled practice [is] to adopt a local time limitation as federal law if it is not inconsistent with federal law or policy to do so." *Wilson v. Garcia,* 471 U.S. 261, 266-67, 105 S.Ct. 1938, 85 L.Ed.2d 254 (1985). The district court relied on *Baker v. Board of Regents of Kansas,* 991 F.2d 628, 631-32 (10th Cir. 1993), to conclude that Rehabilitation Act claims are subject to a two-year statute of limitations borrowed from Kan. Stat. Ann. § 60-513 and that Levy's claims were therefore time-barred. In *Baker,* we concluded that the two-year statute of limitations for claims for injury to personal rights under Kan. Stat. Ann. § 60-513(a)(4)[2] was most appropriate for Rehabilitation Act claims. 991 F.2d at 631-32. "Section 504 of the Rehabilitation Act protects an individual with handicaps from discrimination.... Because a section 504 claim is closely analogous to section 1983, we find that section 504 claims are best characterized as claims for personal injuries." *Id.*

Levy argues on appeal that *Baker* is confusing because it makes repeated reference to Kan. Stat. Ann. § 60-512,[3] which details when a three-year statute of limitation applies in Kansas. He also argues that Kansas caselaw supports the application of Kan. Stat. Ann. § 60-512 to Rehabilitation Act claims because such claims involve statutorily created rights. Aplt Br. at 14-15 (citing *Burnett v. Sw. Bell Tel.*, 283 Kan. 134, 151 P.3d 837, 847 (2007) (concluding that the three-year statute of limitations from Kan. Stat. Ann. § 60-512 applied to ERISA claims because such claims were created by statute)).

Although Levy is correct that *Baker* makes two incorrect references to Kan. Stat. Ann. § 60-512, the opinion itself is not confusing as to which statute we intended to apply. We spent several pages discussing both (1) why the injury to personal rights analogy is the most appropriate for Title VI and Rehabilitation Act claims, and (2) why characterizing § 1983, Title VI, and Rehabilitation Act claims similarly for purposes of a statute of limitations "promotes a consistent and uniform framework by which suitable statutes of limitations can be determined for civil rights claims." 991 F.2d at 630-32. We also repeatedly stated that the two-year limitations period for claims for injury to personal rights under Kansas law applies and we cite the correct statute (Kan.Stat. Ann. § 60-513(a)(4)) three times. *Id.* Lastly, we purported to affirm the district court regarding the applicable statute of limitations, *id.*, which had unequivocally concluded that Kan. Stat. Ann. § 60-513(a)(4) applied. *See Baker v. Bd. of Regents of Kan.*, 768 F.Supp. 1436, 1438 (D.Kan.1991). In short, although the incorrect references to Kan. Stat. Ann. § 60-512 are perplexing, the *Baker* opinion overall is clear that we were applying the two-year statute of limitations for claims for injury to personal rights found at Kan. Stat. Ann. § 60-513(a)(4).

Levy's second argument is somewhat more persuasive, as Kansas courts have explicitly characterized employment discrimination claims as statutorily based and have applied the three-year statute of limitations under Kan. Stat. Ann. § 60-512. *See Wagher v. Guy's Foods, Inc.*, 256 Kan. 300, 885 P.2d 1197, 1204 (1994) (concluding that "the [Kansas Act Against Discrimination] does impose the obligation not to discriminate against women in employment where no obligation previously existed under common law" and that "[t]hus, the liability is created by statute, and Kan. Stat. Ann. § 60-512(2) applies"). And in *Burnett*, the Kansas Supreme Court answered a certified question from the federal district court regarding which state statute of limitations best applied to ERISA claims and concluded that the three-year statute of limitations under Kan. Stat. Ann. § 60-512(2) was most appropriate. 151 P.3d at 838.

However, both this court and the Supreme Court have stated that, although federal courts must look to state law to determine the appropriate statute of limitations for many federal causes of action, the question of how to characterize the federal cause of action is one of federal, not state law. *See Wilson v. Garcia*, 471 U.S. 261, 268-69, 105 S.Ct. 1938, 85 L.Ed.2d 254 (1985). Levy argues that we must reconsider *Baker* in light of more recent pronouncements by the Kansas Supreme Court such as *Burnett* (and in theory, *Wagher*, although he does not cite that case), but he does not explain why we must follow a state court's characterization of a civil rights action as statutory rather than based on a general injury to personal rights. It is the federal court's job to find the most analogous statute under Kansas law, and while the Kansas Supreme Court's pronouncements may be persuasive, we are not bound by them. At oral argument, Levy attempted to distinguish between characterizing the action generally as an injury to personal rights claim, which he claimed was a federal court's duty, and picking the most analogous statute, for which he argued Kansas caselaw should provide guidance.[4] However, nothing in *Wilson* or other caselaw counsels such a fine distinction. Rather, in *Wilson* the Supreme Court affirmed our rejection of a New Mexico Supreme Court case that purported to characterize § 1983 actions as analogous to actions under the New Mexico Tort Claims Act. *Id.* at 270-71, 105 S.Ct. 1938; *see also Baker*, 991 F.2d at 630 ("Characterization of a federal claim is a matter of federal law."); *Garcia v. Wilson*, 731 F.2d 640, 642-43 (10th Cir.1984), aff'd, 471 U.S. 261, 105 S.Ct. 1938, 85 L.Ed.2d 254 (1985).

Although at least one sister court has applied the limitations period from a state statute that mirrored the Rehabilitation Act, the majority of circuits have concluded that Rehabilitation Act claims should be likened to general personal injury claims for purposes of determining a state statute of limitations. *See Disabled in Action of Pa. v. Se. Pa. Transp. Auth.*, 539 F.3d 199, 208 (3d Cir.2008) (collecting cases). *But see Wolsky v. Med. Coll. of Hampton Roads*, 1 F.3d 222, 224 (4th Cir.1993) (concluding that a state statute modeled after the Rehabilitation Act provided the most appropriate statute of limitations and declining to follow other courts that had used personal injury statutes of limitation). Levy offers no Kansas statute that replicates the Rehabilitation Act and we see no reason to depart from what at present is a relatively consistent federal scheme. *See* p.1174 *Owens v. Okure*, 488 U.S. 235, 243, 109 S.Ct. 573, 102 L.Ed.2d 594 (1989) (highlighting "ease and predictability" as important factors in choosing a rule by which federal courts may determine the most appropriate statutes of limitations for § 1983 actions).

Thus, we are bound by our previous holding in *Baker* — not the Kansas Supreme Court's holdings in *Burnett* or *Wagher* — that Rehabilitation Act claims are subject to the two-year statute of limitations under Kan. Stat. Ann. § 60-513. Because Levy joined this lawsuit in March 2011, and his alleged termination from SRS took place in February 2009, his Rehabilitation Act claim is time-barred.

E. Compensatory damages for Rehabilitation Act claims

Because we conclude that Levy's Rehabilitation Act claims are time-barred, we do not address his appellate arguments that compensatory damages are available for such claims.

III

For the reasons set forth above, we AFFIRM the district court's dismissal of Levy's ADA and Rehabilitation Act claims against SRS.

---

[1] In fact, the broad abrogation provisions invalidated under *Garrett* would suggest that Congress did not intend to condition a state's receipt of federal funds on a waiver of sovereign immunity for ADA claims.

[2] Kan. Stat. Ann. § 60-513(a)(4) provides: "(a) The following actions shall be brought within two years: ...

(4) An action for injury to the rights of another, not arising on contract, and not herein enumerated."

[3] Kan. Stat. Ann. § 60-512 provides: "The following actions shall be brought within three (3) years: ...

(2) An action upon a liability created by a statute other than a penalty or forfeiture."

[4] Levy also attempted to distinguish between § 1983 actions and Rehabilitation Act claims at oral argument by arguing that § 1983 does not create substantive rights, but we have already foreclosed that route with our analysis in *Baker*. *See Baker*, 991 F.2d at 631-32 (10th Cir.1993) ("Section 504 of the Rehabilitation Act protects an individual with handicaps from discrimination. It is a civil rights statute ... closely analogous to section 1983") (internal citation and quotation marks omitted).

756 F.3d 1208 (2014)

Tori VARNELL, Plaintiff-Appellant,
v.
DORA CONSOLIDATED SCHOOL DISTRICT; Superintendent Steven Barron; Amber Shaw, Defendants-Appellees.

No. 13-2135.

United States Court of Appeals, Tenth Circuit.

July 1, 2014.

Varnell v. Dora Consol. School Dist., 756 F. 3d 1208 (10th Cir. 2014)

p.1209 Shannon L. Kennedy, Kennedy Law Firm, Albuquerque, New Mexico, for Plaintiff-Appellant.

p.1210 Andrew M. Sanchez, Cuddy & McCarthy, LLP, Albuquerque, New Mexico, for Defendants-Appellees Dora Consolidated School District and Steve Barron.

Desiree D. Gurule (Kevin M. Brown, Keya Koul, with her on the brief), Brown Law Firm, Albuquerque, New Mexico, for Defendant — Appellee Amber Shaw.

Before HARTZ, EBEL, and PHILLIPS, Circuit Judges.

HARTZ, Circuit Judge.

Amber Shaw coached Plaintiff Tori Varnell in several sports while she was a student in the Dora Consolidated School District (Dora Schools). According to Plaintiff, Shaw sexually abused her for more than a year, ending while she was in the ninth grade, sometime in late 2006 or early 2007. On May 24, 2012, when Plaintiff was 20, she sued Ms. Shaw, Dora Schools, and Dora Schools Superintendent Steve Barron under the New Mexico Tort Claims Act, the Civil Rights Act of 1871, and Title IX of the Education Amendments of 1972. She later sought to amend her complaint to add an additional party and additional claims. On Defendants' motion the district court granted summary judgment on the federal claims as untimely, denied the proposed amendment to the complaint as futile, and dismissed the state tort claims without prejudice.

Exercising jurisdiction under 28 U.S.C. § 1291, we affirm. We hold as follows: The applicable statute of limitations on the federal claims is New Mexico's general three-year statute for tort claims; New Mexico's special statute for child sexual abuse does not apply as a statute of limitations or tolling provision because it is not generally applicable. Although the limitations period was tolled by Plaintiff's minority, it was not further tolled by her alleged incompetence because she produced no evidence of incompetence. Plaintiff's contention on appeal that the period was tolled by fraudulent concealment from her mother was not preserved in the district court. And Plaintiff's federal claims accrued when she could file suit and obtain relief, which was no later than when the abuse stopped, not when she allegedly learned the full extent of the resultant emotional injury. In addition, the district court properly dismissed Plaintiff's state-law claims without prejudice once it had dismissed with prejudice her federal claims. Finally, we affirm the district court's denial of Plaintiff's motion to amend because she presents no argument why her new federal claims would not be barred as untimely on the same grounds as her original claims, and it would be futile to proceed with state-law claims that would be dismissed upon rejection of the federal claims.

I. BACKGROUND

We summarize the record in the light most favorable to Plaintiff. *See SEC v. Thompson*, 732 F.3d 1151, 1157 (10th Cir. 2013) (in reviewing a grant of summary judgment, "a court views the evidence and draws reasonable inferences therefrom in the light most favorable to the nonmoving party" (brackets and internal quotation marks omitted)).

Ms. Shaw was coaching Plaintiff in volleyball, track, and basketball when she repeatedly sexually abused Plaintiff. The period during which the abuse occurred is unclear but apparently lasted from January 2005, when Plaintiff was in the seventh grade, until late 2006 or early 2007, when Plaintiff was a ninth grader. Plaintiff "hated every minute of the sexual encounters," Aplt. App., Vol. I at 12, and "wanted to kill herself as she did not see a way out," *id.* at 11. But she did not report the misconduct because Ms. Shaw instructed her not to tell anyone and she feared social repercussions. The abuse ended when Ms. Shaw resigned.

After graduating from high school in 2010, Plaintiff told a spiritual mentor about the alleged abuse. The mentor told her that Ms. Shaw's conduct was criminal and other girls could be abused if she did nothing. At this point Plaintiff "realized for the first time that [Ms. Shaw] could and probably would molest other girls and that what happened was not [her] fault and that [she] had a duty to try to protect others and to tell the people who loved [her] the truth about what had happened with [Ms.] Shaw." *Id.* at 78. She told her mother on July 12, 2010, that she had been sexually molested by Ms. Shaw. Her mother told Superintendent Barron and he reported the abuse to the local authorities. A state grand jury indicted Ms. Shaw for the abuse.

Plaintiff was examined by psychiatrist Gilbert Kliman on May 7, 2012. Dr. Kliman opined that up to the date of the evaluation Plaintiff did not realize that she was being "emotionally manipulated" and did not appreciate the "consequences to her of this two-year training epoch during her years of adolescent personality and sexual identity formation, or upon her anxiety level." *Id.* at 80. Further, Plaintiff did not comprehend how the abuse had "troubled and quietly damaged her," and she only began recognizing the harm done to her after speaking to her spiritual mentor in 2010. *Id.* at 81. Dr. Kliman also said that Plaintiff did not fully comprehend the emotional and physical damage she had suffered and would suffer because of the abuse.

About two weeks after the psychiatric examination, on May 24, 2012, Plaintiff sued Dora Schools, Mr. Barron, and Ms. Shaw in New Mexico state court. At the time, she was 20 years old and in college, pursuing a biology degree. The 16-page complaint raised a claim under the New Mexico Tort Claims Act; civil-rights claims under the Civil Rights Act of 1871, 42 U.S.C. § 1983 (for violations of substantive due process, equal protection, and the Fourth Amendment); and a claim under Title IX of the Education Amendments of 1972, 20 U.S.C. § 1681 (prohibiting discrimination based on sex in federally funded educational programs). Defendants removed the case to the United States District Court for the District of New Mexico. Plaintiff later moved to amend her complaint to add additional claims and an additional defendant (the head coach at her school).

Defendants filed a motion to dismiss under Fed.R.Civ.P. 12(b)(1) on the ground that all claims were time barred. The district court adopted a magistrate judge's recommendation to convert Defendants' motion to dismiss into a motion for summary judgment. It granted summary judgment on the federal claims and declined to exercise supplemental jurisdiction over the remaining state claims, dismissing them without prejudice. Plaintiff did not object to the magistrate judge's recommendation to deny as futile her motion to amend the complaint, and the district court adopted the recommendation.

After the district court dismissed the action, Plaintiff moved under Fed.R.Civ.P. 60(a) to have the state claims remanded to the state court instead of dismissed. The motion was denied.

On appeal Plaintiff contends that (1) her federal-law claims are timely (a) because the limitations period was tolled by (i) N.M. Stat. Ann. § 37-1-30 (a child-sexual-abuse statute), (ii) her mental incapacity, and (iii) fraudulent concealment, and (b) because her claims did not accrue until 2010 when she first understood the injury she had suffered; (2) the district court erred by refusing to remand her state-law claims to state court instead of dismissing p.1212 them; and (3) the court erred in denying as futile her motion to amend the complaint.

II. TIMELINESS OF CLAIMS

The district court granted summary judgment to Defendants on Plaintiff's federal-law claims on the ground that they were untimely. "We review the district court's grant of summary judgment de novo, applying the same standards that the district court should have applied." *Merrifield v. Bd. of Cnty. Comm'rs,* 654 F.3d 1073, 1077 (10th Cir.2011) (internal quotation marks omitted). "The court shall grant summary judgment if the movant shows that there is no genuine dispute as to any material fact and the movant is entitled to judgment as a matter of law." Fed.R.Civ.P. 56(a). A dispute is genuine "if there is sufficient evidence on each side so that a rational trier of fact could resolve the issue either way," and a fact is material "if under the substantive law it is essential to the proper disposition of the claim." *Becker v. Bateman,* 709 F.3d 1019, 1022 (10th Cir.2013) (internal quotation marks omitted). "We examine the record and all reasonable inferences that might be drawn from it in the light most favorable to the [nonmoving] party." *Merrifield,* 654 F.3d at 1077 (internal quotation marks omitted).

The text of § 1983 does not contain a statute of limitations. "When Congress has not established a time limitation for a federal cause of action, the settled practice has been to adopt a local time limitation as federal law if it is not inconsistent with federal law or policy to do so." *Wilson v. Garcia,* 471 U.S. 261, 266-67, 105 S.Ct. 1938, 85 L.Ed.2d 254 (1985). The Supreme Court assumed that "Congress intended the identification of the appropriate statute of limitations to be an uncomplicated task for judges, lawyers, and litigants, rather than a source of uncertainty, and unproductive and ever-increasing litigation." *Id.* at 275. Otherwise, "the legislative purpose to create an effective remedy for the enforcement of federal civil rights [would be] obstructed by uncertainty in the applicable statute of limitations, for scarce resources [would] be dissipated by useless litigation on collateral matters." *Id.* Although national uniformity was not required, there should be "uniformity within each State." *Id.* In particular, the limitations period should not "depend upon the particular facts or the precise legal theory of [the] claim." *Id.* at 274, 105 S.Ct. 1938. As for which state statute should be adopted, the Court held that the one that best fit § 1983 claims as a whole would be the one for personal-injury actions. *See id.* at 280, 105 S.Ct. 1938. And, as the Court held a few years later, if "state law provides multiple statutes of limitations for personal injury actions, courts considering § 1983 claims should borrow the general or residual statute for personal injury actions." *Owens v. Okure,* 488 U.S. 235, 250, 109 S.Ct. 573, 102 L.Ed.2d 594 (1989).

The law was settled in *Wilson* that for § 1983 claims arising in New Mexico the limitations period is three years, as provided in New Mexico's statute of limitations for personal-injury claims. *See* 471 U.S. at 280, 105 S.Ct. 1938; N.M. Stat. Ann. § 37-1-8 (West 2014). We think that Plaintiff is expressing a vain hope when she argues that "the Supreme Court would modify its holding in *[Owens]* to allow an exception for victims of child abuse." Aplt. Br. at 28-29.

Not only the length of the limitations period, but also "closely related questions of tolling and application," are determined by state law in § 1983 actions. *Wilson,* 471 U.S. at 269, 105 S.Ct. 1938. The same reasoning that governed the selection of the applicable statute of limitations should also apply to the selection of tolling statutes. Thus, the state tolling provisions adopted for actions under § 1983 should not depend on the "particular facts or the precise legal theory of the claim." *Id.* at 274, 105 S.Ct. 1938. Only generally applicable tolling provisions — such as those based on minority, incapacity, and equitable grounds — should be incorporated for use under § 1983. *See Sain v. City of Bend,* 309 F.3d 1134, 1138 (9th Cir.2002). As the Ninth Circuit has explained:

> It would no less frustrate the federal interest in uniformity and the interest in having firmly defined, easily applied rules were we to obediently apply the residual statute of limitations, only to then adopt a tort-specific tolling provision. Such a holding would succeed only in transferring the confusion over the choice among multiple statutes of limitations to a choice among multiple tolling provisions.

Bonneau v. Centennial Sch. Dist. No. 28J, 666 F.3d 577, 580 (9th Cir.2012) (brackets, citation, and internal quotation marks omitted) (declining to apply state child-abuse statute to determine timeliness of § 1983 claim).

Although the parties have ignored the point, we must also address the proper limitations period for Plaintiff's claim under Title IX. We agree with the magistrate judge that we should apply the same state statutes that apply to § 1983 claims. That appears to be the uniform rule of the other circuits. *See Stanley v. Trustees,* 433 F.3d 1129, 1134 (9th Cir.2006) ("For other civil rights actions, we have borrowed the state statute of limitations for personal injury. Should we apply the same ruling for Title IX claims? It appears that every circuit to consider the issue has held that Title IX also borrows the relevant state's statute of limitations for personal injury. The rationale of our sister circuits is compelling, and we adopt it." (citations and internal quotation marks omitted)); *Wilmink v. Kanawha Cnty. Bd. of Educ.,* 214 Fed. Appx. 294,

296 n. 3 (4th Cir.2007); *Cetin v. Purdue Univ.*, 94 F.3d 647 (7th Cir.1996) (unpublished table decision). This result is consistent with this circuit's view of the limitations period under Title VI of the Civil Rights Act of 1964, 42 U.S.C. § 2000d. *See Baker v. Bd. of Regents*, 991 F.2d 628, 631 (10th Cir.1993).

A. New Mexico Child-Sexual-Abuse Statute

We now turn to Plaintiff's contention that the timeliness of her federal claims must be determined under New Mexico Statute Annotated § 37-1-30(A) (West 2014). Section 37-1-30(A) provides:

> An action for damages based on personal injury caused by childhood sexual abuse shall be commenced by a person before the latest of the following dates: (1) the first instant of the person's twenty-fourth birthday; or (2) three years from the date of the time that a person knew or had reason to know of the childhood sexual abuse and that the childhood sexual abuse resulted in an injury to the person, as established by competent medical or psychological testimony.

It should be obvious from our above discussion that the statute is irrelevant to § 1983 cases because it does not apply to torts in general. We have already held that a state statute of limitations restricted to child-abuse cases does not apply to § 1983. *See Blake v. Dickason*, 997 F.2d 749, 750-51 (10th Cir.1993). And even if we could do as Plaintiff requests and construe § 37-1-30 as a tolling provision, it still fails the same general-applicability requirement. Insofar as *Cosgrove v. Kansas Department of Social Rehabilitation Services*, 162 Fed.Appx. 823, 827-28 (10th Cir. 2006), says otherwise, we reject it. *See* 10th Cir. R. 32.1(A) ("Unpublished decisions are not precedential....").

p.1214 B. Minority and Incapacity

Plaintiff has better luck, at least at the outset, invoking New Mexico's general statute allowing tolling of the limitations period because of minority and incapacity. The statute states:

> The times limited for the bringing of actions by the preceding provisions of this chapter [including the three-year period for torts] shall, in favor of minors and incapacitated persons, be extended so that they shall have one year from and after the termination of such incapacity within which to commence said action.

N.M. Stat. Ann. § 37-1-10 (West 2014). As noted above, § 1983 incorporates such state general tolling provisions. *See Wilson*, 471 U.S. at 269, 105 S.Ct. 1938; *Fratus v. DeLand*, 49 F.3d 673, 675 (10th Cir.1995).

There is no doubt that Plaintiff qualifies for minority tolling, which would have given her to age 19 to bring her action. But on May 24, 2012, when she filed this action, Plaintiff was 20 years old.

To extend the time further, Plaintiff alleges that she was incapacitated. New Mexico courts have explained that a person is incapacitated when she "is unable to manage [her] business affairs or estate, or to comprehend [her] legal rights or liabilities." *Lent v. Emp't Sec. Comm'n*, 99 N.M. 407, 658 P.2d 1134, 1137 (N.M.Ct.App.1982) (internal quotation marks omitted). Under New Mexico law, "exceptions to statutes of limitation must be construed strictly," *Slade v. Slade*, 81

N.M. 462, 468 P.2d 627, 628 (1970), and the plaintiff invoking a tolling provision bears the burden of persuasion, *see Stringer v. Dudoich,* 92 N.M. 98, 583 P.2d 462, 463 (1978). Plaintiff has not met that burden.

Although Plaintiff's opening brief asserts that she was incapacitated, she offers no evidence that she could not manage her affairs or comprehend her legal rights and liabilities. On the contrary, she had graduated from high school and was pursuing a biology degree in college. Moreover, no later than July 2010 (almost two years before this suit was filed), when, on the advice of her mentor, she told her mother of the abuse, she was certainly able to discuss the abuse with others and she was aware that Ms. Shaw's conduct was criminal, that other girls could be harmed if she did not come forward, that what happened was not her fault, and that she had a duty to tell others what had happened. Any decent person would sympathize with the emotional trauma suffered by a victim of such abuse, and such trauma can certainly impact one's ability to deal with various issues; but a rational trier of fact could not find that Plaintiff had shown that she was unable to manage her business affairs or comprehend her legal rights during the year before suit was filed. *See Eber v. Harris Cnty. Hosp. Dist.,* 130 F.Supp.2d 847, 871 (S.D.Tex.2001) ("The unsound mind exception serves to protect people who are unable to participate in, control, or understand the progression and disposition of a lawsuit."); *Nolde v. Frankie,* 192 Ariz. 276, 964 P.2d 477, 483 (1998) (sexual-abuse victims did not show that they were unable to understand their legal rights and liabilities when they did not allege that they were ever in denial that the abuse occurred or had repressed memories of the abuse but, rather, admitted that they were always aware that the defendant had sexually abused them).

C. Fraudulent Concealment

Under New Mexico law the limitations period is tolled if the party asserting concealment shows "(1) the use of fraudulent means by the party who raises the bar of the statute; (2) successful concealment from the injured party; and (3) that the party claiming fraudulent concealment did not know or by the exercise of reasonable diligence could not have known that he might have a cause of action." *Cont'l Potash, Inc. v. Freeport-McMoran, Inc.,* 115 N.M. 690, 858 P.2d 66, 74 (1993). This is a general tolling provision and is therefore applicable here.

Plaintiff contends that Superintendent Barron had been alerted to the abuse by Plaintiff's teammates but concealed Ms. Shaw's conduct by failing to report the abuse, permitting Ms. Shaw to resign, and dissuading Plaintiff's mother (with whom he was allegedly having an affair) from reporting the abuse. On appeal, she argues that concealment from her mother, who could have sued on her behalf when she was a minor, justifies equitable tolling. But she cites no authority for such a tolling theory and we fail to see how such alleged concealment could have delayed her suit once she reached majority. In any event, she forfeited the argument by not raising it below. *See Lyons v. Jefferson Bank & Trust,* 994 F.2d 716, 721 (10th Cir.1993) ("We have ... repeatedly stated that a party may not lose in the district court on one theory of the case, and then prevail on appeal on a different theory.").

D. Claim Accrual

Finally, Plaintiff argues that her complaint was filed within the three-year limitations period because her claim did not accrue until she had discovered the extent of the injury inflicted on her by the abuse. She contends that "as a teenager and young adult, [she] could not appreciate the damage done to her, nor has she fully discovered the nuances of her chronic psychiatric injury." Aplt. Br. at 20. According to Plaintiff, "[N]ot until after [she] underwent counseling to address manifestations of her injury, was she able to connect Coach Shaw's sexual abuse to its lasting impacts on her life." *Id.* at 20?21. Thus, she argues, the district court erred because she "provided sufficient facts to establish that a reasonable juror could find that until she was twenty years old, [she] reasonably failed to discover she is suffering chronic psychiatric injuries as a result of having been sexually molested by her female coach." *Id.* at 49.

Although some New Mexico court decisions may support Plaintiff's argument, the time of accrual of a § 1983 claim is a matter of federal law "*not* resolved by reference to state law." *Wallace v. Kato*, 549 U.S. 384, 388, 127 S.Ct. 1091, 166 L.Ed.2d 973 (2007). The same is true of a claim under Title IX. *See Baker*, 991 F.2d at 632 ("Federal law controls questions relating to accrual of federal causes of action.") The relevant federal law on accrual is set forth in *Wallace*, which concerned the time of accrual of a § 1983 claim of false arrest contrary to the Fourth Amendment. *See id.* at 387, 127 S.Ct. 1091. Federal law governing accrual of causes of action, said the Supreme Court, "conform[s] in general to common-law tort principles." *Id.* at 388, 127 S.Ct. 1091. And "[u]nder those principles, it is the standard rule that accrual occurs when the plaintiff has a complete and present cause of action, that is when the plaintiff can file suit and obtain relief." *Id.* (brackets, citations, and internal quotation marks omitted). The Court recognized, however, that the common law provides distinctive treatment to the tort of false arrest, delaying accrual until the false imprisonment ends (a rule "dictated, perhaps, by the reality that the victim may not be able to sue while he is still imprisoned"), and it adopted that accrual date for the claim before it. *Id.* at 389, 127 S.Ct. 1091 (citing, among other authorities, Restatement (Second) of Torts § 899 cmt. c (1977)).

Following *Wallace*, we determine the accrual date of Plaintiff's claim by looking to the accrual date for the common-law tort most analogous to her § 1983 claim. That tort is battery, which "occurs when an individual acts intending to cause a harmful or offensive contact with the person of the other or a third person, or an imminent apprehension of such a contact, and an offensive contact with the person of the other directly or indirectly results." *Fuerschbach v. Southwest Airlines Co.*, 439 F.3d 1197, 1208-09 (10th Cir.2006) (ellipsis and internal quotation marks omitted); *see* Restatement (Second) of Torts § 18(1) (1965).[1] As for the accrual of a battery claim, the Restatement § 899 comment c states as a general rule for torts, "[T]he statute [of limitations] does not usually begin to run until the tort is complete, and may not begin to run even then if there has been a series of continuous acts"; and, in the same paragraph cited by *Wallace* as support for the accrual rule for false imprisonment, the comment adds that "[a] battery is complete upon physical contact, even though there is no observable damage at the point of contact." By this standard, Plaintiff's claim accrued no later than the last sexual abuse by Ms. Shaw, sometime in late 2006 or early 2007.

Plaintiff argues that her claims accrued much later because she did not realize the extent of her psychological injury until shortly before filing suit. She relies on what is known as the "discovery rule," which delays accrual of a claim until the plaintiff knew or should have known the facts necessary to establish her cause of action, such as the fact that a surgeon left a sponge in the plaintiff's abdomen after an operation. *See Alexander v. Oklahoma,* 382 F.3d 1206, 1215 (10th Cir. 2004). But even if the discovery rule applies to her § 1983 claim, Plaintiff knew long before she filed suit all the facts necessary to sue and recover damages. Although she may not have known how harmful Ms. Shaw's abuse was, "[t]he cause of action accrues even though the full extent of the injury is not then known or predictable." *Wallace,* 549 U.S. at 391, 127 S.Ct. 1091 (internal quotation marks omitted). "Were it otherwise," explained the Supreme Court, "the statute would begin to run only after a plaintiff became satisfied that he had been harmed enough, placing the supposed statute of repose in the sole hands of the party seeking relief." *Id.*

Moreover, Plaintiff has admitted that she knew from the outset that Ms. Shaw had abused her and caused nontrivial, indeed significant, injury. Plaintiff's complaint alleges:

14. Eventually, Amber Shaw manipulated Plaintiff into performing cunnilingus on her although Plaintiff would try to get out of having to perform cunnilingus on her coach by feigning sickness.

15. Amber Shaw told Plaintiff not to tell anyone so she would not get in trouble.

. . . .

17. Plaintiff was too afraid to disclose to anyone that she was being sexually abused by her female coach.

18. Plaintiff was afraid to report the sexual abuse because she feared being bullied by her peers at a [sic] school for engaging in homosexual sexual acts with her female coach.

19. Plaintiff wanted to kill herself as she did not see a way out.

20. Plaintiff was afraid to disclose that she was being sexually abused by her female basketball coach as she feared p.1217 homophobic retaliation by teachers and other coaches and she needed good school and community referrals for college.

. . . .

24. Plaintiff hated every minute of the sexual encounters with her coach Amber Shaw.

25. Plaintiff did not want to disappoint her coach and feared reporting her coach.

Aplt. App., Vol. I at 11-12. Thus, Plaintiff's § 1983 claim accrued no later than early 2007.

The same is true of her Title IX claim. Plaintiff has not suggested any reason why her Title IX claim accrued at a different time from her § 1983 claim, and we see none. As noted above, the general rule is that accrual occurs "when the plaintiff can file suit and obtain relief," *Wallace,* 549 U.S. at 388 (internal quotation marks omitted); and we know of no reason why Plaintiff could not have brought a Title IX claim as soon as she brought one under § 1983.

Because Plaintiff did not file suit until 2012, her federal claims are untimely and were properly dismissed.

III. MOTION TO REMAND STATE CLAIMS TO STATE COURT

Plaintiff argues that the district court erred when it denied her motion to remand her state claims back to the state court instead of dismissing them without prejudice. She complains that if she refiles her state-law claims in state court, they will now be barred by statutes of limitations. She is wrong. The problem she anticipates has been alleviated by 28 U.S.C. § 1367(d).

Here, the district court had federal-question jurisdiction under 28 U.S.C. § 1331 over the § 1983 and Title IX claims. The court could then exercise supplemental jurisdiction under § 1367(a) over Plaintiff's state-law claims because they "form part of the same case or controversy." 28 U.S.C. § 1367(a). Once the federal-law claims were dismissed, however, the court properly acted under § 1367(c) in declining further supplemental jurisdiction over the state-law claims. *See id.* § 1367(c) (court "may decline to exercise supplemental jurisdiction over a claim under [§ 1367](a) if ... the district court has dismissed all claims over which it has original jurisdiction"). In that event, § 1367(d) provides: "The period of limitations for any claim asserted under subsection (a) ... shall be tolled while the claim is pending and for a period of 30 days after it is dismissed unless State law provides for a longer tolling period." Thus, Plaintiff has at least 30 days after dismissal of the state-law claims to bring suit in state court (assuming that the claim was originally timely filed). State courts have apparently agreed that tolling under § 1367(d) continues until any federal appeal is complete. *See, e.g., Turner v. Kight,* 406 Md. 167, 957 A.2d 984, 993-97 (2008); *Okoro v. City of Oakland,* 48 Cal. Rptr.3d 260, 142 Cal.App.4th 306, 312-13 (Cal.Ct.App.2006); *Huang v. Ziko,* 132 N.C.App. 358, 511 S.E.2d 305, 308 (1999). We are confident that the New Mexico courts would follow suit. The district court did not abuse its discretion by dismissing the state-law claims.

IV. MOTION TO AMEND

Plaintiff argues that the district court erred when it denied her motion to amend the complaint on the ground that adding the new claims would be futile. *See Anderson v. Suiters,* 499 F.3d 1228, 1238 (10th Cir.2007) (a district court may deny a motion to amend a complaint if the amendment would be futile and "[a] proposed amendment is futile if the complaint, as amended, would be subject to dismissal" (internal quotation marks omitted)). Her opening brief on appeal, however, presents no argument why her new federal claims would not be time barred even if the federal claims in her original complaint were so barred. Plaintiff does make such an argument in her reply brief. But arguments for reversal must be presented in the opening brief to be preserved. *See Bronson v. Swensen,* 500 F.3d 1099, 1104 (10th Cir.2007). And it would be futile to proceed with any new state-law claims if they would be dismissed (without prejudice) anyway once the federal claims were dismissed.

V. CONCLUSION

We AFFIRM the district court's grant of summary judgment, the district court's dismissal without prejudice of the state-law claims, and the district court's denial of Plaintiff's motion to amend her complaint. We also DENY Plaintiff's request that we award costs and attorney fees.

[1] The Restatement defines the tort as follows:

(1) An actor is subject to liability to another for battery if

(a) he acts intending to cause a harmful or offensive contact with the person of the other or a third person, or an imminent apprehension of such a contact, and

(b) an offensive contact with the person of the other directly or indirectly results.

Restatement (Second) of Torts § 18(1).

Eleventh Circuit Decisions
Title IX

Doe v. Valencia College, 903 F. 3d 1220 (11th Cir. 2018)......................................453
JS v. Houston County Bd. of Education, 877 F. 3d 979 (11th Cir. 2017) 469
Hill v. Cundiff, 797 F. 3d 948 (11th Cir. 2015)..481
Doe v. School Bd. of Broward County, Fla., 604 F. 3d 1248 (11th Cir. 2010)..515

903 F.3d 1220 (2018)

John DOE, Individually, Plaintiff,
Jeffrey Koeppel, Individually, Plaintiff-Appellant,

v.

VALENCIA COLLEGE, a Florida public college, Defendant,
District Board of Trustees of Valencia College, Florida, Joyce C. Romano, In her individual capacity, Joseph M. Sarrubbo, Jr., In his individual capacity, Thomas Decker, In his individual capacity, Sanford Shugart, Defendants-Appellees.

No. 17-12562.

United States Court of Appeals, Eleventh Circuit.

September 13, 2018.

Doe v. Valencia College, 903 F. 3d 1220 (11th Cir. 2018)

Appeal from the United States District Court for the Middle District of Florida, D.C. Docket No. 6:15-cv-01800-PGB-KRS.

Kimberly C. Lau, Bradley Silverman, Warshaw Burstein, LLP, New York, NY, Connis O. Brown, III, Seth Peter Robert, Brown Robert, LLP, Fort Lauderdale, FL, for Plaintiff-Appellant.

Matthew J. Conigliaro, Carlton Fields Jorden Burt, PA, Tampa, FL, Richard L. Barry, Richard E. Mitchell, GrayRobinson, PA, Orlando, FL, for Defendants-Appellees.

Before ED CARNES, Chief Judge, MARCUS, and EBEL,[*] Circuit Judges.

p.1224 ED CARNES:

Accused robbers, rapists, and murderers have statutory and constitutional rights. So does a college student who is accused of stalking and sexually harassing another student. The question in this case is whether Valencia College violated Jeffrey Koeppel's statutory or constitutional rights when it suspended him for his conduct toward another student at the college. The p.1225 district court did not think so, and neither do we.

I. FACTUAL BACKGROUND AND PROCEDURAL HISTORY

A. Facts

Jeffrey Koeppel met Jane Roe (pseudonym) during the summer of 2014 when they were assigned to the same biology lab group at Valencia College, a public college in Florida. Because they were assigned to work together, they exchanged phone numbers and would occasionally talk out-side of class. As the semester went on, the 42-year-old Koeppel began to develop feelings for the 24-year-old Jane that were not purely academic. He volunteered to do things for her. He tutored her in biology. He offered to give her his old computer. And he asked if he could buy her a gift certificate for a massage. Eventually Koeppel told Jane that he was attracted to her. Jane let him know that the feeling was not mutual. She told him that she already had a boyfriend; that her relationship with Koeppel was strictly related to their role as lab partners in the biology class; and that she did not want him to have the wrong impression. After that the two of them finished the summer semester without incident.

1. Koeppel Messages Jane

A few days before the fall semester began, Koeppel saw something online that made him think that Jane was single. Ever hopeful, on August 3 he sent her a text message telling her once again that he had feelings for her: "So im saying I am interest[ed] in you ... but im not on any mission or anything ... i just don't enjoy feeling conflicted so I would rather talk about it."[1] That message came around 10:00 p.m. on a Sunday night while Jane was at home watching a movie with her son and her boyfriend.[2] Jane responded:

> I have told you that I just want this to be class related [because] I am with someone who I've been seeing for 3 years now .. And we live together ... So I don't know if i gave you the wrong impression or whatever the case may be.. But I do have a serious [boyfriend] and really just thought we were studying and getting through the class.

Koeppel replied that "[i]t really doesn[']t matter [because] you have been very fair with me ..." and that "I just kinda hoped you would come around ... be interested in me." He explained that he had asked her again because after looking at her Facebook page, he thought she had broken up with her boyfriend. And he told her that "U never sent any signals ... I guess i just wanna ask what your plans are."

Jane reiterated: "Listen I have a [boyfriend]. I have been busy with work. [W]hy are u texting me that when we already discussed this[?]" Then: "And saw what exactly on my Facebook? We are not even friends so how did u get on their [sic]...." Jane and her boyfriend then called Koeppel, and Jane asked him why he was texting her, told him he had crossed a line by looking at her Facebook page, and told him that they were not friends.

That apparently was not what Koeppel wanted to hear. He responded with a message to Jane advising her: "Get a nosejob. [Your boyfriend] can pay with his foodstamp[s]." Jane and her boyfriend called Koeppel again and informed him that they were calling the police. Koeppel admits that he then sent Jane a series of "inappropriate" messages and pictures in the hopes of "hurt[ing] her feelings." Each of these quotations is from a separate text:

- "I wondered if u were a hussie and i guess so."
- "Dress like a hooker and now act like it too."
- "Just sucks i didn't wear your pussy out."
- "Them skinny legs i been thinkin about."
- "Believe me i have had plenty of sex with you even if you weren[']t present."
- "What u think i was thinkin bout when ur in them tiny whore shorts."
- "Your little butt cheeks hanging out."
- "Yum yum!!!!!"

- "Ur cute with a LOT of face paint..."
- "But I like that cute little mole by ur titty."
- "A hussie is as a hussie does."

Koeppel also sent her a picture of his bare chest, a picture of himself wearing a costume with his arm around a woman, and a picture of a woman pretending to perform oral sex on another person. He later conceded that given the content and the number of his text messages, it was possible that someone receiving them would have been concerned.

Meanwhile, Jane's boyfriend called the Seminole County Sheriff's Office. Deputy Brenton Rush responded and met Jane outside of her apartment. She told him what had happened and that she was scared. Deputy Rush looked at the messages and, at Jane's request, called Koeppel to recommend that he stop talking to her. Despite his recommendation, Koeppel called her again around midnight from an unknown number.

After midnight that same night, Jane twice messaged Koeppel to "Stop calling me. Do not have any contact with me." But Koeppel kept on texting her until 5:00 a.m.[3] The messages in those later texts included questions about Jane's boyfriend, statements mocking Jane's anxiety disorder, an apology, and, when Jane didn't respond to his apology, this message: "Starbucks date — a 6.5 oz can of expresso [sic] and cream — despite the fact that it is not carbonated when opened it tends to eject some of its contents directly on one[']s face."

On August 6, Koeppel texted Jane again, but she did not respond until August 13, when she once again told him to stop: "You are crazy[. L]eave me alone and my [] life[. S]top stalking my Facebook[. L]eave us alone! The cops already informed u to leave me alone and you haven't." He didn't stop.

2. Valencia Suspends Koeppel

On August 11, 2014, Jane, accompanied by her boyfriend and son, went to Valencia Dean of Students Joseph Sarrubbo's office to complain about Koeppel's messages. At that meeting Sarrubbo noticed that Jane was "visibly upset and shaken," and he recommended that she complete a witness statement with the campus safety and security office.[4]

p.1227 *a.* Sarrubbo's Investigation

Campus security forwarded Jane's complaint and an incident report to Dean Sarrubbo, and he used those documents to create a charge letter listing the potential violations of the Valencia Student Code of Conduct.[5] Sarrubbo emailed Koeppel informing him in writing about the charges against him and instructing Koeppel to schedule a time to meet for an informal hearing. Sarrubbo also told Koeppel that he was beginning an investigation and that until the investigation was concluded Koeppel was under a no contact order with Jane and had been unenrolled from a fall class that Jane was also taking. Koeppel violated that no contact order when he texted Jane later that evening. He admits that he sent Jane 20 messages trying to persuade her to withdraw her complaint with the college.

When he met with Sarrubbo on August 15, Koeppel admitted to sending the messages, explained how he viewed his relationship with Jane, and commented on each allegation in her complaint. A few days later Sarrubbo met with Jane. During that interview Jane appeared "nervous and concerned." She told Sarrubbo that she was "concerned about running into — interacting with Mr. Koeppel on campus" because they were enrolled in the same class in the fall and she didn't "want to be around him."

In addition to meeting with both students, Dean Sarrubbo spoke with Deputy Rush and reviewed documents submitted by Jane and by Koeppel. Jane gave Sarrubbo screen shots of the messages that Koeppel had sent her. Koeppel, who had deleted the messages on his phone, used a text recovery service and submitted a Word document with some of the messages that he had sent to Jane. Koeppel also submitted a receipt for the computer he insisted that he had bought Jane, an image of Jane's Facebook page (showing that she had not blocked him), and the results of a background check that he hired someone to do on himself.

Throughout the investigation, Dean Sarrubbo kept a detailed log of phone calls, meetings, and notes. The phone log listed every call that Sarrubbo made to or received from Jane, Koeppel, and Deputy Rush. The notes log listed each allegation contained in the incident report and in a separate column reported Koeppel's comments about the allegation when questioned by Sarrubbo. The meeting log recorded the date, time, and place of each meeting that Sarrubbo had individually with Jane and with Koeppel. It also included Sarrubbo's comments about each meeting. (To simplify things, we will refer to the phone call, meeting, and notes log as Sarrubbo's log.)

After completing his investigation, Dean Sarrubbo concluded that Koeppel had likely violated the Code of Conduct and sent Koeppel an email informing him that a disciplinary hearing was set for the following week. That email also informed Koeppel that the college was considering disciplining him for having engaged in the following four types of conduct prohibited in the Code:

> [1] Physical abuse, including but not limited to, rape, sexual assault, sex offenses, and other physical assault; threats of violence; or conduct that threatens the health or safety of any person.
>
> [2] Sexual harassment, as defined in College policy ...: Unwelcome sexual advances, requests for sexual favors, and other verbal or physical conduct of a sexual nature constitute sexual harassment when: ... [s]uch conduct has the purpose or effect of unreasonably interfering with an individual's performance or creating an intimidating, hostile, or offensive College environment. In determining whether the alleged conduct constitutes sexual harassment, consideration shall be given to the record of the incident as a whole and to the totality of the circumstances, including the context in which the alleged incidents occurred.
>
> [3] Stalking behavior in which an individual willfully, maliciously, and repeatedly engages in a knowing course of conduct directed at a specific person which reasonably and seriously alarms, torments, or terrorizes the person, and which serves no legitimate purpose.
>
> [4] Disorderly or lewd conduct.

b. Koeppel's Disciplinary Hearing

Dean Sarrubbo, who oversaw Koeppel's disciplinary hearing, met with the Student Conduct Committee 30 minutes before the hearing began. At that pre-hearing meeting, he gave the committee members an overview of the charges and a folder that included his log, Jane's complaint, and the documents that Jane and Koeppel had submitted, including copies of the text messages. Jane did not attend the hearing, and Koeppel did not object to her absence.

The committee members questioned Koeppel for about 35 minutes. Some of them expressed their skepticism about Koeppel and his comments: "[Y]ou're a 42-year-old man, just get over it"; "[H]ow could you have thought that it was in any way appropriate to have offered to buy a massage for Jane?"; and "[W]hen's the last time that you bought a massage for a male friend?" One member said: "I don't see what we even — what's even necessary to discuss. He was obviously stalking."

After the committee finished questioning Koeppel, Dean Sarrubbo told him, "Now is your opportunity to address the committee and wrap things up." Koeppel spoke. Although he contended that Jane's "complaint is 80% willful misstatements and fabrications," Koeppel did not deny sending any of the text messages to her or deny that she had repeatedly asked him to stop. He did ask the committee to let him "go back to the beginning" and "explain chronologically" and to "go over the complaint against [him] line by line," like he did when he met one on one with Sarrubbo. Sarrubbo denied both requests as unnecessary. After deliberating, the committee recommended to Sarrubbo that he find Koeppel responsible for the charged conduct and suspend him from attending the college for one year. Sarrubbo upheld the recommendation and emailed Koeppel to inform him about the suspension and the appeals process.

Koeppel appealed the committee's recommendation and Dean Sarrubbo's decision to the Vice President of Student Affairs, Dr. Joyce Romano. Koeppel contended in his appeal that the committee's conclusions were unwarranted and that the sanction was excessive. Romano denied Koeppel's appeal, explaining that:

> [T]he number of texts is not the main focus in this case as much as the continued behavior you exhibited in not controlling your impulses and continuing to engage with the other student when it was clearly communicated to you that such interactions were unwelcome and that you should have no further contact with her.

B. Procedural History

On October 23, 2015, Koeppel filed a lawsuit against Romano, Sarrubbo, and one other Valencia official in their individual capacities.[6] (Because the claims against them are identical, we refer to the defendants collectively as Valencia.) In his third amended complaint Koeppel claimed under 42 U.S.C. § 1983 that Valencia's policies, on their face and as applied to him, violated the First Amendment and that Valencia's actions violated his right to procedural and substantive due process. He also claimed that Valencia violated Title IX, 20 U.S.C. § 1681.

Valencia moved to dismiss all of Koeppel's claims or, in the alternative, for summary judgment. After the close of discovery, the court granted summary judgment to Valencia on all of the claims.[7] This is Koeppel's appeal.

II. STANDARD OF REVIEW

We review de novo a grant of summary judgment, viewing the facts and "drawing all reasonable inferences in favor of the nonmoving party." Boim v. Fulton Cty. Sch. Dist., 494 F.3d 978, 982 (11th Cir. 2007).

III. DISCUSSION

Koeppel contends that Valencia's policies violated his First Amendment right to free speech, that they were unconstitutionally overbroad and vague on their face, and that he was denied procedural and substantive due process in connection with his disciplinary hearing. Citing Title IX, he also contends that gender bias was a motivating factor in his suspension. We address each of those contentions in that order.

A. Koeppel's As Applied Claim That Valencia Violated His First Amendment Right To Free Speech

The Supreme Court has held that public schools may regulate student expression when it "substantially interfere[s] with the work of the school or impinge[s] upon the rights of other students." See Tinker v. Des Moines Indep. Cmty. Sch. Dist., 393 U.S. 503, 509, 89 S.Ct. 733, 738, 21 L.Ed.2d 731 (1969). Koeppel claims that as they were applied to him Valencia's policies violated his First Amendment rights because his messages to Jane were private, non-threatening speech, which did not cause a substantial interference at the school. Maybe so, but that goes to only half of Tinker's holding.

Tinker held that a public school may regulate student speech not only when it "substantially interfere[s] with the work of the school," but also when it "impinge[s] upon the rights of other students" to be secure and to be let alone. Id.; see also id. at 513, 89 S.Ct. at 740 ("[C]onduct by the student [that] ... materially disrupts classwork or involves substantial disorder or invasion of the rights of others is, of course, not immunized by the constitutional guarantee of freedom of speech.") (emphasis added); see also Brown v. Budget Rent-A-Car Sys., Inc., 119 F.3d 922, 924 (11th Cir. 1997) (explaining that "or" usually "indicates alternatives and requires that those alternatives be treated separately") (quotation marks omitted). We take it as given that when the Supreme Court stated that conduct involving an "invasion of the rights of others" is not constitutionally protected, it meant that conduct invading the rights of others is not constitutionally protected. See CSX Transp., Inc. v. Ala. Dep't of Revenue, 888 F.3d 1163, 1177 (11th Cir. 2018) ("[A] good rule of thumb for reading [Supreme Court] decisions is that what they say and what they mean are one and the same.") (quoting Mathis v. United States, 579 U.S. ___, 136 S.Ct. 2243, 2254, 195 L.Ed.2d 604 (2016)).

Koeppel's conduct invaded Jane's rights, interfering with her rights "to be secure and to be let alone," free from persistent unwanted advances and related insults from another student. See Tinker, 393 U.S. at 508, 89 S.Ct. at 737. He sent her dozens of messages throughout the night making lewd references to her body, and he continued to send unwanted messages over a period of days. His persistent misconduct ignored Jane's repeated pleas that he stop contacting her, Deputy Rush's recommendation that he not contact her, and Dean Sarrubbo's order that he not contact her. As Vice President of Student Affairs Romano explained, the worst aspect of Koeppel's misbehavior was not the quantity of it but the fact that instead of controlling his impulses Koeppel continued to harass Jane, knowing that it was unwelcome and despite being told to leave her alone. He wouldn't leave her alone.

Dean Sarrubbo testified that Jane appeared upset at their meetings and that she was concerned about attending school during the fall term because she was scheduled to be in class with Koeppel. Given Koeppel's persistent harassment as well as the understandable (and intended) anxiety it caused Jane, Valencia reasonably concluded that his conduct invaded her rights.[8] See id. at 512-13, 89 S.Ct. at 740; Hill v. Colorado, 530 U.S. 703, 718, 120 S.Ct. 2480, 2490, 147 L.Ed.2d 597 (2000) ("None of our decisions has minimized the enduring importance of a right to be free from persistent importunity, following and dogging after an offer to communicate has been declined."). Because Koeppel's conduct interfered with Jane's rights, Valencia was free to regulate it under Tinker without impinging on Koeppel's First Amendment rights. We need p.1231 not decide whether Koeppel's conduct also caused a "material and substantial interfere[nce]" with the school's programs or mission. Tinker, 393 U.S. at 511, 89 S.Ct. at 739.

Koeppel's misconduct occurred while he was enrolled at Valencia, although it was during the break between summer and fall classes. He and Jane were scheduled to be in the same class that fall. Still, he protests that the school was powerless to do anything about his misbehavior because he did it all while he was off campus. But Tinker teaches that "conduct by the student, in class or out of it" that results in the "invasion of the rights of others is, of course, not immunized by the constitutional guarantee of freedom of speech." Id. at 513, 89 S.Ct. at 740 (emphasis added). We agree with the Fifth Circuit that "[t]he pervasive and omnipresent nature of the Internet has obfuscated the on-campus/off-campus distinction ... making any effort to trace First Amendment boundaries along the physical boundaries of a school campus a recipe for serious problems in our public schools." Bell v. Itawamba Cty. Sch. Bd., 799 F.3d 379, 391, 395-96 (5th Cir. 2015) (en banc) (quotation marks and alterations omitted); cf. Doninger v. Niehoff, 527 F.3d 41, 48 (2d Cir. 2008) ("[A] student may be disciplined for expressive conduct, even conduct occurring off school grounds, when this conduct would foreseeably create a risk of substantial disruption within the school environment ... [and] might also reach campus."). There is no absolute bar against schools disciplining a student for off-campus conduct that violates the rights of another student.

We need not decide how far Tinker's "in class or out of it" language extends. See Bell, 799 F.3d at 396 ("[I]n holding Tinker applies to off-campus speech in this instance... we decline[] to adopt any rigid standard."). It is enough to hold, as we do, that Tinker does not foreclose a school from regulating all off-campus conduct. And under the facts of this case, Valencia could constitutionally regulate Koeppel's conduct, expressive though it was, which invaded the rights of another student.

B. Koeppel's Claim That Valencia's Policies Are Unconstitutionally Overbroad And Vague

Koeppel also attacks the provisions in Valencia's Code of Conduct about physical abuse, sexual harassment, stalking, and disorderly or lewd conduct. He claims that they are unconstitutionally overbroad and vague on their face and that they are vague as applied to him. The Code of Conduct lists 27 categories of prohibited conduct and provides that a violation of any of them can support any sanction, including suspension. The independent nature of each provision serves to make them severable. See Brockett v. Spokane Arcades, Inc., 472 U.S. 491, 502, 105 S.Ct. 2794, 2801, 86 L.Ed.2d 394 (1985) (stating "the elementary principle that the same statute may be in part constitutional and in part unconstitutional, and that if the parts are wholly independent of each other, that which is constitutional may stand") (quotation marks omitted).

As a result, Koeppel's facial challenge cannot succeed unless all four of the provisions he was found to have violated are overbroad or vague. His attorney conceded that at oral argument, and we agree. See Crowe v. Coleman, 113 F.3d 1536, 1542 (11th Cir. 1997) ("That concessions and admissions of counsel at oral argument in appellate courts can count against them is doubtlessly true."). So long as one of those four provisions can withstand the facial attack, it is not necessary to decide if the other three can as well. See Church of Scientology Flag Serv. Org., Inc. v. City of Clearwater, 777 F.2d 598, 604 (11th Cir. 1985) (recognizing a "long-standing policy of refusing to decide constitutional issues unless strictly necessary").

p.1232 We can begin and end our analysis with Valencia's stalking provision.[9] That provision, at the time this case arose, defined "stalking" as: "Stalking behavior in which an individual willfully, maliciously, and repeatedly engages in a knowing course of conduct directed at a specific person which reasonably and seriously alarms, torments, or terrorizes the person, and which serves no legitimate purpose." Koeppel argues that this provision is overbroad and vague on its face because the words "alarms, torments, or terrorizes" are entirely subjective and set the threshold of harm too low. We address overbreadth first.

1. The Overbreadth Claim

A plaintiff mounting a facial attack must usually prove "that no set of circumstances exists under which the [statute] would be valid." United States v. Salerno, 481 U.S. 739, 745, 107 S.Ct. 2095, 2100, 95 L.Ed.2d 697 (1987). Overbreadth is an exception to that rule. Id. It is an exception because of the concern that "the very existence of some statutes may cause persons not before the Court to refrain from engaging in constitutionally protected speech." Young v. Am. Mini Theatres, Inc., 427 U.S. 50, 60, 96 S.Ct. 2440, 2447, 49 L.Ed.2d 310 (1976).

In a facial overbreadth challenge the plaintiff must show that the statute "punishes a substantial amount of protected free speech, judged in relation to the statute's plainly legitimate sweep." Fla. Ass'n of Prof'l Lobbyists, Inc. v. Fla. Office of Legislative Servs., 525 F.3d 1073, 1079 (11th Cir. 2008) (emphasis added) (quotation marks omitted). "Substantial overbreadth" is not a precisely defined term. Still, we know it requires "a realistic danger that the statute itself will significantly compromise recognized First Amendment protections of parties not before the Court for it to be facially challenged on overbreadth grounds." Members of the City Council v. Taxpayers for Vincent, 466 U.S. 789, 801, 104 S.Ct. 2118, 2126, 80 L.Ed.2d 772 (1984). And the party claiming overbreadth "bears the burden of demonstrating, from the text of the law and from actual fact, that substantial overbreadth exists." Virginia v. Hicks, 539 U.S. 113, 122, 123 S.Ct. 2191, 2198, 156 L.Ed.2d 148 (2003) (quotation marks and alterations omitted). That is not easy to do.

And Koeppel has not done it. The stalking provision, when read as a whole, covers conduct that Tinker allows schools to regulate. It does not prohibit all conduct that "alarms, torments, or terrorizes" someone else. Only that which is also "willful[], malicious[], and repeated[]"; and "directed at a specific person"; and that "serves no legitimate purpose." Although the stalking provision refers to the victim's reaction, it requires that the reaction be both "reasonabl[e] and serious[]," which goes beyond a purely subjective or only minimal threshold of harm. Prohibiting stalking conduct, however expressive it is, that meets all of those requirements does not punish a substantial amount of protected p.1233 free speech, judged in relation to the statute's plainly legitimate sweep. See Tinker, 393 U.S. at 509, 89 S.Ct. at 738. It cannot be said "from the text of [the policy] and from actual fact, that substantial overbreadth exists." Hicks, 539 U.S. at 122, 123 S.Ct. at 2198 (quotation marks omitted). For that reason, the stalking provision is not unconstitutionally overbroad. We turn next to whether it is unconstitutionally vague.

2. The Vagueness Claim

Koeppel contends that the stalking provision is unconstitutionally vague on its face. "[A] plaintiff whose speech is clearly proscribed cannot raise a successful vagueness claim ...." Holder v. Humanitarian Law Project, 561 U.S. 1, 20, 130 S.Ct. 2705, 2719, 177 L.Ed.2d 355 (2010); accord Expressions Hair Design v. Schneiderman, ___ U.S. ___, 137 S.Ct. 1144, 1151-52, 197 L.Ed.2d 442 (2017). Koeppel's conduct was "clearly proscribed" under the stalking provision. He admits that he sent Jane a series of inappropriate messages and pictures hoping to "hurt[] her feelings" and that he continued doing so after she asked him to stop, Deputy Rush recommended that he stop, and Dean Sarrubbo ordered him to stop. That admission shows that his conduct was willful, malicious, and repeated; directed toward Jane; and served "no legitimate purpose," which is conduct that is clearly proscribed by the policy. Any objectively reasonable person would have known that Jane was "reasonably and seriously alarm[ed], torment[ed], or terrorize[d]" by Koeppel's conduct because she repeatedly implored Koeppel to stop contacting her and reported Koeppel's conduct to the police and the school. Yet he continued.

Because Koeppel's conduct was "clearly proscribed" by the stalking provision, his facial vagueness challenge fails. See Village of Hoffman Estates v. Flipside, Hoffman Estates, Inc., 455 U.S. 489, 495, 102 S.Ct. 1186, 1191, 71 L.Ed.2d 362 (1982). For the same reason, to the extent he pursues an as applied challenge, it fails too.

The stalking provision is not facially overbroad, nor is it facially vague or vague as applied to his conduct. We need not and do not address the constitutionality of any of the other provisions that were in place when Koeppel was disciplined.[10]

p.1234 C. Koeppel's Due Process Claims

Koeppel contends that the district court erred by granting summary judgment on his claim that the process Valencia applied to him and the discipline he received violated his procedural and substantive due process rights.

1. The Procedural Due Process Claim

In the school disciplinary setting, procedural due process requires that colleges give students notice and a hearing before suspending or expelling them. See Nash v. Auburn Univ., 812 F.2d 655, 660-61 (11th Cir. 1987) (discussing the type of hearing and notice required when a public college suspended two students for academic dishonesty); Dixon v. Ala. State Bd. of Educ., 294 F.2d 150, 158 (5th Cir. 1961) ("[D]ue process requires notice and some opportunity for hearing before a student at a tax-supported college is expelled for misconduct."). "The adequacy of the notice and the nature of the hearing" required depend on the facts of the case and the "practical requirements of the circumstances." Nash, 812 F.2d at 660.

Koeppel attacks the adequacy of his disciplinary hearing, arguing that he was denied due process because the committee assumed that Jane was telling the truth in her unsworn complaint, denied him the opportunity to cross examine her, and applied the wrong standard of proof. Valencia responds that Koeppel cannot allege a procedural due process violation because he has not pursued available state remedies. Whatever doubts we may have about the adequacy of Valencia's procedures, we agree that because Koeppel failed to take advantage of available state remedies, he cannot show that he was denied procedural due process.[11]

In our McKinney decision we held that "a procedural due process violation is not complete unless and until the State fails to provide due process." McKinney v. Pate, 20 F.3d 1550, 1557 (11th Cir. 1994) (quotations marks omitted). "[O]nly when the state refuses to provide a process sufficient to remedy the procedural deprivation does a constitutional violation actionable under section 1983 arise." Id.; see also Zinermon v. Burch, 494 U.S. 113, 125-26, 110 S.Ct. 975, 983, 108 L.Ed.2d 100 (1990) (explaining that "the existence of state remedies is relevant" in a § 1983 action "brought for a violation of procedural due process" because in those cases the "constitutional violation ... is not complete unless and until the State fails to provide due process"). And in Watts we relied on McKinney to hold that a graduate student who was dropped from a required course p.1235 after being removed from a practicum position could not raise a procedural due process claim because "several Florida Administrative Code sections and state court decisions indicat[ed] that [the student] could seek relief for his procedural deprivations in state court." Watts v. Fla. Int'l Univ., 495 F.3d 1289, 1294 (11th Cir. 2007).

Koeppel argues that Watts does not preclude his federal procedural due process claim because that decision relied on remedies which were available under the Florida

Administrative Procedure Act. That Act no longer provides appellate review in the state courts of a decision by a Florida university because state universities are no longer treated as administrative agencies and now derive their authority directly from the Florida Constitution. See Fla. Const., art. IX, § 7(c), (d) (stating that each state university will be operated by a board of trustees under powers granted by the board of governors and that the state board of governors shall "operate, regulate, control and be fully responsible for the management of the whole university system"); Decker v. Univ. of W. Fla., 85 So.3d 571, 573 (Fla. 1st DCA 2012) ("[W]hen an officer or agency is exercising power derived from the constitution, the resulting decision is not one that is made by an agency as defined in the Administrative Procedure Act.").

Koeppel is correct about the authority of Florida universities now flowing directly from the Florida Constitution. But he is incorrect about the change meaning that the State of Florida no longer provides any avenue for relief from due process deprivations by its universities. Because Koeppel could have sought review as a matter of right through a state certiorari proceeding, see Decker, 85 So.3d at 574 (concluding that appellate review of a university's disciplinary decision was "a matter of right" and that "certiorari [wa]s the proper remedy"), the State provides an adequate remedy for Koeppel's alleged procedural deprivation, see Cotton v. Jackson, 216 F.3d 1328, 1331 (11th Cir. 2000) ("[T]he state must have the opportunity to remedy the procedural failings of its subdivisions and agencies in the appropriate fora — agencies, review boards, and state courts [—] before being subjected to a claim alleging a procedural due process violation.") (quotation marks omitted); id. (noting that "certiorari [to the state courts] is generally an adequate state remedy" for procedural due process purposes).

Because Florida provides an adequate remedy, the district court did not err by granting summary judgment in favor of Valencia on Koeppel's procedural due process claim.

2. The Substantive Due Process Claim

Koeppel contends that he was deprived of substantive due process because he had a constitutionally protected right to continued enrollment at Valencia, and that right was violated when the school acted in an arbitrary and capricious manner during his disciplinary proceedings. But students at a public university do not have a fundamental right to continued enrollment. See Plyler v. Doe, 457 U.S. 202, 221, 102 S.Ct. 2382, 2396, 72 L.Ed.2d 786 (1982) ("Public education is not a 'right' granted to individuals by the Constitution."); see also C.B. ex rel. Breeding v. Driscoll, 82 F.3d 383, 387 (11th Cir. 1996) ("The right to attend a public school is a state-created, rather than a fundamental, right for the purposes of substantive due process."); McKinney, 20 F.3d at 1556 ("[A]reas in which substantive rights are created only by state law ... are not subject to substantive due process protection under the Due Process Clause because substantive due process rights are created only by the Constitution.") (quotation marks omitted).[12] The district court p.1236 did not err by granting summary judgment to Valencia on Koeppel's substantive due process claim.

D. Koeppel's Title IX Claim

Finally, Koeppel contends that the district court erred by granting summary judgment against him on his Title IX claim. Title IX states: "No person in the United States shall, on the basis of sex, be excluded from participation in, be denied the benefits of, or be subjected to discrimination under any education program or activity receiving Federal financial assistance...." 20 U.S.C. § 1681(a). There is some support for the proposition that Title IX's prohibition applies to school disciplinary proceedings when gender bias is a motivating factor in the decision to discipline. See Yusuf v. Vassar Coll., 35 F.3d 709, 715 (2d Cir. 1994) ("Title IX bars the imposition of university discipline where gender is a motivating factor in the decision to discipline."); see also Doe v. Miami Univ., 882 F.3d 579, 589 (6th Cir. 2018); Plummer v. Univ. of Hous., 860 F.3d 767, 777-78 (5th Cir. 2017); Doe v. Columbia Univ., 831 F.3d 46, 53 (2d Cir. 2016). Neither the Supreme Court nor this Court has established a framework for analyzing Title IX challenges to university disciplinary proceedings. But we will assume for present purposes that a student can show a violation of Title IX by satisfying the "erroneous outcome" test applied by the Second Circuit in Yusuf. See 35 F.3d at 714-16; see also Miami Univ., 882 F.3d at 589, 592-94; Plummer, 860 F.3d at 777-78. Under that test, a student must show both that he was "innocent and wrongly found to have committed an offense" and that there is "a causal connection between the flawed outcome and gender bias."[13] Yusuf, 35 F.3d at 715.

Koeppel contends that the out-come of his disciplinary proceeding was erroneous because Valencia could not regulate off-campus conduct, his conduct was protected by the First Amendment, and his conduct did not meet the definition of any of the violations for which he was punished. As our previous discussion makes clear, all three of those arguments underlying his contention fail. Koeppel points to no "facts sufficient to cast some articulable doubt on the accuracy of the outcome of the disciplinary proceeding." Id.; see also id. ("If no such doubt exists based on the record before the disciplinary tribunal, the claim must fail."). He admitted the underlying conduct. That conduct met the school's definition of stalking. Stalking was punishable by suspension under the Code of Conduct. It's as simple as that.

Because Koeppel has not shown that there is a genuine issue about the correctness of the outcome of his disciplinary proceeding, his Title IX claim fails, and we need not decide whether there is a causal connection between the outcome of the proceeding and gender bias. The district court did not err by granting summary judgment to Valencia on Koeppel's Title IX claim.

p.1237 IV. CONCLUSION

The district court did not err by granting summary judgment in favor of Valencia on all of Koeppel's claims.

AFFIRMED.

[*] Honorable David Ebel, United States Circuit Judge for the Tenth Circuit, sitting by designation.

[1] In our quotations from Koeppel's and Jane's messages, all punctuation, including ellipses, appears in the original messages. The bracketed parts we have added for clarity.

[2] It's unclear from the record whether the man was Jane's boyfriend, her ex-husband, her son's father, or some combination of the three. For consistency and ease of reference — and because it doesn't matter anyway — we will refer to him as her boyfriend.

[3] Koeppel asserts that the messages were all sent during a 17-minute span. Although he sent the bulk of the lewd messages from 10:57 p.m. to 11:18 p.m., Koeppel admits that he sent the first of those messages to Jane around 10:00 p.m. on August 3 and the last of them around 5:00 a.m. on August 4.

[4] At the time, Valencia's procedure provided that a student who reported a potential violation of the Code of Conduct was sent to the campus safety and security office to complete a witness statement. That office would create an incident report and forward it to Dean Sarrubbo.

[5] What the parties have consistently referred to as Jane's "complaint" is actually her witness statement in the nature of a complaint. To avoid confusion, we will also call it a complaint.

[6] He also named the college as a defendant, but it was dismissed on sovereign immunity grounds.

[7] Before summary judgment was granted, Koeppel argued that under Federal Rule of Civil Procedure 56(d) it would be premature to do so because he had not had "an adequate opportunity to obtain discovery." The district court then allowed him to depose Dean Sarrubbo and Deputy Rush. Based on those depositions Koeppel sought leave to file an additional 10-page memorandum of law in opposition to Valencia's motion for summary judgment. The district court denied his motion, stating that it did "not require the benefit of additional papers."

Koeppel argues that the district court abused its discretion by denying what he describes as his motion to supplement. But the full transcript of both of those depositions and other evidence collected during discovery entered the record through later motions, including Koeppel's own motion for partial summary judgment. And we consider the entire record, including evidence that came into it later, when we are reviewing the district court's conclusions de novo. There was no abuse of discretion.

[8] Koeppel contends that the district court erred by considering some of the evidence that the committee relied on to reach its conclusion that Koeppel had violated the Code of Conduct. He argues that certain evidence is inadmissible hearsay: the statements in Jane's complaint; testimony by Dean Sarrubbo about what Jane had told him; testimony by Deputy Rush that Jane was scared of Koeppel; images of the text messages between them that Jane had given Sarrubbo; and Sarrubbo's log. We disagree.

The district court did not abuse its discretion by citing the statements in Jane's complaint or considering her statements to Sarrubbo because both were admissible as evidence of what the committee and Sarrubbo considered in reaching their decision. See United States v. Rivera, 780 F.3d 1084, 1092 (11th Cir. 2015) (holding that out-of-court statements offered "only to show their effect on the listener" were not hearsay because they "were not offered for the truth of the matters asserted").

And Jane's statement to Deputy Rush that she was fearful was admissible as evidence of Jane's then existing mental or emotional condition. See Fed. R. Evid. 803(3). As for the text messages she gave to Sarrubbo, all of Koeppel's messages to her were admissible as statements by a party opponent. See Fed. R. Evid. 801(d)(2). And her messages to Koeppel were admissible to show that she had repeatedly asked him to stop. See Rivera, 780 F.3d at 1092. Finally, Sarrubbo's log is a record of a regularly conducted activity, see Fed. R. Evid. 803(6), and the statements in it are admissible as evidence of what the committee considered in reaching its decision, see Rivera, 780 F.3d at 1092.

[9] Valencia argues that Koeppel's overbreadth challenges became moot in 2015 when Valencia updated many of its policies, including its definition of stalking. We disagree. An amendment might moot a claim for prospective relief by a current student, but it can have no bearing on whether Koeppel, a former student who seeks damages, was punished under an unconstitutional policy. For that determination, we must focus on the provisions that Valencia enforced in 2014. See Genesis Healthcare Corp. v. Symczyk, 569 U.S. 66, 77, 133 S.Ct. 1523, 1531, 185 L.Ed.2d 636 (2013) ("Unlike claims for injunctive relief challenging ongoing conduct, a claim for damages cannot evade review; it remains live until it is settled, judicially resolved, or barred by a statute of limitations."); Checker Cab Operators, Inc. v. Miami-Dade County, 899 F.3d 908, 915-16 (11th Cir. 2018).

[10] Koeppel also argues that the Code of Conduct's "jurisdictional" provision is vague because it is "arbitrary and capricious, allowing the school to pick and choose what off-campus conduct it punishes." That provision states: "College jurisdiction regarding discipline is generally limited to conduct of any student or registered student organization that occurs on College premises. However, the College reserves the right to impose discipline based on any student conduct, regardless of location, that may adversely affect the College community." Koeppel argues that the provision is unconstitutionally vague on its face and as applied to his conduct. His argument focuses on two clauses: (1) that Valencia "reserves the right," and (2) that conduct must "adversely affect the College community."

To begin with, the "jurisdictional provision" is not jurisdictional. It does not grant the college authority to discipline students for misconduct, nor does it affect the college's inherent authority to do so. Instead, the provision describes the conduct over which the college may exercise its disciplinary authority.

And neither clause allows for arbitrary enforcement. The two clauses put students on notice that the college may discipline them because of their off campus misconduct (further defined in the 27 grounds for discipline) that adversely affects the college community. And the college community obviously includes other students. Neither clause authorizes or invites application of the Code of Conduct in an arbitrary fashion to off campus or on campus conduct. The fact that Valencia reserved for itself the right to decide when to exercise its authority to discipline students for off campus misconduct that violates the Code is no more unconstitutional than any other type of prosecutorial discretion.

[11] Now for some dicta. See McDonald's Corp. v. Robertson, 147 F.3d 1301, 1314-15 (11th Cir. 1998) (Carnes, J., concurring specially) (recognizing that "dicta in our opinions is not binding on anyone for any purpose," but noting that it "has its place and serves some purposes").

Dean Sarrubbo testified in his deposition that the committee had "taken as true," or assumed to be true, the statements in Jane's complaint and in the resulting incident report. It is not clear whether the committee did that early in the hearing or only after listening to what Koeppel had to say during the hearing. But Sarrubbo also said that he had done the same thing in his investigation subject to Jane's statements being proven false, which they were not.

We would have serious doubts about the constitutionality of decision makers in this type of proceeding basing a decision on an assumption about either side telling the truth. The decision should be based on a fact finding, and if it is impossible to determine what the truth is, it should be based on the burden of persuasion. Not on assumptions. Having said that, we recognize that the facts in this case were not actually disputed. Koeppel admitted all the material ones. The committee's recommendation and the Dean's decision were not based on any assumption about who was telling the truth. Which is why this is dicta.

[12] Ewing and Horowitz are not to the contrary because in those cases the Supreme Court "assumed, without deciding, that federal courts can review an academic decision of a public educational institution under a substantive due process standard." Regents of Univ. of Mich. v. Ewing, 474 U.S. 214, 222-23, 106 S.Ct. 507, 511-12, 88 L.Ed.2d 523 (1985); Bd. of Curators of Univ. of Mo. v. Horowitz, 435 U.S. 78, 91-92, 98 S.Ct. 948, 956, 55 L.Ed.2d 124 (1978).

[13] Yusuf also suggested that a student could prove a Title IX violation by showing that the university selectively enforces its policy. 35 F.3d at 715. Because there is no allegation of selective enforcement in this case, we make no comment (and indulge no assumption) about that part of the Second Circuit's decision.

877 F.3d 979 (2017)

J.S., III, a minor, BY AND THROUGH J.S. JR. and M.S., his parents and next friends, Plaintiff-Appellant,

v.

The HOUSTON COUNTY BOARD OF EDUCATION, Defendant-Appellee.

No. 15-14306.

United States Court of Appeals, Eleventh Circuit.

(October 2, 2017).

JS v. Houston County Bd. of Education, 877 F. 3d 979 (11th Cir. 2017)

Appeal from the United States District Court for the Middle District of Alabama, D.C. Docket No. 1:14-cv-01196-WHA-WC.

William Tipton Johnson, III, Jeffrey Conett Kirby, Kirby Johnson, PC, Birmingham, AL, William L. Lee, III, Lee Livingston Lee & Nichols, PC, Dothan, AL, Stanley Murphy, Murphy & Murphy, LLC, Tuscaloosa, AL, for Plaintiff-Appellant

James Kevin Walding, Jere C. Segrest, Hardwick Hause Segrest & Walding, Dothan, AL, for Defendant-Appellee

Before WILLIAM PRYOR, JORDAN, and RIPPLE,[*] Circuit Judges.

PER CURIAM:

J.S., III is an elementary school student with severe physical disabilities and cognitive impairments. Through his parents, J.S., Jr. and M.S., he appeals the district court's grant of summary judgment in favor of the Houston County Board of Education on his claims under Title II of the Americans with Disabilities Act, 42 U.S.C. § 12131 *et seq.*, and § 504 of the Rehabilitation Act, 29 U.S.C. § 794. J.S. alleges that he was discriminated against on the basis of his disability while attending Wicksburg High School, a kindergarten through twelfth-grade school in Houston County, Alabama. Following oral argument and a review of the record, we affirm in part and reverse in part the district court's order, and remand for further proceedings.

I

When J.S. was in the third grade (2010 to 2011) and fourth grade (2011 to 2012), he received individual education plans (IEPs), under which he was assigned to regular and special education classrooms. The IEPs noted that J.S. had poor balance, used a walker and a wheelchair at school, needed help with using the restroom, and received physical and occupational services while at school. The IEPs specified that J.S. was to spend 80 percent of his time in the regular classroom and 20 percent of his time in the special education classroom. Alicia Brown was J.S.' special education teacher during his third-grade year and part of his fourth-grade year and Angie Boatright was his regular classroom teacher during his fourth-grade year. Drew Faircloth was assigned to work with J.S. as a teacher's aide/special education paraprofessional starting J.S.' third-grade year. Mr. Faircloth helped J.S. with going to the restroom, getting around the school campus, going to lunch and recess, participating in physical education, and completing class work.

In late 2011 and early 2012, Mr. Faircloth began taking J.S. out of his regular classroom and bringing him to the school's weight room, purportedly because J.S. was disruptive in the classroom and because they could do physical therapy and use the private restroom there. Ms. Boatright testified that she never instructed Mr. Faircloth to take J.S. out of the classroom for being a distraction to others or being distracted himself. *See* Boatright Dep., D.E. 28-20 at 24-25, 58.

Matt Barton and Brandon Sunday, both elementary physical education teachers and coaches at Wicksburg, observed Mr. Faircloth and J.S. in the weight room. Coach Barton testified that Mr. Faircloth brought J.S. into the weight room "fairly often" and that on some days J.S. completed class work and worksheets in the weight room, while on other days he would be just "kind of ... hanging out" while Mr. Faircloth was sitting in the coach's office using the computer. *See* Barton Dep., D.E. 28-22 at 23-27. Coach Sunday said that he saw J.S. and Mr. Faircloth in the weight room at least once a week generally, sometimes twice a week. He testified that J.S. would often be doing class work at a small desk, while Mr. Faircloth was on the other side of the p.984 window inside the coach's office talking with Coach Barton, occasionally helping J.S. if he had a question. *See* Sunday Dep., D.E. 28-23 at 32-33.

Ms. Brown testified that she heard from other teachers that Mr. Faircloth was taking J.S. to the weight room and informed Wicksburg Principal Cheryl Smith at least twice. *See* Brown Dep., D.E. 28-26 at 25, 30-31, 38. Principal Smith testified that she spoke with Mr. Faircloth and asked him to stop taking J.S. to the weight room. *See* Smith Dep., D.E. 28-27 at 72. Mr. Faircloth continued to remove J.S. from the classroom.

In March of 2012, a fellow student, R.T., witnessed Mr. Faircloth kick J.S.' wheelchair, while telling him to be quiet, refusing to pick up his pencil for him, and otherwise berating him. R.T. told her parents, who then informed J.S.' parents about what R.T. had witnessed. In response, J.S.' parents placed an audio recorder underneath J.S.' wheelchair for several days. According to J.S.' parents, the device captured verbal abuse by Mr. Faircloth and Ms. Brown, and possible physical abuse by Mr. Faircloth.

J.S.' parents contacted the school district's special education coordinator, Denise Whitfield, to report what they had heard on the recordings. Mr. Faircloth and Ms. Brown were placed on administrative leave and received written reprimands from Principal Smith. Mr. Faircloth ultimately resigned from his position and the School Board decided not to renew Ms. Brown's contract.

J.S., through his parents, originally filed an action in 2012 against the School Board, Mr. Faircloth, Ms. Brown, and others. He settled his claims against Mr. Faircloth and Ms. Brown. The district court granted summary judgment to the School Board because J.S. had failed to exhaust his administrative remedies, but dismissed the suit without prejudice. J.S. subsequently filed an administrative due process complaint with the Alabama Department of Education pursuant to the Individuals with Disabilities Education Act, 20 U.S.C. § 1400 *et seq.*, and J.S. and the School Board resolved that dispute. J.S. then filed this action against the School Board, alleging

Title II and § 504 violations relating to his removal from the classroom and the verbal and physical abuse.

The district court granted summary judgment in favor of the School Board, concluding that (1) regarding his removal from the classroom, J.S. had not shown more than a failure to provide a free appropriate public education (FAPE) under the IDEA; and (2) J.S. had not provided any evidence that the School Board had notice of future verbal and physical abuse. This appeal followed.[1]

II

We review the grant of summary judgment *de novo,* applying the same legal standard used by the district court and drawing all factual inferences in the light most favorable to the nonmoving party. *See Johnson v. Bd. of Regents of Univ. of Georgia,* 263 F.3d 1234, 1242-43 (11th Cir. 2001). Summary judgment is appropriate when "the pleadings, depositions, answers to interrogatories, and admissions on file, together with the affidavits ... show that there is no genuine issue as to any material fact and that the nonmoving party is entitled to judgment as a matter of law." p.985 *Celotex Corp. v. Catrett,* 477 U.S. 317, 322, 106 S.Ct. 2548, 91 L.Ed.2d 265 (1986) (quoting Fed. R. Civ. P. 56(c)). In order to overcome a motion for summary judgment, the moving party must present more than a mere scintilla of evidence supporting his position, and must make a sufficient showing that a jury could reasonably find in his favor. *See Brooks v. Cty. Comm'n of Jefferson Cty., Ala.,* 446 F.3d 1160, 1162 (11th Cir. 2006).

III

Title II of the ADA and § 504 of the Rehabilitation Act forbid discrimination on the basis of disability in the provision of public services. Title II of the ADA provides that "no qualified individual with a disability shall, by reason of such disability, be excluded from participation in or be denied the benefits of the services, programs, or activities of a public entity, or be subjected to discrimination by any such entity." 42 U.S.C. § 12132. Similarly, § 504 states that "[n]o otherwise qualified individual with a disability in the United States, ... shall, solely by reason of her or his disability, be excluded from the participation in, be denied the benefits of, or be subjected to discrimination under any program or activity receiving Federal financial assistance." 29 U.S.C. § 794.

Discrimination claims under the ADA and the Rehabilitation Act are governed by the same standards, and the two claims are generally discussed together. *See Cash v. Smith,* 231 F.3d 1301, 1305 (11th Cir. 2000). To state a claim under Title II and § 504, a plaintiff must demonstrate "(1) that he is a qualified individual with a disability; (2) that he was either excluded from participation in or denied the benefits of a public entity's services, programs, or activities, or was otherwise discriminated against by the public entity; and (3) that the exclusion, denial of benefit, or discrimination was by reason of the plaintiff's disability." *Bircoll v. Miami-Dade Cty.,* 480 F.3d 1072, 1083 (11th Cir. 2007).[2]

J.S. argues that the district court erred by mischaracterizing his Title II and § 504 claim regarding his removal from his regular classroom as merely a claim that he was denied a FAPE, a right guaranteed under the IDEA. The IDEA "guarantees individually tailored educational services," whereas Title II and § 504 "promise non-discriminatory access to public institutions" — specifically aiming "to root out disability-based discrimination, enabling each covered person ... to participate equally to all others in public facilities and federally funded programs." *Fry v. Napoleon Cmty. Sch.*, ___ U.S. ___, 137 S.Ct. 743, 756, 197 L.Ed.2d 46 (2017). Courts have recognized that there is often "some overlap in coverage" across these statutes and that "[t]he same conduct might violate all three statutes." *Id.*

The district court reasoned that, in order to demonstrate discrimination in the education context, a plaintiff must show more than a simple failure to provide a FAPE; he must also demonstrate bad faith or gross misjudgment by the school, or show that he suffered discrimination solely because of his disability. The district court concluded that J.S. had not presented evidence that the departure from his IEP amounted to gross misjudgment, and had not demonstrated that he was treated differently or excluded from something that other students received. We agree that "[t]o prove discrimination in the education context, something more than a mere failure to provide the 'free appropriate education' required by [IDEA] must be shown," *Sellers v. Sch. Bd. of City of Mannassas, Va.*, 141 F.3d 524, 529 (4th Cir. 1998) (internal quotation marks and citation omitted), but disagree with the district court's conclusion that J.S. merely set out an IDEA claim.

In the context of determining whether a claim under Title II or § 504 seeks relief that is also available under the IDEA and is therefore also subject to the IDEA's exhaustion requirement, the Supreme Court has stated that "[w]hat matters is the crux — or, in legal-speak, the gravamen — of the plaintiff's complaint, setting aside any attempts at artful pleading." *Fry*, 137 S.Ct. at 755. Although we are not examining the issue of exhaustion under the IDEA, we find this guidance instructive.

To determine whether a claim seeks relief available under the IDEA, the Supreme Court has proposed that courts ask a pair of hypothetical questions: first, whether the claim could have been brought if the alleged conduct occurred at a public facility outside of a school (such as a public theater or library); and second, whether it could have been brought by an adult at the school. If the answer to these questions is no, then the complaint likely concerns a FAPE violation under the IDEA. *See id.* For example, an allegation that a school building lacks access to ramps would likely state a claim under Title II, whereas an allegation that a student with a learning disability was not provided remedial tutoring in mathematics would likely assert a claim only for the denial of a FAPE. *See id.* at 756-57. Another factor to consider is the history of the proceedings and whether a plaintiff has previously invoked the IDEA's formal procedures to handle the dispute. *See id.* at 757.[3]

The cause of action here does not fit neatly into *Fry*'s hypotheticals. The complaint here specifically alleges that the School Board "allowed J.S. [] to be removed from his regular classroom, based on discriminatory reasons and for no purpose related to his education." Compl., D.E. 1 at 46. Unlike the examples in *Fry*, here we cannot as easily divorce J.S.' claim of isolation from the context of him being an elementary student at a school. Although this claim could be brought as a FAPE violation for failure to follow J.S.' IEP, we conclude that it is also cognizable as a separate claim for intentional discrimination under the ADA and § 504.

In *Olmstead v. L.C. ex rel. Zimring*, 527 U.S. 581, 119 S.Ct. 2176, 144 L.Ed.2d 540 (1999), the Supreme Court concluded that unjustified institutional isolation of persons with disabilities is a form of discrimination based on disability under Title II. *See id.* at 599-600, 119 S.Ct. 2176. The Court considered two important factors in coming to this conclusion: one, that "institutional placement of persons who can handle and benefit from community settings perpetuates unwarranted assumptions that persons so isolated are incapable or unworthy of participating in community life"; and, two, that "confinement in an institution severely diminishes the everyday life activities of individuals." *Id.* at 600-01, 119 S.Ct. 2176.

Isolation via institutionalization is admittedly a more extreme and restrictive action than removal from a school classroom, but the reasoning in *Olmstead* seems to apply here. J.S. has alleged — and p.987 has provided evidence tending to show — that he was, with some frequency, excluded and isolated from his classroom and peers on the basis of his disability. Although the circumstances alleged here do involve a violation of J.S.' IEP, they also implicate those further, intangible consequences of discrimination contemplated in *Olmstead* that could result from isolation, such as stigmatization and deprivation of opportunities for enriching interaction with fellow students. These injuries reach beyond a misdiagnosis or failure to provide appropriate remedial coursework. Compare *K.M. ex rel. D.G. v. Hyde Park Cent. Sch. Dist.*, 381 F.Supp.2d 343, 360 (S.D.N.Y. 2005) (recognizing that "unnecessary social isolation has been considered a form of actionable discrimination" and concluding that, in light of *Olmstead*, a disabled student's isolation during lunch appears to be such a claim), *with Sellers*, 141 F.3d at 529 (concluding that allegations that a school board failed to recognize a student's disability based on test scores were insufficient to state a claim under § 504). Accordingly, the district court erred in analyzing this claim as merely a FAPE violation under the IDEA.

IV

Having concluded that J.S. has stated a claim of intentional discrimination, we must next determine whether the School Board can be held liable for such discrimination under Title II and § 504. We have held that it is appropriate to look to Title IX case law for guidance in examining discriminatory intent under § 504. *See Liese v. Indian River Cty. Hosp. Dist.*, 701 F.3d 334, 347 (11th Cir. 2012). Under Title IX (and, by extension, Title II and § 504), a plaintiff may establish intentional discrimination by showing deliberate indifference. *See id.* at 347-48. "Deliberate indifference is an exacting standard; school administrators will only be deemed deliberately indifferent if their response ... or lack thereof is clearly unreasonable in light of the known circumstances." *Doe v. Sch. Bd. of Broward Cty., Fla.*, 604 F.3d 1248, 1259 (11th Cir. 2010) (internal quotation marks and citation omitted). We may, on a motion for summary judgment, determine that a response was not "clearly unreasonable" as a matter of law. *See Davis v. Monroe Cty. Bd. of Educ.*, 526 U.S. 629, 649, 119 S.Ct. 1661, 143 L.Ed.2d 839 (1999).

Title IX is "predicated upon notice to an 'appropriate person' and an opportunity to rectify any violation." *Gebser v. Lago Vista Indep. Sch. Dist.*, 524 U.S. 274, 290, 118 S.Ct. 1989, 141 L.Ed.2d 277 (1998). So, "[f]or an organization to be liable for Title IX purposes, [a plaintiff must show] the deliberate indifference of 'an *official* who at a minimum has *authority* to address the alleged discrimination and to institute corrective measures on the organization's behalf and who has *actual knowledge* of discrimination in the organization's programs and fails adequately to respond.'" *Liese,* 701 F.3d at 349 (alterations adopted) (quoting *Gebser,* 524 U.S. at 290, 118 S.Ct. 1989).

"[T]he ultimate question of who is an appropriate person is necessarily a fact-based inquiry because officials' roles vary among school districts." *Broward Cty.,* 604 F.3d at 1256 (internal quotation marks and citation omitted). "An 'appropriate person' ... is, at a minimum, an official of the recipient entity with authority to take corrective action to end the discrimination." *Gebser,* 524 U.S. at 290, 118 S.Ct. 1989. "[T]he official with notice... must be 'high enough up the chain-of-command that his [or her] acts constitute an official decision by the school district itself not to remedy the misconduct.'" *Broward Cty.,* 604 F.3d at 1255 (quoting *Floyd* p.988 *v. Waiters,* 171 F.3d 1264, 1264 (11th Cir. 1999)).

J.S. argues that Principal Smith, Ms. Brown (his special education teacher), Ms. Boatright (his regular education teacher), and Coach Barton and Coach Sunday (both physical education teachers), were all appropriate persons who had the authority to take measures to correct Mr. Faircloth's conduct, and that they were each deliberately indifferent to actual notice that Mr. Faircloth was removing J.S. from his regular classroom. We address each individual in turn.

A

J.S. first argues that Principal Smith was an appropriate person who failed to adequately respond to actual notice that Mr. Faircloth was bringing him into the weight room regularly. In *Broward County,* we held that a principal was an "appropriate person" to receive Title IX actual notice because that principal, as "the highest-ranking school official on site" at the school, was "equipped with many... means of deterring or stopping sexual harassment of students, such as admonishing the teacher, conducting a thorough preliminary investigation, swiftly reporting the abuse, and monitoring the teacher's behavior." 604 F.3d at 1255, 1257. Indeed, we noted that the Supreme Court's decisions in *Gebser* and *Davis* "appeared to presume that the principal could be an appropriate person" and that "the majority of our sister circuits addressing the issue have interpreted [those] opinions as standing for the proposition that at least in some circumstances, if not generally, a principal enjoys ample authority to 'take corrective measures' in response to allegations of teacher or student ... harassment." *Id.* at 1256.

Principal Smith specifically testified that she was Mr. Faircloth's immediate supervisor. *See* Smith Dep. at 109. A Houston County high school principal has "direct and primary responsibility for his/her school and [he/she] serves as the administrative and supervisory head of the school." *See* High School Principal Job Description, D.E. 28-25 at 5. The principal is tasked with "[s]upervis[ing] assigned personnel, conduct[ing] annual performance appraisals, and mak[ing] recommendations for appropriate employment actions," as well as "[i]mplement[ing] school board policy, state statutes, and federal regulations." *Id.* at 3. Given our precedent generally recognizing principals as appropriate persons, as well as Principal Smith's responsibilities in supervising staff and implementing regulations, the record establishes, at minimum, that a reasonable jury could determine that Principal Smith, as the "highest-ranking official" at Wicksburg, was an appropriate person with authority to address the alleged discrimination.

As for the failure to adequately respond to actual notice of discrimination, Principal Smith testified that she was informed by Ms. Brown only once, in approximately October of 2011, that Mr. Faircloth was taking J.S. to the weight room. She stated that she told Mr. Faircloth that she would "rather him not take [J.S.] back to that weight room" and that she was never subsequently informed that he had taken J.S. back to the weight room. *See* Smith Dep. at 72. But Principal Smith did not follow up to see if Mr. Faircloth followed her instructions. She acknowledged, moreover, that she did not inform J.S.' parents that he had been removed from the classroom, and did not ask J.S. directly what was happening while they were in the weight room because she believed Mr. Faircloth and his explanation seemed reasonable. Ms. Brown, however, testified that when she later learned Mr. Faircloth was continuing to take J.S. into the weight room, she again told Principal Smith. The record does not show that Principal Smith took any action following the second notice, though she maintains that she was informed of Mr. Faircloth's behavior only that one time in October of 2011.

Viewing the evidence in the light most favorable to J.S., a jury could find that Principal Smith was deliberately indifferent in failing to follow up with Mr. Faircloth, or speak to J.S. or his parents after her discussion with Mr. Faircloth, and in failing to take adequate action when she was informed a second time that J.S. was being removed from the classroom. There is a genuine issue of material fact as to whether Principal Smith had actual knowledge and whether her response was clearly unreasonable, i.e., deliberately indifferent.

B

J.S next argues that both Ms. Brown and Ms. Boatright had the authority to take corrective measures in response to his removal from the classroom, and that they responded to Mr. Faircloth's actions in a manner that was clearly unreasonable. We agree.

1

We have yet to determine whether a schoolteacher can serve as an appropriate person with authority to take corrective measures so as to constitute an official decision from the school district itself. *See, e.g., Hawkins v. Sarasota Cty. Sch. Bd.*, 322 F.3d 1279, 1287-88 (11th Cir. 2003) (declining to address issue of notice and deliberate indifference based on teacher's actions and resting decision instead on denial of access issue). Based on the record before us, we conclude that a teacher can serve as an appropriate person and an issue of fact remains as to whether Ms. Brown and Ms. Boatright were appropriate persons.

In Houston County, both regular and special education teachers are responsible for "instruct[ing] and supervis[ing] the work of volunteers and aides when assigned." *See* Elementary Teacher Job Description, D.E. 28-30 at 6; Special Education Teacher Job Description, D.E. 28-11 at 2. Although Mr. Faircloth was assigned specifically to J.S., and not to a particular classroom, this fact, viewed in the light most favorable to J.S., supports the argument that the teachers held some supervisory authority over Mr. Faircloth as an aide. *See* Denise Whitfield 6-29-15 Dep., D.E. 28-29 at 31-32. Both teachers were also expected to "assist in [the] enforcement of school rules, administrative regulations[,] and [school board] policy." Elementary Teacher Job Description at 6; Special Education Teacher Job Description at 2.

The School Board's expert and special education director, Ms. Whitfield, testified that Ms. Brown was not "totally responsible" for Mr. Faircloth's supervision, but that she was responsible in part as J.S.' case manager, who had to ensure the implementation of the IEP. *See* Whitfield Dep. at 32-33. *See also* Smith Dep. at 109-10, 115-16 (explaining that Ms. Brown did not have any immediate supervisory authority over Mr. Faircloth, but that she was responsible for the implementation, compliance, and enforcement of J.S.' IEPs, including informing school personnel, such as Mr. Faircloth, of their responsibilities under the IEP). Ms. Whitfield also said that Ms. Brown "could have told" Mr. Faircloth that J.S. was not supposed to be in the weight room and that she "had the authority to say whatever she wanted to say." *Id.* at 34-35. When asked whether Mr. Faircloth would have had to comply p.990 with Ms. Brown's instruction or admonition, Ms. Whitfield answered that "he should have complied if she told him that she didn't want him to take [J.S.] to the weight room [and that] if he didn't [comply] she could have gone to her supervisor." *Id.* at 36-37.

As for Ms. Boatright, Ms. Whitfield testified that Mr. Faircloth "should have" been required to follow an instruction by Ms. Boatright to not take J.S. to the weight room, if one had been given. *See id.* at 49. When asked whether Ms. Boatright had the authority by virtue of her position as J.S.' teacher to give such an instruction to Mr. Faircloth, Ms. Whitfield responded "[c]ertainly, I think she could have said that, yes." *Id.* at 49-50.

Viewing this evidence in the light most favorable to J.S., a reasonable jury could find that Ms. Boatright and Ms. Brown had authority to take corrective action to stop Mr. Faircloth from removing J.S. from the classroom. In *Broward County,* we rejected the notion that "final employment decisions such as suspending, terminating, or reassigning an offending [individual] [are] the *only* corrective measures giving an official the power to remedy" harassment under Title IX. 604 F.3d at 1257. Instead, we recognized that there are "many other means of deterring or stopping [] harassment of students, such as admonishing the [individual], conducting a thorough preliminary investigation, swiftly reporting the abuse, and monitoring the [individual's] behavior." *Id.*

A reasonable jury could find that Ms. Brown and Ms. Boatright both held some sort of supervisory authority over Mr. Faircloth given their job descriptions and their designation as persons responsible for the implementation and enforcement of J.S.' IEP, and that they had the ability and authority to take such actions as those contemplated in *Broward County.* J.S., accompanied by Mr. Faircloth, was to spend approximately 80 percent of his time in Ms. Boatright's classroom, leaving her arguably the best-positioned school official to take action to remedy J.S.' removal from her classroom. And although Ms. Brown stated that she did not believe that it was her job to supervise Mr. Faircloth and that she could not have reprimanded or corrected him, the testimony of Ms. Whitfield and Ms. Smith suggests otherwise, particularly given her role as J.S.' case manager and the individual responsible for informing school personnel of their responsibilities under the IEP.

2

The record also contains sufficient evidence from which a reasonable jury could find that both Ms. Brown and Ms. Boatright had knowledge of J.S.' removal from the classroom and that their respective responses were deliberately indifferent under the circumstances.

Although Mr. Faircloth did not usually accompany J.S. to her classroom, Ms. Brown testified that Ms. Boatright told her that J.S. and Mr. Faircloth were not in her classroom when they were supposed to be. *See* Brown Dep. at 22-23. Ms. Brown asserts that she told Principal Smith at least twice that J.S. was being removed from the classroom, but there remains an issue of fact as to whether Ms. Brown spoke with Principal Smith again after learning from Coach Barton, Coach Sunday, and Angela Brockman, another special education teacher, that it was an "ongoing habit." *See Id.* at 30-31; Smith Dep. at 72 (denying that Ms. Brown informed her a second time that Mr. Faircloth was continuing to bring J.S. to the weight room). Ms. Brown testified that she spoke with Mr. Faircloth and informed him that taking J.S. to the weight room was against his IEP, but that she did not speak with p.991 him again because she did not feel it was her responsibility to reprimand him. *See* Brown Dep. at 26, 30-32, 80-81. Moreover, Ms. Brown did not ask J.S. what was happening in the weight room and, although she was in "constant," daily contact with J.S.' mother, she did not inform J.S.' parents of what was happening. *See id.* at 33-34, 118-19. Given these factual disputes and her apparent failure to follow up with Mr. Faircloth or speak with J.S. or his parents, there is sufficient evidence from which a reasonable jury could conclude that Ms. Brown's actions were clearly unreasonable.

As for Ms. Boatright, she testified that J.S. and Mr. Faircloth were often "in and out" of her classroom. *See* Boatright Dep. at 21-23. Although it is unclear whether Ms. Boatright knew that Mr. Faircloth was taking J.S. to the weight room specifically, *see* Boatright Dep. at 29, 43-44, 54, she knew J.S. was often not in her classroom as required. According to Ms. Brown, she and Ms. Boatright had a conversation about the fact that J.S. was not in Ms. Boatright's classroom and Ms. Boatright agreed that she should speak with Principal Smith because she was responsible for teaching J.S. *See* Brown Dep. at 71-72. But Ms. Boatright did not report J.S.' removal from the classroom to Principal Smith. Nor did she ever ask J.S. about what occurred when Mr. Faircloth took him out of the classroom, or speak with Mr. Faircloth about it. *See* Boatright Dep. at 45-46, 85. Viewing the evidence in the light most favorable to J.S., a reasonable jury could conclude that Ms. Boatright had knowledge that J.S. was being removed from the classroom and that she reacted in a manner that was clearly unreasonable under the circumstances.

C

J.S. also argues that Coach Barton and Coach Sunday were appropriate persons that could bind the school district, arguing that they "could have, at the very least, tried to deter Mr. Faircloth from bringing J.S.... to the weight room" and that they had authority to instruct Mr. Faircloth to return J.S. to his regular classroom. *See* Br. of Appellant at 58. Unlike the classroom teachers, however, the record does not contain sufficient evidence from which a reasonable jury could conclude that Coach Barton and Coach Sunday had the authority to take corrective actions to stop Mr. Faircloth.

Ms. Whitfield testified that the coaches had supervisory authority over Mr. Faircloth "to the extent that they were providers of [J.S.'] IEP, and the services in his IEP." *See* Whitfield Dep. at 54. She also testified that either coach "could have" told Mr. Faircloth to take J.S. back to his regular classroom, and that she believed that — based on her "own personal ethical and moral principles" — Mr. Faircloth "should have" complied with such instructions. *Id.* at 50-53. But J.S. has not pointed to any evidence suggesting that physical education teachers and coaches in the school district, like general and special education teachers, maintained a supervisory role over assigned aides. Coach Barton, for his part, testified that he was never told that he was responsible for communicating with J.S.' parents directly. *See* Barton Dep. at 78-79. And although each coach was listed on at least one of J.S.' IEPs, J.S. has not presented evidence that they served a supervisory role similar to, or with the same level of involvement as, Ms. Boatright, the teacher responsible for 80 percent of J.S.' school day, or Ms. Brown, J.S.' case manager.

We recognize that Coach Barton and Coach Sunday could have — and indeed, likely should have — informed someone that they had frequently observed Mr. Faircloth p.992 and J.S. in the weight room. But the record does not reflect that they were "high enough up the chain-of-command" for their actions to "constitute an official decision by the school district itself not to remedy the misconduct." *Broward Cty.*, 604 F.3d at 1255 (quoting *Floyd*, 171 F.3d at 1264).

V

As for J.S.' assertion that the School Board is liable for Mr. Faircloth's alleged verbal and physical abuse of J.S., we again borrow from Title IX deliberate indifference case law to guide our analysis. *See Liese*, 701 F.3d at 347. Having already concluded that there remains a genuine issue of fact as to whether Principal Smith, Ms. Brown, and Ms. Boatright were appropriate persons with actual notice of J.S.' removal from his classroom and whose responses were clearly unreasonable, we must determine whether the "substance of that actual notice [was] sufficient to alert the school official of the possibility" of the verbal and physical abuse. *Broward Cty.*, 604 F.3d at 1254.

J.S. argues that his removal from the classroom created the opportunity for Mr. Faircloth to abuse him. In the Title IX context, we have held that "lesser harassment may still provide actual notice of [] violent conduct, for it is the risk of such conduct that the Title IX recipient has the duty to deter." *Id.* at 1258. For example, in *Broward County*, we held that knowledge of prior instances of sexual harassment of two students by a teacher served as actual notice of the possibility of that teacher's sexual assault of another student. *See id.* at 1259. Similarly, in *Williams v. Board of Regents of University System of Georgia*, 477 F.3d 1282 (11th Cir. 2007), the prior groping of female employees by a college basketball player was sufficient to allege actual notice of the possibility of a later violent sexual assault that occurred in that player's dorm room. *See id.* at 1294-95; *id.* at 1304-05 (Jordan, District Judge, concurring). In contrast, comments made to a group of students during class did not serve as sufficient notice of the possibility of a teacher's sexual relationship with a student. *See Gebser,* 524 U.S. at 291-92, 118 S.Ct. 1989. Nor was there actual notice of potential sexual molestation based on prior allegations of a teacher's touching during a touch football game and perceived imminent touching at a public water fountain. *See Davis v. DeKalb Cty. Sch. Dist.,* 233 F.3d 1367, 1372-73 (11th Cir. 2000).

The record does not establish (or create a jury issue) that knowledge that Mr. Faircloth was removing J.S. from his classroom and bringing him into the weight room would apprise his teachers or the principal of the possibility that Mr. Faircloth was also abusing J.S. *See* Boatright Dep. at 51, 53-54, 60-61; Barton Dep. at 26, 29, 40, 70, 84-85; Sunday Dep. at 33-34. At most, the facts demonstrate that any school officials who could be deemed "appropriate persons" were aware that Mr. Faircloth was inattentive, or even careless, with J.S. But, similar to the incidental touching and inappropriate comments in *Davis* and *Gebser,* no reasonable jury would find that this conduct alerted those school officials to the possibility of abuse.

VI

There are genuine issues of fact as to whether the School Board was deliberately indifferent to discrimination regarding J.S.' removal from the classroom, but there is insufficient evidence from which a reasonable jury could conclude that the School Board had notice of the possibility of alleged verbal and physical abuse against J.S. Accordingly, we affirm in part and reverse in part the district court's order granting summary judgment to the p.993 School Board, and remand for further proceedings consistent with this opinion.

AFFIRMED IN PART, REVERSED IN PART, AND REMANDED.

[*] The Honorable Kenneth F. Ripple, United States Circuit Judge for the Seventh Circuit, sitting by designation.

[1] The district court denied J.S.' motion to alter or amend the judgment based on a Department of Justice Letter of Finding and a decision by this Court that were both issued after the motion for summary judgment was briefed. J.S. does not appear to challenge that ruling.

[2] It is undisputed that J.S. is a qualified individual with a disability.

[3] Justice Alito's concurrence in *Fry* took issue with the majority's hypotheticals, noting that these "misleading clues" "make sense only if there is no overlap between the relief available under" the IDEA and Title II and § 504. *Id.* at 759 (Alito, J., concurring) (internal quotation marks omitted and alteration adopted). As we explain, this may be one of those circumstances in which *Fry*'s hypotheticals could "lead [us] astray." *Id.*

797 F.3d 948 (2015)

James HILL, as guardian and next friend of BHJ, a minor, Plaintiff-Appellant,

v.

Christopher J. CUNDIFF, et al., Defendants,
Madison County School Board, Ronnie J. Blair, Teresa G. Terrell, Jeanne Dunaway, June Ann Simpson, Defendants-Appellees.

James Hill, as guardian and next friend of BHJ, a minor, Plaintiff-Appellee,

v.

Madison County School Board, et al., Defendants,
Jeanne Dunaway, Defendant-Appellant.

Nos. 14-12481, 13-15444.

United States Court of Appeals, Eleventh Circuit.

August 12, 2015.

Hill v. Cundiff, 797 F. 3d 948 (11th Cir. 2015)

p.955 Eric J. Artrip, Dennis Anthony Mastando, Teresa Ryder Mastando, Mastando & Artrip, LLC, Huntsville, AL, Neena Chaudhry, Fatima Goss Graves, Washington, DC, for Plaintiff-Appellant.

Mark S. Boardman, Clay Richard Carr, Boardman Carr Bennett Watkins Hill & Gamble, PC, Chelsea, AL, Howard McGriff Belser, II, Edwards & Besler, Decatur, AL, for Defendant-Appellee.

Before HULL and BLACK, Circuit Judges, and ANTOON,[*] District Judge.

BLACK, Circuit Judge:

These consolidated appeals involve student-on-student sexual harassment. Jane Doe,[1] an eighth-grade student at Sparkman Middle School, was raped[2] in a bathroom after school officials decided to use p.956 her as bait in a sting operation to catch CJC, another eighth-grade student, in the act of sexual harassment. On appeal, Doe argues the district court[3] erred in (1) granting summary judgment to the Madison County School Board (Board) on her Title IX sexual harassment claim and (2) granting summary judgment to the Board, Principal Ronnie J. Blair, Assistant Principal Teresa G. Terrell, Assistant Principal Jeanne Dunaway, and Teacher's Aide June Ann Simpson on her 42 U.S.C. § 1983 equal protection claims.[4] For the reasons explained below, we affirm the grant of summary judgment to the Board and Terrell on Doe's § 1983 equal protection claims. We reverse, however, the grant of summary judgment to the Board on Doe's Title IX claim and to Blair, Dunaway, and Simpson on Doe's § 1983 equal protection claims.

I. FACTUAL BACKGROUND

A. The Parties

At the time of the rape on January 22, 2010, Doe was a 14-year-old girl and an eighth grader. From the time her mother became ill and later passed away in 2007, Doe grew up in foster homes scattered throughout North Carolina. In 2008, Doe moved to Huntsville, Alabama, to live with her siblings' stepmother, Patricia Jones, before starting seventh grade. While in Huntsville, Doe attended seventh grade and a portion of eighth grade at Sparkman Middle School, which is operated by the Board. CJC, a 15-year old male, was also an eighth-grade student at Sparkman.

Four Sparkman officials are named as defendants in this suit: Ronnie J. Blair, Teresa G. Terrell, Jeanne Dunaway, and June Simpson. Blair was the principal at Sparkman. All assistant principals and teachers reported directly to Blair, and Blair retained ultimate authority for operation of the school. Terrell and Dunaway were the assistant principals at Sparkman. June Simpson was a teacher's aide for physical education classes.

B. Board's Sexual Harassment Policies

Prior to and during the 2009-2010 school year, the Board adhered to the following policies concerning the resolution of sexual harassment complaints and the retention of complaint-related documents and student disciplinary records.

1. Investigation and Discipline

Each year, school administrators assigned a team of teachers to instruct the students about Sparkman's sexual harassment policies. Both the 2009-2010 Student Code of Conduct and Board Policy Manual in effect on January 22, 2010,[5] p.957 include sections addressing student sexual harassment.

According to the Code of Conduct, the principal is ultimately responsible for handling all harassment complaints. The Code of Conduct states that students may report harassment to the "[p]rincipal, assistant principal, a teacher, or to whomever he/she feels the most comfortable." Students may fill out a student sexual harassment complaint form, though Principal Blair cannot remember seeing this form or recall a single instance in which a student used the form. The person receiving the harassment complaint "shall make the complaint known to the [p]rincipal," and the principal "shall investigate the complaint and take appropriate action." Similarly, the Policy Manual provides that the school official to whom a complaint of sexual harassment is made "shall make the complaint known to the [p]rincipal of the school, except in cases where the complaint is against the [p]rincipal." The principal "shall investigate the complaint and take appropriate action."

The record contains few details about the training used to implement the sexual harassment policies outlined in the Code of Conduct and the Policy Manual. According to Principal Blair, the Board's central office conducted all sexual harassment policy training. Blair reportedly attended an after-school workshop about sexual harassment conducted at Sparkman, but the record does not reveal any documentation from this workshop, a list of who attended, the year it occurred, or the details of the training. Assistant Principal Dunaway remembers attending sexual harassment training at the Madison County Administrator Academy, but that program has since been discontinued. Again, the record contains no documentation of these training sessions.

At the time of her deposition, Assistant Principal Dunaway was not aware the Code of Conduct had any section addressing sexual misconduct or harassment. Sparkman did not revisit the sexual harassment policy with its employees every year, and no records were kept about sexual harassment training. Principal Blair cannot remember the identity of the Title IX coordinator in 2010; does not know how employees would discover the identity of the Title IX coordinator; and testified students were not told the identity of the Title IX coordinator. Rather than give each teacher a copy of the sexual harassment policy, a large binder containing the entire Policy Manual was kept on file at the media center and principals' office. Despite Teacher's Aide Simpson's entreaties to Blair and other faculty members, she received "no proper training" on how to handle sexual harassment complaints.

Principal Blair testified that when a student alleged another student committed sexual harassment, all school personnel were required to report the allegation up the chain-of-command to him if the complaint was "of significance." Blair was responsible for overseeing the investigation of sexual harassment complaints. The assistant principals and other staff members could also investigate complaints of sexual harassment, but they were required to report such allegations to Blair. Blair was not always the person in charge of disciplinary action with regard to sexual harassment; Dunaway and Terrell, as assistant principals, could also be in charge.

Principal Blair crafted a "catch in the act" policy[6] establishing three exclusive p.958 types of evidence sufficient for the school to discipline a student for sexual harassment. First, if students were "caught and proven" performing a sexual act, that would be grounds for disciplinary action. Second, physical evidence of sexual harassment could be sufficient. Third, discipline was warranted if a student admitted guilt. In contrast, "one person saying" sexual harassment occurred "against another person's word does not work." If a student complained that another student propositioned him or her for sex, that fact alone was not enough to warrant discipline "because you've got one word against another without witnesses."

Principal Blair informed other staff members, including Teacher's Aide Simpson, that students had to be "caught in the act" of sexual harassment to impose discipline. Assistant Principal Dunaway testified that "[s]tudents in middle school, especially with the use of social media, tend to make up a lot of stories about people and if we disciplined every child for every rumor, we would have no children at our school."

2. Recordkeeping

Upon receiving a complaint of sexual harassment or any other disciplinary infraction, school officials conducted an investigation, which often involved interviewing witnesses. An investigation normally produced two types of documents: (1) administrator notes and (2) witness statements.

There was no school-wide policy regarding the retention of administrator notes made during an investigation. Administrators were authorized to arbitrarily destroy or preserve these notes. By contrast, there was a specific policy regarding witness statements. If the sexual harassment allegation was not proven, the witness statements were quickly destroyed. If the sexual harassment allegation was proven, school officials kept the witness statements in a student's paper file located in the principals' office. During the summer shortly after the end of the academic year, all student conduct files (including both administrator notes, if any, and witness statements) were shredded. The identity of the school staff member who performed the shredding is unknown.

After the shredding, the only remaining evidence of a sexual harassment infraction was an entry in the school's disciplinary computer database called iNOW. The database contains a barebones description of each incident, without any accompanying electronic or paper files revealing the precise nature of the infraction. Each entry contains an infraction code noting the nature of offense—such as "sexual harassment" or "inappropriate touching." When asked how the school differentiated between inappropriate touching versus sexual harassment, Terrell testified "one is more serious than the other." The infraction codes were meant to allow administrators to evaluate the cumulative and recidivistic nature of a student's conduct.

The infraction codes were not a systematic method of classifying misconduct, but instead an *ad hoc* determination made solely by Kathy Abernathy, the school secretary. Assistant Principal Terrell testified that she would not tell Abernathy which code to enter, but instead just "hand[ed] her the paperwork." Assistant Principal Dunaway likewise "handed [Abernathy] the paperwork and she . . . filled it out." Terrell believes Abernathy had been trained in the central office about iNOW coding, but she does not know the nature or date of this training.

C. Events Prior to the Rape on January 22, 2010

CJC, a 15 year-old eighth grader, attended Sparkman Middle School during the 2009-2010 school year. Prior to his rape of Doe on January 22, 2010, CJC had accumulated a disciplinary history of violence and sexual misconduct. We break this history into four parts: (1) CJC's recorded disciplinary history in the iNOW database prior to January 2010, the month of the rape; (2) allegations he had been propositioning girls to have sex with him in January 2010; (3) an allegation of "inappropriately touching" a girl on January 13, 2010; (4) and allegations he had repeatedly propositioned Doe to have sex with him for two weeks prior to the rape.

1. CJC's Recorded Disciplinary History Prior to January

CJC's disciplinary record consists of short summaries of incidents logged in the Board's iNOW computer system. Over 18 months preceding the rape in January 2010, CJC had five infractions for sexual misconduct and four infractions for violent or threatening behavior. There is no supporting documentation of these incidents due to the shredding policies described above, and none of the administrators remember any details about the incidents.

The first relevant entry on CJC's record is dated September 24, 2008, when he was a seventh grader at Ardmore High School (Ardmore). CJC received five days of in-school suspension for "[i]napp [p]ublic [d]isplay of [a]ffect," described in the notes as "[t]ouching girls in inappropriate places. Writing inappropriate notes to girls asking them to have sex with him." In another incident at Ardmore, he "[h]it another student" and received three days of in-school suspension.

After transferring to Sparkman during his seventh-grade year, CJC continued to tally disciplinary infractions for violent and sexual misconduct. On December 17, 2008, CJC received an unspecified amount of out-of-school suspension for "[f]ighting" because he "[h]it another student several times on bus." On February 4, 2009, CJC received out-of-school suspension for "[m]aking inappropriate comments to a young lady," coded as "[s]exual harassment."

In September 2009 during eighth grade, CJC received an unspecified amount of out-of-school suspension for "[h]arassment" because he "[o]ffered to pay another student to beat up a girl also stated that would he would like to kill her." On October 23, 2009, CJC was suspended from riding the bus for saying "F ___ You" to the driver. On October 28, 2009, CJC received in-school suspension for "[i]nappropriate touching" coded as "[d]isobedience." On November 18, 2009, CJC was again suspended from the bus for "refusing to obey driver and keep hands off a female student," with the infraction coded as "[m]inor disruption on bus." One week later, CJC received in-school suspension for "[k]issing" coded as "[d]isobedience." On December 15, 2009, CJC received in-school suspension for "[v]erbal confrontation with another student" coded as "[d]isobedience." Three days later, CJC received out-of-school suspension for "[t]hreatening another student" and "intimidation" while serving his in-school suspension.

Assistant Principal Terrell did not know why the school listed CJC's infraction for "[m]aking inappropriate comments to a young lady" as "sexual harassment," but listed his failure to "keep hands off a female student" as "[m]inor disruption on bus." By Terrell's admission, there was "not a normal policy" about "what goes in the infraction box."

2. Propositioning Girls to Have Sex in Bathrooms in January

In the weeks prior to the rape in January 2010, CJC propositioned female students to have sex with him in the school bathrooms. There are two competing versions of CJC's sexual activity in the bathrooms during January 2010.

According to Teacher's Aide Simpson, CJC "had been repeatedly propositioning other female students to have sex in the boys' bathroom." The allegations began shortly after Thanksgiving break in 2009. Simpson reported CJC's sexual harassment to Principal Blair in early January and suggested school officials monitor CJC at all times. Blair responded that school officials "were going to have to catch [CJC] in the act" before taking any disciplinary action.

Blair's recollection differs from Simpson's. According to Blair, he learned that approximately one and a half weeks prior to the rape on January 22, 2010, there was one "alleged incident" involving CJC and female student at the school. Simpson told Blair that CJC and another student were engaged in consensual sexual activity in a bathroom in the special education wing. Blair spoke directly to CJC and the female student about the activity and took notes of the conversations. Though he normally required students to create a written statement about such incidents, Blair cannot remember whether CJC made such a statement. Blair also cannot remember the identity of the female student who made the allegations. CJC and the female student both denied engaging in any sexual activity. Blair did not impose any disciplinary action in response to the allegation because it was a "he say/she say kind of deal." Since he could not confirm the truth of the allegation, it did not count as sexual harassment and all documents relating to the investigation were shredded.

Principal Blair did not examine CJC's disciplinary records as part of his investigation. There was no reason to examine the records because he would "recall" those "big" incidents of sexual harassment that had already occurred. Nonetheless, he told Assistant Principals Terrell and Dunaway to maintain a "heightened state of alert" about CJC's activity. Blair pointed one of the school's security cameras, which had an unmonitored screen in the front office, towards the school's special education bathroom.

3. Sexual Harassment on January 13

On January 13, 2010, there was another allegation that CJC was sexually harassing female students. Assistant Principals Terrell and Dunaway investigated a complaint that CJC "inappropriately touch[ed]" another female student. There are no records of this incident.

Principal Blair cannot recall the exact nature of the allegation, or even whether it involved sexual touching. Assistant Principal Dunaway remembers some students mentioning that CJC inappropriately touched a girl's thigh during class, but she could not identify a witness with personal knowledge of the incident, nor could she remember the identity of the victim. Assistant Principal Terrell described the incident as "middle school drama."

During the investigation, Principal Blair did not review CJC's iNOW record or any other documentation. Assistant Principal Dunaway checked CJC's iNOW record, but it did not inform her decision about how to discipline him. Dunaway did not review the supporting paper documentation in CJC's file regarding the October 28, 2009 "[i]nappropriate touching" infraction, the November 18, 2009 infraction for "refusing to obey driver and keep hands off a female student" infraction, or the November 25, 2009 infraction for "[k]issing." Dunaway chose not to look at this documentation because she "had no reason to believe he was guilty. I had nobody to corroborate the story."

The incident was recorded in the iNOW database. The database entry says CJC received 20 days of in-school suspension for "[d]isobedience" due to "[c]onstant[]distraction continued disruption of learning." When asked why the school listed this incidence of sexual harassment as "[d]isobedience," without any reference to inappropriate touching, Assistant Principal Dunaway explained the allegations had not been proven. Assistant Principal Terrell opined the investigation into the sexual harassment itself was "a constant disruption."

Even though "[n]othing could be proven" regarding the allegation, Principal Blair assigned CJC to 20 days of in-school suspension as a "precautionary measure," but "not as discipline for him." In-school suspension involved, *inter alia*, sweeping hallways and cleaning the lunchroom. A student assigned to in-school suspension was supervised by a custodian or plant manager. When asked whether someone was supposed to be with CJC at all times, Blair responded, "[n]ot necessarily." A student was assigned a particular task in a certain room or hallway and was not watched at all times, but instead occasionally left unmonitored. Blair would not have given CJC such latitude had he been found guilty of misconduct. CJC, however, had been assigned to in-school suspension as a precautionary measure.

4. Propositioning Doe to Have Sex

Over a two-week period prior to January 22, 2010, CJC had been badgering Doe to have sex with him in the bathroom. Doe refused to respond to him. During school on January 21, 2010, Doe told Teacher's Aide Simpson that CJC had been asking her to have sex. That same night, Doe told her guardian, Patricia Jones, that "a guy at school, [CJC], was trying to have sex with me at school." Jones told her to refuse him.

D. January 22, 2010

1. Prior to the Rape

On Friday, January 22, 2010, Doe rode the bus to school, attended classes, and walked to gym class at 2:00 pm. The entrance to the gym sat directly opposite the main hallway where the principals' office was located. CJC was in the hallway performing unsupervised cleanup duties as part of his 20-day, "precautionary" in-school suspension for sexual harassment. CJC began talking to Doe next to the principals' office. CJC asked Doe to have sex with him in the sixth-grade boys' bathroom. Doe said nothing and entered the gym.

Doe lined up for roll call and then, rather than enter the locker room with other students to change into gym clothes, approached Teacher's Aide Simpson. Doe and one of her friends (whose identity does not appear in the record) spoke to Simpson near the entrance of the gym. Doe told Simpson that CJC was still "messing" with her. Simpson said "do you want to get [CJC]" in trouble and Doe said "yes." Simpson said, "Do you want to— you have to go meet him so that we could set him up and get him caught because he's been doing this for a while." Doe responded that she "didn't want to go," and walked to the locker room. Doe and her friend then sat in the locker room a few minutes and conversed. A few minutes later, Doe approached Simpson again and "told her I would do it." Simpson asked if Doe was "sure," and Doe said yes.

Teacher's Aide Simpson escorted Doe to Assistant Principal Dunaway's office, but the precise events that occurred in the office are disputed. The facts recalled by p.962 Doe and Simpson differ significantly from the events described by Dunaway and Andrea Hallman (another teacher at Sparkman).

Doe recollects that, while in the office, Teacher's Aide Simpson "told [an assistant principal] what was going to happen." According to Simpson, Assistant Principal Dunaway and another teacher, Andrea Hallman, were in the office. Since Dunaway was on the phone, Simpson asked for Hallman's advice about the plan to catch CJC in the act of sexual harassment. When Dunaway finished her telephone conversation,

Simpson spoke directly to Dunaway and described the plan to use Doe as bait in a sting operation. Simpson said, "I hope this is legal. I don't know what I'm doing." Dunaway appeared "disinterested" and provided "no direction or advice." Instead, Dunaway showed Simpson some "pictures of some tile on the cell phone." At this time, Doe and her friend from gym class were talking to Hallman in the doorway of the office. Because she had spoken to Dunaway and Hallman, Simpson believed "someone else was handling the situation, so I returned to the gym."

Assistant Principal Dunaway's description of the events in her office is quite different. According to Dunaway, she was speaking to Hallman about student literacy data when she saw Simpson enter the edge of her office and stand near the door. At some point, Dunaway spoke on the phone with her husband. Simpson's back faced Dunaway, and Simpson appeared to be speaking to someone outside the door while looking right and left. Simpson stood near the door for three to seven minutes, but she never spoke to Dunaway. Dunaway claims it was "common" for staff members to stand in her office without speaking to her for long stretches of time because her office is large and sits next to the school's main hallway. She disclaims any knowledge of the plan to use Doe as bait in a sting operation.

According to Hallman's affidavit, she was in Dunaway's office when Simpson arrived. Simpson stated a male student had been asking girls to meet him in the bathroom for sex. When Simpson made this comment, Dunaway was possibly conversing on the phone. Hallman stepped into the hallway and saw CJC working with a school janitor, so she returned to Dunaway's office. Simpson never told Dunaway or Hallman about the plan to use Doe in order to catch CJC in the bathroom.

2. The Rape

After Doe and Teacher's Aide Simpson left Assistant Principal Dunaway's office, Simpson told Doe to inform CJC that she "would do it." Doe found CJC alone in the hallway near the principals' office. There was no janitorial supervisor around CJC at this time. Doe told CJC she would have sex, and he said to meet at the sixth-grade boys' bathroom. Doe walked slowly toward the bathroom where she stood by the water fountain. CJC asked her to go inside the bathroom, and she went in first. CJC told Doe to go inside the most spacious stall. Doe complied and moved to the back corner of the stall.

CJC directed Doe to pull down her pants, but, since she did not do it quickly enough, CJC unbuttoned her pants and then pulled his own pants down. Doe attempted to block the button of her pants, but he moved her hand away. Doe kept trying to "stall" CJC by telling him "the teachers are going to come," but CJC said they would not arrive in time. When CJC pulled his own pants down, Doe told him "I don't want to do this" and attempted to pull her pants back up. CJC, however, pulled them back down and said "I thought p.963 you wanted it." CJC anally raped Doe. Doe kept telling him to stop.

3. The Aftermath

After leaving Assistant Principal Dunaway's office, Teacher's Aide Simpson returned to the gym. Shortly thereafter, Doe's friend told Simpson that Doe had left to meet CJC. Concerned for Doe's safety, Simpson returned to Dunaway's office. Simpson asked Dunaway and Hallman to search the sixth-grade bathroom. Dunaway said nothing, and Hallman said she didn't want to catch students "with their clothes off." Simpson called Kennedy, another teacher at Sparkman, and asked him to search the boys' bathrooms. She returned to the gym and asked the gym teacher to also search the boys' bathrooms. In the meantime, Hallman checked the hallway, saw a teacher checking a bathroom, and returned to her own classroom.

Within approximately one minute of receiving Simpson's phone call, Kennedy arrived in the sixth-grade boys' bathroom and saw two pairs of feet "close together" beneath the stall. He did not feel comfortable saying anything without another adult present, so he left the bathroom, saw another teacher, Campbell, and motioned for her to help him. Kennedy and Campbell entered the bathroom. Campbell asked if anyone was there and told the students to come out. CJC and Doe exited the stall. Kennedy observed CJC was noticeably erect. CJC told Kennedy he and Doe "were not doing anything but making out." Campbell spoke to Doe in the hallway and asked her what had happened, but Doe could only answer that he had "touched" her.

The school receptionist learned about the incident and told Assistant Principal Terrell that a boy and girl were found in a bathroom. Terrell approached the bathroom, located Doe, and told her "you'll be suspended." Terrell walked outside the school and spoke to Principal Blair, who was performing bus duty. Terrell said Doe had been instructed to enter the bathroom, but "things had changed a little bit— or a lot in the situation." Terrell walked back inside the school to escort CJC and Doe to the principals' office.

Assistant Principals Terrell and Dunaway interviewed Doe. Terrell asked Doe why she had been in a boys' bathroom. Terrell cannot remember Doe's response, other than "[i]t was some wording in defense of herself." Both Terrell and Dunaway claimed Doe appeared calm during this meeting. Teacher's Aide Simpson entered the office and made a "fist pump" gesture, saying, "I sent [Doe] and we got [CJC]." After Simpson's entrance, Terrell and Dunaway asked Doe to leave the office and remain seated in the lobby.

Principal Blair interviewed Simpson in his office. Teacher's Aide Simpson said she devised the sting operation with Doe in order to catch CJC in the act of sexual harassment. According to Blair, Simpson said the plan went awry because Doe failed to meet CJC at the correct bathroom where Simpson had originally planned to catch him.

Principal Blair also interviewed CJC. CJC claimed he and Doe had only kissed consensually in the bathroom. Blair cannot recall whether he and CJC discussed any of the prior allegations of sexual harassment against CJC.

Finally, Principal Blair interviewed Doe. She initially cried and could not tell him what happened. After her guardian, Jones, and Teacher's Aide Simpson entered the office, Doe explained that CJC had raped her. During this interview, Doe wrote a contemporaneous statement describing the rape in vivid detail.

p.964 Before the police arrived, the administrators conferenced to determine whether to punish CJC for the rape. They decided to suspend CJC for five days, subject to a subsequent disciplinary hearing at the central office. According to the "Suspension Notice" provided to CJC's guardian, the administrators imposed the suspension for "[i]nappropriate touching."

After speaking to the police, Doe was transported to a child advocacy center where nurses performed tests and provided medical treatment. The medical records from the examination were consistent with anal rape. Doe suffered anal lacerations, rectal bleeding, redness, and swelling, all of which are well-documented with photographs. For reasons undisclosed by the record, the Madison County District Attorney's Office never filed charges against CJC.

E. The Board's Response to the Rape

After contacting CJC's parents about the sexual assault, Principal Blair referred CJC's disciplinary proceeding to Dr. Jim Nash, the Student Support and Personnel Director for the Board. Nash scheduled an expulsion hearing on Wednesday, January 27, where he presided as the "Hearing Officer." There is virtually no information in the record about this hearing. There are no minutes, no description of the evidence before Nash, nor an explanation of Nash's reasoning. Nash allegedly wrote a report documenting the research and conclusions of his investigation, but the Board has not produced this report.

The only evidence about the hearing is a one-page form. The form says Nash sentenced CJC to "Alt[ernative] School Placement/duration of school year unless results of investigation suggest [unintelligible] punishment." Later documents show CJC was assigned to alternative school "pending investigation" of the rape.

CJC attended alternative school at the "Promoting an Alternative Commitment to Excellence Alternative Education Program" (PACE) beginning on February 4, 2010. On February 24, 2010, while at PACE, a teacher caught CJC viewing pornography on a school computer. CJC claimed he looked at the picture "to impress a classmate." PACE gave CJC two days of out-of-school suspension for this infraction.

CJC stopped attending PACE on April 2, 2010, and returned to Sparkman on April 5. The record does not explain why CJC returned to Sparkman, other than a discharge notation from PACE stating "Dr. Nash approved return due to outcome of investigation." The precise nature and findings of this investigation are unknown. The record also does not show that school officials placed any additional restrictions on CJC when he returned to Sparkman Middle School.

On May 5, 2010, Sparkman had, according to an email from Assistant Principal Terrell to Principal Blair and PACE, "additional problems with [CJC]." Among other things, CJC "kept moving to the table with his girlfriend" and "hugged a girl in front of the cafeteria." As a result, Terrell suspended him for three days and placed him in alternative school the rest of the school year from May 10 to May 26. This disciplinary infraction was never recorded in Sparkman's iNOW database.

CJC's January 22, 2010 rape of Doe is listed in CJC's iNOW record. The database entry says CJC received out-of-school suspension for "[s]exual [o]ffenses" due to "[i]nappropriate touching a female in boys bathroom." Assistant Principal Terrell contends the report describes the incident as inappropriate touching, rather than rape, because CJC admitted to "making out" with Doe, whereas no one actually p.965 witnessed the rape. Thus, the rape was not definitively proven. No one appears to remember who told Secretary Abernathy to describe the rape as inappropriate touching.

Principal Blair does not know whether he believes CJC actually raped Doe. Assistant Principal Dunaway never formed an opinion on whether CJC raped Doe because the police never arrested CJC or charged him with rape. Dunaway believes a rape cannot occur unless prosecutors bring criminal charges against the alleged student rapist. Dunaway also believes Doe's decision to enter the bathroom makes CJC's conduct "different" because, in her mind, he was not "dragging a cave woman by the hair and pulling her into your cave as opposed to someone saying sure, I'll go with you."

Assistant Principal Terrell also never formed an opinion on whether CJC raped Doe because "[w]e turned it over to the police department for them to investigate it. That was not my place to make that decision." After examining the medical photographs documenting Doe's anal injuries, Terrell had no opinion on whether Doe was raped.

With one exception, the Board has not changed a single policy in response to CJC's rape of Doe. The Board decided to discontinue the one-day sexual harassment training workshop for administrators at the Madison County Administrator Academy. Otherwise, the Board has not changed its sexual harassment disciplinary policy and recordkeeping policies, nor has it altered the way it investigates sexual harassment complaints. Sparkman has not changed its practice of assigning students to unsupervised janitorial duty as punishment for alleged sexual harassment. Principal Blair would not change any policies because "we did as good a job I think as you could do under the circumstances."

F. Effect of Rape on Doe

After the rape on January 22, Doe continued attending Sparkman until she withdrew on March 26. She returned to North Carolina to finish eighth grade. Doe never received any assistance from the Board, in the form of counseling or otherwise, to deal with her trauma. Upon her return to North Carolina, Doe attended mental health counseling sessions and was prescribed medication for depression. Doe discussed the rape with her counselor and how it has affected her.

In seventh and eighth grade at Sparkman, Doe played intramural basketball. She stopped playing basketball at the end of her eighth-grade year because "I just didn't feel like I could do it anymore" and "I was just depressed." Doe has not participated in any extracurricular activities since leaving Sparkman. Due to the rape, Doe prefers to "be by myself" and does not "trust being at school anymore." Her grades have suffered because, even though she was diagnosed with bipolar disorder prior to the rape, her depression has been exacerbated. Doe's grades have gone up and down, sometimes earning As, Bs, and Cs, but sometimes receiving Fs.

G. Destruction of CJC's Paper Disciplinary File

In a letter dated April 30, 2010, approximately three months after the rape, Principal Blair received from Doe's counsel a letter notifying him to preserve certain records relating to the January 22, 2010 personal injuries of Doe. The letter stated:

> As you may be aware, my law firm represents [Doe] as a result of personal injuries resulting from an incident which occurred on January 22, 2010 at Sparkman Middle School. We specifically request that the following evidence be maintained and preserved and not be p.966 destroyed, modified, altered, repaired, or changed in any matter [sic]:
> 1. Any videos or documents pertaining to the above referenced incident.
> 2. Any communications, including e-mails, regarding the incident.

Blair says he preserved all the records stemming directly from the January 22, 2010 rape of Doe. Blair preserved no documents, other than the iNOW records, related to CJC's other alleged or proven infractions during the 2009-2010 school year.

II. PROCEDURAL HISTORY

A. Doe's Complaint

On September 23, 2010, Doe filed a complaint against the Board, CJC, Blair, Terrell, Dunaway, and Simpson.[7] The complaint alleged (1) negligence against Blair, Terrell, Dunaway, and Simpson; (2) recklessness/wantonness against Blair, Terrell, Dunaway, and Simpson; (3) negligent/reckless/wanton hiring, training, retention and supervision against Blair, Terrell, and Dunaway; (4) the tort of outrage against Blair, Terrell, Dunaway, and Simpson; (5) a violation of Title IX, 20 U.S.C. § 1681, against the Board; and (6) a violation of the Equal Protection Clause and Substantive Due Process Clause, 42 U.S.C. § 1983, against all Defendants. The complaint sought declaratory relief, injunctive relief, and damages.

B. Motions for Summary Judgment

The Board, Principal Blair, Assistant Principal Terrell, and Assistant Principal Dunaway collectively moved for summary judgment. The district court granted summary judgment to the Board on the Title IX claims because CJC's sexual misconduct and violent behavior did not "constitute[] sexual harassment so severe that it was depriving female students of educational opportunities." According to the district court, CJC's disciplinary history was not enough to give the Board actual knowledge of CJC's harassment of female students. The district court found that, even if the Board had actual knowledge, it was not deliberately indifferent because the disciplinary response to CJC was not clearly unreasonable.

The district court granted summary judgment to the Board, Blair, Dunaway, and Terrell on the § 1983 claims. The district court granted summary judgment to Blair, Dunaway, and Terrell on the Alabama negligent/wanton hiring claims, as well as the tort of outrage claims. The district court also granted summary judgment to Blair and Terrell on the Alabama negligence/wantonness claims because they were entitled to state-agent immunity. The district court denied summary judgment to Dunaway on the negligence/wantonness claims, however, because she acted beyond her authority by ratifying the sting operation.

In her own motion, Teacher's Aide Simpson moved for partial summary judgment on the tort of outrage and § 1983 claims. The district court granted the motion for partial summary judgment. After the district court's rulings on the two motions for summary judgment, the only pending counts were negligence/wantonness claims against Dunaway and Simpson.

Dunaway timely filed an interlocutory appeal from the district court's denial of summary judgment on the negligence/wantonness p.967 claims.[8] The district court subsequently dismissed without prejudice the pending state law counts against Dunaway and Simpson because all claims over which the district court had federal question jurisdiction had been dismissed and the state-agent immunity issues were not settled under Alabama law.[9] Doe timely appealed the orders granting summary judgment in favor of Defendants. This Court granted the parties' joint motion to consolidate the appeals of Doe and Dunaway.

III. STANDARD OF REVIEW

We review de novo a grant or denial of summary judgment, viewing all facts and reasonable inferences in the light most favorable to the nonmoving party. *Bridge Capital Inv'rs, II v. Susquehanna Radio Corp.*, 458 F.3d 1212, 1215 (11th Cir.2006). The propriety of summary judgment on state-agent immunity and qualified immunity grounds is a question of law to be reviewed de novo. *Taylor v. Adams*, 221 F.3d 1254, 1256-57 (11th Cir.2000); *Johnson v. Clifton*, 74 F.3d 1087, 1090 (11th Cir.1996). "Summary judgment is appropriate only if there is no genuine issue of material fact and the moving party is entitled to judgment as a matter of law." *Hallmark Developers, Inc. v. Fulton Cty., Ga.*, 466 F.3d 1276, 1283 (11th Cir.2006); *see* Fed.R.Civ.P. 56(a).

IV. DISCUSSION

Doe raises five issues on appeal. Doe argues the district court erred in granting summary judgment (1) to the Board on the Title IX claim; (2) to the Board, Blair, Dunaway, Simpson, and Terrell on the § 1983 equal protection claims; (3) to Simpson on the § 1983 substantive due process claim; (4) to Blair on the negligence/wantonness claims; and (5) to Simpson on the tort of outrage claim.[10] In p.968 her consolidated appeal, Dunaway raises a single argument: the district court erred in denying her state-agent immunity against Doe's negligence/wantonness claims. We first address Doe's Title IX claim.

A. Legal Standard for Title IX Student-on-Student Sexual Harassment

Title IX states, in pertinent part, that "[n]o person in the United States shall, on the basis of sex, be excluded from participation in, be denied the benefits of, or be subjected to discrimination under any education program or activity receiving Federal financial assistance." 20 U.S.C. § 1681(a). Although Title IX does not expressly permit private enforcement suits, the Supreme Court has found an implied private right of action for individuals to enforce Title IX through monetary damages actions. *Franklin v. Gwinnett Cty. Pub. Sch.*, 503 U.S. 60, 76, 112 S.Ct. 1028, 1038, 117 L.Ed.2d 208 (1992); *Cannon v. Univ. of Chi.*, 441 U.S. 677, 717, 99 S.Ct. 1946, 1968, 60 L.Ed.2d 560 (1979).

The Supreme Court first addressed Title IX claims in the context of teacher-on-student sexual harassment. In *Gebser v. Lago Vista Independent School District*, 524 U.S. 274, 277, 118 S.Ct. 1989, 1993, 141 L.Ed.2d 277 (1998), the Court held § 1681 creates a private cause of action against funding recipients for teacher-on-student sexual harassment when "an official of the school district who at a minimum has authority to institute corrective measures on the district's behalf has actual notice of, and is deliberately indifferent to, the teacher's misconduct." The Court described the deliberate indifference standard as "an official decision by the [funding] recipient not to remedy the violation." *Id.* at 290, 118 S.Ct. at 1999.

One year later, in *Davis v. Monroe County Board of Education*, 526 U.S. 629, 633, 119 S.Ct. 1661, 1666, 143 L.Ed.2d 839 (1999), the Supreme Court held § 1681 creates a private cause of action for student-on-student sexual harassment. A Title IX funding recipient is liable for student-on-student harassment if it is "deliberately indifferent to sexual harassment, of which [it] has actual knowledge, that is so severe, pervasive, and objectively offensive that it can be said to deprive the victims of access to the educational opportunities or benefits provided by the school." *Id.* at 650, 119 S.Ct. at 1675. The standard for student-on-student sexual harassment claims is far more rigorous than a claim for teacher-on-student harassment. *See id.* at 650-53, 119 S.Ct. at 1675-76.

Student-on-student sexual harassment rises to the level of actionable Title IX discrimination only if the harassment is "sufficiently severe." *Id.* at 650, 119 S.Ct. at 1674. The plaintiff must establish not p.969 only that the school district was deliberately indifferent to known acts of harassment, but also that the known harassment was "so severe, pervasive, and objectively offensive that it denie[d] its victims the equal access to education that Title IX is designed to protect." *Id.* at 651-52, 119 S.Ct. at 1675.

The Court imposed this high standard to guard against the imposition of "sweeping liability." *Id.* at 652, 119 S.Ct. at 1675-76. Unlike an adult workplace, children "may regularly interact in a manner that would be unacceptable among adults." *Id.* at 651, 119 S.Ct. at 1675. Due to their immaturity, children at various ages will invariably engage in some forms of teasing, shoving, and name-calling that "target differences in gender." *Id.* at 651-52, 119 S.Ct. at 1675. Some risk of sexual harassment is inherent to the enterprise of public education, in particular, because public schools must educate even the most troublesome and defiant students.

We begin by clarifying the correct legal standard for student-on-student sexual harassment claims under Title IX. The parties dispute whether the district court applied the appropriate standard for evaluating the actual notice requirement of Doe's student-on-student harassment claim. The district court required Doe to prove the Board had actual notice of sexual harassment "so severe, pervasive, and objectively offensive that it can be said to deprive the victims of access to the educational opportunities or benefits."

Doe, with support from the United States Department of Education and United States Department of Justice (collectively, DOJ) acting as *amicus curiae*, argues the district court erred in applying a "heightened" notice requirement unsupported by law. According to Doe, a plaintiff must show only that allegations of sexual harassment alerted the school district that the harasser posed a "substantial risk" of engaging in "severe, pervasive, and objectively offensive" harassment against other students. After this showing, a plaintiff may then prove the harasser's conduct culminated in sexual harassment that was "so severe, pervasive, and objectively offensive" that it harmed the victim by depriving him or her of educational opportunities.

Doe's and the DOJ's proposed "substantial risk" standard lacks merit. The "substantial risk" standard emanates from teacher-on-student Title IX cases, whose requirements are not as rigorous as student-on-student cases. *See Davis,* 526 U.S. at 653, 119 S.Ct. at 1676 (noting that "[p]eer harassment, in particular, is less likely" to breach the Title IX guarantee of equal access to education than "teacher-student harassment"). All of the cases cited by Doe and the DOJ applying a "substantial risk" standard or similar language involved teacher-on-student harassment. *See Doe v. Bd. of Broward Cty., Fla.,* 604 F.3d 1248, 1254 (11th Cir.2010) (teacher-on-student harassment); *Bostic v. Smyrna Sch. Dist.,* 418 F.3d 355, 360-61 (3d Cir.2005) (same); *Williams v. Paint Valley Local Sch. Dist.,* 400 F.3d 360, 362 (6th Cir.2005) (same); *see also Baynard v. Malone,* 268 F.3d 228, 240 (4th Cir.2001) (Michael, J., dissenting in part) (same).

We hold a Title IX plaintiff must prove the funding recipient had actual knowledge that the student-on-student sexual harassment was severe, pervasive, and objectively offensive. The plain language of *Davis* dictates this result:

> "[F]unding recipients are properly held liable in damages only where they are deliberately indifferent to sexual harassment, *of which they have actual knowledge,* that is so severe, pervasive, and objectively offensive that it can be said p.970 to deprive the victims of access to the educational opportunities or benefits provided by the school."

Davis, 526 U.S. at 650, 119 S.Ct. at 1675 (emphasis added). The high burden of *Davis* ensures school districts are not financially crippled merely because immature kids occasionally engage in immature sexual behavior. Simply put, "[t]he Supreme Court has applied a more rigorous standard when a Title IX plaintiff seeks damages against a school district for student-on-student harassment." *Sauls v. Pierce Cty. Sch. Dist.,* 399 F.3d 1279, 1284 (11th Cir.2005). Accordingly, the district court applied the correct standard to Doe's Title IX claim.

B. Application of Legal Standard for Title IX Student-on-Student Sexual Harassment

We now apply this legal standard to Doe's Title IX claim. In *Williams v. Board of Regents of University System of Georgia,* 477 F.3d 1282, 1292-99 (11th Cir. 2007), this Court applied *Davis* and held a plaintiff seeking recovery for a Title IX violation predicated on student-on-student sexual harassment must prove five elements.[11]

First, the defendant must be a Title IX funding recipient. *Id.* at 1293. Second, an "appropriate person" must have actual knowledge of the alleged discrimination or harassment. *Id.* (quotation omitted). Third, the discrimination or harassment—of which the funding recipient had actual knowledge under element two—must be "severe, pervasive, and objectively offensive." *Id.* (quotation omitted). Fourth, the plaintiff must prove "the funding recipient act[ed] with deliberate indifference to known acts of harassment in its programs or activities." *Id.* (quotation omitted). Fifth, the plaintiff must demonstrate the discrimination or harassment "effectively barred the victim's access to an educational opportunity or benefit." *Id.* at 1298 (quotation and internal alterations omitted).

Applying this test, the district court concluded no reasonable juror could find the Board had actual knowledge that CJC's behavior constituted sexual harassment so severe, pervasive, and objectively offensive as to deprive Doe of educational opportunities. For the reasons explained below, we disagree and reverse.

1. Is the Board a Title IX funding recipient?

The first element requires Doe to prove the Board is a Title IX funding recipient. *See id.* at 1293. The parties do not address and therefore appear to agree the Board is a Title IX funding recipient. Doe succeeds on the first element.

2. Did the Board have actual knowledge of the sexual harassment and discrimination Doe faced?

The second element requires Doe to prove an "appropriate person" capable of putting the Board on notice had "actual knowledge" of CJC's sexual harassment and discrimination. *See id.* We begin by identifying the appropriate persons capable of putting the Board on notice of CJC's sexual harassment. We then discuss whether the Board had actual knowledge of CJC's sexual harassment.

p.971 a. Appropriate persons

The Supreme Court has explained that an "appropriate person" is an official of the recipient entity who "at a minimum has authority to address the alleged discrimination and to institute corrective measures on the recipient's behalf." *Gebser*, 524 U.S. at 290, 118 S.Ct. at 1999. In *Floyd v. Waiters*, 171 F.3d 1264, 1264 (11th Cir. 1999), this Court elaborated on the "appropriate person" requirement, stating the school official must be "high enough up the chain-of-command that his acts constitute an official decision by the school district itself not to remedy the misconduct." Applying this standard, this Court held a school security guard was not an appropriate person. *Floyd v. Waiters*, 133 F.3d 786, 788, 793 & n. 15 (11th Cir.1998), *vacated by* 525 U.S. 802, 119 S.Ct. 33, 142 L.Ed.2d 25 (1998), *reinstated in* 171 F.3d 1264 (11th Cir.1999).

The parties agree Principal Blair, Assistant Principal Dunaway, and Assistant Principal Terrell were appropriate persons capable of putting the Board on actual notice of sexual harassment and discrimination. The parties dispute, however, whether Teacher's Aide Simpson was an "appropriate person" such that her knowledge is attributable to the Board.

We conclude Teacher's Aide Simpson was not an "appropriate person" who could put the Board on notice of sexual harassment and discrimination. No evidence in the record suggests teacher's aides at Sparkman have the authority to discipline students for sexual harassment. *See Gebser*, 524 U.S. at 290, 118 S.Ct. at 1999. The principal and assistant principals alone possessed that authority. As a teacher's aide, Simpson had to answer to a teacher, the assistant principals, and the principal, and she was not high enough on the chain-of-command at Sparkman for her acts to "constitute an official decision by the school district itself not to remedy the misconduct." *See Floyd,* 171 F.3d at 1264. Accordingly, in evaluating whether the Board had notice of CJC's sexual harassment, we evaluate only the knowledge of Principal Blair and Assistant Principals Dunaway and Terrell.

b. Actual knowledge

We now ask what the Board knew—vis-à-vis Principal Blair or Assistant Principals Dunaway or Terrell—about CJC's alleged harassment and discrimination. Under element two, we are concerned only with the Board's knowledge. *Williams,* 477 F.3d at 1293. The analysis of whether CJC's alleged harassment was sufficiently severe, pervasive, and objectively offensive is reserved for element three. The determination of whether the Board's response to CJC's alleged harassment was deliberately indifferent is reserved for element four.

The Board knew—again, vis-à-vis Blair, Dunaway, or Terrell—the following facts. The Board admits it had knowledge of CJC's disciplinary history that was tersely recorded in the iNOW database. The Board does not contest it had actual knowledge of CJC's unrecorded instances of alleged sexual harassment in January 2010. Administrators learned weeks before the rape that CJC had been propositioning girls to have sex in bathrooms. On January 13, 2010, ten days before the rape of Doe, the administrators learned CJC had allegedly inappropriately touched a female student. We recognize there is a dispute of fact as to whether Teacher's Aide Simpson informed Assistant Principal Dunaway a few minutes before the rape about her proposed sting operation and CJC's propositioning of Doe to have sex in the boys' bathroom. Construing the facts in favor of Doe for purposes of summary judgment, the Board (through Dunaway) p.972 had actual knowledge of the use of Doe as rape bait for CJC in the sting operation and CJC's propositioning of Doe to have sex. And it is undisputed that the Board became aware of the rape-bait scheme and the rape when Principal Blair interviewed Simpson and Doe and discovered these events. At that point, the Board also definitively knew CJC's verbal harassment of Doe led Simpson to implement the sting operation.

3. Was the sexual harassment and discrimination Doe faced, of which the Board had knowledge, severe, pervasive, and objectively offensive?

As to the third element, we ask whether the sexual harassment and discrimination, of which the Board had actual knowledge, was sufficiently "severe, pervasive, and objectively offensive." *Davis,* 526 U.S. at 651, 119 S.Ct. at 1675; *see Williams,* 477 F.3d at 1294. "Whether gender-oriented conduct rises to the level of actionable [Title IX] harassment . . . depends on a constellation of surrounding circumstances, expectations, and relationships, including, but not limited to, the ages of the harasser and the victim and the number of individuals involved." *Id.* (quotations and citations omitted). To be severe, pervasive, and objectively offensive, the behavior must be serious enough to have a "systemic effect" of denying equal access to an education. *Id.* at 652, 119 S.Ct. at 1676. A "single instance of sufficiently severe one-on-one peer harassment" cannot have such a systemic effect in light of "the amount of litigation that would be invited by entertaining claims of official indifference to a single instance of one-on-one peer harassment." *Id.* at 652-53, 119 S.Ct. at 1676.

This is a unique case because the administrators effectively participated in CJC's sexual harassment by setting Doe up in a rape-bait scheme involving CJC in order to "catch him in the act." Thus, in considering the third element, we examine and count (1) CJC's past sexual harassment of Doe and others; (2) Doe's complaints about CJC to the Board (through Simpson and Dunaway) to which the Board responded by having Doe participate in a sting operation with CJC; (3) the Board's "catch in the act" policy that motivated Simpson to conduct, and Dunaway to approve, a rape-bait scheme with CJC as a participant that directly harassed, injured, and impacted Doe further; and (4) after the rape, the Board's utter failure to respond to Doe's traumatic injury and experience orchestrated by the Board.

In *Williams*, this Court reversed the dismissal of a Title IX claim brought by a female student at the University of Georgia (UGA), who was gang-raped by three student-athletes in a dorm room. The *Williams* plaintiff alleged UGA had actual knowledge of the following forms of discrimination or harassment that she faced. 477 F.3d at 1294. UGA had actual knowledge of prior sexual harassment of women by the ringleader of the gang-rape, and then despite that conduct UGA recruited him to play basketball and admitted him as a student. *Id.* The plaintiff also alleged UGA had actual knowledge of the rape and the subsequent discrimination of the plaintiff caused by the university's own inadequate response to the rape. *Id.*

This Court concluded that UGA's failure to supervise the ringleader on campus was deliberately indifferent in light of UGA's knowledge of his prior sexual misconduct at other schools. *Id.* at 1296. This Court also concluded that UGA again responded with deliberate indifference by waiting almost a year after the rape to conduct a disciplinary hearing, and by failing to take any precautions to prevent future attacks by, for example, removing p.973 the rapist from student housing or implementing a more protective sexual assault policy. *Id.* at 1296-97. As *Williams* shows, a school's deliberately indifferent response to sexual harassment can create Title IX liability.

Here, a jury similarly could find the Board's knowledge of CJC's prior sexual harassment on multiple occasions; the Board's catch in the act policy; Doe's complaints about CJC; the Board's knowing use of Doe as rape bait in its sting operation with CJC; and the Board's failure to respond at all, much less adequately, to Doe's allegations or the rape itself, were sufficiently "severe" and "objectively offensive" to satisfy the third element.

These facts differ markedly from the "rarely actionable, theoretical single incident mentioned in *Davis*." *Williams*, 477 F.3d at 1298. We conclude the harassment here is materially different because the physical act of penetration in the bathroom was (1) preceded by CJC repeatedly propositioning Doe for sex for two weeks and (2) orchestrated by school officials during a botched rape-bait scheme with CJC. Like the rape in *Williams* where the ringleader conspired with his friends beforehand to commit sexual assault, a jury could find CJC's rape of Doe was the culmination of "a continuous series of events," *id*, at 1298, and was therefore pervasive. These are highly unique and extreme facts that will hopefully never again be repeated. A jury could find CJC's rape of Doe was the culmination of CJC's two weeks of harassment and the school's choice to use Doe as bait for CJC's sexual harassment, and thus satisfies the third element.

4. Was the Board deliberately indifferent to the sexual harassment and discrimination Doe faced?

As to the fourth element, funding recipients are deliberately indifferent "only where the recipient's response to the harassment or lack thereof is clearly unreasonable in light of the known circumstances." *Davis,* 526 U.S. at 648, 119 S.Ct. at 1674. A clearly unreasonable response causes students to undergo harassment or makes them more vulnerable to it. *See Williams,* 477 F.3d at 1295-96. To survive a summary judgment motion, a Title IX plaintiff must present evidence from which a reasonable jury could conclude "the Title IX recipient's deliberate indifference to the initial discrimination subjected the plaintiff to further discrimination." *Id.* at 1296. We therefore ask whether the Board's decision to use Doe as bait in a sting operation with CJC, a known and already disciplined sexual harasser, combined with the Board's failure to change any sexual harassment policies after CJC's rape of Doe, was clearly unreasonable in light of the known circumstances. *See, e.g., Williams,* 477 F.3d at 1297 ("[The School] acted with deliberate indifference. . . when it responded to the January 14 incident [of rape.]").

We conclude a genuine dispute of material fact exists as to whether the Board's deliberate indifference to Doe's "initial discrimination subjected [Doe] to further discrimination" that prevented her from continuing to attend Sparkman. *Id.* at 1296. As outlined above, the Board's knowledge of CJC's sexual harassment, its catch in the act policy, its orchestration of a sting operation using Doe as bait for CJC's sexual activities, and its failure to help Doe in any way was patently odious. In addition, the Board made only one policy change: it discontinued a one-day sexual harassment training workshop for administrators at the Madison County Administrator Academy. Although Principal Blair believes the Board did not need to change any policies because "we did as good a job I think as p.974 you could do under the circumstances," a reasonable jury could disagree.

In evaluating whether the Board's above conduct was deliberately indifferent, a jury might conclude the Board's failure to revise its iNOW recordkeeping policy was clearly unreasonable. After the rape, a jury could find the Board should have known it needed to develop a more accurate system for recording sexual harassment in order to adequately monitor and respond to student misconduct and complaints of sexual harassment. As an example, the Board recorded CJC's rape of Doe in CJC's disciplinary file as "[i]nappropriate touching a female in a boys' bathroom." In response to the allegations that CJC was harassing female students by propositioning them to have sex in bathrooms, the Board recorded the incident as "[d]isobedience" due to "[c]onstant[]distraction continued disruption of learning." The evidence reveals school officials never recorded CJC's placement in alternative school for "hugg[ing] a girl in the front of the cafeteria." School officials apparently did not find this incident worth recording, even though CJC had raped Doe three months earlier.

A jury could find the policy of entrusting the school secretary to make iNOW database entries through an *ad hoc,* rather than systematic, method of classifying sexual misconduct was flawed. As Assistant Principal Terrell conceded, the Board did not have a "normal policy" about iNOW recordkeeping. A jury could find the Board's failure to create an accurate and systematic iNOW database policy after CJC's rape of Doe was clearly unreasonable.

Additionally, a reasonable jury could find the Board's decision to continue shredding students' disciplinary paper records at the end of each year impeded school officials' ability to adequately respond to sexual harassment allegations against CJC. A jury could conclude the Board's policy prevented school officials from "draw[ing] a connection" between CJC's January 2010 incidents and prior sexual harassment complaints. *See Doe v. Bd. of Broward Cty., Fla.*, 604 F.3d 1248, 1261 (11th Cir.2010).

The Board also has not revised its policy of assigning suspected sexual harassers to unsupervised janitorial duty. In response to complaints that CJC was inappropriately touching girls, Principal Blair assigned CJC to 20 days of in-school suspension during which he was occasionally unsupervised. A jury might find that, after CJC's rape of Doe, continuing to allow suspected sexual harassers to roam a middle school's halls unsupervised—as punishment for covertly attempting to have sex with girls in bathrooms—was clearly unreasonable.

A jury could find it was clearly unreasonable for the Board to decline to remedy the school administrators' practice of ignoring paper disciplinary records when deciding how to respond to sexual harassment allegations. Principal Blair did not examine CJC's disciplinary records as part of his investigation of CJC. Assistant Principal Dunaway did not check the supporting paper documentation that would have been in CJC's file regarding the October 28, 2009 "[i]nappropriate touching" infraction, the November 18, 2009 "refusing to obey driver and keep hands off a female student" infraction, and the November 25, 2009 "[k]issing" infraction. A reasonable factfinder might conclude the Board's refusal to direct its officials to consider all the known circumstances, including the nature, pattern, and seriousness of a student's conduct, was clearly unreasonable. *See Doe*, 604 F.3d at 1263 (stating funding recipients do not "satisfy their obligations under Title IX without ever evaluating the known circumstances at all").

p.975 A jury might also find it was clearly unreasonable for the Board not to improve its sexual harassment training. Teacher's Aide Simpson stated that despite her entreaties to Principal Blair and other faculty members, she and other teacher's aides received no training on how to handle complaints of sexual harassment. *See Simpson v. Univ. of Colo. Boulder*, 500 F.3d 1170, 1178 (10th Cir.2007) (holding funding recipient demonstrates deliberate indifference by failing "to provid[e] adequate training or guidance that is obviously necessary for implementation of a specific program or policy of the recipient"). Blair admitted the Board does not have a policy for annually revisiting its sexual harassment policy, and no records are kept about sexual harassment training. Further, there are genuine questions of fact and credibility regarding the quantity and quality of the Board's purported training. The Board has failed to produce any official documentation of staff training sessions. Blair can remember one workshop on sexual harassment over the past few years, but cannot remember the approximate date or details of the program. Assistant Principal Dunaway, despite being integrally involved in disciplining students for sexual harassment, was not aware the Code of Conduct had any section addressing sexual misconduct or harassment. Blair could not remember the identity of the Title IX coordinator in 2010; did not know how employees would discover the identity of the

Title IX coordinator; and students were not told who the Title IX coordinator was. *Cf. Williams,* 477 F.3d at 1296 (holding plaintiff adequately alleged deliberate indifference when school "fail[ed] to inform its student-athletes about the applicable sexual harassment policy"). When the Board's sexual harassment policies are considered collectively, a reasonable jury could find the Board's choice to do nothing to improve its sexual harassment policies was clearly unreasonable.

Given all these events and circumstances considered cumulatively, there is a genuine issue of fact as to whether both the Board's action and inaction were deliberately indifferent. We do not say that any one action or inaction suffices. The deliberate indifference standard is rigorous and hard to meet. But the cumulative events and circumstances here, viewed in the light most favorable to Doe, are enough to establish deliberate indifference under Title IX.

5. Did the Board's deliberate indifference to the harassment and discrimination effectively bar Doe's access to an educational opportunity or benefit?

Turning to element five, a genuine dispute of material fact exists as to whether CJC's sexual harassment, combined with the Board's use of Doe in a rape-bait scheme involving CJC, "effectively bar[red] [Doe's] access to an educational opportunity or benefit." *See Davis,* 526 U.S. at 633, 119 S.Ct. at 1666.

A reasonable jury could find the Board's overall conduct and its clearly unreasonable response to the rape prevented Doe from continuing her education at Sparkman. Although Doe unenrolled and moved to North Carolina approximately two weeks before CJC finished his stint at alternative school and returned to Sparkman, Doe's withdrawal does not bar a finding that the Board denied her an opportunity to continue attending Sparkman. In light of the incomprehensible rape-bait scheme and the resulting severe suffering Doe endured on January 22, combined with the refusal of school personnel to acknowledge the rape or begin implementing new sexual harassment prevention or recordkeeping policies, her withdrawal was p.976 reasonable and expected. *See Williams,* 477 F.3d at 1297 (holding student's withdrawal after rape was "reasonable and expected" and did not foreclose fact that defendant's deliberate indifference denied her an opportunity to continue attending the school). A person in Doe's position could have no confidence in a school system that orchestrates a rape-bait scheme and whose disciplinary file describes CJC's rape of her as "[i]nappropriate touching a female in a boys' bathroom." Indeed, her choice to withdraw now seems prescient because, only one month after CJC returned to Sparkman, school officials had "additional problems" with him, including "hugg[ing] a girl in the front of the cafeteria." Had Doe declined to withdraw from Sparkman, she might have again been CJC's victim.

Drawing all reasonable inferences in favor of Doe, a jury could find CJC's sexual harassment, combined with the Board's rape-bait scheme involving CJC, "had a concrete, negative effect" on her ability to receive an education. *Davis,* 526 U.S. at 654, 119 S.Ct. at 1676. Doe missed time at school due to the rape and had to transfer due to the school's clearly unreasonable response. She now attends counseling sessions, takes medication for depression, no longer participates in extracurricular activities like basketball, and her grades have suffered. Doe has satisfied element five.

Doe has satisfied all five elements necessary to create a genuine dispute of fact on her Title IX student-on-student sexual harassment claim. We therefore reverse the district court's grant of summary judgment to the Board.

C. Section 1983 Equal Protection Claims

Next we consider Doe's 42 U.S.C. § 1983 equal protection claims against the Board, Blair, Dunaway, Simpson, and Terrell. Section 1983 allows persons to sue individuals or municipalities acting under the color of state law for violations of federal law. One such law is the Equal Protection Clause, U.S. Const. amend. XIV, § 1, which confers a federal constitutional right to be free from sex discrimination. *See, e.g.*, *Pers. Adm'r of Mass. v. Feeney*, 442 U.S. 256, 273, 99 S.Ct. 2282, 2293, 60 L.Ed.2d 870 (1979).

Although Title IX and § 1983 sexual harassment claims are similar, our resolution of Doe's Title IX suit does not dictate the result of our § 1983 analysis. The differences in Title IX and § 1983, in addition to the parties' framing of the issues, may lead to results that are seemingly inconsistent. For instance, in this case we concluded the Board may be held liable under Title IX, but, as explained below, we conclude the Board may not be held liable under § 1983.

Doe has framed her § 1983 equal protection claim against the Board differently than her Title IX claim. Under Title IX, Doe has asserted the overall conduct of the appropriate school officials—Blair, Dunaway, and Terrell—whose conduct was attributable to the Board, was deliberately indifferent. By contrast, under § 1983 where *respondeat superior* is unavailable, Doe has alleged only that (1) the Board's allegedly inadequate training policies and (2) the "catch in the act" policy amount to deliberate indifference. In contrast to her Title IX claim, Doe has thus narrowly framed her § 1983 claim against the Board.

Title IX and § 1983 are different. As the Supreme Court has said, Title IX's and § 1983's protections "are narrower in some respects and broader in others." *Fitzgerald v. Barnstable Sch. Comm.*, 555 U.S. 246, 256, 129 S.Ct. 788, 796, 172 L.Ed.2d 582 (2009). For instance, p.977 Title IX is enforceable against institutions and programs that receive federal funds, but does not authorize suits against individuals. *Id.* at 257, 129 S.Ct. at 796. Section 1983 equal protection claims, by contrast, may be brought against individuals and municipalities. *Id.* The standards for establishing liability under each mechanism also "may not be wholly congruent." *Id.* at 257, 129 S.Ct. at 797. Under Title IX, for example, a plaintiff can establish school district liability by showing an appropriate school official responded to sexual harassment with deliberate indifference. *Id.* A plaintiff bringing a similar § 1983 claim must show a municipal custom, policy, or practice caused the harassment. *Id.* at 257-58, 129 S.Ct. at 797.

Now that we have discussed the relationship between § 1983 and Title IX, we analyze Doe's § 1983 claims. Doe argues the district court erred in granting summary judgment to Defendants on her § 1983 claims because Defendants violated her federally guaranteed right to equal protection by subjecting her to sexual harassment. Specifically, Doe contends Defendants exhibited deliberate indifference by failing to adequately prevent and respond to CJC's sexual harassment. We first analyze the Board's municipal liability. We then examine the individual defendants' liability.

1. The Board

The Board, which is a municipality, may not be held liable for constitutional deprivations on the theory of *respondeat superior. Denno v. Sch. Bd. of Volusia Cty., Fla.,* 218 F.3d 1267, 1276 (11th Cir.2000). Instead, "municipal liability is limited to action for which the municipality is actually responsible." *Pembaur v. City of Cincinnati,* 475 U.S. 469, 479-80, 106 S.Ct. 1292, 1298, 89 L.Ed.2d 452 (1986). A municipality therefore may be held liable "only if such constitutional torts result from an official government policy, the actions of an official fairly deemed to represent government policy, or a custom or practice so pervasive and well-settled that it assumes the force of law." *Denno,* 218 F.3d at 1276.

Doe contends the Board is subject to municipal liability for adopting the "catch in the act" policy and allegedly inadequate training policies that led Simpson and Dunaway to formulate the rape-bait sting operation. Assuming, without deciding, that these policies are attributable to the Board, the district court did not err in granting summary judgment.

"[I]t is not enough for a § 1983 plaintiff merely to identify conduct properly attributable to the municipality." *Bd. of Cty. Comm'rs of Bryan Cty., Okl. v. Brown,* 520 U.S. 397, 404, 117 S.Ct. 1382, 1388, 137 L.Ed.2d 626 (1997). The plaintiff "must show that the municipal action was taken with the requisite degree of culpability and must demonstrate a direct causal link between the municipal action and the deprivation of federal rights." *Id.* The Supreme Court has noted the "deliberate indifference" standard under § 1983 is a "stringent standard of fault, requiring proof that a municipal actor disregarded a known or obvious consequence of his action." *Id.* at 410, 117 S.Ct. at 1391. A court must "carefully test the link between the policymaker's inadequate decision and the particular injury alleged." *Id.* at 410, 117 S.Ct. 1382. The evidence must show the deprivation of the constitutional right is a "plainly obvious consequence" of the municipal action. *Id.* at 411, 117 S.Ct. at 1392.

The Board could not have foreseen a rape-bait scheme that required an eighth-grade student to voluntarily subject herself to sexual harassment as a "known or obvious consequence" of the "catch in p.978 the act" policy or its training policies. *See id.* at 410, 117 S.Ct. at 1391. While the Board's policies may have made a violation of Doe's rights "more *likely*" by motivating Simpson to engineer the rape-bait operation, that alone does not give rise to an inference that the policies "produced a specific constitutional allegation." *See McDowell v. Brown,* 392 F.3d 1283, 1292 (11th Cir.2004) (quoting *Brown,* 520 U.S. at 411, 117 S.Ct. at 1382). It is not obvious a teacher's aide would craft a sting operation like the one here in response to (1) the Board's allegedly inadequate training policies or (2) a policy requiring witnesses, physical evidence, or an admission of guilt before disciplining a student for sexual harassment. We accordingly affirm the grant of summary judgment to the Board on Doe's § 1983 claim.

2. Principal Blair

Doe asserts the district court erred in granting summary judgment to Principal Blair on her § 1983 claim. She says Blair's inadequate response to CJC's known sexual harassment deprived her of equal protection, and he is not entitled to qualified immunity because he had fair warning his actions violated the Equal Protection Clause. We agree and reverse.

"[A] governmental official . . . may be held liable under section 1983 upon a showing of deliberate indifference to known sexual harassment." *Murrell v. Sch. Dist. No. 1, Denver, Colo.,* 186 F.3d 1238, 1250 (10th Cir.1999); *see Williams v. Bd. of Regents of Univ. Sys. of Ga.,* 477 F.3d 1282, 1300-02 (11th Cir.2007) (discussing government officials' liability under § 1983 arising from "right to be free from sex discrimination"); *Hartley v. Parnell,* 193 F.3d 1263, 1269 (11th Cir.1999) (applying "deliberate indifference" standard for § 1983 deprivation of constitutional right to be free from sexual harassment). In order to prevail on a claim of deliberate indifference to sexual harassment, a plaintiff must prove the individual defendant "actually knew of and acquiesced in" the discriminatory conduct. *Murrell,* 186 F.3d at 1250 (quotation omitted). Qualified immunity, however, offers complete protection for individual government officials performing discretionary functions "insofar as their conduct does not violate clearly established statutory or constitutional rights of which a reasonable person would have known." *Harlow v. Fitzgerald,* 457 U.S. 800, 818, 102 S.Ct. 2727, 2738, 73 L.Ed.2d 396 (1982).

When a court concludes the defendant was engaged in a discretionary function, "the burden shifts to the plaintiff to show that the defendant is *not* entitled to qualified immunity." *Holloman ex rel. Holloman v. Harland,* 370 F.3d 1252, 1264 (11th Cir.2004). The parties do not dispute that, at all times relevant to this appeal, Blair acted in his discretionary capacity. Doe consequently bears the burden of showing "(1) [Blair] violated a constitutional right, and (2) this right was clearly established at the time of the alleged violation." *See id.*

With regard to the first prong of qualified immunity analysis, there is a genuine dispute of material fact as to whether Principal Blair violated Doe's constitutional right to equal protection. For the reasons explained above in our Title IX analysis, *supra* Section IV.B(4), a jury could find Blair's actions after CJC's rape of Doe amounted to deliberate indifference. The evidence shows Blair crafted and implemented Sparkman's sexual harassment and recordkeeping policies. A jury could find that despite these policies' glaring inadequacies that were exposed by CJC's rape of Doe, Blair did virtually nothing in response. The only change was to discontinue the one-day sexual harassment training p.979 workshop for administrators at the Madison County Administrator Academy. Viewing the evidence favorably to Doe, doing nothing was a deliberately indifferent response that subjected Doe to further sexual harassment by depriving her of the opportunity to continue attending Sparkman.

As to the second prong, when viewing the evidence favorably to Doe, Principal Blair violated a clearly established right. A right may be clearly established for qualified immunity purposes in one of three ways: "(1) case law with indistinguishable facts clearly establishing the constitutional right; (2) a broad statement of principle within the Constitution, statute, or case law that clearly establishes a constitutional right; or (3) conduct so egregious that a constitutional right was clearly violated, even in the total absence of case law." *Lewis v. City of W. Palm Beach, Fla.,* 561 F.3d 1288, 1291-92 (11th Cir.2009) (citations omitted). Doe has confined her argument to the second of these methods. Under this method, "every objectively reasonable government official facing the circumstances would know that the official's conduct did violate federal law when the official acted." *See, e.g., Vinyard v. Wilson,* 311 F.3d 1340, 1351 (11th Cir.2002); *see also Hope v. Pelzer,* 536 U.S. 730, 741, 122 S.Ct. 2508, 2516, 153 L.Ed.2d 666 (2002) (the "salient question" is whether the state of the law gave "fair warning" the conduct was unconstitutional).

The relevant question is whether a reasonable government official in Blair's position as principal could have believed that "doing nothing" to reform Sparkman's sexual harassment and recordkeeping policies in response to CJC's rape of Doe was lawful, in light of clearly established law. *See Cross v. State of Ala., State Dep't of Mental Health & Mental Retardation,* 49 F.3d 1490, 1503 (11th Cir.1995). Viewing all reasonable inferences in favor of Doe, we conclude an official in Blair's position would not have believed doing nothing was lawful in light of the clearly established principle that deliberate indifference to sexual harassment is an equal protection violation. *See, e.g., Doe v. Sch. Bd. of Broward Cty., Fla.,* 604 F.3d 1248, 1261 (11th Cir.2010) (finding deliberate indifference when the principal "effectively did nothing" in response to sexual harassment). We reverse the district court's grant of summary judgment to Blair on Doe's § 1983 equal protection claim.

3. Assistant Principal Dunaway

The district court also erred in granting summary judgment to Assistant Principal Dunaway on Doe's § 1983 equal protection claim. The district court found Dunaway was entitled to qualified immunity because it could not identify sufficiently similar case law involving a sexual harassment sting operation. This was error. Drawing all reasonable inferences in favor of Doe, Dunaway acquiesced to and ratified Teacher's Aide Simpson's plan to send Doe alone into a bathroom with a known sexual harasser and have Doe pretend to initially welcome the harasser's sexual advances. It is not surprising the district court could not find similar case law. That is because "every objectively reasonable government official facing the circumstances" would know this irresponsible plan violated the Equal Protection Clause. *See Vinyard,* 311 F.3d at 1351. We therefore reverse.

4. Teacher's Aide Simpson

Teacher's Aide Simpson is not entitled to qualified immunity for the same reason as Assistant Principal Dunaway: she participated in using Doe as rape bait for CJC's sexual harassment in the sting operation. p.980 The only difference between their conduct is that Simpson contrived the sting operation, whereas Dunaway ratified it. We reverse the district court's grant of summary judgment to Simpson on Doe's § 1983 equal protection claim.

5. Assistant Principal Terrell

We affirm the district court's grant of summary judgment to Assistant Principal Terrell. Terrell is entitled to qualified immunity because the record does not show she violated Doe's constitutional right to equal protection. *Holloman,* 370 F.3d at 1264 (stating official is entitled to qualified immunity if plaintiff fails to show "the defendant violated a constitutional right"). Unlike Principal Blair, Terrell was not ultimately responsible for Sparkman's sexual harassment policies. As a subordinate to Blair, she could not dictate the response to CJC's rape of Doe. Blair's deliberately indifferent response consequently cannot be attributed to Terrell. Unlike Assistant Principal Dunaway and Teacher's Aide Simpson, there is no evidence Terrell acquiesced to or ratified the plan to use Doe as rape bait for CJC in the sting operation. Thus, Dunaway's and Simpson's deliberate indifference also cannot be attributed to Terrell.

D. Section 1983 Substantive Due Process Claim

The district court did not err in granting summary judgment to Simpson on Doe's substantive due process claim. This Court has held deliberate indifference is not, without more, a basis for finding substantive due process liability in cases arising in the school context. *See Davis v. Carter,* 555 F.3d 979, 983-84 (11th Cir. 2009). Doe's effort to state a claim for a violation of her right to substantive due process fails. Simpson is entitled to qualified immunity, and we affirm the district court's grant of summary judgment.

E. Negligence/Wantonness Against Principal Blair

We now turn from Doe's federal claims to her Alabama state law claims brought pursuant to the district court's supplemental jurisdiction. *See* 28 U.S.C. § 1367(a). Doe argues the district court erred in granting summary judgment to Principal Blair for state law negligence/wantonness. The district court held Blair was entitled to state-agent immunity under Alabama law. Doe contends Blair is not entitled to state-agent immunity because he (1) acted beyond his authority by failing to comply with his Title IX obligation to prevent, eliminate, and address the effects of sexual harassment; (2) acted in bad faith by failing to impose effective discipline when he assigned CJC to unsupervised in-school suspension; and (3) mistakenly interpreted Title IX by improperly conducting investigations of sexual harassment allegations. We affirm because, as discussed below, Doe has not shown any of the exceptions to Alabama state-agent immunity apply to Blair's conduct.

Under Alabama law, "[s]tate-agent immunity protects state employees, as agents of the State, in the exercise of their judgment in executing their work responsibilities." *Ex parte Hayles,* 852 So.2d 117, 122 (Ala.2002). The Alabama Supreme Court has established a burden-shifting framework for application of the state-agent immunity test. *Ex parte Estate of Reynolds,* 946 So.2d 450, 452, 454-55 (Ala.2006). A state agent initially bears the burden of demonstrating that she was acting in a discretionary function that would entitle her to immunity. *Id.* If the state agent makes such a showing, the burden shifts to the plaintiff to show the state agent "act[ed] willfully, maliciously, p.981 fraudulently, in bad faith, beyond his or her authority, or under a mistaken interpretation of the law." *Ex parte Cranman,* 792 So.2d 392, 402 n. 13 (Ala.2000).

Doe concedes Principal Blair has met his initial burden because his handling of student disciplinary matters is a discretionary function. The only question is whether Blair lacks state-law immunity because he (1) acted beyond his authority by violating Title IX, (2) acted in bad faith, or (3) acted based on a mistaken interpretation of Title IX. We consider each exception in turn.

1. Acting beyond authority

First, Doe contends Principal Blair is not entitled to state-agent immunity because he acted "beyond his authority" in failing to comply with his Title IX obligation to prevent sexual harassment. Even if we accepted the dubious proposition that Title IX imposes obligations on Blair—who is an individual school official, not a Title IX funding recipient—he did not forfeit state-agent immunity by acting beyond his authority. As the Alabama Supreme Court has explained, a state agent acts beyond his authority when he "fail[s] to discharge duties pursuant to detailed rules or regulations, such as those stated on a checklist." *Ex parte Butts,* 775 So.2d 173, 178 (Ala.2000). The rules or regulations must be so "detailed" as to "remove a State-agent's judgment in the performance of required acts." *Ex parte Spivey,* 846 So.2d 322, 333 (Ala.2002) (quotation omitted).

Doe has not alleged how Title IX creates rules or regulations so detailed as to "remove a State-agent's judgment in the performance of required acts." *See id.* Doe cites only generally to Title IX's directive that funding recipients eliminate sexual harassment, prevent its recurrence, and address its effects. Indeed, Doe has not cited to any specific rule. The failure to abide by a "broadly stated, general safety policy," as opposed to a "detailed rule or checklist," is insufficient to abrogate state-agent immunity. *Bayles v. Marriott,* 816 So.2d 38, 41-42 (Ala.Civ.App.2001).

2. Bad faith

Moving to the second exception to state-agent immunity, Doe contends Principal Blair acted in bad faith because he failed to discipline CJC harshly enough. Bad faith, however, requires more than a showing of incompetence. Bad faith "is not simply bad judgment or negligence. It imports a dishonest purpose and means a breach of known duty . . . through some motive of self-interest or ill will." *Gulf Atl. Life Ins. Co. v. Barnes,* 405 So.2d 916, 924 (Ala.1981); *see also Ex parte Turner,* 840 So.2d 132, 136 (Ala.2002) (applying state-agent immunity where, even though state official exercised poor judgment, evidence showed he acted in "good faith"). Doe has not pointed to evidence from which a jury could infer Blair's disciplinary response to CJC was motivated by self-interest or ill will towards her.

3. Mistaken Interpretation of Law

Third, Doe argues Principal Blair is not entitled to state-agent immunity because he acted under a mistaken interpretation of the law. Even assuming Title IX imposes a personal obligation on Blair, and even further assuming Blair's allegedly inadequate disciplinary response to CJC's conduct was caused by a misinterpretation of Title IX's requirements, this exception does not remove Blair's state-agent immunity.

Not every innocent misinterpretation of the law revokes an official's state-agent immunity under Alabama law. If nothing more were required than an innocent misinterpretation of the law, "that exception would 'swallow' the whole of the general rule of immunity itself" because "any misstep by any state employee or other state agent that wrongs another can be said to be beyond his or her authority and/or committed under a mistaken interpretation of the law." *Segrest v. Lewis,* 907 So.2d 452, 456 (Ala.Civ.App.2005). For that reason, the misinterpretation of the law must be coupled with willfulness, maliciousness, or bad faith to "pull the agent out from under the umbrella of state-agent immunity." *Id.* The evidence does not show Principal Blair acted with willfulness, maliciousness, or bad faith.

None of the exceptions to Alabama state-agent immunity are applicable to Blair. We accordingly affirm the district court's grant of summary judgment to Blair on the negligence/wantonness claims.

F. Negligence/Wantonness Against Dunaway

In her consolidated interlocutory appeal, Assistant Principal Dunaway argues the district court erred in denying her state-agent immunity for negligence/wantonness on the basis that she acted beyond her authority. The district court found that, viewing the evidence in the light most favorable to Doe, Dunaway ratified Teacher's Aide Simpson's plan to use Doe as bait to catch CJC in the act of sexual harassment. The district court concluded Dunaway exceeded her authority by ratifying the rape-bait scheme rather than reporting CJC's sexual harassment to Principal Blair in accordance with the Policy Manual, which required a school official who receives a complaint of sexual harassment to report that complaint to the principal.

We affirm the district court's denial of state-agent immunity to Assistant Principal Dunaway. Again, under Alabama law, a state official acts beyond her authority when she fails to comply with a policy that has "remove[d] a State-agent's judgment in the performance of required acts." *Ex parte Spivey*, 846 So.2d at 333. The Alabama Supreme Court's decision in *N.C. v. Caldwell*, 77 So.3d 561 (Ala.2011), is particularly instructive on the application of this standard when, as here, a school official has allegedly contravened a school policy.[12]

In *Caldwell*, the plaintiff, a seventh-grade girl, was raped by an older male student after gym class. *Id.* at 562. Defendant Caldwell, the girl's gym teacher, had assigned the male student to serve as a student aide during the gym class, despite evidence that other female students informed Caldwell the aide had directed inappropriate sexual comments toward them. *Id.* at 562-63. Caldwell moved for summary judgment on the basis of state-agent immunity. *Id.* at 563-65. Plaintiff responded Caldwell was not entitled to immunity because he "acted beyond his authority" by appointing the male student as his aide and by failing to report previous complaints of sexual harassment. *Id.* at 566.

The Alabama Supreme Court reversed the grant of summary judgment to Caldwell because he failed to follow two school policies. *Id.* at 568-69. First, the faculty handbook said, "Any student not scheduled for a class should not attend that class." *Id.* at 569. Since the male student had not been assigned to Caldwell's gym class, there was a genuine issue of material fact as to whether Caldwell acted beyond his authority by appointing the student as an aide for that class. *Id.* Second, the school's code of conduct provided "it shall also be a violation of board policy for any teacher to tolerate sexual harassment." *Id.* (alterations in original omitted). The court held there was a genuine issue of material fact as to whether Caldwell acted beyond his authority by failing to report the other girls' complaints of sexual harassment. *Id.*

Based on *Caldwell*, the terms of the Policy Manual are sufficiently detailed under Alabama law to create a genuine issue of material fact as to whether Dunaway acted beyond her authority by failing to report Doe's sexual harassment complaints to

Principal Blair. Under the Policy Manual, the school official to whom a complaint of sexual harassment is made "shall make the complaint known to the [p]rincipal of the school, except in cases where the complaint is against the [p]rincipal." The principal "shall investigate the complaint and take appropriate action." This language is certainly more narrowly focused than the directive in *Caldwell* that no teacher may "tolerate sexual harassment," *id.* at 569. Because the district court did not err in denying Dunaway state-agent immunity, we affirm.

G. Tort of Outrage Against Simpson

Doe next argues the district court erred in granting summary judgment to Teacher's Aide Simpson on her Alabama state law claim for the tort of outrage. We agree and reverse.[13]

Under Alabama law, the tort of outrage requires the plaintiff to show "(1) the actor intended to inflict emotional distress, or knew or should have known that emotional distress was likely to result from his conduct; (2) the conduct was extreme and outrageous; (3) the defendant's actions caused the plaintiff distress; and (4) that the distress was severe." *Harris v. McDavid*, 553 So.2d 567, 569-70 (Ala. 1989). We consider each element in turn.

1. Known or Should Have Known

First, a reasonable jury could conclude Teacher's Aide Simpson "should have known" emotional distress was likely to result from her decision to send Doe into the bathroom alone with CJC to act as bait for his sexual harassment. According to Simpson's own affidavit, she knew CJC "had been repeatedly propositioning other female students to have sex in the boys' bathroom." On January 21, 2010, Doe told Simpson CJC had been asking her to have sex, and Doe sought Simpson's guidance again on January 22 about how to stop the harassment. In her meeting with Assistant Principal Dunaway regarding her plan to use Doe as bait for CJC, Simpson said, "I hope this is legal. I don't know what I'm doing."

From all this evidence, a reasonable jury could conclude Simpson knew the significant danger CJC posed to Doe and severely doubted the legality of her conduct, presumably due to the risk the plan could misfire and an attack or rape could occur. Despite her consciousness of this risk, Simpson proceeded with the sting operation. Moreover, she did not even help personally oversee the operation because, after speaking to Dunaway and Hallman, Simpson believed "someone else was handling the situation, so I returned to the gym." A jury could find Simpson should have known that sending Doe to meet CJC alone in a bathroom and using Doe as bait p.984 to catch CJC was likely to cause emotional distress, especially when Simpson declined to personally monitor the sting operation.

2. Extreme and Outrageous Conduct

Moving to the second element of Doe's tort claim, a reasonable jury could find Simpson's conduct was extreme and outrageous. The Alabama Supreme Court's decision in *Henry v. Georgia-Pacific Corp.*, 730 So.2d 119 (Ala.1998), illustrates the type of behavior that is considered extreme and outrageous under Alabama law. In *Henry*, the defendant-employer required the plaintiff-employee to attend counseling sessions. *Id.* at 119. After the counselor made improper sexual comments and solicitations during these sessions, the plaintiff notified her employer of the harassment. *Id.* at 120. Nonetheless, the employer told her the sessions were mandatory, which led her to continue the sessions until the counselor stopped visiting. *Id.* The court reversed the grant of summary judgment to the employer, stating a reasonable juror could conclude that requiring the plaintiff to attend counseling sessions with a known sexual harasser constituted extreme and outrageous conduct. *Id.* at 121.

Likewise, a reasonable jury could conclude Simpson's conduct, like the employer's conduct in *Henry,* constitutes extreme and outrageous conduct. Simpson, with prior knowledge of CJC's harassment, pressured a vulnerable middle school student to subject herself to his sexual advances alone in a bathroom, despite the obvious risks accompanying the plan. As in *Henry,* a jury deserves to decide this issue because "[e]gregious sexual harassment can amount to the tort of outrage." *Id.*

3. Causation

With regard to the third element, a reasonable jury could find Simpson caused Doe's emotional distress. Under Alabama law, foreseeability is the "key" to proximate causation. *Vines v. Plantation Motor Lodge,* 336 So.2d 1338, 1339 (Ala.1976). A person who "by some act or omission sets in motion a series of events[ ] is not responsible for consequences of intervention of another agency, unless at the time of his original act or omission, the act of the intervening agency could reasonably be foreseen." *Id.* In simple terms, where the act of an intervening agent is reasonably foreseeable, a defendant may be held liable for damages caused by that agent. *See* Restatement (Third) of Torts: Liability for Physical & Emotional Harm § 19 cmt. d(Am. Law Inst.2010) ("[R]isk is evaluated by reference to the foreseeable . . . probability of harm of a foreseeable severity."). A jury could find Simpson proximately caused Doe's emotional distress because CJC's rape of Doe was a reasonably foreseeable consequence of the sting operation. Any plan that involves placing a middle school student alone in a bathroom with a known sexual harasser and asking the student to feign sexual interest in the harasser poses a high risk of emotional distress.

4. Severity of Emotional Distress

As to the fourth element, a jury could conclude the emotional distress Simpson caused was severe. It is hard to imagine what could cause emotional distress more severe than the psychological trauma of rape, and the record is replete with evidence about the anguish Doe has suffered. We reverse the grant of summary judgment to Simpson because her conduct satisfies all four elements of the tort of out-rage.

V. CONCLUSION

We reverse the grant of summary judgment to the Board on Doe's Title IX claim. p.985 To prevail on a student-on-student sexual harassment claim, a plaintiff must prove the funding recipient had actual knowledge the sexual harassment was severe, pervasive, and objectively offensive. Applying this standard, there is a genuine dispute of material fact as to whether Doe has satisfied all five elements necessary to succeed under Title IX.

Under element one, the parties do not contest the Board is a Title IX funding recipient. Under element two, Blair, Dunaway, and Terrell were appropriate persons capable of putting the Board on notice of sexual harassment and discrimination, but Simpson was not. A jury could find the Board learned all of the facts leading up to the rape and the fact that CJC had raped Doe.

As to element three, the harassment and discrimination Doe faced—of which the Board had knowledge—was severe, pervasive, and objectively offensive. CJC's sexual harassment of Doe was pervasive because he propositioned Doe for two weeks, school officials orchestrated the sting operation, and the sting operation resulted in the rape.

With regard to element four, a jury could find the Board clearly acted unreasonably and therefore was deliberately indifferent to the sexual harassment and discrimination Doe faced. Under element five, a jury could find the Board's deliberate indifference barred Doe's opportunity to continue her education at Sparkman. Since there are genuine questions of fact, the district court erred in granting summary judgment to the Board on Doe's Title IX claim.

We affirm the grant of summary judgment to the Board on Doe's § 1983 claim. Simpson's rape-bait scheme was not a known or obvious consequence of the "catch in the act" policy or the Board's allegedly inadequate training policies.

We reverse the grant of summary judgment to Blair on Doe's § 1983 equal protection claim. There is a genuine dispute of material fact as to whether Blair violated Doe's constitutional right to equal protection by acting with deliberate indifference to the rape of Doe. Viewing the evidence favorably to Doe, Blair violated clearly established law. No reasonable official in Blair's position would have believed doing nothing to reform Sparkman's sexual harassment policies was lawful in light of the clearly established principle that deliberate indifference to sexual harassment is an equal protection violation.

We reverse the grant of summary judgment to Dunaway on Doe's § 1983 equal protection claim. Viewing the evidence favorably to Doe, Dunaway acquiesced to and ratified the sting operation. She is not entitled to qualified immunity because every objectively reasonable government official facing the circumstances would have known the plan to use Doe as rape bait violated the Equal Protection Clause. For the same reason, we reverse the grant of summary judgment to Simpson on Doe's § 1983 equal protection claim.

We affirm the grant of summary judgment to Terrell on Doe's § 1983 equal protection claim because Terrell is entitled to qualified immunity. Unlike Blair, Terrell could not dictate the school's response to CJC's rape of Doe, and, unlike Dunaway, there is no evidence she ratified the sting operation.

We affirm the grant of summary judgment to Simpson for the alleged § 1983 substantive due process violation. Simpson is entitled to qualified immunity because deliberate indifference is not, without more, a basis for finding substantive due process liability in cases arising in the school context.

p.986 Moving to the state law claims, we affirm the grant of summary judgment to Blair for negligence/wantonness because he is entitled to state-agent immunity. Doe has not shown any of the exceptions to Alabama state-agent immunity apply to Blair's conduct. We affirm the denial of summary judgment to Dunaway. She is not entitled to state-agent immunity because there is a genuine dispute as to whether she acted beyond her authority by failing to report CJC's sexual harassment to Blair and instead ratifying Simpson's sting operation. Finally, we reverse the grant of summary judgment to Simpson for the tort of outrage because a jury could find Simpson should have known that emotional distress was likely to result from the sting operation, using Doe as rape-bait was extreme and outrageous, the sting operation caused Doe's distress, and that distress was severe.

In light of the foregoing reasons, the district court's summary judgment orders are affirmed in part and reversed in part, and this case is remanded.

AFFIRMED IN PART, REVERSED IN PART, AND REMANDED.

[*] Honorable John Antoon II, United States District Judge for the Middle District of Florida, sitting by designation.

[1] We grant James Hill's (the father of BHJ) motion to substitute BHJ, who has now reached the age of majority while this matter has been pending, as the named plaintiff and allow BHJ to proceed anonymously as Jane Doe.

[2] We refer to this incident as a rape, rather than an alleged rape, because in reviewing a motion for summary judgment "we are required to view the facts in the light most favorable to the nonmoving party." *See Sauls v. Pierce Cty. Sch. Dist.,* 399 F.3d 1279, 1281 (11th Cir.2005).

[3] All parties to this proceeding jointly consented to the exercise of full dispositive authority of the magistrate judge handling their case, pursuant to 28 U.S.C. § 636(c) and Federal Rule of Civil Procedure 73. We refer to the magistrate judge as the district court.

[4] Doe also appeals the district court's grant of summary judgment to Simpson for § 1983 substantive due process; to Blair for negligence/wantonness; and to Simpson for the tort of outrage. In her consolidated appeal, Dunaway argues the district court erred in denying her state-agent immunity for Doe's negligence/wantonness claim. We discuss these issues after resolving Doe's Title IX and § 1983 equal protection claims.

[5] Two policy manuals are in the record. The first was approved "June 1997" and titled "STUDENT SEXUAL HARASSMENT." The second was approved "June 24, 2010" and titled "6.10 *Student Anti-Harassment Policy.*" Blair testified he "believe[d]" the June 24, 2010 Policy Manual was in effect on January 22, 2010, but that is obviously a temporal impossibility. He also believed the June 1997 policy was in effect as of January 22, 2010. Viewing the facts in the light most favorable to Doe, only the June 1997 policy was effective as of January 22, 2010.

[6] We refer to this policy as the "catch in the act" policy because the parties have used that phrase in their briefing.

[7] The complaint also named CJC as a defendant. The district court dismissed the claims against CJC because he was an unrepresented minor and numerous attempts to appoint a guardian *ad litem* had proven unsuccessful. That order of dismissal is not on appeal.

[8] We have jurisdiction to consider a public official's interlocutory appeal from an order denying her state-law immunity where the disputed issue is whether the official acted outside her discretionary authority. *See Taylor v. Adams,* 221 F.3d 1254, 1260 n. 9 (11th Cir.2000).

[9] *See* 28 U.S.C. § 1367(a) (authorizing a district court to decline to exercise supplemental jurisdiction if, *inter alia,* "the district court has dismissed all claims over which it has original jurisdiction").

[10] Doe also argues the district court erred in failing to draw a spoliation inference against all Defendants for the school officials' destruction of CJC's disciplinary record. The district court did not abuse its discretion in denying Doe's request for an adverse spoliation inference. *See Mann v. Taser Int'l, Inc.,* 588 F.3d 1291, 1310 (11th Cir.2009) (reviewing district court's decision regarding spoliation sanctions for abuse of discretion). Under our precedent, "an adverse inference is drawn from a party's failure to preserve evidence only when the absence of that evidence is predicated on bad faith." *Bashir v. Amtrak,* 119 F.3d 929, 931 (11th Cir.1997). As the district court held, the timing and content of Doe's preservation letter do not establish Defendants destroyed CJC's 2009-2010 school year records in bad faith. Instead, the Board continued to follow the customary document retention policy by which disciplinary files were shredded each summer.

With regard to timing, Blair received the preservation letter from Doe's counsel in early May 2010, but the original complaint was not filed until September 23, 2010. Blair therefore received the letter roughly five months before Doe put the Board on explicit notice that she was bringing a Title IX claim whose success hinged on school officials' knowledge of CJC's sexual harassment history. Furthermore, it is undisputed that the summer—the time period between the submission of the preservation letter and the filing of the complaint—was the customary time of year when school officials shredded paper disciplinary files.

The content of the preservation letter likewise supports the district court's denial of sanctions. Notably, the letter did not request all of CJC's disciplinary records, but instead only the evidence "pertaining to" the "incident which occurred on January 22, 2010 at Sparkman Middle School." Defendants did, in fact, preserve records stemming directly from the rape of Doe. We note the narrow request for information in the preservation letter is not dispositive of Doe's spoliation claim because "the common-law obligation to preserve relevant material is not necessarily dependent upon the tender of a 'preservation letter.'" *Cache La Poudre Feeds, LLC v. Land O'Lakes, Inc.,* 244 F.R.D. 614, 623 (D.Colo. 2007); *cf. Thompson v. U.S. Dep't of Housing and Urban Dev.,* 219 F.R.D. 93, 100 (D.Md. 2003) (holding a party's failure to request the preservation of documents "does not vitiate the independent obligation of an adverse party to preserve such information"). A poorly worded preservation letter does not necessarily shield a defendant from spoliation sanctions solely because she complied with the letter's narrow request. In this case, however, the Board's compliance with the plain meaning of the preservation letter is another factor pointing against bad faith.

[11] In *Williams,* we described this test as comprising four elements, with the fourth element containing two parts: 4a and 4b. *Williams,* 477 F.3d at 1293, 1297-98. For purposes of this appeal, we apply *Williams* as a five-element test, designating 4a and 4b as separate elements. For the sake of clarity, we also rearrange our discussion of the elements in the following order: 1, 2, 4a, 3, 4b.

[12] Dunaway contends on appeal that *L.N. v. Monroe County Board of Education,* 141 So.3d 466 (Ala.2013) (per curiam) (no opinion), overruled *Caldwell.* Her reliance on that decision is misplaced. *See* Ala. R.App. P. 53(d) (stating "no opinion" affirmance orders "shall have no precedential value and shall not be cited in argument or briefs and shall not be used by any court within this state").

[13] Simpson has not asserted a state-agent immunity defense. *See Ryan v. Hayes,* 831 So.2d 21, 27-28 (Ala.2002) (stating state-agent immunity doctrine applies to "*asserted* State-agent-immunity defense") (emphasis added).

604 F.3d 1248 (2010)

Jane DOE, by and through Jane Doe's Mother and Father as parents and natural guardians, Jane Doe's Mother, Jane Doe's Father, individually, Plaintiffs-Appellants,

v.

SCHOOL BOARD OF BROWARD COUNTY, FLORIDA, Dr. Sam Scavella, Defendants-Appellees.

No. 09-10394.

United States Court of Appeals, Eleventh Circuit.

April 27, 2010.

Doe v. School Bd. of Broward County, Fla., 604 F. 3d 1248 (11th Cir. 2010)

p.1249 Stuart S. Mermelstein, Mermelstein & Horowitz, P.A., Aventura, FL, for Plaintiffs-Appellants.

Michael T. Burke, Johnson, Anselmo, Murdoch, Burke, Piper & McDuff, Debra Potter Klauber, Haliczer, Pettis & Schwamm, P.A., Ft. Lauderdale, FL, for Defendants-Appellees.

Before WILSON and ANDERSON, Circuit Judges, and RESTANI,[*] Judge.

p.1250 ANDERSON, Circuit Judge:

Jane Doe brought this action, by and through her parents, against the Broward County School Board ("the School Board") and Dr. Sam Scavella, former principal of her high school ("Scavella"), alleging that she was the victim of sexual harassment by her math teacher. Her complaint included claims under Title IX of the Education Amendments of 1972 ("Title IX"), 20 U.S.C. § 1681 *et. seq.*, and 42 U.S.C. § 1983. The district court granted summary judgment in favor of both defendants. Doe now appeals, arguing that disputed issues of fact remain as to the School Board's liability under Title IX and § 1983, making summary judgment improper, and that Scavella is not protected by qualified immunity from liability under § 1983. Because we find that a reasonable jury could conclude that the School Board responded with deliberate indifference to actual notice of sexual harassment, we reverse the district court's grant of summary judgment with respect to Doe's Title IX claim. We affirm the district court's grant of summary judgment in favor of both the School Board and Scavella with respect to Doe's § 1983 claims.

I. FACTS AND PROCEDURAL HISTORY

In reviewing a grant of summary judgment, we are required to view the facts in the light most favorable to the nonmoving party. *Sauls v. Pierce County Sch. Dist.*, 399 F.3d 1279, 1281 (11th Cir.2005). Therefore, we set forth the facts in the light most favorable to Doe.

Jane Doe was a fifteen-year-old ninth-grade student at Blanche Ely High School ("Blanche Ely") during the 2006-2007 school year. During that year, Doe was a student in Conraad Hoever's math class. According to Doe's complaint, in March

2007, Hoever sexually assaulted her in his classroom.[1] Blanche Ely's current principal requested a formal investigation, which resulted in Hoever's administrative leave and ultimate termination. Although this was the first instance of sexual harassment by Hoever of Doe, two other female students had previously filed complaints against Hoever for sexual harassment and misconduct. It is the School Board's and Principal Scavella's response to these complaints that forms the basis of Doe's Title IX and section 1983 claims.

The School Board first hired Hoever as a full-time math teacher at Blanche Ely in December 2002. At the end of the 2003-2004 school year, Blanche Ely's principal decided not to renew Hoever's annual contract because of poor teaching and classroom management skills. Dr. Scavella became Blanche Ely's principal at the beginning of the 2004-2005 school year and recommended to the School Board that Hoever be reinstated. It was during the 2004-2005 school year, when Scavella was acting principal, that two different female students filed complaints against Hoever.

A. First Complaint Against Hoever — The K.F. Incident

K.F. was an eleventh-grade student in Hoever's math class. In October 2004, she filed a complaint with Blanche Ely about three incidents occurring in Hoever's classroom. According to her written complaint, during the first week of school K.F. visited Hoever's classroom to ask for assistance with homework. During their meeting, Hoever made inappropriate comments to her, telling her she was "beautiful," "sexy," had a "flat stomach," and a "beautiful smile," and then gave her his phone number. K.F. told another student, Cassandra, p.1251 about Hoever's conduct the day after the incident. The second incident occurred a few weeks later when Hoever asked K.F. to remain after class. While alone with K.F. in his classroom, Hoever told her that he loved her, wanted to do "business" with her, and wanted her to be his girlfriend because she needed someone "special" to take care of her. When K.F. said she had to go to lunch, Hoever approached her, lifted up her shirt, and commented on her "flat stomach" and her "sexy" physique. K.F. told her cousin about Hoever's advances, and the cousin in turn told K.F.'s legal guardians. Her cousin gave her a tape recorder to secretly record Hoever's comments but her attempt was unsuccessful. Finally, in late October, K.F. alleged that she approached Hoever about her "D" grade in his class, and Hoever told her that she "couldn't have a good grade" because she did not "want to do business." That day, K.F. reported all of Hoever's alleged sexual advances to Principal Scavella.

Principal Scavella responded by conducting an informal on-site investigation of the alleged misconduct and requested written statements from K.F. and Hoever. In his written statement, Hoever admitted that on one occasion K.F. had asked him to help find her a sponsor for her modeling career, and he had stated that she was "tall, slim, and sexually appealing" for the job, but that finding her a sponsor was "strictly business." Hoever also stated that he had removed K.F. from his class earlier that day for being disruptive and that K.F. had threatened to go to Scavella on numerous prior occasions, saying "You don't know what I can do."[2]

Scavella then contacted the School Board's Special Investigative Unit ("SIU") and requested a formal investigation through the filing of a Personal Investigation Request, which classified the incident as "sexual harassment." The following day, SIU

Executive Director Dr. Melita assigned the investigation to Officer Wollschlager. The School Board also provided Hoever with notice of the formal SIU investigation and directed him not to "engage the complainant ... in any conversation regarding the matter under investigation"; placed him on administrative leave pending the outcome of the investigation; and banned him from returning to the high school premises.

Investigator Wollschlager interviewed K.F. and obtained her sworn taped testimony about the incident, which largely tracked her prior statements except for the inclusion of an additional incident in which Hoever told her if she "did business" with him then she would not "ever have to work hard" and could have a "B" grade in his class. In his taped sworn statement, Hoever stated that K.F. was a poor student with behavioral problems who had threatened to go to Scavella on several occasions if she did not get a good grade in his class. He also denied ever commenting to K.F. that he wanted to take care of her, "do business," or that he picked up her shirt and commented on her stomach.

Wollschlager also met with two other students who both stated that they had not seen K.F. and Hoever ever speaking after class. Wollschlager did not interview K.F.'s friend Cassandra, her cousin, or her guardians, the only individuals who allegedly knew of the incidents, because he determined that they had no first-hand knowledge of the events and could only report what K.F. told them. A senior staff member at SIU reviewed the Wollschlager p.1252 report that the evidence was inconclusive as to whether any sexual misconduct occurred, and the report was sent to the Professional Standards Committee, of which Melita was a member, for a "probable cause" or "no probable cause" finding. The Committee recommended that no probable cause existed for additional disciplinary action against Hoever due to the inconclusive results of the investigation and the fact that the incident was "1 on 1 — no video — no eyewitnesses." Pursuant to school policy, Hoever returned to teach at Blanche Ely for the second semester of the 2004-2005 school year.

B. Second Complaint Against Hoever — The S.W. Incident

Upon his return, Hoever taught an algebra class in which S.W., a tenth-grader, was a student. S.W. filed a complaint against Hoever in May 2005 regarding two incidents of sexual harassment. According to her complaint, some time during the semester Hoever asked her, in response to a question about a math problem, if she wanted to "ride around with him" over the weekend. She declined. Then in May, she and four other female students were listening to music at Hoever's desk during class. Some of the students departed, leaving only S.W. and one other student, Naomi, with Hoever in the classroom. Hoever started making a compact disc of music for S.W. and Naomi, and he allegedly touched S.W.'s leg while trying to hold her hand. At some point, Naomi left, and Hoever and S.W. remained in the classroom alone. He commented that S.W. seemed "very grown up," that he liked how "soft" her hands feel and how her "lips look." Then, according to S.W., Hoever "came around his desk to where I was standing and told me to pull up my jacket and my shirt so he can see my stomach." Hoever followed S.W. as she left the classroom, gave her the compact disc, and appeared to be waiting for her "to give him a hug."[3] She reported the incident immediately. In her deposition, S.W. testified that she had not reported the first incident because she knew that Hoever had gotten in trouble for the same thing before; the school had "only suspended him" in response; and the school was "not going to do anything about it because he's friends with the principal."

In response to S.W.'s complaint, Scavella testified that he directed the Assistant Principal to conduct an informal on-site investigation.[4] Several students, none of whom were named in S.W.'s complaint, were asked to give written statements about the incident, and Scavella called Hoever for a statement. Notably, the students interviewed did not include S.W.'s friend Naomi, the only student named in her complaint, and included some male students, even though S.W.'s complaint reported that "four girls" were with her at Hoever's desk on the day of the incident. The interviewed students denied witnessing anything improper between Hoever and S.W. In his statement, Hoever denied the allegation, claiming that he had only pushed S.W.'s hand away when she reached toward his lap top computer, but admitted to using class time to make compact discs for students. No one interviewed S.W. about the incident after she filed her written complaint.

p.1253 Scavella then called Dr. Melita, the SIU Personnel Director, and reported that the school's informal investigation did not support S.W.'s complaint or the allegation that Hoever made inappropriate comments or touched her leg. Melita testified that Scavella did not inform him that Hoever was the teacher involved. Scavella testified that he did not remember whether he told Melita that Hoever was the accused teacher and that he did not draw a connection between the similarities in the K.F. and the S.W. complaints at the time. After hearing from Scavella that he thought students were ganging up on a teacher, Melita concluded that the complaint did not warrant formal investigation. Scavella handled the matter on-site by giving Hoever a letter of reprimand for using class time to make compact discs. No one ever advised S.W. about the final disposition of her complaint. Because the S.W. incident occurred at the end of the school year, S.W. was permitted to take her final exam in the front office. No other administrative action was taken.

After the 2004-2005 school year, Scavella resigned as Blanche Ely's principal. Before resigning, Scavella gave Hoever a "satisfactory" performance evaluation and recommended that he be retained for the 2005-2006 school year. The new principal was not informed of the prior complaints against Hoever. There is no record evidence that any continued monitoring of Hoever occurred. The record contains no additional complaints against Hoever until Doe's sexual assault in March 2007.

C. The Instant Suit

Doe filed this federal lawsuit in the Southern District of Florida, alleging various claims under Title IX and § 1983 and requesting relief in the form of compensatory and punitive damages. Doe's Amended Complaint alleged that the School Board sexually discriminated against her in violation of Title IX by exhibiting deliberate indifference to known prior harassment by Hoever against female students at Blanche Ely High School (Count III). She also alleged that the School Board and Scavella violated her constitutional right not to be sexually abused by a state official acting under color of law pursuant to § 1983 due to the School Board's policy, practice, or custom of conducting cursory investigations of student complaints

(Count I) and Scavella's deliberate indifference to the risk of sexual abuse of Blanche Ely students (Count IV).[5]

The School Board and Scavella filed separate Motions for Summary Judgment, with Scavella asserting the defense of qualified immunity. The district court granted summary judgment for both defendants. The district court held that the evidence could not support a finding that the School Board acted with deliberate indifference under Title IX or that it had a policy, practice, or custom in violation of § 1983. The court also determined that Doe failed to show a causal connection between Scavella's actions and Doe's sexual assault. Therefore, the court determined that Scavella was entitled to summary judgment with respect to Doe's § 1983 claim. This appeal ensued.

II. STANDARD OF REVIEW

We review *de novo* a district court's grant of summary judgment, applying the same legal standards as the district court. *Johnson v. Bd. of Regents of Univ. of Ga.*, 263 F.3d 1234, 1242 (11th Cir.2001). These legal standards dictate that we are required to resolve all reasonable inferences p.1254 in favor of the non-moving party and that summary judgment should be upheld only if the pleadings show that there is no issue as to any material fact and the moving party is entitled to judgment as a matter of law. *Hawkins v. Sarasota County Sch. Bd.*, 322 F.3d 1279, 1280-81 (11th Cir.2003). Therefore, "[i]f a reasonable fact finder evaluating the evidence could draw more than one inference from the facts, and if that inference introduces a genuine issue of material fact, then the court should not grant the summary judgment motion." *Samples ex rel. Samples v. City of Atlanta*, 846 F.2d 1328, 1330 (11th Cir.1988).

III. DISCUSSION

A. The School Board's Liability under Title IX

Title IX provides that "[n]o person in the United States shall, on the basis of sex, be excluded from participation in, be denied the benefits of, or be subjected to discrimination under any education program or activity receiving Federal financial assistance." 20 U.S.C. § 1681(a). The Supreme Court has recognized an implied right of action for money damages in Title IX cases of intentional sexual discrimination and has held that a teacher's sexual harassment of a student constitutes actionable discrimination under Title IX. *Franklin v. Gwinnett County Pub. Schs.*, 503 U.S. 60, 75-76, 112 S.Ct. 1028, 1037-38, 117 L.Ed.2d 208 (1992). In the case of teacher-on-student sexual harassment, our analysis is governed by the Supreme Court's decision in *Gebser v. Lago Vista Independent School District*, 524 U.S. 274, 118 S.Ct. 1989, 141 L.Ed.2d 277 (1998).

In *Gebser*, the Supreme Court made plain that not all sexual harassment by teachers is sufficient to impose liability on a school district. Because "Title IX is predicated upon notice to an 'appropriate person' and an opportunity to rectify any violation," *id.* at 290, 118 S.Ct. at 1999 (citing 20 U.S.C. § 1682), the Court explained that school districts may not be held liable on a theory of *respondeat superior* or mere constructive notice, *id.* at 285, 118 S.Ct. at 1997. Rather, Title IX liability arises only where "an official of the school district who at a minimum has authority to institute corrective measures on the district's behalf has actual notice of, and is deliberately indifferent to, the teacher's misconduct." *Id.* at 277, 118 S.Ct. at 1993.

Therefore, applying the *Gebser* framework to the summary judgment context requires three related inquiries. First, the plaintiff must be able to identify an "appropriate person" under Title IX, i.e., a school district official with the authority to take corrective measures in response to actual notice of sexual harassment. *See Floyd v. Waiters,* 171 F.3d 1264, 1264 (11th Cir.1999). Second, the substance of that actual notice must be sufficient to alert the school official of the possibility of the Title IX plaintiff's harassment. *See Gebser,* 524 U.S. at 291, 118 S.Ct. at 2000. And finally, the official with such notice must exhibit deliberate indifference to the harassment. *See Sauls,* 399 F.3d at 1284.

i. Appropriate Person

Because the district court concluded that the School Board did not act with deliberate indifference, it found it was "not necessary to reach the issue of whether [the School Board] had actual notice of Hoever's misconduct." Likewise, the court did not address "who, within the school system, must have notice of the harassment for the school board to be considered to have actual knowledge." *See Hawkins,* 322 F.3d at 1285.

The Supreme Court has not clearly delineated which school officials are appropriate persons for purposes of Title IX p.1255 actual notice. Nor has our circuit. In a pre-*Gebser* decision, we held that actual notice to a direct supervisor of a school janitor, who was "at least three levels removed from the superintendent of schools position," could not expose the school district to Title IX liability. *Floyd v. Waiters,* 133 F.3d 786, 793 & n. 15 (11th Cir. 1998), *vacated by* 525 U.S. 802, 119 S.Ct. 33, 142 L.Ed.2d 25 (1998), *reinstated in* 171 F.3d 1264 (11th Cir.1999). In reinstating our decision in light of *Gebser,* we articulated our only elaboration of the Supreme Court's "appropriate person" requirement, commenting that the official with notice of the harassment must be "high enough up the chain-of-command that his acts constitute an official decision by the school district itself not to remedy the misconduct." *Floyd,* 171 F.3d at 1264, *cert. denied,* 528 U.S. 891, 120 S.Ct. 215, 145 L.Ed.2d 181 (1999). A janitorial supervisor was plainly not "high enough up the chain-of-command" for his deliberate indifference to known harassment to impose liability on the school district. *See id.* Our subsequent panels facing the question have elected to rest their Title IX holdings on other grounds, bypassing the issue. *See, e.g., Hawkins,* 322 F.3d at 1288 (refraining from addressing the question of whether a teacher could be a source of actual notice to the school board in a student-on-student sexual harassment case); *Davis v. DeKalb County Sch. Dist.,* 233 F.3d 1367, 1372 (11th Cir.2000) (stating it was "unnecessary to decide whether Duncan, as principal of Knollwood Elementary, was a supervisory official with authority to take corrective action on behalf of the school district").

Here, it is undisputed that the principal of Blanche Ely High School, Sam Scavella, had actual notice of the K.F. and S.W. complaints. Both K.F. and S.W. filed written complaints with Blanche Ely of Hoever's alleged harassment, which Scavella reviewed and acted upon. Doe has litigated her case on the theory that Scavella is an "appropriate person" to receive Title IX actual notice, although neither party has briefed this issue. Neither the School Board nor Scavella has contested — before the district court or on appeal — Doe's assertion that Scavella's actual notice of the prior complaints could form the basis of the School Board's Title IX liability. More importantly, both the School Board and Scavella conceded at oral argument that Principal Scavella could "initiate corrective action" or place "other restrictions" on an offending teacher in response to a sexual harassment complaint, even if he could not take final adverse employment actions such as terminating the teacher. Therefore, we treat Scavella as an "appropriate person" to receive actual notice under Title IX for purposes of this appeal.[6]

Even if the parties disputed this issue, we would not hesitate in concluding that Principal Scavella, as the highest-ranking school official on site at Blanche Ely High School, was "high enough on the chain-of-command" to impute liability to the School Board. This position is in harmony with the Supreme Court's treatment of Title IX claims. *See Davis v. Monroe County Bd. of Educ.,* 526 U.S. 629, 653-54, 119 S.Ct. 1661, 1676, 143 L.Ed.2d 839 (1999) (extending Title IX liability and *Gebser*'s actual notice and deliberate indifference requirements to the context of student-on-student sexual harassment); *Gebser,* 524 U.S. at 291, 118 S.Ct. at 2000.

In both *Gebser* and *Davis,* the school principal was the highest school district official with knowledge of the alleged sexual harassment. And in both cases the Court appeared to presume that the principal could be an appropriate person under Title IX's enforcement scheme. In *Gebser,* it was the substance of the actual notice to the principal, not his identity, that was fatal to the plaintiff's Title IX claim. *See* 524 U.S. at 291, 118 S.Ct. at 2000 (affirming summary judgment because a teacher's inappropriate comments were "plainly insufficient to alert the principal to the possibility" that the teacher was involved in a sexual relationship with a student). In *Davis,* the Court held that the plaintiff had sufficiently pled a claim for relief under Title IX where she alleged that her daughter was the victim of repeated acts of sexual harassment and no disciplinary action was taken by the school or school board. 526 U.S. at 653-54, 119 S.Ct. at 1676. Significantly, the Court found that "[t]he complaint also suggest[ed] that petitioner may be able to show both actual knowledge and deliberate indifference on the part of the Board." *Id.* at 654, 119 S.Ct. at 1676.

Moreover, the majority of our sister circuits addressing the issue have interpreted the *Gebser* and *Davis* opinions as standing for the proposition that at least in some circumstances, if not generally, a principal enjoys ample authority to "take corrective measures" in response to allegations of teacher or student sexual harassment. *See Plamp v. Mitchell Sch. Dist. No. 17-2,* 565 F.3d 450, 457 (8th Cir.2009) ("It is apparent from Supreme Court precedent, however, that school principals are considered 'appropriate persons' in the Title IX analysis."); *Warren ex rel. Good v. Reading Sch. Dist.,* 278 F.3d 163, 171 (3d Cir. 2002) ("[W]e think that a school principal who is entrusted with the responsibility and authority normally associated with that position will ordinarily be 'an appropriate person' under Title IX."); *Vance v. Spencer County Pub. Sch. Dist.,* 231 F.3d 253, 259 (6th Cir.2000) (upholding jury verdict and concluding that student satisfied actual notice requirement where student informed the principal about a teacher's sexual misconduct); *Murrell v. Sch. Dist. No. 1, Denver, Colo.,* 186 F.3d 1238, 1247 (10th Cir.1999) (finding "little room for doubt that the highest-ranking administrator at GWHS exercised substantial control of" a harassing student during school hours so that her "knowledge may be charged to the School District"). *See also Doe ex rel. Doe v. Dallas Indep. Sch. Dist.,* 220 F.3d 380, 384 (5th Cir.2000) (assuming without deciding that the principal was an official with the power to remedy discrimination on behalf of the school district). *But see Baynard v. Malone,* 268 F.3d 228, 239 (4th Cir.2001) (holding over a vigorous dissent that a principal cannot be the recipient of actual notice where the principal has "no independent authority to suspend, reassign, or terminate" offending teachers).

However, we also note that the ultimate question of who is an appropriate person is "necessarily a fact-based inquiry" because "officials' roles vary among school districts." *Murrell,* 186 F.3d at 1247. Nonetheless, we find ample support in the specific factual context here to accept the parties' concession of Scavella as an appropriate person within Title IX's administrative scheme. The record reflects the School Board's express delegation of authority to district principals to take corrective measures in response to sexual harassment complaints. According to the School Board's "Incident Process for Administrative Action," the principal, as p.1257 school administrator, is imbued with absolute discretion at a "key decision point" in the administrative process. It is the principal who has responsibility to conduct the first on-site investigation; who enjoys discretion to request formal investigation or proceed informally; and who can determine that a complaint is meritless and requires no further inquiry. In other words, the School Board policies in this case delegated to Principal Scavella the authority to conduct the first on-site investigation, to decide that the complaint had no merit, and to terminate the investigation at that point. This is what Scavella did with respect to S.W.'s complaint.

Furthermore, we do not think that the Supreme Court, in recognizing a private right of action under Title IX against school districts for sexual harassment of students, intended to insulate school districts from liability where the "highest ranking school official present at the school every day" who is typically "the first line of responsibility for ensuring that the students in her school are safe" has actual knowledge of a teacher's sexual harassment of students. *See Baynard,* 268 F.3d at 242-43 (Michael, J., dissenting in part). Nor are we persuaded by the Fourth Circuit's minority position that the Supreme Court intended final employment decisions such as suspending, terminating, or reassigning an offending teacher to be the *only* corrective measures giving an official the power to remedy sexual harassment. *See id.* at 239. Here Scavella, as principal, is equipped with many other means of deterring or stopping sexual harassment of students, such as admonishing the teacher, conducting a thorough preliminary investigation, swiftly reporting the abuse, and monitoring the teacher's behavior. Therefore, we treat Principal Scavella as an "appropriate person" to receive Title IX actual notice for purposes of this appeal.

ii. Actual Notice

We now turn to our second inquiry under Title IX's actual notice requirement: whether the K.F. and S.W. complaints were sufficient in substance to alert Scavella to the possibility of Doe's sexual assault. Although the district court found it unnecessary to reach this issue, it stated in dicta that the K.F. and S.W. complaints were insufficient to provide actual notice to the School Board of Doe's harassment for two reasons: Doe's sexual assault was the first incident of harassment by Hoever against Doe specifically; and the K.F. and S.W. complaints alleged only inappropriate conduct that did not rise to the level of Doe's violent sexual assault. We agree with Doe that the district court too strictly construed *Gebser*'s actual notice requirement in emphasizing these two distinctions.

First, no circuit has interpreted *Gebser*'s actual notice requirement so as to require notice of the prior harassment of the Title IX plaintiff *herself*. *See, e.g., Escue v. N. Okla. Coll.*, 450 F.3d 1146, 1154 (10th Cir. 2006) ("Although *Gebser* makes clear that actual notice requires more than a simple report of inappropriate conduct by a teacher... the actual notice standard does not set the bar so high that a school district is not put on notice until it receives a clearly credible report of sexual abuse from the plaintiff-student.") (internal quotation and citation omitted); *Baynard*, 268 F.3d at 238 n. 9 ("We note that a Title IX plaintiff is not required to demonstrate actual knowledge that a particular student was being abused.").

Notably, we have held in a Title IX student-on-student harassment case that the plaintiff sufficiently alleged actual notice where the primary substance of that notice differed significantly from the circumstances of the plaintiff's harassment. *See Williams v. Bd. of Regents of the* p.1258 *Univ. Sys. of Ga.*, 477 F.3d 1282, 1288-90, 1294 (11th Cir.2007). In *Williams*, we held that a Title IX plaintiff who suffered a violent sexual assault in a UGA basketball player's dorm room sufficiently alleged actual notice to UGA and its Athletic Department to withstand a motion to dismiss. *Id.* at 1294-95. Relevant to the court's analysis of actual notice was the basketball player's prior sexual harassment of a female store clerk and employees from the player's former university, which were both out-of-state incidents occurring two years before the plaintiff's assault. On the authority of *Williams*, we reject the School Board's argument that the substance of the complaints with respect to K.F. and S.W. differed from Doe's to the extent that the prior incidents provided no notice, and we further reject the School Board's contention that, because there was no additional harassment in the intervening twenty-one months between the S.W. complaint and Doe's sexual assault, there could be no actual notice of the possibility of Doe's sexual assault.

With respect to the district court's second point, *Gebser* does hold that some prior allegations of harassment may be sufficiently minimal and far afield from the conduct underlying the plaintiff's Title IX claim that they would not alert a school district official of the risk of a Title IX plaintiff's sexual harassment. 524 U.S. at 291, 118 S.Ct. at 2000 (holding that a teacher's sexually suggestive comments during class were "plainly insufficient to alert the principal to the possibility that [the teacher] was involved in a sexual relationship with a student"). Similarly, we have held that there was no actual notice of the potential sexual molestation of plaintiffs where the only prior complaint against the teacher alleged an "incidental touching" during a touch football game and a "perceived imminent" touching at a public water fountain. *Davis*, 233 F.3d at 1373. However, the K.F. and the S.W. complaints alleged far more than an incidental touching or mere inappropriate comments.

Unlike the harassment allegations in *Gebser*, which consisted solely of comments made to a group of students during class time, K.F. and S.W. both alleged overtly sexual conduct with both a verbal and physical component, directed at them individually, occurring while the students were alone with Hoever in his classroom.[7] Both students accused Hoever of propositioning them on more than one occasion for dates and sex and commenting on their bodies in a sexual manner. In the case of K.F., she alleged that Hoever physically lifted up her shirt to look at her stomach. In the case of S.W., she alleged that Hoever told her to lift up her shirt and touched her leg while trying to hold her hand. Moreover, unlike the prior allegations of harassment in *Davis*, these alleged touchings did not occur in a context in which touching a student may have been appropriate or accidental, such as an athletic event. Nor did the prior allegations against Hoever involve only a single complaint of a targeted incident against a student.

Moreover, as our decision in *Williams* demonstrates, lesser harassment may still provide actual notice of sexually violent conduct, for it is the risk of such conduct that the Title IX recipient has the duty to deter. In *Williams,* the plaintiff, who was p.1259 a victim of a violent sexual assault and rape in a UGA basketball player's dorm room, did not allege that the University had actual notice of the player's history of raping female students. *See* 477 F.3d at 1294. Yet we still found her complaint sufficient to withstand a motion to dismiss where she alleged that the University actively recruited the player and failed to sufficiently monitor his behavior despite actual notice of a history of lesser sexual harassment. *See id.* The player had allegedly groped female employees by "putting his hands down their pants" and "whistled at and made lewd suggestions to a female store clerk." *Id.* at 1290. If these unrelated incidents could state a Title IX claim, the harassment alleged in the K.F. and S.W. complaints, which resembled Doe's assault in significant respects — all incidents occurred in Hoever's classroom, between classes, and with his female math students — could provide actual notice to the School Board.

We also do not find it determinative of the School Board's liability that the results of the K.F. and S.W. investigations were ultimately inconclusive as to Hoever's actual sexual misconduct. Even if prior complaints by other students are not clearly credible, at some point "a supervisory school official knows ... that a school employee is a substantial risk to sexually abuse children." *Escue,* 450 F.3d at 1154 (internal citation and quotation omitted). *See also Williams v. Paint Valley Local Sch. Dist.,* 400 F.3d 360, 363 (6th Cir.2005) (requiring actual notice that a teacher poses a "substantial risk of sexual abuse to children in the school district"). A reasonable jury could find that Scavella had such knowledge. The K.F. and S.W. complaints, when viewed collectively, provided actual notice to Principal Scavella of a pattern of sexual harassment and a series of related allegations occurring over a period of nine months in Hoever's math classroom. We think these allegations are sufficient to satisfy Doe's burden of raising a material issue of fact on the issue of actual notice. The simple fact that these prior incidents were unconfirmed and did not escalate to a violent sexual assault akin to Doe's cannot as a matter of law absolve the School Board of Title IX liability.

iii. Deliberate Indifference

In addition to requiring that an appropriate person have actual notice of the teacher's misconduct, a Title IX plaintiff must show that the official was deliberately indifferent to that misconduct. *Gebser,* 524 U.S. at 277, 118 S.Ct. at 1993. Deliberate indifference is an exacting standard; school administrators will only be deemed deliberately indifferent if their "response to the harassment or lack thereof is clearly unreasonable in light of the known circumstances." *Davis,* 526 U.S. at 648, 119 S.Ct. at 1674. In essence, Title IX's premise "is an official decision by the recipient not to remedy the violation." *Gebser,* 524 U.S. at 290, 118 S.Ct. at 1999.

The district court concluded that the School Board was not deliberately indifferent to Hoever's misconduct because "Scavella confronted Hoever, obtained statements from each student who lodged complaints against Hoever, and informed [the Special Investigative Unit] of the sexual misconduct allegations." The district court reasoned that although these actions were ultimately ineffective in preventing Hoever's assault of Doe, as a matter of law they were not "clearly unreasonable in light of the known circumstances." We disagree.

Although it would be mere speculation to conclude that a perfect investigation and more vigorous response to the complaints would have prevented Doe's sexual assault, that is not our inquiry here. We only face the question of whether the district court erred in concluding that a jury, as a matter p.1260 of law, could *not* find that Scavella's response to the K.F. and S.W. complaints was clearly unreasonable under the known circumstances. Viewing the facts in the light most favorable to Doe, we conclude that she raised a material issue of fact as to whether the School Board was deliberately indifferent to Hoever's alleged sexual misconduct. *See Sauls,* 399 F.3d at 1287 (affirming summary judgment for school district because plaintiff failed to create a genuine issue of material fact that it acted with deliberate indifference). Therefore, the district court erred in granting summary judgment to the School Board.

We reach this conclusion even though it is undisputed that Principal Scavella and the School Board took *some* action in response to K.F. and S.W.'s sexual harassment allegations. Granted, this is not a situation in which a school district "made no effort whatsoever either to investigate or to put an end to the harassment." *Davis,* 526 U.S. at 654, 119 S.Ct. at 1676. In *Davis,* the Supreme Court had no trouble concluding there that a failure to take *any* disciplinary action in response to a student's "severe, pervasive, and objectively offensive" harassment of a peer could constitute deliberate indifference under Title IX's standard.[8] *Id.* at 653, 119 S.Ct. at 1676 (reversing district court's dismissal of plaintiff's Title IX complaint). Here, in fact, the School Board's response to the *K.F. complaint* was thorough, albeit deficient in some respects. After K.F. filed her complaint regarding three incidents of sexual harassment by Hoever, Scavella obtained written statements from Hoever and K.F., timely reported the incident to the School Board's Special Investigative Unit, and in his discretion requested a formal investigation. The School Board placed Hoever on administrative leave for the remainder of the semester. An investigator interviewed both K.F. and Hoever, obtained their sworn statements, and filed a report with the School Board's Professional Standards Committee. The Committee reviewed the investigative report and concluded that there was insufficient evidence to support "probable cause" for further disciplinary action against Hoever.

If we were examining the School Board's response to the K.F. incident alone, it is unlikely that this investigation, though imperfect, could be viewed as "clearly unreasonable in light of the known circumstances." Even though the investigator arguably should have interviewed other witnesses, including K.F.'s guardians, her cousin, and her friend Cassandra — who could have corroborated K.F.'s claim that the sexual harassment was ongoing and not just a fabrication to dispute her "D" grade in Hoever's class[9] — this omission cannot be said to represent a decision by the School Board effectively "not to remedy the violation." *See Gebser,* 524 U.S. at 290, 118 S.Ct. at 1999. K.F.'s complaint was the first allegation of sexual misconduct against Hoever by a Blanche Ely student. Therefore, even the School Board's failure to institute informal corrective measures such as admonishing Hoever to avoid his female students between classes or monitoring his classroom for the appearance of any impropriety probably p.1261 would not, as of this stage, render the School Board's response clearly unreasonable "in light of the known circumstances."

However, the "known circumstances" from which we evaluate the reasonableness of a School Board's response changed significantly once S.W. filed her complaint. It is the School Board's response to this complaint, in light of the known circumstance that a prior female student had also accused Hoever of sexual harassment in the same school year, that we conclude raises a sufficient fact issue of deliberate indifference to overcome the School Board's summary judgment motion. Although we have recognized that a school district is not deliberately indifferent simply because the measures it takes are ultimately ineffective in stopping a teacher from harassing the plaintiffs, *Davis,* 233 F.3d at 1375, we also agree with the Sixth Circuit that "where a school district has knowledge that its remedial action is inadequate and ineffective, it is required to take reasonable action in light of those circumstances to eliminate the behavior," *Vance,* 231 F.3d at 261 (affirming jury verdict for plaintiff and denial of school district's Rule 50 motion for judgment as a matter of law). Once Scavella had actual notice of a second complaint, his failure to institute any corrective measures aimed at ferreting out the possibility of Hoever's sexual harassment of his students could constitute deliberate indifference.

Although S.W.'s allegations against Hoever were not as serious as those alleged by K.F., they still constituted sexual harassment. Taking reasonable inferences from the summary judgment record in Doe's favor, Hoever asked K.F. to "ride around with him" during the weekend, essentially asking a student for a date; he tried to hold her hand; he made sexually suggestive comments about her lips; and asked her to lift up her shirt to show him her stomach. In response to a complaint containing these allegations, and with the knowledge of their similarity to K.F.'s prior allegations, Principal Scavella effectively did nothing other than obtain a written statement from S.W. and Hoever. There was no investigation, formal or informal. No one interviewed S.W. No one interviewed Naomi, S.W.'s friend who was named in her complaint. Instead, an unidentified person obtained written statements from five students who appeared to have no connection to S.W.'s allegations. Notably, these students included males, despite the fact that S.W.'s complaint stated that four girls surrounded Hoever's desk the day of the incident.

Most unreasonably, and almost incredibly, however, is the fact that when Scavella made a telephone call to Dr. Melita regarding the S.W. complaint, he did not advise Dr. Melita that Hoever was the accused teacher. Dr. Melita did not question Scavella as to whether the teacher had a prior history of harassment complaints, and Scavella admitted in his deposition that he did not at the time draw a connection between the K.F. and S.W. incidents.[10] Thus, a reasonable jury could conclude that Scavella had full knowledge of the K.F. complaint and the subsequent investigation of Hoever yet he knowingly failed to apprise Dr. Melita that the S.W. complaint involved a sexual harassment allegation against the same teacher who had been the subject of a formal investigation just months earlier. Instead, Scavella recommended that no further investigation occur, and his only subsequent remedial actions taken were permitting S.W. to take her final exam in the school office instead of Hoever's classroom and placing a letter p.1262 in Hoever's file admonishing him for using class time to make students compact discs of music. Scavella completed his tenure at Blanche Ely High School by giving Hoever a "satisfactory" performance rating and recommended his retention for the following school year. The incoming principal was never informed of Hoever's history, no informal warning was issued for Hoever to avoid female students, and no recommendation was made to monitor Hoever's classroom.

In granting summary judgment for a school district in our prior decisions, we have repeatedly recognized that a school district's reasonable response to sexual harassment may include corrective action such as monitoring and admonishing an accused teacher or student despite the inconclusive nature of the school's investigation into the misconduct. *See Sauls,* 399 F.3d at 1285-86 (explaining that school officials "investigat[ed] the allegations," "interview[ed] the relevant parties," and "also consistently monitored Blythe's conduct and warned her about her interaction with students"); *Davis,* 233 F.3d at 1373-74. In *Sauls,* after a first incident, "[e]ven though Williamson failed to find any evidence supporting the allegation, he nonetheless issued a warning to Blythe. He directed Blythe to avoid any situation that could be construed as inappropriate and warned that her interaction with students must always be beyond reproach." 399 F.3d at 1286. After a second incident, "[a]lthough PCSD still did not have any evidence of misconduct by Blythe, Dr. Williams took corrective action[,] ... admonish[ing] Blythe both orally and in writing, and direct[ing] her to avoid even the appearance of impropriety when dealing with students." *Id.* And finally, after a third incident, a school official instructed the new high school principal "to closely monitor Blythe and Dustin, to prevent any unnecessary contact between the two, and to report any suspicious behavior." *Id.* at 1287. Similarly, in *Davis,* we explained that "[e]ven though the investigation failed to reveal reasonable evidence of inappropriate conduct by Mency, Duncan took immediate corrective action." 233 F.3d at 1373. "Duncan instructed Mency to avoid all contact with Burrell other than class;" "Duncan also forbade Mency from being alone with Burrell or any female student;" and "Duncan also monitored Mency for any indiscretions." *Id.* at 1374.

These school districts seemed to recognize that inconclusive investigations are common, especially when alleged harassment occurs behind closed doors. Therefore, a reasonable response under the known circumstances may include taking informal corrective action in an abundance of caution to ensure that future misconduct does not occur. Here, once it was a known circumstance that Hoever had been accused of multiple acts of sexual harassment in his classroom behind closed doors, such cautionary measures could have contributed to the reasonableness of the School Board's response.

In the summary judgment posture of this case, we of course take all reasonable inferences in Doe's favor. After a careful review of the record and for the foregoing reasons, we conclude that Doe has adduced sufficient evidence to create a genuine issue of material fact as to whether Scavella's response to the cumulative complaints of K.F. and S.W. was clearly unreasonable in light of the known circumstances. Additionally, we find that Doe has sufficiently alleged causation. As we concluded in

Williams, a reasonable jury could also find that these deficiencies caused Doe's sexual harassment by "substantially increas[ing] the risk faced by female students" at Blanche Ely. *See Williams*, 477 F.3d at 1296 (reversing the district court's dismissal of plaintiff's Title IX complaint because "placing Cole in a student dormitory and failing to supervise him in any way or to p.1263 inform him of their expectations of him under the applicable sexual harassment policy ... substantially increased the risk faced by female students at UGA").

In sum, we cannot say that as a matter of law it was reasonable for Scavella to ignore an alleged pattern of sexual misconduct by one of Blanche Ely's teachers, failing to even inform the SIU of Hoever's identity in relation to S.W.'s complaint. Nor can we accept the district court's conclusion that merely because school officials "confronted Hoever," "obtained statements" from the complaining students, and "informed the SIU of the sexual misconduct allegations" (while omitting material details), the School Board's response was reasonable. To do so would permit future school districts to satisfy their obligations under Title IX without ever evaluating the known circumstances at all. The Title IX inquiry is contextual: it does not require school districts to simply do *something* in response to sexual harassment; rather, they must respond in a manner that is not "clearly unreasonable in light of the *known* circumstances." *Davis*, 526 U.S. at 648, 119 S.Ct. at 1674 (emphasis added). We conclude that the district court erred in holding that despite these serious deficiencies the School Board's response was not deliberately indifferent as a matter of law.

B. The School Board's Municipal Liability under § 1983

Doe further argues that the School Board should be held liable for her injuries under § 1983. As in Title IX, municipalities may not be held liable for constitutional deprivations on the theory of *respondeat superior*. *Denno v. Sch. Bd. of Volusia County, Fla.*, 218 F.3d 1267, 1276 (11th Cir.2000). Instead, "municipal liability is limited to action for which the municipality is actually responsible." *Pembaur v. City of Cincinnati*, 475 U.S. 469, 479-80, 106 S.Ct. 1292, 1298, 89 L.Ed.2d 452 (1986). Therefore, a municipality may be held liable "only if such constitutional torts result from an official government policy, the actions of an official fairly deemed to represent government policy, or a custom or practice so pervasive and well-settled that it assumes the force of law." *Denno*, 218 F.3d at 1276. In addition to identifying conduct attributable to the municipality, a plaintiff alleging municipal liability under § 1983 must show that the "the municipal action was taken with the requisite degree of culpability, i.e., that the municipal action was taken with deliberate indifference to its known or obvious consequences." *Davis*, 233 F.3d at 1375-76 (internal quotation and citation omitted).

In this case, Doe does not point to an official School Board policy or a "custom or practice so pervasive and well-settled that it assumes the force of law." Instead she argues that the School Board is liable under § 1983 for the deprivation of her constitutional right to be free from sexual abuse due to the actions of Principal Scavella and Dr. Melita, "officials fairly deemed to represent government policy."[11] p.1264 In other words, Doe's argument rests solely on the final policymaker theory of liability. According to Doe, Scavella's and Melita's actions reflect a School Board policy of ignoring standard investigative measures and presumptively resolving "he said, she said" complaints in the favor of the teacher.

The district court granted summary judgment because it concluded that the School Board did not act with deliberate indifference in responding to the K.F. and S.W. complaints. We need not address deliberate indifference in this regard because Principal Scavella and Dr. Melita are not "officials fairly deemed to represent government policy" under our circuit's standard for § 1983 municipal liability. Therefore, Doe's § 1983 claim against the School Board fails as a matter of law, and the School Board is entitled to summary judgment. *See United States v. $121,100.00 in U.S. Currency,* 999 F.2d 1503, 1507 (11th Cir.1993) ("This court will affirm a grant of summary judgment if it is correct for any reason.").

Municipal liability from a single action or decision may only "be deemed representative of the municipality" if "the acting official [is] imbued with *final* policymaking authority." *Denno,* 218 F.3d at 1276 (emphasis added). Determining the persons or bodies that have final policymaking authority for the defendant is a matter of state law to be determined by the trial judge and not the jury. *See Jett v. Dallas Indep. Sch. Dist.,* 491 U.S. 701, 738, 109 S.Ct. 2702, 2724, 105 L.Ed.2d 598 (1989); *Owens v. Fulton County,* 877 F.2d 947, 950-51 (11th Cir.1989). Doe argues that Dr. Melita has final policymaking authority because the School Board delegated Dr. Melita the discretion to develop disciplinary guidelines and procedures for conducting personnel misconduct investigations. Doe also argues that Principal Scavella is a final policymaker for the School Board because he had the discretion under these procedures to make the initial decision whether or not to investigate a student complaint. This authority, though representing a vesting of discretion in both Melita and Scavella, is insufficient to imbue them with final policymaking authority for purposes of § 1983 municipal liability.

We have strictly interpreted "*Monell*'s policy or custom requirement to preclude § 1983 liability for a subordinate official's decisions when the final policymaker delegates decisionmaking discretion to the subordinate, but retains the power to review the exercise of that discretion." *Scala v. City of Winter Park,* 116 F.3d 1396, 1399 (11th Cir.1997). In other words, final policymaking authority over a particular subject matter does not vest in an official whose decisions are "subject to meaningful administrative review." *Id.* at 1401. *Compare Hill v. Clifton,* 74 F.3d 1150, 1152 (11th Cir.1996) (accepting concession that city police chief was not final policymaker with respect to employment decisions where police chief's decisions could be reversed by the city manager) *with Martinez v. City of Opa-Locka, Fla.,* 971 F.2d 708, 714-15 (11th Cir.1992) (finding final policymaking authority where "the City Manager's decision to hire or fire administrative personnel is completely insulated from review"). Doe has not shown that Melita's and Scavella's decisions are not subject to meaningful administrative review.

According to the School Board's "Event/Incident Process for Administrative Action," Melita, as a member of the Professional Standards Committee that reviews SIU investigations, makes "non-binding recommendations" of "probable cause" or "no probable cause" to the Superintendent of the School Board. Although Melita may have authority to make key decisions at various "decision points" in the administrative review process, the Superintendent has ultimate authority to veto or override the Committee's "no probable cause" finding or recommendation of a specific disciplinary action in the case of a "probable cause" finding. It is the Professional Standards Committee's "no probable cause" finding in K.F.'s case that Doe argues reflects the School Board's policy of deliberate indifference to "he said, she said" complaints. Because the Superintendent had the authority to veto this recommendation, this decision was "subject to meaningful administrative review" under *Scala,* and Melita was not a final policymaker that can subject the School Board to § 1983 municipal liability.

If Dr. Melita is not a final policymaker for the School Board, it follows *a fortiori* that Principal Scavella's decisions do not reflect final School Board policy under our circuit's § 1983 municipal liability standard. Doe contends that Scavella's decision not to pursue a formal investigation of the S.W. complaint reflected a School Board policy to favor a teacher's version of an alleged incident of harassment. Scavella's authority to make a mere recommendation to a superior, which that superior is free to accept or reject, does not equate to the final authority to make School Board policy. Therefore, the School Board may not be subjected to municipal liability under § 1983 for the single acts of Principal Scavella.

C. Principal Scavella's Liability under § 1983

Doe's final argument on appeal is that Principal Scavella is individually liable for Doe's injuries under § 1983. Principal Scavella pled the defense of qualified immunity before the district court in response to this claim. Qualified immunity offers complete protection for individual government officials performing discretionary functions "insofar as their conduct does not violate clearly established statutory or constitutional rights of which a reasonable person would have known." *Harlow v. Fitzgerald,* 457 U.S. 800, 818, 102 S.Ct. 2727, 2738, 73 L.Ed.2d 396 (1982). The parties do not dispute that at all times relevant to this appeal Scavella was acting in a discretionary capacity. When the court concludes that the defendant was engaged in a discretionary function, "the burden shifts to the plaintiff to show that the defendant is *not* entitled to qualified immunity." *Holloman ex rel. Holloman v. Harland,* 370 F.3d 1252, 1264 (11th Cir. 2004). To satisfy this burden, the plaintiff must show that: "(1) the defendant violated a constitutional right, and (2) this right was clearly established at the time of the alleged violation." *Id.* "The judges of the district courts and the courts of appeals should be permitted to exercise their sound discretion in deciding which of the two prongs of the qualified immunity analysis should be addressed first in light of the circumstances in the particular case at hand." *Pearson v. Callahan,* 555 U.S. ___, 129 S.Ct. 808, 818, 172 L.Ed.2d 565 (2009). The district court did not address the second qualified immunity inquiry, holding that Scavella was entitled to summary judgment because Doe failed to establish that Scavella violated her constitutional rights, clearly established or not.

Section 1983 "provides every person with the right to sue those acting under color of state law for violations of federal constitutional and statutory provisions." *Williams,* 477 F.3d at 1299. Section 1983 does not create any substantive federal rights in and of itself; it is merely a vehicle to bring such suits. *Id.* Therefore, a § 1983 plaintiff must allege a specific federal right violated by the defendant. Here, Doe asserts that Scavella violated her constitutional right not to be sexually abused by a state official acting under color of law, a substantive due process right grounded in the Fourteenth p.1266 Amendment.[12] Scavella appears to concede that Doe has this right and that Hoever's sexual assault deprived her of that right. We assume so for the purposes of this appeal. *See Hartley v. Parnell,* 193 F.3d 1263, 1268 (11th Cir. 1999) (assuming for purposes of appeal that plaintiff had constitutional right not to be sexually abused by a state official). Scavella argues, and the district court held, however, that under the circumstances of this case, he cannot be held liable under § 1983 for Hoever's acts because he did not cause that deprivation. We agree.

Scavella did not personally participate in Hoever's sexual assault of Doe. Therefore to impose liability on Scavella for Hoever's constitutional violation, Doe must establish Scavella's liability in a supervisory capacity. *See id.* at 1269 (holding that a school district superintendent was not liable under § 1983 for the sexual abuse of a student at the hands of her teacher where plaintiff failed to show that he either personally participated in the abuse or that he was supervisorily liable for the teacher's violations). She cannot do so. "It is well established in this circuit that supervisory officials are not liable under § 1983 for the unconstitutional acts of their subordinates" unless the "supervisor personally participates in the alleged constitutional violation" or "there is a causal connection between actions of the supervising official and the alleged constitutional deprivation." *Id.* This requisite causal connection can be established in the following circumstances: (1) when a "history of widespread abuse puts the responsible supervisor on notice of the need to correct the alleged deprivation, and he fails to do so" or (2) when a supervisor's "improper custom or policy results in deliberate indifference to constitutional rights." *Id.* (internal quotation and citation omitted). For a history of abuse to be sufficiently widespread to put a supervisor on notice, the abuse must be "obvious, flagrant, rampant and of continued duration, rather than isolated occurrences." *Id.*

We agree with the district court that Doe cannot show the requisite causal connection between Scavella's actions and Hoever's sexual assault of Doe based on his notice of Hoever's "history of widespread abuse" or his "custom or policy" of deliberate indifference. "The standard by which a supervisor is held liable in her individual capacity for the actions of a subordinate is extremely rigorous." *Braddy v. Fla. Dep't of Labor & Employment Sec.,* 133 F.3d 797, 802 (11th Cir. 1998). First, Doe's conclusory assertion of a "history of widespread abuse" is clearly insufficient to put Scavella on notice of an ongoing constitutional deprivation. In evaluating the existence of widespread abuse, we have stated that "[a] few isolated instances of harassment will not suffice." *Id. Cf. Valdes v. Crosby,* 450 F.3d 1231, 1244 (11th Cir.2006) (denying prison official's summary judgment motion where "inmate abuse at the hands of guards was not an isolated occurrence, but rather occurred with sufficient regularity as to demonstrate a history of widespread abuse"). Unlike the two instances of sexual harassment alleged here, in *Valdes* there was evidence that the prison warden received at least thirteen complaints and inquiries in the year and a half preceding the plaintiff's son's death at the hands of prison guards, along with repeated warnings p.1267 from the outgoing warden concerning the prison's problems with specific guards using excessive force on prisoners. *Id.* at 1241-43. Here, there is no basis for claiming that the two complaints against Hoever prior to Doe's sexual assault rose to the level of sexual harassment similarly "obvious, flagrant, rampant and of continued duration." *Hartley,* 193 F.3d at 1269.

Also insufficient is Doe's conclusory assertion of a custom or policy resulting in deliberate indifference to Doe's constitutional right to be free from sexual assault. Even if Scavella's decisions contributed to the fact question of the School Board's deliberate indifference and liability under Title IX, we cannot conclude that Scavella had a "policy in place prior to the sexual abuse which could have led [Hoever] to believe that sexual abuse of students was permitted." *See id.*

Accordingly, in the absence of evidence that Scavella personally participated in Doe's sexual assault, was on notice of a history of Hoever's widespread abuse of female students, or had a policy in place permitting such assaults, Doe cannot show that Scavella has supervisory liability for Hoever's deprivation of her constitutional right to be free from sexual abuse.[13] Although Scavella's acts and omissions reflect serious deficiencies that may be "clearly unreasonable in light of known circumstances" for purposes of Title IX liability, Doe has not established that these acts and omissions could subject Scavella to supervisory liability for the acts of his subordinates. Therefore, the district court did not err in granting summary judgment to Scavella, and we need not reach the second step of our qualified immunity analysis — whether Scavella was on notice that his conduct violated clearly established constitutional rights at the time of the alleged violation.

CONCLUSION

In conclusion, we REVERSE the district court's summary judgment in favor of the School Board on Doe's Title IX claims. We AFFIRM the district court on all other rulings.

[*] Honorable Jane A. Restani, Chief Judge of the United States Court of International Trade, sitting by designation.

[1] Doe claimed that Hoever pinned her against a classroom wall, lifted her skirt, digitally penetrated her, and then rubbed his penis against her vagina.

[2] K.F. admitted in her deposition that Hoever ejected her from class that day and that she had been "fighting for her grade."

[3] In her deposition, S.W. also testified that Hoever seemed to be attempting to block her from leaving the room by getting in front of the door. However, because this was not included in her written report and because she was not interviewed as a part of Scavella's informal investigation, we cannot be sure that this fact was known by Scavella at the time he evaluated the seriousness of her complaint.

[4] The Assistant Principal denied being involved in any investigation.

[5] Doe does not appeal the dismissal of her § 1983 failure-to-train claim against the School Board (Count II).

[6] Because the School Board concedes that Principal Scavella could institute "corrective measures" in response to known harassment, we need not address whether other school district officials, such as Dr. Melita as Executive Director of the School Board's Special Investigative Unit, also had actual notice of the complaints. Although Dr. Melita had actual knowledge of the K.F. complaint, he

lacked notice of material facts surrounding the S.W. complaint, such as Hoever's identity as the accused teacher, due to Scavella's lack of disclosure.

[7] The *Gebser* plaintiff alleged that the teacher with whom she ultimately had a sexual relationship also directed his sexually suggestive comments to her both in class and when they were alone together in his classroom. 524 U.S. at 277-78, 118 S.Ct. at 1993. However, she did not report this harassment; it was other students' complaints that she alleged provided notice to the principal of the harassment. *Id.*

[8] In *Davis*, a male student attempted to touch a female student's breasts; spoke in vulgar language to her; told her "I want to get into bed with you" and "I want to feel your boobs"; and placed a door stop in his pants and acted in a suggestive manner toward her. 526 U.S. at 633-36, 119 S.Ct. at 1666-68. The school did not discipline the student, separate the plaintiff from the student, or establish a sexual harassment policy or procedure. *Id.* at 634-35, 119 S.Ct. at 1667.

[9] According to the School Board's Special Investigative Unit's Enforcement Procedures for Personnel Investigations: "All witnesses or persons mentioned in the initial investigation should be contacted and interviewed."

[10] The School Board's "Recommended Guidelines for Preliminary at the Site Investigations" requires principals to "Locate any past complaints regarding the employee and their disposition."

[11] Before the district court, Doe also argued that the School Board could be subjected to municipal liability due to a pervasive and well-settled custom with the force of law. It appears that she has abandoned this argument on appeal. Regardless, Doe also cannot establish the School Board's § 1983 municipal liability on this basis. As a general rule, an "isolated incident, however unfortunate, does not demonstrate evidence of the County's 'persistent' or 'widespread' policy," *McDowell v. Brown*, 392 F.3d 1283, 1290-91 (11th Cir.2004), and will not be considered "so pervasive as to be a custom or practice," *Grech v. Clayton County, Ga.*, 335 F.3d 1326, 1330 n. 6 (11th Cir.2003). Even viewing Doe's allegations surrounding the K.F. and S.W. complaints collectively, they do not evidence a widespread or pervasive practice of disregarding student complaints.

[12] Doe does not allege Scavella's individual violation of Title IX. We have previously held that because Title IX expressly prohibits claims against individual school officials, permitting plaintiffs to use § 1983 to assert an individual Title IX claim "would permit an end run around Title IX's explicit language limiting liability to funding recipients" and is therefore prohibited. *Williams*, 477 F.3d at 1300.

[13] Doe's brief on appeal bases its assertion of Scavella's § 1983 liability solely on the theory of his supervisory liability. Therefore, we need not, and do not, express opinion with respect to the possibility of Scavella's § 1983 liability based on a direct causal connection between his actions and omissions and Doe's sexual assault distinct from his potential supervisory liability. Even if we considered such a possibility, Scavella would probably be entitled to qualified immunity. Doe has not cited a single case showing that Scavella violated her clearly established Fourteenth Amendment rights by failing to vigorously investigate prior sexual misconduct allegations against Hoever. Therefore, she has not satisfied her burden under the second step of our qualified immunity analysis. *See Williams*, 477 F.3d at 1301 ("Williams has failed to present any cases that show the three defendants violated her

clearly established equal protection rights by recruiting and admitting an individual like Cole."). Although a plaintiff does not "have to show that the precise conduct in question has been held unlawful," for a federal right to be clearly established "its parameters 'must be sufficiently clear that a reasonable official would understand that what he is doing violates that right.'" *Id.* at 1300 (citing *Anderson v. Creighton*, 483 U.S. 635, 640, 107 S.Ct. 3034, 3039, 97 L.Ed.2d 523 (1987)).

Doe v. School Bd. of Broward County, Fla., 604 F. 3d 1248 (11th Cir. 2010)

Made in the USA
Las Vegas, NV
06 August 2024